T0093154

# A Practical Guide to Level Design

Written by an AAA industry expert with over 20 years of experience, this book offers comprehensive coverage of the practical skills that all successful level designers need to have. It covers everything from practical production skills to the social and soft skills required to thrive in the gaming industry.

This book begins with a theoretical and abstract approach that sets a common language for the later hard-skill applications and practical examples. These later chapters cover a wealth of practical skills for use during the concept phase, while creating layouts, scripting, and working with AI. This book includes essential chapters on topics such as social skills, soft skills, world-building, level design direction, production, as well as how to gain employment in the industry.

This book will be of great interest to all level designers, content leads, and directors looking to enhance their skillset. It will also appeal to students of level and game design looking for tips on how to break into the industry.

**Ben Bauer** has been working in the gaming industry since 2003. He previously held lead roles at Crytek and Ubisoft and is currently the Creative Director at Plan A Collective.

# A Practical Guide to Level Design

## From Theory to Practice, Diplomacy and Production

Ben Bauer

CRC Press
Taylor & Francis Group
Boca Raton London New York

CRC Press is an imprint of the
Taylor & Francis Group, an **informa** business

Designed cover image: Cover Art: Noud van Miltenburg

First edition published 2023
by CRC Press
6000 Broken Sound Parkway NW, Suite 300, Boca Raton, FL 33487-2742

and by CRC Press
4 Park Square, Milton Park, Abingdon, Oxon, OX14 4RN

*CRC Press is an imprint of Taylor & Francis Group, LLC*



*Library of Congress Cataloging-in-Publication Data*
Names: Bauer, Ben, author.
Title: A practical guide to level design : from theory to practice, diplomacy and production / Ben Bauer.
Description: First edition. | Boca Raton, FL : CRC Press, 2023. | Includes
bibliographical references and index.
Identifiers: LCCN 2022041410 (print) | LCCN 2022041411 (ebook) |
ISBN 9781032230894 (paperback) | ISBN 9781032230986 (hardback) | ISBN 9781003275664 (ebook)
Subjects: LCSH: Video games–Design. | Level design (Computer science)
Classification: LCC GV1469.3 .B395 2023 (print) | LCC GV1469.3 (ebook) |
DDC 794.8—dc23/eng/20221025
LC record available at https://lccn.loc.gov/2022041410
LC ebook record available at https://lccn.loc.gov/2022041411

ISBN: 9781032230986 (hbk)
ISBN: 9781032230894 (pbk)
ISBN: 9781003275664 (ebk)

DOI: 10.1201/9781003275664

Typeset in Times
by codeMantra

*I dedicate this book to my father—He was my undying inspiration and idol.*

*A huge thanks and hugs go out to my supporting wife Edit, who probably was even happier than I was that this book is finally out.*

# Contents

## Section II Production and Social Skills

## Section III Level Design Theory

## Section IV Practical: How to Get Started

## Section V Practical: Layouts

## Section VI Practical: Technical Aspects and Game Design

## Section VII Closing Topics

# *Acknowledgment*

I learned many things from many people, a lot inspired me, some are fantastic colleagues, and some I just must thank for the opportunity to be where I am. Below is a list of those people:

Alex Felton, Alexandre Parizeau, Andrew Wilson, Avni Yerli, Christian Carriere, David Footman, David Grivel, Denny Borges, Derek Patterson, Eric Felten, everyone else I forgot because you always forget some important people in such lists, Francois Roy, Gordana Vrbanc Duquet, Gregor Kopka, Guido Kuip, Hanno Hagedorn, Jack Mamais, Kyle Kotevich, Manfred Nerurkar, Martin Walsh, Martin Nerurkar, Matt West, Michael Khaimzon, Navid Khavari, Pat Ingoldsby, Patrick Redding, Paul Dobson, Peter Gelencser, Philipp von Preuschen, Rima Brek, Roger Liu, Russ Flaherty, Sophie Caramigeas, Sten Hübler, the rest of the old NS:CO mod crew, Tom Roller, and Will Bateman.

# Section I

# Book and Level Design Introduction

# 1

# *Book Introduction*

## 1.1 Preface

I based everything I wrote in this book on my practical experiences. Just to set the right expectations, I am not an academic, nor do I have an academic degree. Due to my experience, I can write in more detail, be always practical-oriented, share the aspects that work, and mention the ones that did not. I do like to make a lot of cooking analogies, so you can compare this book to a cooking book written by a chef, and not only by someone who only tastes food. To a large extent, I believe this is what makes this book so unique and motivating for me to write it. However, this limits the book's content since my experience is primarily rooted in the realm of 3D action games. If there is anything I have less experience with, yet is important to share for the bigger picture, then I prefer to keep it brief. Still, I strongly believe that many lessons in this book can carry over to other genres and more about my background further on.

Most of what is written here comes from me as an autodidact because there was not much theory or shared practical experience about level design back in my days—and certainly no schools or universities in Germany. Therefore, I consider it almost a duty of mine to share my knowledge and experience, just to set an example. I sincerely hope more people in my craft will do the same because each person can only share and experience so much. Only if we all share our unique perspectives, the younger generation can get a more complete picture of our craft. Of course, I also learned a lot from mentors and peers. Unfortunately, it is difficult to give accurate credits to each one of them. Therefore, if anyone wants to reach out to me then please do so for hopefully future editions of this book. Additionally, this also includes many lessons on how not to do things by myself or others. Further on, my sincere hope is that by sharing those especially negative lessons, you do not ever have to repeat them—it is enough if I have done them. Just do not expect any dirty details because non-disclosure agreements (NDAs) prevent me to talk about any corporate, personal, or very project specific secrets.

I tried to write this book as entertaining and on point as possible. I am not a huge fan of adding unnecessary "fluff," but I understand that sometimes it lightens the mood, especially regarding "drier" topics. I will also have to touch on more "complicated" issues because our industry, especially in recent years, was not without its failings—or at least they became more public. However, this is still a book about level design for designers, so do not expect a lengthy editorial piece about anything too controversial. Instead, it very briefly touches on mental health and conflict avoidance.

Related to that, I have experienced many designers in my professional and mod-community career who struggled because they only focused on the hard skills. I had my own fair share of such lessons to learn because back in the early 2000s, there was not much knowledge, teaching, or standards about social skills and such—just everyone had their own expectations, and sometimes it worked out, and sometimes it did not. Therefore, I did not write this book just to talk about level design. Instead, I firmly believe that a book about level design should include all the other elements affecting most level designers, especially social skills. After all, this book aims at professional level designers or those who want to become one and in this reality just making levels is only half the job because making games is a team effort.

Still, at heart, this book is about level design theory and especially practical applications based on my 20+ years of experience as a level designer, lead, and director. The first bigger impact I had on the industry was in 2004 when I published "Ben's Small Bible of Realistic Multiplayer Level Design." I'm still impressed that this article's relevance is still mentioned almost 20 years later and it is a testimony

DOI: 10.1201/9781003275664-2

that many core principles of level design stay relevant for decades to come. I truly hope the same can be said about this book. Moving on, I had a lot of positive reception with my YouTube channel "Bauer Design Solutions" because it felt there was a need for more practical, experience-based knowledge exchange about level design, instead of often just very academic. Outside of those public knowledge sharing, professionally I always took a strong focus on mentoring and coaching anyone from juniors to directors.

Ultimately, I do not believe in common sense, especially not when it comes to the games industry at large. Unfortunately, the term "common sense" is too often used by experienced people to separate themselves from others, often in a rude way. However, if it truly would be a thing, then we would have no need for most tutorials or articles, yet they are more popular than ever. Most of my positive reception of my articles and videos come from level design novices, who are hungry for more knowledge because there isn't much out there, especially nothing as comprehensive as I try with this book.

Many professionals and academics alike created some great articles, videos, or books about level design. Thanks to CRC press and especially Will Bateman (the Commissioning Editor who found me), I thought it was my take on this topic in a larger volume, listing as much experience and knowledge I managed to gather over the decades.

## 1.2 Chapter Overview

My goal was to organize this book as logically as possible and therefore divide it conceptually into larger categories. Those categories do not appear in the book formatting-wise but should help understand the structure of my thinking categorizing this volume.

### 1.2.1 Book and Level Design Intro

The first two chapters, "Book Introduction" and "Definition of Level Design and Level Designers," are meant to give you a foundation about this book and what it means to be a level designer. Essentially it sets the expectations for further reading because my background might be long but not all-inclusive; for example, I never worked on an RTS or side scroller, but again more about my background a bit later. Also, this chapter establishes what I expect from level designers or what defines as one because there is no real standard in the industry.

### 1.2.2 Production and Social Skills

The next three chapters, "Level Design Production," "Diplomacy of Level Design," and "Teamwork & Leadership Tools," are covering primarily the previously mentioned social skills. It also gives an overview of a typical level design development cycle because it ties in very well with diplomacy and leadership topics.

### 1.2.3 Level Design Theory

This category includes the five chapters "About Vision, Direction, Pillars, and DNA," "Abstract Level Design," "The Big Picture," "High-Level Layouts," and "Connective Tissue." Essentially it covers a wide range of ideas, concepts, or abstract tools and how I design/analyze levels or games. They all have practical applications but remain on a higher, theoretical level.

### 1.2.4 Practical: How to Get Started

I decided to split the practical part of the book into three parts, initializing with how to start levels in the "Concept Phase" and then transition to the "First Steps" in the editor. I will cover crucial topics on how to transition from a plan to reality or documentation and also include a few topics like world-building or benchmarks.

### 1.2.5 Practical: Layouts

The following practical category includes the two big chapters, "Cover, Flow and Player Leading" and "Scenarios and Location Types." Here we talk a lot about where we place our beloved crates, guide the player through our space, or create exciting stealth layouts. The layout is at the heart of level design for many people, so expect a lot of graphics and level design "geekiness."

### 1.2.6 Practical: Technical and Game Design

The last practical category encapsulates the two chapters, "Scripting & Technical" and "Working with Ingredients." The first one includes, as the name suggests, a lot about scripting and how to handle technical limitations. The second acts as a bridge to game design from which we level designers get most of our gameplay mechanics.

### 1.2.7 Closing Topics

In the end, we talk about how to close a project as a level designer in the chapter "Closing & Shipping" since this is one of the most crucial, rarely crazy creative, and sometimes it is the most challenging step. I also added the chapter "Becoming a Level Designer" because it is the topic I get the most common questions about after I held a presentation to industry outsiders.

## 1.3 About Myself

### 1.3.1 How It All Started

#### *1.3.1.1 Before the Internet*

Since I read "Lord of the Rings" from J. R. R. Tolkien and had my first tabletop roleplay experience on my 10th birthday in 1990, I was hooked on world-building and making games. Originally, I started writing my roleplay games on an old-school typewriter, but it all changed once a PC got into my life. In 1994, the first game I bought with my own money was "Forgotten Realms: Unlimited Adventures" by MicroMagic, which is essentially an AD&D level design editor to make your own adventures and share it with your friends. Of course, exchanging dungeons on 3½-inch floppy disks was not very popular, plus not to mention my limited design skills back then.

However, with the rise of LAN parties and "Duke Nukem 3D" by 3D Realms, my levels got a lot more popular. Later on, "Quake 1" id Software was a massive yet daunting game-changer in my perception of level design. Keep in mind that such games were perceived with very critical eyes in Germany in the 1990s, which should explain why games like "Doom" by id Software showed up so late in my life.

#### *1.3.1.2 Joining the Mod Community*

I do not know anymore exactly what year I discovered internet access in our home, but it took my parents a massive bill to realize that I had found it. Still, thanks to my loving parents, it all got sorted out, and soon I joined a mod team for "Quake 2" by id Software. The team was "Team Mirage," and our first multiplayer mod, or rather total conversation, was "Navy Fortress." If I remember correctly, this was the first tactical round-based game with classes, but please do not quote me from ~25 years ago on my foggy memory. The mod was not massively popular, since it was released more at the end of Quake 2s era, and I still had to learn a lot about what it means to be a level designer, especially releasing my first levels while still learning the ropes as a teenager was quite an experience.

However, it all got a lot better with our team's next project, "Navy Seals: Covert Operations," which was a multiplayer total conversation for id Software's "Quake 3." Of course, as hardcore Quake players, we all thought that making round-based tactic mods for Quake 3 would be way more popular than for "Half-Life 1" by Valve - Yes, we could not have been more wrong, but more about that another day.

Anyhow, the mod was way more popular, way better executed, and I think we even won a few awards. I not only designed levels as the Lead Level Designer but was also deeply involved in the game design of the mod's unique ability system. I especially tried to focus on creating natural-looking environments, for which the engine was not very known for, like rock arches or even trees you could climb in. I had to do my own textures, write my own shaders, do minor audio work, helped out with organizing the work of more local friends and was something like the team's "weapon and realism expert." It was a fantastic time, even though school and homework paid their unfortunate price. Still, by buying a separate level compiling workstation, my parents supported me massively. Without that support I doubt I could have gotten even close to releasing around 20 levels in the loosely two years.

I also wrote my first article "Art'n'Level Design" and my practical part of the final exam was to translate art from the 20th century into 3D using the "Quake 3" engine. Long story short, after 9/11 it was difficult for a German (without any prior work experience or university degree) to get a job in the USA, so the mod's fans pushed me to apply at Crytek for a level designer. All in all, I would not be where I am today without my great parents, team members, and fans.

### 1.3.2 My Professional Career

#### *1.3.2.1 Joining Crytek*

After a grueling six-hour-long interview at the beginning of 2003, I got an offer as a junior level designer at Crytek working on the very first "Far Cry." I also did something like a trade school to become a print graphic designer next to the job. It is a special German thing, and I will not bore you with all the details.

Working on the first "Far Cry" with CryEngine was a crazy unique experience, even though it only lasted about a year for me. The switch from multiplayer to singleplayer was initially challenging, but I quickly became accustomed to it and focused primarily on interior levels, lighting, environment art, visual special effects (VFX), and placing artificial intelligence (AI), meaning enemy and friendly non-player characters (NPCs). In the end, I was promoted to intermediate level designer and even got an art credit next to level design. Before the next bigger project, I worked on a few smaller projects like tech demos and multiplayer packs.

Then working on "Crysis" by Crytek was another wild ride. Initially, I worked on the alien ship interiors but then switched to the second and third outdoor terrain levels. I have created two levels, including terrain, AI setup, scripting, and environment art. Additionally, I was closely working with AI programmers on the design for the human-AI and therefore touched pretty much every other human-levels' combat/cover setups and scripts. At the end of the project, I also got deeper involved in mentoring junior designers. Something I had little experience in, but I started to enjoy it a lot. Looking back, I can certainly say that my mental health suffered a lot during the few years of development. I crunched for more than a year non-stop, and in a combination of various other things, I had two burnouts, from which I luckily recovered. At the end of the project, I got promoted to senior level designer.

Following "Crysis," I had the opportunity to join a newly founded Crytek studio in Budapest as a Lead Level Designer working on "Crysis Warhead." I can definitely recommend switching from senior to lead on a familiar brand. Not only did I have to mentor the local team in the engine, genre, and IP, but I also had to learn what it means to be a lead. Following "Crysis Warhead," we started to work on the initial version of "Ryse" by Crytek. I learned a lot about leadership during my years in Budapest, including what not to do.

#### *1.3.2.2 Joining Ubisoft*

In the middle of 2011, when the development of "Ryse" switched from Budapest back to Crytek's HQ in Frankfurt am Main (Germany), I took a job offer to join Ubisoft Toronto to work on "Splinter Cell Blacklist" as one of the Level Design Directors focusing on the singleplayer campaign. It was a great opportunity to switch country, city, and continent and experience a completely new company and culture—something I can only recommend to everyone who was at his first company for 9+ years. Working on a blockbuster Splinter Cell is a fantastic experience, and it certainly enhanced my stealth and third-person skills. All levels used for marketing, after the initial showcase, came from my team.

Then followed a few unannounced/unreleased projects (protected by NDAs), but that is nothing common in the industry. Luckily, I could again work on a released game called "Far Cry Primal" by Ubisoft. I was a Level Design Director responsible for the Great Hunts, which are epic open-world boss fights against massive, majestic creatures. The project was co-developed with the lead studio in Montreal. Designing and developing something like the Great Hunts, which was new and unique to the franchise, is undoubtedly a thrilling experience.

After this Far Cry game came "Far Cry 5," which was also co-developed with Ubisoft Montreal. I had the role of an Associate Game Director, directing the other directors in the Toronto team. We were responsible for developing the northern open-world art, characters, missions, fishing, and narrative, about one-third of the game's world content. Leadership and diplomacy essentially covered my primary learnings during this game's development.

In 2018 Ubisoft opened up a new studio in Berlin. I decided to move back to Europe and join the studio as a Content Director, responsible for Art and Level Design direction. My close connection to the Canadian Far Cry teams was one of the important reasons the studio gained a large content mandate for "Far Cry 6" by Ubisoft. We had the unique opportunity to design, direct, and develop the Special Operations, which were large, highly detailed, complex, open-world missions separated from the main world. Besides directing most of the team and designing the core direction for the project, I focused mainly on leadership, team building, and studio topics.

#### *1.3.2.3 Joining Plan a Collective*

I started to write this book in the middle/end of 2021, close to the release of "Far Cry 6." After the exciting journey working 10+ years for Ubisoft I decided that it was finally time to switch to the indie company Plan A, co-lead by a good old friend of mine.

Looking back, I have directly worked on three new IPs (more if I count all the unannounced projects), successfully shipped seven AAA titles, worked on countless prototypes and new game concepts, and have helped build four new studios. I made my dream job a reality, which can sometimes be a blessing and a curse, but after +20 years of making games, I still could not imagine anything else. In my opinion, the satisfaction of finishing a challenging project, together with some outstanding individuals/teams, is something no day-to-day job can even come close to. It remains my primary motivator to keep pushing myself and to inspire and mentor others continuously.

### 1.3.3 Other Side Gigs

Below is a brief list of other smaller side projects I did next to my professional career

- 2004: I wrote my second article, "Ben's Small Bible of Realistic Multiplayer Level Design." I know it is quite a mouthful of a title, but it was my way of leaving my multiplayer past behind. The article was a bit of a slow burn initially but soon became recognized all over the industry. Even today, people still bring it up occasionally and how much of an impact it had on their level design career. The article's reception was one of the primary motivators to keep sharing level design knowledge, which ultimately resulted in writing this book.
- 2009: I started writing and designing my own tabletop roleplaying system called "Dark III" (working title). Up to this day, it has been my ongoing creative outlet ever since a project is in a more "uncreative" phase like closing. I have kept working on multiple worlds and used it to develop different world-building methodologies, which I then refined in the professional work context.
- 2014: I had the unique opportunity to be a panel speaker at "Walt Disney Imagineering Ideation" in Los Angeles. I was the only one representing the digital medium to share my thoughts about "Playful Environments" to enrich their future park designs potentially.

- 2014: Based on the impression I left at Disney, one of the peer panel speakers, Chad Oppenheim, invited me to hold a guest lecture at Harvard University for his course "Immersive Landscape: Representation through Gaming Technology." Once a year, he invites one game developer to give a speech about their work, lessons learned, and inspirations. I have held a few university presentations, but that one so far is undoubtedly the most memorable one.
- 2010: In the playful spirit of "If you work on so many shooters, you should kind of know what it means a bit to be in a firefight," I started to play airsoft first in Hungary and then more extensively in Canada. However, it quickly escalated around 2014–2015 when our team and I began to go nuts with the equipment replacing as many parts, clothing, and equipment with the real ones, as long as it stayed 100% legal and safe. Extended hardcore milsims or a massive amount of CQB firefights with night vision, IR lasers, real optics, and thermal scopes can never replace the real thing. However, it was insanely fun, sometimes grueling, but you learn a ton of lessons and gain friends for life. In 2015 I decided to start my own YouTube channel about my activities and learnings called "Dark Gray Project." Unfortunately, I had to discontinue the channel since I do not play airsoft anymore after moving to Germany.
- 2016: I started another YouTube channel called "Bauer Design Solutions," where I shared some of my level design and world-building thoughts. Essentially, it was a continuation of writing articles because I thought to reach a broader/different audience by making videos. The reception was excellent so far, and it ultimately led to this book deal. However, I should apologize that the update rate of the channel was not very high in recent years and, unfortunately, stopped while I was working on this book. Still, I certainly plan to continue working on it later on again.
- 2020: I had the unique opportunity to have access to some exceptional mentors, and therefore I decided to write a fantasy novel, learn how to code, and started drawing concept art. However, I would not dare to call myself a writer, coder, or concept artist! Ultimately it was a combination of lockdown occupation, providing material for my tabletop roleplay game "Dark III" and primarily taught me some empathy for writers, narrative designers, programmers, and concept artists. My respect for their craft increased even further by walking in their shoes—something I can only recommend to anyone if such an opportunity arises.

# 2

# *Definition of Level Design and Level Designers*

Long story short, there is no clear-cut definition of a level designer. The job has drastically changed its role and what it entails over the last decades and is still evolving because the game industry as a whole is constantly changing, too. Pretty much every company or studio I worked for had variants of the job description, and often it changed over the years. It goes so far that some companies have no level designers by title but call them mission/quest/world designers or use game designers instead, and this is all fine and good.

However, this chapter should help to understand better what the role means in broad terms and what you can expect of becoming a level designer or a variant—regardless of the actual title at the end.

## 2.1 The Level Designer

### 2.1.1 Introduction

End of the 1990s and early 2000s, it was challenging for me to explain, especially to my parents or my now wife: What is a level designer? What do we actually do? The primary problem was that the game industry, and in particular the big-budget blockbuster (AAA) action game development, was not established in Germany.

Typically, an explanation included something like: "we build worlds or games and make them fun, but there are also artists who build the worlds, and then there are game designers, too." It was not a very convincing description for an outsider. For the longest time, my parents did not believe that it was an actual job with career options supporting sustainable living. Of course, it all changed with time for the better, and after over 20 years of level design, I would like to now share my refined definition. However, if it will be a game-changer in the dating game, it has to be seen.

### 2.1.2 What Is a Level Designer?

Without going into the wide range of level design variations, for me, the broad definition of a level designer is: We are world builders. We are assemblers. We are diplomats.

The "world builder" aspect is pretty straightforward since we create the space, levels, maps, and ultimately the worlds for the players to experience in some form or another. Often, we work closely with artists and narrative people to define or craft those worlds, but in the end, it is our job to make the worlds as exciting and fun as possible. To be clear, we are typically not writing long documents of lore or creating individual assets. However, we need to take all such aspects, and many more, into careful consideration when collaborating with all the surrounding departments and the game's direction. Still, some level designers lean more toward an artistic or narrative role but more about variants later on.

Too often, when people, including some senior developers, think about level design, they think about us creating just layouts. While this is true for some level designers, there are many other ways for us to create worlds and experiences. Some level designers, especially particular quest, technical, or mission designers, do not even touch layouts. Nevertheless, their designed worlds and realities are just as wonderful because they enrich and shape them with characters, events, and generally speaking: player experiences.

The "assembler" notion is another clear one because, after all, we take the elements from all the surrounding developers and combine them in our levels. I like to compare level designers with master

DOI: 10.1201/9781003275664-3

chefs, who cook stunning meals with the produce of all the other departments. After all, cooking is just another way to show creativity. In our levels, the ingredients are, for example, art assets, game features, AI characters, audio, backdrops, VFX, cinematics, animations, or lore. Every game has a different set of ingredients, and it is the level designers implementing them. However, as a minimum, we are the ones who provide the canvas. The better we can combine all the elements, the more fun will be the level, or the tastier the meal.

To say it in simple terms: in levels, most of the game's content comes together, and it is your responsibility to make sure that each component shines. It is crucial to show deep respect and understanding for each element that other developers have created and give it the presentation/treatment it deserves. I consider it disrespectful to your colleges if they have spent weeks working on a feature, asset, or element and players only experience it for seconds in your level. In cooking terms, it is like butchering an entire delicious cow, throwing everything but the filet away, and then only using it for meatballs in a cafeteria. A great chef, or level designer, can create a stunning experience with the simplest of ingredients.

The "diplomacy" facet is the surprising one for most people when I explain my level designer definition. However, it is the most underrated one and one of the key differences between an okay and a great level designer. I want to believe that, by explaining the previous two aspects, it is clear that level designers do not work in a vacuum. Instead, every day we collaborate with a wide range of developers, and its intensity changes continuously throughout the production stages.

I met so many level designers who only defined themselves by their hard skills, but it quickly went downhill when working with peers. Therefore I want to spend some dedicated effort in this book to dig deeper into the production of levels, show supporting departments, and highlight why diplomacy is vital for us level designers. I would go so far as to state that establishing rapport with the people around you is more important than your level-editor knowledge. After all, it takes hundreds of people from all around the globe to make modern AAA games, and level designers are in the center of it all. Further on, in smaller non-AAA teams it is even more vital because you have to count on the support of a lot less people.

### 2.1.3 Variants of Level Designers

#### *2.1.3.1 Introduction*

When I started making levels for a Quake 3 total conversion, I was not just making the layouts. I also wrote shaders, drew my textures, created small models, designed the architecture, scripted, defined the narrative, added audio, and took care of the lighting and performance—to name a few. Many of those jobs would not even fall under level design anymore, at least not in bigger AAA production.

Even once I had my first professional level design job in 2003, I still wore many different hats, which nowadays would fall under many different developers' responsibilities. All I am saying is that the industry is continuously changing, and specialization is undoubtedly a trend, especially in large AAA teams. It simply becomes challenging to find enough talents that are good in a wide range of disciplines. It is simply not realistic anymore for projects which require 30+ level designers. Instead, it is a lot easier to find people who are very good in a narrow field.

The previous definition of a level designer was still very broad and hinted at the wide range of level designer variants. Therefore, I would like to dive a bit deeper into the common types of level designers to define the role further. Please note that the terms I am using here are only those I'm more or less familiar with. The exact titles and exact details may heavily vary between companies and sometimes even between the studios of the same enterprise. Additionally, please keep in mind that my classifications below do not fully represent the actual titles. However, instead, I use them to differentiate specialization of what often is just called "level designer."

This understanding is critical when you apply for a level design position. Therefore, ask exactly what your job would entail and if it fits you. After all, most job ads are just called "level designer."

The four primary factors for level designers are technical, art, narrative, and game design. All the variants below trend toward a specific direction in the industry's ongoing trend of specialization.

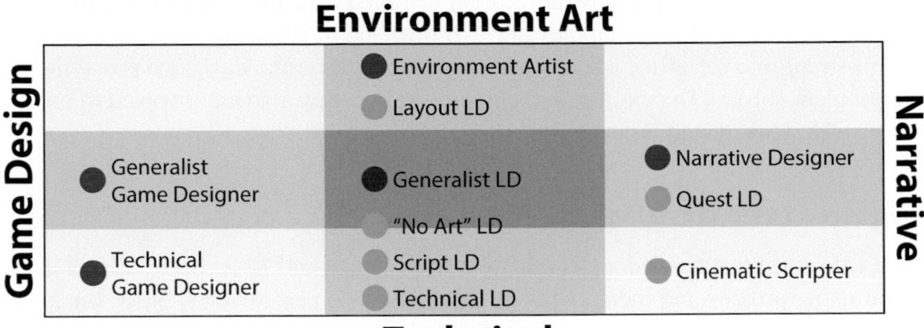


**FIGURE 2.1** Positioning the different job expertise is only a loose guestimate to sell the idea because their interpretation severely varies between studios.

### *2.1.3.2 Generalist Level Designer*

The "classical" level designer, who has a good understanding of layout, can script well and understand narrative and game design. The better ones are certainly no "masters of none." As I mentioned previously, the good, well-rounded ones are rare. However, most level designers nowadays specialize themselves in their strength and passion, without a title change. It is common to start more as a generalist, and then throughout your career, you grow in one direction or another.

They need to have a good understanding of pretty much anything related to level design ranging from layout, world-building, environment art, scripting, technical limitations/possibilities, and game design. The smaller the team, the more likely you are to fulfill most of those requirements because you will have to wear many hats and work with a wide range of different developers.

### *2.1.3.3 Layout Level Designer/Level Builder*

They are the ones who primarily focus on layout and sculpting/arranging the play space. In some instances, they are variants of environment, track, or terrain artists. They implement a wide range of elements, but especially art assets and game ingredients. It is not uncommon for some layout level designers to script some simpler cases like basic AI or mission implementation.

They need to be good at world-building, environment art, and, of course, layout. They need to have an eye for composition, know how to translate concept art into the game's reality and what it takes to create a believable world within their game's context and technical restraints. Additionally, an excellent understanding of the behaviors of the game's ingredients is vital. Otherwise, you cannot design environments that make them shine.

### *2.1.3.4 Mission/Quest Designer*

They primarily focus on implementing quests and missions in an essentially already existing world/environment. This can range from main missions to side quests. Often, they are also the ones creating the narrative of their missions, especially if it is smaller or side quests. Their impact on environments and layout heavily varies from project to project.

They have to be good scripters and know how to use script possibilities creatively. A deep narrative understanding is also key, at least good enough to work well with writers or narrative designers. They also need to be very aware of the worlds and environments they work with, especially if they have little ways to adjust them to their needs.

### *2.1.3.5 Script Level Designer*

They are comparable with mission or quest designers, but in my experience, they are more versatile in their scripting assignments and often are less narrative-oriented. They would be involved in bigger scripting tasks such as big AI implementations, complex missions, or complicated puzzles. Depending on the team composition, it is likely that they are still involved in some layout design.

Their obvious strength is scripting, a deep understanding of the technical/game possibilities, and being very creative problem solvers. Depending on the game/engine, they also are involved in profiling, performance, or other technical-related tasks.

#### *2.1.3.6 "No Art" Level Designer*

This is no real title, but I just needed a classification for this variant! Essentially, a level designer builds the level layout using proxies and then scripts the necessary elements/events. Next, the art team comes in to make it all pretty without ideally affecting much of the original layout. I am not very familiar with working with this type, but several bigger studios/companies work in that fashion.

#### *2.1.3.7 Technical Level Designer*

They are a further specialization of the script level designer. They are responsible for tackling the most complicated technical level design tasks. They establish (script) standards, tech scripting, and other technical knowledge, maintain sensitive databases, define/enforce the metrics, and take care of the most central or most complicated scripts. Typically, they are the default bridge between programmers and level design. They are the first to experiment with new features, and once approved, teach them to the other level designers. Writing technical documentation is also one additional common task for them.

Their requirements are very similar to those of a script level designer. However, they have to be even more reliable because they often work on very central, potentially game-breaking parts. To some extent, they also have to understand that they are no longer part of the creative process. They are a support team that comes in when there is a particular high profile need or serious problem.

#### *2.1.3.8 Cinematic Scripter*

They are another variant of the script level designers but specialized in implementing cinematics in the levels. In this context, we are talking about in-engine scenes which play in levels. Even though they typically work within the cinematic teams, there are many touching points with the other level designers. After all, before or after a cinematic scene, the player is in a level.

### 2.1.4 Level Design Senioritis

#### *2.1.4.1 Introduction*

Like with the level design variants, there is no global industry standard for level design seniority. However, what I write below are typical standards I have encountered so far and should fit well enough. As usual during an interview, check in detail what seniority means and what your growth possibilities are.

Of course, the industry is also full of other seniority variants like senior experts, senior leads, senior directors, or associate/assistant directors. However, they are so company or project-specific that they do not have a place in this broader overview.

#### *2.1.4.2 Intern/Junior Level Designer*

The key difference between intern and junior level designers is that interns have a time-restricted contract; typically, this is a few months and often connected to a university program. They have only little to no previous industry experience or experience in the upcoming genre—more about how to become a level designer in later chapters.

The main expectations for them are learning a lot, being a sponge for new knowledge, and listening to the more experienced developers. They will make mistakes, but that is okay, especially if they only make a mistake once or twice. It is not expected from them to already have a specialization. Instead, they should try out as much as possible so, later on, they can make a more educated decision.

#### *2.1.4.3 Regular/Intermediate Level Designer*

The key definition and expectations toward an intermediate or regular level designer is "independence." They should not need much regular oversight anymore like a junior and mostly know the basics of their craft. Like all of us, they can and must still learn, but they should be trusted developers in most cases. If they need daily task breakdowns and daily reviews and seem to keep making the same mistakes, they are not ready yet.

The transition from junior to regular is not clearly defined and often is a friction point. In my experience, two to three years of experience or shipping a larger project are common requirements for the promotion. However, it is incredibly complicated and arguably unfair if the company's requirement is: one shipped game. Because if the game takes seven years to make or never ships, then the junior has no chance to step up in a reasonable time frame. Therefore, I highly recommend this particular requirement and instead replace it with a combination of time and show of "independence."

#### *2.1.4.4 Senior Level Designer*

The key definition and expectations toward a senior level designer is "affecting others." Essentially, they positively impact other developers, especially in mentoring juniors, setting standards, or being a role model. I understand that many see senior level designers just as regular level designers with more experience. However, if this experience does not reflect on others, it is not easy to justify the promotion in my opinion. Eventually, they might all end up being seniors, but that does not mean they could have it earlier if they made a bigger difference within the team.

The promotion requirements for seniors are similarly shrouded in mystery and friction, like becoming an intermediate. Common requirements you hear is a mix of five to seven years of total experience as a level designer or two to three bigger projects shipped. However, again, the same unfair issues apply.

#### *2.1.4.5 Expert/Principal Level Designer*

There is no difference between an expert or principal level designer. Different companies use different names for the same seniority. Essentially, they are very experienced senior level designers, sometimes with an additional strong specialization. However, their type is still scarce today because the industry is not that old yet. Therefore, there are no explicit requirements, but often you look here at around 15 years of experience, plus minus a few.

The position of an expert became a topic in the industry when it became clear that not every level designer could become, or want to be, a lead or director. However, many level designers had the impression that they had to become leads or directors to grow and ultimately earn more money. Therefore, they established the role of preventing too many designers from fighting for the same position or avoiding developers lacking leadership skills to become leaders. Another reason was that several level designers wanted to keep making levels and were not interested in a lead or director role. Now, the expert/principal role still gives them the option to grow and ultimately justify a higher salary and status.

#### *2.1.4.6 (Team) Lead Level Designer*

The definition of a lead level designer heavily varies from studio to studio, sometimes even within the same project. Essentially the main difference is how creative or managerial their responsibilities are. In some cases, they are "mini-directors," in some companies, more project managers for the level design team, and sometimes half and half. Team lead level designers are typically more managerial, but otherwise, the definitions are as plentiful as we have game studios on this planet. Some leads are still occasionally hands-on, while others are not at all. Again, it heavily depends on the project, team size, the lead itself, and the studio. However, keep in mind that you will work less and less in the levels once you are a lead, especially later on as a director.

The requirements are a mix of basic managerial skills, a respectable amount of experience in the field, solid communication abilities, and a very good understanding of leadership. In my opinion, you do not have to be a senior level designer for many years to become a lead as long as you have strong leadership skills. You also do not necessarily have to be a better designer than a senior. It is not uncommon for senior level designers to be better designers than their leads, but the lead has the edge in leadership. For a lead, good social skills can easily compensate for the lack of perfect hard skills. One of the base definitions of good social/leadership skills is to use the available resources wisely while not forcing your will over others. However, more about social and leadership skills is discussed later in this book.

#### *2.1.4.7 Level Design Director*

The core definition for a level design director is to define the level design direction and then maintain its execution. They work closely with their peer directors, producers, and creative directors, and together they shape the high-level vision for the game. More about level design direction later on in this book. Some directors still have managerial responsibilities or occasionally are hands-on, but it is rarer, especially in bigger teams.

The prerequisites to become a level design director are excellent communication skills, a good understanding of the genre/game, strategic thinking, even greater leadership skills, and ideally were excellent level designers. Again, they will likely be less and less hands-on, but I highly recommend having a fundamental understanding of the tools and workflows. Otherwise, you cannot counter a potentially wrong estimate, or you have trouble negotiating with management.

## 2.2 Level Designers as Experts

### 2.2.1 Introduction

Level designers have to be experts in many fields because their job descriptions are diverse in the industry. They work with so many different departments because creating highly entertaining worlds is inherently complex. Level designers touch on so many aspects that only being experts in a handful of aspects is usually not enough.

Of course, the amount of expertise per field varies depending on what type of designer you are, but it certainly speaks to the generalist level designer as a whole. Also, when I am talking here about "experts," I do not mean Ph.D. level of expertise. However, you need to know a lot more than the basics. For example, connecting with a trained professional during the research should not start with establishing the lingo. You should explain the foundation and the "why" of everything you do, and you could easily have a chat about any of those fields during a cocktail party without anyone noticing that you are "just" a level designer.

### 2.2.2 Experts in Architecture

Creating layouts for houses or any urban structures is a staple skill for most level designers. I'm not just talking here about your average townhouse, mansion, or apartment, but definitely also corporate and industrial spaces like beer breweries, flower shops, the headquarters of despotic rulers, or Berlin warehouses occupied by ravaging punks.

You should tackle common questions like: What is the relationship between hallways, rooms, and stairs in a house, and how much space should they take? How many bathrooms does a mansion need, and where should they be located in relation to the bedrooms? How to create an inviting/intimidating/repelling corporate entrance space? What type of space can you find on the different floors of a skyscraper? What is the order of rooms in an industrial halal butchery?

Multiple times, designers and artists presented me mansions without hallways or even bathrooms in my professional career. You do not have to have an architect or engineer degree to realize such basic issues. The difference between creating a believable world and something implausible starts with good research about the different elements and knowing why the relationships between the different types of spaces are the way they are. I am still slightly embarrassed that I had to delete once all interior bathrooms from a game because we could not afford them memory-wise.

Often it is not important to fully recreate a realistic representation of a space. Still, the important aspect is to create a believable environment that your players can relate to or at least somewhat makes sense. For example, the public view of the Guantanamo prison is closer to the, now closed, Camp X-Ray with its outdoor cages and not necessarily of the nowadays present high-security prison buildings.

### 2.2.3 Experts in Landscape Architecture and City Planning

It does not just stop knowing how to layout a building. The next step is to integrate the structures in the bigger picture of the space around. This topic does not only include basic cities and towns and, but also for example the layout of, industrial complexes, harbors, airports, amusement parks, or large military bases occupied by communists pixy mutants.

What is the balance between traversal, administration, leisure, representation, and production space? Where would you place a church, strip club, grocery store, or flower shop in a small rural town in Kentucky, compared to Las Vegas or Chengdu? How do harbor layouts change between Seattle, Havanna, or Venice? What are the main elements of a nuclear power plant, and in what relationship are they with each other?

You can quickly tell if a level designer or environment artist has done their research about the bigger picture of their fictional space. They often forgot to add parking lots for industrial complexes, skipped the fence going around a nuclear power plant, or did not think that a lumber mill needs office space. However, for example, when they have done their homework well, you could really immerse yourself in a liquid gas terminal at the Gulf of Mexico, even if the game and tech required us to alter the scale or skip a few less known elements.

Back in the days, I got schooled by our art director because I placed huts too close to the road on a rural pacific island. My thinking was still related to German villages, where I grew up, where available space was limited. However, on rural pacific islands, property space is more abundant, and the properties are often more extensive. So, when the kids run out of the house, they do not get instantly hit by a car because there is a bigger space between the house and the main street. Of course, kids do not get constantly hit by cars in German villages, but I had to research the reference space better and apply a different mindset.

### 2.2.4 Experts in Geography

Urban environments are only one facet of designing an environment, but the terrain is another essential aspect. Essentially it includes the form factors of your landmasses and why they look in specific ways. It includes any other related aspects ranging from rivers, bridges, roads, hydro dams, or caves inside your standard floating islands filled with shiny sugar crystals formed after a gigantic space raccoon mating rampage.

What are the erosion patterns of wind, water, sand, or glaciers? What is the difference between mountains created by tectonic shifts, volcanic eruptions, or humans? How does water, wind, animals, or time affect terrain? How does a river realistically flow through your swampy, mountainous, or urban environment? How big would a bridge be in rural Kosovo compared to Chile or Germany? Does it make sense here to have a tunnel, or would they instead build a road around? What different types of islands exist and what are their origins?

Not everyone connects level design with geography and the design of vast open spaces, including how they affect connected elements like roads, bridges, or rivers. However, I spend many long, geeky nights chatting with artists and level designers about erosion patterns. Especially designing or crafting yourself in a vast outdoor environment requires a deep understanding of what makes particular terrain look the way it is. Even if you have terrain specialists in your team, you still need to know enough to set them a solid foundation, or otherwise, they have to change too much from your design to make it look and feel believable. Plus, for me it is a certain calming feeling to sculpt a beautiful piece of terrain.

### 2.2.5 Experts in Biology

After terrain, the next significant factor is knowing what grows on it and what lives here. Placing the correct fauna and flora is essential to make a believable world. Those facets do not stop with a few trees, types of grass, or wolves but include domestic animals and plants, small insect swarms, fish in the water, your classic wild mix of Norwegian trolls, and Irish leprechaun, and of course birds. In outdoor first-person games, a large junk of your screen is the sky, and birds are a great, and often cheap, way to bring your world to life. The same counts of third-person games, but then, of course, more focus on critters on the ground.

Which trees grow close to saltwater and which ones do not? What crop makes sense to grow in your season? At what heights do trees, bushes, and ultimately grass stop growing? Does it make sense to have tigers and cows live in the same forest? How far inland can you still use seagulls? What is the difference between Pacific and African palm trees? Do all domestic animals in your part of the world live in enclosures, or can some roam freely? What is the realistic ratio of predators and prey in your world? How many predators can you still spawn without losing believability?

During my second game, I learned some tough lessons from my director when I placed the wrong tree next to a saltwater coast and had some entertaining experience when the boar and tiger spawning ratio was off. Especially when you want to breathe some life in your world, you have to be very careful and well-versed. When you create a fantasy ecosystem, make sure that the balance between food and "consumers" seems right. Still, most games do not require a detailed wildlife simulation, and to be honest, a perfect simulation might not be enjoyable for the player. For example, I worked on enough games where there were almost more predators than prey. This crooked mix was all fine because especially showing the conflict between the two types brought the world to life. However, there is a fine line; once you cross it, it becomes funny at the beginning and transitions to ridiculous and then eventually frustrating. Lastly, please do not forget to add animals into urban environments, and I do not just mean a few rats, pigeons, pettable dogs, and cockroaches. Instead, I was thinking of memorable moments caused by the more elusive ones like foxes, raccoons, escaped giraffes, and mutated sewer crocodiles.

### 2.2.6 Experts in Chemistry, Physics, Engineering, Mechanics, etc.

After geography and biology, the remaining natural sciences are essential. However, in most games, they do not directly shape the majority of your world; they just exist and are mainly expected by the players, like gravity. Of course, physics plays a significant role and not just sci-fi or realistic games. However, you need to understand all the factors that define your environment's remaining rules for me. They can be helpful to explain some odd encounters or phenomena, but they are critical when you create puzzles. Please keep in mind that especially the interactive and simulated aspects of those sciences are very game and engine-dependent.

Can water extinguish a fire in your game? What happens if this 9-ton truck crushes into this flimsy hut? Is there a difference when I shoot a rope or chain, and what happens to the attached container? How do portals or time travel work in this world? How well do crates float in this game, and do the streams have a simulated currency? Can a giant rolling boulder crush an overconfident archeologist?

Yes, physics engines and other game-related features answer the majority of those questions. Still, for me, they are separated from typical game design ingredients because they are strongly defining the look and feel of your world. Consistency is key here, and I strongly advise you to stay away from one-use hard-scripted moments which break the rules expected by the player. It is always odd when in-game events can crash cars through house walls, but then your driven tank gets stopped by a rusty street sign. Unfortunately, I scripted enough falling trees in a game that otherwise had no large, destructible trees. Looking back, it was just odd. Available tech and time constraints are significant factors, of course, but especially modern games give us way more possibilities to create consistent acting worlds. Moreover, no, I do not mean every game needs to have destructible trees; there just should not be inconsistent exceptions.

### 2.2.7 Experts in Culture, History, Geo Politics, etc.

Social topics are other aspects that are fundamental to create a believable civilization and environment they live in. Every world-building level designer has to understand the fabric connecting the inhabitants of their world. We are talking about the balance between rich and poor, how gangs show their presence in the hood, or how the local populations show their love/hate to their overseas occupants. Also, how ravenous the local gang of alien toads celebrates their daily tea party.

How old is the location, and what are the significant events in its time? Who occupies the area, and how do they show it? What factions exist in your world, and how do they express themselves? How is injustice or oppression displayed at your level? What hidden global factions play a hidden role in the local conflict, and how can you still hint it? What are the details of an essential local ceremony, and what are the steps or preparations for it?

In my experience, it is a sign of a mature, experienced development team if they take their time to hash out their factions, non-player characters (NPCs), timelines, or cultural differences. If you do not do your homework, what makes your world tick, then at best, you end up with a very inconsistent experience. In the worst case, you keep running in circles trying to fix something which nobody understood, to begin with. Of course, it is impossible in most action or shooters to expose every NPC's background story to the player, and many unfortunately also do not care. However, as long as it helps an environment artist or designer dress the NPC's environment consistently, it is worth it. Finding the balance between defining too much or too little is high art, but a bit too much hurts less.

### 2.2.8 Experts in Level Design Tools

Of course, mastering your level design editor is one of the primary skills of any level designer. Sometimes it is a publicly available editor uniquely created for one engine like Epic's Unreal Engine or Crytek's Sandbox. Then many in-house engines have their editors and tools, and occasionally programs like Autodesk's Maya or 3ds Max are used as level design tools.

How can multiple developers work efficiently and frictionlessly on the same level at the same time? How well is any version control software integrated into the editor? Are there any ways for you to speed up the loading process? How quick and easy is it to create a simple combat scenario? How rich are the debug tools? How quickly can I test the level? How stable and forgiving is the tool? How easy is it to script complex prototypes with it? Can I easily export parts of the level in another software? Is it a level design exclusive tool, or how many other departments are using it too? How good and fast is the tech support for the tool and its future development?

The list of expertise is not in a particular prioritized order. However, I am always surprised how many level designers consider their advanced editor knowledge the primary and only skill they need. Please keep in mind that most better, modern editors are not crazy complex to learn anymore. They are stable enough, easy to collaborate with, and you can quickly and easily test your level. Of course, editor skill remains a key component in every level designer's arsenal. However, other skills step into the foreground, especially in the social and attitude realm, and many of them are way more difficult to learn than software.

### 2.2.9 Experts in Scripting

Next to layout and general editor knowledge, scripting is another primary level design hard skill. We are talking about basic triggers that turn on a light, spawning a group of patrolling AI, prototyping some wacky ideas with fire and turtles, or implementing the backbone of the entire game's mission structure. Then there is the occasional scripting of entire massive floating, wet, fully lit alien spaceships, which also act as the game's final three-stage boss fight.

What is the difference between text, visual, and "3D" scripting? How do I keep my script clean? What are good and what are useless comments? What nodes work well over the network and which require extra safety measures? Do I need to add extra buffers or other backup scripts to ensure the original intentions work 100% in every circumstance and platform? How well do I have to script to become a senior level designer?

I have worked with some insanely creative and impressive scripters who managed to get the best out of occasionally questionable engines. I know some level designers who created scripts that made professional coders blush because what they have created was not supposed to be possible. On the flip side, I know accomplished senior level designers who do not script well or do not like it—and that is fine! Specialization is not a sign of weakness, but to harness your strengths and make them work within the team's context. I love to script, and I think some of my bigger visual ones became company internal memes. It is a daunting topic initially but incredibly rewarding once you have some success.

### 2.2.10 Experts in Layout and Arrangement

The definition of layout is to arrange or lay out parts. As I have stated previously, we level designers are masters of arrangement and creators of exciting, cohesive experiences. We might not know the individual ingredients like an AI character, weapon, crate, or a tree as good as their original creators, but it is our job to know how well they work best combined. Of course, we must know each element by heart. However, one of the few key aspects of a great level designer is to see the totality of all the elements combined in our levels, including guidance and flow through this carefully crafted entirety/experience.

What AI archetype works great or bad with an attack dog or sniper? How do I ensure that the player does not miss that cool animation on top? In what other crazy ways can I combine the wingsuit and grapple hook? How can I make the medkits stand out more in the current environment? Can I expect the players to know the combination of truck, C4, and vehicle-takedowns? How can I improve the flow through my space without changing the number of cover objects? Can I retouch the lighting without affecting difficulty or player leading? Will the players know that this is a good spot for sniping and drone gameplay? How else can I use those art assets in a different context to cover up the flaws in a different modular art kit?

I am always amazed about the creativity of the level designers when you let them loose. They create sections that feature the wildest combinations of environments, game features, any art elements, or AI. Undoubtedly, it is one of the most prominent expertise of level designers, and it is the one most people think of what defines a level designer. Of course, the topic is a bit more complicated, and therefore I will cover the whole topic a lot more later in this book.

### 2.2.11 Experts in Progression and Difficulty

Every level has its internal progression, and it is part of the game's progression. It gets more complicated when levels shuffle around during production or look at very open game structures. This unpredictability means you as a level designer not only need to be well aware of your level's position within the difficulty curve, but you also need to know how to adjust it quickly. Level reviews and playtest become key components during this process.

How difficult should the game be in total, and where do my levels fit in? What are good and bad ways to make the experience more difficult or easier? When should I start to worry about balancing? How can I avoid frustration and confusion for the players? What testing tools do I have? How many playtests do we get? Where within the game's progression are my levels located, and what does that mean?

Designing an initial plan for your game's progression is easy. However, I've yet to work on a game with no cut levels, locations switched around, features got shuffled or cut, and then the playtests still proved us all wrong. The same counts for the progression within levels because iteration is not a sign of a bad initial plan, but if done right, it shows improvement, humility, and growth. The difficulty is to keep the original good intentions intact, despite all the changes. It does not matter how you start; it matters how you finish. I've worked on games that were primarily successful because the blend of all its facets was spot on, despite similar games with more resources but noticeable shortcomings in their mix and progression. You noticed it when most of your friends loosely agreed when a game became stale.

### 2.2.12 Experts in Art and Technology

Just making a fun game is not good enough anymore, especially in the AAA games industry. Games have to look good, and that certainly includes squeezing the maximum out of your engine and technology. However, the only thing which trumps fun and beauty is performance. Nobody cares if your game is the most captivating experience if it does not run smoothly.

Do your assets look good in the shadows, and if not, how can you avoid large encapsulating shadows? What is my maximum AI count, and how can I "fake" a larger amount? What are my streaming limitations, and what does it mean for level design? Do I have an overdraw, drawcall, or polygon limit? What are the best-looking shaders you have access to, and how could you incorporate them to stunning effect? What are the strengths and weaknesses of your art and tech team, and how can you, as a level designer, make them only shine?

I think the last question is one of the most important ones. I have worked with some world-class artists and tech developers, but no team was ever perfectly staffed or had no weaknesses due to human nature. We level designers rely so much on those two departments that I firmly believe that it is our responsibility to support them as much as possible. If, for example, the art team does not have many good organic artists but brilliant hard surface ones, then do not push for substantial outdoor terrain levels. If you know your engine is not the best to make large patches of shadow look great, then make sure that your chosen time of day is not making it worse. You all need each other to make the best-looking, most fun, and smoothest running game.

### 2.2.13 Experts in Creativity and Fun

Being experts in creativity and fun sounds like a no-brainer; we are designers for games, after all. However, you do not follow a simple, mysterious methodology, and suddenly you are super creative and know how to make the most "fun" every time. However, there are a few methods that at least prevent the worst. After all, basic creative concepts, avoiding the most boring/frustrating aspects, and combining it with some staple always-prepared ideas go a long way. I often rely on those basics because nobody serious can always have the best ideas for everything.

What are your go-to methods if you are stuck creatively? What are easy and quick modifiers to create more ideas? What are your big no-goes to guarantee at least a solid foundation? If a mission just does not get exciting, what are your default backup solutions? What are your handful of basic game, mission, or layout ideas which you can use as a base in a pinch? What are your standard questions/patterns to hopefully find the right answers if a level is just dull and unexciting?

We all have our moments where we shine, but they are unfortunately not the everyday norm. I recommend constantly looking out for patterns, refining our backup ideas, thinking about solid foundations, knowing what to avoid, and improving the processes. What we cannot expect is to be the always switched on brilliant creative masterminds. I mean, some do believe they are, but they do not last very long. I think a quote from Chuck Close best sums it up: "Inspiration is for amateurs. The rest of us just show up and get to work. If you wait around for the clouds to part and a bolt of lightning to strike you in the brain, you are not going to make an awful lot of work. All the best ideas come out of the process; they come out of the work itself." Or in other words, "Amateurs wait for inspiration, designers go to work."

### 2.2.14 Experts in Time and Work Management

At least in the AAA game industry, levels or missions are rarely made in days, sometimes in weeks, but mostly it is a matter of months. If you count in iterations, debug phases, re-works, and general maintenance, it is not uncommon to work on a level for years. Now hopefully, you do not end up working on the same level non-stop for so long, but that only means you probably work on multiple levels. That is why time and work management is such a fundamental skill for level designers. As you have seen in the breakdown above, it is not about scheduling your daily work—no, it is about planning and pacing your work effort over months, if not years.

From start to finish, how long does it take to finish the different stages of your level? What could go wrong, and how much buffer do you need? What are my current blockers, and when and how do I communicate them to my leads or managers? When is the right time to put in the extra effort, and when is it best to recharge your batteries? Do you have a task list, and how often do you update it? What does my manager need from me to support me efficiently? How can a manager help me? How can other developers help me, and how can I help them?

With enough production experience, you can answer most of the example questions above. The more often you go through an entire production cycle, the better you know how to manage your own time and workload over the years and months to come. However, if you don't have that experience, ask others in your team. Do not make the mistake and just stay silent. You show more seniority if you ask for help, than staying a quiet junior. Another important factor is well-timed, clear communication without drama. The more right people within the team communicate effectively, the more information is available to make better estimates, which leads to more actions than time-costly reactions. If you have everyone in your proximity focusing first selflessly to remove blockers for others, then you have an excellent production foundation, team work, and can manage your work with a lot less stress.

### 2.2.15 Experts in Diplomacy

Lastly, we are briefly covering the already mentioned diplomacy angle of a level designer. However, it is not that simple because you have to foster relationships with many people. It starts with your closest contacts, like your feature team. Then you have your level design peers and peers in other departments. If you are lead, director, or maybe senior, then you have people "under" you. Then there are the more distant contacts or departments, people directly "above" you and the ones even further above—This is not a small order.

I have a strong tendency to establish rapport with certain groups better than with others. Everyone in the industry knows a few people who seemingly rise in their careers effortlessly because they might be brilliant to report upwards, despite arguably lacking hard skills. Then, few are not great to report upwards but are carried by the team because they deeply respect them as great leaders.

I worked with enough developers who had solid hard skills but seemed to struggle with the social ones. It appears unfair that you can make a career as a level designer without being as good as they are. The reality is it is not unfair per se because social skills, especially in any team context, will play a more significant, not a minor, role in the future. The fact is you will struggle in your professional life without soft skills in any team bigger than one. In my experience, more people were let go due to lacking soft than hard skills. Therefore, I put extra emphasis on them in this book as well.

# Section II

# Production and Social Skills

# 3

# *Level Design Production*

This chapter aims to give you an overview of level design productions and their different common steps. I will introduce typical AAA production and go in more detail about the different steps. Lastly, I will detail work pace and effort, essentially avoiding tiring yourself out too fast, and from personal experience, how I experienced certain mental health issues and how you hopefully can avoid them. I firmly believe all those aspects are essential for a smoother and healthier level design production.

## 3.1 Overview of Level Design Production

### 3.1.1 Introduction

The primary reason shipping games is such a highly regarded professional "currency" in our industry is that you know what to expect. So you know when to focus on what aspect and avoid as much waste of energy and nerves. It all comes down to pacing yourself as much as possible, so you have the strength when needed.

Therefore, understanding the different stages of production is crucial. However, no game production is ever the same. There are too many factors ranging from project type, team composition, funding, time, team seniority, game scope, company philosophy, studio situation, and many more. It is a very complex matter not only concerning the initial setup. However, so much can happen during production, such as budget cuts, developers leaving, project direction pivoting, and industry-wide paradigm shifts. It would take too long to list all the unforeseeable possibilities.

Essentially it means there is no clear-cut standard, and therefore I try to keep the different level design production phases below as general as possible. Many companies give them different names, have more or fewer steps, and even studios working on the same project treat them differently. I worked on sequels where the production steps were different from their predecessor because the new people in charge changed and saw things differently. Those changes are often for the better, but still, I believe the steps I list below are as universal as possible for AAA action game level design and likely similar for many other game types. Keep in mind that below I am talking about ideal cases, because for example, in reality, you rarely reach a perfect alpha for big AAA projects on time. Also expect that indi or mobile game development to be even more vastly different than what I outline below.

### 3.1.2 Initial or Pitch Phase

Nobody should think about individual levels or maps during this phase because the focus is on the broader game itself. Overarching elements like high-level gameplay, unique selling features, original art direction, business/marketing plan, and the game-wide narrative are at the center of attention. Essentially it is everything that is required to get an early pitch signed. I could reluctantly call it a concept discovery phase, but I am cautious because I heard the phrase also used for certain pre-production phases.

It can include an early estimate of the number of levels or missions, with maybe a few key examples. However, any high-level details or examples are not necessarily binding and only function to sell the pitch. It should include a first guestimate about the game's playtime and, of course, what types of levels you are thinking of.

You should have a good answer for questions like: Is it an open world, or consists of separate maps? Is it singleplayer, multiplayer, or co-op? How strong is the online component, and how much offline?

DOI: 10.1201/9781003275664-5

As a level design director or lead at the end of this phase, you should understand how the game could be structured or split into levels and how they could look like. Nothing is set in stone at that point, but it should initiate the first constructive conversations with art, tech, narrative, and game design. The goal is to have a solid, theoretical, prepared foundation to build on for the next step. Most importantly it should get everyone excited about the project, especially whoever pays your bills.

### 3.1.3 Pre-Production Phase

The goal of pre-production is to get production-ready. During this phase, developers should have finished all the main planning and documentation. Typically, it is a very intense prototype and benchmark phase. Ideally, you should be confident that if you go into production, you are ready and keep experimentation and surprises to a minimum. The experiences during this phase are crucial for managers to make estimates for production. The learnings also include observations about team chemistry and the resulting future team composition.

Essentially this means all the tools are ready, the level designers know how to make great levels, artists know how to make beautiful objects, and game design is confident that their mechanics will be fun and unique. Certain companies have gates and pitches to complete to get a green light for the final production budget approval.

The following high-level or blueprint phase happens ideally at the start of pre-production. Any bigger master design documents like game or level design are the foundation for more detailed documentation like the individual levels. Therefore, the documentation phase further below is a fundamental part of it, but it is typically more at the end of pre-production.

### 3.1.4 High-Level Phase

Some companies also call it the blueprint phase. If it is a linear game, you hash out the high-level idea for each level, the order of levels, and how they fit together in the game. If it is a less linear game, then the main core missions should be addressed with some early concepts for less relevant side missions. If the project is huge, it is not unusual to split up such phases in multiple chunks, like regions of the game world or different game stages. Still, if you split it, there should be a master phase or a wider umbrella encapsulating the smaller ones.

This step commonly happens during an offsite with the core team's directors, which can last for days, if not weeks. In my experience, the result is many filled-out tables covering as many high-level aspects for the whole game as feasible at that given time.

Each mission or level should have an internal production name as a reference. You should have an answer for the high-level narrative for each level. Set the gameplay focus for game and level design, especially what unique mechanics are featured or introduced in each level. The map's location and what key locations it contains should be determined, same as the time of day if not open world. I highly recommend having early discussions about technical risks or challenges. Ignoring them too long is very dangerous because it might ruin your creative dreams and is not helping anyone.

Most importantly, the reason for each level or mission's existence should be very clear! What is the unique, memorable aspect of each map, or why do we have it? If a level only exists to drive the narrative forward, how else can we boost it with some unique gameplay moments or a very cool, unique environment? Every level or mission should have a severe value for anyone to later work on it, and especially worthy for players to experience it. You should make early production estimates and see if they are actually doable with your expected resources. Cutting maps now is cheap and relatively painless.

In an ideal world, you can give the results of this phase to the level design leads and teams, and they can easily fill in further details following this blueprint. However, there is no ideal scenario, and game development is inherently complex. The truth is that such a plan is crucial to have a foundation for wider teams to start working and planning, but like any plan, it needs continuous adjustment—after all, no plan survives the first contact with reality. Even the best directors will not develop the perfect plan in a few weeks, defining the foundation for years to come. Be especially worried if directors believe they can come up with the perfect plan. Accept change and iterations—within limits and up to a point, but more about that later.

Typically, such high-level or blueprint phases happen at the beginning of pre-production or ideally shortly before. It is always tricky to get all the directors and other important people in a room for weeks, but the process is fundamental. The later in production you have that phase, the more likely production will get very messy, and you will find fewer issues. In my experience, most problematic productions did not have a solid high-level phase or restarted that phase again and again late in production.

### 3.1.5 Document Phase

It is typically time for the level designers to get involved at that stage because before, it was mainly directors and leads. As the name suggests, it is about writing the documentation for the individual, upcoming levels.

The amount of detail, type, and content of documentation heavily vary between projects and companies. Additionally, it also depends on what directors and leads expect. Even the used software and document style heavily varies. I've started my professional career writing huge Word documents and scribbles on paper. Then, later on, it was a bit of Excel sheets and lots of PowerPoint presentations with the additional support of SketchUp, Photoshop, and Visio. Lately, other projects work more in Confluence or even directly in task-tracking tools like Jira. My point is that level design documentation is continuously evolving and changing, but you can be sure that it will always include some maps, pictures, and text. However, regardless of the format, type, or use of software, the level design documentation has two key purposes.

The first purpose is to sell your level—it is a pitch document foremost. After all, only if you get approval for your level design, you go into production with it, and your primary medium is your document and commonly a presentation. Therefore, your documentation needs to convince all the stakeholders of your level, like peers, directors and leads from multiple departments. However, typically you do not create the documentation alone. Commonly for bigger projects, you work together with at least environment/concept artists and potentially also narrative and game designers. Everyone needs to buy-in that this level can go into production.

The second purpose is to communicate the level intentions to QA and QC. Ideally, they use your documentation to base their walkthrough tests on, instead of creating their own test plans based on what they think the level is. However, this also means you need to keep your documentation updated throughout the production, and maintainability is typically the pitfall of level design documentation.

However, I have dedicated a special chapter about level design documentation later in this book, with more details.

### 3.1.6 Production

This phase is typically not a real phase because it is simply way too big and long. It makes more sense to break it down into alpha, beta, and reaching gold, with their further steps in between. However, the start of production is a vital milestone.

### 3.1.7 Skeleton Phase

As the name suggests, you implement the "skeleton" of your level into the game engine. However, the primary focus for it is technical and production preparation but now it is not theory anymore, it is now happening in your game engine.

First, you create the physical foundation for the level or world, with primarily scale and distance in mind. An open world should have the space for the mission carved out even if it is just some flat terrain and loosely the right height and marked with a placeholder object. For non-terrain levels, it commonly would just be enough floor plates, stairs, and possibly a few walls to represent the intended floor plan's scale. If it includes some more fancy navigation types which are not available at that stage during production, then a teleport is just fine, or even a cheat to fly as a last resort. The goal is to judge the size and distance early on. Start playing the level early on and get a feeling for your space, so you can answer the essential questions now when it is still cheap to tweak the level's physical foundation.

Secondly, implement all the main objectives with placeholder triggers. Such placeholder triggers can be a simple proximity trigger or a button to press. No complex gameplay, AI, mechanics, events, etc., have to be implemented yet. However, the level should be playable from start to finish, trigger all the essential beats and be completable. If that means running through some invisible trigger and some placeholder objective texts change, then this is just fine. Once the skeleton phase is complete for all levels, it should be possible to play the entire game from start to finish, or at least other departments have a solid foundation to keep stitching it all together and have the right hooks.

Lastly, set up all layers. From now on, all other developers working in the same space have their correct layers. All naming/color conventions are established and followed right from the get-go. Changing them later is too much of a waste.

At the end of the skeleton phase, you can play through the whole level/mission; it is just incredibly bland, which is fine. Plus, all other departments have what they need to work on the level of space. Now it is a matter of filling all the still almost empty scripts and locations, but you have a solid foundation that already works from start to finish. More about the skeleton phase later on in this book.

### 3.1.8 First Intention Pass

The level's skeleton is not really creatively reviewable, at least not from a serious gameplay perspective. Therefore, the next step is to get the primary intentions across, so feedback makes sense and iterations are based on reason and less gut.

You would start adding the real gameplay elements, so far they exist already. So, for example, you add the to-be-killed VIP, but the (placeholder) object to destroy at the right spot, or have an early prototype implementation of your puzzle. Then you populate the level with an estimated amount of AI and their types, plus their enable triggers/conditions. Essentially you should have all the main gameplay elements of the level implemented. However, it can still be rough. Placeholders are fine if the actual elements are unavailable from other departments and it is acceptable if you only focus on the main intended path. Alternative paths, secondary objectives, edge cases, making it fool-proof, or any other additional ideas which popped up during development are not required, yet.

Secondly, you add all the supportive layout elements, but they can still be block-outs, depending on what is available at that production stage. AI needs covers, puzzles need environmental context, and vehicle sections need roads. Without fine-tuning in mind, it should be possible to play and traverse the entire level now from start to finish with all the intended gameplay ingredients; no more fake teleports or debug-ghosting. The layout intentions are clear, so if you want much verticality, add all layout elements at the right height, or if a section should have a lot of cover then place many blocks representing the right size and density.

The final goal is that creative reviews and feedback are now possible from knowledgeable reviewers like directors, leads, or peers. Sure, they can happen before already, but then many assumptions are needed to fill in the blanks. The reviewers have to be "knowledgeable" because too many unjustified assumptions/opinions can likely ruin the level for good. Also, it is fine that the level has to be played as the designers had it in mind, and not yet how a player would approach it because probably most of the level is not water tight. After all, it is a check if the intentions outlined in the level design document start to come together and not a stress test on how you can break the level.

The jump from first intentions, or sometimes called "first pass," to alpha is often big. This big gap is an old level design problem because any stage in between is difficult to quantify. However, many games have then a "second pass," or "pre-alpha" stage. I favor such a step because otherwise, there is no goal for weeks or months to strive toward. Still, it is important to define that in-between step clearly, or it just becomes a purely managerial or very weak level design stage. This in-between step is very game-dependent and requires careful planning with experienced leads, designers, and managers.

### 3.1.9 Alpha

The goal of the alpha milestone is to be content-complete. This means everything you planned to be at the level should be there. So this includes, for example, all AI placement, AI patrols, idle actions, lighting intentions, vantage points, cover, art assets, gameplay features, at least cinematic placeholders, or narrative elements. Alternative paths, secondary objectives, bigger edge cases, and especially known walkthrough breaks are all now considered. Essentially the level is refined enough that it is now external playtest ready.

It is important to mention that you can only bring a level to content-complete, if the rest of the game is feature-complete prior to this stage. After all, you can only add all the elements if all the ingredients are done, working as intended and you have enough time to implement them correctly.

It should not be easy to break the level, and you can get relevant feedback from directors, leads, or peers without anyone imagining all the remaining parts. It makes sense to have the first performance tests because your environment is very advanced, and you implemented all main performance taxing ingredients.

However, nobody should expect that the level will not change anymore after alpha. After all, at alpha, ideally, it is the first time anyone can get a feel for the totality of the whole game, including your level. Therefore, the feedback is now more relevant because they base on the game as a whole. Expect to change your level, add rooms, cut houses, move cover, rework AI, or even redo a large chunk of your level. Serious performance risks can also be another factor for potential changes. At that stage, alpha typically has no stringent performance goals, but if it runs very choppy or anything points in a very wrong direction, then you should make adjustments now.

Change is part of this iterative industry where it is impossible to predict perfect fun months or years ahead of time. However, changes have a limit, and they have to fit in available production capacities. Further on, feedback has to come in now fast, and it has to be precise, or your production capacities are shrinking fast to allow bigger changes. Further on elements like balancing, bug finding & fixing, and polish are just starting now.

### 3.1.10 Beta

The goal of the beta milestone is to have a "first shippable" version of the level and the entire game. It does not mean it is a great version of the game, but it would be "okay" if you had to ship it now. Meaning, bugs are still present, some polish is missing, and the balancing should be close to perfect, but the game as a whole is there as intended and well playable.

To complete this stage, it, first of all, goes through an iteration phase based on the alpha feedback. Feedback comes in from various internal, sometimes external, and playtest sources—bug testing and fixing increases continuously to root out as many bugs as possible, especially walkthrough breaks. A big focus is to address anything which would give the game and the levels a lower rating or a negative review. More and more content and features are finalized and polished. Balancing is an additional strong focus because all the major components are in place post alpha, and from then on, ideally, avoid any more extensive changes. Unfortunately, it is not uncommon that more considerable local changes still have to be done because only around alpha can the game be seen as a whole. Massive AAA productions are so inherently complex that you can only give certain feedback once you see the complete picture.

Another huge aspect of beta is performance and compliance with third parties. For example, at beta all platforms should run smoothly with the targeted frames per second, fits into memory, no more warning messages, or the levels load fast enough. The compliances are related to third parties such as Microsoft, Sony, or Nintendo which require games to fulfill certain standards, like a maximum level loading time, minimum frame rate or online connections work. This book won't go into such details, because it is more a production, tech, QC/QA, and management topic, but they need to inform level designers about potential consequences. Every platform and every generation of them has changing compliances, so it is important to stay aware and up-to-date.

The phase toward the beta milestone is also when cutting features or big level segments can ultimately cause more production issues. It often takes more effort to patch up the cut in an already well-developed coherent game than leaving it in and maybe massaging it so it does not stand out too much. This realization is an important consideration, or in other words: cut early.

### 3.1.11 Closing

Closing is a crucial phase within the beta phase. During this phase, the number of creative changes reduces, and slowly production and tech become the sole decision-makers if a change or task should still happen. The goal is to aim for a shippable product, and ongoing changes are then counterproductive. Any feedback, especially from directors, has to get approved by production with a risk assessment by technically focused developers.

For level designers, this means that the number of tasks is getting less and less, while at the same time, the number of bugs should increase because of intensified testing. This transition is commonly a fluid process and is handled differently by companies, but it is necessary. It can be painful to accept an end, especially if you keep having so many wonderful ideas. Therefore, it is vital for most creative-type directors to eventually step away from the project before the game is final. It is normal that close to beta, more and more developers step away from the project, and only the most reliable and tech-oriented developers focus solely on bug fixing without introducing more problems.

### 3.1.12 Until Gold

From beta to the final gold master, it is essentially a strict version of the previous closing. Any tasks or changes have to go through a strict approval process by project and tech stakeholders, but they should remain the exceptions. Typically, only glaring issues from playtesting, low-risk balancing adjustments, or very high-up director feedback should still go through. Avoid at all costs any changes which could introduce more issues or bugs. The time of introducing new features or experimenting with new ideas has ended long before during beta already. Otherwise, you will have a hard time shipping a solid product.

Therefore commonly, only senior or tech level designers are left to work on the levels. Of course, the primary focus is only on bugs and, depending on bug numbers and risk, not even the small ones anymore. This process intensifies until you run out of time. Close to the end, fix only critical bugs, stop messing around, and hopefully, you will end up with a great game. Often many developers are already working on the day-one patch in parallel.

### 3.1.13 Closing Words

Keep in mind that what I have described above is an ideal case. In reality, nothing runs smoothly, and every company or project has different interpretations. For such complex and long-lasting projects, I can only recommend prioritizing the mindset of resilience over highly efficient, yet often fragile, plans.

Things will go wrong because perfect predictability is impossible, so learn to roll with the punches and adjust your plans when necessary, but not too often. The balance between stability and flexibility is the high art of game development.

## 3.2 Work Pace and Effort

### 3.2.1 Introduction

Making games is more a matter of years or at least many months, and therefore pacing yourself is fundamentally essential. Game development is a marathon (or even a few) and not a sprint. Unfortunately,

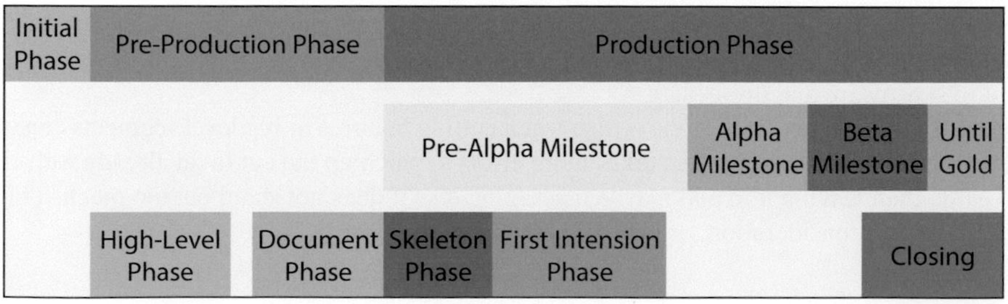

**FIGURE 3.1** The size and time of the phases are not to scale! The graphic should only show which phases are part of which overarching ones and how they are connected.

not every level or even every game you work on will be released, and that can understandably be very frustrating and taxing. I have worked on my fair share of games that were not released or had big blocks of my work getting cut. I had to fight with two burnouts, a lot of negativity, disappointments, and frustration. Therefore I would like to dedicate this chapter to those crucial topics and offer my personal view and, more importantly, my personal solutions.

It is also crucial to state that this topic does not cover any level design specific topics but game industry-wide ones. Still, I consider such topics to be essential, and they, of course, affect level designers, leads, and directors like myself. Also worth noting that those observations are my very personal views and opinions and that I am not a professional doctor or alike.

### 3.2.2 When to Push and When Not

#### *3.2.2.1 The Premise*

One of the key differences between a seasoned and a junior developer is that the seasoned one typically knows better when to push hard and when not. Seniors commonly know when extra effort is more in vain and when it pays off because they have already been through a few production cycles. To be clear, I am not talking here about extended periods of crunch (more about crunch below), but about investing extra energy, focus, dedication, attachments, cutting down longer breaks a bit, and maybe staying a bit longer just to finish the current task.

For example, you have the incredible opportunity to work on a level for a new game mode. That sounds pretty exciting, right? So you pour your heart and soul into this project to show everyone how great you are and that you totally earned it to be here. You are 100% dedicated, have passionate arguments about the mode and level, sneak in a few extra hours, maybe even come in on the weekend, and you are very much attached to your work. Then, surprise, after a few months of hard work, your level and the entire game mode get cut. Of course, you are understandably devastated. Sure, that sounds a bit drastic, but it does happen. Maybe it is not always so huge and impactful, but comparably no concept artist expects that every sketch leads to the final product without any change or iterations.

Now I'm not advocating to have no passion, ownership, or attachment to your work. Of course, we need those; it is an essential part of our industry and a huge factor why it can be so fantastic. However, it is also a professional industry, with the final goal to create a product.

#### *3.2.2.2 When Not to Push*

The common mistake juniors make is that they push too early and then are too tired, lack focus, or are too frustrated/negative when the time comes. If you are new to the industry, you, of course, want to prove yourself, especially when it is your dream job, and that is perfectly fine. This fresh wind of energy can be quite uplifting and refreshing to see for the more seasoned developers. It is one of the reasons why I genuinely enjoy working with juniors myself.

At the start of a game's development cycle, or during pre-production, companies ideally hire most developers. Now, as a newcomer, you want to prove yourself. The problem is that this is the phase that is defined by the most experimentation and preparation. This fact means many things will be thrown away or completely changed.

Again, do not attach yourself too early to a product, feature, idea, or level. Enjoy that you might work on a wide variety of prototypes, ideas, or level concepts. However, it might sound cruel, but never get too attached to anything, especially in this phase. Sure, you might have liked a cut candidate, but more importantly, try to understand the reasons for the decision within the bigger picture. Take your time, learn why something did not work out, and use that learning for the next one. Post-mortems exist for a reason, and even if you do not have an official one, at least have your own.

It is worth mentioning that this is not only a pre-production topic. It can easily come up again during long extended periods toward alpha or beta. Too long milestone periods of +9 months can often lead to fatigue if developers do not pace themselves or the team does not push well together as a unit. This issue is another reason why I am an advocate of in-between milestones such as pre-alpha.

#### 3.2.2.3 Leadership Responsibility

For leads, directors, and managers, it is vital to clarify what can easily be thrown away, what is just an experiment or likely to change a lot. It all comes down to managing expectations, or in the long run, people will lose faith in you as a decision-maker. Always saying something like "This is it now," and yet it keeps changing, just builds up frustration and negativity among your fellow developers.

The best leaders I have worked with were transparent, owned their mistakes, and communicated expectations clearly. They tried to cut as early as possible and felt genuinely sorry, especially when bigger changes had to happen. Sometimes one of my better levels had to drastically change for the greater good, but in the end, I felt okay.

Once, two-thirds of my levels got cut because of a very high-up managerial deal or agreement. Of course, I cannot go into details, but it hurt, and I wished I would have known earlier, or at least I expected my leads to stop me in time. Unfortunately, I know too many seniors to whom such cases happened too often, and they stopped pushing or stopped developing any passion for game development. In such situations good leadership and seasoned management come into play to prevent such avoidable cases.

#### 3.2.2.4 When to Push

Okay, now when is a good time to push? Essentially every time there is a deadline, or team-wide high stakes are involved. Classic deadlines are any bigger milestones like alpha, beta, and the occasional pre-alpha, a build for a press event, or pre-production benchmark. Still, keep in mind that especially pre-production benchmarks or anything for early press-release builds is vastly throw-away. They are essential, no doubt, and everyone involved will learn a lot from them, but it is common for most of the level design work not to transition into the final product.

I limited it to "team-wide high stakes" to prevent a too personal attachment. Losing something as a team is a lot less taxing than if it is all on your shoulders. The less drastic impact is especially true if you have a good team dynamic and health. All major milestones are, of course, team-wide deliverables.

Lastly, make sure you rest after such pushes. Recharge your batteries, or you will run out of fuel. Just because you might be young or drink many energy drinks does not mean you can do it forever. You know best how to recharge. Some do it best alone; some need social contacts, and some need to travel or cuddle with their cats and dogs. It is all very individual but make sure that you do, and take your time. This restoration is not something that happens in a few days. Without the energy recharged, you cannot do the next push well, and you will wear out.

### 3.2.3 About Crunch or Overtime

This industry has a bad reputation for applying a lot of crunch or overtime. So, let us cut it short: avoid any crunch at all costs. In the vast majority of the cases, especially extended crunch is not worth it, or instead, it is counterproductive. A well-rested developer performs more efficiently on average 8 hours than a developer who continuously works 10+ hours a day. It gets even worse when we consider the

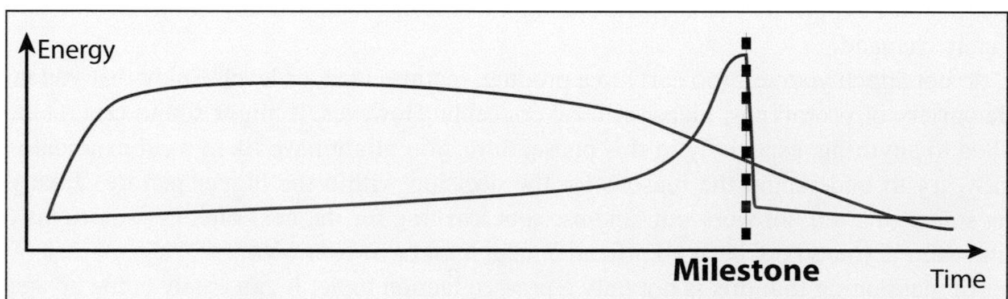


**FIGURE 3.2** A simplified example: Common junior energy pacing curve (red) vs. common senior pacing curve toward a milestone.

social aspect. Tired people are commonly more snappy or more likely to behave in less ideal ways. At that moment, the team, and not just the individual, has to pay the price.

However, I might say something potentially controversial now, but crunch can have its place. It needs to have a clear purpose, a team event, time-wise limited, not forced, and never be part of the managerial plan all along. It needs a clear important purpose, like any push (see above), so overtime does not become the norm and stays an exception. It should be a team effort because we create levels with other departments, and supporting each other is vital in such taxing times. Limiting the crunch time is absolutely crucial because otherwise, it quickly gets out of hand. Especially people with families need to plan and need time for their partners, kids, and pets.

Management that expects crunch time, or even plans with it early on, is one of the banes of our industry. Therefore, it should never be forced on a team or especially selected individuals—This includes any kind of "soft" or peer pressure. If you cannot crunch for any reason, then it has to be fine. Almost every management-rooted crunch is because of bad planning, but it is a lot more complicated case by case. Still, avoiding crunch is by most means the responsibility of production and management.

I will not detail the legality or crunch or compensation because it differs vastly between companies and countries, plus it certainly is not my expertise. However, it is an industry with much passion. I can fully understand when people want to do overtime, just to push their own work. You should be proud of your achievements and contribution, so it is reasonable to want the opportunity to put in some extra time and energy. Still, it should come from you and your team, and more importantly, you need time to rest in between. Especially weekends should be well protected, never crunch several days consecutively, and after two to three hours extra, the extra effort drastically wears off.

### 3.2.4 Let's Talk Burnout

As an important disclaimer, I am not a psychologist or therapist, so when I talk about burnout then it only comes from my own personal experience, and nothing more. However, the topic of mental health is too important to skip; not just in our industry, but we have too many cases because we are not talking enough about it. Therefore, I would like to share, just a bit, my own personal story and what I've learned out of it.

In my first ten years as a developer I had two burnouts, in times where the topic was not very common. Back then the perception was more that it was a sign of weakness, which made it even worse, of course. For weeks I could physically not touch a keyboard, severe sleeping problems, or got anxiety just moving the mouse cursor close to the editor icon, just to list a few symptoms. For a level designer, like myself, that was devastating and I was close to quitting the industry.

What led to my burnouts was, of course, connected to a large amount of overtime. I have worked for months ten to fourteen hours a day, including most Sundays. However, what was for me personally the primary kicker, was the lack of appreciation. I was not in a safe environment where I believe receiving the necessary support and protection. I felt I was the only one who could do it, I was the best one to do it, and if I felt tired, it was because I was not strong enough—a vicious circle.

Luckily later I had leads and managers who helped me with the desperately needed change. If you have a burnout, then I do not believe that a few weeks or even months vacation is the cure because you just go back to the old work and habits. Wide encapsulating change in your work is fundamentally important to cope with a burnout. For the first burnout I switched my level design specialization and team. For the second one I moved to another city, country and studio, with a strong effort to find a better work-life balance.

Now, I know it might sound controversial again, but I do not believe that working a lot of long hours alone leads to burnout. It can certainly accelerate it and often plays a crucial factor. However, the common expression that a person will burn out because they work a lot is not correct in my opinion. Of course, every person is very different and this topic is immensely complex, but with the right genuine support you can work long and hard, for extended periods of time without burning out right away. I would not recommend it of course, but it is possible.

The key factors to prevent people in your team from burning out are a good mix of appreciation, support, and protection. I'm proud to say that after my burnouts, to my knowledge, nobody in my teams ever had a similar experience, despite the occasional crunch periods. We, as a team of managers, directors, and leads, made sure that their work was very much appreciated and gave them all the support. We sat together with them a lot, tried to cater to all their needs, were there for them, and never left them alone. If it got too late or they wanted to work too much, we forced them to go home. It sounds dramatic but sometimes that is required. You need managers who prioritize your mental health over the product. After all, you can't make a great product if your people are burned-out. I believe that the primary responsibility to prevent people from burning out lies in the hands of the closest leads and managers. They should be the people the developers can trust and talk to, and they are the ones creating such a safe and supportive environment.

If you start to feel constantly tired, don't enjoy work that much anymore, start to get depressed, or are constantly negative, then I recommend you seek help. It might still be very early, it might be nothing, but just talking about it with someone is the first necessary step. Find someone you can trust. Denial is a tricky slope and by definition we don't notice it ourselves. It is never a sign of weakness to open up about mental health issues! Do not convince yourself that you have to show strength overcoming it yourself. I thought the same and it didn't end well.

### 3.2.5 About Work-Life Balance

I wrote a lot about pushing yourself, overtime, and even burnout. Therefore, I would like to share a few thoughts about another crucial yet more positive aspect: a healthy work-life balance.

I had to learn it the hard way, but if you make your work your life, then your life goes to hell if your work has extended dark times—and it will happen because nobody is in happy, fulfilling production for his entire life. I don't want to paint a dark picture, but it is better to prepare for some tougher production cycles or phases.

Now everyone is different. Some have families; some live alone, some are introverts, and some are extroverts. We all recharge our batteries differently, and that is perfectly fine. However, my vital recommendation is to develop such a balance. Young developers especially can walk into this trap. If their dream job completely absorbs them, they might forget about that vital balance.

Now it is too easy to tell everyone to do some sport and go out with people, we are all very different after all. However, I do recommend looking for some physical, creative and social activities in your free time. It does not mean everyone should run to the gym or join a soccer club, but even some extended walks can make a difference. Moreover, as horrible as the whole covid-19 crisis was, I think most nerdy introverts started to miss socializing. Everyone has a different balance, but we all need to have some. Too often, we underestimate physical and especially mental health. Otherwise, you end up like me, paying thousands of dollars for physiotherapy and burnouts. I wish I would have listened more in my beginnings, and now I only hope I affect at least one person.

# 4

# *Diplomacy of Level Design*

As I stated previously, one of the three pillars that define a level designer is being a diplomat. However, I am well aware that this is not one of the defining aspects when most people think of level designers. Therefore, I would like to explain this pillar more in this chapter and introduce why it is so important to be a good diplomat. Later on, in this book, I will detail how to hone your basic social skills to be an actual good diplomat.

Diplomacy here is all about building rapport through empathy with other surrounding developers. Not everyone is an absolute master of social skills or a charismatic extrovert. In my experience, instead, the opposite is the case, and this is okay. It is unrealistic to expect that everyone is friends with each other. However, it is reasonable to expect that egos can take a step back, communication is respectful, and the primary goal of everyone is to support each other.

However, suppose you define yourself as a level designer only by your hard skills. In that case, I can guarantee you that you will very likely have a very rocky road ahead of you—trust me, I speak from personal experience. Therefore, I am writing this chapter based on my journey and hard lessons learned, and I hope you do not have to repeat them.

## 4.1 Level Design in the Center of Production

### 4.1.1 Introduction

In this subchapter, I explain why it is so essential for us level designers to be diplomats. That might be clear for some more seasoned developers, but I am always surprised how little this aspect is known to juniors or students or some very reluctant seniors. Still, it is not easy to comprehend the full complexity of an AAA development cycle without experiencing it a few times.

Therefore, to showcase the complexity at least a bit, I will list what departments level designers commonly deal with during a production cycle. It is important to note that this is a showcase based on my experience and will likely differ for other companies, projects, studios, and level designer specializations. I mean, it keeps changing for me as well for each new project. Still, even if it is different, it will show the diplomacy requirement very well.

### 4.1.2 Departments Level Designers Work With

The following Table 4.1 covers the multiple production phases and lists which departments you work with. This table is written from the perspective of a level designer and not from a lead or director.

When I write "directors" or "leads" below, I mean the direct director/lead responsible for level design primarily. However, it often includes the director/leads of other departments such as art, narrative, game design, creative, audio, game code, or production.

I applied no priority to the sorting of the table entries. The main difference here between "Close Collaboration" and "Occasional Collaboration" is that the first group is the one you very likely work with a lot on a very regular, if not daily. The second group lists the ones you might only work with infrequently, not very long, or maybe not at all.

Let us also keep in mind that each entry here is usually not a single person but typically an entire team of two to ten people. I hope to reinforce the understanding that level designers work with a vast number of people throughout a development cycle.

DOI: 10.1201/9781003275664-6

**TABLE 4.1**

This Table Shows Who Level Designers Collaborate Closely With, and Who Occasionally With, at Different Phases of Development

| Production Phase | Close Collaboration | Occasional Collaboration |
|---|---|---|
| Pre-Production | Level Design Peers Environment Artists<br>Game Designers<br>Technical (Level) Designers<br>Leads/Directors | Concept Artists<br>3D Artists<br>Production/Managers<br>Audio Designers<br>Game/AI Programmers<br>Engine/Tools Programmers<br>Animators<br>QA/QC |
| Document Phase | Level Design Peers<br>Environment Artists<br>Narrative Designers<br>Leads/Directors | Concept Artists<br>3D Artists<br>Technical (Level) Designers<br>Production/Managers<br>Engine/Tools Programmers<br>QA/QC |
| Skeleton Phase | Level Design Peers<br>Environment Artists<br>Technical (Level) Designers<br>Leads | 3D Artists<br>Cinematic Scripters<br>Production/Managers<br>Game/AI Programmers<br>Engine/Tools Programmers<br>QA/QC<br>Directors |
| First Intention Phase | Level Design Peers<br>Environment Artists<br>Narrative Designers<br>QA/QC<br>Leads/Directors | Concept Artists<br>3D Artists<br>Cinematic Scripters<br>Technical (Level) Designers<br>Game Designers<br>Production/Managers<br>Audio Designers<br>Game/AI Programmers<br>Engine/Tools Programmers<br>Animators |
| Alpha Milestone | Level Design Peers<br>Environment Artists<br>Narrative Designers<br>QA/QC<br>Leads/Directors | Concept Artists<br>3D Artists<br>Cinematic Scripters<br>Technical (Level) Designers<br>Game Designers<br>Production/Managers<br>Audio Designers<br>Game/AI Programmers<br>Engine/Tools Programmers<br>Animators |
| Beta Milestone | Level Design Peers<br>Environment Artists<br>Narrative Designers<br>QA/QC<br>Leads/Directors | 3D Artists<br>Cinematic Scripters<br>Technical (Level) Designers<br>Game Designers<br>Production/Managers<br>Audio Designers<br>Game/AI Programmers<br>Animators |
| Closing | Level Design Peers<br>Environment Artists<br>Technical (Level) Designers<br>QA/QC<br>Leads | 3D Artists<br>Cinematic Scripters<br>Production/Managers<br>Audio Designers<br>Game/AI Programmers<br>Directors |

Further on, there are clear patterns. In my experience working in a more agile-oriented production, you work a lot, almost daily, throughout the entire production cycle with fellow environment artists, QA/QC, and of course, level design peers. Narrative and technical (level) designers are a close second. The consistent daily presence of leads and often directors should not surprise anyone since it is essentially their job to keep a tab on your work. Production or manager folks are typically in the daily mix, but I moved them in the "occasional" category because it is often not more than morning stand-ups if you work in sprints.

The "technical (level) design" entry in the table needs some brief clarifications because not every company works with specialized roles. Instead, you can see them as any technical role which bridges the connection between the code and level design department. So, it can also be a tech-savvy game designer, a design-oriented programmer, or a fellow level designer with tech affinity.

I sometimes split the leads and director in the "close" and "occasionally" because directors are not as frequently working with the level designers throughout the production cycle. Some directors work even less with the team directly, not necessarily by choice but because of their busy schedule or too large teams. Still, I always enjoyed it and hope more directors find the time as well.

### 4.1.3 Closing Words

So again, I hope it is clear now that we level designers work a lot with many people from a wide range of disciplines. Now, let us not forget that it is widespread in the industry to work in international teams where developers come from various countries, cultures, and backgrounds. Then add additional aspects like age, seniority, gender, sexual orientation, social status, and it quickly gets very complicated. Co-development with different teams/studios in remote locations and time zones or, generally speaking, work-from-home adds additional challenges. Lastly, I did not include politics and religion since, in my opinion, they should stay out of the workplace when possible.

Therefore, unfortunately, friction, misunderstandings, and miscommunications in some form or shape are pre-programmed. However, it is in anyone's interest to reduce it to an absolute minimum. Therefore, central developers like managers or level designers have an additional special responsibility to keep the overall work climate as welcoming, friendly, smooth, and productive as possible by applying diplomacy and empathy.

## 4.2 How to Work with Different Departments

### 4.2.1 Introduction

First of all, there is no strict difference between dealing, for example, artists or programmers, because they are all humans after all. Therefore, I am starting with diplomacy basics, and first, then transition to more department specifics. The more distinct departments are not covering clichés like all programmers are quiet, math geniuses, and introverts, but instead should give you a brief of their craft to develop further empathy.

### 4.2.2 Game Developer Diplomacy 101

#### *4.2.2.1 Do Not Treat People How You Like to Be Treated*

I heard it a billion times: "I am great working with people because I treat them how I like to be treated." What can go wrong? In reality, people do not want to be treated like you do because they are not you! You might like to communicate directly and not shy away from curse words, while others can consider this as off-putting or even rude. Add, for example, a bit of cultural difference to the mix, and you quickly have some friction and a bad reputation on your hands.

Instead, treat people how they like to get treated. It sounds way easier than done because you do not know them well enough when you start working with someone. Therefore, the first step is to really get to know them. This step takes time and requires effort from you, and realistically is only applicable to people you work with a lot.

It goes a long way to get to know them outside of work. For example, go out for some drinks, visit the cinema together or spend some time having casual chats around the desks or common rooms. Have some private, maybe even candid, conversations with them. If you open up more about yourself without consistently annoying them too much about your private life, it increases the chance they will open up about you, too.

For example: Are they more the visual or text type? Do they prefer bullet points, examples, or both? If directness is not their preferred way of communication, how else can you adjust? If they have a strong stance about certain social aspects, then you better avoid such topics or certain phrases/words. By default I strongly recommend staying away from politics, religion, and arguably sport.

Ultimately, in my experience, the best way to bond with someone and get to know them better is to go through a development cycle or at least a tougher milestone. United experience is a great glue and offers many possibilities to get to know each other. Moreover, it is okay if not everyone becomes friends with each other, but at least you know where you stand and how to treat them.

Now, what is the case when you do not work with someone very often or only meet them a few times? This case is where it gets tricky, of course. My main advice is to be very careful, be overly respectful, and not make assumptions. Assumptions are the mother of all screw-ups! You need to know yourself well enough to know how much you can be yourself with strangers. Therefore, you have to swallow the bitter pill and avoid being too much of yourself when you meet people for the first time. With time this can change but remember those bad first impressions have the ugly tendency to stay.

#### *4.2.2.2 We All Sit in the Same Boat*

I cannot stop stressing to people that we all sit in the same boat. I mean by this expression that it is in all our interest to make a great game. However, if the boat sinks, then we all drown. Yes, that sounds a bit drastic, but too often, developers only think for themself or for a few people around, but the great work of an individual, especially at the expense of other developers, does not make a great game.

If one rows in a different direction, then the ship/production slows down, and if more row in the opposite direction, the ship/production might get off course, rotates on the spot, or causes a standstill. Of course, the ship/production needs a clear direction which typically comes from the top, but the team also plays a part in it. Further on, even if the higher-ups are rowing too, the majority of the rowing/productivity comes from the team.

It all starts with a team-oriented mindset. Selfishness is not a way to succeed in a team and is often rooted in an unsafe work environment or personal insecurities. We all need to help each other and see the complex totality of our product in order to succeed.

This mindset is especially prevalent in the common small pairs of environment artists and level designers. The old belief that, for example, gameplay trumps art is a matter of the past. Modern big AAA games need to both look and play great without sacrificing one or the other. Technical limitations are the only real showstoppers.

For the level designers, in the context of diplomacy, we need to support our fellow developers as much as possible so their work can shine in our great levels. Again, it comes down to understanding that we all sit in the same boat with the same goal. If that means we occasionally have to jump over our shadows and welcome other developers' needs and desires, so be it. After all, if we do it, they hopefully return the favor, but it should start with us level designers since we row in the very middle of the boat.

#### *4.2.2.3 About Empathy*

The original definition of empathy is to understand and share the feelings of others. In the context of game production, for me, it is about understanding the other surrounding departments. Their impact, the struggles they go through, what is easy/difficult for them, and generally show interest in their craft. Essentially, what does it mean to walk in their shoes? For us level designers, this is especially crucial since we interact with so many different departments, and our requests and work can significantly impact their work and sometimes well-being.

Now, it does not mean that we all have to become, for example, programmers, concept artists, or writers. Still, some basic knowledge about their craft goes a long way. For example, the understanding that a specific feature request means a major time-consuming code restructuring or that you cannot simply drastically change the lighting in a complex piece of concept art. It is often enough to believe them and listen and potentially change the request accordingly.

Another classic example is the narrative designer's request to implement lengthy radio dialogs in a level. Then we usually do not have the space for such a lengthy non-combat moment playing in the background. However, once we take our time and understand that this dialog is crucial for a character arc, then we might not brush it aside easily. This outcome, of course, requires us to understand enough about narrative to understand the importance of a character arc. With that knowledge, we can work a lot easier with the narrative designer, find some compromises, and clearly feel we have their best interest in mind. Ideally, they also understand your struggles from a level design perspective and try to help as well. Empathy, after all, goes best both ways. Still, do not be afraid to be the first one opening up, and if you help them understand better level design concerns, try your best not to come across as condescending.

The more we show true interest in their craft, the more they hopefully are interested in our needs and desires. Also learning about other departments is exciting in my opinion, too. Only together we can find solutions which make every involved party happy, and ultimately a better game.

#### *4.2.2.4 About Teamwork*

It is easy to say that you are a great team worker, and it is easy to state that a team has great teamwork if everything goes smoothly. However, true teamwork shows when things do not go as planned. Especially when team internal dependencies, blockers, or unbalanced workload show up, things start to get challenging.

Therefore, if everyone as the top priority is genuinely and knowingly trying to unblock and help everyone around, you have a productive foundation for solid teamwork. If you are done with a task or have time in between, then check if anyone needs your help, or maybe you can even unblock them because they wait for you. In an Agile production environment, such blockers are typically heard and said during the daily stand-up. However, ideally, you work so closely with most people anyhow that they know it already.

If developers do not prioritize unblocking or supporting another, we are back to the selfishness I wrote about previously. Development starts to stall, frustration rises, and likely nobody will want to support or unblock you anytime soon, too, but it should not go so far.

Again, we level designers have a special responsibility because we implement a lot of the work from others. It is not uncommon for other developers to wait for our work to keep moving forward, especially if you work closely together in the same tight space of a level.

### 4.2.3 How to Work with Artists

#### *4.2.3.1 Environment Artists*

In my recent agile-oriented development experience, it is common practice to pair up a level designer with one or more environment artists. In practice, daily, you might see and talk to them more than your partner/pet. Therefore, it is crucial to develop a good rapport with them.

However, it is not surprising that this collaboration is often loaded with friction potential due to the arguably opposing goals. Both of you work in the same space, while one has the goal to "just make it fun" while the other "just make it look pretty." This limited, selfish, and outdated view is the core of the issue. Instead, to achieve a functioning and harmonic collaboration, both parties should have the goal to "make a great level" while respecting each other's strengths. After all, you all sit in the same boat.

Getting to know each other, empathy, and teamwork are the keys to success here. Learn a lot from each other, not just the basics of the craft but also about the intentions, possibilities, and especially the limitations of each other to find succeeding compromises without sacrificing one or the other. Weak compromises do not help anyone. Only if you truly know the other developers' possibilities can you find good compromises. As a level designer, it goes a long way to genuinely try to help the environment artists to make a great-looking level and making them shine; since then, they will more likely return the favor. I have yet to find an artist who wanted the level to play badly.

I recommend learning some of the basics of art like composition, commonly used software, color theory, or set dressing. Even just going through some tutorials or watch some videos can go a long way. Such knowledge or practical experience sets a good foundation to develop empathy toward artists.

Working with other "3DArtists" is very comparable to working with environment artists.

#### *4.2.3.2 Concept Artists*

Traditionally, if concept artists provide concepts for locations, their goal is comparable with one of the environment artists. However, the problem is that they often do not work as closely with level designers like the environment artists. Therefore, empathy for each other is harder to achieve. Therefore, ideally, before they start painting, sit together with them, plus the specific environment artists, and explain your level design intentions. Why you have done what, but also listen to their thoughts. The more you can sort out before anyone spends time on a concept, the less frustrating iterations you hopefully have.

Lastly, it is essential to talk to the artists to understand the essence of the concept. For example, you usually don't have to place every crate exactly where the artist painted it. However, they might have wanted to indicate something specific here like a transport/storage location, specific colors, or just wanted to fill the space with objects and had no better idea due to the time pressure. Concept art rarely has to be followed exactly one to one, but that assumption is the primary friction. The good news is that you can easily avoid it with friendly, empathetic chats before and after the concept's creation. If such chats are not possible for whatever reasons, then at least try to talk to the respected leads/directors.

### 4.2.4 How to Work with Narrative

#### *4.2.4.1 Narrative Designers*

Even if your game only has a light narrative layer, I highly recommend regularly and closely working with narrative designers. After all, narrative elements like characters, world, or events can significantly impact your levels and you better want to be aware of them before it is too late. Like the environment artists, I do not advocate for trumping one or the other; instead strong collaboration, teamwork, and especially empathy are key here again.

Try to understand why the individual narrative elements are important to the designer. For example, I suggest having chats together with the environment artists because all three of you are the key people who bring your game world to life. It should be everyone's best interest to tie together art, world-building, and level design harmonically.

I recommend learning some of the fundamentals of narrative, like character arcs, character bio creation, or narrative structures. Such basic knowledge is quick and easy to learn and sets a solid foundation to develop empathy with narrative designers.

#### *4.2.4.2 Cinematic Scripters*

The primary goal of cinematic scripters is to implement cinematic cutscenes or events in a level. Therefore, you both work closely in the same space, which by default can result in friction. The primary issue is with the transition between cutscenes and gameplay. Commonly both parties agree on a hand-over in the scripts, which guarantees a smooth and stable connection. However, expect that such events can break during production. For example, a cutscene causes a walkthrough-break because it does not trigger the end-event, or the cutscene assets are still present in the gameplay space. The first case is especially frustrating in bigger reviews and trust me; it still happens more often than we like to with many smart people involved.

Of course, ideally, the engine and its tech allow for robust implementations. However, if there are any such crucial issues occasionally, I recommend adding backup scripts/commands that can trigger your gameplay after a cutscene and vice versa. So even if a broken cutscene would normally mean a walkthrough-break, you can still jump ahead and review/play your level section. It can also speed up testing in case the cutscene is non-skippable initially. To be very clear, this is not a sign of distrust to your fellow cinematic scripters but instead only a tool to reduce friction and frustration. The same, of course, counts for similar problems and solutions, not just connected to cinematics.

### 4.2.5 How to Work with QC/QA

QC, QA, or DevTesters are one of the most important members of any development team! They are crucial for any quality product, and the sheer complexity of modern games makes them an absolute necessity. It does not matter if it is a large remote team or embedded testers in your local team. However, realistically the ones you interact with the most regularly are the local ones, of course.

Empathy is your best approach with them. Their job can often be quite frustrating, testing the same content over and over again, especially early on when it is typically not the smoothest ride. See what you can do to make their life easier with workaround scripts, jump points through the level, or decent documentation. The more you involve them in the level's creation, the better, because then, their level test cases will be more accurate, and soon they will know your level better than yourself. Additionally, they might have some good early insights from an advanced player's perspective. They will figure out the wildest/exotic ways to play and especially break your work, and it is your job to adjust/fix accordingly. I always enjoyed having a good relationship with them, having the occasional late-night laugh, and just watching them with awe as they breeze through our levels. They are irreplaceable, especially when it comes to pushing the difficulty limit to the absolute highest bearable limit. You know if something is off when they start relying purely on exploits or get bored on the highest difficulty.

### 4.2.6 How to Work with Other Level Designers

Essentially how do you work with your peers? They are your primary source of knowledge exchange and legitimate level design feedback. Empathy between each other should be a given, even though not guaranteed. If there is good harmony, collaboration, and teamwork among the level designers, it is a blast to work in such a team. Playtesting each other's levels, sharing old stories, exchanging new concepts/ideas/editor-tricks are all fantastic and highly recommended.

However, the relationship can quickly be tainted when strong egos, unfairness, insecurities in a non-safe work environment, hiring policies, or "friendly competition" come into play. First of all, this is not a problem unique to level designers, of course. Instead, it is a matter of studio/company/project culture and would go outside this book's scope. Still, I would like to leave a few brief hints to the individual developer.

- Self-reflect a lot, and do not be afraid to ask for 360-feedback to get a check on your ego. It is important to get an outside perspective as long as strong egos can come with denial. However, make sure that you can truly trust them and not play their own manipulative game with you.
- If you plan to join a new company/studio/project, do your research about their work culture. Do they provide a safe work environment where you can speak up about unfairness, express your insecurities, or otherwise cover touchy private subjects? Of course, every company will tell you that they have a safe work environment, but the industry is small, and the potential toxic truth is coming out eventually.
- Do companies hire for hard skills only and how truly important are team fit and social skills for them?
- Team internal, professional, and friendly competitions are loved by many misled bosses to squeeze the best out of their teams seemingly. However, instead, the opposite is the case. They can often be the foundation for growing toxicity, frustration, and jealousy. Respectful and friendly collaboration always beats friendly competition.

### 4.2.7 How to Work with Managers

Managers or any production staff come in many forms and shapes, but first of all, they hopefully are not your controlling enemy and on the flip side you should not treat them like your secretaries. Their responsibility is to overview aspects like the timeline, team progress, communication, project/team representation, budget, and ideally, team health. Therefore, they rely on your input to be effective, not the way around. Of course, if they spot a problem or negative trend, they will approach you, but again their data is based on your communication and collaboration.

Keeping them out of the loop, not giving even rough estimates, fighting their processes, treating them as pure task managers, or only using them to order pizza is not helping anyone! It might sound drastic, but none of the listed examples were novelties in my experience, and unfortunately, there are way more. Empathy, teamwork, and realizing you all sit in the same boat is once again the beginning of successful collaboration.

I can only recommend learning as much of the smaller managerial tasks as possible, especially when it comes to meeting organization, note-taking, task database updates, or helping to carry up pizzas. For example, I consider it embarrassing if level designers (or any other developers) refuse to set up meetings or even pretend that they do not know how to do it.

### 4.2.8 How to Work with Game Designers

Unlike public belief, game designers are not the ones designing the game. In my experience, game designers are primarily responsible for developing features and mechanics. No design "caste" stands above the other. However, the lack of this basic collaboration principle is often the root of friction between the level and game design.

On the one hand, it is "easy" to have an opinion or idea about a feature or mechanic. However, the actual skill lies in making a good idea work well in the game's context and project's/team's limitations. If you find a game designer who can do that while also being a great respectful collaborator, keep him close because they will be a great ally. Working with such designers can be a fantastic experience because you can truly inspire each other to new heights without any egos involved.

On the other hand, it is "easy" for game designers to have demands on level design to use or showcase their features mechanics how they see it. In reality, the implementation of any elements in the levels should be the responsibility of the level designers.

However, playing stubbornly without empathy will not bring anyone forward. You need to understand each other's needs, problems, and intentions, or otherwise, you end up with an "okay" level with a "bad" feature or a "bad" level with an "okay" feature—none is acceptable. If the design goals, even after extended respectful talks, do not match up, then I recommend making a calm step back and respectfully involving the specific leads and ultimately directors. Starting a bad relationship with a fellow designer is not worth it—you sit in the same boat after all and will do so for a while.

### 4.2.9 How to Work with Programmers

Directly working with programmers can be a very pleasant experience. I will not repeat common clichés since most of them do not match up with reality anyhow. However, one root of such perception is that programming and level design are often quite alien to each other. Especially when you, as an absolute non-programmer, see those strange-looking, endless colorful lines of code. Teamwork and realizing you sit all the same boat should be clear by now, but empathy is, therefore, a bit trickier.

Learning how to code, even just a bit certainly won't hurt. However, more importantly you should learn how annoying—yet vital—seemingly less productive activities like merging, refactoring, or cleaning-up code are. Hopefully, by working with coders over an extended period, you should learn how they tick individually, what annoys/excites them, and show some understanding of why you cannot get your feature-tweak the next day already.

The better you establish rapport with programmers, the more you will be surprised how much is truly possible to achieve with code. Otherwise, you will hear many times "No," and you honestly will not have the knowledge/expertise to argue against their statement. Not that every programmer is moody, of course, but a good relationship opens doors and increases motivation to look twice for a solution.

### 4.2.10 How to Work with Audio

You do not need to be an audiophile person to enjoy working with the audio department. Unfortunately, there is a famous saying in the industry: "Everyone forgets about audio." Even though it is not really true anymore, one origin of this issue is that they can first start implementing a lot of their work when the levels are relatively stable and done. This reality means that, by definition, it happens at the end of the project when everyone scrambles to still get as much work/tweaks/fixes as possible.

It should go without saying; that you should take your time to support them during such stressful times because they usually have it worse. The earlier you can involve them, the less pressure is on both departments at the end of the project. There was a drastic difference in player experience when a level was designed together with audio or without! After all, you two might inspire each other for some cool audio-based ideas. You can prove everyone wrong by thinking about them from the very beginning.

# 5

# *Teamwork and Leadership Tools*

We have already established that level designers have to work with a wide range of developers and that levels are at the center of game development because here, most elements come together. Therefore, every level designer has the responsibility to be a diplomat and a leader because leadership at its core is about affecting people. So even a junior level designer has to learn about leadership.

Being a leader does not mean that you should rule with an iron fist and tell everyone what and how to do their job! Instead, it is about getting people inspired and motivated together with a shared goal and often this goal is set in your level. To say it in simple terms: Leaders are there for the people, managers for the project, and bosses command people around.

Still, please keep in mind that this is not a leadership book. However, regardless I think it is important to cover some of those few topics. Especially basic leadership principles, feedback, and decision-making are at its core, while the remaining subchapters are more good practices to unite teams. All the practices listed here are ones I deployed very successfully in the context of level design. I hope to inspire anyone to tweak them further or develop their own.

Lastly, even if you are not a lead or director, I can highly recommend reading a few good leadership books. You do not have to read many or continuously reading such books, but one to three certainly will not hurt. Ask around your trusted colleagues about what they recommend, and look around what might fit you.

## 5.1 Basic Leadership Principles

### 5.1.1 Introduction

Again, this is not a leadership book, and I do not attempt to write a complete list. However, I strongly believe that the few general topics I will cover in this subchapter are genuinely helpful for every developer and, in particular, level designers. All of the ones below did help me a great deal in my career, and I wished I would have known them earlier in many cases.

### 5.1.2 Make Others Better Than You

I absolutely believe in the mantra: "You should always make others better than yourself." When I learned it for the first time, I was in a quite competitive environment, and I initially struggled with the idea, but then it started to make all sense.

First of all, typically, you can only advance in your career when someone can take your old spot. Therefore, to grow, you have to become replaceable, and if you train the one who replaces you, the better.

Secondly, people who genuinely felt that you try to make them better, the ones you seriously invested much energy to grow, will care back. If they are no sociopaths, then they should not forget what you have done for them. It might take some time, but they might honestly return the favor—the industry is small after all. Further on, it is a good start for them to trust you back when you trust in their abilities.

This principle does not only apply to leads or directors but to any position. Even juniors eventually have some knowledge to share or at least can show genuine interest to help others.

I know that this idea can be tricky for alpha personalities or people with insecurities, especially in a competitive or unsafe work environment. However, I firmly believe that is one of the better

DOI: 10.1201/9781003275664-7

principles to live and work by. You might have to jump over your shadow, and it will not be easy, but it benefits you in the future! Start small and grow it with time; remember, it is a win-win for all parties involved.

### 5.1.3 Own Your Failures

If you make a decision and it fails, it is crucial to stand up for it. Especially if you are deciding in the absence of your peers or team, it disqualifies you as a leader or trusted peer when you blame others instead.

It takes much strength to admit failure, especially if it is a big mistake or you are in a leadership position. However, we are all humans, and humans make mistakes. People do not rise to responsible positions without ever making mistakes, except they are narcissists living in denial, and then you should stay away from them.

Ultimately you have a choice between either becoming someone who always blames others and has excuses or someone who shows strength by admitting screw-ups. Regardless, you will gain a reputation in your team/studio/company and ultimately in the industry, and it is not good to be known to excuse and shift blame. Especially if you are in a higher-up position, blaming the ones below is a clear sign of weak leadership. If you cannot take such responsibility, then you should not be a leader.

However, you do not show weakness if you admit a mistake and take responsibility for it. It is a good indicator that you own your insecurities or have less, to begin with. You can only gain strength and respect among your peers, leads, and team members, but you lose it all if you excuse yourself.

### 5.1.4 Acting Under Stress

Being under bad stress is not enjoyable but often unavoidable in our industry. Sure there are always people who can never get stressed, but let us talk about the majority of humanity. Many people under stress start to talk louder, make irrational decisions, make no decisions, and make more mistakes because they rush or panic.

You cannot tell a stressed person to calm down and then expect them to actually calm down. That is not how it works. However, how the perception others have about you is crucial and, by default, more valid than you think you acted. If people tell you that you panicked, then accept it; fighting the perception of your people around is just making it worse. Telling people that they felt wrong about you is gaslighting. In my past, I had to deal with some very toxic narcissists who continuously lived in a world of denial while acting like headless peacocks.

The key is to find the right balance between overreacting and not acting at all. Forcing yourself to either slow down or make a decision can help to break the cycle. After a while, you learn what the signs that you are getting stressed are. Learn what triggers your reptile brain, and you act and talk with less rational conscious decisions. It is a fascinating topic, and I recommend you research it, especially which ones affect you and how.

Especially anyone in a leadership role is under special observation by the team, and they expect a sane, respectful, reasonable, and calm acting leader, especially in stressful times. Leaders are mood multipliers. If the leader is panicking, it negatively affects the entire team because they either start panicking, too, or lose respect for the leader. However, if done well, a good leader reassures the team that they are in good hands and that everyone can remain focused. Still, lying about it is even worse, so do not even try because it will all come out eventually.

A continuously panicking or very stressed developer runs the risk of getting a bad reputation up to the point where nobody wants to work with them anymore. It gets worse if they are in a leadership position and when they add more excuses. However, let us relax and remember that everyone can have a bad day or even a week. Apply empathy to others and remember that tragic or stressful events in private life can significantly impact work stress. Staying calm and reasonable is not something you can learn by reading a book or watching a video. Instead, get real-world experience and grow with it.

## 5.2 About Feedback

### 5.2.1 Introduction

I believe that giving and receiving feedback effectively and respectfully is an art form. After all, giving and receiving feedback is at the very core of most game developers' daily communication. Yet, it is one with many potentials to cause misunderstanding, friction, and it can severely harm production. As leads and directors, you continually give feedback since it is part of their job description, but in reality, every member of the team receives feedback and gives it in the context of teamwork. Ultimately the goal of every feedback should have the purpose to improve the recipient, not just the product. If they can't learn from the feedback, then likely they will do it again and that only results in wasted time and potential.

### 5.2.2 Giving Feedback

#### *5.2.2.1 Clarify Feedback and Opinion*

First of all, make it very clear if you give an opinion or direct feedback. An opinion can be anything from initial thought, impression, or just a hunch. It is totally okay to have an opinion about something because we often do things for the first time in our creative industry without being an expert on everything completely new. You would be surprised how many people consider themselves experts about all sorts of things without actually having experience with such topics. Opinions are by default open for discussion and do not become a task, except the receiver agrees with it. If you do not make it clear, then occasionally thinking out loud becomes a lot of unnecessary tasks, which can cause more confusion and frustration.

On the flip side is feedback, things you expect to happen or see as an apparent problem that needs action. Feedback needs to be clear, candid, set expectations, and easy to understand for the feedback receiver. Keeping feedback vague or you appearing very indecisive is equally causing confusion and frustration.

Of course, generally speaking, I recommend keeping feedback more for leads and directors and not necessarily for peers, except it is acceptable given the circumstances like a senior mentoring a junior. Otherwise, I recommend primarily giving opinions to peers.

#### *5.2.2.2 Feedback as Questions and Problems*

My preferred way to give feedback is to give the designer an open question or problem. This means a problem or question is not a simple yes or no answer. It should also include the reason why you have a problem or question. For example: "My problem is that we do not have enough cover on the left side, which results in less flanking possibilities on all sides." or "How would you create more flanking options on the left side because we appear not to have enough cover."

This approach has multiple advantages:

It gives the designer ownership of the solution. This ownership is crucial, avoiding designers feeling like "drones" who only have to follow orders. After all, why do you want to hire experienced developers if you do not care much about their creative solutions?

It creates a conversation between the designer and the feedback giver, potentially unraveling reasons on both sides, or creates a better understanding of why the designer has done certain things.

Adding the reason for the problem/question is ultimately teaching your way of thinking and designing. It shows that you care about the designer's thoughts and want them to improve.

It helps with cross-department communication because not everyone would have a level design solution, but of course, still a valid one. Often you can better fix some level design problems with, for example, art, game design, or code.

When you see a problem, the classical issue is that you instantly want to give a solution, especially as a lead and director with more experience. However, holding back with giving a precise solution is key here. Think about what you would do, then think about the issue, and first then announce the issue as a question or a problem. Start the question with "How," "Why," and "What" to keep them open. It takes practice, and occasionally you snap back by saying the solution immediately. Do not worry; it happens to all of us occasionally, but it is the mindset that counts, self-reflect when it happens, and you should always keep trying to improve.

A closed question or problem is when the answer is essentially given or a simple "Yes" or "No." For example: "Don't you think we need more cover on the left side?" or "My problem is that the door is not 10 meters to the left." Arguably, it is a bit better than a precise task, but often not by much.

The tricky part with working with open questions and problems is that if they are too vague or, no communication exchange happens, the designer comes up with a solution that is very different from yours or might even cause further issues.

First of all, if the solution fixes your problem or answers your questions, but it is not what you had in mind, I recommend accepting it. If not, your open approach might be considered hypocritical since you still want exactly what you want to happen. You might want to be more careful and precise next time.

Secondly, if it does not fix your problem or causes new issues, be open about it, and potentially admit that you did not word the problem or question precisely enough. State a new open problem/question, but explain it in more detail, maybe narrow down the window of solutions/answers or try to come up with a solution together.

Giving example solutions or answers is another problem because designers are often inclined just to do what you suggested. It might be okay working with less experienced designers, dealing with a very complicated issue, or when the time is limited. Then giving "bad examples," which explain the question/problem better but is clearly not applicable, is not ideal either. Then sometimes, designers either get frustrated because they do not know how to move forward or get confused. In the end, it depends on how the receiving designers prefer it. Some truly work better with examples, some do not like them, and a "bad example" might be okay in a pinch. As I stated previously, get to know the people you give feedback to and adjust to them.

### *5.2.2.3 Direct Tasks*

Open questions and problems are the ideals for most cases. However, below is a list of situations when a straightforward task is perfectly fine as well.

Less experienced developers might benefit more from direct solutions because they lack, by definition, the experience to come up with good solutions. This case applies to most junior developers, but I would be careful treating them like that all the time. Therefore slowly give them the option of ownership and problem solving as well. However, if you notice that they struggle, give them a supportive hand with some more precision from your side, but make sure that you clearly explain your reasoning, so they learn something from it.

A bug should never be a big discussion because the problem is clear. Of course, finding the right solution can require a conversation or when the bug is huge/complex.

When there is a tight deadline ahead, close to a milestone, or generally during the closing phase, I recommend switching to direct tasks with clear solutions. During such times you do not have the time and the luxury for much time-consuming creativity. It is not empowering, but the project has priority in such times.

Some developers simply do not like open questions or problems. They just want to know what to do and act upon it. That is perfectly fine and should be respected. However, on the flip side, some developers think that open questions mean their lead/director doesn't know what to do. At the end of the day, it comes again to get to know your people.

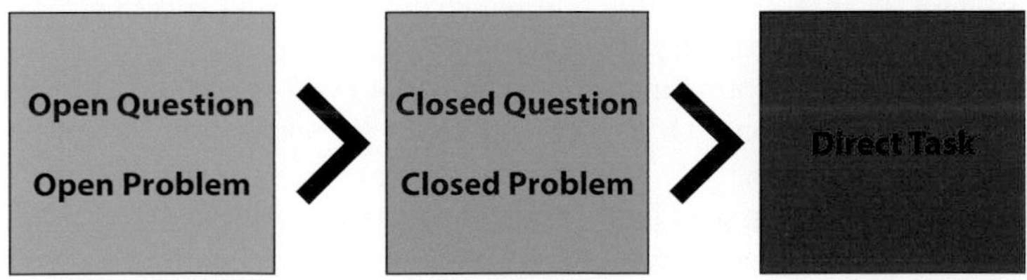


**FIGURE 5.1** Open questions/problems are better than closed questions/problems, and direct tasks are the least ideal.

### 5.2.3 Receiving Feedback

#### *5.2.3.1 Introduction*

If the feedback is all reasonable, you had maybe even a good chat about it, and you react well to it then everything is fine of course. However, for many people receiving feedback can be tricky if they are, for example, stressed, the feedback is very confusing, badly worded, easy to be misunderstood, personal issues are affected, or some egos are involved. Once the "less ideal" feedback is stated then you can't do much, except react professionally. Jumping the gun, overreacting, getting very emotional, or even responding in a personal way isn't helping anyone.

Below I have listed a few ways, based on personal experience, how to deal with problematic feedback.

#### *5.2.3.2 Written Feedback*

Getting written feedback can be one of the most difficult ones because you do not know the writer's mood, you lack context, you might not be in the most positive mood, and all that can lead to assumptions. However, even if you know the writer or only believe you know them, it can lead to misleading assumptions. Therefore by default, try to battle your urge to make any assumptions.

Suppose you are lucky and work with professionals. In that case, the written feedback is primarily factual. It includes enough context of how/why they came to the feedback and other circumstances like what people were present, time constraints, bugs, or misunderstandings on their side. Be especially careful if the ones who write you feedback are not developers close to your content! By definition, they lack the in-depth knowledge you possess and will consequently likely make unfortunate assumptions, which can lead to less-than-ideal feedback.

If separate note-takers wrote the feedback and not the ones giving the feedback, then in my experience, the feedback is more neutral and hopefully still factual. However, it often misses the important context of the how and why. On the flip side, if the feedback-givers wrote the feedback, then it could be less neutral, or at least you might feel like it. Ideally, it includes a bit more context, but it might make you think that the feedback had an agenda or that there is something more personal. Especially if there is a history between the two of you or any other reputation/rumor topic is involved. It should go without saying that such an urge is human, yet we need to resist it as much as possible. The increase in remote work and co-developments between studios make it even more important.

If you sense a lack of neutrality, not factual, or lack a lot of needed context, then you still have a few options. After all, any feedback can be useful, and you can only benefit from it, even if it is potentially wrong.

First, try to read it as neutral as possible by removing any personal perceived tones or wording. Essentially you have to translate it into something which does not lead you to any negative assumptions. Trust me; it is not easy if the first read already puts you in a bad mood.

Secondly, it makes sense to ask other people to read the feedback. It is common and recommended to involve some leads, directors, or managers. The second pair of eyes might spot something which can lead to assumptions, misunderstandings, or miscommunication, just to keep it as professional, neutral, factual, and contextual as possible. They might be more distant from the topic and make more reasonable assumptions. Together, you can decipher the feedback into something more useful to improve your level or reinstate your feeling to not act on all or most points. However, do not influence them in any way before they read the feedback, or their support is likely negatively tainted. It is in your best interest to keep them as neutral or positive-oriented as possible.

If you already even have the slightest sense that some negativity might taint your written response, then involve a trusted lead, director, or manager. If the stakes and blood pressure are high, I highly recommend that they write the feedback instead. Their title alone carries more weight than yours typically. They are potentially more distant from the topic and are more experienced in responding to complicated feedback. However, if you respond, then at least let them read the email before you send it. Any of such steps is not a sign of weakness or inexperience! The opposite is the case because it shows maturity. Any harm you could cause with a response based on assumption not only likely backfires to you and your reputation but also your peers and team.

#### 5.2.3.3 Verbal Feedback

Now let us look at verbal feedback. The advantage of verbal feedback is that you should have the possibility for a conversation and you also have a lot more context.

The conversation aspect is crucial because it allows you to dig deeper into the reasoning of the feedback. Especially the "why" and the background of the feedback are key here because, after all, ideally, you learn something from it. Therefore in a healthy and safe feedback relationship, certainly ask for "why" and clearly show interest to improve further. Making one mistake should be okay, making it twice is not. Another positive side effect is that the feedback giver, hopefully with time, includes the "why" right away in his feedback or might even become more considerate with their comments.

If such a conversation is not possible, because, for example, it is a large review or not enough time, then try your best to get such vital additional information later on, potentially through your leads, managers, or director. If they reject such a request, or the additional information is unsatisfying, try to interpret it with peers or leads/directors, just as usual, be wary about assumptions.

If the feedback triggers any irrational responses, then first, of course, try to hold them back because you will not benefit from a very unprofessional reaction. However, controlling irrational responses is very difficult because often they are too strong or sudden to be easily controlled. Hopefully, you can make a genuine apology later on, and it helps you understand your triggers better. Then, the next time you sense such triggers are showing up or you sense hints in the conversation, it might allow you to counteract the reaction. Take at least three slow and deep breaths, which will likely just appear as you are thinking, and hopefully, it allows you to break the cycle or at least reduce the reaction. Now, I am not implying that everyone is constantly a rage-triggered, mentally unstable threat to society (joking here!), but we are humans. Humans can have a bad day, we have our baggage, and since I have seen otherwise the calmest zen people getting loud on rare occasions, I see it beneficial to mention here.

Now, you hopefully got the feedback's context, but the second advantage of verbal communication is explaining yourself. In many cases, it certainly helps the feedback giver to understand your point of view or, of course, your context and reasoning. Having a respectful, fair, constructive, and ideally, short argument about feedback should always be fine. Potentially the feedback changes based on what you say. However, you need to fight three urges: To excuse yourself, be too defensive, and to be too apologetic.

Excusing with less than rock-solid, factual, and short reasoning is just a waste of time, and the same counts for always long, tiring defensive arguments. It makes you look bad, gives you a bad reputation, and likely annoys the feedback giver to the extreme point that they prefer not to communicate with you anymore. If you do not like the feedback, but you have no seriously good counter-argument, try to learn from it, maybe ask for advice for the future, and then let it be. It should be okay to voice that you do not like it but that you accept it. Trust me, dealing with uncomfortable feedback with professional manners gives you more credit than trying to excuse yourself. However, from your perspective, it might not appear a lot like an excuse, of course, but as a valid argument. Again unknown triggers or under-dwelling insecurities can play a factor here, unfortunately. If you sense that you talk too much or get too defensive, try to take a step back. You would be surprised how well it works if you ask your conversation partner, "Hey, am I too defensive?." Any too strong defense can get especially counterproductive if people see you as passive or defensive aggressive. In no scenario do you benefit from a scenario where people avoid giving you feedback! Therefore occasionally genuinely ask how people perceive you, even if you think everything is right because denial can be strong for reasons. More importantly, if the feedback is negative, do not continue with even more excuses. Take it by heart and seek help if you struggle.

Lastly, let us talk about being too apologetic. Classically the root is somewhere between insecurities and wrong expectations, but I do not want to dive too deep into my pseudo-therapist role. It is also not the end of the world, compared to excusing yourself. However, you might be seen as insecure, which by definition is not a sign of strength. If the reviewer is a decent human being and keeps trying to reassure you that everything is fine, mistakes happen, and how could you know all of it, then try your best to accept it. I know it is not as easy as it sounds! See what you can do to open up, maybe during one-on-ones. Try to express your concerns, your expectations to yourself or others. After all, maybe it is all not that bad, and that is just your type? I know, especially if insecurities, knowingly or unknowingly, play a factor here, worrying about how others see you isn't helping. The best advice is to have several chats with the affected people and try to manage their expectations about you. If you know they should adjust, then maybe it helps you, too.

## 5.3 About Making Decisions

### 5.3.1 Introduction

You do not have to be a lead or director to make decisions. Even junior level designers have to make countless decisions daily. Easy decisions are not a big problem, by definition. Therefore I only want to write about difficult decision-making in this chapter. As a note ahead, most of what you can say about decision-making can also apply to acting in general.

### 5.3.2 No Decision

Making no decision is the worst-case scenario. A good decision is justifiable, by definition, even if it has painful consequences for certain people. Unfortunately, rising responsibility also comes with a rising expectation and duty to make the occasional painful decision. Especially undeceive leaders are a serious problem for the project and team morale.

However, just because you want to avoid making no decision, it should not result in rushed or "hip-shooting" decision-making. Instead, it makes you appear frantic, less controlled, unprofessional, irresponsible, and potentially insecure. I mean, sure, if the answer is dead simple because it is your field of expertise, and you know it certainly, then do not start adding artificial five-minute breaks. We are still talking here about difficult decision-making, after all.

It is okay to take your time, consult others, and gather enough information to make a grounded call. Still, there is no clear-cut time recommendation for how long certain decisions are allowed to take or a reasonable timeframe to make a verdict. Typically, you have a bit more time as long as not many people wait for it, it does not happen all the time, or it does not harm production.

If you make no decision, two things happen: You do not learn from it, and you potentially stall production. You will never know if your decision might have been right or wrong. Nobody benefits from it, neither yourself nor the team. Both consequences are problematic for obvious reasons. It is okay to ask for help. If you cannot decide, ask others because jumping over your shadow shows way more strength than the damage you do with not making a call! Additionally, it shows a healthy team dynamic if it is not continuously one-sided.

### 5.3.3 A Decision

Typically, two things happen when you decide: You learn from the positive/negative outcome, and production keeps moving forward. However, that negative outcome, especially on a larger scale, is why so many people prefer not to make any decision. However, there are a few ways to mitigate this issue and hopefully motivate people to make decisions.

The first one is a safe team environment where it is safe to make mistakes within the context that everyone can make mistakes. Nobody should be afraid to get punished or even fired if they make a bad call. However, such a privileged environment is no excuse to make a lot of hasted or unthoughtful decisions! Exploiting such a scenario is the reason why they can fail and vanish. Of course, making bad calls should not be the norm either. Still, if you did your diligence, involved others, tried your best to gather enough information, and made a call within a reasonable time frame, then there is rarely a reason for grave consequences. Likely most people would have acted similarly and ignored all the people who (easily) talk trash afterward or say "told you so." Sure, looking back, if the decision-making process was questionable, it is the primary starting point to take some lessons.

Secondly, if you have even the slightest doubts about the call, start establishing safety measures. Trust your guts, as long as they do not tell you to make any decision. Establishing a plan B, C, and D with the team/peers is the basic recommendation. Applying an adversarial mindset to your decision can be helpful by exploring everything which could go wrong and developing backup plans for all possibilities. Just make sure that it does not spike your insecurities and doubts, and you still make a call. Be open about your concerns and make everyone aware. The more eyes are on the upcoming development, the sooner you can catch it if it goes wrong. Potentially with enough people aware, the resulting damage is smaller than a stall.

If the decision turned out to be a bad one, you and others learned from it. That learning will reduce the chance for another bad call, and ultimately it helps you and others to grow. It is way more difficult to learn from only successes compared to failures. However, it is that burden of those huge impactful consequences which freeze us. I know it can be freakingly scary to make a tough call with an unknown outcome, even if you have the previously covered possibilities to soften the blow. So let us look at how you can hopefully make more right decisions.

### 5.3.4 The Right Decision

The key is having the right amount of information, enough experience, and some gut feeling. Having an opinion without experience is not a valid strategy! It might sound a bit harsh, but pretty much anyone can have an opinion about design. I do not believe in people whose opinion is always right, without enough knowledge and experience to back it up—neither should you.

Do not rush big decisions; ask people or do some research. Ask some questions which dig deeper into the problem you want to solve. Especially the "why" you have the issue is a good start or can you split up the decision into smaller chunks?

Secondly, if the information is not available yet, it is okay to make conditional decisions. Clearly state what exact information you are waiting for. For example: "If case A kicks in, then my decision is X, and in case of B, then it is Y." Then team members can act without you being present if the cases kick in. Additionally, it can be good learning for them. It is also reasonable to set a timeframe for how long you wait to decide if it is unsure when or if the information becomes available.

Thirdly, always state your reason for your decision to the team or present people. They might find a flaw in your logic so you can adjust, or they buy-in. It is a lot easier to execute on a call when you believe in it. It also allows them to adjust when you are not around because they know the "why" and can act upon it. Lastly, it is again a learning opportunity, and they get to know your way of thinking.

If there is still a bit of doubt, then apply the points from the previous subchapter. Still, none of the points here are not necessarily helping to make tough calls that have painful consequences independent from the outcome, like cutting an entire level. Good reasoning can help, but the rest is a matter of empathy and emotional intelligence, but it is the wrong book to cover such a tricky yet crucial topic.

### 5.3.5 About Acting

As I stated already previously, acting is very similar to deciding. By default, not acting is worse than reacting, and proactively acting is better than reacting. Not acting is the same as not making a decision. If you cannot act, then at least find someone who can. Stalling and not learning from the outcome is never a good idea.

Reacting is not ideal because you are already at a disadvantage and a step behind. Likely, it gets you more stressed, you make mistakes, and you will never stop running behind the problems. Often teams or developers just feel stressed or tired without understanding why. Potentially it is because they are in a constant reacting loop. Then as much as possible, try to break the vicious circle by applying as much push, experience, and resources to the team and project.

All points from the previous subchapters, "A Decision" and "The Right Decision" apply. Prepare for the worst case, have backup plans, gather enough information, and do not rush. Prioritize experience over just opinion, involve the team, always state your reasoning, avoid assumptions, and lastly, never plan to be lucky. If none of the points applies or helps, then you have nothing left other than to listen to your guts. The more you stay aware of what is going on in the project and team, the more likely you spot issues ahead of time. Keep an eye out for trends or bad tendencies. If you can identify a potential problem ahead of time, then create a list with possible actions. If you can act proactively, then do so. However, not every

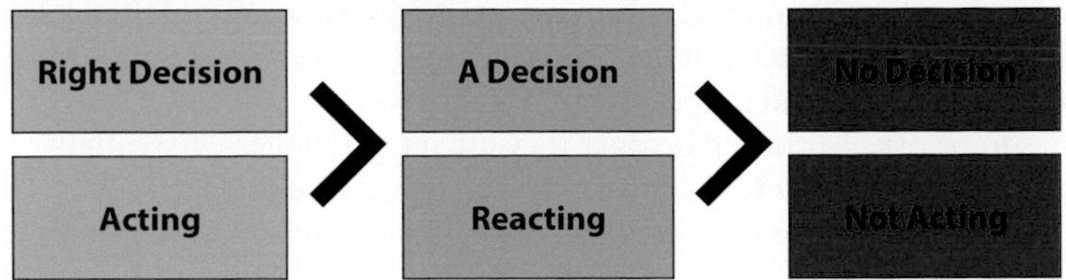


**FIGURE 5.2** Of course, the right decision is ideal, but any decision is still better than no decision. Similarly, acting is always better than reacting, but the worst is not acting.

issue requires assaulting it with full force instantly! Sometimes just being aware of slightly steering it in the right direction is all that is needed, especially if it is more of a social/team issue. Project topics should be dealt with swiftly and clear, however.

## 5.4 Emotions as a Common Language

### 5.4.1 Introduction

First of all, this is not a chapter about emotions or emotional intelligence. Instead, it is a tool to unite a team, especially a team consisting of multiple different departments. Therefore, it is also a method to establish direction because, ideally, then all members pull in the same direction.

### 5.4.2 The Problem

Let us start with an example problem to showcase why this tool is necessary. Imagine, we have an exciting new type of level with some really cool new gameplay. It could be a unique take on a racing section, exotic play with gravity, or a different take on boss fights.

The team working together on this level could consist of level designers, environment artists, narrative designers, game designers, gameplay programmers, animators, and audio folks. The concepts, tasks, and designs for all involved departments are clear. The teams go back to the desks and start working on them. However, when it all starts coming together, it seems that they are not harmonizing well.

The level designer tried to make it very difficult, the artists preferred more of a dire/dark look, narrative thought it is funny to add and write some witty dialogs, game design interpreted it as a tutorial to their feature, audio infused a lot of uplifting sounds and music, and animation kept it short and snappy.

I know it is a bit of an extreme chaotic example, but even if you establish aspects like mood and theme, it does not mean that everyone interprets it similarly enough. Concept art, examples, character bios, and alike can help, but they still leave much room for interpretation and assumptions.

### 5.4.3 The Solution and Process

The solution is relatively simple: You get a representative from each involved department in a room, and you together agree on an emotion you want the player to feel when playing the level.

A representative from each department is significant because you want to speak in unity, after all. I recommend limiting it to only one representative because you want the group to stay small. It is already challenging to agree on such topics with a small group and almost impossible in large ones. It can also be that not everyone deeply cares or not every involved department makes sense to include if their involvement is just very light.

However, it is crucial that once you are done, you speak the same "language." From now on, all of you are united "ambassadors" of the level's emotion. As a bonus, the process itself can be a great bonding experience for different departments working together, which they might not do daily.

Essentially, you sit together till you find an agreement. Be prepared that this can take a while because everyone should be equal here. Forcing it on the group or any power plays only disrespects the idea of the exercise, threatens the unity, and ultimately the belief in it.

The emotion has to be player-oriented because they are our consumers. Essentially, how do you want the player to feel? How can the different departments help to achieve this feeling?

For example, if we talk about the emotion "awe," level design and environment art can aim for stunning vistas and nicely framed reveals. Game design can make the feature very impactful yet gives the players the time and opportunity to be deeply impressed. The animations could be majestic, narrative foreshadows its allure, and audio looks into its monumental repertoire. As you see, now all different departments pull in the same direction with their expertise and knowledge.

The advantage of using a binding emotion is that it typically has only limited room for interpretation. Of course, there is some wiggle room, but it is a lot less than with other methods in my experience. Especially if you consider that we often work in international teams where different phrases or words have different meanings. However, if translated correctly, emotions can work universally.

### 5.4.4 Additional Hints

Below is a brief list of additional hints, based on my experiences running this exercise many times:

I recommend having a thesaurus or lists available, ideally online. When you are stuck, they are a great resource to come up with new ideas.

I recommend staying away from negative emotions, which are associated with bad gameplay like frustration or boredom. However, other negative emotions, like sadness, disgust, or fear, can work quite well.

You can repeat the same emotion for different levels or missions; just avoid repeating them too close to each other, or they are less impactful.

Avoid any longer "emotional constructs" like "the fear of drowning in dark water." There might be some rare instances where this is the best candidate, but otherwise, I recommend keeping it as short as possible, ideally just one word.

Try to avoid getting back in the habit of using terms like "Phantom of the Opera," "Jack the Ripper," or "Ghostbusters," because everyone interprets such terms very differently.

The same counts for nouns. Calling a level the "ghost" level could mean many different things for many people. I mean, some people like ghosts or some particular individuals even have sexual desires with them—the world is a fascinating, surprising, and exciting place, after all.

Try to avoid emotions like "fear" or something like "in power." They are the most basic emotions in games. Players are either afraid of dying/losing because they are not powerful enough, or they are/become an almighty entity. They are too close to the classic, and often already present, player progression where they start weak and gain more power with time. Try to find something fresher, even if it is just "frantic," "dread," or "romance."

The emotion should be easy to understand, especially again in the context of working with international teams. Not everyone might instantly connect with emotions like "disquietude," "consternation," or "gaiety."

## 5.5 "The Triumvirate of Practical World Building"

### 5.5.1 Introduction

This methodology is one of my proven concepts of practically applied empowerment. I know "The Triumvirate of Practical World Building" is a bit of a mouthful, but let us break it down.

It is a world-building leadership tool because it empowers the teams to act and change the game world without constant close oversight and approvals by leads and directors. It allows them to act independently, up to a point, essentially saving the precious times of anyone involved. Additionally, it is practical because it is easy to understand and executable by most world-building teams and their members.

It is a triumvirate because it encapsulates the three most common key departments of world-building: level design, art, and narrative. Of course, there are way more departments involved, and it can quickly change depending on team composition and the production stage of the level. Still, too many people involved will bloat up the process and ultimately quickly become counterproductive.

### 5.5.2 The Application

The initial, important idea is when the "three" main developers of a level always talk to each other about any change and come to a united agreement; then it is less likely that leads or directors have much to add later on.

This idea sounds a bit too easy, but in my experience, when for example, only level design and environment art agreed on a change, without involving narrative, then often things went wrong. More adjustments were needed, and directors and leads had to point them out, which resulted in more approval meetings. Those extra circles and approval cost quite some time for everyone involved.

So essentially, we made a verbal agreement with the level-feature teams: "Only bring up change suggestions to leads and directors when all three of you agreed on it."

When we, leads or directors, heard about a proposal, we first checked if all three indeed had the agreement. If it was not then, we kindly send them back to have a chat first. It sounds a bit harsh, but sooner than later, it became automatic, and the team noticed the positive change.

Once they did involve everyone, then the proposals from the team were way more solid, mostly requiring only a few or no adjustments, and it certainly raised the team spirit and feeling of belonging and empowerment. The benefit for leads and directors is clear: you save much time. Of course, it adds some more initial time for the teams, but it should be manageable, especially if they are sitting close together.

In my experience, the results often got so solid that we often did not even ask the changes to be approved, especially for the ones with a small or medium impact. Instead, we asked them to execute right away, saving even more time for everyone. In the vast majority of the cases, any adjustments which still had to happen had way less time impact than going through a more rigid approval circle. However, this required a certain level of earned trust, maturity, and proven autonomy of the team.

### 5.5.3 Closing Words

This process does not work with every team or in any team-composition context, especially if the workflow is more Waterfall than Agile or no level feature teams in any form or shape exist. For example, it could add an extra burden on the narrative designers, who now have to allocate more time talking to the teams.

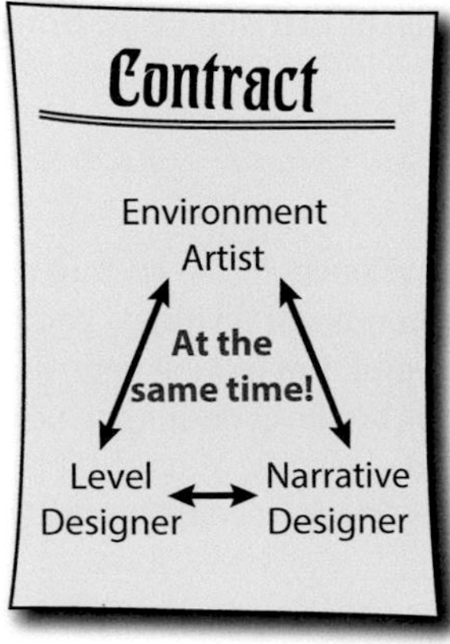


**FIGURE 5.3** The contract between environment artists, level designers, and narrative designers is to always agree together on a world change before talking to higher-ups.

However, even if you cannot translate the methodology to your situation, then I still hope that it inspired you in some form or another. It might spark another idea on practically applying empowerment while saving everyone's time and reducing stress. I am not a big fan of throwing buzzwords like "empowerment" around, but in this case, I am confident.

## 5.6 "The 10th Man"

### 5.6.1 Introduction

This exercise aims to get a deep, respectful insight into your product while also boosting the team's ownership. In this book's context, I primarily talk about a level designed and developed by a mix of multiple disciplines. However, I even ran that exercise with a single level designer. Also, feel free to adjust this exercise to other creative products.

It allows the team to openly talk about the problems they see with the levels, develop solutions, and own them. Essentially it is another practical and proven method of empowerment.

This exercise is especially useful with new developers or if the developers have doubts about their levels. This situation is not uncommon and nothing shameful. Especially in big productions, with tricky tech or time pressure, the number of issues can be huge and discouraging. Giving some ownership back to the developers can make a huge difference.

This method requires a moderator, whose job is to organize the meeting and then run the meeting's moderation. They should, of course, be very familiar with the process and are ideally familiar with the level. Typically this is a lead, director, or senior developer.

Initially, I kept the details of the exercise a secret till I've run it with the developers because I believed the process works better if they do not know all the steps. However, later on, the team approached me again and asked me to rerun them because they knew their benefits. Overall, I had only a positive reception about it, so I would like to share it here.

### 5.6.2 Origins

The original inspiration came from the exercise of the same-named exercise, which I learned from the blog www.redteams.net. It has a military background where a fireteam of nine men/women would develop a plan and then invite a "10th man" to poke holes into the plan.

Essentially the "10th man" would bring in a fresh perspective from an adversary point of view. For example, how would he attack their plan, where to set up an ambush, or how to disrupt it. The original team would then adjust their plan accordingly, develop countermeasures, or at least come up with backup plans.

To my understanding, the "10th man" does not have to be a single individual. Also, my variant is only loosely inspired by the original and has no militaristic vibes. However, I thought I would share the origin story and give credit.

### 5.6.3 Step 1

It all starts with inviting all involved developers of the level in a meeting room with a whiteboard. The suggested meeting time is one hour. I recommend inviting a good mix of disciplines, even if they are not necessarily responsible for creating the level. I'm talking here, for example, the level designers, environment artists, technical developers from art or level design, game designers, narrative designers, relevant leads, occasional managers, and embedded testers. You would be the best judge of who should be present. However, as I mentioned previously already, it could just be the single designer if availability is tight or you are under time pressure.

You, as the moderator, then ask the single developer who is the most involved in the design of the level to come to the whiteboard. They then sketch out the level on the whiteboard. They are essentially drawing a map with writing some of the key aspects/moments. The sketch should be in the left third of the whiteboard, not bigger. The reasons for this spatial restriction become clearer in the following steps.

The goal of this step is for everyone to familiarize themselves again with the level and to establish an equal playing field. Without this step, it easily happens that everyone has their views on the level, and it might sincerely impact the next steps.

Then make sure that everyone agrees with the correctness of what the developer drew on the whiteboard. If they disagree, you have a very different problem, which seriously affects proceeding with step 2. You can only proceed to step 2 if everyone agrees.

## 5.6.4 Step 2

The first step was easy and hopefully only a formality, but now it gets more interesting. Everyone should sit down again, and you, the moderator, take over the whiteboard. Now every developer has to voice their problems, fears, issues, or concerns—Everything goes, and everyone should voice their opinion freely. Nobody should judge anyone, and it is not the time to discuss or especially devalue anyone's points!

Your job as a moderator is to write down each point on the second third of the whiteboard. Again, you are not here to judge but rather to encourage everyone to speak freely. Of course, you can add your problems with the level. Further on, it is perfectly acceptable to skip, group, or modify points if very similar ones are already on the board. It is advantageous to keep the list well organized and easily maintainable.

Once everyone lists all their worries, even the smallest ones, then still wait a bit. Give them some extra time to think about it, especially if they are not familiar with the exercise. It is your responsibility to ensure that everyone understands that this is a safe environment to speak openly. This agreement is especially critical about problems originating from people's decisions in this room or higher up!

Honesty and trust are essential to establish such an open and safe environment. If such a foundation does not exist, you again have a different problem, and this exercise will likely not be as effective.

## 5.6.5 Step 3

In this last, most crucial step, you, the moderator, assign each problem an owner. Every issue needs to have an owner at the end. Ideally, the owner is in the room and can directly work on the solution. However, if this is not the case, then at least they should be responsible for following up on it. That is the reason why the composition of the meeting's attendees is so critical.

In my experience, you can assign the majority of the problems to the team working on the level—this includes leads and directors. Essentially giving the team ownership of the problems, and more importantly, the solution. After all, it is in their best interest to fix the issues of their level—hence the aspect of true practical empowerment. I recommend assigning any problems which the team members cannot address to leads, directors, or managers for follow-up. It reinforces the feeling that everyone is in the same boat.

It is up to you and your company's practices if they directly translate to tasks. It is also up to you how you follow up on the solutions. It was often much appreciated if the team had a way to voice their concerns and be part of the solution.

It is essential that this meeting does not turn into extensive discussions about the solutions already. This meeting is about identifying the problems and finding owners for the solutions. Any more significant further conversations will derail the meeting and likely will last way longer than one hour.

## 5.6.6 Closing Words

Besides the positive effect of empowerment, true ownership, and speaking out, another big result of the meeting is the hopeful feeling that solutions are coming, or at least managing expectations. The result can make a huge difference, especially if the stress within the team is high.

This exercise is initially for groups or at least pairs, but I can also recommend running this exercise alone. Essentially it helps you to self-reflect and to break down an overwhelming problem into smaller, manageable chunks.

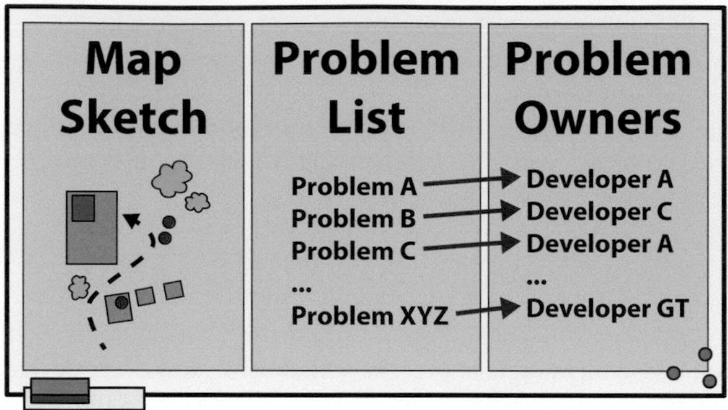


**FIGURE 5.4** The three stages of "The 10th man."

Further on the origin of this exercise is all about an "outsider" coming in to poke holes into the plan. However, in the steps I listed above this is not the case. The reason for this is because it takes a lot of time to explain one or multiple "outsider" the unknown level well enough so they can really list enough relevant and new problems. Very quickly the meeting might take one and a half up to two hours. Of course you can add "outsiders" to the participants, but in my experience the teams were already more than capable of listing a huge amount of problems. Occasionally I added leads from different departments, who are familiar enough with the level, but are not directly responsible for it. Another consideration is your team composition and the feedback culture; not every team appreciates feedback from every "outsider."

I recommend running this exercise somewhere between the initial conception of the level and shortly after the production start of the level. It is not always easy to find a good time slot, especially with a tight production schedule where everyone is always fully booked. However, the team needed to understand the issues at hand fully, and if you do this meeting too late, it gets harder and harder to apply solutions.

Feel free to adjust this methodology to your context and team. I firmly believe in its benefits, but it is hard to know every team's context. So, for example, I prefer to use a whiteboard, but it could also work digitally on a screen, especially with many developers working remotely.

# Section III

# Level Design Theory

# 6

# *About Vision, Pillars, and Direction*

When most people read vision, direction, and pillars, they might think this is a topic for only directors or maybe "creative" producer roles. However, I do believe they can be a strong tool for individual level creation. Still, the perception, use, and interpretation of such a theoretical high level concept vary hugely between companies. Therefore, I will not go into too crazy detail and focus more on their mindset and my personal take on them. Remember, especially when it comes to such methodologies, there is no industry-wide standard, and writing in too much detail about each person's approach would exceed the scope of this book.

## 6.1 Vision as a Starter

### 6.1.1 What Is a Vision?

The vision is the initial idea or spark, the one which inspires and motivates the developers to work on the game or level. Really good vision statements cause increased heart race or goosebumps. Everyone should get excited and start to smile like a child in a candy store. Everything which follows the vision is based on it, and therefore it is the defining foundation for the entire game or level.

I prefer a vision to be short, just about two to three sentences long, or a short paragraph. If you need five pages to get people excited, something went wrong, and they are likely all asleep.

### 6.1.2 How to Create a Vision?

#### *6.1.2.1 Step by Step*

First of all, start with simply writing down your description of the game/level in your own words. Don't worry too much about the length. Just list all the parts you consider important to sell the idea, what is essential for the unique selling point, and what gets you excited. It is okay if the first draft is still a bit tiring, but it must include all the essential information.

Then start reducing and compressing your sentences, so it is just two to three sentences, and you can speak them aloud, and clear with normal talking speed in about 20–30 seconds. The length is not a crazy hard rule and is more a guideline. If it is too long according to your feeling, then cut everything which is not absolutely necessary. I recommend rather use emotional words than simple descriptions. However, you need to list several aspects after each then don't list more than three to four in a row. More detailed descriptions can come later in the pitch presentation or design documents. After all, the more the audience (game developer) fills in the blanks themselves the more they could get excited to work on the mission. The more ideas your vision sparks the better, even if they might clash with your more detailed ideas later on. Creative people "desperately" want to fill gaps and this excitement is giving you more wins in the end. It is all a matter of balance and a lot of try and error—expect to refine your vision a lot before you feel ready to present it.

Now it is time to refine individual words and maybe add some more. It should not make the pitch much longer. I am thinking here, especially about words that impact strongly, carry lots of information, set high expectations, trigger emotions/experiences/memories, or strengthen your message. I recommend avoiding spamming it artificially with too many cliché buzzwords like synergy, holistic, emergent, systemic, or awesome. Working with a thesaurus is undoubtedly helpful here.

DOI: 10.1201/9781003275664-9

Ideally, you then have a short paragraph of something which at least excites you. Speak it aloud a few times and sense how it rolls over your tongue and refines it if necessary. Then I highly recommend involving some other people, but not yet right away the whole team! Start with a small group of people, peers you know want to support you, want a great pitch, too, and are close to the context. The game's or level's core group is a good starting point. Essentially use them as your "test-puppies." How impactful, motivational, or inspirational was it for them? What were their thoughts/associations when they heard it? Refine based on their reaction.

Ideally, after those four steps, you are done. You started with a raw version, refined/shortened it, enriched it, and ultimately adjusted it based on feedback.

#### *6.1.2.2 Idea Creation*

However, this process does not explain how to come up with a cool, mind-blowing idea to begin with because that is a matter of raw creativity. Now there is not a simple to-do list you follow, and you have a fantastic idea, but below are some of my typical hints for levels to avoid anything awful—and that is already a good start.

Do your research, watch movies, read books/articles, check Wikipedia, play similar games, explore with Google Maps, essentially anything you can get your hands on. Become an expert on your topic. A lot of ideas will spark here already and research is fundamental for the next step, too.

What is very common and very obvious? Make a list of them and add them to your level design banned list like warehouses, crate factories, construction sites, or sewers. If you want to stand out, avoid this list at all costs. Some examples could be churches, graveyards, harbors, farms, gas stations, or trailer parks. It all depends on your game and game world, and they will likely exist in your world, but again we are looking for something memorable and outstanding. Knowing the no-goes is already a huge step forward!

Based on your research, you should know your topic's trivia, the niche, or obscure. If it is not too crazy outlandish, draw your inspiration from them. For example, it could be a ski resort built in the desert, a copy of an Austrian village in China, a forgotten WW2 submarine harbor in Africa, or a swinger club in a decommissioned rocket silo.

If the base idea is a bit dry, because maybe she was given to you to make it exciting, then think about adding layers to it. For example, adding the swinger club to the previously mentioned decommissioned missile silo or a rocker gang turning a French cathedral into their clubhouse. It is absolutely crucial not to add more than one or two layers to your base location/idea! The more layers you add, the more difficult it will be for you to expose/explain/show all of them clearly to the average non-exploratory player with not a long attention span. You end up with a "brown sauce" (=mixing all watercolors together) where you cannot identify the individual colors anymore.

Essentially the steps help you to find something which is not generic, too boring, or obvious. However, the steps are primarily applicable for levels in semi-believable environments on Earth. For sci-fi or fantasy games, you would need to adjust them, but then you have the luxury to define a lot of it yourself. However, this either means more world-building and this can stall people because they do not know where to start.

By no means does this have to be a solo exercise. Especially if you work closely with a few peers on a level, then work together to create the pitch. It is very rarely a one-person show! However, I can also understand keeping the group small because the vision or pitch is more difficult to create the more ideas and "personalities" floating around. Still, especially for the level's core group, it is a great bonding experience; you will more likely speak with one supportive voice for the level from then on.

### 6.1.3 How to Use a Vision

I said multiple times that the vision is especially important for pitching and to get people excited, inspired, and motivated at the beginning. This is correct, but the vision has another important use.

The second use of a vision is as a gauge, something you should check regularly if what you are working on is still within the game's or level's vision. Every time you add anything bigger to the game/level do yourself a favor and check if it still fits within the vision. If it still makes sense, then it is all good.

However, if it doesn't fit then either adjust the new element or change the vision. If you change the vision you need to check every other previously created element if it then fits in the new vision or needs changing. This step is incredibly crucial because so many times, developers notice too late that their game or level deviated too far off the original vision and various elements are inconsistent and messy holding together.

The vision is comparable with a character bio. For example, if the bio describes the character fighting like a standard gladiator but then someone wants to add a samurai move then either something crucial is missing in the bio, or the move doesn't fit.

### 6.1.4 Closing Words

In many, the vision is your starting block and foundation. It gets everyone excited, and you build everything on it. Therefore, the vision has a social and a production function. Adjusting the vision early on is easy; it is fine and can happen. Changing it, later on, is likely to be way more costly and potentially less exciting. The irony is that especially games or levels that go through a long production cycle end up changing the vision, later on, increasing the already high stress and frustration. However, the reasoning for such changes is way too complex to give easy and short advice here.

Also, the process I described does not have to be followed by the letter! It is one way for people who are a bit stuck or less experienced. Ultimately it only means the result has to make people excited, and ideally, it is short. How short is up to you at the end, and a pitch presentation is, of course, way longer again. However, if a vision fails, in my experience it is when it was too long or did not excite the room or key people, and the last point is subjective.

## 6.2 Pillars as a Safety

### 6.2.1 Introduction

The pillars are commonly two to five (typically three) words or phrases that describe your game or level. They define the most dominant aspects. For example, you could say: "Our game's pillars are horror, freedom, and time travel." You loosely know what to expect if you hear the pillars, yet it lacks any detailed description. They are often very wide open for interpretation, with a purpose. Early in production, all the details are unknown, and therefore any pillars are by definition looser. The pillars have to match the vision, and typically the vision is first. You could compare the pillars to the composition of a painting to give it a basic structure, but first, you needed an idea/vision.

The pillars for games count for every department. Typically, there can be sub-pillars for a single department like in the art direction, occasionally for a bigger sub-element of a game like different multiplayer and singleplayer parts. However, for individual levels, I have not seen them used very often.

### 6.2.2 How to Create and Use Pillars

#### *6.2.2.1 Introduction*

The reason for combining both the use and creation is because you first need to understand the use in order to create them effectively. Another important fact is that the use of pillars can widely vary between companies. What I wrote below is what I understand under them and how I made use of them. Some have a more or less strict approach, but I am not a big fan of creating something that has no practical application for most developers, especially non-directors.

#### *6.2.2.2 The Use*

Suppose we have three pillars, then the principal use of pillars is to check every new idea of your game against them. If a new idea fits only one or no pillar, the idea likely does not fit your game. If it serves two, then the idea might be okay, and, of course, three means the idea seemingly fits very well. Ideally it should fit at least 50% of the pillars as a bare minimum.

The pillars act as a tool for developers to check if one of their new ideas fits into the game. Since ideally, the pillars are modeled after the vision, you can check if the new idea is within the vision. It is not a very strict rule, but again a strong supportive guideline. In that way, it is an independent guideline of empowerment. Still, since the interpretation is often subjective, it is no guarantee that the idea gets approved!

For example, our previous pillars were: horror, freedom, and time travel. Suppose one level designer has an idea for a level featuring a widespread sunny forest and a puzzle jumping between the seasons. In that case, it could fit because it serves two of the pillars (freedom and time travel) but lacks the horror one. However, I would not be surprised if the idea gets rejected because the horror one might be a game-wide defining pillar. This example also shows that not every pillar is always equally weighted. I mean, ideally, they should, but every director/developer could have their interpretation. Subjective topics often quickly get confusing and complex.

On the flip side, not everything should be checked against the pillars. If an artist creates a table, it is hard to incorporate horror, freedom, and time travel. However, if the same artists create an important scene using that table, it ideally covers most if not all pillars.

Another critical aspect, in my interpretation, is that the pillars, as a tool, are, first of all, developer-focused. Of course, they could include player-oriented terms like "horror," but their primary function is to support the developers as a pre-safety check and orientation.

If developers do not follow the pillars, they likely end up with a confusing and incoherent product. Therefore the pillars are part of the direction, in my opinion, just with a more explicit use. Especially when a team struggles with creative consistency, then pillars are a great tool to introduce. However, it can also mean the existing pillars are not helping, nobody really follows them, or they are not inspirational. Then it is time to revisit them. I would not say that the pillars' primary function is to motivate/inspire, but they should certainly not repel anyone.

#### *6.2.2.3 The Creation*

The creation is quite simple but often difficult to execute: Come up with a few words/terms that define most future ideas following the vision.

My recommendation for the creation is to look at your vision, already existing ideas/examples, or sources of inspiration. Come up with terms/words which encapsulate/describe them. Check them against your already existing ideas and see if the examples would serve the pillars. Sometimes, I changed my example ideas because I liked the pillars more than the initial examples. Otherwise, go back and search for better pillars.

It is not a surprise if you come up with only one or two initially, and the third one has seemingly no place but sounds "cool." For example, in our previous "horror, freedom and time travel" example, it could be that the "time travel" one is only a dominating flavor but not necessarily present everywhere.

The more example ideas or even real features you already have when you think about the pillars, the better, but I would not wait too long with the pillar creation because otherwise, you have many ideas to check against the pillars. Plus, ideally, the pillars should exist very early on because they should guide the development of the features. Therefore, I recommend creating the pillars with the core group so everyone buys in. They should represent their own ideas and more refined ideas in their heads.

Sometimes, I first created the pillars with only some loose ideas in my mind. Essentially I thought of my terms, which I wanted to define the ideation process of the product.

Ultimately the more you are used to working with pillars, the easier it is to create them because you can quickly make some pre-checks and see how they fit, why they might not fit and what part has to be changed. Starting with the core definition of your game is always solid. However, make sure that the terms are helping developers. For example, if a pillar is "fantasy," "awesome," or "pencil," then it could mean way too much or nothing. It is the difficult balance between being loose enough to give freedom while being tight enough to be useful.

#### 6.2.2.4 Hints for the Creation

Below is another list of hints to create good pillars.

Keep the pillars short. A sentence or even a short paragraph is not a pillar. If it is too long, it gets too difficult to remember, or they are not catchy enough.

If a pillar needs a lengthy description, it typically does not serve well as an easy-to-remember development tool and can cause many interpretations again. Therefore, keep them short and easy to understand by everyone.

I recommend staying between three to four pillars. Fewer pillars and they are not defining enough of a product. More pillars are hard to remember, or it is tiresome to use them. Therefore, people might stop using them, and ends up just as a nice printout hanging behind the director's desk.

Skip obvious/general pillars like "accessible," "fun," or "make money." They might sound essential, but I have yet to work on a game that tried not to be accessible, fun, or did not want to make money. Sure they are always exceptions, but I recommend putting in some effort and picking pillars that describe your game closer, or the whole exercise is quickly useless.

### 6.2.3 Closing Words

I have heard about and worked on games that had seven to nine pillars, and some pillars came with a lengthy one-page description. I know many developers who use pillars differently, cannot comprehend the idea, or do not care much about them. For some, it is an essential creative tool defining their vision, while for others, it is just something like "marketing fluff and buzzwords." I can understand where both sides are coming from; therefore, I need to reinforce the practical application of pillars. If they are not applicable for most developers, then they will indeed quickly become forgotten by most.

Honestly, if you have to preach them at every team meeting or talk about them during project closing, you also do not understand their use. There are many opinions about pillars. However, I often found them not used well and they ended up more of a director-toy for pitches than a developer tool. It is up to us to make the change.

## 6.3 Direction as Guidance

### 6.3.1 Introduction

The purpose of direction is to orientate all developers to work with the same orientation, stay close together, and move forward at a similar speed. Bad or the lack of direction means the game's production is chaotic, messy, and unclear. Everyone interprets the vision differently, and the difference can create an incoherent mess further down production. That's where a good direction comes in.

For me, a direction is more of a strong guideline, not a law or a loose guideline. The difference for me is that you should not break laws, but guidelines can be bent. However, just because I see them more as guidelines should not act as an invitation and bend them all the time—hence the added "strong" guideline. I mean, as a director like myself, you are always conflicted because, on the one hand, you meant to create and ensure the direction, but on the other hand, we know that sometimes much creativity lies in breaking the rules. Therefore, I cannot recommend you trying to show off creativity by always being the rule breaker. Still, first master the rules before you even consider breaking them!

Direction can exist for the whole game, for a department, like level design, or for a bigger sub-part of a game like multiplayer or singleplayer. They provide the specific team with a set of guidelines. If developers follow them, they establish a coherent consistency among the product. For example, art direction could define how stylized the characters should look, not that some artists go entirely cartoony and some hyper-realistic.

In a perfect world, the direction would allow the directors to go for months on vacation and come back and enjoy a game that is still very consistent. As opposed to "dictating," the direction provides controlled creative freedom. I like to say that it puts creativity in a "grid." It gives the team's creativity much-needed structure, in which they can express their creativity, while the grid prevents a chaotic mess. If done very well, it is a tool of empowerment because it requires less frequent micromanagement.

You know a direction is good when it fulfills the following brief:

- A good direction achieves a consistent product.
- A good direction is applicable and easy to understand.
- A good direction gets everyone to work toward the same goal at a similar pace.
- A good direction inspires and motivates developers even if you are not around.
- A good direction will make every developer believe in it, resulting in them using all their knowledge and power to achieve it.
- The better the direction is, the less often it needs re-adjustments.

If developers cannot apply the direction or misunderstand it, it is useless for them. However, it is almost worse if the direction is so unclear that developers interpret it differently and work in opposing directions. If the direction is not inspiring, then much motivation is lost, but it is that extra individual push of passion that adds the magic to your product. Additionally, if they are motivated, they want the product to succeed, they believe in it, and they will use all possibilities to ensure that the game/level is a success. Lastly, constantly readjusting your direction will only result in eroding your reputation as a good director. Essentially it means you do not know what you want, and nobody wants to follow a lost leader. However, sometimes the "reality" catches up with us, and we have to adjust the direction or cause more harm than good. In the end, it comes down to a matter of reasons, timing, and frequency.

I have worked on games or heard about some which changed the direction every new month because the top-dog had some new ideas or where the final direction came together a few weeks before the beta milestone. You can imagine how the production went and what the reputation of the top leaders ended up being.

### 6.3.2 When to Create Direction

Before we start talking about the "how," I think it is essential to set clear expectations about the right time to create the direction. The primary problem is that the direction has a practical use. However, early on in a development cycle, there is not much practical experience to base a rock-solid direction on.

You can make estimates or a first draft showing your intentions, experience, and ideas early on, but make it clear to everyone that those are not the final directions and that they will evolve. Honesty pays off. Once the team faced practical realities and gathered some early production experience, it would make sense to revisit the direction. Check what the team needs, where the direction already works, and need some more guidance. Retrospectives exist for a reason.

Ideally, it would be best to have a more or less finished direction at the end of pre-production so the team can go full steam ahead. However, suppose you could not create enough benchmarks, demos, or prototypes, I believe it is acceptable if the refined direction comes in the first quarter of the alpha milestone. Such a case is not great, but a guideline is just guesswork without enough practical reality/experience. Some directors believe they have all the experience already early on, based on previous projects. However, except the new game is very similar to previous ones, it remains honestly just guesswork. Good for them if it works out, but staying a bit humble with realistic expectations is recommended. Also, never rely on luck that your direction is now final.

The trick is to find the right time to adjust/define the direction. Wait long enough to base it on some practical reality, but not too long, or your direction will not provide creative stability reducing costly reworks. Therefore, I believe it is okay to create one early-ish, see how it holds up with reality, and have more critical eyes look at it with time. Again, run as many retrospectives as possible. Then be honest that it will change, reason your timing plus the changes itself, and re-adjust once enough experience is collected, but soon enough that it still matters for the bulk of production.

### 6.3.3 How to Create Direction

#### *6.3.3.1 Step 1: Start with Mistakes to Avoid*

With the vision in mind and the team's practical experience/results, I typically start with something maybe unusual: I first write down all the things the team has done wrong or they might do wrong. I essentially list their mistakes in my view, and then I turn them into positively worded guidelines.

For example, the level design team often does not provide enough vantage points for the open-world locations. Then a direction could be "Provide three to five vantage points around your open-world location." It is an easy-to-follow/remember guideline, hard to argue against, and will make the product consistent and better.

Most points listed in my YouTube video "Open World Coop Level Design Guidelines" on my channel "Bauer Design Solutions" came from issues I saw with early levels.

I start with the team's issues because we are already a huge step in the right direction if they make a lot fewer mistakes. If the primary audience for the direction is the development team, then starting with the parts they need the most help with is only reasonable. It is up to you to filter out the issues worth defining the direction and which do not. A small mistake or bug is not worth it, and a one-time problem may not be as well, but if you see patterns or more than one developer making the same mistake, it is worth considering. They are issues, trends, or less ideal designs which will cause problems now or later on, based on your experience.

#### *6.3.3.2 Step 2: Observe the Team*

Now, often I observe bigger, "direction worthy" design choices the teams have done well. Often those are aspects I have not thought about myself! For example, during prototyping, the team discovered that certain AI archetype combinations are highly effective or unrewarding. It is not uncommon that while directors keep a more theoretical, strategic view, we lose the view of the practical reality. Therefore, it is crucial, in my opinion, to base direction on practical past or present experience to stay applicable for the team.

#### *6.3.3.3 Step 3: Add Your Vision*

Now that you have a solid initial list based on problem avoidance or practical team findings, it is time to add everything you believe is still missing to fulfill your vision. This step means adding elements that define and guide the production within your scope, expertise, and craft.

For example, in your game, an open-world location is defined as being approachable from all sides, then a new direction is "All open-world locations should be approachable from all sides." If the open world can only lead to linear missions, then the direction would be: "Every mission location has a clear start point within the open world."

However, you would be surprised how many directions you already have after completing Step 1. Then many defining ones now might not be necessary. If, for example, our last point, "Every mission location has a clear start point within the open world" has a technical origin. Arguably this could be in the technical level design direction or simply a technical rule/metric and not necessarily a level design direction.

Another angle is to list the creative requirements, for example, a level, a stealth section, or a new gameplay experience. For example, a stealth section should feature no "avoidance path," have no AI standing around waiting to get killed, feature clear vantage points, not feel random or way too difficult, etc. This list foreshadowed parts of my later topic on stealth sections, which lists problems I have experienced with such.

#### *6.3.3.4 Step 4: Spot Patterns and Fill the Grid*

After the last steps, you should have a lengthy list of essential directions. Now it is time to start organizing them and look for patterns.

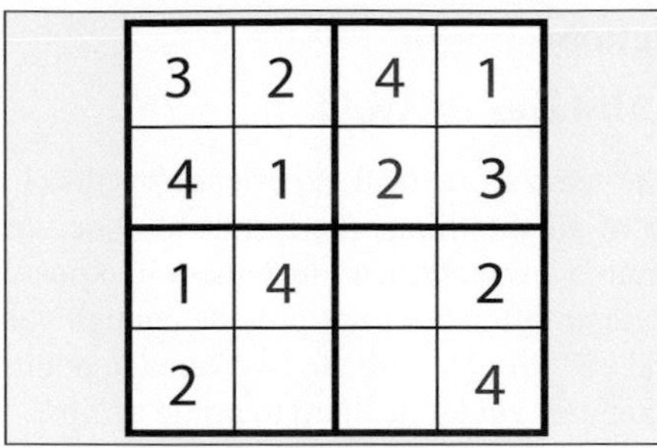

| 3 | 2 | 4 | 1 |
|---|---|---|---|
| 4 | 1 | 2 | 3 |
| 1 | 4 |  | 2 |
| 2 |  |  | 4 |

**FIGURE 6.1** Filling out the abstract "Direction Grid" visualization Sudoku style (simple 4×4)/Black: came from practical experience/Red: came from logically filling in the gaps/Empty: still needs to be figured out.

For example, we have a few points about the outside of an open-world location and the inside. Therefore, we order them in the way the player approaches them. Then we might notice that we lack any direction for the wider approach of such locations or the transition between the surrounding vantage points to the center location. We now need to make a call if we need any additional direction for those two steps or not.

I call it "filling the grid" because it always reminds me of playing Sudoku. Step 4 is like playing a logic puzzle—I have a few set fields, and then I need to fill in the missing ones based on my experience and knowledge. Just staring at a screen and magically creating a whole level design direction in one go is unrealistic. You will have gaps initially, and that is fine because you focused on the important aspects first: Avoid mistakes and what is important to your vision. Step 4 helps you to fill in the gaps.

It helped me the most to create such patterns or grids by following the players' actions. For example, as a concept for level design I have one path is from the outside into an open-world location; the second is to stay outside. I can now check the two paths and if I have covered every step and can consider covering them with a direction. However, I can also decide which path I prefer the players to take. If I want players to rather go inside the location instead of staying outside, I have to develop a level design direction that motivates the players to do so. Occasionally this thinking might spot future problems ahead of time, and I can proactively trigger bigger discussions within the team.

By laying out our direction in patterns and filling out the grid, you will likely spot obsolete directions, similar ones, or any which are not necessary anymore in the bigger picture. Essentially step four is also a much-needed cleanup pass. Any unnecessary noise will only weaken your direction as a whole.

By defining the direction, you guide the developers, but the result should also result in a better player experience. A consistent product is more pleasant for players, but so is also, for example, good pacing, well-balanced rewards, no frustration, no boredom, excellent player-leading, and solid entertainment.

#### *6.3.3.5 Step 5: Bring It to Paper*

We now have a nice list of directions, and we collected them in categories and patterns. Now it is time to bring them all together in a presentable form. The form itself depends on your liking or how your company/studio/project functions. Some prefer PowerPoint presentations with nice big pictures, some still prefer a more text-heavy approach, and I prefer larger graphical one-pagers.

Start with the categories and patterns which you have already identified during step four. For example, combine all directions about your open-world location on one page. Compartmentalizing brings order, helps you explain to the team the "why," helps to remember them easier, and highlights the connections.

As much as possible, present them in order and especially look out for loops. The more often a direction collection is applicable for the same or similar gameplay sections, the more likely you have a clear order or even loops. Designers love loops after all.

Loops, clear order, categories, or other patterns are ideal for graphical treatment. Even just showcasing them connected is already a great help. Any visualization is highly beneficial for the common visual types among us designers and artists. My channel's previously mentioned YouTube video "Open World

Coop Level Design Guidelines" is a good example. Just imagine it as a large one-meter by one-and-a-half printout on the wall.

Lastly, it is okay to add some additional explanations here and there. Ideally, your direction does not require a more detailed description, but for example, not everyone might know what you mean by an "avoidance path." As long as the clarification is not too long, it is fine. Otherwise, your direction might be too confusing and needs a revisit, or maybe it is better to split it up into clearer chunks.

### 6.3.4 How to Use Direction

Obviously, it starts with a presentation and some explanations and examples to a wider audience affected by the direction.

If only small parts get adjusted or added occasionally then it should be no big deal. Making games is primarily an iterative process, especially massive AAA projects, and it certainly counts for the direction. However, it does not hurt to acknowledge it from time to time. Still, if severe/bigger changes or bigger reworks occur, it should be presented again in a more extensive meeting/presentation format, ideally as fast as possible.

Once you establish the direction and gave a presentation, it should remain accessible to everyone within the project. However, I would not count on the individual developers to read it daily or know each part by heart. Therefore, especially use any review to reinforce it or to remind people. For example, use it as part of your reasoning when giving feedback; it does not matter whether it is a small desk review or a bigger build review.

However, if you notice that your reasoning with direction is standing on shaky ground, facing the game's current reality, then likely, your direction needs some attention. Again, the frequency and scope of the changes are what matter here.

### 6.3.5 Closing Words

Creating a direction can be daunting to its wide and potentially costly implications. Experience and routine are key factors here, which make it incredibly daunting for first-timers. However, if you have ever worked on a game with an excellent or horrible direction, you know this step is important.

The last thing I would like to add at the end is that any direction, especially for level or game design, is not a design document. A design document describes WHAT a specific design is. The direction defines HOW the designs, features, or assets should be used/treated/created to establish team-wide consistency. Therefore, whoever writes a design document is not defining direction. They have to go hand in hand, and the design document has to follow the direction, but I believe that separation in mindset is crucial.

However, the biggest damages in my experience came from massive, game-wide, top-down design changes. Entire games can get revamped overnight, often completely ignoring any previous direction. In my personal experience, this was often the case for very unclear, weak, or often non-existing directions. If the concept of properly used direction is understood and team-wide established, then such massive changes are rare or at least can be reasoned a lot better. As much as it hurts, sometimes reality kicks in hard, and much more extensive changes are unavoidable, but good directions and directors can certainly soften the blow. It puts the consequences in context or even makes them self-explanatory to the team.

# 7

# *Abstract Level Design*

For me, anything abstract in level design is the underlying pattern that sets the foundation for typically a good or bad level. Of course, it is not the only aspect which makes a great level, but more about it later.

A good abstract level design concept is comparable to the golden cut of art, the three act structure for storytelling, or the 12-bar blues for music. They are not the only ones and do not always work, but they exist for excellent reasons, and in their own realm, they work very well. However, for level design, such abstract conceptions do not exist, because our craft is only a few decades old. Secondly, it still keeps changing drastically, a lot faster than music, art, and storytelling.

In this chapter, I am sharing my view on this topic because I was always fascinated by the topic. I was always looking for that hidden "golden rule" because I thought as long as level design is an art form, there should be such rules. By no means do I claim that I found it, but hopefully, it helps others by sharing my mindset. After all, we again have to reinvent the abstraction concepts (and much more!) each time we make a brand new game. Therefore, I do not know if we should desperately look for that "golden rule" instead of rather internalizing a general, abstract mindset.

However, before diving too deep into the joy of intellectual level design theory, let us be clear about one fundamental truth: The best theory does not matter if you cannot translate it into practice. Therefore, it does not matter much what sophisticated terms you know, what fabulous ideas you present, and how many nights you spend theorizing about abstract design if you do not have the finished levels to prove it. Without any practical application, a theory is a waste for me. I mean, it is great to have a casual chat about it over a beer or coffee, but if it does not turn into reality, then it just remains a chat.

## 7.1 About Theory

### 7.1.1 Introduction

I genuinely enjoy working with or developing new-level design theories because it always feels like walking on new ground. I do not know when or if it will ever end, but it was and remains a great time to be a level designer so far. I am well aware that not everyone is deeply into level design theory and they prefer the pure practical application, which is fine. Still, if you are one of them, I still hope you are interested enough to have a sneak peek behind the curtains.

### 7.1.2 Creation of Theory

#### *7.1.2.1 Introduction*

I am writing below not necessarily an easy step-by-step description of how to create a theory, but instead, those are my steps to establish a mindset. It is my way of thinking when I need to create a new concept, which can transform into a level design direction, theory, or the foundation for more.

#### *7.1.2.2 Step 1: Stating the Problem*

You need to have a problem to fix; typically, a problem too complex lacking any clear-cut solution. For example: "why does this level flow so well?" or "Something is off with this level, but I cannot put my

DOI: 10.1201/9781003275664-10

finger on the exact cause." In such cases, there is usually no simple answer. Therefore, we need to do a bit more digging into the root of the issue or cause.

Typically, I would say that you need to state the problem clearly. However, often you only have a gut feeling that something is wrong, like in one of the upper examples. Fortunately, this approach works for both clear and unclear stated issues because you reveal the underlying fabric step by step, always looking for a logical explanation or pattern.

#### *7.1.2.3 Step 2: Simplify*

Instead of listing all the parts which have, for example, a good flow or cause issues, I take a step back. I start to look at the level from a higher level. I split it into simplified parts like connections, battlefields, objective spaces, stealth/assault parts, tight space, open space, or crossroads. I compartmentalize the level in junks as a step of abstraction. Then I draw or imagine connections. I am looking for any connective tissue or network which might reveal itself. The goal is to abstract it far enough so I can see patterns in Step 2.

However, when you apply the next step for the first time, do not go too high-level immediately with Step 1. Approach it slowly, keep it small scale, layer by layer. For example, there is no need right away to strip the level to its three main lanes or turn it into a circle. You might spot something different at every "zoom" or rather "abstraction" level, and each one could be important to solve your problem.

#### *7.1.2.4 Step 3: Patterns*

When turning the level into something abstract, the simplification allows me to look out for patterns that are otherwise potentially hidden under the surface. I look for the logic which explains why something is maybe good or bad. I might spot a hidden symmetry or a rhythm of ingredients/pathing. After all, it is all about peeling off the upper layers and investigating the underlining fabric. I might notice poorly distributed options, there might be too much, not enough, a bad mix of certain space types (like stealth, combat, tight, open), or there is no clear separation between the battlefields and connections.

I once had the case that the root of the issue was that abstracting the level showed that it had no clear underlying structure, to begin with; it was all just mess thrown together. As a result, I could quickly define a simple level design direction, put it in a nice graphical format, and the team had a clear path forward. However, without Steps 1 to 3, I would not have found it so quickly/easily. I could not so quickly define a theoretical root for the issue and a helping fix that stayed general enough to be applied to all other levels of the same type. It then turned into the general level design directions for those levels.

#### *7.1.2.5 Step 4: Repeat*

During Step 2, I mentioned that you should do the abstraction slowly, layer by layer. If you have not found what you needed during Step 3, it is time to repeat the process, starting with Step 2 just more abstract, then Step 3 until you hopefully find what you were looking for. However, not finding anything can also reveal a lot, as mentioned previously in the example of Step 3. Even if you found something intriguing, I would still recommend simplifying further because you might reveal even more or something that connects the issues you found at a lower level of abstraction.

#### *7.1.2.6 Closing Words*

The irony is that those steps to create theory are incredibly theoretical. They are also constrained to levels because this book is, after all, about level design. It might read as if it is limited to layout topics, but I prefer to draw out other aspects as well, like level progression, game loops, or any gameplay meta layers in or around the levels. I start in detail and then apply a similar simplification process, always looking for patterns and signs.

The process I described in large is initially a process of abstraction and simplification. However, the process of developing a theory is in Step 3, looking for patterns. What looks odd, is there a certain rhythm, what good/bad underlying elements repeat a lot, or are there any exciting/worrying correlations? There is no magic solution to develop a theory from it, but keep distilling your data or layout till something stands out. Then see if it is applicable for more than one case, and maybe it leads to a broader applicable theory or a solution to your problem.

Later in this book and even in this chapter, I show more case studies or situations with the same thinking, either by example in the abstraction of a level's layout or the composition of a game in levels. This chapter is merely an introduction to level design theory. Further on, I do believe, with some adjustment but a similar mindset, you can apply the same thinking to other design fields.

### 7.1.3 Balance between Theory and Practice

#### *7.1.3.1 Introduction*

As I stated previously, theory without practical application tends to be useless for many level designers, but creating levels without some theoretical foundation also stands on shaky grounds. It is a bit like building a space rocket without knowing physics, maths, and chemistry. You might get lucky eventually, but as long as engineers/designers have to go work every day, relying on luck for a multi-million-dollar rocket/AAA game is never a good start. Essentially, it means that a solid level design theory establishes consistency and reliability in level creation. In that matter, it is comparable to direction. The main difference is that direction affects a larger scope and more people, while a theory can be very isolated at times. However, it is not a guarantee for any freaking, genius, mind-blowing creation—that is an additional layer of talent and luck on top, but of course a lot easier to achieve on a good foundation.

In this chapter, I want to go a bit deeper into the two questions, "how and when" to use theory, because answering both might warm up some theory critics or make the theory fans even more effective.

#### *7.1.3.2 When and How to Use Theory*

First, any level design theory is just a tool that I can apply if I believe I or the level would benefit from it. It is rarely a rigorous guideline or even a "law." However, it often gives a certain comfort, so I can focus more on other things, like how I can elevate the level idea more, make it more memorable, or push certain boundaries to the absolute limit. It is a bit like running a marathon and not having to worry that your pants rip any second—it keeps you focused on the important topics.

Secondly, you cannot force a theory on anyone who does not believe in it or considers it useless. You can try to be a bit convincing, but it might quickly turn awkward. Therefore, if the designer who should apply the theory in his level creation is not buying into it, then look for another "tool in the box." If they do, then it is all good, of course.

Thirdly, developing any theories is essential early on in a project, best until the end of pre-production. In that context, any theories are comparable to direction, based on the practical experience of your own team or competitors.

Developing any theory in the vacuum of practical reference is possible. However, it requires a lot of discipline, tons of experience in the specific field, little to no guesswork, no big egos present, and a good portion of respectful roleplay. The roleplay portion is crucial. It requires you to predict as close as possible what would happen in a practical application. Therefore, without the experience, it turns into guesswork, and you are back dangerously basing a theory on luck and guts. However, if you develop a compelling theory, turn it into a prototype as fast as possible to get some empirical data to back it up or refine it further. It is a bit trickier if the theory lives the game's meta-layer or requires multiple, larger chunks to be feature complete.

Therefore, bigger theory creation is still valid until Alpha and a bit beyond. When all the game's different elements come together, you can have a more realistic, closer look at the actual product. Now is the time to look if the theories that defined how all should work together were correct or not. This evaluation means now is the critical time to adjust any theories and look at what else is affected by them as a consequence. The complexity of large AAA projects is often so huge that it can take weeks until all effects are clear to everyone.

However, it is a bit complicated to still call it theory at that stage since it turned into reality. Reality means many people invested a lot of work and passion into it. Therefore any more extensive changes have a steeper price than just money and time, making any careful previous considerations so much more important. However, even the best estimates early on go through iterations, but what separates the okay from the great theories is that the great ones can adjust at a lower price.

When you enter a closing phase, the time of bigger theories comes to an end, or at least their use outside of a post-mortem. You can still theorize, but ideally, major reworks come to an end, which means any still applicable theories have a much smaller scope. It is about that one feature or level, and the closer you get to beta, it gets even smaller. The risk of changes is simply increasing the risk of introducing even more or bigger bugs. Of course, you can still develop new theories and analyze the now more complete game, but be prepared that production/management and tech teams should give you severe restrictions to execute the changes. The more the creative folks phase out of a project, the more they either focus solely on bug fixing or leave the project completely and with them theory creation.

## 7.2 Success for the Player

### 7.2.1 Introduction

In this chapter, I would like to cover some more theoretical thinking about the player's success and its importance. However, instead of going deep into game theory or design, I will stay in the level design realm as much as possible. This essential mindset was my foundation for feedback, direction, theories, or basic reasoning on countless occasions.

### 7.2.2 The Player and the Developer

First, let us accept the non-surprising realization that most players play games to succeed in some form of shape, and let us not all come up with a list of niche exceptions. Therefore failure is part of the equation, and success feels more satisfying the more difficult the challenge. It is like heroes in movies are perceived as more badass the stronger their villain. A group of average teenagers beating intergalactic gods is pretty epic, but the way around is certainly not heroic.

The tricky part for us, game developers, is that we do not know who our heroes, or rather players, exactly are. Sure we have focus groups, playtests, but that provides a trend at best and certainly does not cover all cases. Therefore, I try to treat the player in this chapter as neutral as possible—Just a theoretical entity without any judgment. I know it sounds crude or cruel. However, I have to stress that it is often too easy/tempting for developers to blame players rather than themselves, and occasionally such developers get rightfully bad press for it.

Therefore, the first lesson is: "If the players fail, we developers are to blame." We did not explain the situation/feature well enough. We failed at player-leading. We poorly balanced the challenge, skipped options, hid the consequences, or potentially a combination of multiple causes. Of course, especially during playtest, there can always be that one guy who lied about his previous gaming experience, showed up intoxicated, or is undoubtedly, seriously a horrible player. However, funny enough, you can learn a lot from those exceptions because they also reflect reality in the real world. Therefore, I would not wholly dismiss such cases and still be very careful putting such players too fast in the "dismissal category." Sure, if the intoxicated players keep getting lost in the first hallway of the tutorial level, then you can dismiss them or, better, send them home.

However, your "average bad" players are very common. Just take your average players as a base and then accept, by definition, that 50% of all players are worse than them. Nevertheless, they still deserve to enjoy the game and your level because they hopefully paid good money for it.

### 7.2.3 Player Options and Choices

#### *7.2.3.1 Introduction*

In this book, I often write about player options and choices because I consider them as one of the core principles of a good game and level design. Making active choices is one of the principal differences between interactive mediums like games, in contrast to movies or theater. Players can make right or wrong choices which should have different consequences. We want players to make the right choices with just enough challenges associated with success having meaning, and bringing satisfaction. Happy players will hopefully buy your next game and tell their friends to buy it too, which ultimately makes you as the developer happy again.

However, unfortunately, it is not that easy as it sounds. Therefore, in this chapter, I will focus on the difficult balance between choice, challenge, and player ultimately satisfaction in the context of level design.

#### *7.2.3.2 Make the Player Feel Clever*

As I previously stated, we want players to feel happy by overcoming a challenge. One way to achieve this is by making the players feel smart by making the right choice.

First of all, a meaningful choice should be related to a problem or challenge for the player. For example, choosing a left or right door outside an irrelevant building gives the player no problem. Therefore he cannot feel clever picking any of the two because he did not know about the problem. However, if they accidentally pick the correct one, the accomplishment feels lucky, not archived. Therefore, such cases without problem or based on luck should not be about a right or wrong choice or good or bad consequences.

Secondly, the options need to be available to the players. When you give the player problems, like "How to attack the enemy group ahead?", "How do I reach the upper floor?" or "How to solve this puzzle?", then the options should be accessible. Depending on the intended difficulty, the options do not have to be crystal clear, but players should have a fair chance of finding them.

For example, if the players circle the enemy group, they could spot an explosive barrel or an inviting stealth route. In case of the navigation challenge, the route to the upper floor might be outside, hinted at with an open window and light outside. Lastly, the puzzle's solution might be hinted at in a note on a shelf, or color-coded cables lead toward the machines to turn on.

However, adding big waypoints, any other game elements, or any other super obvious hints take away the players' chance to feel clever. It can be easy, especially early on in the game, but never expect the player to feel smart reaching the waypoint on the other side of the room. However, more about waypoints later in the book under "player-leading." Essentially it means, anything subtle and in the game world has a better chance to make the player feel clever than anything which is on-the-nose, especially if it is gamy or comes from outside of the game world.

Before we go to the next point, it is crucial to consider that not every game needs to always make the player feel clever, especially if the attempt could cause frustration. For example, not every game is about long-distance navigation challenges, yet they have long-distance travel. Therefore, it might be okay to use a waypoint in this game's context because not providing the player one could lead to player frustration. Here, the frustration of long-distance navigation challenges could be based on player expectations (especially if it is a sequel), or the developers did not spend enough time in pre-production to find entertaining ways to make the challenge work well. Typically, by default, avoiding player frustration beats the notion to make the player feel clever.

Thirdly, it is vital to make the consequences of a choice clear to the player. If they do not know what is behind the left or right door, then the consequences feel random, and random success or punishment can never make the player feel clever. At best, they feel happy, or at worst cheated and frustrated. Additionally, they will blame or give credit to the game for the outcome, not themselves. However, we want the player's action to lead to success or failure, so they blame/congratulate themselves and never the game. I will talk more about randomness further below.

Fourthly, the known positive consequence needs to have an impact, meaning, purpose, push the progress forward or be rewarding. If any positive player action's outcome is in vain, then why would they do it in the first place? This issue is often present in a games' later progression. The core systems like shooting AI might be fun, but after a while, that is not enough to mow down enemies for some currency or XP, which players might not need anymore or overall it feels too much like an endless grind.

Fifthly, the difficulty of the challenge has to be correct. If you consider stealing candy from a baby a severe challenge and entertainment, then I recommend at least therapy; for everyone else, we only value our achievement based on the challenge we succeeded. If a boss fight was very difficult, but we finally managed to beat that dude, we feel great, relieved, and pretty epic. However, if the boss fight was over after a few accidental shots in his direction, we feel at best "meh."

#### *7.2.3.3 Closing Words*

Those five steps sum up my approach to make the player feel happy. If something does not feel right or rewarding, then I typically go through this list in my head and see if one or more points could be the reason.

The tricky part is that some points can be subjective, such as the difficulty or impact. The other problem is that aspects like available options or clarity can be tainted for us developers because we know the level. In all those cases, reviews with mixed reviewers and internal or outside playtests are an excellent way to get a fresh opinion.

### 7.2.4 Fairness, Frustration, and Difficulty

#### *7.2.4.1 Introduction*

When a challenge feels unfairly difficult, then it leads to player frustration. However, difficulty and resulting player frustration are complex topics that developers might dismiss, especially when they are under stress or pressure. Still, there is no benefit as a developer trying to convince the players or peers into believing the opposite, especially blaming or gaslighting players is never a good idea. Therefore, if frustration even becomes a remote topic, then take it seriously.

However, often it is not the challenge itself that is the problem, but its presentation. All the right ingredients are often present to make a challenge solvable in the intended difficulty, but they are not clear to the players. Therefore, do not make the mistake and as the very first step change the challenge itself, but instead make your solutions clearer to the players.

The ideal goal is for players to consider the difficulty "just right" and above "just right" in later levels. As long as they feel that a challenge is difficult but not frustrating, you hit the jackpot for serious milestones like boss fights or critical challenges. However, even if you have made all messaging clear and correct, serious abusive difficulty will ultimately lead to frustration. Then you need some more data, or potentially the recording of the playtest, to make an educated call for the true root of the issue.

I will talk more about practically applied balancing later on. This chapter is more about avoiding unfair setups and the mindset to tackle player frustration.

#### *7.2.4.2 About Random and Luck*

As I stated previously, I am not a big fan of randomness in level design if connected to player choices. Especially random consequences, messaging/clarity, or problems often lead to the players feeling cheated. A player who feels cheated will not feel clever and ultimately not enjoy the game as much. Even if the player keeps getting lucky, it will wear off eventually because it can lead to meaningless success. Therefore, I recommend avoiding randomness whenever possible in such contexts.

However, there are cases where randomness has its place. Below is a list of examples where I consider randomness to be okay. I doubt I can list every possibility, but I hope they bring the mindset across.

- Random game design aspects in certain games are acceptable, like dice rolls in RPGs or random card drawing in deck-building games.
- Random AI spawn positions if replayability is important for your game/level and players have enough time to adjust to the new AI position.
- Random AI patrol paths, if replayability is important for your game/level if the patrol paths do not include any unfair paths like turning around on the spot in stealth sections/games.
- Random layout modifications, if replayability is very important for your game/level and your engine/AI supports it.
- Random AI spawn positions or patrol paths if the intention is to establish a frantic feeling of chaos—typically in faster-paced games where players do not die/fail instantly.
- Random codes for doors are always better than fixed ones, so players don't get the codes from the internet.
- Random amount/position of lesser important pickups for flavor, like certain resources or some money/ammo.
- Random art elements like lights, texture patterns, and shader effects are okay if it is in line with the art direction.
- Random filler AI like civilians, traffic, wildlife, or small amounts of enemies if it is in line with the game's creative or level design direction.

I have mentioned replayability a few times. Randomness unquestionably plays a crucial role in any game with replayability. However, replayability and the connected randomness come with an increase in production cost. The cost is not just you supplying all the scripts. However, it also increases the costs for reviews, testers, and potentially other departments like artists, game coders, designers, and managers. Therefore, if your game is not severely about replayability, I recommend not playing a lot with randomness. It might be easy for you, but it can lead to high hidden costs, surprises and consequences. Further on, especially in singleplayer games without a replayability focus, it is often not even noticed by many players. Usually, game code is more suitable for covering many randomization topics like loot distribution or certain AI setups/encounters than level design. Random layouts always sound super intriguing initially, especially for us level designers, but then too often get cut by production/managers because the gain is too little compared to the likely huge risks and costs.

### *7.2.4.3 Blame Yourself—Not the Game*

Okay, the headline of this little chapter might sound a bit harsh for some, but it encapsulates a goal we as designers should thrive for: "Players should blame themselves in case they failed/die and never the game/level." If players acknowledge that they, for example, did not aim well enough, did not shoot fast enough, could choose a different load-out, dodge quicker or try a different strategy, then they typically do not blame the game. Instead, they hopefully remain motivated to try again, keep enjoying the game, and maybe even explore/discover new ways to play.

However, if, they instead blame the game rather than their skills, then we developers could have done a better job. For example, if we suddenly throw a huge horde of crazy difficult enemies at the players, deadly traps are randomized and undetectable, or we spam the players with surprise artillery strikes. Essentially we kill them seemingly randomly, often connected with a surprise. It is the clear definition of unfair gameplay.

It is essential to keep in mind what is predictable for us developers of the game/level and what is for the players. Again, we know the levels, and especially late in development, we likely have tunnel vision and see such cases not as problematic anymore. As usual, playtests are a good solution. More often than none, it pays off to be nice to the players.

## 7.3 Abstract: High-Level

### 7.3.1 Introduction

For me, seeing high-level compositions of maps is comparable to compositions of paintings, just in a different medium. They are very abstract and essentially a simplification. They are visual patterns that can make or break a picture; the same applies to levels.

In my old article "Ben's Small Bible of Realistic Multiplayer Level Design," I referred to it as the "strategic plan." It is the underlining placement and arrangement of visual elements. Ultimately in paintings, they can help to guide the viewer's eyes, and well in levels, the composition guides the players. My previous article focused primarily on multiplayer maps, but in this book, I will extend it to singleplayer level design.

### 7.3.2 Thinking High-Level

When you simplify or abstract a layout far enough, you hopefully reveal the underlying "essence" of a level layout. Successful maps which play great usually have a great conceptual foundation. Of course, the high-level composition is not the only reason for a level's greatness, but it is a lot harder to make a map play fun based on a flawed foundation. Therefore every level should start with a basic understanding of the high-level layout. Researching and reverse engineering such patterns, especially of multiple successful maps of the same game mode, can show a universal composition, leading to a solid level design direction.

When abstracting level design layouts, the first common observation is how simple most basic layouts are once you analyze them in-depth. I am not talking here about mid-level design, details like cover placement, small shortcuts, or curve angles. I am just talking about the primary player lanes, aka the high-level. They are your layout foundation, and they must be executed and planned excellently since they are your base skeleton of the entire level. Otherwise, way too late and way too expensive to change, your level's appreciation crumbles like a house of cards. For clarification: mid-level are the additional options which complement your high-level layout, but more about them later on.

High-level layouts often go back to basic geometrical forms and shapes. At that stage, there is no focus yet on balance or path length; instead, focus on the base idea or form. Just picture all the possible paths of the player as simple lines, and you will begin to see a basic layout composition. However, at that stage,

**FIGURE 7.1** Golden cut composition of the Mona Lisa.

try to hold yourself back to go into details. Instead, merely draw the main lanes, ideally stay in a large grid, and keep it simple! There is a certain beauty in simplicity.

### 7.3.3 Getting Started with Simplification

Let us assume we have two opposing teams, and they should have an exciting and action-packed experience in your level. However, both players and AI need choices because meeting in an empty corridor or field is very boring. For example, a few falloff paths along the way or flanking routes, go a long way at that stage. In multiplayer, players want to be unpredictable and show clever tactics. In singleplayer too predictable AI is no fun to fight either, and players want to outsmart AI.

The symmetry of your high-level layouts vastly depends on the opposing partys' goals. Therefore, for example, capture-the-flag (CTF) maps are commonly symmetrical because both teams have the exact same goals. In asymmetric bomb defusal game modes, the layout options for both teams are asymmetric because the teams have very different objectives. Singleplayer is vastly by default defined by asymmetry and so are their layouts.

However, regardless of symmetry or not, the thinking is similar: What do the teams want at the start or when they spawn? Where should or could they meet? Furthermore, what choices do they want in between? Do not forget that every AI in your level should have a goal and purpose as well. They should not just spawn and exist to get shot.

At that stage, "roleplay" your level as a player, even AI, and or as a team. What would you or they do? What is the best way to ruin your level? What are all the wrong things the worst and least attentive players could do? Such considerations are important early on and at each planning step, and it starts here when you are still in a very abstract phase. Do you like that you only have one or two options here? Is it cool to run in a dead-end? Isn't that path too long without any other options? Is it a good idea to have such a fast connection between the teams' bases or objectives? Answering such questions now and acting upon them is a lot cheaper than later on.

### 7.3.4 Closing Words

I know this sounds all a bit too theoretical and "easier said than done." After all, it is not that easy to reinvent the "golden cut" for your level every single time. However, I would like to keep stressing recurring patterns, especially when we go very simplified and abstract. Most smaller-scale symmetrical multiplayer game modes follow a similar pattern; so are many asymmetrical ones, open-world singleplayer maps, or linear chain of sandbox levels.

In my opinion, the problem in many ways is less the simplification process but the sheer complexity of game modes, game world requirements, or lack of clear level-based goals/objectives. For example, it is easy to state a base pattern for CTF maps, but it is not easy for deathmatch maps, which typically do

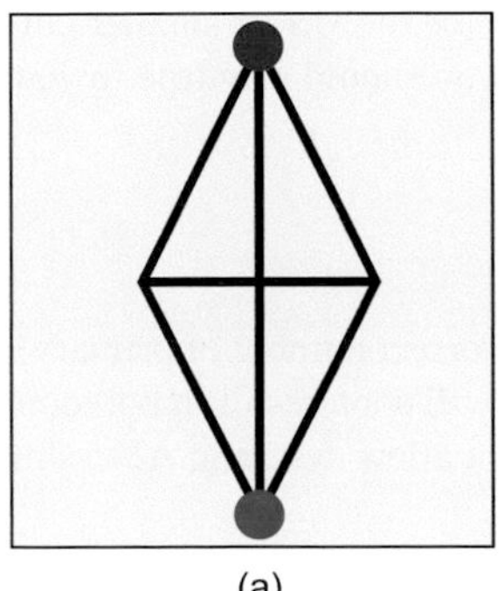

(a)

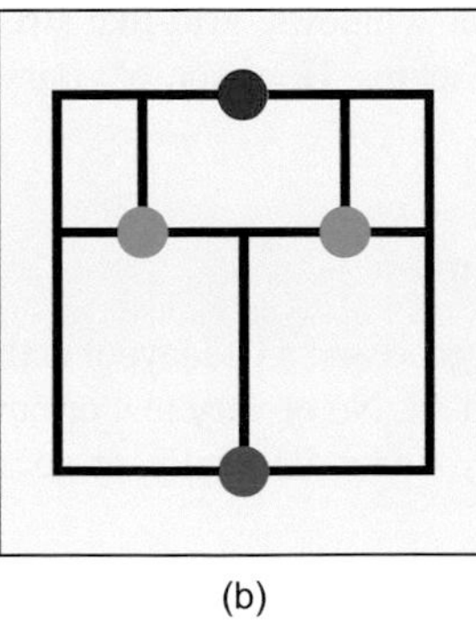

(b)

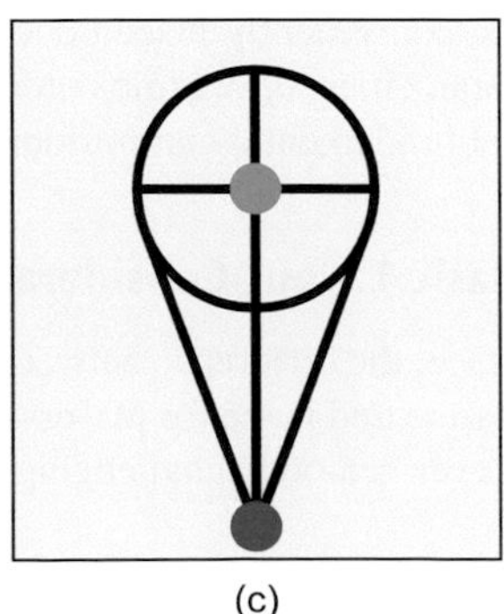

(c)

**FIGURE 7.2** (a) Classic capture-the-flag high-level abstract simplification. (b) Classic round-based objective-based high-level abstract simplification. (c) Classic singleplayer open-world objective location high-level abstract simplification.

not have a level-based objective. Then add, for example, different map sizes, game speeds, vehicles, or pickups to the mix, and you understand the difficulty of the task.

At that stage, ahead of an unknown, I can only recommend taking a big step back. Do some research, analyze, and simplify similar maps till you find several patterns you like. Prototype these few patterns till you find one which your guts tell you is a great foundation—something you feel very comfortable with and alter further. However, if you do not have a solid foundation, changing the level later will make you unaware of the greater impact of such changes. Instead, you rather design "blind," which results in a more time-consuming and frustrating "try & error" design approach.

Please visit my YouTube channel "Bauer Design Solutions" for a case study of abstraction. The specific video is called "The Abstract Deconstruction of de_dust2." In this video I explain step by step how to make the original map more abstract until we just have a basic high-level layout or, in my opinion, the layout essence. Then I see what we can learn from it, and try to create some new layouts from its original high-level lane composition.

## 7.4 Abstract: Mid-Level

### 7.4.1 Introduction

The transition from your previous abstract high-level composition to the mid-level is about adding more player options between and within the main lanes. First, this transition makes your map more unique, especially if you share the core composition with other maps. Secondly, it should closely represent your map's final pathing layout because the abstract high-level layout is only about the core essence.

### 7.4.2 Cover Your Tracks

Now, let us transition back from the very abstract, grid-based mid-level layout sketches to something more tangible. Of course, your map layout stays too simple if you just focus on building the main lanes from the abstract, high-level sketches. Furthermore, if we only build them alone, with no other supporting mid-level lanes, the design becomes too obvious and simple—you want to avoid that, of course. The more your layout design has a subconscious impact and feel to it, the better.

It is a bit like the layout of a traditional English landscape garden. Lots of thought went into the layout and flow, but you do not see the protractor of the park designer. Strict geometrical layouts are great to get the basics right, but it ends there. Imagine how unnatural the world would be if everything built followed a strict grid. There is a good reason why I believe too planned out cities lack soul. Additionally, do not think that you have to translate these geometric lines precisely in 3D. Without a doubt, you should, for example, change the angles of the corners, adjust rotations, or shift hallways when you build it for real.

That means you are finally ready to start adding extra mid-level paths and shape them to the environment. For example, you could consider adding thin alleyways between houses, shortcuts through buildings, conveniently placed doors or windows, grid-like streets for the US or smaller curvy routes in European cities, or organic outdoor setups. However, of course, you should stay true to your abstract high-level fundamental composition.

### 7.4.3 Basic Layout Considerations

At that stage, the difference between a good and a bad layout is the correct number of primary options at the right time and place for players and AI. No or very few options will soon result in boredom, frustration, not even remotely challenging anyone intellectually, or does not allow systemic AI to shine.

#### *7.4.3.1 Number of Options*

If the players have too many options, they could get confused/frustrated quickly, and it can take them way longer to learn the multiplayer map. Remember that any option the players cannot explore can leave them feeling that they have missed out. This situation can lead to much backtracking and only increase frustration or confusion. Therefore, too many mid-level options are often unnecessary. Slower and more systemic games often ask for more options, while faster and simpler games ask for less.

#### *7.4.3.2 Frequency of Options*

However, it is not just about the number of options; it is also about the frequency of options. Spending too long without any options is bad. However, as usual, context is key. A high-speed section does not need many options because you travel at high speed, but the opposite is the case for slower sections or stealth games.

#### *7.4.3.3 Right Place for Options*

Next is the right place for options. Players and AI should have options right away when they spawn or when they enter a new area or part of the map. Then letting them traverse for a while is okay, but at places where they meant to face off each other, they need options again for maneuvers. Keeping a healthy balance between simpler traversal sections and areas filled with options for encountering foes is important.

#### *7.4.3.4 Rhythm of Options*

Lastly, let us also not forget the rhythm of options. If, for example, you have two hallways going left and right every 50 meters, then the whole map feels too constructed, too artificial, and boring because it is all the same everywhere. So it is fundamental to consider the right frequency and rhythm of game objectives, and layout options. The composition is not just limited to visual mediums, but instead, I would consider music composition, too.

### 7.4.4 Options Are Key

The origin of new paths rises from the need for options at the right places. In general, this should result in fewer long paths where players have no options to change routes. I have previously written about it in this chapter, but as a reminder, it is not a very elegant level design to create long lanes without player options to change them.

It is quite simple: You need more choices the longer the lanes and the more players/AI you build your map for. Especially around combat encounters, you need a good amount of get-out paths for players and potential ways for AI reinforcement. Imagine enemies pin you down in a hallway, or you have trouble breaking through the enemy defense, and the only options you have left are: wait to get shot or make a suicide run. To make things worse, you have the same situation every time you take that hallway. I would

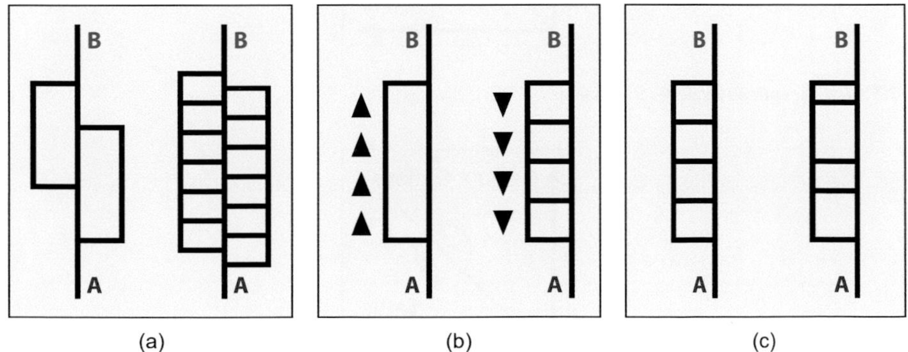


**FIGURE 7.3** (a) Number of options: (left) good amount; (right) too many. (b) Frequency of options: (left) fast section; (right) slow section. (c) Rhythm of options: (left) repetitive; (right) infrequent.

bet you would enjoy the level design a lot more if you had ways out. The same desperation, or rather boredom, kicks in if all AI reinforcement comes down the same single tunnel.

However, create additional paths carefully because the need for them changes from case to case. Sometimes you do not want many choices. So, for example, if players go against the enemy spawn point. Players will try it regardless, but there is no reason for you to support any such non-sportsmanship moves or making your AI look bad. Sometimes it should be harder here or there or requires a specific tactic like a long-range approach. So if you designate a lane to be a sniper section, then it does not need many shotgun close-quarter-battle (CQB) tunnels, but instead a lot of cool sniper spots and ways to travel between them. If players then still run through it with a shotgun, they have to deal with the consequence. Remember, you know the level very well. Therefore, it is up to you to teach the players all the possibilities to enjoy your work, just in a very subtle way without forcing it on them.

### 7.4.5 Basics of Additional Paths

As I have already mentioned, there are locations in your map where you want more player and AI options than your original abstract high-level plan. Typically those locations are where most of your fighting is happening. For example, for CTF maps, this means around the flags and the map's center. For single-player or multiplayer attack and defense scenarios, this means primarily around the objectives and a few lane-swapping options. Those are the locations the players fight the most or where they stop and plan. Those are the "layout-hearts" of your maps. If you have to or want to treat your whole map like that, unfortunately, your life got a lot harder. Additionally, it is a lot trickier to create a nice contrast between traversal parts and combat sections, let alone trickier player-leading.

Having enough options does not just reduce frustration but, importantly, reduce boredom and predictability. If you always know the main paths of your enemies or they know yours, you cannot surprise each other anymore, and the level/game quickly becomes boring.

If you add any additional routes in your identified areas, it is a simple rule of risk vs. reward. A longer path should reward players with some safety because they spend more time here. A shorter path can be riskier because it is obviously faster. On top of that rule, ensure that routes with a high frequency of battle possibilities have more get-out options, while a less frequent lane can live with fewer get-out paths. Lastly, as much as possible, avoid dead ends.

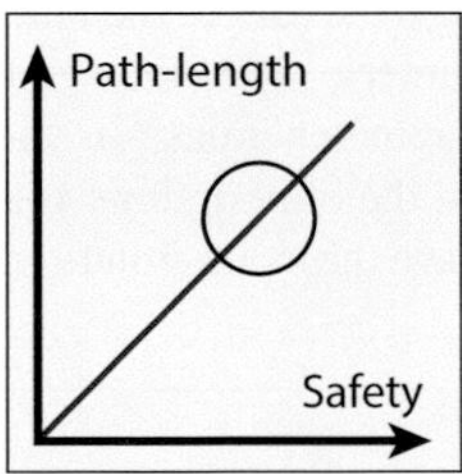


**FIGURE 7.4** Path length and safety relationship.

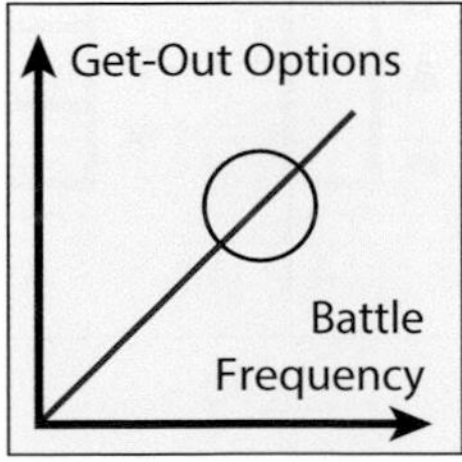


**FIGURE 7.5** Get-Out Options and Battle Frequency relationship.

### 7.4.6 Game Mode Considerations

When we get more detailed, we should start thinking about further game mode specifics. So, for example, a team defending two bomb spots in Counter-Strike needs at least one path, if not more, to travel in between the spots. In Team Deathmatch maps, players need quick ways away from the spawn points to important spots like weapons, upgrades, sniper spots, general map control areas, or armor. For fairness reasons, the distances to those special spots should roughly be similar between the different spawn points.

In singleplayer, it makes sense to consider the different available playstyles. Identify and mark which paths are more like stealth, assault, sniping, explosive, speedy, or vehicle-based. Ideally, already find and document ways how those paths can fulfill their designed intention. For example, sniper paths should lead to sniper spots, stealth paths to some shadowy takedowns, or a fast assault route should be straight with just the right amount of cover. Following the playstyles, it is now time to consider AI. What path-layout and path-types do they need to be a decent challenge for the players?

For example, if you plan with much reinforcement but do not like monster closets, you need to consider that early. Can you bring them in by helicopter or parachutes if you do not have enough layout options for the AI to run in? If neither works, then you might have to rethink your entire layout or concept for the level? Maybe you can stretch out the location further to gain some more space for reinforcement routes? Do I need even more routes if my game is in Coop?

### 7.4.7 Think 3D

So far, we only sketched in 2D, and I know spending a long time in an abstract view can make us forget, but let us not neglect the fact that we most likely work on a 3D game nowadays. Meaning, for example, a previous flanking route can be moved below the ground level without sacrificing much length. Investigate what paths or lanes can overlap instead of running parallel or as a corner route. Further, crossroads do not always have to intersect on the same horizontal plane, but they can be two separate lanes connected with a vertical tunnel/stairs instead. What paths can include stairs or ramps? How will it affect sniping, cover, or grenade throwing?

In general, anything which does not feel like playing a boring pure 2D map translated into 3D is already a step in the right direction. Verticality in any form and shape can be a huge factor but keep target platform controllers in mind. Looking up and down is still more comfortable with a mouse and keyboard than a typical console controller. How aggressive vertical you can get heavily depends on your target platform and game mechanics. I strongly recommend researching and prototyping your verticality metrics early to have a good feeling for it later when you want to push the envelope.

### 7.4.8 Balance of Complexity

To understand what I mean with "balance of complexity" in this context, let us look at cases of two bomb-defusing objectives in a round-based tactical multiplayer map.

In the first one, we have a complex staging area before the objective, which is easy to control. To balance this, the layout directly around the objective makes it harder to attack.

In the second case, a somewhat predictable and straightforward staging area is compensated with an easy-to-attack objective.

Approaches to objectives cannot be all easy or all difficult but should contrast the difficulty of the objective space itself. Furthermore, naturally, with multiple objectives in a map, ensure there is variety.

Okay, what does that mean now? A team now has to think a bit more to execute their plan: In the first version, the approach is "We all have to be at the right spot to execute this difficult attack, but getting to those spots is not the problem." In the second version, it is "Attacking should be pretty straightforward, but we have got to be on our toes getting into position."

If both options exist in the map, what is the preferred tactic of the team? Can I predict the enemy team because I know them, or are they one of those unpredictable ones? Will the defending team take the risk and leave the objective area and attack us during staging? You see, there are already some good stories in the layout without fancy expensive features.

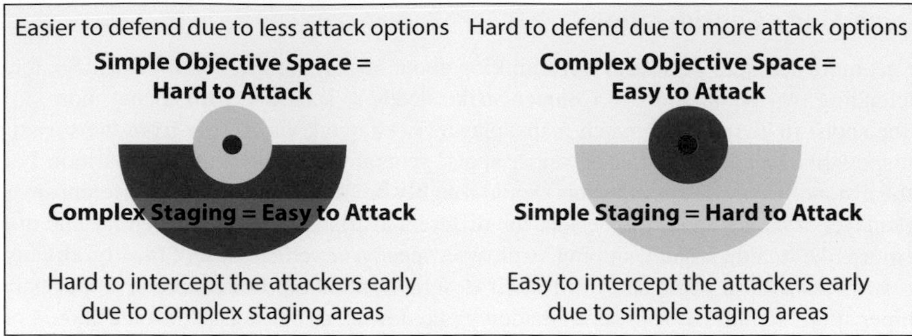


**FIGURE 7.6** The balance of complexity affecting the difficulty of two objective spaces and their staging areas.

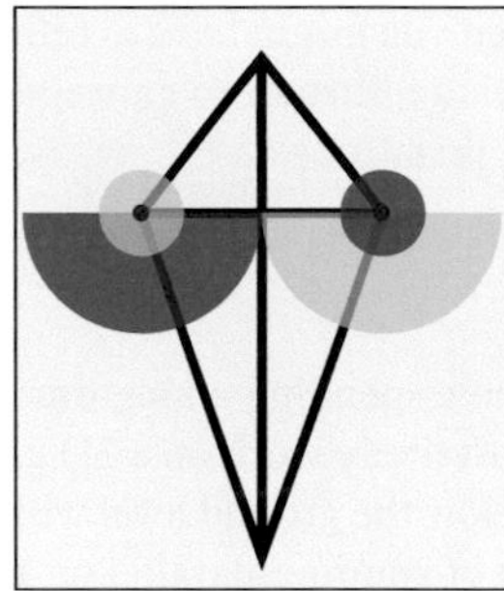

**FIGURE 7.7** Two same objectives create variety in one map due to different balance of complexity.

Singleplayer maps can apply similar thinking, but it is less about fairness. Instead, the right balance of complexity supports a rich gameplay experience. In a more linear game, you should switch up the balance to create variety. Occasionally, a section could be simpler, yet easier, just to change things up because players will get bored if they know that you always have exactly two flanking or stealth routes next to the main paths.

In a more open-world game, use the balance of complexity to support different playstyles. For example, the straight-up assault path into a base might be easy to grasp but difficult to execute. Then the stealth path for the same base might be more hidden, but once found, it should be easier to execute since you have many options to play hide, seek, and stab with the AI. However, it could also be entirely different for another base. Here, for example, the assault path requires careful planning; you have to blow up gates at the right moment and must place mines precisely to deal with the reinforcement. However, then it gets a lot easier. The important consideration is never to be repetitive, yet keep the options balanced between each other and within.

### 7.4.9 Closing Words

As long as you only design in an abstract world, it is easy to make such changes if mentioned before. When analyzing a level, especially an early sketch or document, many problems can be identified when analyzing a level more abstractly because less noise and details cover the potential core issues.

Like for the high-level, I highly recommend studying and analyzing great classic maps of your game mode. Create more and more abstract versions of them and try to find why the maps work so well. This consideration especially counts for the number, frequency, placement, and rhythm of the mid-level options. Start writing down all their good, and maybe sometimes bad, elements in layout and add them to a checklist. Over time you create your collection of well-working elements, and when you apply them, you can be sure that it is not a copy because it came from a very abstract origin and went through a unique mid-level pass.

Simplifying any map to a very abstract level helps find hidden issues, especially high-level and mid-level ones. However, it can also be an excellent foundation for planning and sketching maps. I would not always recommend detailing each aspect of each map. Though, I would consider sketching out the abstract high- to medium-level foundation and lanes, especially for multiplayer maps, linear singleplayer maps, or main missions in an open-world game. Regardless of the scope of your level, even if it changes, you have done the abstract-thinking exercise already. Now you know how any changes affect the overall layout composition, for the better or the worse.

## 7.5 The Concept of "Points of Advantage"

### 7.5.1 Introduction

When I review or analyze a level, I often notice that something is off, but it is hard to point my finger at the issue instantly. So, I try to envision the level more and more abstract and observe when I stumble over a problem. However, back in the days, I could not even really formulate the exact process in my head, but over the years, I think I now can share one of my views on level design layout fundamentals. I am calling it "Points of Advantage" or simply POA. I consider it simply another tool in my toolbox, and I suggest everyone study as many different methodologies from as many different designers as possible.

### 7.5.2 What Is a Good Level Layout for Me?

I have asked many designers this question, and the vast majority said something like: "a fun space for the player(s)." However, I think many problems start here, even if what I said above is distilled and could be answered way more complex. Sure, "fun" is very relative, but that is not the problem with this definition. Instead, the problem is considering layout as space.

I am well aware that this view might be controversial, but let me explain. In real modern combat, there is a saying: "If you worry about your stance, then you are doing two things wrong: You are not moving,

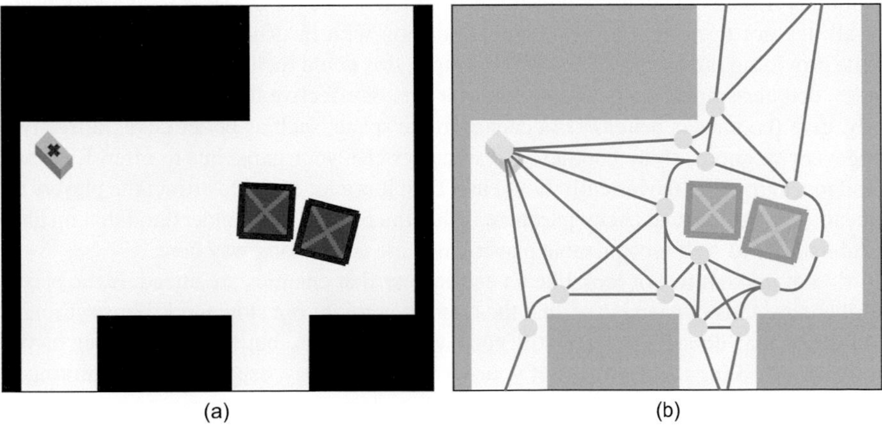


**FIGURE 7.8** (a) A simple layout sample. (b) The same layout with a detailed POA network overlay—The top left corner is only relevant because of the medkit, and the other POAs are cover.

or you are not behind cover." It is not that much different in action games, except we tend to shoot a lot more while moving.

If the combat difficulty is not ridiculously low, it is strongly advised not to stand around in the open. Instead, in a layout, points are attractors, which give you an advantage, in short, POAs. Those POAs can include cover, objectives, flanking opportunities, dynamically changing advantageous shooting positions, sniper spots, power-ups, weapon pick-ups, keys, anything to interact with, moving platforms, or other special navigation spots. We move between those points, and standing around in between is less than ideal.

So essentially, in short, I consider layout as "points and their connections." The space in between is primarily a matter of theme and setting. However, in the context of evaluating if a layout is working or not, space itself matters very little.

It is important to consider that not every POA matters because they are not relevant enough for your analysis or scale. For example, it does not help to count every cover pointing in every direction when you only care about the player coming from one or two directions—It just gets too cluttered. This view or weighting of POAs is fundamental if you look at justifications for paths, branches, or loops. Just because a loop has a tiny cover object might not mean the entire path is justified. On the flip side, if the cover is, for example, essential against a boss enemy, then the loop is relevant enough—more about the scale of the POA method further below.

Additionally note that the points and their connections are not necessarily static. In many instances, they are dynamic, move, appear, disappear, or change context. How good a layout depends on the relationship between the said points and connections. Easier said than done, of course, but more about that below.

### 7.5.3 Player Motivations

To fully engage in the concept of POAs, we first need to understand why players move from points to points? To keep things simple for now: "Players move, because of player-facing layout motivations."

Let's also add the notion that we, in most cases, want the players to move through our designed space. Generally speaking, we do not want players to stand still at one POA for extended periods.

We all know the cases where it is more comfortable to stay at a room's entrance and use the door-frame as cover until every enemy is dead, rather than explore and use the space ahead. I know the door-frame is a classic one which hopefully brings my point across very well. The door-frame topic also represents any other situation where a single cover space at the beginning of a combat space is overly powerful.

From a level design perspective, a player staying at the door-frame, luring every enemy toward them, and killing everyone from here is a bit of a disaster. We wasted all the time and effort to make an excellent combat space, which the player never utilizes. It is safe to say that a heavily underutilized layout is not a good one.

The solution is simple but not easy: the entrance should not be a POA or at least a very weak one.

First of all, try not to make it a good combat position with insufficient cover and bad player attack angles while providing the enemies POA. For example, this could include good, well-protected places to lob grenades, counter-sniping spots, indirect mortar fire, or effective flanking routes.

Secondly, give the players better POAs deeper in the space, such as better cover, attractive positions to use gadgets or weapons, shiny goodies, and whatever else your game has to offer. Especially if your features and mechanics are intrinsically fun to use, then it is a lot easier to attract the players to use them at spots ahead. The critical and tricky part here is that the players must understand that up ahead is such a spot. Established and well-recognizable player language goes a long way here.

Thirdly, do not make it feel or look like an entrance or that enemies are ahead. If the player does not know that there are tons of enemies behind the door, they might not stop and kill everything from here. This could mean that door-frames are still good vantage points, but they are deeper in your overall gameplay space. Masking the gaminess of your layouts is not easy, especially with limiting tech, but it is certainly worth the effort.

Finally, since we lured the players deeper into our space, try not to give the player a reason to run back to his favorite entrance at the first sign of danger. Then, your only option is to prevent it physically, and that is not elegant. Closing the door behind the player is not an exquisite solution, but it has its merit in more arcade games, of course. Jumping down an unclimbable cliff is the classic go-to solution, but you can only do it so often before the players feel cheated. Better solutions are to flush the player forward using AI or other events or keep attracting him even more forward by providing more attractive POAs ahead.

With that example in mind, let's return to player-facing motivations. We want to motivate the player to move from POA to a new POA. Essentially a good layout is a dynamic network of POAs.

No POA should be perfect. A cover POA is only good against specific directions, a pickup POA is only good while the pickup is there, and a good shooting position POA is, of course, only suitable when an enemy is at the right spot.

Ideally, there is always a need to move to the subsequent POA because the current one became less advantageous. The pacing of switching POAs depends on your game. Things are a bit faster in arcade arena shooters or high-speed tactic shooters than in your classic stealth game.

### 7.5.4 Arenas

Let us continue with the first of primary dynamic POA networks: the arena.

Many level types use an arena network, ranging from boss fights, multiplayer maps, sandbox bubbles, or an ample space with an open objective. Essentially anything in which the player has free movement and the objective is not a singular linear point.

An arena's basic shape is a loop, typically a circle, square, or triangle with at least two, but ideally three POAs. A loop with one or no POAs does not give the players enough real reason to move.

Empty space has very little chance to generate relevant POAs, and it is often a sign of wasted potential in your layout. Playtest or reviews highlight such spaces if rarely anyone goes there. Such cases appear if there is no value for the players or they do not know of anything important there. Therefore, right at the beginning, during the arena's planning, think in terms of POAs to justify why you add every loop.

The square or circle shape is the fundamental shape for any arena, but it is essential to remember that such a shape does not mean an empty room unless the player has the motivation to go to each corner. An empty corner is not a POA except if there is, for example, some cover, a relevant pickup, or an advantageous shooting position.

After establishing the basic form, you can go ahead and expand it with more loops. They can overlap; they can be bigger vertically or horizontally. For example, two overlapping squares are a classical basic arena layout, which you can interpret vertically and horizontally.

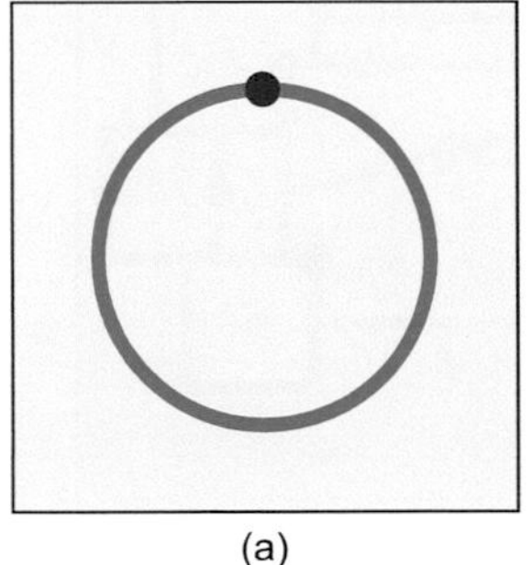

(a)

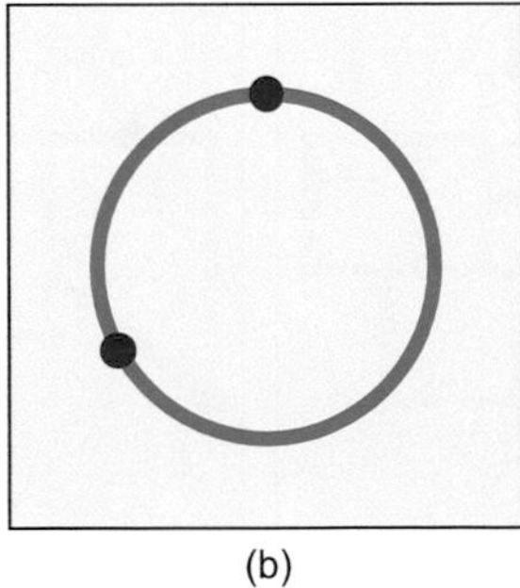

(b)

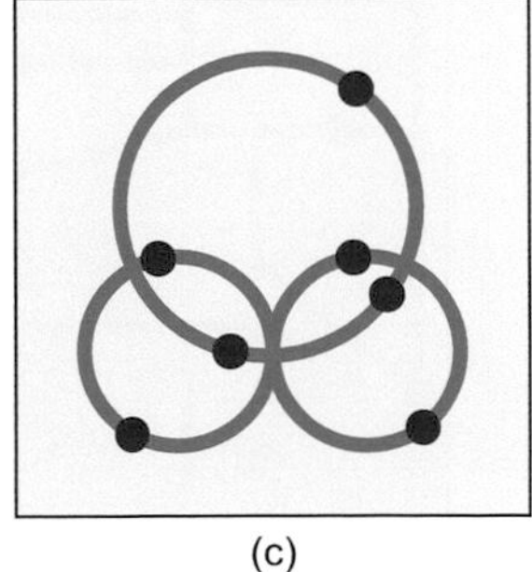

(c)

**FIGURE 7.9** (a) This arena is incomplete because it only has one POA. (b) This arena has the minimum amount of POAs. (c) Arena out of connected loops with enough POAs for each.

So far, I have only talked about looping structures, but I have to talk about dead ends now. Dead ends can be tricky and who knows me well enough knows that I am not a big fan of them. However, they have their place, and in the end, it comes down to "risk vs. reward" and sometimes tech or design constraints.

So, for example, a railgun in an arcade arena shooter might be in a dead-end because it is a powerful weapon. Going there and back exposes you to the enemy or makes you more predictable since everyone knows where you have to come back. However, in a boss arena, a dead-end means the player might get stuck in a corner with little to no way out. Depending on your AI, game mechanic, or tech, this is a bad thing.

Again, in general, I recommend keeping the movement fluid in an arena structure and only break this rule if risk and rewards are clear to the player.

### 7.5.5 Linear Structures

Let us continue with the linear POA networks. The most simple layout under this model is a single POA, but this, of course, is a bit too simple, and it does not keep the player moving. The next most straightforward solution is two connected POAs. However, the players now only have one option at each POA, and it is not exciting going back and forth.

However, when I am talking about linear structures, I do not see it as that simplified. Instead, very straightforward objectives typically define them, like reaching a point, killing someone, pushing a button, or chasing someone.

From a layout perspective, a direction or chain of POAs defines them. However, that does not mean it is a single path without any branching options or preventing the player from going back. Depending on your game, branches create small loops that always bring the player back to the main linear direction. The loops make it feel less linear, but that is not the focus here.

The critical aspect is that each branch must feature a POA. Ideally, the POA or at least the idea of a possible POA must be clearly understood by the players before they choose to switch branches. If there is no advantage, then the branch is meaningless.

The way you present multiple options, the number of options, and how far spread out they are, are quite important. Think of each option as the angle of the player's field of view. The faster your game or sequence, the smaller you should make the option's angle.

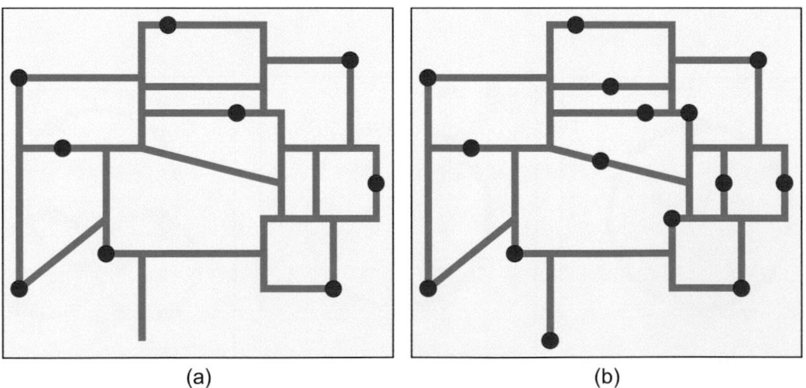


**FIGURE 7.10** (a) Arena layout with some loops less relevant because they have no POAs. (b) Arena layout with all loops relevant because they have at least one POA.

So, for example, in a fast-paced chase, I would stay away from any options presented larger than 45 degrees and certainly have none at 90 degrees or more. This allows the player to keep their options in view easily. Now in linear stealth or slower puzzle navigation games, the pacing means you can hope that players look all around, including behind or up. How many options you want to give to the player primarily depends on your game's pacing in conjunction with the environment.

You would imagine in an underground tunnel, you typically have fewer options than in a scrapyard. However, slower-paced stealth games often give the players more pathing options in a tunnel than some more fast-paced action games give you in the mentioned scrapyard.

The distance between paths depends on your game's pacing, environment, and tech limitations. For example, if your game engine is not open-world ready, then a short distance between paths makes sense. A very dense jungle valley with all paths being ten meters away from each other is likely fitting, but if they are 1 kilometer apart then it doesn't sound entertaining.

More than anything, it just has to make sense from a fun and production level while meeting the technical limitations of your engine. It all comes down to finding the right balance and being aware of it before jumping in the editor. Fixing a bad layout too late is just too expensive to not care about early enough.

### 7.5.6 Connections

Now to be fair, if we only focus on the points itself then we forget the second most important aspect of this theoretical model and that is the connections between POAs.

Connections can be short, long, difficult, risky, easy, fast, slow, safe, and so on. The connections are obviously critical because they affect important aspects in the context of combat, navigation, stealth, driving, coop, or time. So a fast and safe way to a pickup or objective is obviously weighted very differently compared to a long and risky connection.

Now connections can be a fundamental part of level design direction. For example, you could declare that for your Coop mission each connection between gameplay bubbles requires Coop or a risky navigation puzzle. But when you work on an arcade arena shooter all connections ideally are fast and easy because that better suits the game direction.

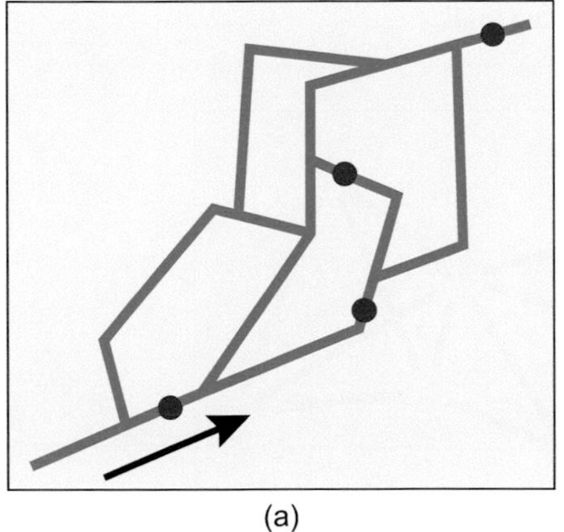

(a)

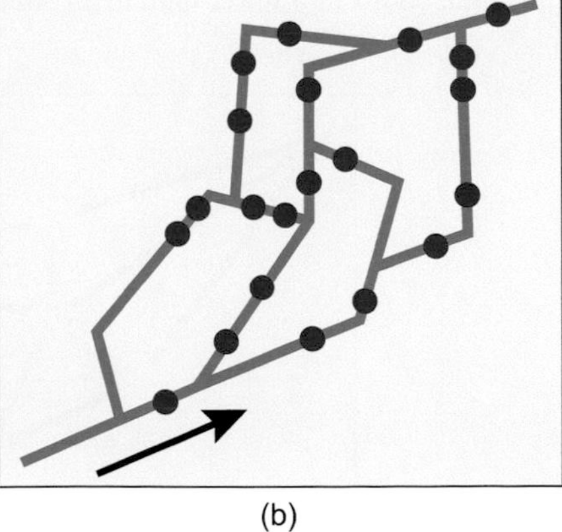

(b)

**FIGURE 7.11** (a) Linear section with unnecessary branches because they have no POAs. (b) Linear section with relevant branches because they have POAs.

The risk associated with a connection is crucial as well. So for example a connection exposing you to potential enemy sniper fire is quite different from a tight shotgun-heavy sewer connection path. Essentially connections are key tools to translate the creative direction into pacing and level design direction.

I recommend keeping the number of connection types small per level, section or activity. So for example if you build a 15-minute open-world mission, then ideally don't mix vertical navigation, flying vehicle sections, normal walking, grappling, driving, swimming, diving, risky minefields, coop gates, chasing and forced stealth sections in one. A good mix and a memorizable highlight are important, but too much of everything will just dull the impact.

Another different example was when I designed the level design direction of large sandbox maps which can be played in Coop and singleplayer. There, during the planning, we strictly separated the connection between the two modes. The coop-only connections had different advantages, travel speeds, or navigation compared to the ones available in singleplayer and coop-only. This differentiation allowed us to make the maps feel and play significantly different in Coop compared to just singleplayer. Playing in Coop wasn't just a better experience with your friend but also gave you new and different options, tackling even harder challenges.

Additionally, some connection types are defined by POAs like teleporters or jump plates because they start and or end at a designated place. What exactly is now a connection or a POA ultimately depends on your game's features and honestly how you prefer to plan it. This isn't really strict science, just an abstract personal thought model.

### 7.5.7 Filling the Gaps

I stayed for quite a long time in a very abstract space of just points and lines. Now, it is time to briefly talk about how to translate all that into actual space. While I have focused on POAs, and despite my original statement about space, the space surrounding points and connections is not completely irrelevant.

The required space around your POAs and your connections depends on your environment and type of game. Arena shooters where players jump around dodging grenades and rockets typically need more space around POAs than a game where a few bullets already kill you. Of course, we are talking here about a general state with exceptions coming with the usual risk vs. reward balance.

The environment type is the second leading factor, and I hope you decided on it with intent and awareness of the consequences. First, for example, it should go without saying that you have less space at POAs and around connections in a sewer than in an American mall.

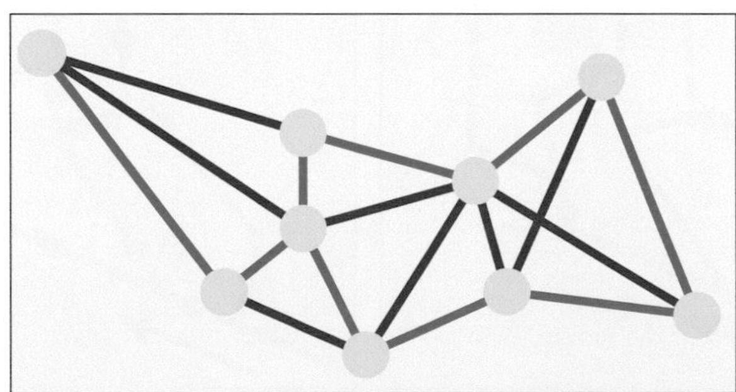

**FIGURE 7.12** Solo (green) and coop-only (purple) connections between small groups of AI (yellow), which are our POAs in this context in a larger sandbox arena.

Secondly, your gameplay intentions have to match your chosen environment. So, if you want a sniper-heavy map and you picked a sewer instead of a desert, then I guess you misunderstood me.

### 7.5.8 Meta Level and Scale

At this point, some designers will think this is all a bit too much detailed work and thinking for their type of game or level, and they are right. This methodology can easily be scaled up or down, depending on your needs.

So, for example, in an open-world mission, it might be enough to first plan out mission locations, and then per location, primarily plan the "golden" routes with vantage points, playstyles, and objectives in mind. It is perfectly okay to plan the rough cover locations instead of pre-planning each option, especially cover—as important it is—should rarely be planned in such detail. There is rarely much need to think that each crate means at least four POAs, except if you work on, let us say, a tactical CQB multiplayer map.

A more cinematic linear experience needs more detailed planning than your standard systemic open-world game, yet you will always find exceptions. Arena shooters might not take every small corner as cover-POA in consideration as well, but instead each powerup. Stealth games or other cover-based games are pretty much the opposite. When I work on classic open-world locations, I primarily look at vantage points, the cover paths originating from them, and determine their types instead of planning each cover object.

Especially with more modern engines, where you can quickly jump in-game, I do not recommend planning too long and too detailed on paper. Get your intentions across on paper, plan your main paths, communicate it well to your fellow artists, designers, or leads, but once agreed on, finish your details in the editor. Moreover, with "paper," I mean anything from PPTs, sketch-up, fancy animated vectors, drawing on a napkin, or even on actual paper.

The possibility of quick iterations nowadays is a blessing compared to the old 7+ hour long compile times. So, make use of the speed and your hopefully good tools. We all know that once you go in-game, especially with many systemic mechanics around, your best plans quickly fly out of the window. However, what always stays are your intentions.

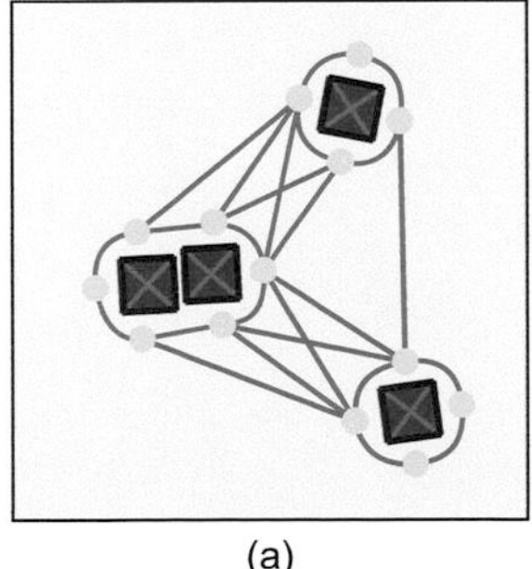
(a)

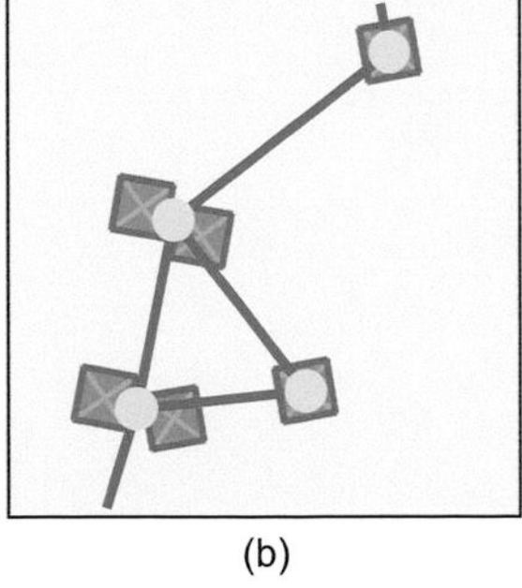
(b)

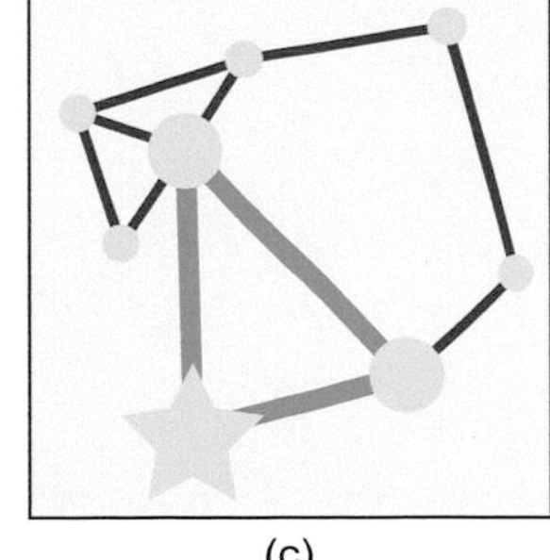
(c)

**FIGURE 7.13** (a) POA scale: covers in a stealth game. (b) POA scale: lose cover network in an FPS. (c) POA scale: open-world locations with different connections.

### 7.5.9 Closing Words

Once again, the idea of seeing layout strictly only as points and connections instead of space is just one method of many. It helped me to keep things abstract, high-level when needed, handy to build a direction upon it, and allowed me to sell my intentions to the developers around me. I use it to dig deeper on why one layout might work better than others: both during private research and when I review the work of other designers as a director.

Further on, many modern systemic AIs in action games are very similar. So, what works for players can be quickly translated to some sort of an AI model. After all, many AI systems are very point-oriented, too.

It can easily be expanded based on your game and game mode. So, for example, it can be helpful to plan a chase with some additional rules about angles and speed. Adjusting its scale helped me plan large missions between many locations or an entire open-world network, including their connections, history, and different world-building layers. It is all a matter of scale. Instead of having a different methodology, just adjust the detail, zoom, and context.

It all started with my origins in small-scale tactical multiplayer maps, where I had to plan every piece of cover and connection carefully. A lot of what I wrote in my old article "Ben's Small Bible of Realistic Multiplayer Level Design" is based on this thinking and further expanded in the last 20 years, working a lot with AI and open worlds. Modern engines can reduce the impact of much detailed pre-planning, but it is hard to replace a convincing idea or intention, especially in a team context.

# 8

# *The Big Picture*

On a broad high-level, one definitive aspect for most singleplayer games is that they are a chain of levels or a collection of missions. Chaining missions is typical for rather linear games, while a collection of missions describes more free games that have, for example, an open world.

Therefore, it is crucial for level designers, leads, and directors to see games from a higher perspective. It is about understanding the "big picture," the high-level, to set up success for any lower level from then on. This high-level is also where all the planning for further levels originates from. The right mix of level design, game design, narrative, and art ingredients guarantees that the hour-to-hour experience for the player follows an entertaining pattern and mix.

We all know games that had great levels, but the overall experience of how they are tied together was lacking. It could be a sign for a less developed understanding of the big picture fun, or beloved elements start to be left behind. After a third or half of the game, such games only focus on less developed features, art, or narrative. Remember that such a bad pattern can also come from trouble during production when big cuts profoundly impact the overall experience but they never had the time to rearrange their high-level foundation and mix.

The better you understand the big picture, its patterns, connective tissue, and why certain elements are where they are, the better you are prepared to make still meaningful decisions if such often unavoidable cuts appear. The better you understand the "why" of the high-level, the more resilient you can react to an unforeseeable production reality. However, sticking to a rigid plan that often crumbles under the bespoken pressure of unforeseeable production reality leaves you only with the too-late choice to make tough, avoidable, less-than-ideal decisions.

Lastly, this chapter covers the topic of tutorial levels because each game usually starts with them. Sure, not all games have an apparent tutorial segment; some hide it better than others, but all games teach players about their game and world in some form or shape.

## 8.1 The Game as a Progression of Levels

### 8.1.1 Introduction

When I describe the big picture of games in this chapter, I first talk about the linear type, hence the "progression" in this chapter's title, because it is easier to understand and to explain. Later on, I cover how to approach it for the open type.

### 8.1.2 Progression in the Big Picture

#### *8.1.2.1 Introduction*

In order to get an understanding of the bigger picture, we need to get a good overview of the game's totality. In our case, that means all the levels and what they entail. The best way to show the big picture is to put it, well, on one picture or one (large) page. Such a format is essential to spot potentially problematic patterns and plan a good progression. It is also a great way to communicate the game's progression to peers and the team.

Keep in mind that the creation of such an overview is not the responsibility of one person. There might be one person mainly responsible for creating the document, but its content is a matter of a bigger team. Typically, in my experience, it is a matter for the game's creative core team like level design director,

DOI: 10.1201/9781003275664-11

game design director, narrative director, art director, and of course, the creative director. Every discipline represented in this document is part of the process and core tech people should evaluate it for an early reality check.

Ideally, you start working on such a document early on during pre-production, during or after the high-level or blueprint phase. A close-to-finished version is required to start the individual level documentation phase and then production. This high-level document should be easy to maintain because likely changes will happen even during production.

### 8.1.2.2 Progression Table Creation

In my experience the best way to create such a "big picture," one-pager document is to create a big table that lists all levels and all of the game's relevant factors that affect the levels.

In theory, any software which can create tables or table-like graphics is suitable, but I suggest keeping large printouts in mind. I'm talking here about larger plotter-type formats. Printing them and hanging them on the wall of your studio is always a nice touch and a great way to present the whole game. If you want to keep things good-looking, I suggest vector graphic software like Adobe Illustrator, InDesign, or similar.

Filling out the table should not start from scratch. You should have most of the information following the high-level or blueprint phase. Do not expect that every field already has an answer. However, most empty ones should be easy to fill out because they follow logical consequences. The ones that are self-explanatory might require you to make a guesstimate at first. Then typically, you need a follow-up meeting where every stakeholder gives their green light, which is also a good place to discuss your previous guesstimates. Another option is that you go into the high-level phase with an early, empty table and use it as a guide for the meetings of that phase.

I suggest, the columns are the levels and the rows are the elements, so we read the levels going from left (first) to right (last level). The content of the rows is very game dependent, so the list below is just an example of potential candidates.

- Level number
- Level name
- Chapter name (spreading over multiple columns)
- Level connectivity (in case you have branching levels, spreading over multiple columns)
- Location/setting
- Time of day
- Interior or exterior
- Difficulty
- Level structure type (linear, arena, a chain of sandboxes, etc.)
- Gameplay pillars (long-range, stealth, action, puzzle, navigation, etc.)
- Enemy/friendly faction
- Dominating AI archetypes (including animals)
- First appearance of AI archetypes (including animals)
- Player weapon/feature unlocks or rewards
- Dominating player features (vehicle, abilities, weapons, level design ingredients, etc.)
- Other unique features specific for the level, unique selling points, or memorable moments
- Gameplay modifiers (limited weapons, time pressure, forced stealth, etc.)
- Narrative meaning/hook
- Key NPC presence
- Tone/mood/emotion
- Art thematic/focus

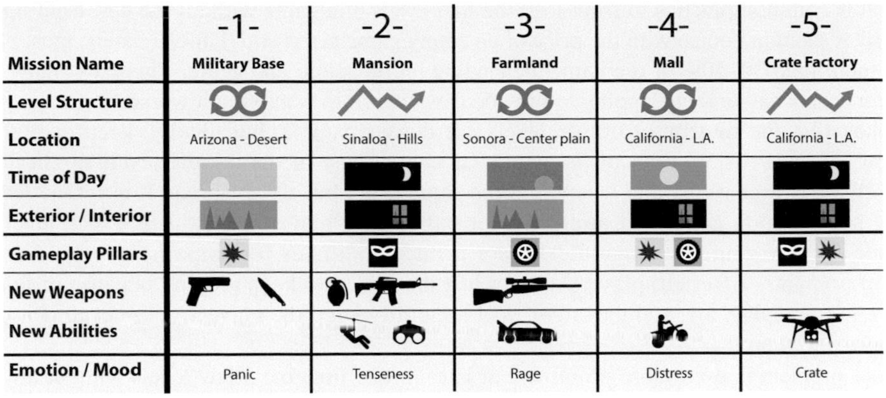

| Mission Name | -1- Military Base | -2- Mansion | -3- Farmland | -4- Mall | -5- Crate Factory |
|---|---|---|---|---|---|
| Level Structure | | | | | |
| Location | Arizona - Desert | Sinaloa - Hills | Sonora - Center plain | California - L.A. | California - L.A. |
| Time of Day | | | | | |
| Exterior / Interior | | | | | |
| Gameplay Pillars | | | | | |
| New Weapons | | | | | |
| New Abilities | | | | | |
| Emotion / Mood | Panic | Tenseness | Rage | Distress | Crate |

**FIGURE 8.1** Example progression table (simplified, incomplete, not a UI artist/designer).

- Key concept art (only one)
- Length/time of the level (in minutes)

Sometimes you cannot avoid it, but as much as possible, avoid text, especially longer ones. Even if you use a single or a few words, try to give the background of the cell/box a color indicating its category. As much as possible, try to find similarities and showcase them with colors, or at best, icons. Remember, it is a graphical format and a tool to spot patterns. Therefore, the more you can use icons, colors, categories, and fewer words, the better.

For example, time of day, interior/exterior, or gameplay pillars are primary icon candidates. However, you can even transform anything like difficulty, AI archetypes, weapons, abilities, level length, modifiers, or NPC presence in a graphical format; just ask your fellow, friendly UI artist/designer for some help. The more you transform to graphics, the faster anyone can read this table, grasp the bigger picture and see how it is all connected.

One common mistake when developers create such a table for the first time is to add too many rows and elements. Only focus on what is essential for your game. Depending on your context, you might want to have, for example, more or less level design, narrative, game design, or art elements. If you add too many elements, you run the risk of overcrowding the table with unnecessary data. You make it harder to spot patterns or any other type of problems while leaving less space for the essential elements. A good indication that a row might be unnecessary is if you notice that you fill out rows just for the sake of completing it. If you sense it doesn't add any more value or that the data is better suited in other documentation, cut it.

### 8.1.3 Patterns in a Progression Table

#### *8.1.3.1 Introduction*

I have talked a lot about spotting patterns in progression tables, and below I will cover some of the more common ones. In my experience, I would consider all of them as potentially problematic, but again context is key. Those patterns described below are not exclusive to progression tables but for others as well. Therefore, feel free to apply similar thinking if you work with comparable tables listing ingredients.

#### *8.1.3.2 Too Many Ingredients per Level*

If a single level, mission, or map has many new or unique ingredients, then this would only mean that others could have little or even none. It creates a noticeable imbalance in the game's distribution, leaving other levels likely feeling unexciting, unattractive, and empty gameplay-wise.

While it is common practice to front-load the first levels of a game with all the new exciting features and "toys," it shouldn't come with the price of an empty game afterward. Unfortunately, most players do not play more than 30–50% of the game, depending on the game and genre. There are many complex reasons for this behavior, but stopping to provide new attractors is making it worse.

It is okay that the first two to three levels are denser packed, but ideally, keep enough for the later game, at least till 50–60% of the game. Of course, any of the middle levels might not reveal a new ability, AI archetype, and weapon at the same time, but try to spread it out. One level could feature a new weapon, a new AI archetype, or only a new player ability. Also, such levels, which get lighter on new gameplay ingredients, are prime candidates for some unique art or narrative treatment/moments. After all, players are not just motivated to keep playing because of features. A good mix of gameplay, art, and narrative, will hopefully keep the players going even if it gets a bit lighter here and there.

The core problem is even more prominent at later levels. Imagine a few levels without any new AI archetypes and then comes a level that suddenly has three new types. Even if you introduced a new faction or elite variations of previous archetypes, I would try to spread them out more. Leave something for the upcoming levels. Sure, you can be less strict, with variations like pure visual differences, helmets, grenade throwing, or plate carriers.

Still, one risk is that level designers of earlier levels experiment with, for example, some later scheduled AI archetypes and notice that they play well in their maps. After all, creating early levels with a limited set of ingredients can be taxing. They might be very right, but I can only recommend staying a bit strict here and apply empathy for the later levels and their designers. After all, early levels already get a lot of attention and new "toys."

#### *8.1.3.3 Dominating Patterns per Row*

A classic and easy-to-spot pattern is if you chain up too many levels with the same ingredient, without much variety. For example, your game's creative or art direction asks for a night and day mission balance. However, now the first half of the game is entirely at night, and the rest during the day. So technically, the distribution follows the brief, but the execution leaves much to desire.

However, the solution cannot force a strict change of ingredients (day, night, day, night, day, night) because it feels artificial again. There are many design, narrative, and art considerations that make it unreasonable for a perfect regular mix. Where applicable, show early on, in the first two or three levels, that you have day, dusk, or dawn missions, then it can be okay to have longer, darker stretches again.

Therefore, avoid any extremes. Avoid excessively long stretches of a single ingredient, perfect seemingly predictable/artificial/forced/regular patterns, and show early on in the game that you offer variety.

#### *8.1.3.4 Dominating Patterns per Column*

You might have a perfectly natural feeling distribution per row, but you might also have problematic patterns in the columns. For example, almost every time you introduce a new AI archetype, you introduce a new ability or you only have long-range sections in linear level structures. Another example is that you barely feature the navigation gameplay pillar in outdoor levels. Those cases might sound rare at first, but they can still happen on a smaller scale and with some variation. It can stand out, especially in the midsection of your game's progression, when the number of new ingredients gets lower and such patterns become more prominent. Early on in the game, shiny new stuff might cover up such patterns, but they can appear there as well.

Essentially you need to compare every possible variation of ingredients per level and see if they appear in other levels. It might sound daunting, especially if the table is large, but trust me that a solid iconographic treatment can do wonders to spot such patterns.

However, if you spot such a pattern, check if it is actually a bad thing. Especially check pattern distribution, because if they are far apart from each other, it might not be a glaring issue and too costly to fix and renegotiate with all the creative stakeholders. For example, it should be okay to introduce a new AI archetype with a new ability three times, but they are not right after each other, and you have 15 levels in total.

For me, another exciting aspect of looking for such patterns is less player but developer-oriented. For example, you notice that most of your vehicle-centric missions are outdoors. Sure, that all makes sense, but wouldn't it be a cool, memorable challenge to have a vehicle section indoors for a change? Of course, the tech team needs to be okay with it but if that sparks new ideas like a motocross section through a massive burning mall, then, by all means, go nuts.

### *8.1.3.5 Too Many Ingredients too Early*

I have already mentioned the imbalance of individual levels earlier, but it is also essential to look at it from a broader perspective. When, for example, the first third of your game sits on the vast majority of all cool moments, feature introductions, and attractive locations, you have a problem. As I said earlier, it is okay if later levels get a bit lighter in overall relative production cost, but that should not mean they dry out completely. Do not get me wrong, but just basic level design, narrative, and art elements can carry an AAA game only so far. Without some fresh wind or some memorable/unique moments, the game might quickly feel stale.

Even if you run out of new player abilities/ingredients which make sense to introduce early, try keeping some of the level ingredients (for example, zip lines, repelling, turrets) or even some AI variations for the later levels. Even if that does not work out, do not stop supporting some more crazy memorable moments (for example, riding on a train, big burning sections, rappelling down a skyscraper while getting shot at by helicopters) for the later levels. Players can undoubtedly sense if a section (at least on the surface of the final game) was high on production cost and which ones were not. It also does not mean that you cannot make a great game with just plain yet amazing levels, art and narrative, but the competition is fierce. If you like it or not, such unique moments are attention-grabbers, often truly memorable/fun, serious respectful achievements of some awesome developers, and excellent marketing material, which ultimately can lead to more sales.

### *8.1.3.6 Ingredients Late in the Game*

I have written a lot now that early levels should not be too front-loaded, at least to leave some for the mid-game, but it is a bit trickier with the late game. The player will only use any new player ingredient introduced late, like a new weapon, vehicle, or ability, for a limited amount of time. The worst example would be that the most powerful weapon gets available after defeating the final boss.

Therefore, I recommend giving the vast majority of new player ingredients in the early and mid third of the game. In the late game, I would focus on aspects like, for example, new memorable moments, AI

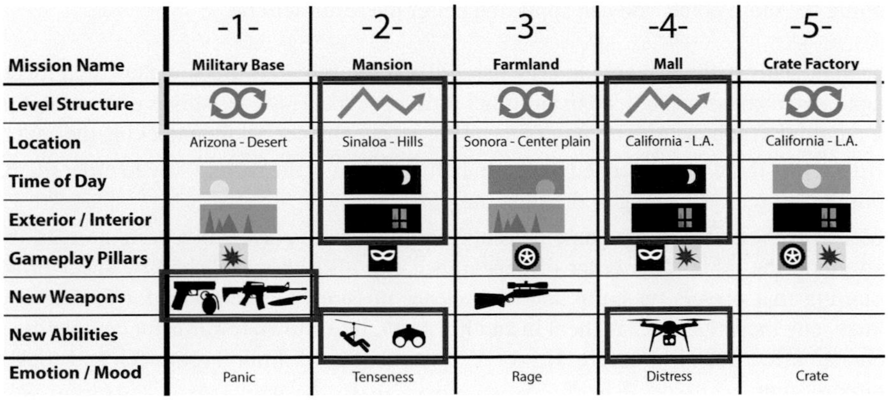

| | -1- | -2- | -3- | -4- | -5- |
|---|---|---|---|---|---|
| **Mission Name** | **Military Base** | **Mansion** | **Farmland** | **Mall** | **Crate Factory** |
| **Level Structure** | | | | | |
| **Location** | Arizona - Desert | Sinaloa - Hills | Sonora - Center plain | California - L.A. | California - L.A. |
| **Time of Day** | | | | | |
| **Exterior / Interior** | | | | | |
| **Gameplay Pillars** | | | | | |
| **New Weapons** | | | | | |
| **New Abilities** | | | | | |
| **Emotion / Mood** | Panic | Tenseness | Rage | Distress | Crate |

**FIGURE 8.2** **Yellow:** Dominating pattern per row (linear and arena structure alternate). **Red:** Dominating pattern per column (every linear level is indoor, at night and only they introduce new abilities). **Blue:** Too many ingredients too early (almost all weapons in the 1st level).

archetypes (especially variations), new narrative/art elements/twists, or an exciting mix of ingredients. However, they need to be truly unique in order to have an impact.

#### *8.1.3.7 About Rational Design*

As much as I'm not a devoted fan of rational design, I do believe it is fine to optionally apply it on progression tables, case by case; so far, it fits. This table is so high-level that rational design is unlikely to lead to a significant negative experience for the player.

For example, you introduce a new exotic archetype in one level, but you remain on the easy difficult side with their implementation. Then in the following one or two levels, you go a bit more complex/difficult in their use or require the players to combine more and more features or level design opportunities to defeat them. You can also combine the enemies in more lethal combinations like other AI archetypes or more challenging environments. The same, of course, counts for anything else like new weapons, abilities, or vehicles. At later levels, make the players experience the full potential of their new "toys."

### 8.1.4 Mission Progression in Open Game Types

#### *8.1.4.1 Introduction*

Open game types are any games whose missions are not in a particular linear structure. Essentially players can do the missions in any order, or there is freedom in groups of missions before it unlocks the next one. Open-world games are the most typical example. This case can apply to freely available (side) missions or a loose yet still semi-controlled chain of main missions.

Of course, their loose order makes it difficult to easily put them in a table suited for linear content. In this chapter, I will explore various options for approaching such a situation while still providing the ability to spot patterns and showcase them in an easy-to-understand, readable format.

#### *8.1.4.2 Progression Table for Open Games*

The first option is to put them still in a table, regardless of their non-linear order. The advantage, of course, is that you can still apply everything from the previous chapters about patterns and the creation of such tables. However, if there is some branching, I recommend adding a level connectivity chart to the table. This chart should give you enough structure to put them in an order, close enough to the real experience.

If there is no structure providing branching, then the most difficult part is putting them in any order. Below is my checklist of how I would approach putting open-structured missions still in a linear format. The checklist is sorted by priority, starting from the most important one. The checkpoints are cumulative, meaning the more points you can apply, the better the result will be.

1. Chapters: This is the first step to establish order if the missions are somehow tied together in chapters or compartmentalized in any other form or shape. However, this is only valid if players are required to complete all or most of the missions per chapter before unlocking the next bunch.
2. Difficulty: If there is an intended increase in difficulty, it is the second way to order them. Start from the left (easiest), going to the right (hardest).
3. Order of Appearance: If the game presents the missions to players in a certain order, this can also guide the table. This order of appearance can also be established by sheer proximity, assuming that players typically approach closer missions before going for further ones. Of course, any incentives to play them in another order, like known rewards for completing a mission, can affect such a structure. However, I would not overthink it too much and stick to one simple system.
4. "Golden Path": The "golden path" describes your ideal order of how the missions should be played if you could put them in a linear order. Of course, players will deviate from it, but it can also guide/direction of how you subtly, "soft-push" players to play the missions in your ideal order.

Still, this checklist can only give you an approximation. However, it can still give you a foundation to apply the advantages of a table, even if it is just for planning and team communication.

#### *8.1.4.3 Progression Sheet for Open Games*

The word "sheet" is not descriptive enough, but in this context I mean the map of your game world (or just a sub-section) with the boxes, which include a brief mission description and pointing at their start locations. It gives you less pattern-recognition possibilities and likely you run out of space quickly, leading to a lighter amount of information per mission-box. However, it contextualizes the missions within the game world, which can help to spot other issues and it is a great tool to visually communicate a mission overview to the team.

Location-related issues are of course the easiest ones to spot on such a sheet. Are there too many/little missions in one part of the map? Is there an imbalance of distribution of certain missions, like too many missions of a certain faction, NPC, or game mode anywhere? If streaming is a topic for your game engine then this is also a good starting point to plan out the necessary distances between memory heavy activities/locations.

The information you put in the mission's box surrounding the map is crucial. For readability and pattern comparison I recommend to use the same formatting, content, and layout for each box. Essentially I found two box-types to be working well.

The first variant is similar to the table, where icons and short descriptions sum up the high-level information of a mission. However, first of all you might end up with less information than the table if space is sparse or the boxes become unreasonably large. Secondly, focusing on iconography and very short text (ideally just a few words) becomes even more important to keep a clean and compressed look. Thirdly, the icons and text itself should be so self-explanatory.

The second variant for such a mission-box is more mission design or narrative oriented. Essentially it would list the major story or gameplay blocks of the specific mission and how they are connected. I recommend you still try your best to categorize/colorize those blocks in for example broader gameplay types (for example, vehicle, stealth, open, exotic), cinematic or in-game events. The best foundations for such blocks are focusing only on the major objectives or most impactful narrative beats like cinematics, reveals, or important NPC interactions. For example: Drone flight introduction (cinematic) → Infiltrate Mansion (gameplay) → Locate Drug Lord (gameplay) → Interrogate Drug Lord (exotic) → Exfiltrate w/ unconscious Drug Lord (gameplay) → Defend Exfiltration Location (gameplay) → Van Exfiltration (cinematic).

Of course, the first variant makes it a lot easier to still detect and work with patterns. More difficult than in an easy-to-compare table, but still possible. Using the second variant it is way more difficult to

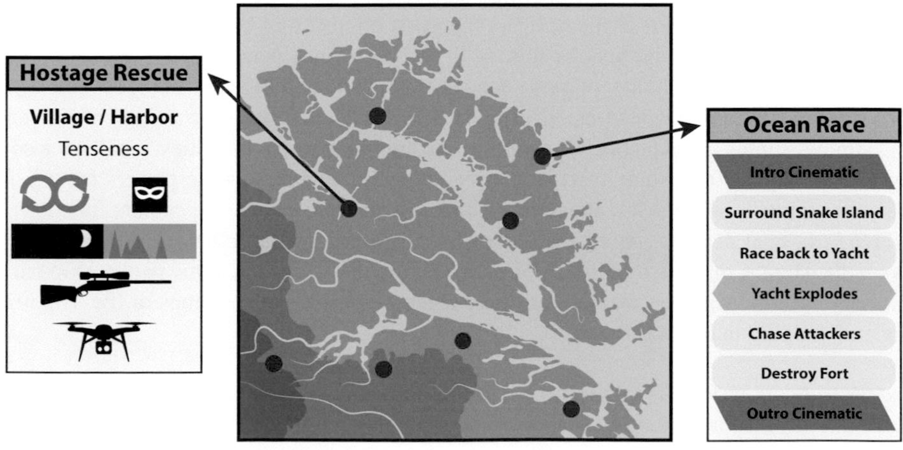


**FIGURE 8.3** Showcase of two types of boxes around a map filling out an open world "progression" sheet.

find patterns, even if you apply some graphical categorized iconography. It certainly has its advantages conveying a lot more actual gameplay and narrative of the individual mission. In contrast to the first variant which keeps things more abstract. However, if you chose the second model, then I would still recommend additionally creating a progression table at the side. Even if the missions are only in a loosely defined order, it still allows you to analyze patterns. If you have too much pace you can of course also combine the two methods.

## 8.2 About Tutorial Levels

### 8.2.1 Introduction

In the context of any game's progression, the very first level holds a very unique, exciting, yet challenging place. It has so many roles to play, like teaching the player the game's basic controls and abilities, hooking the player into the entire game/world, establishing a core narrative, astonishing people with technical/artistic possibilities, and so much more. Therefore, despite the limited space of the first level, almost every department has a high stake in the first level. However, it gets even more complicated that a lot of the presented aspects can keep changing wildly during a development cycle. The narrative changes can have a significant impact on the level. New core mechanics get cut or added and need to find a new home in the already tight level or tech-specs change requiring complete reworks. It is not unusual that more of those challenges appear simultaneously and multiple times throughout a production cycle. However, everyone has high expectations at the first level, from developers to players, since so much depends on its success.

I will only cover basic tutorial considerations in this book. More complex or very different forms of tutorials are very game dependent and can easily go beyond the scope of this book.

### 8.2.2 Gameplay, Art, and Narrative Considerations

#### *8.2.2.1 Introduction*

This chapter covers some of the basic ways to introduce game design, art, and narrative ingredients in the first level. Keep in mind that tutorial levels are so complex and highly game-specific that I can only share general aspects.

#### *8.2.2.2 Gameplay Teaching: Basics*

Players typically first learn basic navigation in classic tutorials, such as look/rotate, movement, jump, climb, or crouch. Following or still, part of the navigation portion often comes basic interactions like picking up items, opening doors, pressing buttons, or talking to an NPC. Since none of these are the most thrilling first impressions of any action game, players soon get to shoot something very harmless like a cardboard cutout or a super easy enemy. Depending on the game, it typically includes more aspects like grenade/knife throwing, aiming/sniping, introduction into some exotic moves, or special abilities. Ideally, it also includes anything else which sets the game apart from its competition and makes the players hungry for more. Essentially, the player learns the 3Cs, meaning character, controls, and how the camera functions.

The classic (rational design) way to teach players a feature is by the following three to four steps. It depends on the game if that has to happen for every feature. For example, some games skip basic movement tutorials by now. Another variant here is to teach players multiple things at the same time, like attacking and dodging in one training fight.

1. Safe Introduction: Players can use the feature in a 100% safe environment to get a feel for it. For example, they are shooting some cans or cardboard cutouts.
2. Easy Challenge: Players have to use the feature in their first challenge, but the difficulty is very low. For example, shoot your first enemy, who can (badly) shoot back.

3. Difficult Challenge: Players have to use the feature in a challenge with difficulty closer to the upcoming sections, but typically the challenge stays very "clean" with no other features potentially confusing the player. For example, shoot three (same as before) enemies who can shoot back. Some games skip this step for some/all features.
4. Combination: Players have to use their recently learned feature in combination with another feature they learned before, or the challenge is a combination of multiple features. For example, shoot three enemies while jumping between poles or shoot three enemies, but some can throw grenades (players have to dodge). Some games skip this step for some/all features.

Depending on your game's audience it might be interesting to hide as much of the tutorial nature as possible, either by, for example, detecting how experienced the players are and then skipping basic steps or by smoothly integrating into the game's initial narrative. The whole topic can be controversial because for some players tutorials are very boring. For some very necessary, and skipping tutorials always gives the feeling that you might have missed something important. However, I do believe we can be a bit more experimental with tutorialization of games and don't have to rely too much on old-school methods for everything.

#### 8.2.2.3 Art and Narrative Introduction

When we talk about art and narrative, the first level is less a tutorial than an introduction. Narratively it should give the player a combination of what to expect, introduction to the world, plus ideally makes them hungry for more. Art-wise, it should showcase something awe-inspiring, highlight the game's production value, and introduce the world through artistic means while looking stunning.

There are two classical ways to introduce art or narrative in the first level. The first variation is to start slow and build up tensions and then have a big reveal, while the second one is to start right away or very quickly with a big bang and then calm down at the end of the level. Of course, you can combine them in any order or at the same time.

If the story takes a backseat initially, then at least at the end of the first level or mission, players should have an idea of what the game's narrative is (at least what you as a developer want them to believe). It is comparable to a very slow prologue, which has more world-establishing elements, or in the case of a game, it can also have a very strong initial gameplay focus. It can create great narrative tension because, of course, players are eager to know what is going on. A classic example is waking up with amnesia, wandering around in an empty, devastated hospital/bunker/spaceship. Then it takes the first 15 minutes to realize that a zombie apocalypse happened, and now the actual game starts. This last narrative reveals also acts as a cliffhanger, motivating them to hopefully keep playing.

On the flip side, if the narrative starts with a big reveal right at the start of the game, then it typically calms down afterward, leaving some space for gameplay and art introductions. However, at the end of the first level, you need to have a narrative cliffhanger again. It does not have to be as big as the initial reveal but still strong enough to make the player hungry for more. A classic example is a longer initial intense cutscene or in-game event that introduces the current situation. Then finally, the later cliffhanger reveals what is going on or what players are actually about to do about the initial, high-tension narrative introduction. For example, it starts with a barrage of TV announcements, a presidential speech, and military briefings about an apocalyptic zombie outbreak. At the end of the level, players learn that their job, as part of an elite undercover unit, is to investigate the plague's origin and find the guy who caused it all. Of course, while hinting at some conspiracies or twists.

On the art side, a calm start allows for an even more impressive artistic reveal a bit later in the first level or mission. A classic example is the stunning vista players see when opening a door after walking through dark tunnels, bunkers, sewers, or any other tame interiors for the first few minutes. Of course, the vista is perfectly framed, composed, your prime example of visual player leading and long-distance environmental storytelling. Depending on the game, you have the obligatory plane/helicopter crashes, big dinos stomping through the mid/background, massive explosions, or an alien fleet mowing down New York. However, the often underestimated part is the "boring" part before. Ideally, it is the absolute opposite of the vista, with only a few small teasers about what to expect, like notes to read, light coming through cracks, graffiti on the walls, screen rumbles, and any other subtle audio clues. The more you can surprise the player when opening an ordinary door, the better. However, the surprise and impact of the vista is stronger, the more the previous section is "boring." Of course, it can be anything other than a door that triggers the reveal like an exploding/crashing wall, a glass surface suddenly turns transparent, a falling curtain, surprise teleportation, or whatever else sci-fi and fantasy games have to offer. You should absolutely fight the urge to take away the player's control when they open the door and turn it into a mini in-game cutscene. Yes, some players might not look in the ideal direction the art director wants. However, if you take away control of players in such a crucial moment, they know that they also likely do not have agency about the most stunning-looking parts for the rest of the game. These breathtaking moments are wins/rewards for players; never take it away from them.

Last version is the big, initial, impressive art reveal, which leaves players breathless and ideally forget that the gameplay part started at some point. It sets the tone and expectations for the rest of the game, and it better sets it high. Of course, you cannot keep up such a high fidelity for the rest of the game/level, but the interesting aspect is that you do not have to. If you set a high standard early on, players likely apply the same standard for the rest of the game, even if it dropped. The same can be observed not just about visual quality but also gameplay and overall production effort. A classic example, besides the action-packed James Bond intros, is the classic plane crash. On the way down, the plane crashes along a few skyscrapers/mountains, it breaks into parts, a few passengers get sucked out, the player almost flies out, too but hangs in, and then the plane slides brutally over the ground. All of it happened in-game, and now the player stands up and can move around in a devastated, burning hidden Tibetan temple landscape.

I will write more about combining them in conjunction with gameplay in the next when I cover the tutorial's level design implications.

### 8.2.3 Level Design Considerations

#### *8.2.3.1 Linearity*

A classic tutorial level is linear. You, as a designer, want to make sure that players experience everything step by step, carefully orchestrated based on your teaching strategy. The artistic and narrative introduction to the world has to go hand in hand with the gameplay tutorial, but also it must leave players hungry to keep playing. Finding this balance in a linear level is already difficult and likely to end up with many iterations. However, applying an open structure to the tutorial is not beneficial for both developers and players.

The players do not benefit from potential confusion of too much early freedom or unknowingly missing out on important information for the rest of the game. The irony is that many players say they want freedom, but too much and too early is not helping anyone. Till players are familiar with the very basics, a bit of handholding early on can be okay. Opening up the order in, for example, an open-world context is doable but it comes with a cost which is often not reasonable. You could also think about splitting up the tutorials. Start with a shorter linear tutorial segment, but then give players more and more freedom till they are done with learning.

I believe giving players more space in tutorials is perfectly fine, especially if large open environments are part of your game's DNA. After all, a linear level does not mean a tight tunnel. The linearity is more about the required linear steps to complete the tutorial sections. A linear structure is necessary, especially if art, narrative, and gameplay aspects build upon each other or are tightly connected. For example, it requires a narrative event for the player to unlock a unique ability.

#### *8.2.3.2 Combining Art, Narrative, and Gameplay*

I have alluded to it previously, but one of the key aspects of tutorial levels and the important responsibility of level design is the right balance and pacing of art, narrative, and gameplay.

Introducing new, essential gameplay in narrative-heavy parts is typically bad because you want players to focus on the narrative and vice versa. A good example is that barely anyone remembers a radio dialog in the middle of a heated firefight. However, narrative and gameplay can go after each other in

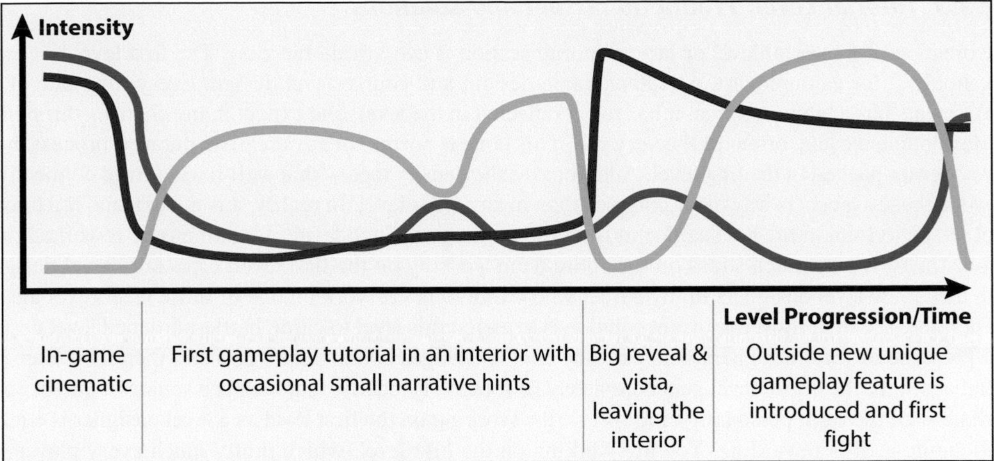


**FIGURE 8.4** Tutorial level narrative, gameplay, and art pacing graph—Example A: **Narrative (Blue)**: Strong narrative start, few more hints along, and narrative cliffhanger at the end. **Art (Red)**: Strong start with narrative, lower till big reveal/vista. **Gameplay (Green)**: High during narrative lows, low during art reveal or narrative moments, unique feature introduction at the end.

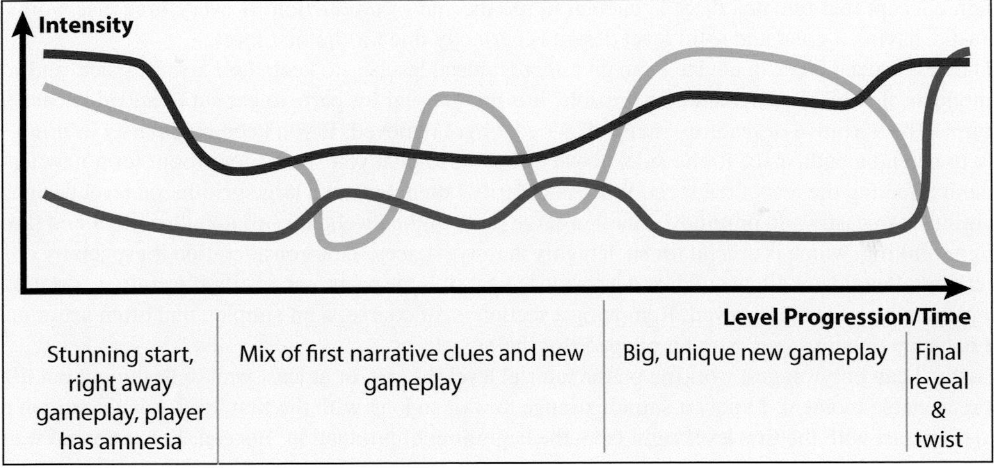


**FIGURE 8.5** Tutorial level narrative, gameplay, and art pacing graph—Example B: **Narrative (Blue)**: Low narrative start due to amnesia, just a few hints with final reveal and twist at the end. **Art (Red)**: Strong start with gameplay, stays medium, goes back up again with big, new gameplay and even higher during narrative reveal. **Gameplay (Green)**: Right away gameplay but safe and easy tutorials, first easy fight in between narrative hints, final big spike during big, new feature introduction, before dropping low during narrative reveal and cliffhanger.

tight intervals, with some mild overlaps. They just should not peek at a similar time to give players time to soak it all in.

Art, on the flip side, can go well with both at the same time. However, I would still reserve art its own unique peeks, vistas, and reveals. At least wait a bit after a stunning moment before you bombard players again with gameplay tutorial messages or important dialogs. Still, majestic artistic events which are part of world-building are perfect ways to combine those two crafts—the same counts for impressive artistic consequences or introductions to gameplay moments.

#### 8.2.3.3 Tutorial Level: Production Issues and Solutions

The creation of a tutorial level or larger tutorial section is everything but easy. The first level has many stakeholders, for example, art, narrative, game design, and course level design. Every time one of the departments has a bigger change, it has to get reflected in the level, and expect many changes throughout the development cycle, often till the very end. This issue is normal in any creative, iterative process, but it is way denser packed in the first level. Additionally, the density means that well-harmonized connectivity between those aspects is way more complex than in any other level. In reality, it is not unusual if a tutorial level or section sits in the hot seat for most of the production. Such levels are commonly reworked three to four times. It puts much stress on the entire team working on the first level, especially level design. I have met a few level designers in my career who swore to never work on one of those levels ever again.

Therefore the first, most important solution is to assign this level to calm, battle-hardened level designers. The type of level designers who can stay cool if changes come, a part gets cut, then a bit later gets added again, or the entire level gets completely reworked. Typically, that means a senior or maybe intermediate with the right personality and soft skills. Working on the first level as a level designer is equally challenging as it is rewarding. You are working on the first level, which pretty much every player will experience. However, you need a very thick skin, need to be very flexible with your design, and ideally, your diplomatic skills are way better than average.

One way to keep the stress down for level designers is to avoid any crazy, risky, or experimental design. I am not saying it is impossible, but depending on the type of game, production, and team, I cannot recommend reinventing level design in the first level. I am always an advocate of pushing the boundaries, and of course, if your game defines new ground in the industry, then so will be the first level. However, you will likely be busy enough while going through so many iterations and dealing with so many stakeholders. At the same time, it will be even more challenging to develop a mind-blowing level design concept that remains flexible enough to see the end of production. If everything else works out fantastic, having a great and solid level design is perfectly fine for the first level.

The next crucial piece of advice I can give about tutorial levels is to keep their layout, space, and script as modular, flexible, and dynamic as possible. It is not unusual for parts to get cut or added because, for example, the narrative or features changed, added, or got removed. If you keep modularity in mind, it is easy to extend a path/space to the side, above or below, to give you some more room for a new feature without affecting the rest of the level. With modularity I do not mean a large grid-based level design, but the mindset to easily add or remove small or large parts of the levels. It is all about resilient and flexible design thinking, which is crucial for such highly iterative spaces. This consideration is especially crucial for engines that do not allow quick and easy movement of large parts, especially if terrain, vegetation, or complex architecture is involved. Removing a section is, of course, a bit simpler, and often art or narrative is happy to gain some extra bit of space for their craft.

Lastly, I can only suggest working on the tutorial level the last, or at least wait to fleshing it out till the last reasonable moment. I know it sounds strange to wait so long with the first level, but a common mistake is to start with the first level right from the beginning of production. Instead, I recommend waiting some time until the game, design, narrative, tech, and art have settled a bit. If you do not wait then, you might add a few unnecessary iteration loops, which could be better spent on later levels. Working on the first level has much potential for waste, so reducing it and the associated frustration is critical. However, it certainly makes sense to have a rough, very modular version early. The goal would be to get a feeling for creating a tutorial section or sketching out key art/narrative moments. You also might need the first level to test the overall gameplay or a tutorial level for early playtests. Just do not refine it too far, and especially do not polish it too soon.

# 9

# *High-Level Layouts*

In this chapter, I want to start stepping away from pure theory and explain how to apply the previous mindset from abstract level design and the concept of "points of advantage" (POA) onto something more practical-minded. Therefore, at first, I want to start with high-level layouts. However, arguably anything high-level, even in a practical context, will always remain partially theoretical. Still, creating an actual high-level layout remains at the core of level design and sets the foundation for anything even more practical building upon it.

High-level layouts only refer to the main lanes and core player options. To some extent, it touches mid-level layouts when I talk about adding options depending on the situation/gameplay, but the principles of flow and dead-ends remain. However, it does not include low-level individual cover placement. The basic mindset of the circle applies to multiplayer, arenas, and linear singleplayer maps alike.

## 9.1 Circle to Complex Arena

### 9.1.1 Introduction

I believe that at the heart of any good flowing layout is a circle, or rather a combination of circles. However, let us first get a basic understanding of the circle itself before we get complex.

Level layouts should maintain a good flow, including not only movement but also options to act or react. If players run out of visible options, it only leads to frustration, and then they blame us developers and not themselves. Therefore, the circle is the most basic building block for well-flowing layouts.

### 9.1.2 The Circle

First of all, a circle, by definition, is a loop, which means players have an unlimited number of options theoretically. They either run away forever (given they are equal or faster than the threat) or move to the threat and eliminate it. A circle can be anything from a path, like a hallway, walkway, or connection of floating rocks on a lava sea. However, it can also be a large enough space, where a continuous loop defines the outer borders. The space just needs to be big enough for reasonably running in circles.

For example, imagine a big, static alien in the middle of a large circular room shooting at the player. The space starts to be reasonably big enough when players can run along its borders and can still dodge the alien's attacks. If the space is too small, and they cannot dodge the attacks then it is not really a loop. Of course, many factors play a role here, like the enemy's attack/projectile speed and player movement, and other abilities. Still, let us keep it simple and more general. Another interpretation of a circle in high-level layouts is negative space, aka running around a circular object.

Secondly, when I say loop, I do not mean a perfect circle strictly. It can be anything that defines a loop. So, for example, it can be rectangular, octagon, or a wired mix of concave or convex corners as long as they form a loop at the end. As long as players have at least one continuous path, you are good. However, for the sake of simplicity and consistency, I keep referring to it as the circle or loop.

Combining those two important points can already give us a large number of possibilities, and you likely recognize their use in many levels you played. Sure, the scale will vary wildly, but it is everywhere. Also, just running in a circle all the time is not very exciting either. After all, we need to give the players meaningful options. Therefore, let us get a bit more complicated.

DOI: 10.1201/9781003275664-12

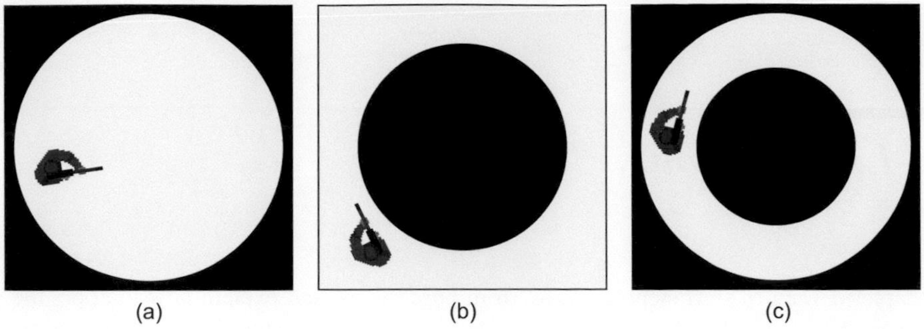


**FIGURE 9.1** (a) Circle as positive space. (b) Circle as negative space. (c) Circle as tubular space (a variation of positive and negative space).

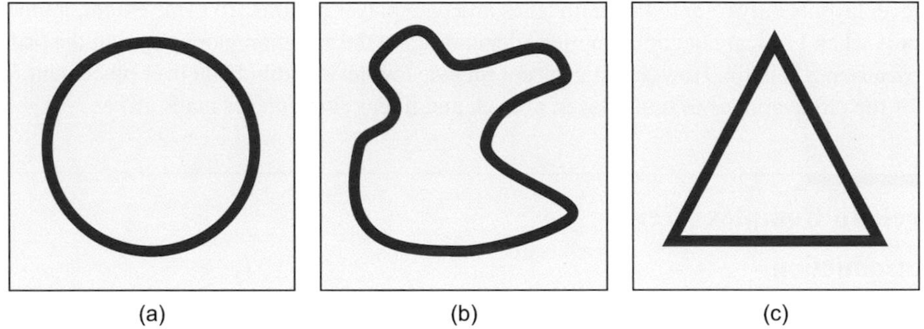


**FIGURE 9.2** (a) A circular loop. (b) A wobbly loop. (c) A triangular loop.

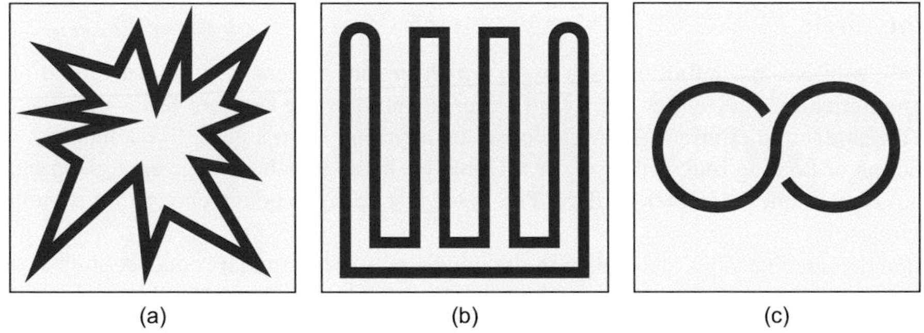


**FIGURE 9.3** (a) A spiky loop. (b) A long loop. (c) An overlapping loop.

## 9.1.3 More Circles

### *9.1.3.1 Introduction*

When I teach designer layout, I always start with one circle on the whiteboard, but then keep expanding it quickly. It becomes clearer as soon as I add a few more circles, some overlap while others just touch at one point. Then we apply both points from the previous subchapters about adjusting the shape and changing the meaning of the loops between positive, negative or tubular space. However, the hard rule, to always think in loops, must remain.

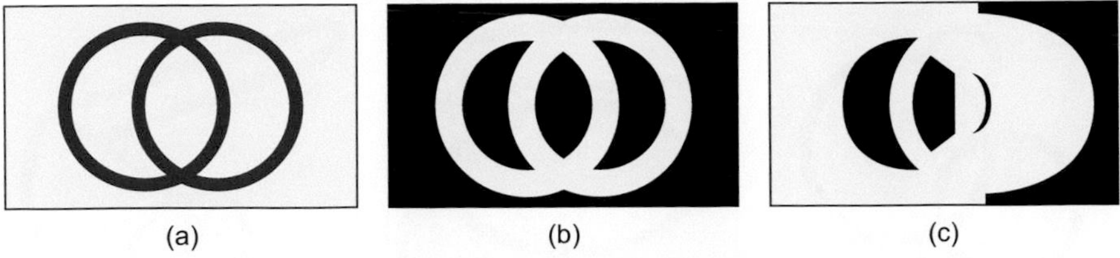

**FIGURE 9.4** (a) Base high-level layout. (b) A simple variation translated into primarily positive (tubular) space. (c) Another variation with a mix of negative and positive space.

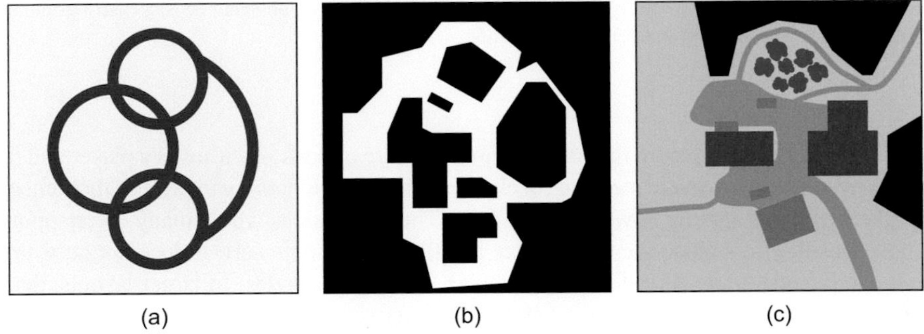

**FIGURE 9.5** (a) Base high-level layout. (b) A variation translated into space. (c) Another variation translated into a more realistic space.

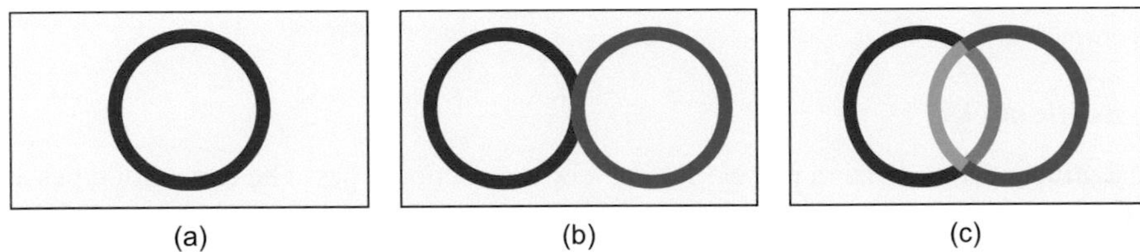

**FIGURE 9.6** (a) One loop. (b) Three loops. (c) Six loops.

Another interesting observation is that each circle you add, it creates even more loops. Two touching circles create three loops (the two original loops and then both combined). If only two circles overlap, you create six loops (the two original loops, the inner one, the outer one, and the two loops minus the overlap). Enjoy adding more circles and count the loops, and very quickly it gets complicated because the number of overall loops increases rapidly.

### *9.1.3.2 Circle Size, Weight, and Density*

When you start playing around with different sizes of added circles, you notice that they change weight. A large circle needs to have a justifiable POA or its value/weight for the player drops. Why run all the long way if it does not reward me for the time spent? If it is just another yet longer tunnel that allows players to run away from the charging threat, its priority drops toward a side path while the smaller loop stays the main, preferred loop. However, suppose the long loop includes an important powerup, weapon, or other significant option to defeat the threat. In that case, it becomes the priority, and players do not mind the long run.

Now, let us switch to the more likely reality that you deal with multiple threats or threats that can do more than run after players. I have already covered the principal thinking of options in the chapter "Abstract:

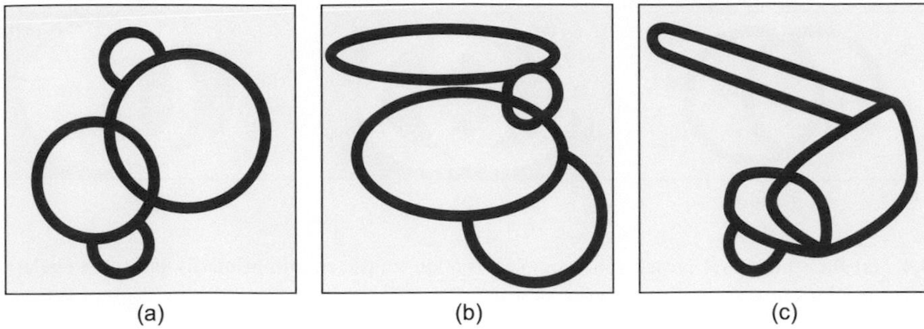


**FIGURE 9.7** (a) Base high-level layout. (b) A variation with different path weights and density distribution. (c) Another variation with different path weights and density distribution.

Mid-Level." It is safe to say the more threats there are, the more options you want as a player and developer. Again players need options to make meaningful choices, while developers try to prevent their enemies from appearing like lemmings coming down only one lane. Therefore, areas where many (overlapping) circles create a high density of options typically indicate a battlefield of some sort. It does not have to be about fighting but can include things like stealth or complex navigation puzzles. In larger layouts, denser areas can create hubs. Often they are central, but hubs in the outer rims of your layout can create an interesting tension and relationship between them, while a central one leads to a more consistent contestation.

Lastly, within your network of several loops, it might soon get messy. Therefore, think about giving some loops more weight and purpose. Some loops become the main streets or the upper main walkways, while others become service tunnels, air ducts, or side alleys. Not every loop should be equal. This clear separation, weighting, and clear identity of loops are essential for player orientation, player recognition, and environment art.

### *9.1.3.3 Bottlenecks*

The next significant consideration is the different loop connection types. The two main types are bottlenecks and anything else. The bottleneck is an isolated connection between two separate, significantly large networks.

Controlling or just alone crossing bottlenecks is key in many layouts. They hold significant tactical importance, and therefore you should design them very cautiously. Bottlenecks can slow down the player's movement or even deny complete progress. Putting them at the wrong spot can completely slow down or eliminate flow. However, at the right spots, they create interesting peek challenges. In a multiplayer context: Suppose alternative routes around the bottleneck exist, then a good spot for bottlenecks is in the center of a map like in a capture-the-flag (CTF) map. However, if little or no alternative routes exist, bottlenecks could act as a disadvantage for any spawn-camping team. In a singleplayer context, bottlenecks controlled by AI act as difficult peeks. I suggest treating them as "action puzzles" where the obvious approach can be very difficult. However, smart players should find alternative solutions to overcome it.

Another variant of bottlenecks is the connection or crossroad between two long lanes. The length creates essentially something like two "soft" dead-ends ahead and behind the player. Ahead is the potentially contested or dangerous crossroad, and behind is another long path. This case is not as severe as the previous one but should still handle it with care, especially in central or primary locations within the layout.

Despite the difficulty of dealing correctly with bottlenecks, I like to include them in most of my high to mid-level layouts. They are an essential tool to give a layout rhythm, provide clear, recognizable compartmentalization for players and developers, and a great way to affect the game's pacing. If all connections are weighted similarly, quickly navigating the layout becomes a dull, almost meaningless experience.

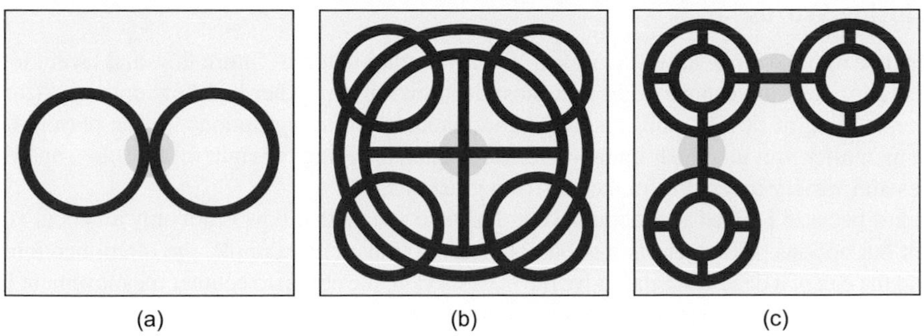

FIGURE 9.8 (a) Simple bottleneck (yellow). (b) Central bottleneck due to long path. (c) Bottlenecks between sandbox bubbles.

### 9.1.4 Dead-Ends

I keep mentioning that dead-ends are generally bad. Therefore, let's dive a bit deeper into the topic and unravel some of its myths by initially looking where they are applicable before thinking about solutions.

- If a player reaches a dead-end and there is no threat, then there is, of course, no problem. Dead-ends as part of exploration, navigation, or any other puzzle are perfectly fine.
- Dead-ends can work in a pinch if combat is static and does not rely too much on movement. For example, they can work in some melee-centric fighting games.
- Suppose the dead-end provides the players with the solution or safety from a threat. For example, you are jumping up on a tall rock when chased by wolves.
- Dead-ends might be less of an issue if its path is so wide or gives enough micro-options along its path that it does not create a trapped feeling.
- If the risk-vs-reward is correct, for example, reaching the rocket launcher at the end of a longer dead-end might be worth it, even if enemies can abuse my limited escape options.

This list also defines where dead-ends are bad: In combat situations where freedom of movement is important, or risk vs. reward is highly disadvantageous.

However, when you look closer, the dead-end path is not at the core of the issue—the end spot is the problem. When you are stuck at the end without options is the main frustrating part. Therefore, a solid way to reduce this issue is by providing space at the end by applying the concepts of circles.

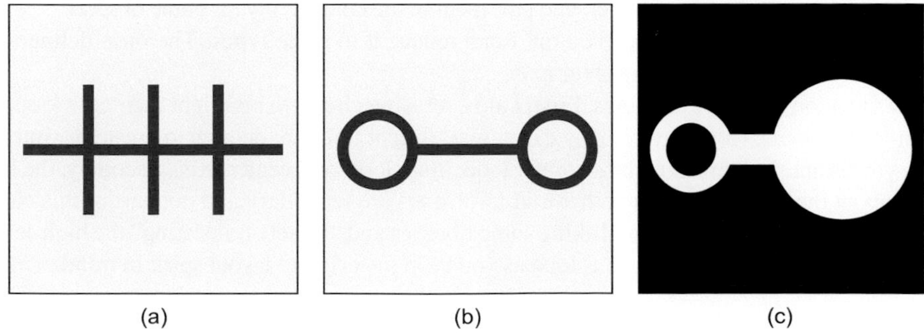

FIGURE 9.9 (a) Bad use of dead-ends. (b) How to fix dead-ends purely with layout. (c) A variation of the solution translated into space.

### 9.1.5 Closing Words

This deep dive into the circle mindset aims to set the foundation for all future flow and layout topics. The circle mentality described above addresses most dead-end or any other bad flow options. After all, my core understanding of flow in games is about continuously providing options for the player. Therefore, the circle mentality provides the foundation for flow. Then applying the right mix, pacing, and rhythm of challenges and variety to the flow makes a flow a great one.

Lastly, just because I talked a lot about layout, I have to restate that flow is not only all about continuous movement but options. Movement is just one of many options. For example, the often-mentioned rocket launcher at the end of a dead-end might give the player a valuable option to counter the movement limitation either by force or by a rocket jump. Options come in many forms and shapes—it is just a matter of context.

## 9.2 Sandbox, Multiplayer, and Boss Arenas

### 9.2.1 Introduction

I decided to combine sandbox, multiplayer, and boss arenas because at a high-level the core understanding is similar. A sandbox in most games is a large enough space which provides players with a wide range of options with typically at least one open objective. An open objective just states what players have to do as a result, without providing detailed steps to achieve it, for example, "Kill general X in the village." Players now have the whole sandbox arena available to locate, reach, and ultimately kill this general. A closed objective chain would give the player a detailed order of objectives to locate, reach and kill him.

Multiplayer maps are not far off from large sandbox arenas solely in the context of high-level layouts. Of course, context, enemies, and objectives are completely different. However, they also need to provide enough options for all present players, and their objective is often even more open and less predictable or defined. This chapter covers more "free" and symmetric types of multiplayer modes like deathmatch, team deathmatch, domination, or alike. Asymmetric multiplayer modes are more a mix of this chapter and the next one about linear levels. However, the exact mix heavily depends on the game and the details of the mode.

Boss battle arenas are again similar but are, of course, highly contextual to the actual boss design. If the boss works best in a big flat arena and has trouble navigating anything more complex, then this chapter is the wrong one. However, if the boss can navigate properly or players benefit from using a more complex space, this chapter should help. Good boss battle design is inherently very difficult, and even a good layout can only do so much if the boss design has flaws.

Before we move on, the term "arena" must be clear. In the context of this chapter, an arena is a large space, defined by paths, options, and negative and positive space. An arena is not just one huge room. An arena can be anything from a village in a sprawling open world to, of course, a walled-off space-gothic cathedral. For simplicity, I will primarily focus on the paths/lanes. How you translate those lanes into options and positive and negative space is then up to you when you pull them in the context of your game or level.

If I look at all the arena types I worked on; I can reduce it to three types: The ones defined by a surrounding circle, an inner circle, or a center axis.

Quick clarification about the drawings: First, I am overusing circles to highlight their core loop-principle in the high-level layouts. However, in many cases, just straight lines are enough to create the intended network once you establish dominating lanes (outer loop, inner loop, and center axis). Secondly, the high-level layouts are about the main lanes. Any other mid-level lanes are secondary and not part of this chapter, but you see them in the example drawings. Taking some liberties and "loosely translating" the high-level sketch into a closer reality is perfectly normal as long as you keep the original layout spirit in mind.

### 9.2.2 Surrounding Circle Layouts

#### *9.2.2.1 Introduction*

As the title suggests this arena type is defined by a surrounding loop, which players can follow uninterrupted. Again, it doesn't have to be a perfect circle, is completely safe or trivial to find/follow—it just has

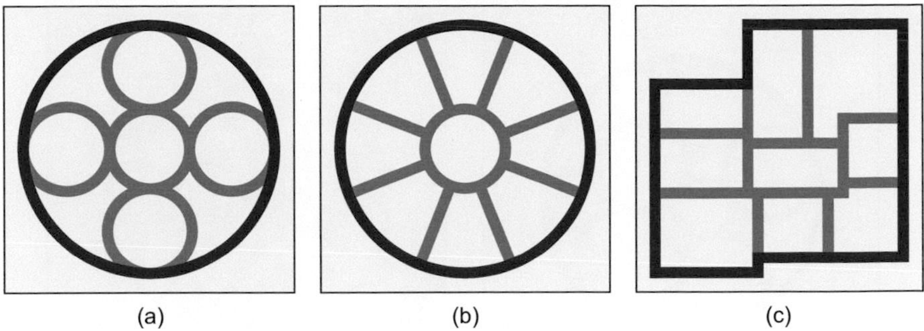


**FIGURE 9.10** (a) A version just made of circles. (b) The same but now a combination of circles and lines. (c) Still the same, but now just using lines and took some more liberties.

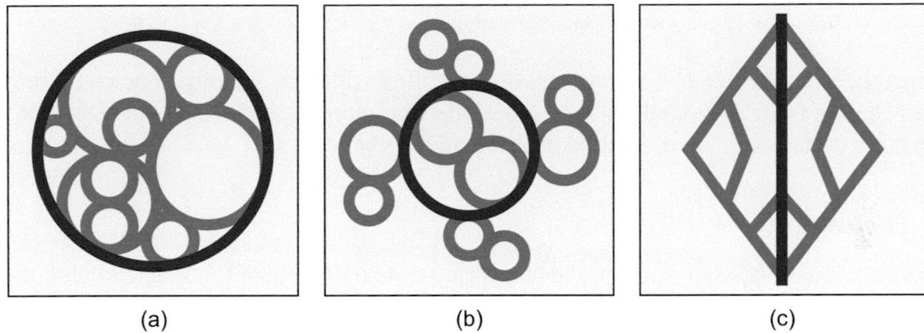


**FIGURE 9.11** (a) Surrounding circle; base high-level layout. (b) Inner circle; base high-level layout. (c) Center axis; base high-level layout.

to be there in a fair manner. Depending on your game, occasionally climbing, swimming, some risk of detection, jumping, or running over open ground should all be acceptable.

### *9.2.2.2 Open*

In this context, "open" means there is much space around the actual arena, without a close, walled-up feeling around. This case can be in an open world, large sandbox, or multiplayer map.

The surrounding circle is close enough around the location that you can see any actors inside, let it be other players or AI. Essentially, it is close enough to see the location being "alive" or have targets/NPCs/players to interact with. Along this path, we have the often bespoken vantage points that give you an overview of the location and observe what is going on ahead—more about vantage points later on when we go more detailed.

Now from the vantage points or the surrounding loop, paths lead to the heart of the location. Those connections are crucial and have to be inviting because that is when players commit to the inner part of the arena. Otherwise, they stay outside, keep circling and stay at a distance. There is nothing bad about some sniping action around such a location, but ideally, there are valid/fair counters against such tactics for any actors inside. However, depending on engine limitations, not every surrounding circle layout means there are vantage points and open ground all around. Negative space leading to the outer ring and essential resources, objectives, counter-sniper spots inside are valid solutions to create some tension and variety between the outer and inner parts.

Once inside, away from the outer ring, you keep going with circles to your liking. You can have more circles and make it look completely like an onion, or you can get more complex with more intersecting or connected circles. However, keep in mind that there is a dominating circle around. This loop means at any moment players or AI can let go of the likely tighter space inside, reset the fight, go out, and re-enter from anywhere! This layout reset option is huge. It can keep a very interesting and always fresh balance and tension going for a long time. One example could be that it leads to a wild chain of hits and

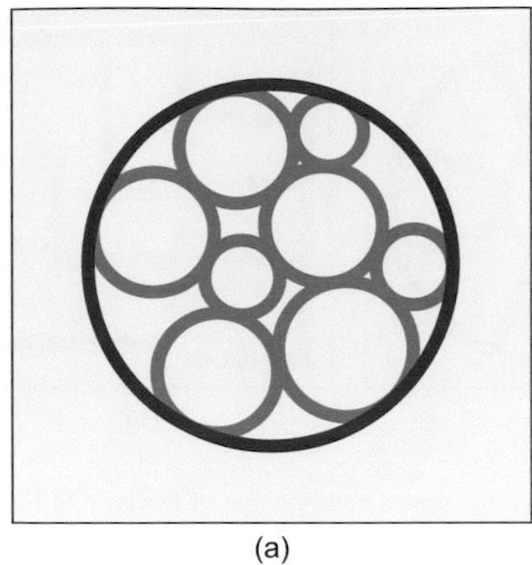

(a)

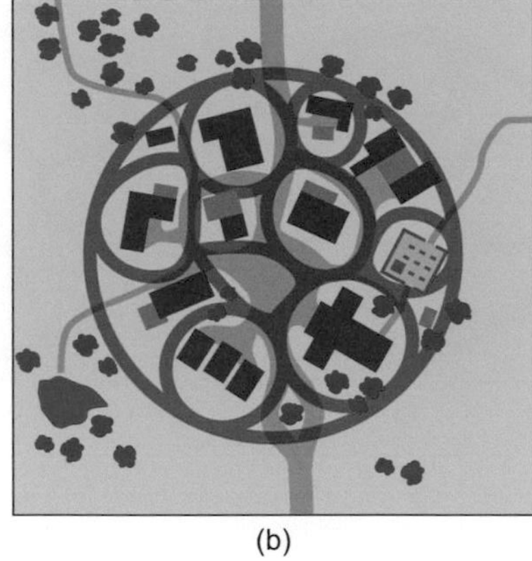

(b)

**FIGURE 9.12** (a) Base high-level layout. (b) Open surrounding circle example (took a few liberties).

runs against the overwhelming strong defenders, crumbling with time. Another one could be a barrage of enemies coming from all around, creating a 360° defense moment, but because of the circle, they can switch up lanes at the last minute, creating a varied mix of challenges.

### *9.2.2.3 Enclosed*

As soon as an arena is enclosed, it means the players are essentially trapped. The surrounding circles still allow for a reset, but it does not always feel the same. Instead of being a safety net, it can feel more like being pushed to a hard border, leaving no way to escape.

Controlling the outer circle still means that you can strike to the center part from any side, and you can typically navigate here fast. It is a bit like a big street around a building block, just that you cannot move further away. If players cannot dominate or navigate the majority of the surrounding loop, you might have an inner circle layout, which I describe further below.

If controlling the surrounding loop has more advantages than being inside, you have a dominating surrounding loop. This advantage can be a combination of resources here like powerups, ammo, or weapons, but also tactical like seeing enemies at greater distances, easy/quick/surprise strikes to the inside, controlling the inside or objectives, or generally any initial unpredictability. The classic besieged mansion, in both single and multiplayer, comes to mind. Attackers can control/engage a large part of the mansion from the outside, semi-safe circle it to find weak spots, and strike when the time is right.

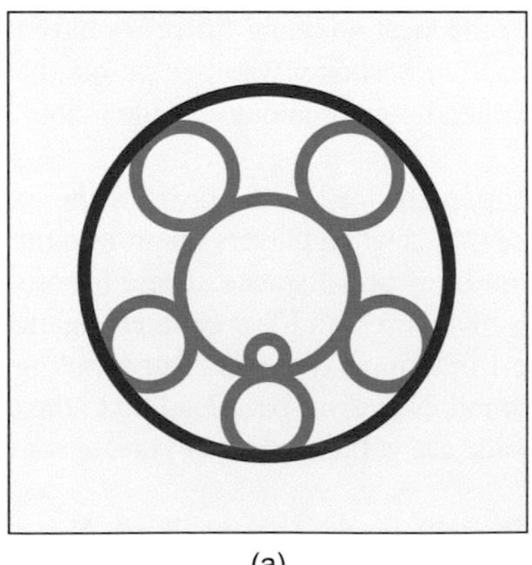

(a)

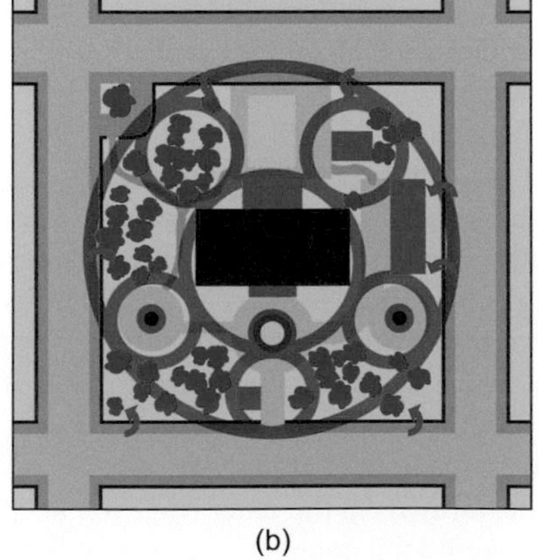

(b)

**FIGURE 9.13** (a) Base high-level layout. (b) Enclosed surrounding circle example with only one-way entrances from the outside to the inside yard (excluding interior, very symmetrical).

Any defenders inside have limited space and are, therefore, more predictable than anyone on the larger outside perimeter.

### 9.2.3 Inner Circle Layouts

#### *9.2.3.1 Introduction*

This layout type has a loop inside the arena, which is advantageous to dominate as a player or actor. One example could be a semi-obvious route in a deathmatch map that controls all the major pickups with the perfect respawn time. Another one is that street inside the larger village controlled by a tough tank. Those lanes are dominating and defining the layout. However, they do not have to have a continuous look, width, or style. That previous tank route can be two separate asphalt streets, but the tank creates its own dominating loop, connecting the streets by cutting through some unfortunate gardens or graveyards.

The main difference between an inner and a surrounding loop is the dominating loop and what loops are secondary. The inner loop has "compartment-loops" toward the outside connected to the inner dominating lane. These outside lanes should hold relevant POAs, but navigating the very outside lane is disadvantageous compared to the inner one. Such disadvantages could be the ease of navigation (lots of concave corners), exposure to inner POAs, inherent complexity, or simply its pure boring length. A dominating surrounding loop means you dominate the inside. However, an inner loop means you can dominate both the outer compartment loops and the potential additional inside. For example, in a multiplayer map, players can stay on it, pick up a weapon in one outer segment, and then use it to engage anyone inside before switching to another outer extension for some armor or another good shooting position. The inner loop connects all those outer and inner POAs and is therefore so dominant. A classic singleplayer example is a defense scenario with a bigger central object. Enemies come from multiple angles all around. Players keep circling the central object, running from shooting position to shooting position, scrambling to keep health and ammo high, and occasionally making a sortie. However, they always come back to this inner circle.

#### *9.2.3.2 Open*

The open case of an inner circle layout happens if a location in an open world, large sandbox, or other bigger space has a dominating inside loop. This inner loop can be in combination or relationship with a surrounding one, but it does not have to be. It could also be that the surrounding circle is not continuous or very disadvantageous to be on. If you have multiple dominating loops inside each other you have what I call a "layout onion."

A dominating inner loop can act as a strong player magnet to quickly draw the player from the outside to the inside. However, this is only valid if the player very well knows about it and its strong advantage. Vantage points, NPC, or maybe even narrative means are some better ways to message this to the player,

(a)

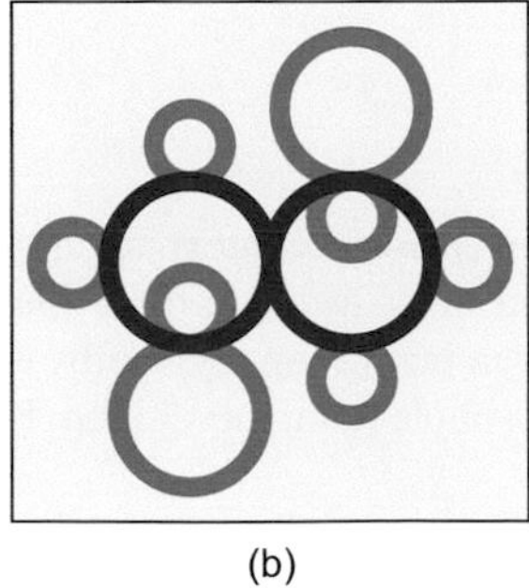

(b)

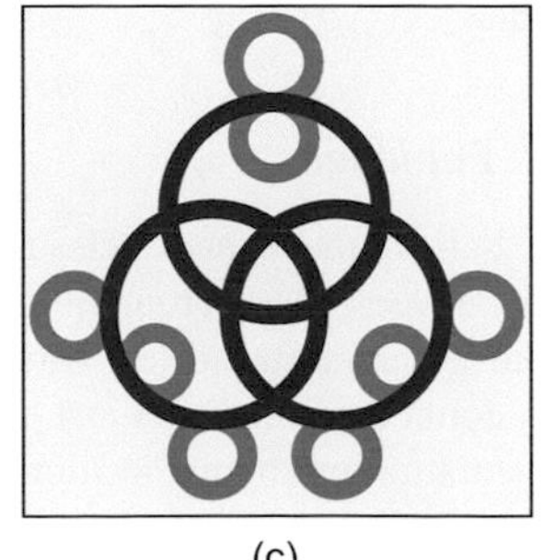

(c)

**FIGURE 9.14** (a) Simple dominating inner loop (b) More complex dominating inner loop(s). (c) Probably a too complex dominating inner loop(s).

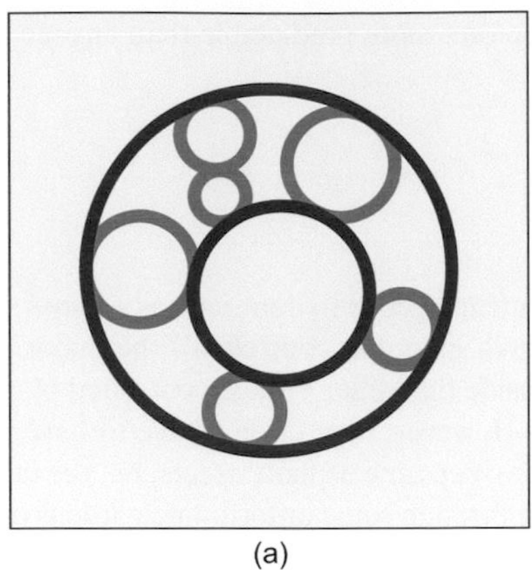
(a)

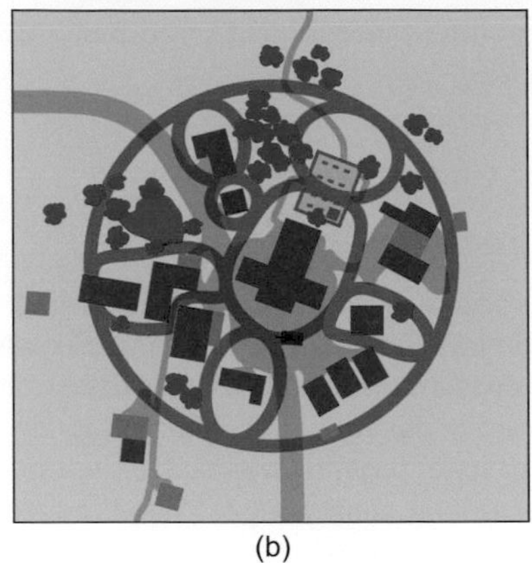
(b)

**FIGURE 9.15** (a) Base high-level layout. (b) Open inner circle example as tank path (with an outer circle, too).

but it is quite tricky to tell the player something like, "Hey, there is an advantageous loop inside that location ahead."

For example, a player-centric inner loop inside an open-world location could be a chain of connected rooftops. Some connections are simple jumps, some wooden boards, and some zip-lines. The player can stay up high, controlling the surroundings while continuously going all around. The same principle from the example can easily be applied to other settings with teleporters, jump-pads, zero-gravity fields, speed-boosts, double jumps, or inviting wall running opportunities.

However, it has to have an advantage to dominate this inner lane. Controlling roofs is just one case. Others could be, for example again POAs like resources, objectives, stationary mounted weapons, stealth ambush spots, or excellent sniper positions. The nature of the advantage defines the type of loop. So, for example, if it is about striking from the shadow to take down opponents silently, then the loop might be less about roofs all the time but could include sewers or dark alleys as well.

Now, when I wrote above about the outer circle going around a location, it is by definition just one circle. However, inside, things can get a lot more complex. It can be more than just one loop, like, for example, two intersecting loops or an eight. However, I would be careful making it too complex or it water downs its impact and clarity.

Another advantage of inner loops is that you can have multiple ones in the same space. A surrounding one is limited and defined by, well, being the surrounding one. However, inside, you could have your dominating tank lane, for example, but the player has connected ambush POAs. Especially the tension between a few paths can be exciting and provide for a good flow yet challenging player experience for various play styles. However, as above, I would be careful if you have more than two to three such paths in one space, or they might reduce each other's clarity. A hard-to-recognize path is hardly a very dominating one.

### *9.2.3.3 Enclosed*

I want to believe that inner circles in an enclosed context are a lot clearer than in an open setting, where the lines between the surrounding and inner loop are often blurred. Levels for Deathmatch, or maps for similar game modes, often feature an inner loop. Typically, especially larger maps of this kind have multiple, connected ones, not just one simple dominating loop. Players switch between them depending on their situation or enemy position.

Another good example is building interiors where hallways, walkways, and stairways create such inner loops, while the inner and outer rooms are the extensions. If you dominate the hallways, you control the movement and reduce options from anyone in the rooms. This approach works for both single- and multiplayer.

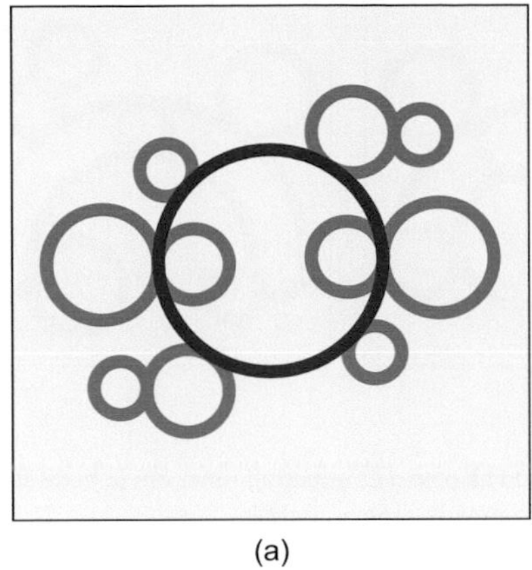

(a)

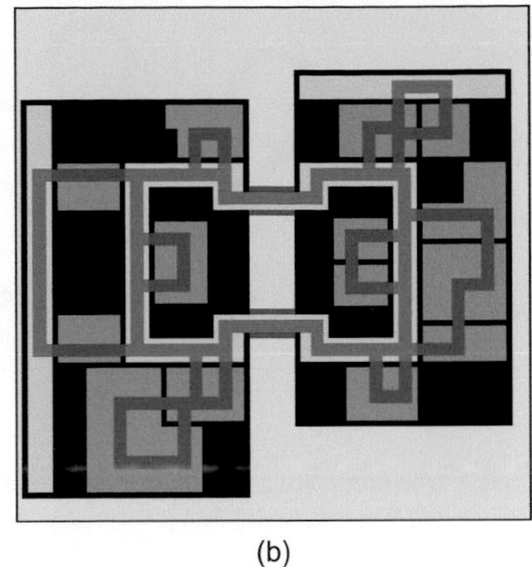

(b)

**FIGURE 9.16** (a) Base high-level layout. (b) Enclosed inner circle example (two skyscrapers connected by bridges).

Extensive, complicated networks of inner loops need careful consideration because they quickly become overwhelming and frustrating to navigate clearly. Especially interiors with limited overview and visibility are hot spots of such issues. In such cases, I recommend clear styles for the different settings, bottlenecks to funnel player attention/focus, and especially a clear separation between the main dominating lanes and secondary ones. Additionally, any player-leading elements to establish orientation are highly supportive here, but more about such elements later.

Let us quickly go back to building interiors, especially believable ones with a real-world reference. The issue is that hallways and rooms define most buildings, and most of their rooms are dead-ends. Anyone ill-advised to transform their school into a level might have quickly realized that it often is not the most fun layout. As a result, many level designers develop creative solutions to connect the rooms somehow to create alternative, secondary paths, and loops (insert scaffoldings or construction sites here). However, if it happens too much, then you create a very messy and confusing network. Instead, I recommend closing off rooms and focusing on those who have interesting inter-connections and interior space setups. However, if, after closing off many rooms, hallways become too long or boring and create problematic bottlenecks, then simply take the liberty and shorten the hallways. If the hallways are your dominating inner loops, then you need to ensure that they are indeed dominating and not a long, frustrating death zone. Realistic environments rarely provide consistent fun looping spaces.

### 9.2.4 Incomplete Loops

Granted not every arena can provide a dominating loop of any kind. Reasons for such a case could be an engine limitation, production limitation, a conscious gameplay consideration, or related to world-building restrictions. Not every engine or game allows for large open space with potentially long connected sightlines. You might not have the time or resources to create all the space. Gameplay reasons are typically connected to a wish to control player movement in some sort. Lastly, for example, not every space allows for a bigger loop surrounding a location if there are large cliffs or lava lakes involved.

Essentially an interrupted circle means a few things. First of all, they can feel more like a linear section than an easy-flowing arena. In that case, I recommend considering aspects from this chapter and the next about linear high-level layouts. Secondly, secondary routes can still establish loops, but due to their nature feature a less smooth flow. Still, especially if the limitation is engine or world related it is better than nothing. Thirdly, after some closer consideration you might end up with only a heavily dented loop and not with an incomplete one. Often, I've encountered designers wanting to create a more linear flow, but then the nature of the game added so much space and routes around that it was still one or two separated arenas connected by a bottleneck. In reality it is difficult to create a true incomplete circle flow in games which has a reasonable amount of free roaming. If it is a good flow is a different question.

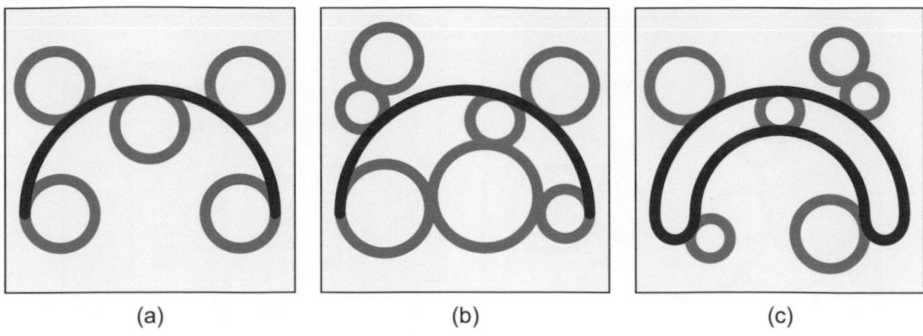


**FIGURE 9.17** (a) A true dominating incomplete loop. (b) Could also be a dominating inner circle but it is a stretch since there is a non-dominated loop below. (c) Just a very squeezed dominating inner circle.

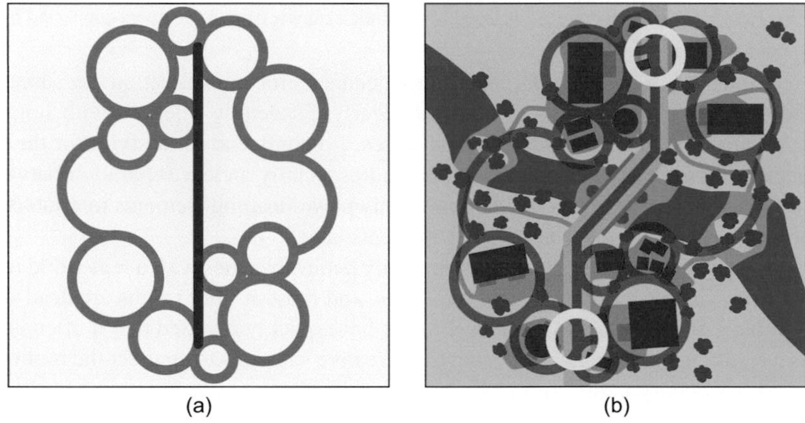


**FIGURE 9.18** (a) Base high-level layout. (b) Center axis example (semi-symmetrical variation, mission area is yellow).

### 9.2.5 Center Axis Layouts

Not every good flowing layout is dominated by a loop; some are dominated by a central lane. However, this is typically more the case in multiplayer maps, given a consistent back-and-fore between two teams. For singleplayer maps or other game modes, which are more about reaching a point and then keep on moving, I recommend looking at the next chapter about high-level linear layouts. It is possible for singleplayer, but more of a rare special case.

For center axis layouts, the flow is established by the consistent push and pull of two teams throughout the layout. You do not have a circular flow throughout the entire layout, as long as each team is consistently spawning at their side and, therefore, stays in control of each side.

A classic example is CTF, where both teams have the same objective to capture their flag from the opposing side and bring it back to theirs. The effective route between the two flags establishes the central lane. Of course, the central lane has other important supporting lanes, but it all starts with the main one. Similar game modes like Payload or Escort can benefit from similar thinking.

More than one dominating lane is possible as well, of course. However, the shortest and easiest route will always remain the most dominating ones. Other lanes might come very close in importance, and it is not uncommon that matches are won or lost here. Still, losing control of the fastest and most direct route between objectives is always a significant disadvantage. I am not a MOBA (multiplayer online battle arena) developer but looking at the standard MOBA map layout is a good starting point for a multi-lane layout approach.

As a level designer, you can look for other advantages for the longer lanes, but I would not expect a perfect balance. Another way to see it is that the other alternative main routes serve different purposes or playstyles. Some lanes might be more stealth or long-range oriented, while the central one is more about direct confrontation. Speed will play a factor for both the side and the center lane; you either want to keep up the pressure in the middle or compensate for the longer path somehow.

## 9.3 Linear Levels

### 9.3.1 Introduction

The core definition of a linear level is that players have to get from A to B. This progression is either achieved by a linear objective chain, a linear physical space, or a combination of both. However, this does not mean just a singular lane or exclude loops in between. This chapter will focus more on the physical layout aspect; later chapters will cover the entertaining mix/order of ingredients like objectives, pacing, and connecting the pieces.

This chapter covers the most common type of linear high-level layout types, which are branching and mixing in sandbox sections.

### 9.3.2 Compartmentalizing

Before we jump into the different types, let us first cover one of the most important considerations, or it can quickly get messy planning out any linear level. The easiest way to design a linear experience is to split it into explicit segments. Each segment is different from the next gameplay-wise and very often visually as well. They have a clear start and end, typically defined by an objective or progression milestone for the player. I will cover pacing a bit later, but separating the experience into smaller pieces is essential for a well-orchestrated experience.

You define each segment or beat by the player's time spent here and less about the size of space per se. A beat is a similar intense experience, like a single and simple objective or similar intense fight. Each beat should not be longer than two to ten minutes for a regular playthrough, with a bit of slack and no strict science attached. When I previously stated that they should have a clear start and end, it does not necessarily mean a physical entrance and exit, but more a clear start of a beat and end of the experience before the next one starts. This difference means that you can have multiple beats in the same space.

Still, looking strictly at the layout, this means that the individual segments typically only have one, sometimes two or three connections to the next one. Those bottlenecks help you focus the layout to a few focal points—the less, the easier. At those points, you can easily switch up the theme, pacing and especially run all your next scripts for the segment.

In classic linear levels, those connection points between segments were points of no-return. The original reason for this was often streaming. During the transitions, you unload anything from the previous segments and load the next segment into memory. It was not a matter of space but time. Therefore, those transitions often had other time-consuming elements like slow-moving doors, or they always required all coop-partners to be present. Nowadays, games still feature points of no-return even though streaming is becoming a smaller and smaller reason. The primary reason is to prevent players from going back to the

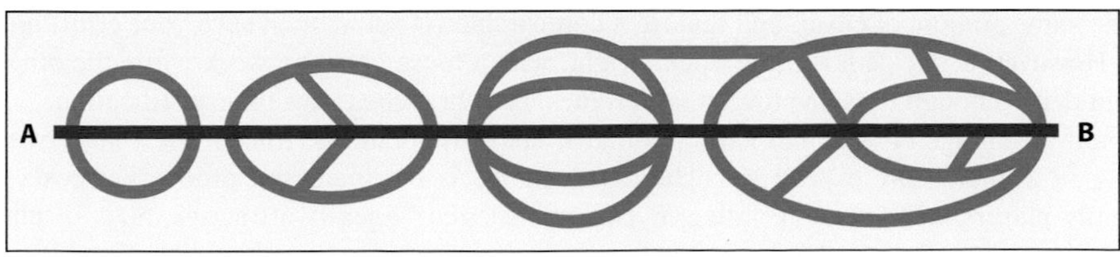


**FIGURE 9.19** Linear level compartmentalized into five segments with increasing complexity, last two segments have more than one connection.

previous segment for baiting AI or similar gameplay reasons. However, we will cover that low-level topic several times further down in this book.

This compartmentalization makes it easier to create and design, but it also gives players a meaningful sense of progression. If everything feels very similar, it is hard for players to understand moving in a new direction. However, the requirement is that, of course, each segment is noticeably different. For example, one segment is on rooftops, the next in interiors, and then on the street level.

However, just because you compartmentalize the linear level, it does not mean that the transitions have to be jarring or abrupt. Smooth transitions are a must, and carefully balancing the contrast between the segments is highly recommended. However, the contrast is contextual and is a careful case-by-case consideration. For example, an oil refinery switching from peace and quiet to suddenly a burning inferno can make sense. However, switching from the oil refinery to a natural beauty segment is a bit of a stretch, without some heavy magic, sci-fi, or mind-trick lifting.

### 9.3.3 Linear Branching

#### *9.3.3.1 Introduction*

The most common segment type within a high-level linear layout is a linear branching one. Typically, it starts with one line connecting the start and end, but if you want to give the player more than one path, you add additional ones, branching off the layout. However, since we are still on a high level, a branch has way more weight. I am not talking here about the small little, close side-corridor or going left or right of your shipping container. Each branch has to have at least one, or ideally more, significant POAs. At best, each branch offers a different gameplay/visual experience or supports a different play style. If the POAs or a branch is not strong enough or the difference between the branches is weak, you might simply cut it. Each branch needs to have a strong reason to exist, or it is a production waste and not giving the player a significant enough experience. It is better to spend production efforts on one good path than two mediocre ones.

Therefore, I split branching into two categories: wide and tight. Each of them has its justification and challenges.

#### *9.3.3.2 Wide Branching*

For me, wide branching means that the branches of a segment are so far apart that they are not in direct connection or proximity. While on the one side it allows for a truly different experience worthy of a proper branch, it also comes with challenges.

The primary general challenge is production. Creating two very different separate branches is not necessarily right away double the amount of time and effort. However, it certainly adds up, especially if you have three or more such branches. It is not just your time creating the additional lanes, but also, for example, set-dressing it and testing each branch, especially for QA/QC that can very quickly add a lot of daily workloads! It is a serious consideration, and you should not just add branches just to show some options alone. It needs to add serious value to the game and your level, or otherwise, I recommend putting the effort in fewer branches.

This issue is crucial if the different branches are not different enough. For example, you have a large building, and the player could go around it left or right. If both paths feel and look similarly clean, have almost the same amount of cover, and feature a comparable AI setup, then save your effort and cut one of them. However, if one path is more open, bright, with a loose cover network while the other is dark, dingy, and dense enough for some nice stealth routes, both branches have their justification.

The main advantage of wide branching is that it helps to create the illusion of a large world while remaining in a linear core experience. The disadvantage is the increased production costs for paths which many players will not even notice. If two branches are equally attractive, 50% of players will never experience one of the paths. It obviously gets worse with more branches. Therefore, if you decide to create wide branch high-level setups, make sure that every developer can finish them in time and that they are worth it.

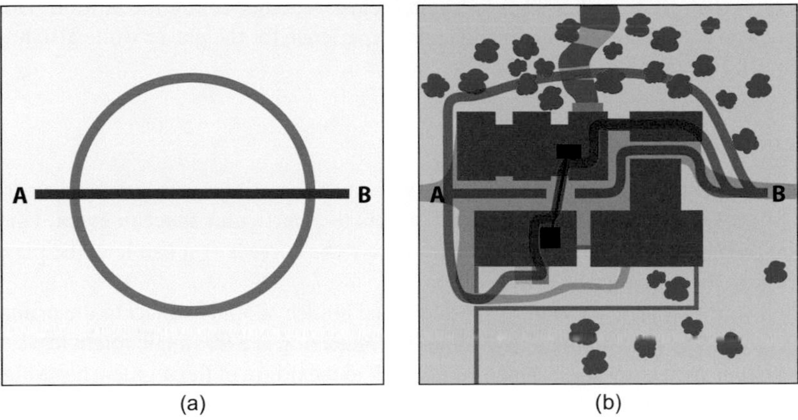


FIGURE 9.20 (a) Base high-level layout. (b) Wide branching example (the lower path overlaps now the center one).

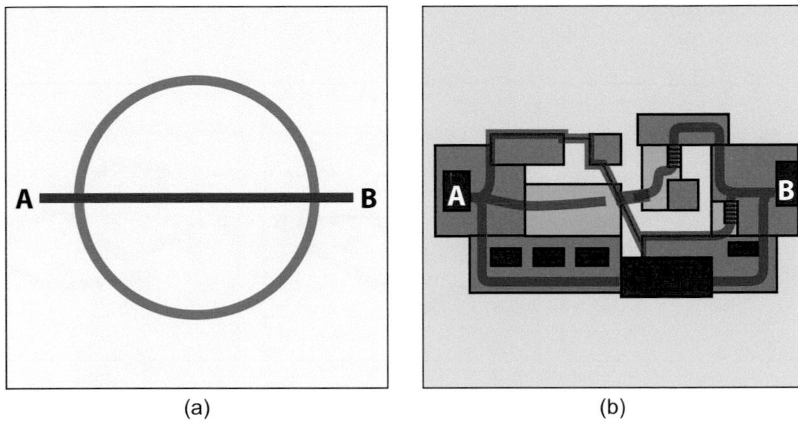


FIGURE 9.21 (a) Base high-level layout. (b) Tight branching example (rooftops, the upper navigation path overlaps the center one, the center path is straight up action, the lower path is stealth going through interiors)

### 9.3.3.3 Tight Branching

When wide branching means completely separate spaces, tight branching means one or more lanes going through the same space. The production advantage is clear because often, creating one space is easier than multiple ones. However, squeezing in two separate high-level lanes through the same space is the primary challenge. Like with the wide branches, each branch here has to be very different from the others to be justified. Otherwise, they are just options within the mid-level.

A very good application for tight branching is when a space or segment supports multiple playstyles. For example, your rooftop section has a central path for all the action-oriented parkour speed-freaks, but it also has a stealth path woven around, below, and above the central one.

Most spaces, which feature tight branching, struggle to create the feeling of a larger world. Their use has its place, but be aware of the drawback. If you try to compensate for this and the space for your tight branching grows larger, you potentially cross into wide branching or create an arena. Depending on the game and your intentions, this transition does not have to be bad; just be aware of the consequences. I know this whole topic can quickly turn into a subjective argument. However, I recommend sticking to the strict differentiation between arenas, wide and tight branching, because it allows you to better plan and manage expectations.

The risk is high that different branches merge too close together or are too similar. However, if you take it seriously, you can create a genuinely different experience for the player while also hopefully keeping production efforts reasonable.

#### *9.3.3.4 Branch Connection Angles*

One key difference between arenas and linear spaces is that arenas try to keep the player freely roaming inside, while linear spaces try to guide or attract players to a particular space or event. For linear levels, this means that the connection angles of branches have to be correct or it can lead the player backward, potentially keeping them in unwanted loops.

After creating your first primary path, every additional branch should connect to the primary one pointing in the target direction; the "pointier," the better. Reconnecting at a 90° angle might leave players guessing to either go left or right. Any angle which points back to the origin of the segment has a high potential of sending players on a confusing and frustrating journey, especially in a wide branching scenario. Of course, certain player-leading elements such as signs, lighting, and waypoints can help to compensate. However, the more in-world player-leading elements you implement instead of relying on gamy waypoints, the better.

I bring up connecting angles already at high-level because the sooner you consider them, the more likely you properly implement them. It is about getting in the right flow mindset, right from the get-go, during high-level planning.

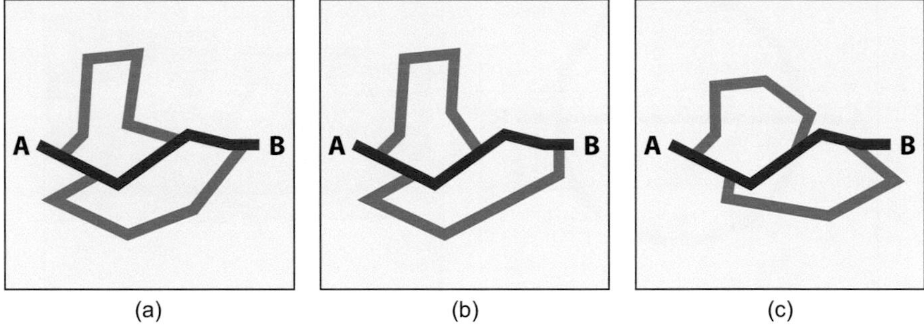


**FIGURE 9.22** (a) Branches (pink) point toward the target B. (b) Branches (pink) reconnect with the main path in 90°. (c) Branches (pink) point backward, away from B.

# 10

# *Connective Tissue*

I wrote a lot about high to medium-level layouts and theory. However, before I go into more details about the nitty-gritty and how to get started in practice, let us cover one severely underestimated aspect: How it is all connected.

When the high and medium-level concepts are your foundation or skeleton, your action areas are the muscles; then the connections are your tendons—if they are weak, it all falls flat. Therefore, I will first talk about the actual connections in various design and world contexts. I'll follow it up with a brief dive into the verticality. Then, the progression within a level is about the right mix and order of major ingredients within a mission flow. The last chapter is about pacing. Understanding pacing is essential, or all ingredients won't flow well together at the wrong speed and it all feels like a big incoherent mess.

## 10.1 Inner-Level Connections

### 10.1.1 Introduction

I guess we all know a few movies with some pretty intense action scenes, but how they are stitched together in the movie's narrative does not make sense or is not coherent. Now there are many reasons for bad movies, but one vital aspect is how all the main beats are all connected. How the heroes got from A to B and especially how they used the time is crucial to create a coherent experience. In level design, this is even more important because here, players have to move themselves and do not have the luxury of a sudden cut jumping from, for example, Kairo's buzzing streets to a dodgy bathroom in Hong Kong.

Each of the main world or level types has different requirements described below. However, I recommend you read them all, regardless of what game you are working on because they are not as exclusive as my categorization makes them appear. Finally, transitions in and out of cutscenes are crucial because otherwise you end up with a jarring experience.

### 10.1.2 Connection within Linear Levels

#### *10.1.2.1 The Classic Usage*

In the past, and occasionally still today, levels were linear because of streaming. Due to hardware restrictions, there was not enough memory to load all the assets, textures, animations, audio, scripts, and much more of the entire level. Therefore, levels had to get cut into chunks that individually fit into memory. In simple terms, the previous chunk was unloaded during the next transition, and the next chunk was put into memory. Therefore, the transition or connection had to take a certain amount of time (not long space per se), and often they had to be points-of-no-return. Planning in one direction was already not easy, but continuously allowing it both ways just made it extra difficult or not always enjoyable for players.

However, one particular problem is that when you start working on the level, you do not know how heavy each segment's memory load will be and how well the engine or tech might still get optimized during development. Therefore, you do not know till sometimes between Alpha and Beta (rather the later) how long or time-consuming your connections have to be. As a result, you need to build your connections with flexibility in mind, and you can only start with a guesstimate. I would recommend starting with rather too-long and curvy/corner transitions because making them shorter than longer

DOI: 10.1201/9781003275664-13

is typically easier. However, this seriously depends on the context and available space. Another factor is if your tools allow a safe movement of large chunks of your levels to adjust the length so late in production.

Another important consideration is how you create the unload and load time. The easiest way is simply a long path and some type of point-of-no-return, like an automatic locking door behind you, a deep jump down, or a one-way teleport. Fancier solutions are procedurally generated hallways that adjust their length based on the load time or often longer transition animations like a really heavy door or an NPC providing (slow) entrance.

Depending on the engine and underlining online tech, in Coop, it is often crucial that all players are at the points-of-no-return and progress simultaneously, or it can lead to technical difficulties.

With time, memory, and storage, mediums got faster and faster, reducing the severe impact of streaming. As a result, it allowed for way faster transitions to almost instantly switching entire worlds. Still, I believe understanding streaming as a concept remains vital for every well-rounded level designer.

#### *10.1.2.2 Control and Hide the Transition*

Now, such transitions give you much control, yet they can appear jarring for players. This case can happen regardless if you utilize a transition for streaming or ideally compartmentalize your linear level (as mentioned in the previous chapter).

Let us start with the control aspect. You have to set up the entire next segment during the transition, or at least the initial part. So, we are talking here, especially about scripts that, for example, activate all the AI, update mission objectives, play dialogs, or set anything else into motion. The timing and placement of this script activation are crucial, and ideally, it happens a good time before players fully experience the next segment. No player traveling at the highest possible speed should experience any assets popping in the scene or AI just "waking up." I recommend playing safe with the placement because those activation times tend to change during the production cycle. The transition is also a good place for any master scripts for the entire upcoming segment.

Secondly, the jarring or boring experience often happens because the transitions are just bland transition corridors and are not utilized for something else. They are very gamey when players clearly feel that they just play a game instead of an immersive experience. Therefore, your goal as a level designer should be to mask or hide the transitions as much as possible or at least use them for something meaningful.

Once players reached the end of the segment and entered the connection, they hopefully accomplished something. Now, whatever the previous segment had to offer as a gameplay challenge is not present anymore during the transition. Additionally, the transitions are not high-octane action sections because then they would not be a transition but the next segment already. Therefore, we typically cannot use gameplay to fill the void, but we still have navigation and narrative. Narratively closing the previous segments and teasing the next one with (radio) dialogs is a good starting point, especially because they are otherwise ill-placed in the middle of the action. Low memory environmental storytelling is another solution to give players some alluring hints about what is going on in the world. Art that is very heavy on memory is not a good idea for transitions because it would defeat the purpose of streaming. Finally, suppose your game has a good amount of navigational features. In that case, you can always use them to build small puzzle sections in between, especially in conjunction with collectibles or other achievements. Essentially it boils down to taking away one "candy" from the player, but replacing it with another one, just with a different "flavor."

### 10.1.3 Connect between Sandboxes Arenas

#### *10.1.3.1 Introduction*

Transitions between sandbox arenas are typically a mix of either linear segments or comparable to open-world connections. So in this chapter, I want to focus on what makes them unique. Additionally,

I believe most of the points here could also work for both open-world and linear transitions with some slight adjustments.

### 10.1.3.2 Foreshadowing and Leading

If you connect sandbox areas, it is typically not through a tight tunnel, but at the same time, it does not offer the complete freedom of an open world. It is normally something like a wide tunnel or wide-open field. However, this mix of loose leading yet some light control allows for some interesting teasing and leading options.

Since you know the rough direction of travel, you can foreshadow the next location with much small environmental storytelling along the way. Signs, smoke ahead, and NPC conversations are obvious, but they can also get more exciting. Think about the consequences of what happened at the upcoming location and show hints of those results. For example, the next location is a village taken over by some cruel enemies, and you could show some luggage lost in haste along the way with a teddy bear. Factories can be hinted at by toxic waste and poisoned animals, or on a more positive note, a festival by a firework, singing drunks stumbling home, or happy kids with cotton candy. The advantage of doing it in such wide "tunnels" between sandbox arenas is that it does not feel forced, you can pace them out how you want, yet you do not have to cover a massive area like in an open world.

Let your fantasies go wild, and rather place a few too many according to your guts because very likely most players will not find all hints anyhow. The fantasy and ideas players build up in their minds are often the crucial, powerful key to making your target location come to life. Think about the anxiety of approaching a haunted house, planning your first date, or before performing a public speech. Without that anxiety or foreshadowing, it is just half the "fun."

As much as teasing is excellent in such semi-controlled/loose connections, it also allows you to give direction without making it feel forced. Of course, likely some borders left and right provided some direction already, but ideally, they are not too apparent due to foliage, architecture, or generally believable world-building. However, I am talking more about the little aspects like small seemingly hidden trails, a suspicious-looking tunnel entrance, no birds singing getting closer, or a sign which clearly states something like "GET AWAY" or "TRESPASSERS WILL GET SHOT." Essentially anything in real life would send an unequivocal uninviting message, but in many games, they achieve the exact opposite. However, once players overcome their fears or do it regardless, they might feel clever or rebellious. Regardless, it is a good thing because players feel they acted and not the game told them to do something. At that moment, it does not matter that you, as a game developer, have placed them precisely for that noble purpose.

### 10.1.3.3 Where and How to Connect

It can be difficult to block off connected sandbox arenas because of their usual semi-open game environment. Below are a few examples of how you can still get players to a specific point or area and control the unlocking to the next sandbox arena. Even if they are likely not applicable for your specific game, I hope they give you enough inspiration to find solutions that work for you.

- Players have to get close to an NPC (or interact with them) who only open up the next transition after completing the last objective.
- Players can only interact and open up the transition to the next arena after completing the last objective. However, make it logically connected; for example, the previous objective gave you a key for a door, the code to call for helicopter pick-up, or the correct disguise to enter a club.
- Arriving AI opens up/allows the transition to the next sandbox arena after completing the last objective. For example, an arriving elephant or tank crashes through a gate, or players can use the arriving boats to cross over to the next island.
- An in-game event opens up the next transition after completing the last objective; for example, planes blow open a gate, a huge ape places a tree as a bridge, or your allied NPC can now crack the safe.

- A cinematic event opens up the next transition after completing the last objective; for example, the game's nemesis lures you into his dungeon, a certain woman lets her hair down, or a transport helicopter picks you up (more about cinematic transitions further below).
- The objective in the next sandbox area is not present yet. However, this can be a bit tricky if it should not appear too gamey. For example, the enemy helicopter fleet only arrives if players previously caused much trouble, or the big mean boss dragon only shows up if the player is covered in the blood of the previously slain dragons. However, avoid anything contrived, like the next, already physically present interaction is only active after completing the last objective.
- The next objective location does not exist yet before players have not completed the previous objective. So players can visit the next arena, but not the next objective because the entire objective location is missing. This case typically requires magic, fantasy, expensive, or sci-fi elements like teleporting cities, giant worms coming out of the earth, or big spaceships landing.
- The current objective gives you the only/best weapon to defeat the enemies in the next sandbox arena. Sure, players can skip the previous arena, but they might regret it.

Below are a few points of ideas you ideally avoid:

- Coincidences like players complete an objective, and now an NPC remembers that he had a key the whole time.
- Disconnected consequences, for example, you free some hostages, and then an earthquake opens up a cave.
- The opening secretly appears because the developers hope that players do not snoop around in that corner of the sandbox arena and will not notice that, for example, the ladder was not there previously. Variants of this case are typically last resort solutions to cover up edge cases, noticed late in production—happens to the best, but good planning can avoid them.

### 10.1.4 Connection between Open-World Locations

#### *10.1.4.1 Introduction*

First of all, in this chapter, I want to write about open-world connections covering large distances. Shorter distances are closer to sandbox arena or even linear level connections. Secondly, player-leading is a crucial factor for such long-distance connections, and I strongly recommend you agree on the types of player-leading before starting to work on most of the game. Changing in too late will only create lukewarm results, and you might end up with waypoints again—however, more about the player leading in later chapters. Therefore, I want to solely focus on some unique aspects of such long travels through an open world.

As a quick clarification, connections between open-world locations can also cover the transition between the questor mission giver and the quest or mission location. It does not have to be only about transitions between two quest or mission locations. Also, this chapter is more about very loose or non-orchestrated connections. Later chapters cover the more production-heavy case when the transition is its own challenging mission segment.

#### *10.1.4.2 How to Embrace No Control*

One of the striking aspects of an open world is that they commonly do not provide tunnels between their locations. Sure, there might be leading world elements like valleys, streets, tunnels, or rivers, but they typically exist because of world-building considerations. However, they can exist for transition purposes, or locations were picked due to their existing transitions. For example, if you want a severe high-speed connection between two locations, you typically pick two connected by roads and not mountain wilderness. Still, strict control of the player movement does not exist.

However, if players have a clear sense of direction provided by a waypoint or compass direction, most will follow it almost blindly. I saw enough playtesters crushing down cliffs despite a bridge 50 meters to the left. Therefore, an open world is more an illusion of no control because most players follow such gamey markers often more strictly than in even linear levels.

Let us look at how you can approach this contractionary control and lack of control to our advantage. As a starting point, provide a semi-straight direct connection between the two locations. This connection does not have to be all safe, but you should give players a fair chance to spot dangers ahead of time, especially when traveling at high speed. For example, no surprise cliffs after a few dense bushes. Then in the areas where they can detect the danger ahead show them an alternative route. However, keep in mind that both the areas to spot and the alternative route are not clearly forced by the game. Therefore, they have to be quite large and stand out. Do not expect most players to study maps or spot little clues. If you as the developer think it starts to be a bit too obvious, then it might start to be okay for most players. Depending on the distance, you can do this approach multiple times.

Additionally, roads or trails can be player magnets, but only if they "convince" players not to go off-track. It is almost as if they have to establish first some trust with players before they drive on them. Therefore, initially, try letting the roads go in the perfect direction for quite some time before going a bit off-course. When their direction goes too far off, then provide a new route, an inviting opening in the vegetation, or a new road/trail.

All the locations along this main route and where players adjust their course are great spots to foreshadow the target location, the current state of the world, or anything else connected to world-building. Their concentration is high at those spots and hopefully more open to looking around and taking the stimuli. Other alternatives are, for example, hints for further quests, missions, achievements, collectibles, cool locations to do some stunts, small or bigger world events, or impressive-looking vistas to take pictures.

Essentially in my experience, the best way to embrace free travel through an open-world is to nudge it a bit. Players are so attracted by straight-up traveling directly to any location that we as developers should take advantage of this. Provide them a good time, use them for world-building, consider player magnets, build up trust to not make it too straight, but without making it too frustrating. The challenge factor depends on your game.

#### *10.1.4.3 How to Embrace Long Distances*

Another relevant aspect of open-world connections is that they often take a long time. So how do we make them still exciting for the players without making it another too orchestrated and production-heavy transition? Below are my classic go-to solutions on how to make long travels more enjoyable.

- If you have any leading elements like roads, rivers, or tunnels, try to curve and angle them to reveal epic vistas or otherwise stunning art/environments. Especially consider this if you can control the time of day.
- Radio/phone calls from NPCs are perfect during long rides. You have an extended period where the player's character and NPCs can hopefully have a long uninterrupted conversation for world-building, character development, or background information. Narrative moments are, of course, even better if the NPCs are sitting in the same vehicle. However, ensure that the dialogs can stop if accidents happen because it is usually a bit off-putting if two people chat while drowning or burning in a car.
- As previously mentioned, travels through the open-world are good opportunities for world-building. Placing many advertising signs, generally relevant world events, or hints of world state can work not just for this one mission but also for any travel through the open-world.
- Investigate if you have means to increase the challenges or threats along the way for specific missions; for example, a higher rate of police cars, more helicopters, or more wild animals populating the roads. Essentially anything which can give the transition not just a bit more challenge but also some unique theme. It is even better to have such adjustments only to specific regions instead of potentially the whole monotonous track.

- Plan long travels to go close to other distractions along the way. For example, quick side missions, something to take over or collect, or NPCs with additional information or quests. Essentially anything which enriches the player's understanding of the game's world or gameplay. Of course, ideally, do not distract players with anything major because ultimately, they should focus on the current main quest, but some occasional distraction does not hurt either.

Last quick point if you plan your connection with a specific vehicle: Travel with it through the open-world as early as possible. Just because the vehicle sounds fun, like flying or speed-boating, does not mean it is fun in the world's or game context. For example, on paper, an epic world-crossing helicopter, wingsuit, or plane section might sound fun. However, ten minutes of just pressing a button while flying gets quickly boring without any obstacles or real challenges.

## 10.1.5 Connection between In-Game and Cutscenes

### *10.1.5.1 Introduction*

Cutscenes are scenes where the player loses control over their action and camera. They provide no player agency but, depending on the game, are important narrative tools. Consider their implementation very carefully and early on because they are in such a stark contrast to pure gameplay. If the direction for their implementation gets defined too late, it can lead to much avoidable friction between cinematic/narrative and level design teams.

### *10.1.5.2 Intro Cutscenes*

If there is a good collaboration between the cinematic team and the level designers, I typically do not foresee any complications with intro cutscenes. They are a classic staple of level design and games in general. The main challenge is the smooth transition, but that is more of a matter of tech and resources.

The primary and most important aspects of level design are what the cutscene foreshadows and where and how it ends. Do you want to reveal parts of the level already, or shall they remain a secret? If you want to foreshadow, what are the important parts? Ideally, they are from an angle where players in-game can recognize them again. The final gameplay start angle and position are also key and ideally set or defined by the level designers, not the cinematic team.

### *10.1.5.3 Mid-Level Cutscenes*

By default, I have to strongly advise against using any cutscenes in the middle of a level. The classic issues are:

- Enemies could still be around. Of course, you usually could turn off all AI during cutscenes, but activating them is not just a jarring experience in the middle of a firefight or can be used as an exploit.
- The cutscenes area could be covered by, for example, vehicles, wrecks, debris, physicalized props, dead/alive NPCs, and VFX. Again, cleaning it up by script creates a jarring experience.
- It breaks the immersive flow from free gameplay to losing control and back to free gameplay. Some people tend to downplay it and refer to other games that have done it, but something bad others have done does not make it better in your game.

It all gets even worse with the wrong transitions or triggers. I consider it a cardinal sin to start a (mid-level) cutscene with a surprise invisible trigger, either spatial or by an event. The player has no idea what could happen suddenly and gets ripped out of the immersive experience into losing all his agency. Those triggers have to be avoided at all costs, especially if the result of the cutscenes means the player travels to a new location or all pick-ups disappear. You never know what players still want to do here, like exploring, collecting, or otherwise enjoying your game world. Robbing them from this experience or possibilities is the worst cutscene transition.

If you really have no choice against a mid-level cutscene, then ideally, have the transition in a new, safe, non-combat space. Depending on the game, the player, for example, cannot drive into the location with their vehicle or litter it accidentally with physicalized props or dead bodies before triggering the cutscene. Accidental is the keyword here, just to avoid any unforeseeable loss of their favorite car, crate, or corpse.

I recommend starting the cutscene with a conscious player (inter)action like pressing a button, talking to an NPC, or activating a radio. It should be an action they do not do all the time without triggering a cutscene like opening a door or picking up ammo. The player should expect a cutscene to happen and can still finish the area beforehand.

Another problem of invisible, spatial/event-based triggers is that you do not know where the players are at that moment. If the space is relatively large, there is a noticeable jump between where they initiate the cutscene and where the players are at the beginning of the cutscene. Depending on the distance, this can be jarring, or even worse if players teleport to a completely different location out of nowhere. Therefore, if you really have to use such triggers, make the trigger space as small as possible. Again, a player (inter)action removes this problem completely.

Finally, the frequency of mid-level cutscenes is crucial. If one of them is terrible, more is worse, and it was likely lousy planning if they happen back-to-back.

#### *10.1.5.4 End-Level Cutscenes*

Cutscenes at the end of a level face the same challenges as mid-level ones. However, they have a few advantages.

- A bigger jump, for example, in a helicopter or back to the base, is more forgiving when it is at the end of the mission.
- Typically, players kill all enemies at the end of a mission before the mission-complete-cutscene triggers.
- Often you move away from the last location during the cutscene, so any devastated or littered environment is no big problem.
- Picking up ammo or other pick-ups is not that important once the mission is over but can still be a topic for collectibles, achievements, or similar ones.
- In general, it is not a complete surprise if defeating the last big boss/objective triggers a cutscene. However, ideally, manage the players' expectations.

## 10.2 About Verticality

### 10.2.1 Introduction

Verticality simply adds another (third) dimension to your level, giving you many more options, especially in layout. I am not talking here about just some softly rolling hills or mild height differences, but about overlapping spaces or lanes and anything where players have to consciously look up or down. However, verticality does not come without its challenges. So in this chapter, I want to cover high-level layout and input considerations before we jump into some of the most common tools which create verticality.

Quick disclaimer: Most of the level sketches in this book primarily display 2D landscapes with few elements of verticality besides some houses, towers, or rocks. This simplification is not because I am not fond of verticality, but it is clearer to bring certain aspects across on paper without its complexity.

### 10.2.2 Importance of Verticality

For some, it might sound trivial, but if we think about it, without this extra dimension, we would only care about looking left and right or navigating on a 2D plane. Every time you create an ample space without verticality, you severely limit the players' options and waste potential.

Additionally, it offers a lot more possibilities for you as a level designer. For example, often flanking routes can be replaced with a short underground tunnel or an overhead zip-line connection. Another example is that adding stealth paths in an office interior would be close to impossible without the conveniently placed air ducts, cable shafts under the floor, or ceiling pipes.

Let us also not forget world-building. Often verticality is not a matter of pure level design but comes with the world's reality, for example, anything in the high mountains. If the world's reality forces verticality on level design, we, especially with art and game design, have to find creative solutions to turn it into an advantage instead of a hindrance.

Always think of how you can add verticality, making players enjoy and comprehend the world and game further. First of all, if players in a city never have to look up or down, then most of the potential to showcase an exciting urban environment is wasted. Secondly, it is usually okay challenging to engage targets at a different axis, other than left and right, and let us also consider other threats, paths, hints, or pick-ups up or down there. Thirdly, it is simply quite dull for players never to need to look around, not just from a challenging perspective. However, I recommend not forcing verticality where it makes little to no sense, especially to add suiting verticality. For example, adding random towers on a frozen lake is not always fitting.

### 10.2.3 Planning Vertical Levels

Typically, I start sketching out any level-sketch 2D first, but then I try to add as much verticality as reasonable. Can I overlap any lanes? Does verticality make sense from a world-building perspective, or does it add anything to the level?

The presence of verticality alone is not a reason for any potential design, planning, or sketching complications. Especially not if it is, for example, just a few zip-lines, small tunnels, or hills. However, if a level has many or large overlapping parts, sketching or planning such a level is tricky, for example, multiple floors of a building. Therefore, plan out each floor separately and just mark the connecting staircases. If it gets a bit more complex, I recommend providing an isometric wireframe sketch of the high-level—the same counts for anything more detailed, but more about documentation a bit later in this book.

However, even if it is not easy to plan the high-level of a complex 3D space, any connection is part of the flow. Every staircase is a bottleneck and acts as a connection. In many ways, they are even more important than most hallways and other basic bottlenecks because they can unlock/control access to entire new playing fields. More about staircases and other aspects of verticality is further below.

### 10.2.4 Controller, Height, and Angle Considerations

#### *10.2.4.1 The Controller*

When I switched from making exclusive PC shooters to designing console games, I had to learn the hard way that both platforms handle verticality differently. Mouse and keyboard make it a lot easier to look up/down while moving, while many players struggle to do the same with the same ease using a common console controller. Many playtests I've observed have confirmed my own learnings.

Especially tight small turns, including an upwards or downward viewing angle, are tricky. The tight spiral staircase is a classic example, but it can also affect fast engagements at ledges. Therefore, I recommend avoiding any extreme cases where you mix dangerous movement and steep viewing angles. Try to make your staircases a bit wider, or ledges with many fights not very deep/high. Console players can, of course, handle verticality, but with only a few adjustments, we can make their experience a lot more comfortable.

#### *10.2.4.2 Anything Up There*

Another big problem of anything very far up is that players do not see it because it is outside their field of view. Most players, especially on consoles, are used to scanning left and right, but constantly looking up and down is uncommon. So, for example, you added a vital hint up on a cliff, but players continuously do not see it?

The first solution would be to frame a wider view previously, so players have a realistic chance to see it in their field of view. For example, vistas, along paths, or previous navigational challenges guide players looking at a specific point and direction. Secondly, you can add something at the bottom which motivates players to look up. For example, this could be climbing ropes, a corpse/item which fell, or simply a painted arrow pointing up. If it is a common problem in your game, I recommend adding it to the game-wide player language.

Architectural or other art elements can motivate players to look up as well. Especially vertical lines in geometry, bend-upwards features, or similar drawings on walls are way more subtle than anything gamy or a big arrow pointing upwards. Another way is to involve game designers and develop certain features with height in mind. For example, (high-up) snipers make themselves known with laser beams or tend to miss the first shot.

#### *10.2.4.3 Angles*

Check how well your game's features support navigation angles. Many features, such as building small structures or specific animations, are not supported on slopes or stairs. Most games have restrictions on how steep navigable angles can still be or how slopes affect cover—more about cover at slopes in a later chapter.

It gets particularly tricky when terrain is involved. As a player, you do not clearly see when a slope starts to be non-navigable or when certain features are not supported anymore. Therefore, it became a norm to stay away from any angles close above the navigable limit. For example, if the game only supports navigation up to 40°, then stay away from any angles above 40° till ~70°–80°. Essentially eliminate any frustrating assumptions and make it very clear where to navigate and where not.

### 10.2.5 Types of Verticality

#### *10.2.5.1 Introduction*

Below I am briefly covering common verticality types with a few important considerations, but keeping it light since changing technology and your game's context can be wildly different to my personal experiences.

(a)

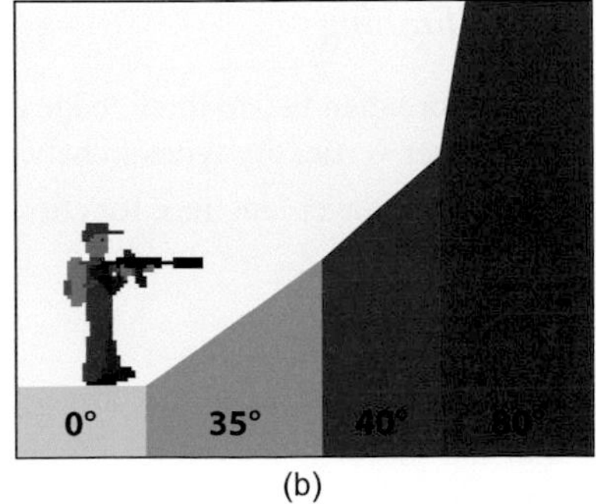

(b)

**FIGURE 10.1** (a) Example: provide hints at the bottom of cliffs for players to look up for opportunities. (b) Example: If your game allows a max slope angle of 35° then players won't notice the difference to the 40° one.

#### 10.2.5.2 Plain Height/Steep Slopes

- AI can be kited around slopes/cliffs because players can jump down and AI cannot. Therefore, if possible, keep the slopes/cliffs short and provide fast ways for AI to navigate up and down.
- If your game has falling damage, stay below the height lethal limit or go clearly above it.
- If the height is vast and players have to navigate or balance close to it, do not forget that vertigo is quite powerful for some people, even if it is just a game.

#### 10.2.5.3 Stairs, Ramps, and Slopes

- Slopes, stairs, or ramps are the default way to move up or down, and pretty much every 3D game has them. If the world allows it, try to use them as your default over other types.
- They are critical because you can still fight and act on them, but consider which features are affected by angles.
- Try to break up long (non-road) serpentines with other verticality types in between or switch from going outside to a short inside section.

#### 10.2.5.4 Interior Staircases

- If possible, avoid tight interior staircases, and if you cannot, avoid combat around and in them.
- They are death traps because they provide little to no cover, offer no space to dodge attacks, and enemies have many attack angles. If you cannot avoid combat, try to make them as big, even if it slightly bends realism.
- Avoid more than two to four continuous floors of tight staircases, or keep them as absolute exceptions.

#### 10.2.5.5 Ladders, Vines, and Pipes

- Don't be too tempted to place them everywhere where you need a quick and easy height transition. Think twice if a ladder makes sense at your location, if the length is reasonable, and the number of ladders in a location.
- Be aware of potential game limitations on ladders, for example: Can AI use them? How many AIs can use them at the same time, and what happens to the other waiting AI? Can players jump on or off a ladder? Can an AI/player engage while hanging on a ladder?
- Ladders are your last resort option if you need a vertical connection. First, try everything to avoid them since they are very limiting for players and AI. Plus, too many of them in one space just look ridiculous.

#### 10.2.5.6 Ledge Climbing

- Do not place more than two to three ledge climbs after each other, or it gets repetitive. Instead, mix in some other verticality types in between if you have to cover much height.
- Make sure that the player language for climbable ledges, especially non-climbable ones, is very obvious to players.

#### 10.2.5.7 Free Climbing

- Ensure that the player language for climbable areas, especially non-climbable ones, is very obvious to players.
- Developer tools to create such spaces need to be very easy and fast to use; ideally, automate their creation as much as possible.

- Free climbing is a massive, expensive, and often game-defining feature. Therefore either do it right or spend the resources for something else.

#### 10.2.5.8 Elevators/Moving Platforms

- Understand the physics engine and AI/player navigation/combat limitations of your engine's moving platforms. Allowing big AI fights on moving platforms is not a given by every engine.
- Otherwise, you can still keep "elevators" as "monster closets" (= AI spawn rooms) or secretly teleport the player once the door is closed.

#### 10.2.5.9 Rope Actions

- I am talking here about grappling hooks, repelling, or zip-lines.
- If they are not free-to-use, then all three are very contextual and often require a lot of careful metrics considerations. Still, try to use them as much as possible because they change up the "monotony" of just moving around.
- Grapples (free or restricted) are not only a means to get up or down, especially considering the momentum when releasing from it. It gets even more exciting when the rope wraps around vertical (sideways) or horizontal (upwards) objects.
- You can top it even further when combining with movement types like double jumps, gliding, short teleports, or continuous grapple usage.

#### 10.2.5.10 Long Falls

- Jumping down from great heights typically means two things: You navigate very fast downwards, and you likely die.
- Be very mindful if you seriously expect players to master long falls and survive, such as hitting small pools of water, piles of hay, or big teddy bears because failing means likely a frustrating re-load.

#### 10.2.5.11 Jump Pads

- Jump pads are gamy and arcadey, but they can be great fun for players and developers if it fits your game. The explosion of speed, getting catapulted through a level, is quite exhilarating.
- I can only encourage pushing the boundaries of what is typically possible with jump pads because they open up some quick connections on a horizontal and vertical plane, which otherwise would be slow, long, and way duller.
- Be careful with too-long jumps because it might feel boring at one point. Test in-game what starts feeling too long for you, and then cut another 25% of the flight time to get your maximum length.

#### 10.2.5.12 Zero Gravity

- Handling large parts of zero gravity is not easy. It requires extremely good 3Cs and a lot of solid features, or players quickly lose orientation and breakfast.
- The visual player leading is crucial to establish rotation and direction. Ideally, the whole room/space visually has a clear start and end and other supporting elements, such as lines or lights, pointing toward the exits. I recommend focusing more on player-leading than simply providing a sense of up/down.
- Be careful with too large rooms because when players fly through the middle, they do not have any close reference points to feel how fast/slow they fly.
- Be careful with too small rooms because it is more difficult to establish a clear sense of direction, especially after players perform a few quick spins.

#### *10.2.5.13 Wall Walking*

- Players can comfortably walk on walls or only specific parts of the walls. A classic example is walking on walls with magnetic boots in a zero gravity environment.
- Every new plane players walk on requires their own player-leading and player-orientation pass.
- Wall walking is a very complex and confusing experience for some players. Carefully establish the connections between the different planes, especially when players switch planes or they quickly lose the relationships between the completely different view-angles.
- Be especially incredibly mindful when players can freely walk on almost all walls instead of selected paths/sections.

#### *10.2.5.14 Wall Running*

- Typically, wall running is a great tool to commit players to a navigation section because they can be a point of no-return.
- Experiment combining this feature with other verticality tools such as grapples, climbing types, ladders, or any jumps/teleports your game has to offer.

#### *10.2.5.15 Portals and Teleportation*

- Pre-placed portals are a convenient and instant way to connect two parts of your level. However, I would be careful using too many of them in your level, or it quickly becomes a messy experience because players quickly lose their orientation.
- If players have a short-distance teleportation or "blink" ability, then work closely with your QA/QC department if you do not want players to break your level design! Players very likely will put them to extreme use, especially in combination with potentially other navigation features.

## 10.3 Progression within a Mission

### 10.3.1 Introduction

Multiple experiences, for example, attacking, defending, or escort, are the basic building blocks of any longer singleplayer mission or level. Some of such blocks have additional modifiers such as time limits, limited weapons, or forced stealth. Planning the progression through the right mix of such blocks is key to creating an entertaining mission experience. A bad mix will likely lead to a very monotonous or boring experience. Therefore, it is essential to set up the correct order based on the initial high-level pitch. Ideally, you created the high-level pitch with a good mix of building blocks already in mind. Otherwise, splitting up a mission into building blocks will deviate too. Mission blocks do not necessarily translate to objectives one to one. Instead, mission blocks are core player experiences which can be split up into multiple objectives in-game.

This methodology only works for missions or levels with a minimum amount of complexity, length, and often some narrative depth. Typically, such missions are at least 15 minutes long. If the entire mission only has one focus, for example, a race, quick assassination, or simple kill-all, then you should, of course, not apply it.

### 10.3.2 Basic Building Blocks and Objectives

#### *10.3.2.1 Introduction*

I'll only cover here briefly the basic, classic building blocks of action games. Feel free to add or remove building blocks depending on your game's context. Each of the blocks I list here is the main one, followed by a list of a few common subtypes. For example, you can split an attack-block into "kill all," "destroy five items," or "kill boss NPC."

Each block is typically between five to ten minutes long, depending on your game and mission needs. As an exception, you could have longer ones, but after 15 minutes of average playtime, it starts to get monotonous again, and I recommend you split and change it up again.

Another big advantage to split missions into such blocks is that the base script of each type can be pre-created. Such template script groups can then get open or broken and become unique per individual mission. Alternatively, they stay closed in the mission, just with unique inputs. The base script stays in a central database, with enough modifiers to adjust for each mission's needs, while a few crafty technical developers (for example, technical level designers) maintain the library throughout production. It might be a bit more limiting for some, but it allows for a way more consistent script quality and faster script progress.

### 10.3.2.2 Attack

First of all, attack essentially means either "Kill" or "Destroy." It is "Kill" if the targets are NPCs such as humans, aliens, animals, or anything else which at least moves with some intelligence and typically can fight back. "Destroy" covers the destruction of items, which are typically static and non-organic. However, the items can, of course, still move around, for example, on a train or conveyor belt. The difference between "Kill" and "Destroy" is a narrative differentiation to give the block more context.

Secondly, players either Kill/Destroy "All," or "a selected amount X." Both of them can be limited to a certain area and type, like "Kill All Blue AI in the Warehouse," just "Destroy 10 evil Mushrooms" or "Kill General Bauer." Ideally, the area is somehow clearly marked, or if no area is required, it is clear where to find the targets. The progression is either shown as a number or a bar if the numbers get too high. Bars can, of course, also be used, for example, like a boss enemy's health bar to motivate players through progression.

One of the biggest problems of this block is to give AI a clear objective or goal. It is tricky to make AI look smart with the primary goal just to stay alive. Defensive strategies like retreating, deploying turrets/shields, or asking for reinforcements only work so far and are not always suitable.

### 10.3.2.3 Defend

The defend block is more passive and reactive compared to Attack. You either defend an area, keep items/NPCs alive, or essentially just survive as a player. The area-defend block can be one or multiple ones, with or without the option to re-take them again and different types of timers involved to switch the area's ownership. Sometimes an interaction like a button press or putting up a flag is involved as well. Domination or King of the Hill is classic multiplayer example of this objective, but they can fit well into a singleplayer context.

Defending one or multiple items/NPCs is another typical application of this block. Typically, the fewer items/NPCs you have, the higher the chance the design asks for a health bar instead of a frustrating one-hit-fail criteria. A special variant of this subtype is the infamous escort objective, where one or multiple NPCs have to reach a location alive. The basic escort types are either the one where the NPCs move by themselves, the one where they move based on player actions (for example, players have to kill X enemies ahead), and finally, where they follow players directly.

The one where players just have to defend themselves is essentially just basic survival. Typically, there is a specific condition attached like a timer. The primary problem is that you need a sound AI system to make searching AI work well because players just hiding in a corner for extended times is often not very fun. Therefore, I would not necessarily recommend this version.

I like the defense block quite a lot because it gives AI a clear objective and makes them look smart. Any time AI has to do something other than killing the players is typically a good thing, especially when there is some type of tug-of-war associated with it.

#### *10.3.2.4 Interact*

In its simplest form, the interact block is where players just have to interact with one or multiple items/NPCs and are done, for example, talking to NPCs, press a few buttons, or stand on a few platforms. They might sound simple but can quickly become more challenging if threats exist, the NPCs run away, or a puzzle is associated with it. Essentially the action itself is simple, but the HOW or WHERE to interact is the key here. Interacting does not have to be always a simple press of a button, but can also be connected to a skill challenge, for example, if players have to hit a small item to activate, like a rope for the piano to drop. It could also be a Destroy block, but the more "puzzly" it is, the more I prefer to keep it in the interact category.

Collecting is another variation, even if it is just walking over the items. Again, the lines get blurred if players first have to kill enemies for the items to drop, but I recommend looking at the dominating player-facing aspect. Collect objectives are often associated with a search component if the item's location is unclear, comparable to a puzzle.

Any interact blocks are typically very player-centric because it primarily focuses on player actions. Any AI or other threats are simply said to be just a hindrance. It is rare that there is a competition with AI without turning it into a defense block.

The interact block has the most exhaustive options due to its sheer huge amount of variations. You can distill so many game objectives into the interact block, yet none of the objectives are incredibly similar in execution.

#### *10.3.2.5 Navigation*

At its core, the Navigation block requires players to reach one or multiple target locations or areas or reach a certain distance away from an entity. The locations, entities, or areas can dynamically change or even move in case of, for example, a chase. However, the player challenge factor here typically comes from threats or a puzzle. The puzzle variant can be to find the target spot or figure out the way to the location because the path might be blocked or otherwise unreachable. Again, the HOW to reach the target or WHERE the target is are the key aspects. The primary difference between a navigation and an interactive puzzle is the last action players are required to do in order to complete it, and that gives them a different vibe. The navigation vibe is often associated with the notion of "get out," "get to," "get away," or "get through."

Another huge factor for this block is distance and, with this comes potential vehicle usage. The question is can players pick their vehicles freely, or are they tied to a specific one? Is one vehicle better than the other, or maybe just one can do the job? Also, do they drive the vehicle themselves, or do they, for example, just handle the mounted weapon? The more limited the choices, the more essential it is to prevent the vehicle from blowing up, which often becomes one of the primary core design challenges. Again, in such cases, it blurs the lines with defense blocks.

Typically, I recommend not using any "Go-To" objectives, except it is required for technical reasons or by the mission system. Ideally, you give players the next objective at the target location right away and let them figure out how to get there. Especially chaining up "Go-To" objectives can feel very demeaning and redundant. However, they do have their place if the navigation is a challenge or a bigger experience in itself, like a chase, running away from a horde of lemmings with rabies, or sitting behind the mounted grenade launcher of a stolen get-away vehicle breaking out of a military base.

#### *10.3.2.6 Narrative Blocks*

Narrative blocks are an exception because they are often shorter than five minutes. However, I highlighted them here separately because they are unique, require special attention, are crucial for pacing, and typically include other departments. Classic examples are cutscenes, bigger in-game events, or NPC walk-and-talks. I would not add every smaller narrative event here, just the big and major ones for the story; the same counts for any narrative events that happen during gameplay. For example, a long drive with a lengthy radio call or an NCP on the driver seat talking is still rather a navigation block instead of a narrative one. The walk-and-talks are a bit special because they primarily exist for the player to listen to the NPC.

#### 10.3.2.7 No Blocks

Quick reminder, I would not make a block out of everything just to create a seamless coverage of the mission in your level design document. Minor transitions do not require a particular navigation block. I recommend adding any smaller pieces to either the previous or next block and be good with it.

### 10.3.3 Modifiers

#### 10.3.3.1 Introduction

Modifiers are an additional layer of complexity you can add to a mission building block to create more variety between them, affect their difficulty, or make them narrative or world-building-wise more fitting. In theory, you can stack as many modifiers as you want, but there is a reasonable limit case by case before it gets silly. Also, some objectives require a mission block to have a modifier, or, for example, a checkpoint race without a timer is not a checkpoint race.

Modifiers are especially great if you have to use the same building blocks with only minor variations between them. In order to still create some exciting differences between them, you can investigate using modifiers.

#### 10.3.3.2 Time

Applying a time limit is one of the most classic modifiers. Essentially it puts time pressure on completing an objective. The time pressure can come from a failure at the end of a timer, it has to happen at a specific time, or the timer needs to finish for success. Classic examples are any checkpoint-races, disarming a bomb before it explodes, completing a download, hitting the hostage taker when he raises the gun, or reaching the antidote before the poison kills you. I recommend connecting the time pressure with a tangible reason to cause death or absolute failure. For example, the arrival of reinforcement in five minutes is not time pressure which should trigger an objective failure because players still have a chance to fight and escape. Alternatively, you can apply "fake narrative time pressure," where you stress out players by giving them hints and messages about the impending threat or danger without instant failure when the time runs out.

#### 10.3.3.3 Forced Stealth and Stealth

Another classic modifier is forced stealth, which triggers an objective failure upon detection by the player. However, I would be careful linking a complete failure to this objective in general, even if you have a very stealth-centric game. Detection is often a very black&white experience, and you need very well-tuned game mechanics to be exciting and fair for players. Instead, I generally suggest letting the players deal with the consequences of their detection, even if it is a very harsh one.

However, if a mission block is instant failing on detection consider a slim chance of redemption. For example, if a hostage taker still needs to run to the hostages to kill them, or someone has to run to an alarm box to activate. In such cases, you still have a chance to take out whoever would then trigger the actual mission failure.

#### 10.3.3.4 Limited Tools

This modifier limits the tools players are allowed to complete an objective. It either reduced the action to one specific item or group. Alternatively, it states which items or item types/categories you are not allowed to use. Player-facing this can also force a certain playstyle if, for example, the objective requires using a sniper rifle or bow and arrow. Common examples are killing an evil man with his own gun, not being allowed to use explosives because the body should stay unharmed, or only using non-lethal force. It is a good modifier to spice up otherwise simple action blocks. However, I would be careful not to overuse it because players typically prefer to use their full earned arsenal.

#### *10.3.3.5 Specific Order*

This modifier specifies the order in which to complete certain aspects of an objective. Some examples are buttons that have to be pressed in a specific order, kill the family of evil gnomes starting with the youngest, defend the shield pylons from the outer to the inner ones, or cut the wires in the correct order to prevent the bomb from exploding. I recommend only using this modifier if the context is clearly justifiable and does not come across as arbitrary.

#### *10.3.3.6 Other Modifiers*

Below is a brief list of other, less often used modifiers.

- Distance: Adding a minimum or maximum distance required to complete an objective is an occasional good way to spice up mission blocks. A few examples are sniping targets above a certain distance, staying within a minimum distance to a fleeing target, or shadowing a VIP without getting too close or far away.
- Speed: An objective has to be completed above, at, or below a certain movement speed. A few examples are driving slow for the unstable chemicals not to explode, not getting caught by the police for exceeding the speed limit or keeping a bus above a minimum speed to prevent a bomb from exploding.
- Light: Sunlight or darkness has to take into consideration failing or succeeding an objective. Some examples are defending a vampire, staying in the light because flesh-hungry demons lurk in the shadows, handling some light-sensitive chemicals, or staying in the sunlight to prevent instant depression.

### 10.3.4 How to Mix Them

#### *10.3.4.1 Basics of a Good Mix*

I believe that it is more complex than simply stating a good mission should be all about variety, like always mixing attack, defend and interact blocks. First of all, it starts with the narrative premise of the mission, which sets the initial mood or theme of the mission, but it does not have to stay like it for the entire duration. Instead, I recommend breaking the initial player expectation of a mission to create drama and excitement. It is a bit like starting to watch a movie, and you soon predict the rest of it. Some simple twists and turns are always a good starting point.

For example, the mission asks for a hostage rescue, which makes the initial theme more sneaky and calm. So, in this case, it would start with a forced-stealth-interact mission block to free the hostage ideally undetected, or they would shoot him. Then you can add a defense block to protect the hostage till the get-away vehicle arrives. Finally, the initial pick-up location is compromised and we have a wild ride vehicle-block while you are behind the mounted gun while the hostage drives. It started stealthily and gradually went more action with a nice progression.

Now, depending on the mission's briefing, the example might not surprise players or break their expectations because it might have been the plan all along. So an alternative example could be that the freed hostage turns against the player as the twist, and then we could follow up chasing the hostage through a hornet's nest ending with him giving up. Finally, we have a big shootout till your get-away car arrives gun blazing.

At the same time, the example could have stayed stealth-oriented by changing the defense block to a stealth escort one and maybe even a driving sequence where the player drives but has to stay undetected in traffic till they are far away.

A good piece of advice is to see your mission as a movie and how it could play out in an ideal scenario. Think about turning it into an exciting movie to watch, with some interesting plots, twists, and memorable moments. Of course, for example, turning an action movie about fast cars into mainly a soap opera is not the kind of surprise most would enjoy. However, a few love scenes and relationship trouble will not hurt just to break up the monotony. Also, the more freedom players have, the less likely they will follow your ideal scenario, but it sets the foundation and potential.

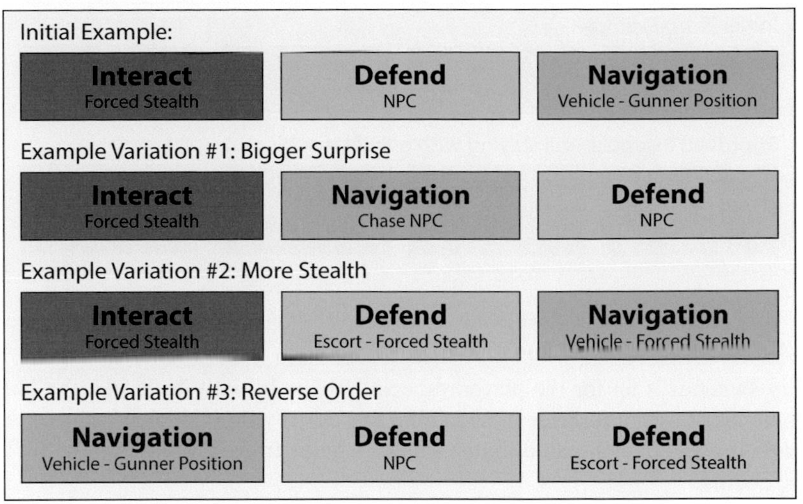


**FIGURE 10.2** A three-mission-block level and three alternative variants.

I will cover pacing in the next bigger chapter, but it is already important to note that not every mission has to end loud and action-oriented. Sure, it leans toward a high intense ending, but there are many other options to establish an increasing intensity and end with a highlight. Let us take the previous example and see how we can start with an explosive vehicle entry, then a defense, and end with a stealth-interact block. We could start with initially freeing a VIP from a heavily guarded prison truck with an NPC buddy driving and you controlling the mounted gun. Then we must defend our NPC buddy till he managed to weld open the prison truck's door. Of course, something goes wrong, and we then have to escape on foot while the buddy carries the unconscious VIP. The only escape route is through a dense forest at night, swarming with cops and corrections officers. If we do not sneak or take out enemies undetected, they quickly kill your slow/unarmed buddy and VIP. This intense cat & mouse game, breaking through the enemy lines chased by dogs, finally ends by reaching the door to a safe-house. Of course, the initial car chase/attack is likely quite intense, but I hope the example showed that you could end up with an intense sneaky ending by pulling the right levers. Also, that now the last block is rather defense than interact is more semantics, but you still "interact" by reaching the safe-house.

### *10.3.4.2 Monotonous Block Usage*

It is not always possible to add up a nice variety of blocks and add some twists to break up player expectations or even to surprise them. For various reasons, it can be that a mission, for example, is dominated by attack or interact blocks. First of all, the good news is that the blocks allow for much variety in themselves already. Secondly, applying one or multiple modifiers is the next obvious option. Otherwise, the same goals to break expectations and add surprises remain.

For example, we have a mission where the players have to take over a village. Instead of applying some interesting blocks with variety, I make it purposely monotonous and then see how we can improve it. We start with a kill-all-block of all enemies in the village, followed by three more kill-all-blocks to take out three troop reinforcement waves. Without changing the attack blocks to another type, I could start with first a kill-VIP-block to take out the commanding officer, who would flee upon detection, adding a bit of a stealth incentive or even a systemic chase. Up next, we do not change much and still keep the kill-all-block of the enemies in the village; we have to clean it somehow. However, I could add the modifier only to take them out non-lethally because the regular troops do not deserve to die for later diplomatic talks. An alarm mechanic or time modifier could also work here in a stretch to potentially affect future reinforcements. The first reinforcement wave is a fanatic special forces recon platoon consisting of primary snipers and sneaky and fast guys. This very long-range and fast

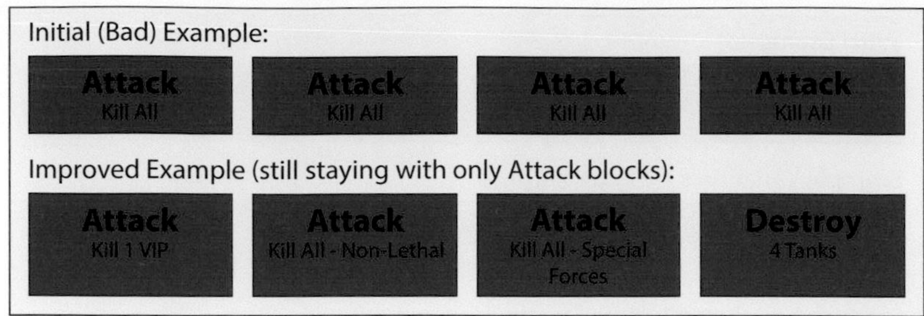


**FIGURE 10.3** First, a very repetitive four-mission-block level, with then an improved alternative.

focus certainly switches it up for the player, especially if he initially feels like the hunted. Finally, we send in some tanks as reinforcement, switching to a destroy-tank block which requires players to change playstyle drastically compared to just killing regular troops. A big tank battle also acts as a nice explosive ending.

Sure, I played a lot with changing enemy archetype composition to give them a clear/clean focus, and the VIP-kill block could also be an optional one. However, it succeeded in breaking up the monotony without changing any attack-block to another type. In reality, I would try to change one or two to a defense block or another type, but that was not the point of this example.

However, missions with primarily monotonous blocks have their place. One reason could be the game's dominating theme or the lack of production resources to create enough variety. There is only so much pure level design can do in such cases, except maybe some custom scripting. Another reason is to add monotonous blocks to the overall mission mix purposely. The irony is that always having well-mixed missions with surprises and twists can be monotonous as well. Sometimes some predictability can be refreshing and give the true twists more weight. Therefore having a few missions in between with a very dominating block type can break that pattern.

## 10.4 About Pacing and Timing

### 10.4.1 Introduction

The pacing defines the intensity of the player's experience at any time during the mission or level. Planning out a good pace is essential for level designers to avoid, for example, classic mistakes like a long boring middle part, players getting tired of too much, non-stop high intensity, or the highlight of a level is more at the beginning than the end. It can also help balance out gameplay with narrative or singleplayer with coop experiences.

The origin for pacing comes from story writing, where pacing determines how fast or slow the viewer gains narrative information or how fast/intense the plot is moving forward. The classic example is from the three-act structure. Act one exposes the viewer to the overall situation, sparks the protagonist's adventure, and ends lower in intensity when the protagonist makes their first bigger decision moving forward. In act two, we have the bulk of the story with the rising action, leading to a big confrontation that goes wrong. Then again, pacing drops again, reflecting on or dealing with what went wrong. Finally, in act three, we start with some doubt to ensure that the final climax is even more impressive. We close with the aftermath, which is usually also a lot slower-paced again.

This book is not about narrative, but I highly recommend reading up on the three-act narrative structure or similar models if you are interested in such topics. There is certainly an advantage for level designers to have basic narrative knowledge. You will find other different-looking graphs, but that is the variant I prefer to bridge to pacing within level design. I hope you will see the similarities, but in an interactive medium driven primarily by gameplay, I am replacing "the speed of narrative" with "gameplay intensity." Essentially a non-scientific measure of the player's heart rate or sweaty hands.

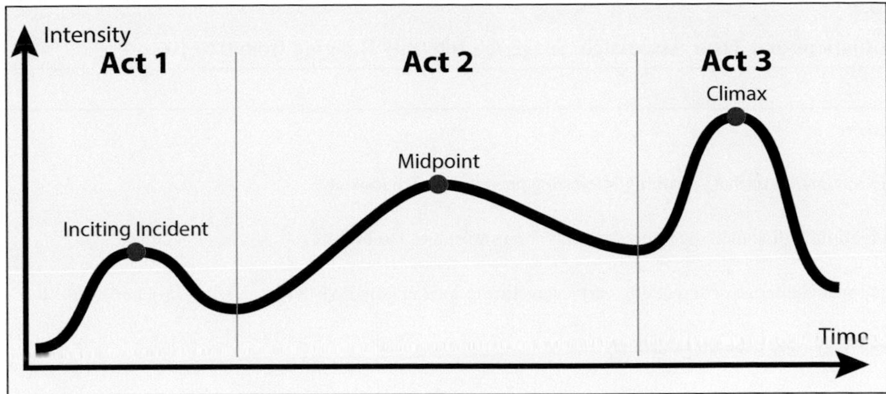


**FIGURE 10.4** It shows a classical pacing graph, which is often used in narrative forms.

I recommend working with a pacing graph for any bigger mission, which requires some more detailed planning. As I said, it is not something highly scientific, it is very subjective, and not every player will have the same experience. However, it gives safety and sets expectations for the level designer about the journey through the level. For example, early on, they might spot issues of not enough "breathing" points, clearly set the pacing expectations for any major moments before the finale, or spot that the highlight might not be as impressive as initially intended. Also, a good-looking pacing graph always looks good in level design presentations and shows your confidence in the design.

## 10.4.2 The Beat and Intensity

### *10.4.2.1 Introduction*

The beat is the smallest element I would compartmentalize a player experience in a level or mission. A new beat starts whenever the intensity changes, by either going up or down. Each beat has a certain length. I recommend seconds because it gives you more flexibility. You can still easily calculate minutes out of seconds but working with, for example, "6.75 minutes" can be odd.

Therefore, a beat is defined by its intensity and length of time. The time is another guesstimate but should be close to the time you want an average player to spend here, close to the golden path or maybe a tick slower. Then the pacing graph shows the rising and lowering intensity curve over the different beats.

### *10.4.2.2 Intensity Estimation*

The recommended maximum intensity is ten, which should be your absolute highlight of the mission. I do not recommend comparing the intensity between missions. Keep it simple and look at each mission individually. The lowest intensity is zero, and that is when the mission loads and ends. Otherwise, even the most boring walking beat has an intensity of one. Now since we know the maximums and minimums, the remaining intensity levels are about gut feeling. However, remember we are still in the planning phase. Therefore, your intensity levels are about your intentions to make sure you have enough low points as a breather and that none of the previous beats are putting the highlight to shame.

Another important consideration is that difficulty does not directly link to intensity. I know that might be confusing because, of course, a difficult section is more intense. However, other aspects raise intensity, for example:

- Speed (even without extreme difficulty)
- Narrative closure (finally catch that bad guy)
- A lot of not so dangerous and near-miss explosions

**TABLE 10.1**

Various Situations and Their Associated, Suggested Intensity Ranging from 0 to 10

| Situation | Intensity |
|---|---|
| Loading screen | 0 |
| Very simple navigation without anything interesting happening or to look at | 1 |
| Simple navigation with something interesting (art or narrative, etc.) to look at | 2 |
| Mild navigational challenge or something very interesting to look at (small vista reveal, small in-game even, etc.) | 3 |
| Very small or very easy firefight / skirmish | 4 |
| Easy firefight, difficult navigational challenge, or something stunning to look at (bigger vista, medium in-game event, etc.) | 5 |
| Medium firefight, very difficult navigational challenge, or something incredibly stunning to look at (massive vista, big in-game event, etc.) | 6 |
| Challenging firefight or very difficult navigational challenge with an extra component (explosions, time pressure, etc.) | 7 |
| Very challenging firefight, it starts to get intense but remains conservative (= no severe extra components) | 8 |
| High intense firefight with an extra intense extra component (extra navigational factor, limited cover, time pressure, lots of explosions, difficult AI archetypes, or mix, etc.) | 9 |
| High intense firefight with an extra intense extra component (extra navigational factor, limited cover, time pressure, lots of explosions, difficult AI archetypes, or mix, etc.) | 10 |

- Running through a burning house (without extreme difficulty)
- For some people, lots of spiders
- Really cool loud heart-pumping music.

Table 10.1 shows some example intensity as a guideline. Feel free to adjust the situations and their intensity to your game's context.

### 10.4.3 The Pacing Graph

#### *10.4.3.1 Introduction*

The pacing graph is the visual representation of your mission's intensity. Typically, it is an initial intention and not something clearly measurable. The height (x) of the graph represents intensity, while the length (y) represents time. The graph is split into all the individual beats of the mission with their heights and length of time. Drawing a curve between the top-middle points of each beat is the pacing graph.

#### *10.4.3.2 Basic Rules*

The ideal way to work with a pacing graph is to work with Microsoft Excel or a similar program where changing table entries right away affects the curve. Below I list the basic rules, what you want the pacing graph to look like and what to avoid.

- Each level typically should only have one highlight with one beat at intensity ten. Ideally, the last high-beat is the highlight and the memorable moment. If it is different, then expect the level to feel anticlimactic.

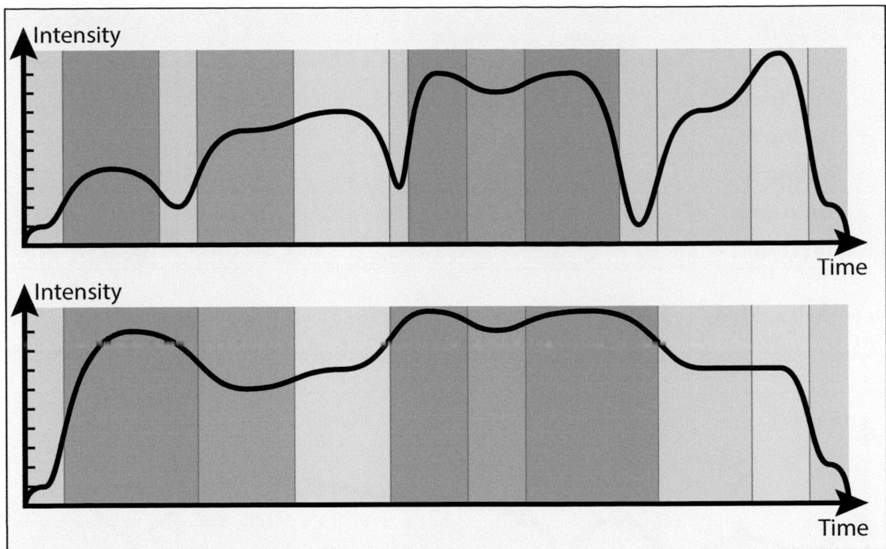


**FIGURE 10.5 Top Graph (good)**: Occasional breaks, beats, and higher blocks raise gradually, clear highlight at the end. **Bottom Graph (bad)**: No clear breaks, highlight is in the middle of the mission, way too steep raise at the beginning of the mission, and the last two beats have equal intensity.

- You can combine more than one higher beat, for example, three beats with an intensity of six, seven, and nine. However, I do not recommend such blocks to be longer than ten minutes, fifteen at most, before you have a lower intensity beat as a break. Otherwise, you likely tire out many players, and they might not feel an intensity increase anymore that drastic.
- Any intense beats or blocks should ideally go up gradually toward the final highlight. It does not have to be crazy strict, but I recommend overall growth of the higher points.
- The intensity breaks are crucial every five to fifteen minutes. They allow players to have a breather, and without them, the next intensity spike will not feel as powerful. For example, if you would have a continuous increase, then the rise from six to eight is barely noticeable, but if you have a drop-down to a two in between then, there is a noticeable spike. Without breaks, players not only get exhausted, but they also become callous and indifferent for any highlights.
- The height of the breaks does not have to increase gradually, but in order to be a break, it certainly should be around one to three and at least 30 seconds long.
- Two following beats should never have the same intensity because by the core definition a new beat is a change in intensity.

Arguably you could have two connected beats with the same intensity because you change the mission block. However, I would recommend seriously considering changing the intensity between the two blocks because otherwise, it might be dull. It is just a lazy design if you cannot find anything that changes the player's experience.

The background coloration of the beats according to their mission block color is optional, but it can help show good or bad patterns. However, remember that you can cut a mission block into multiple beats like multiple defense waves, and the small little break-beats in between are not mission blocks either. So, I am just using the colors without a strict mission-block analogy. Also, keep in mind that there is no direct correlation between objectives and beats. An objective can have multiple beats if, for example, a defense has increasingly difficult waves.

After all, the pacing is not a very strict science since it largely shows just an intention and cannot be precisely measured. I bet there are great levels with a very bad-looking pacing graph. Therefore, I recommend using it, especially for more linear experiences, to set expectations and not be too stifling. It might

| | A | B | C | D | E | F | G | H | I |
|---|---|---|---|---|---|---|---|---|---|
| 1 | | **Beat 0** | **Beat 1** | **Beat 2** | **Beat 3** | **Beat 4** | **Beat 5** | **Beat 6** | **Beat 7** |
| 2 | **Mid Time** | 0 | 5 | 160 | 325 | 445 | 610 | 835 | 1010 |
| 3 | **Pacing A** | 0 | 2 | 5 | 1 | 6 | 7 | 8 | 2 |
| 4 | **Pacing B** | 0 | 6 | 1 | 6 | 2 | 2 | 1 | 7 |
| 5 | **Time (sec)** | 0 | 10 | 300 | 30 | 210 | 120 | 330 | 20 |
| 6 | **Total Time** | 0 | 10 | 310 | 340 | 550 | 670 | 1000 | 1020 |

**FIGURE 10.6** **Yellow Fields**: Level Designer fills out those cells. **Blue Fields**: Those cells get calculated.

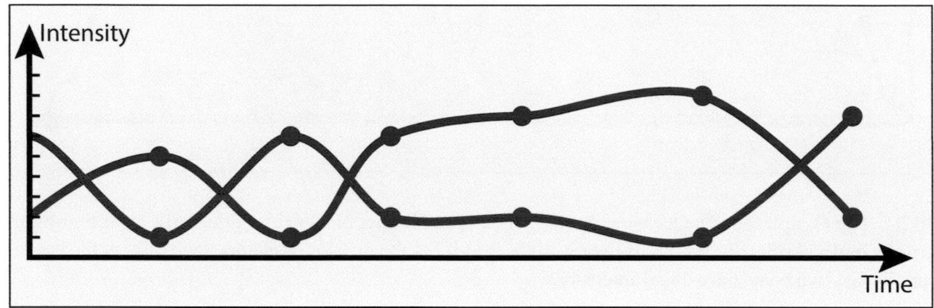


**FIGURE 10.7** If everything worked out fine your graph should look similar to the one above.

even be helpful for some level designers or directors to create them for very open missions planning the golden path—even if it is just a whiteboard sketch.

### *10.4.3.3 How to Create a Pacing Graph Using Excel*

The easiest way to work with a pacing graph is to use Microsoft Excel or similar programs. Below I describe a quick way how to create such a graph for two pacing graphs using Excel.

1. Create a table where the columns are the individual beats, starting with an empty beat zero (all numbers zero here for a nicer looking graph), then your first beat of the mission, till your final beat.
2. The first-row call "Mid time," second row "Pacing A" (your first pacing graph, like "Gameplay pacing"), third-row "Pacing B" (whatever your second pacing graph should be, see further below), fourth-row "Time," and last sixth-row "Total time."
3. Start filling in the two pacing rows and the one "Time" row. We will calculate the other ones.
4. Calculate the "Total time," which takes the previous total time and adds the current time, for example, D6=C6+D5.
5. Calculate the "Mid time," which is the middle time of the current beat within the context of total time. Otherwise, the graph will show the intensity at the end of the time and not in the middle. The total time context is important to show a continuous graph. It is the previous beat's total time plus half the current beat's time, for example, D2=C6+D5/2.
6. Mark the rows "Mid time," "Pacing A," and "Pacing B" and insert a "Scatter Chart with Smooth Lines." Feel free to change the formatting or naming of your now hopefully visible pacing graph.

Ideally, if you change the timing and intensity, the pacing graph should change accordingly. You see that longer beats take more space while, for example, a short break is just a quick dip.

If you add or remove beats, you might have to adjust the graph's data or make a new one quickly. If you are fancy, you could add a new graph ("Stacked Column" rotated by 90°) behind the current one showing just the individual time to highlight the beats. However, that can quickly get finicky.

### 10.4.4 Alternative Pacing

#### *10.4.4.1 Introduction*

The beautiful aspect of pacing graphs is that you can display more than one graph in the same graphic showcasing even more information and to showcase their relationship. It is also a great tool to communicate different intentions or spot issues in more than just gameplay intensity.

The two types of additional graphs I'm most used to are for narrative and coop. Based on your game, you might come up with your own pacing graph types, but I recommend not having too many graphs in one graphic and not going too granular; otherwise, it is less helpful and just an exercise for the sake of an exercise.

Usually, I do not see a reason for any additional graphs to follow similar strict rules like the gameplay intensity graph. For example, a narrative graph will always start pretty high if the level starts with a cool cinematic.

#### *10.4.4.2 Narrative Graph*

The narrative graph shows where you transmit more or fewer amounts of narrative to the players. That can include anything ranging from cinematics over radio dialogs to environmental storytelling. It is ideal because it communicates clearly when the narrative has more space and opportunity and where less. Typically, it would be best not to trigger relevant radio messages in very heated gameplay beats but instead use the break in between. However, you could sprinkle some lower narrative-dense environmental storytelling in some more intense scenes. Looking at your graph narrative design might claim early on that they need more or less time to bring their narrative across. It might also tell them that they only have two or three bigger moments for radio dialogs or cinematics, and otherwise, it is just environmental storytelling. Expectations can go both ways. Sure, we are still in the realm of guesstimates, but it is better to sort it out now and set base expectations than make adjustments later in production.

#### *10.4.4.3 Coop Graph*

The coop graph shows where the players have to work more together and where they usually act more individually. For example, they commonly act more as one unit in a smaller space than in a wide space with many flanking opportunities. Other examples are strict purpose-built coop-sections or where players work individually without relying much on each other. Especially for coop-centric games, it can highlight if you have long segments without any coop-centric gameplay or too much after each other.

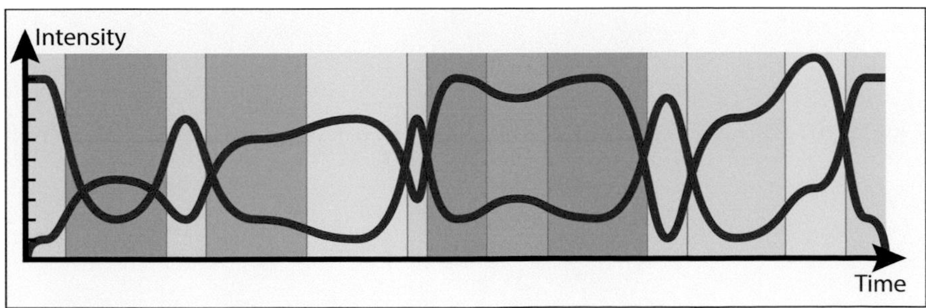


**FIGURE 10.8** **Blue Graph**: Gameplay intensity. **Red Graph**: Narrative density.

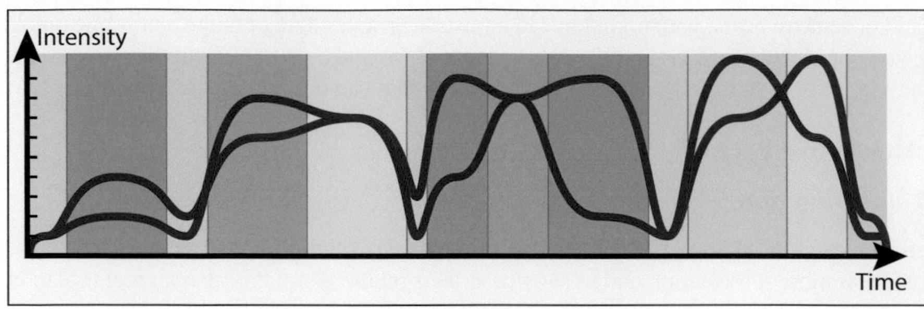


**FIGURE 10.9** **Blue Graph**: Gameplay intensity. **Red Graph**: Coop density.

# Section IV

# Practical: How to Get Started

# 11

# *Concept Phase*

After a lengthy part about theory, managing expectations, and intentions, I will finally start with the more practical part, and we start with the very beginning: the level's conception phase. At first, I will cover information gathering and then the often argued level design document topic. Before I jump to two world-building methodologies, I will briefly talk about how to approach finding the right location because understanding how to combine art, narrative, and level design happens exactly during this phase. Lastly, instead of going into the depth of world-building, I wrote about two of my most used best practices or methodologies applied for level design or environment art.

## 11.1 It All Starts with Research and Reference

### 11.1.1 Introduction

At the start of most level creations, you should always have a research phase, where everyone involved gathers as many references as possible and reads as much as possible about the subject matter. Big companies spend thousands of dollars organizing several research trips, interviewing experts in the field, or hiring consultants. In this book, I stay a bit more old school, cheaper and therefore, explain things we all can do with a computer and an internet connection.

Essentially it is way more than just collecting a handful of reference pictures and browsing Wikipedia. As I stated at the beginning of this book, you, as a level designer, have to become an expert yourself about what you are about to design and create. For example, if you plan to use an old Alaskan radar station from the cold war, then you have to become an expert in the cold war, radar stations, Alaska, and all its combinations, simple as that. I know it sounds daunting, and you likely can skip a few chapters here and there, but a severe and focused research phase is important to create a coherent level.

### 11.1.2 Searching Correctly

As usual, if we want to know something, we google it, and if we want to find a related image, we use Google's image search. That is not a bad start, and many research phases started using that simple yet proven method. However, in many cases, it just skims the surface of the topic you are looking for, or when it gets a bit more exotic, you often barely find anything useful. I worked with enough level designers or environment artists who struggled with this phase because the specific topic was so rare or exotic. After all, we typically do not want to make boring vanilla locations.

Below are my basic hints on how to maximize your search results. In the continuous example, I am using below, I want to research for a "haunted village" level, and I already used the usual google and image search for this term. The hints below are in no particular order.

- Use alternative search engines, for example, Bing or DuckDuckGo.
- Use a thesaurus or imagination to replace your search query. In our example, you could search for "hamlet," "city," "suburb," "location," "place," or "town." Instead of "haunted," you could look for "ghost," "cursed," "ghastly," "forgotten," "abandoned," "weird," or "eerie." Any combinations of the two terms are now possible new search candidates. However, you will find many duplicates or find some rather obscure, irrelevant, yet sometimes entertaining results in many cases. Still, this method is often wholly worth it.

DOI: 10.1201/9781003275664-15

- Read as many articles as possible to learn more about the subject matter. You might find exact locations or alternative terms you have not known previously. Then searching for those terms or locations likely reveals even more. For example, just looking around for "abandoned villages" (see alternative terms above) might lead you to "abandoned saxon villages in Romania." Digging a bit deeper, you might stumble over the Romanian village Viscri. This village is not necessarily haunted, yet it might offer a lot of exciting reference pictures because it is also a big tourist attraction. Sometimes it is worth going down the rabbit hole.
- Translate your search query and its alternatives in different languages. For example, "Spukdorf," or "verfluchtes Dorf" (both German) will get you very different results than your previous "haunted village." Especially when I was stuck with some rather specific terms, I could still find something new looking in different languages. You would be surprised how many crazy good references are hidden on non-English sites.
- Search on Google Map in specific areas. Occasionally you might find some interesting gems or it might lead you to another trace.
- Combine it with additional terms which focus the search further. For example, "haunted village Lovecraft," "haunted village Stephen King," "haunted village top 10," or maybe even try "haunted village game reference." They can all lead you to new clues; especially somehow, the internet is fascinated by "top 10" or other numbers.
- Follow search suggestions. For example, Google suggested "haunted village houses" or "haunted village in Rajasthan" when I wrote this book.
- Remove certain terms from your search query like: "haunted village" – "concept art" – "site:artstation.com."
- Search on picture-collection pages like Tumblr, Pinterest, Artstation, DeviantArt, or Instagram. Those are just some quick common ones, but many more pages do not show their search results efficiently using Google Image search.
- Take your time to scan "Related images" when you find something interesting, using, for example, Google Image search. Even if they just lead you to another webpage for new clues.

Those are some quick ideas; I bet there are many more. The essential idea is always to keep digging and reading. The more you become an expert, the more terms you know to search for.

### 11.1.3 Research the Why

When you research a topic, collecting thousands of pictures and learning many facts is one thing, but that should only be the beginning. I mean, it is fun to impress people with your in-depth knowledge about Canadian lumber mills, German WW2 submarines in the pacific, or disturbing, hopefully fictional, steroid-infused, illegal, underground raccoon fight arenas. However, in the vast majority of cases, when you make a level, you will likely not translate your knowledge one-to-one into the game, not even mentioning copyright.

Instead, what you have to learn are not facts, but the interconnections—essentially, "why" are the things the way they are. So when you then make your version, it is still a coherent experience or location, without too closely resembling the original. If you don't have a good understanding of the "why," players will feel that something is off, even if they cannot say precisely what.

For example, if you plan to design the previous "haunted village," you must first learn why villages look the way they are. Why is the church sometimes more central, and why sometimes on the village's edge? So, if you now want to move the church around, you know how to adjust the surrounding buildings. Is a monastery involved, or was it originally just a chapel? Also, not all graveyards are close to the church, or their position has changed over the centuries. Additionally, each culture and region handles it once again differently. Unless you have extensive comprehension, you might end up with a pig farm and gas station next to the church. Every factor counts, and your expertise is essential. Again, the interconnections are the absolute key here.

Once you understand all the "why's" of your environment, you can look into the "how." How would they have built a church in the center or edge of the village during the specific era? How would surrounding buildings, roads, and places look like in both cases? How would they have extended an original small chapel in south France compared to midwest America? How would both cases look different in the 18th century compared to the 19th century?

Once you master "why" and "how," only then "what" comes into play; for example, what stone do they use to build the church? However, most of the "what's" are already answered in your original research, facts, and references.

If you work on something completely fictional, you should still follow the same order, but then you have to define the "why" yourself. Write down the interconnections for your own later work and for other developers to connect their work coherently with yours. Again, more about world-building processes later on.

### 11.1.4 Collecting Reference Correctly

#### *11.1.4.1 Introduction*

It is always the same. Teams of level designers, environment artists and narrative designers start their research phase and everyone starts to frantically download all kinds of pictures and save a ton of bookmarks of interesting articles. However, once they realize that they should collect it all together at a central location it gets messy. Still, once they overcome that initial hurdle, it gets even messier. Different people have different ideas on how to sort all the data, the same pictures show up multiple times and everyone adds new folders according to their idea of a super logical folder hierarchy.

In this chapter I would like to share a few common and practical oriented hints on how to avoid the usual chaos. It all sounds so easily avoidable, yet every project fights with similar issues.

#### *11.1.4.2 Pictures*

Collecting or storing pictures is the origin story of reference collection chaos. Below I have listed a few simple rules for everyone to follow.

- Everyone agrees on a central location for storing pictures, either using version control software or somewhere on a server.
- Only one experienced person makes the initial proposal of a folder structure. Then have a brief meeting, maybe a few adjustments, but then it stays.
- Only the initial person can create new folders—no self-initiative, or it gets messy again. If the project is big, you can have a few more people with folder-creation rights, but they have to stay in close contact to follow their own rules.
- If you need a new folder, you can request it and keep the pictures locally till the new one exists. Alternatively, the initial owner approves you to create the folder.
- A folder structure overview exists somewhere accessible by everyone, for example, on a Confluence page with some basic guidelines and rules.
- I believe that using a database for reference pictures is often overkill. Instead, you can rename pictures and use basic search in the folders. However, even that is often unnecessary and likely not followed by many developers. Still, a good folder structure that people follow is the minimum you can expect, and it typically functions well.

A common mistake, which leads to the bespoken mess, is a folder structure that mixes picture types and locations or the same picture type exists at multiple locations. For example, you have in your original folder one folder called "props" and "location A." However, it gets messy once someone creates another "props" folder in its later sub-folders of "location A." Now, if someone looks for props references, they might miss some. One way to address the issue is to clearly label one folder "generic props" (for all locations) and the other one "unique props" (unique to this location or building). Therefore, everyone who finds a new prop reference picture has to think if it is generic or specific and place it in the hopefully correct one. Other alternative structures are possible, whatever fits your project and team, but I hope the base is clear and shows why not everyone should have the liberty to create their own folders and structures.

#### *11.1.4.3 Links and Articles*

It is best practice to store all relevant articles or links on, for example, a central Confluence page. However, in my experience, most developers somehow never really click on them or even read them. The reality is that you should be lucky if they read some—developers are busy humans, no hard feelings. By no means do I recommend not having a link collection somewhere. It remains relevant for any later research when you want to check something or for new team members.

However, I recommend small little presentations of the research experts. You can present it alone or as a group and share your findings with the team. The short presentation can be completely improvised just by going through pictures or scrolling through interesting articles. There is no reason to have a fancy presentation, just share it with the team and talk about it. It might lead to exciting conversations, good questions to dig deeper, it trains your public speaking even if your audience is small, and certainly improves team coherence. Additionally, you often learn and remember it a lot more when you present it, forcing you to really think about it and its interconnections. Also, your listeners tend to remember it better than quickly scrolling through random links posted on a Confluence page.

## 11.2 Documentation Basics

### 11.2.1 Introduction

Right away, I need to say that I am a firm supporter of light level design documentation. The times of massive, detailed documentation are over in times of modern level editors. Sure, it took us hours to compile a level back in the days, so quick iterations were not a feasible option, and we had to plan a lot more carefully. Still, even when we had editors which allowed us to jump in-game with the press of a button, we had to write endless text documents with crude graphics. Nowadays, we should spend more time experimenting in-game utilizing this amazing technology and opportunities. For example, AI patrol paths should not be planned on paper, then wait to get it approved and finally realize that it has to change anyhow.

My love-hate relationship with level design documentation comes from this time, and since then, I have been trying to reduce designers' workload as much as possible. Of course, the documentation phase is crucial, but it has to go with the time, and their purpose has to be clear; otherwise, we do not have time for more important things. Therefore, in this chapter, I want to sort out the clear purpose of documentation to reduce unnecessary workload.

Another essential aspect of such documentation is that each game and project has different needs and requirements. Therefore, I will cover two different styles of level design documentation that can act as a foundation for you.

Lastly, we need to briefly cover time estimates because at the end or during the document phase, managers will likely ask how long it will take to create all that, and many, especially younger level designers, struggle with that.

I write everything in this chapter based on the idea that level design documentation is a collaboration between level design and environment art, with some narrative and game design involvement. Feel free to adjust it to your team composition, especially if less specialized developers are involved.

Important: Do not follow the "very light" approach when taking a level design test for an interview! I recommend staying instead too detailed and stating that you went into more detail for the sake of the test only—better be safe than sorry. Remember when you normally present your level design documentation for approval, you are talking. In the context of a design test, all that matters is what is in the document. Then going very abstract and high-level might not get you very far. As much as

I love that stuff, I had to dismiss level design tests because what we got is a far cry from what we asked for.

### 11.2.2 Document Purpose and Audience

#### *11.2.2.1 Introduction*

In my opinion, level design documentation only has two purposes:

1. Show your intentions: Pitch your level and show confidence in the design so you (or a team) can start working on it
2. For externals: External or new developers can get a quick understanding

That is it.

As you see, there are no crazy detailed plans of AI patrols, cover positions, or anything else mentioned. Once you go 3D, most of the details will change anyhow, so do not waste time now.

Another well-known fact in the industry is that barely anyone keeps their original level design documents updated. Nobody has time to keep it updated once the level is playable and the first intentions are visible. It is not ideal but somehow a reappearing pattern. However, sometimes it is seriously required. Then it is easier to convince even the most disgruntled or busy level designer to update a light document than a crazy detailed one.

#### *11.2.2.2 Intentions*

You, or the level's team, need to convince whoever approves it that you could start production. Therefore, the primary key is to establish confidence. How you achieve this largely depends on the approvers.

If you work with reasonable leads or directors, then the base criterion for the documentation is that your documentation brings across your clear intentions. Why is your design (and all the individual parts) the way it is? How do you plan to do so, and is this plan realistic given the available time and resources? Typically, people try to poke holes into the design and you need to be prepared for it. Also, the amount of detail they expect might differ from my opinion. If you work with them for the first time, it is best to clarify such topics beforehand.

Of course, the intentions require you to do a decent design! It is pretty difficult to pitch a bad level to qualified directors or leads. Therefore, the documentation needs to answer key questions, show an interesting mix of ingredients, events, or experiences in addition to exciting layouts and world-building—essentially everything else I wrote in this book.

Another important aspect of the intentions is to act as a base for further evaluation, especially for production and tech teams. After all, the sooner you get at least an early okay that the level is technically feasible or what it would take to get it done, the better. More about time estimates for production a bit later in this chapter.

#### *11.2.2.3 For Externals*

The second use for level design documentation is for any external or new members joining your team. Instead of giving everyone new or external presentation about the level, they can just have a quick look at the document and get a good idea. If they still have questions, they can ask you. Of course, later on, massively outdated documentation is a problem here.

A primary, recurrent client for level design documentation is QA/QC when they later in the production cycle have to write their test cases/procedures for your level. Hopefully, if you have an embedded QC member in your team, they will take care of it; otherwise, it usually falls back to the level designers. Other occasional clients are writers who write walkthrough books or online versions and trust me; it gets awkward if they base it on the pre-alpha version of your mission. Lastly, more separate teams like cinematics, publishers, or audio often also reference those documents.

### 11.2.3 Documentation for Linear Levels

#### *11.2.3.1 Introduction*

I prefer to stick to a beat foundation for linear levels because pacing is crucial for such levels and more realistically achievable compared to more open types. Also, among other aspects like mission blocks or objectives, they are the smallest unit. Further on, for linear levels, I prefer to take a document format that suits this purpose and is more of an easy-to-work type of document than a pure presentation type. Therefore, my preferred program is Excel or similar software. I can list all the different beats nicely to do some calculations and some simple linking to reduce my workload.

The second aspect I like about Excel is that I have multiple tabs. Each tab has a different purpose or is created for a different audience. The first tab is the high-level, typically filled out by the level design director or lead level designer during the high-level phase of production. The second tab is the level sketch or drawing with the connected beats shown. The third tab is the medium level, the main table with all the information, primarily filled out by the level designer. The last tab is for details if I really need it.

#### *11.2.3.2 Tab One: High-Level*

The first tab contains all the high-level information for the level. If you want to get a quick understanding of the level, then you look here. It has five major elements:

First comes the name of the level, which gets linked throughout the file from now on.

Second, the level's global stats come, like the level's file name, level's location within the world, time of day, weather and season, and the level's narrative position (for example: "act 3, mission 2"). You can add anything else important for your game here, like game modes, rewards, or coop/singleplayer.

Third, add some concept art or reference pictures, scaled small, to fit the page; typically, not more than one to three.

Fourth, some mission blocks breakdown in a table. Ideally, the level design director or level design lead translates those blocks directly from the high-level or blueprint phase, from early in pre-production. Each column is a mission block, while the rows are the categories. I prefer to group the rows into level design, narrative, game design, level art, and misc comments. The Table 11.1 should give you an idea of what classical categories are per group. However, feel free to remove or add categories that fit your game.

Fifth, add a pacing graph below because it helps to get a quick understanding of the level.

As you see, it is not much, and you do not have to fill out everything. However, this is typically the starting information the level designers and environment artists get coming out from the high-level phase, plus, of course, a lengthy verbal introduction. Ideally, they can then use this information to fill out the medium level (tab three) and the level sketch (tab two).

#### *11.2.3.3 Tab Two: Level Sketch*

You can use any software you like to create your level sketch, like Photoshop, scanned pencil drawing, Illustrator, SketchUp, or any similar software. It does not really matter as long as it is clear and clean for anyone to understand the level's size, scope, scale, and totality.

**TABLE 11.1**

High-Level Documentation Table for the Mission Blocks with Main Categories and Subcategories. Each Subcategory Can Be One Row

| | |
|---|---|
| **Level Design** | Time estimate, Dominating gameplay pillars, Modifiers, Quick walkthrough, Special moments |
| **Narrative** | Story description, Cinematics or in-game events, Emotion, Narrative context/consequences |
| **Design** | Tutorial, New ingredient, Ingredient focus |
| **Level Art** | Level art direction |
| **Misc Comments** | Must comments, Should comments, Can comments (essentially other random ideas which came up during the high-level phase for the mission blocks) |

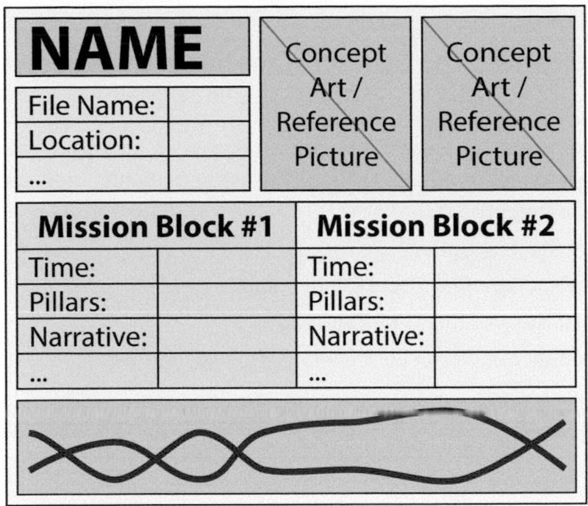


**FIGURE 11.1** Linear high-level documentation mockup (not to scale).

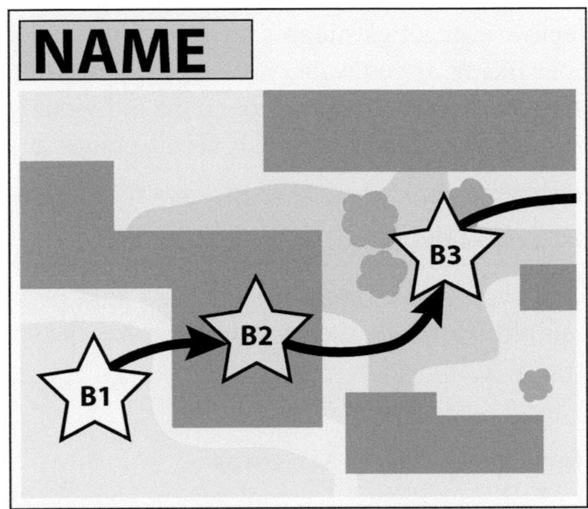


**FIGURE 11.2** Linear level sketch mockup (not to scale).

I do recommend using, for example, Excel's shapes to show where in the sketch the beats are. Then add their beat number inside, give them the same color as the beat in tab three and connect them using the arrow connectors.

It does not hurt to add a separate text list of beats below for quick reference. Also, if the sketch is very colorful and it might interfere with the visibility of the beat-shapes, then just change the sketch's opacity and saturation.

I cannot recommend going into too much detail here! There is no need to carefully pre-plan every cover placement. It is crucial so the viewer gets an idea of the space, the type of locations, intended architecture, the overall scale/scope, and how it is all connected. If the layout intentions are not clear from one big picture, you might have to break it down into multiple ones or have close-ups. I would rather state in tab three what your space, cover, or layout intentions are instead of proving it already in the sketch. Otherwise, you did it twice, and one was a waste of time. As long as it all makes sense and looks reasonable and convincing, it should be all fine. However, if you have a very complex space that really needs more careful planning, you still have tab four.

#### *11.2.3.4 Tab Three: Medium-Level*

Here happens the bulk of the documentation work. Essentially the whole tab is one huge table, but the table gives a solid starting point for anyone to get started. The columns are the beats, translated by the

**TABLE 11.2**
Mid-Level Documentation Table with Main Categories and Subcategories. Each Subcategory Can Be One Row

| | |
|---|---|
| **Level Design** | Beat type (gameplay, in-game event, etc.), Location, Linearity/Openness, Dominating gameplay type, Dominating gameplay pillars, Difficulty, New ingredients, Ingredient focus, AI archetypes, Special moments, Comments |
| **Narrative** | Objectives, Story description |
| **Pacing & Time** | Time (per beat), Gameplay pace, Other pacing |
| **Level Art** | Environmental Storytelling, Lighting, Mood |
| **Tech** | Streaming comments, Script comments, Misc tech comments |
| **Audio** | Music, Unique sounds |
| **Animation** | Unique animations |

level designers from the original mission blocks, now just, of course, more granular. Ideally, each beat has a unique name, too, plus of course, a number. The rows are again many different categories, but way more detailed, of course, compared to the high-level. Like on tab one, Table 11.2 shows groups and their categories.

Again, feel free to add or remove categories suitable for your game and team. I purposely kept it light so you could adjust them to your liking. If you want, you can showcase the pacing graph here as well.

The audio, animation, or other team fields are a way to tell the individual teams if you have any special requests or ideas here. Alternatively, they fill out the fields after a conversation with the level's core team.

#### *11.2.3.5 Tab Four: Detail/Low-Level*

This tab is optional and, in my experience, rarely used. Like I said previously, it is rare that a more detailed sketch of a beat is required. However, the level designer has the space if they need it, for example, for a complex puzzle or tricky script/action setup.

### 11.2.4 Documentation for Open World Missions

#### *11.2.4.1 Introduction*

For open-world missions, I decided to show how to use PowerPoint for level design documentation. Such missions often don't require as detailed planning as linear missions due to their typically looser structure. However, if your open-world essentially just leads to a strict linear mission, then, of course, stick to a more precise document type. Still, of course, PowerPoint is way more suitable to present

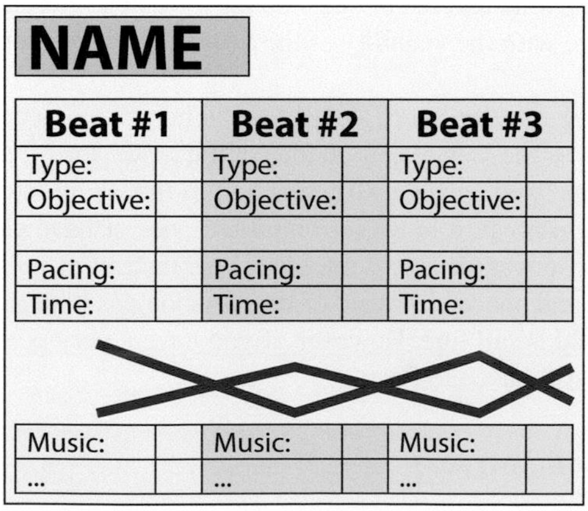

**FIGURE 11.3** Linear mid-level documentation mockup (not to scale).

and pitch your level than an Excel sheet, catering toward one of the primary functions of level design documentation.

Comparable to the Excel sheet, the documentation is split over multiple pages, following a similar order, structure, and thinking, however, of course, without the interactive aspects of Excel. Ideally you have a supporting document that shows how all the open-world missions are connected together.

### 11.2.4.2 Intro Page: High-Level

The first page is the introduction to the mission, giving every reader a brief understanding. It typically has the following ingredients.

- Mission Description: A brief overview of the mission explaining what is happening. I recommend writing it from the player's perspective. Additionally, it should include the narrative context so the reader can locate the mission within the game's narrative structure.
- Outcome: Why is the player doing this mission? What is their reward? How will it impact future narrative? I like to list this information here because it allows you to better understand the mission within the bigger picture, especially in less-linear narrative structures of open-world games.
- Concept Art/Reference Picture: Simply, one good, big picture that gives the best artistic impression of the mission. You do not have much space on one page so make it count.

Feel free to add anything else you see fit for your game, but I recommend keeping the first page rather light. You can do a lot using the mission description and highlighting keywords, like essential gameplay ingredients or focuses. PowerPoint is a visual medium, and huge walls of text or tables are typically off-puttingly.

### 11.2.4.3 World Map

The reader needs to understand where to locate and place the mission within the bigger picture of an open world. It is about contextualizing it. Therefore, the next page should show where to locate the mission on your world map. If you have multiple locations, then show them all and how they are connected. I recommend using a light version of the mission blocks here already, foreshadowing them for the next page. It is also a good page to show more reference pictures or concept art pointing at various locations on the map.

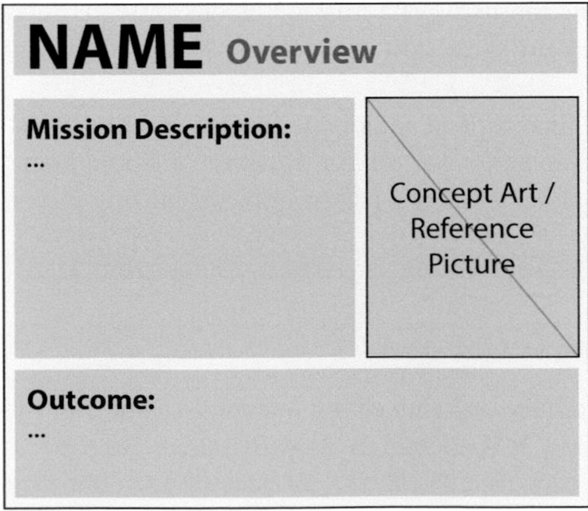


**FIGURE 11.4** Open-world high-level documentation mockup (not to scale).

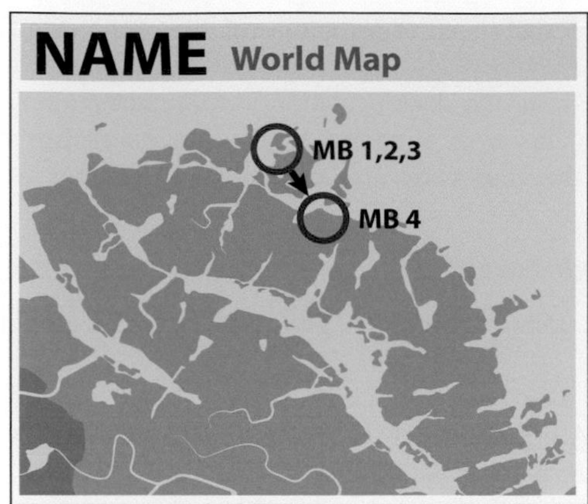


FIGURE 11.5 Open-world map mockup (not to scale).

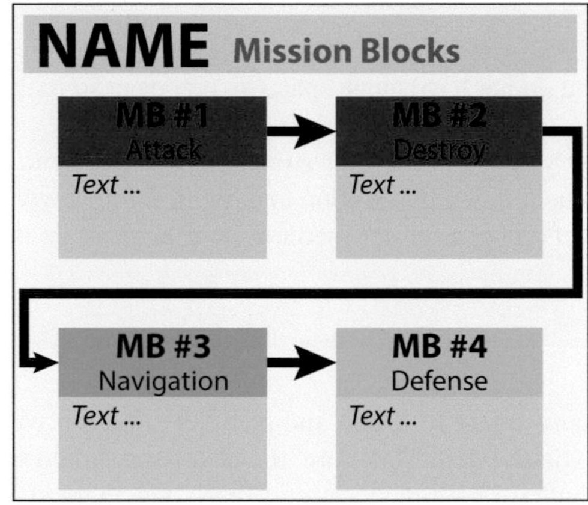


FIGURE 11.6 Open-world mission block flow mockup (not to scale).

#### 11.2.4.4 Mission Blocks: Mid-Level

For open-world missions, which are typically less orchestrated like linear missions, I recommend not going into the details of beats but using just mission blocks instead. Secondly, I would not use a table but connected text boxes here to show how the mission blocks are connected, especially if you have branching.

Under the mission blocks, you can add additional information like quick descriptions, time estimates, locations, gameplay focuses, or gameplay pillars. However, I would keep it light again, and if you can work with icons or other graphical elements (shape of boxes, different types of connecting arrows, etc.), then even better.

#### 11.2.4.5 Detailed Location: Low-Level

Like every level, you need to have a sketch of the intended layout. For the sketch, the same rules from the linear level document apply. It is enough to show that there are a few trees instead of arguing about the exact trunk placement of each tree. However, just because I say not to go into great detail, you cannot ignore one aspect: scale. You cannot just suddenly make an open-world location twice the size because you underestimate the size of your buildings. There are many technical reasons but also world-building

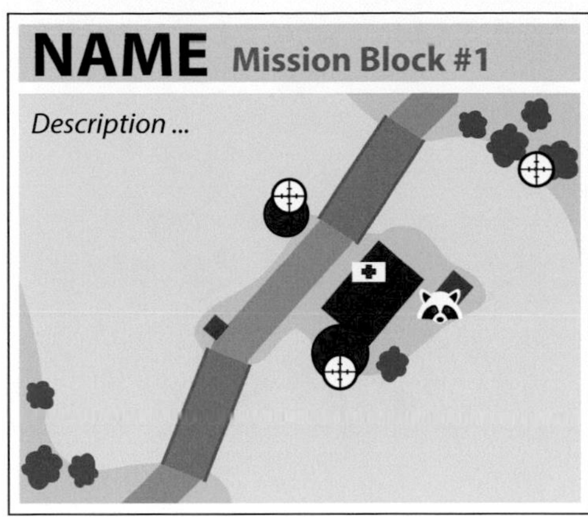


**FIGURE 11.7** Open-world location sketch mockup (not to scale).

restrictions. Open-world locations are often very restricted in how big they can be, and their maximum space is often fixed.

With gameplay ingredients, you can be a bit looser. It is typically enough if you indicate on the towers are snipers, in the building is a health-box, and at that corner are some mean attack raccoons. There is no need to detail out every single patrol path or cover. Once you build the levels, you have to figure out those details, but your intentions have to be clear and make sense in the sketch. However, what intentions are crucial depends on your game and can quickly vary from my examples here.

The low-level page should indicate which mission block they cover. If you have multiple locations or your location goes through multiple stages, then simply add more pages. Large missions might require a low-level pager per mission block.

#### *11.2.4.6 Supporting Pages*

Additional pages are typically for supporting teams, additional detail information, or more reference pictures/art collections.

Commonly there is a page for animation, audio, or assets where the level's core team writes what they would like to request from the other teams. Alternatively, of course, the supporting teams fill them out after a chat with the level's team. Those pages heavily depend on your team composition and how you work together. Therefore adjust them to your needs.

Additionally, you could add more lore or other details in an appendix.

### 11.2.5 Documentation for Multiplayer Maps

My recommendation for multiplayer maps is one massive one-pager, like one by one meter large, using Illustrator or InDesign, setting all its compartments together. A big sketch shows the entire map in its center, following the same sketch guidelines from linear levels or open-world missions. However, especially for smaller maps, it does not hurt to go into a bit more detail indicating visually where you, for example, plan to use less cover, big cover, high density of cover, doorways, windows, or ladders. For multiplayer maps, such details are crucial to show your intentions and thinking behind the map. However, the centimeter/inch precise placement of your crate is not.

Surrounding the sketch, I would add a huge amount of reference pictures pointing at various points in the map, so any viewer very quickly gets a clear artistic understanding. If needed, add some text under some references.

Feel free to add your high-level lane sketch or other relevant sketches in a corner to show where you originally came from. It will help a lot to get your original base concept across. Further on, add

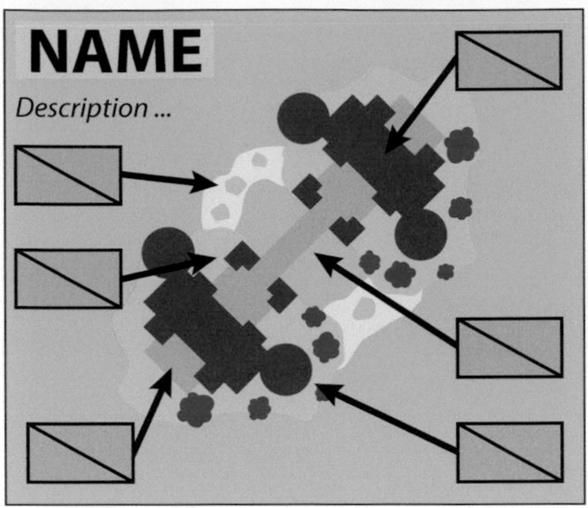


**FIGURE 11.8** Multiplayer map sketch mockup (not to scale).

information like the map's name, file name, descriptions, underlying narrative, locations, time of day, weather, lighting, unique selling points, special events, mood, or other misc comments.

I have a certain penchant for massive big one-pagers, and I believe it fits very well for multiplayer maps. Still, you might need additional supporting documentation or multiple versions of the large maps for external team requests and alike.

### 11.2.6 Time Estimates

It has nothing strictly to do with documentation, but managers often ask for time estimates of how long it would take to create the level when you work on level design documentation. This production estimate is crucial to, for example, eventually cut parts of the level—and that can be understandably scary. However, the more precise you make the initial estimates the less painful cuts happen later on during production.

First of all, giving time estimates is not optional; you have to give them, no argument. Saying that you do not know it is not an option. It is better to give some than none. Even senior developers keep trying to avoid them, but in truth, it does not help anyone, and it is not professional. Managers are not your enemy, and in the end, it will hurt you, the team, and your level if they cannot plan the project.

However, if you do not know or feel not very confident, speak to some more experienced developers about what they would estimate. In the end, with all the advice, follow your gut or experience, make an estimate and add some buffer of at least 25% to 33% because things will go wrong, you might want to have a vacation, or you might get sick. However, check with the manager if they add a buffer anyhow. There is no benefit for both of you to add 25%.

Further on, it always helps to break down the different stages of a level's production cycle. How long will it take to create the skeleton version, first intention pass, and so on? If you break down the level's production into smaller goals, you can extrapolate the following ones after you finish the first two to three stages. It is the absolute perfect method either because each stage has different conditions, but it is a start and might show trends.

Most importantly, straight from the beginning in your mind, what sections or parts of your map could be cut and build the level accordingly. Always have not just one but multiple backup plans ready if things go wrong. No time estimate will be perfect. Therefore resilient planning is the key. It will give you, and especially your manager, some peace.

### 11.2.7 Closing Words

All three main document types I listed here are essentially just basic archetypes. They are primarily inspirations for you, and you should adjust them to your needs, projects, and liking. I only slotted them for the different types as examples. For example, there is a realistic chance that you prefer to use the PowerPoint approach for linear or certain multiplayer maps. Alternatively, you could craft parts of the linear level Excel sheet for your open-world mission or use the one-pager approach for your linear levels. Sandbox-style levels might take a combination, as well. Mix, match, and modify however you feel fit.

Level design documentation changes for every project, game, studio, and of course, within time itself. It is a never-ending evolution. Even sequels of a game often had completely different approaches to documentation. Level documentation should not be an annoying chore but instead a quick and easy thing that enables everyone involved to do their best and to get started. Keep documentation as light as possible yet as detailed as needed.

## 11.3 Approaching Location Ideas

### 11.3.1 Introduction

Being tasked to come up with a new location can be daunting, even for senior designers. Level designers have some exciting layout and gameplay ideas, narrative wants to include some exciting story ideas or crazy NPCs, and artists want to make it look stunning. Then on top of it all, you hear something like from your director/lead: "The new location must be totally unique, exotic, stunning, and play awesome." I have been in such a situation way too many times, and typically two mistakes happen: First, the location is way too generic due to a lack of imagination or too many compromises. Secondly, the location gets so complex and convoluted that none of the visions or layers are clearly visible, and it just feels like a confusing mix. This chapter will cover both cases and then some basic ideas on how to hopefully find the right location concept.

### 11.3.2 The Generic Location

A generic location is any location that is not unique to a certain region. Essentially a location you can find in many parts of the world, such as gas stations, warehouses, churches, or farms. However, it can also be generic in the context of your game or setting. For example, a supply depot, forward operating base, or road checkpoint is generic in any military context. Alternatively, trailer parks, shooting ranges, or meth labs are generic in some wacky version of an American backcountry. It is all a matter of perspective and ultimately subjective.

The reasons for generic locations are plentiful. I already mentioned a lack of imagination or too many compromises. However, other reasons could be world-building limitations or considering it a challenge to make a generic location exciting. Sure, any believable world has to have generic locations in order to be believable. For example, any world with cars but without gas stations just feels wrong. Therefore they have, of course, a reason for existence, especially in open-world games. However, it does not mean you have to make them all to your primary mission locations.

If you end up with a generic location and you cannot do much about it, then, first of all, do not fall into the trap about making it overly complex. Secondly, go back to the roots. What is the essence of this location, and then how far can you extend it without going too messy? For example, churches are well known for a few things: a massive big room, tall towers, and catacombs. Therefore, you could put effort into its verticality and move the action under ground and under the roof. You could also play with a creepy network of tunnels, crypts, hidden doors, and underground connections to multiple other buildings in the neighborhood. None of the ideas means that you had to turn the church into another rave club, hidden dolphin foster home, and zeppelin station owned by three diabolic, narcissistic twin sisters with a disturbing presence on OnlyFans.

As a level designer, if you focus on the location's core aspect, then both narrative and art should also find ways to shine; ideally, they overlap, of course. Still, sometimes a very solid location executed well is still better than burying it under tons of glitter born out of insecurity.

### 11.3.3 The Overly Complex Location

There is often this urge to make every location, especially the generic ones, somehow extra memorable and unique by adding many narrative or artistic layers. For example, you worked on so many farms in your open-world game, so you decided that the next one would be special. So your next farm shows the injustice between rich and poor, the previous Russian occupation, a rising movement of graffiti spraying cultists, and environmental pollution from a local chemical plant. Not to mention the owner is howling on the roof to pray to some obscure moon-gods of his dead ex-wife. It might sound like a crazy example, but I walked into a similar trap myself and so many of my colleagues.

If you make a location incredibly complex by adding too many additional layers, it will not set you up for success because, first of all, you cannot show them all correctly. The layer ideas individually might sound fine, but you likely do not have the space and time to give them all enough exposition. It is the "jack of all trades, master of none" problem, just applied to a location. Secondly, likely it will all turn all into an indistinguishable, convoluted, and confusing "brown sauce," like when you mix all watercolors together. None of the layers will show; now, all of them together is making it way worse. Let us not forget that many players are not the exploring type, catching all the subtle clues you, the environment artists, and narrative designers have placed. Instead, most players will run through your space with inhuman speed and understand nothing.

Therefore, focus on one or two layers, maximum. Make those two layers unique, bold, and then you have a realistic chance that even the fastest players catch it. For example, if toxic green foam, dead cows, sticky slime, and a layer of greenish fog cover half the farm, then you made it quite clear that there is an environmental pollution problem. Sure, you might not have to go that extreme, but by no means be too subtle. If you think it is enough, then keep adding more till you think it just starts to get too much. In my experience, you have to be a bit more on the nose than what you as developers believe is necessary. When we thought we overdid it, then we got good scores back from the playtests that players understood what was going on.

### 11.3.4 The Right Location

I hope I will not disappoint too many, but there is no magical formula to find the right, non-generic location. However, some ways hopefully help you. The first, often underestimated step is defining what you consider generic within the game's context. After all, even a gas station might be quite unique in a game located in the 24th or 1st century. Obviously, avoid any of those generic locations if you want to go more unique or memorable, but keep them at hand for world-building.

Secondly, do your research—Go deep into the rabbit hole, read about the past, future plans, the obscure, the wired, the surprising, or simply odd. For example, in Berlin, you have a complete underground tunnel network from the cold war mixed with world war two, an eerie abandoned amusement park, a deserted NSA listening station, a strange tree-like building in German brutalism architecture style, a futuristic-looking saltwater spa with techno music, and of course a David Hasselhof museum. However, that list about Berlin is still tame and far from complete. You can easily go down a way more obscure, exciting yet often dark path. Many locations in this world have a past, the current people prefer to forget, but they are still often listed somewhere. That is why in-depth research is so essential to unravel the obscure and unique.

Alternatively, many level designers I know have their own "cool" locations list in their heads. I can only recommend never to stop researching and start growing your list of locations you would love to take as level inspirations. You never know when you need it, even if it is just for interviews.

## 11.4 World Building: Translating

### 11.4.1 Introduction

It is common practice to get inspired by reference when designing a location. Sometimes closer, sometimes a bit looser. However, for many reasons, we cannot just copy a location one-to-one. Ignoring legal reasons, the primary ones are technical limitations, space restrictions, production costs, and layout requirements or needs.

Therefore, we translate a location from reference into our game without losing its essence, yet adjusting it to all our needs. In this chapter, I cover a method to do exactly that, going over four simple steps. Lastly, I will cover the case when no reference exists because we also often have to create completely fictional places.

### 11.4.2 The Four Steps

#### *11.4.2.1 Step 1: Reference*

The first step is, of course, to find a reference. However, the critical factor here is to find a reference which you understand. It does not help if you look at a castle map and then do not know what is in each building or tower or why the castle's builders arranged the walls in a certain way. Once again, this is why it is so essential to becoming an expert in your subject matter. Once you know, for example, the types and purpose of farm buildings, you can just look at one and make some solid guesses.

The example above is from a farm I happen to know well enough. It is a cow milk farm that maintains a few fields to grow crops to feed their cows. Building #1 is the main living house. The large building #2 is the barn where they keep the cows and the milk tanks with the pumping machines are in the southwest extension. Their tractor garage is building #3, while #4 is the food silo for the silage (food fermentation for winter). Building #5 is just an open roof with multiple smaller machinery and generic storage under it, next to the back courtyard #6 at the back surrounded by various materials, bags, small huts, or construction materials. Close to the front courtyard entrance is a small vegetable and flower garden #7 for private use.

The living building is about 17.5 by 11 meters, the main barn is 22.5 by 17,5 meters, the garage 7.5 by 9 meters, and the open roof is 27 by 6 meters. The red square is 50 by 50 meters. Noting the scale of the main structures is very important to keep everything in balance later on.

The information above is enough to cover the main parts. You could go into more detail when going into the interiors of the barn and the farmhouse. The cow waste process is especially essential for such a farm operation because it acts as a fertilizer. However, they store the waste in underground tanks connected to the back courtyard.

#### *11.4.2.2 Step 2: Note Coherences*

After you have studied your reference, the following crucial step is to note down all major coherences, connections, workflows, and the relationships between the main parts. You have to understand the

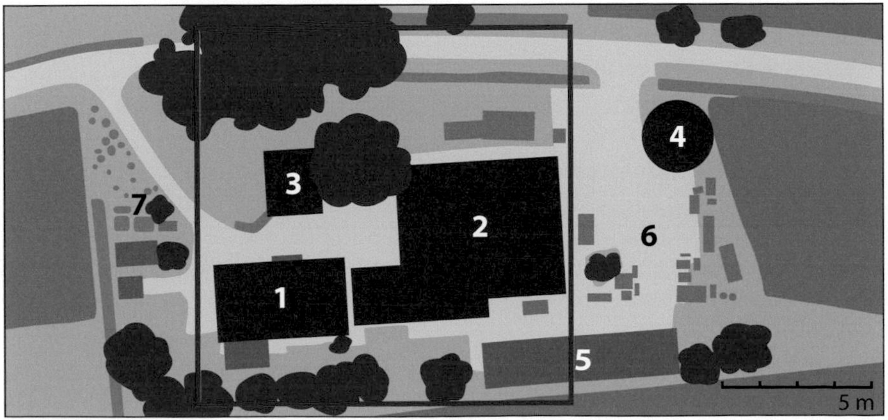


**FIGURE 11.9** Original location map.

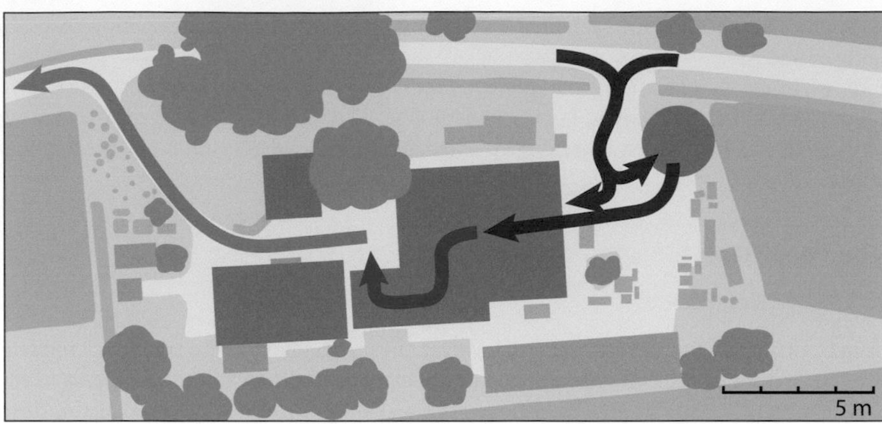


**FIGURE 11.10** Original location map with economy flow.

essential parts of the location and why they are where they are. Essentially you have to understand the world logic and effective flow of the place.

A good start is to ask essential questions like: Where do people sleep, eat, work, hang out or go to the bathroom? Where do goods arrive, where are they stored, how and where they are processed, and finally, how and where do they leave? What connection is between the local people and the goods? Why are certain parts further away from each other, why are some closer, and when is a specific order essential and when not? Also, size comparisons are crucial. For example, the building for the cows is way bigger than the living house.

In our example, let us start with the main workflow of this milk farm. The vegetables, mainly mangelwurzel, arrive from the fields, coming over the main northern road into the back courtyard. The leaves of the mangelwurzel and other suitable vegetables come into the silo for silage (red arrow) to have food for the cows during winter (blue arrow). The food cows can eat right away goes in the barn upon arrival (the other red arrow, pointing west). In the barn, the cows produce milk pumped to storage tanks toward the southwest building extension (green arrow). There the milk stays till a tank truck arrives to transport it away (orange arrow).

Then let us note down a few more coherences:

- The silo is the furthest away from the farmhouse because it smells worse than the cows.
- The vegetable and flower garden is close to the main farmhouse because walking a long distance to your garden is inconvenient, and it looks nice at the front of the property.
- The back courtyard is full of garbage and construction materials because nobody really sees it in the back.
- The barn is in the center because everything rotates around the cows.
- The hedges block the view toward the road and most visited sides because a village is in the west.
- The open roof is the main storage space for other machines because the tractor garage is not huge.
- The tractor garage position is not ideal because most of the tractor use happens in the back courtyard. However, that might have had historical reasons for how the farm was built and grew over time. It gives the farm some personal touch. However, don't excuse your world logic mistakes for a similar reason.
- They load the cows' waste on distribution trailers in the back courtyard.

As you see, we now have an excellent understanding of the coherences, and if we had to translate it into our game, we could keep the main parts believable.

#### 11.4.2.3 Step 3: Delete, Adjust, or Close

During step number three, you have to think about what parts can be cut, changed in size, or what locations remain inaccessible by the player. The reason for cutting or changing anything is typical because of limited available space, performance concerns, or simply not enough production resources available.

However, if anything changes, it should not affect the location's believed functionality in players' eyes. The problem is that at that stage, we have to make assumptions because we have to assume what "most players" will not miss or notice if it changes. That assumption about the knowledge of "most players" can be seen as demeaning. Secondly, it might be tricky for you because you know so much about the space that you might consider every aspect critical.

By default, I would look to cut less iconic steps in the center of a workflow. We shipped a few games where we cut officially essential steps of processing resources, but they were, for example, in a boring-looking gray building which we hoped most players would not know much about. However, be prepared that there will always be a few players who are even bigger experts than you and that's fine.

When you look into changing the size of a location's parts, you have to keep the direct comparisons intact. For example, a smaller building cannot suddenly be the biggest one. However, a bit of adjustment is always possible, especially when it is about seemingly less relevant or even optional structures.

When we look at our farm example, we could consider the following changes:

- The barn and especially the milk pump building can be smaller, as long as it clearly stays the biggest building.
- You can make the open roof significantly smaller because it is just storage.
- You can completely cut the vegetable or flower garden because it is unnecessary for the primary workflow, yet it has some charm.
- You can completely cut the silo because the assumption is that many players might not know silage as winter food. However, it is a great sniper spot and adds verticality, so it should stay, in my opinion.
- The farmhouse is not huge. Therefore, I would recommend closing it off. The only way to make a very cramped interior work well would be to make the building a lot bigger, which might be the opposite of what we are looking for.
- The barn should have an accessible interior because it is spacious and sells the location's purpose and workflows.
- The back courtyard could become smaller, but the rubble and garbage is great for cover.
- You can cut the cow waste pipes and tank because it is barely visible and noticeable. However, it might also be cheap to keep and used for some narrative reference.

It does not mean we have to do all the steps, but being aware of what is possible is crucial in conjunction with step #2 when translating it to our game world.

#### 11.4.2.4 Step 4: Translate

We are finally at the last stage where we translate our space into your game world. Commonly the scale has to be adjusted but often also the context or even the setting changes. For example, the nearby roads, buildings, or vegetation could be very different, affecting the location's logic. Similarly, a castle from the middle ages needs adjustments to become now a tourist attraction. Another crucial reason for the translation is gameplay. Most real-world locations do not have the most exciting layout or flow. For example, it is not uncommon to close off or add a path. However, you can only do this safely if you do not ruin the location's believability.

I recommend starting with the most central part of your location, which gives it purpose and meaning. Then look at the start and end parts of your workflow and logically arrange them. It is okay if a few paths are now shorter, longer, or more crooked as long as the order is correct. The same applies if the original

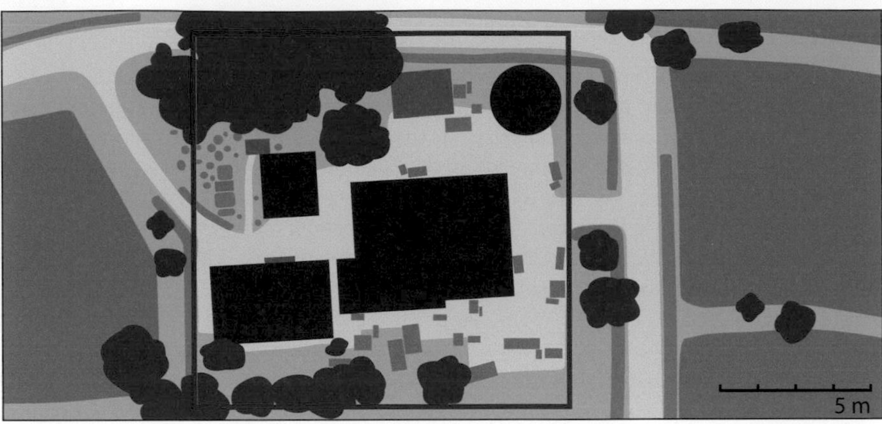


**FIGURE 11.11** Previous location now translated in a 50-by-50-meter space.

positions had to move around, or their scale had to be adjusted as long as they kept their relative proportions compared to other location parts.

Remember the reasons and coherences from step #2 when rearranging the location and if you have space issues, go through your list from step #3. Never cut or remove anything iconic or what most players would associate with the location's core identity. For example, a gas refinery needs some chimneys with fire flares above to be recognized by most people because it is iconic. However, it gets tricky if the reality is less ionic than what you assume people would consider iconic. For example, many people might imagine snow, mountains, and maple syrup when thinking about Canada. However, when you visit Canada's biggest city Toronto you likely experience a brutally warm and humid summer, very flat land all around, and way too often just corn syrup with your pancakes.

After going through those steps, the translation will allow you to create locations that keep the original spirit and believability yet in a much smaller space or after required gameplay, resource, or performance adjustments.

In our example, I had to squeeze our farm into a 50-by-50 meter space (the red square) for streaming reasons. Outside of the square, I can only use terrain and vegetation. Additionally, the northern road is now making a bend instead of staying straight. Luckily the required transformation is not too drastic, but it should still highlight the translation. Below is a list of my changes.

- The farmhouse and the barn got a bit smaller, but the barn remained the largest, central, dominating building. Especially the number of milk tanks and the size of the pumping machines shrank.
- The northern road had to move further north to give the farm more space.
- The silo had to move in the northeast corner within the red square.
- The silo's move also meant to adjust the courtyard further north, now going all around the barn.
- Since the courtyard got overall a lot smaller on the east side, I had to drastically cut down the size of the open roof and move it from the south to the north side.
- It is now possible to drive around the barn with the tractor, which is convenient and more logical compared to the previous layout.
- Much rubble and hedge adjustments to accommodate the new roads and courtyard layout and some early cover considerations.
- The flower and vegetable garden moved west of the garage and changed entirely in layout and size. Its original garden shed is now only one and at the back of the garage.

Overall, all the fundamental aspects and workflows of the original layout remained intact. For example, the silo is far away from the farmhouse, the back part remains the dirty one, while the front retains its charm. The food arrival, storage, then feeding, and milking process may be more curvy and dense now, but the order stayed intact. The hedges kept doing what they meant to do, we took the liberty and extended the amount of rubble for cover reasons, and I bet nobody would seriously notice that the open roof storage is now too small for such a farm. I could have squeezed out even more space, but if you move too many structures too close to the edges of such a square, it loses its natural look and feel.

### 11.4.3 Fictional Locations

#### *11.4.3.1 Introduction*

The steps I described above are for the case you work with a reference. However, often you will not have this luxury if you work with fictional locations. In such a case, you have to start with the previous step #2 and define all the workflows, coherences, and interconnections yourself. The important aspect is that you stay as logical as possible. Even if you work with obscure sci-fi or fantasy processes or locations, try to keep some logical order. It will give your location structure and purpose, which otherwise might feel like a complete random mess.

#### *11.4.3.2 How to Create Fictional Coherences*

Below is a list of questions that should help you create the world logic of your fictional locations and smaller regions.

- What is the purpose of the location? What is the primary (unique/iconic) aspect(s) that sells the location's purpose to players?
- What are the entrances and exits of the location?
- What is the service/production order of the location's workflow? What are the priorities of the service/production workflow?
- If you have multiple services/production workflows in one location or region, how do they interconnect or rely on each other? What are the dependencies, and how are they typically resolved? Are there any mid-production storage facilities or waiting rooms?
- If goods/people arrive, where are they stored, wait or park their vehicles/animals? What happens with goods/people after finishing the process? Is the flow throughout the workflow convenient or convoluted?
- What are the outer, border, and inner security/advertisement/warnings of the location or region?
- How many resident factions exist in the location/region? Are they in conflict, partnership, coexistence, or not aware of each other? Where and how do they interact? How do they interact with the purpose(s) of the location/region?
- Where do the factions sleep, rest, hang out, recover, heal, eat, drink, party, pray, work, go to bathrooms, or do other relevant activities?
- What are rewards, propaganda, or punishments for the factions, and how do they express it within the location?
- Is the life/work cycle of the factions convenient, logical, or convoluted?

The above basic set of questions should give you a solid foundation for most locations or regions. However, I highly recommend modifying and extending them according to your setting or game's context. For example, high reproductive raccoon mutants in a high-magic fantasy setting or sci-fi necromancers from Uranus will likely have to answer different questions for their locations' world logic. The critical point is that you do ask such questions. You need to establish some order, structure, and priorities. Write them down; make them part of your documentation and consistent team standard.

If you do not create a coherent world, logic players will notice it. They will arrive at a place, and even if they do not understand what exactly each machine is doing, they likely sense that some logic was behind its order. There is always some logic behind the chaos, even if a very messy, illogical, lunatic, drugged madman created the location.

## 11.5 World Building: Working in Layers

### 11.5.1 Introduction

This world-building methodology is a distilled, quick, and light version for especially video game locations. However, with some extensions, you can apply it for larger worlds, for example, for books and tabletop roleplaying games.

It is a hard world-building tool to create coherent environments to avoid significant loopholes while allowing players to emerge fully. When we create locations for games, speed is of the essence, but at the same time allows collaborative world-building in a larger team. This methodology's goal is to achieve precisely that. It is not an in-depth world-building structure or necessarily meant for soft-world building.

### 11.5.2 Start with Vision

Any world-building starts with a vision, an original idea. Please refer to previous chapters about vision creation. The vision is layer zero. Each time we add another layer to your world during its creation, you must check it against the vision. Is the new layer in line with the vision? If so, proceed, otherwise either revisit the layer or vision. If the vision has to change, you have to check all previous layers if they are still in line with the new vision and modify them if necessary. This process continues till you align all layers and the vision.

The vision is the one core aspect that unites all layers. It is not the foundation; it is more; it is the glue that holds them all together collectively. For example, the vision for your location is to showcase the brutality of gladiator fights, then turning most of it into a spa is in contradiction. However, if it is less a spa for relaxation but more a hospital to treat savage gladiator wounds, then it fits the vision.

However, not all layers have to be deeply affected by the vision directly. For example, if your location's vision is about an orc-invested vegetable farm, then the farm's produce might only be loosely connected to this vision. Of course, only if the orcs did not attack the farm because of the vegetables but let us remain in our classic fantasy tropes.

### 11.5.3 The Layers

#### *11.5.3.1 Introduction*

Each layer is a working step within this world-building process. It is part of a workflow that enables you to keep coherence and keep various aspects of your locations logically connected. Adding a new layer means going through a specific process to keep the world logic intact.

The first two layers in my model are more workflow than world-building oriented, but it does not change the process, and I hope it all makes sense if it all comes together.

#### *11.5.3.2 Basic Layer Use*

Every time you add a new layer, you must first check it against layer zero, the vision. Then check how it could affect the next layers, continuing with layers one, two, three, and counting up. If no layer had to change, it is all good. However, if a layer had to change, check how this change affects all layers again. Every new layer is below the previous one.

The principle idea is that upper layers are the base for the lower ones hanging on, and hopefully if you picked the proper order, the number of changes for higher ones stays limited. For example, a higher layer is about natural resources that attract certain factions. However, the factions do not affect the natural resources. Therefore, factions should be a layer below.

Ultimately you check any layer changes or new layers against all other layers, and adjust them if necessary till they are all aligned and coherent. When you check layers against each other, you analyze if the new one impacts the established ones. For example, you add a new layer because you defined the natural resources of a region. If you check it against the timetable (layer #1), there is typically no need to set the date when the natural resources appeared. However, comparing it against the map as the next layer certainly impacts it because the natural resource location should have a presence on the map (layer #2).

Of course, lower hanging layers can impact the higher ones. World-building can very quickly get incredibly complex because so many aspects are interconnected. However, by keeping a strict order and the resulting simplification reduces this complexity. The goal is to stay as fast and light as possible.

Not every new layer is necessarily directly based on the higher ones, and that is fine. However, when you think about the order of layers, it helps to think about what was first? What layers drive another? For example, take the sectors of the economy. The primary tier is raw material, which is the foundation for the secondary manufacturing tier. Once that is established, the tertiary tier is the service industry, including selling the manufactured goods. There is a clear order of how the first sectors affect the second and third sectors more than the way around.

This simplification and forced order are vital to keeping this methodology clean, fast, and easy to use in practice. You still have to come up with most of the layers yourself, but the process itself always forces you to think with connectivity and world logic and the overall world's connected economy without losing sight of your vision. It is a reassuring process that should prevent a vast majority of flawed world logic holes. You can make this process as complicated and intense as you like, but most game environments do not need a huge amount of layers. With time you develop your rhythm and workflow, making this process even faster.

Additionally, this methodology is especially suitable for working in a team. As a group, you agree on the next layer, check it against the vision, and hopefully, the hive-mind will catch any interference with the other layers.

#### *11.5.3.3 Always Start with the Timetable*

The primary first layer, after the vision, which is the foundation for everything below, is always the timetable. Everything is rooted here, and every significant impact or event has a place in time. Keeping track of events and their time between is a major factor for all hard world-building endeavors. For example, it makes a huge difference for environment artists and level designers if the orcs attacked the farm one

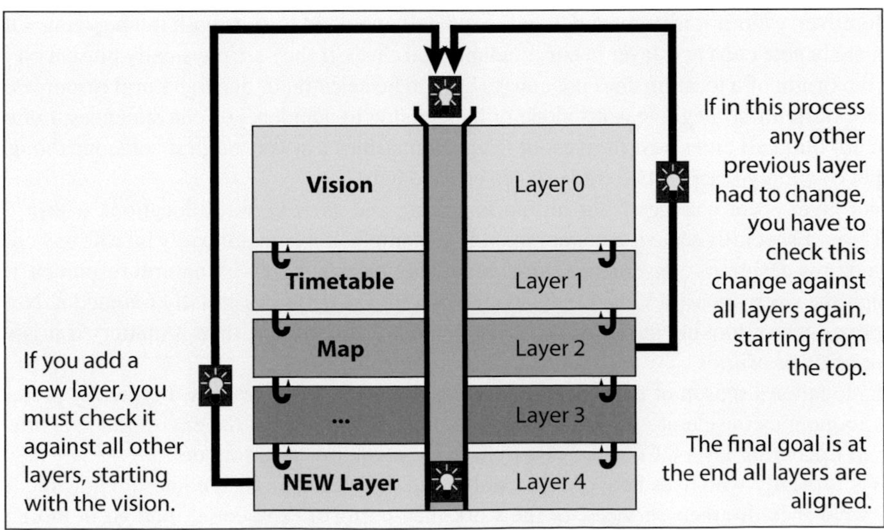


**FIGURE 11.12** Diagram showing the flow of new ideas or changes pass through the different layers.

minute, one hour, one day, one week, or one month ago. If different people have different ideas of how the events unfold, then an incoherent mess is preprogrammed.

Additionally, every major event of the upper layers should have a place in the timetable, which means, by default, you have to check their impact on all higher hanging layers again. For example, if the orcs attacked the farm four months ago, and consequently, once you re-check the natural resource layer, you will likely notice that nobody maintained the fields for months, compared to a very recent attack.

As a first step, I would note down all events in the timetable, which you can already distill out of your vision. Just note them all down how you see fit, and do not worry too much about accuracy at that stage. Once you work your way through lower layers, they might change, and that is fine. In the case of our previous example of the orcs attacking the farm, you might want to shift the time of attack around. For example, suppose you originally envisioned that the attack happened a long time ago, and the orcs are still there. In that case, this could mean that the closest protective/retaliating force is far away; however, once you draw the map you might feel that this remoteness does not fit. Therefore, you again change the timetable for a more recent attack.

### 11.5.3.4 The Second Layer Is a Map

When the first layer makes sure that everything has a place in time, the second layer has to be a map, so everything has a physical place. Sure, not every timetable entry or lower layer has a physical presence, but for level designers and environment artists, they are still critical, of course. Therefore, it is the second layer.

At that point, I had a few debates about why the map is not the first layer because, after all, we world builders love to start drawing a map early on. We also often believe that the world is the ultimate foundation for everything else. However, as long as we create vastly fictional game environments, the map reflects our needs. Remember, the higher layers drive the upper ones. For example, if one of your factions in the lower layers nuked a city, you should first note it in the timetable to know how present the destruction is still visible in your map. Vision beats time, and time beats space.

### 11.5.3.5 The Next Layers

All following layers are more what you would typically imagine being world-building-related and are arguably less administrative like a timetable or a map. I typically recommend starting with the origin of your world or being more precise about what is relevant for your world's creation. For example, if you have a grounded contemporary setting, your third layer does not have to be about gods or celestial beings. Moreover, even if it is grounded, there is typically no need to start with the big bang. Of course, we continuously note each new layer in our timetable and check if they are physically present on our map. However, the origin of a location does not always have to be celestial or due to natural resources. Certain locations are built for strategic reasons alone or happen due to accidents or conveniences. For example, people did not build all cities next to rivers or lakes. Sometimes it was enough if someone thought it was a pretty spot or simply because two trade routes crossed here.

The exact layer order changes from setting to setting and even between locations within the same game or region. Especially scale is a major factor. For example, if a tsunami badly hit a sleepy coastal village and you now design its convenience store, you do not have to start with natural resources. However, if you design the sleepy coastal village, you should look into why they originally founded it. Now, if you zoom out, even more, looking at the surrounding terrain of the village, then it matters if it is volcanic, tectonic, or of other origins.

After the location's reason of existence, natural resources, or other origins, I typically prefer to continue with economic considerations. The richness of other advantages of the environment is often a huge driver for all upcoming layers. Consider researching the economy sector model.

Next up is typically who lives here or who established the location. Then comes up how the local factions live, what they do, their services, or the work they perform. You could then go in more granular detail and detail out key NPCs, food, transportation, or other world-defining new layers. Major factions could split into more sub-groups, families, or splinter movements depending on your setting and need.

In reality, you do not need many layers for smaller locations, and you very quickly have your patterns, and then it all starts to click into place with some practice. For smaller locations like a singular property, I would recommend the following layers as building blocks:

0. Vision
1. Timetable
2. Map
3. Reason of existence / Origin / Natural resources
4. Economy (primary, secondary, or tertiary sector)
5. Factions
6. Unique events

For bigger locations like a small village, industrial/business complex, or a simple, smaller region, you could go a bit more complex:

0. Vision
1. Timetable
2. Map
3. Natural resources
4. Primary economy sector
5. Secondary economy sector
6. Tertiary economy sector
7. Factions
8. Key NPCs
9. Unique events

I have yet to create two worlds using the same layers, even for the same scale. I keep having new ideas, and the vision is often a big driving factor for the layers. For example, I am a big fan of cooking and eating, so I often have a special food layer between the economy layers. Some people or settings are more about marketing, brands, electric grid, waste disposal, recycling, or occult research. Depending on the setting, I often split natural resources into inorganic resources like ores, stones, and plants, followed by animals. Now, animals can be once again briefly separated into herbivores, carnivores, and omnivores. The list goes on, but, again, in reality, in the day-to-day job of creating smaller environments for video games, we often do not need it so granularly. Still, I hope to paint you a good picture of both the possibilities and how much you really need.

#### *11.5.3.6 Multiple Layer Constructs*

We typically do not have to go very granular for each location because the groundwork already happened at a larger scale. For example, we established most major factions early on during the game's conception phase; the same counts for your animals, kingdoms, or terrain origin.

Depending on your game's scope, I recommend doing the process for your world, then regions, settlements, and smaller unique locations. Each of them is built and connected with the same layer concept. For example, if your world changes but you have already created a few cities, you must check if the change impacted the cities once again. However, a city rarely impacts the larger world to a large extend, excluding some more significant events, major world shaping constructions, and other exceptions, of course.

Yes, that means you have to track multiple timetables and maps for each location and scale. However, in my experience, this compartmentalization is more a blessing than a curse. First of all, you save time, because you can skip repeating yourself a lot. Secondly, it frees up your headspace when you can create something more isolated from the bigger picture. Constantly checking many layers within a whole world's context can be highly taxing and prone to mistakes. However, every time you start a new environment when scaling down, it is like a fresh chapter. The foundation comes, of course, from the previous scale, but mostly everything is separate, and the few connections you have or come up in the process are manageable.

### 11.5.4 Example Layer Workflow

#### *11.5.4.1 Step #1: Vision*

I have picked a simple example that should be close to the day-to-day reality of many level designers and environment artists: "During a zombie apocalypse, a struggling gas station in a rural forest in Oregon turned into a biker gang's headquarters."

It is a simple location with a few twists. All other aspects like the biker gang faction or the main events of the zombie apocalypse were already defined previously.

#### *11.5.4.2 Step #2: Layer 1—Timetable*

Based on the vision and previous declaration, we can already fill out parts of the timetable (Table 11.3). I need to set dates for the biker gangs and the zombies. I also know there is a gas station, so I should define when they built it.

I decided to give the gas station some longer past to later on have some room to give the space some depth and personal touches. The bikers showed up just two weeks after the zombies came by and they have been settling in for two months already.

There is no need for consistent use of time formatting. You can use whatever suits your purpose and change it when it is no longer convenient for the developing team.

#### *11.5.4.3 Step #3: Layer 2—Map*

I took a fairly standard and generic rural American gas station layout as a base. It has a main gas station building with a small shop, the pumps with a roof above, a big sign attracting travelers on the road, and a bigger parking lot.

#### *11.5.4.4 Step #4: Layer 3—Reason of Existence*

I'm adding some origin story to the location: Back in the 1960s, three long roads connected three small towns. The resulting t-junction was between the three towns, in the middle of a deep forest. As a result, Mr. Moore thought it made sense to build a gas station here, 40 miles away from the closest settlement. Due to the long distance to the nearest town, Mr. Moore thought it made sense to attach a garage to fix any cars that have trouble in the forest. Additionally, he bought a tow truck.

The addition of the garage and tow truck should be both added to the timetable and the map (Table 11.4).

**TABLE 11.3**

Initial Timetable Based on the Original Vision

| Date | Event |
|---|---|
| Now (30 January 2020) | |
| 2 months ago | Biker gang finished headquarter |
| 3 months ago | Biker gang started to take over gas station |
| 3.5 months ago | Zombies arrived and kill everyone here |
| 52 years ago (1968) | Gas station construction is finished |

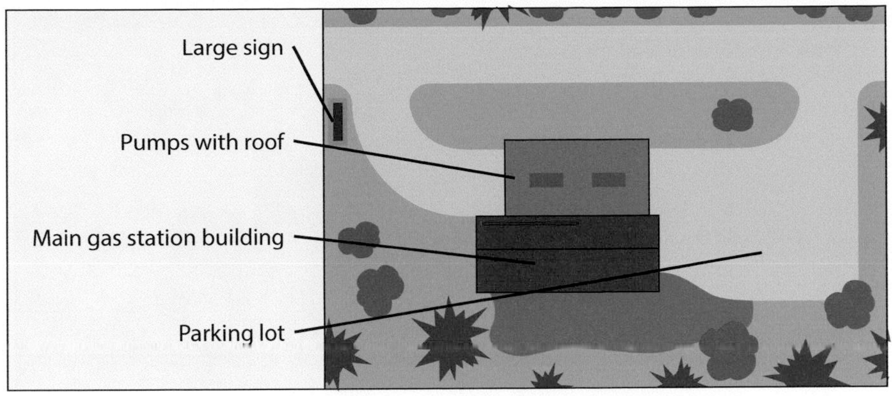


**FIGURE 11.13** The first original sketch of the gas station location based on the original vision.

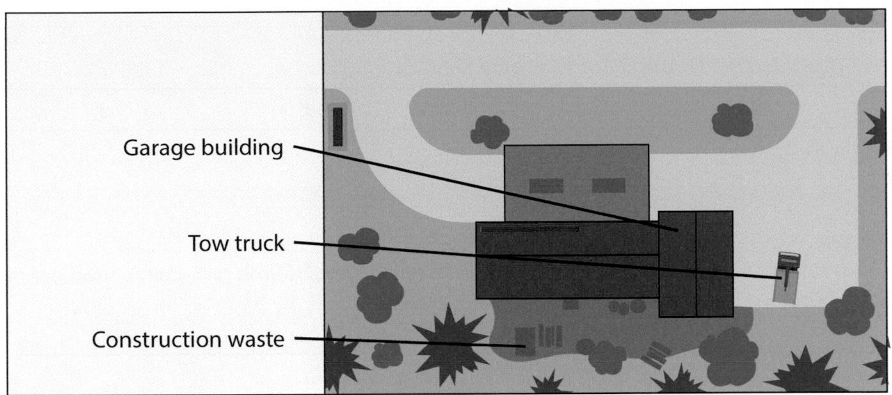


**FIGURE 11.14** Updated gas station sketch after detailing the "reason of existence."

**TABLE 11.4**
Updated Timetable after Detailing the "Reason of Existence" Step

| Date | Event |
|---|---|
| Now (30 January 2020) | |
| 2 months ago | Biker gang finished headquarter |
| 3 months ago | Biker gang started to take over gas station |
| 3.5 months ago | Zombies kill everyone here |
| 49 years ago (1971) | Small garage attachment finished, tow truck bought |
| 52 years ago (1968) | Gas station construction is finished |

### *11.5.4.5 Step #5: Layer 4—Economy (Tertiary Sector)*

I am adding some depth to the economy: The gas station is a service provider because it sells gas and offers construction. However, to make it a bit more interesting, Mr. Moore's son thought it made sense to turn the struggling garage into a small supermarket. After all, he heard that many gas stations nowadays make more money selling goods than selling gas alone. At the same time, he took a loan to modernize the already 26-year-old gas station.

The modernization and new supermarket should both be present on the timetable and the map (Table 11.5). Unused construction materials and old cars they failed to sell are covering the surrounding property.

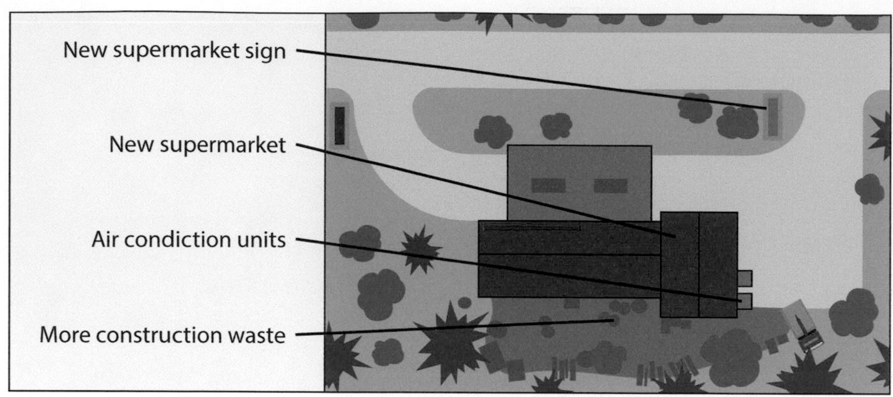


**FIGURE 11.15** Updated gas station sketch after detailing the economy steps.

**TABLE 11.5**

Updated Timetable after Detailing the Economy Step

| Date | Event |
|---|---|
| Now (30 January 2020) | |
| 2 months ago | Biker gang finished headquarter |
| 3 months ago | Biker gang started to take over gas station |
| 3.5 months ago | Zombies kill everyone here |
| 26 years ago (1994) | Gas station gets renovated/modernized, changed small garage into a small supermarket |
| 51 years ago (1969) | Small garage attachment is finished |
| 52 years ago (1968) | Gas station construction is finished |

#### *11.5.4.6 Step #6: Layer 5—Factions*

Two factions are essential when we look at the gas station: The family of Mr. Moore and the bikers. The zombies are a faction in the world, but they are more an event than a consistent faction that had a severe, permanent impact on the location.

The Moores did not live at the station but in one of the nearby towns. Mr. Moore built the gas station in 1968 when he was 34 years old. In 1994, his 26-year-old son built the supermarket attachment to take over the gas station eventually. They didn't have much money, so the father and son did most of the construction themselves. In the year 1994, Mr. Moore was already 60 years old. The son completely took over the gas station five years later, and the old Mr. Moore retired. When the zombies came in 2019, the son was 51 years old but did not die at the gas station. The zombies killed only three staff members at the station.

When the bikers arrived at the gas station, they liked it because the remoteness meant little to no zombies, plus the underground gas tanks were still almost full. The supermarket products were another big plus. However, they know the gas station is only a temporary solution because once the tanks are empty, the station loses its main attractiveness. Till then, their main fear was other marauding gangs, and they barricaded the gas station accordingly.

Most of the Moore family background is nice to have but not necessarily worth an entry in the timetable or the map. However, you must display the biker gang's barricades and other transformations on the map, of course. The other relevant dates of the bikers are already part of the timetable.

#### *11.5.4.7 Step #7: Layer 6—Unique Events*

The primary event which affected the locations was the zombies. However, it was just a small swift visit of a medium-sized group roaming the forests. Within the last months, barely any zombies are still around.

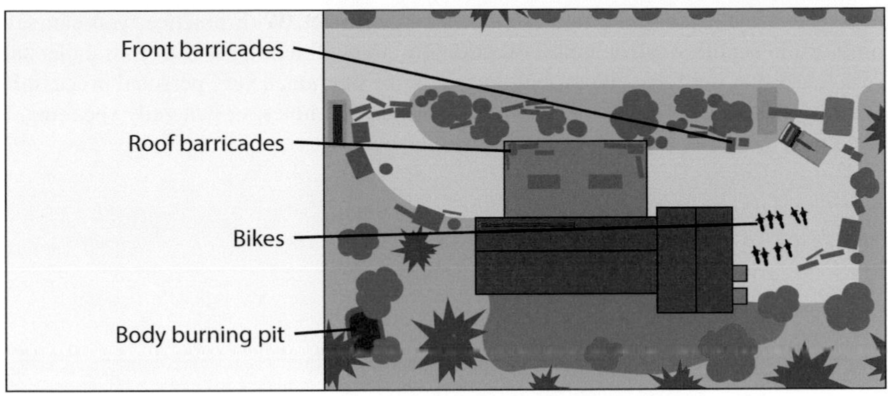


**FIGURE 11.16** Updated gas station sketch after detailing the impact of the present biker faction.

The zombie event is already on the timetable. The only addition on the map is a remote place where the bikers burn their bodies, but I have already added it to the previous map since it is only a tiny change.

#### *11.5.4.8 Final Observations*

Now, since we finished this process, let us look at the relevant information to build this gas station.

- Most of the gas station's look and architecture originates from the 1960s, while the renovations in the 90s were more of a patchwork. The tow truck is from the 1970s. For example, we should expect to see lots of paint chipping off, revealing older color pallets, lots of unused construction material or building waste still lying around, and a wild mix of old-school ice machines, freezers, and one modern monitor on the wall.
- You can still recognize the old garage architecture under the self-built facade of the supermarket.
- The gas station does not belong to a chain. Therefore, the Moors added a lot of personal touches to it, like their name on the sign, some family pictures in the back office, or generally a lot of personal trinkets. Of course, the bikers did not care much and threw out a lot, but it is still there for exploring players and excellent bits of environmental storytelling.
- The barricades are more toward the main road, geared to fight off enemies arriving on vehicles.
- The bikers took the fortifications and settlement seriously since it took one month to build.
- They started to feel quite homey and took even more effort to decorate it with personal touches because they had already been here for two months.

All in all, we now have a solid, consistent foundation that aligns level design, environment art, and narrative design. We have answers for most major questions, and we have a coherent location within the more extensive world logic/narrative. The gas station has enough charm and details for neat environmental storytelling to show some vital depth at such horrible times.

### 11.5.5 Final Worlds

In reality, I would not go through the steps like that for such a small location I have covered in the previous example. Instead, I would still start with the timetable, but right away go through the different steps: vision, origin, economy, factions, special, and note all their relevant dates and events. First, I would make one map reflecting all the entries. It is just a matter of scope and practice. However, if I create large fantasy worlds for tabletop games, I go through such steps slower and stricter due to the sheer complexity and size of the task ahead. If you do it for the first few times I still recommend you to do it step by step till you feel very comfortable with the process.

In the end, it is a methodology, a mindset, not a strict ruleset. With practice, you can safely skip steps for simpler and smaller environments. Additionally, you will modify it with your understanding of world-building, and that is all fine. World-building is, in my opinion, a very personal process. However, I prefer sticking to such processes not to lose track, oversee plot holes, or generally speaking, keep my worlds as coherent, plausible, and immersive as possible.

# 12

# *First Steps*

We spend a long time theorizing, planning, and documenting level design. Now it is time to get our feet wet, open your level editor, and start to work. However, the transition from documentation to practical reality is a very crucial one. Many things can go wrong during this time, which are costly to correct later on. Many aspects have to be considered, like scale, the impact of perspective, and how to plan resiliently. Therefore, I dedicate this chapter to this crucial phase.

## 12.1 From Plan to Reality

### 12.1.1 Introduction

Everyone can have fantastic ideas, and it is easy to get excited about a great idea. However, the actual skill of a talented developer is turning them into reality! The transition from theory to reality is exceptionally crucial for various reasons. First of all, it is the time to check if the idea is as great as imagined. Secondly, if the idea is feasible given existent production restraints, and thirdly does the idea fit within the larger context of the game's totality of the world. Therefore, this chapter covers the most critical first steps and best practices to reach the first intention phase.

### 12.1.2 Layers and Teamwork

Ideally, you set already unified crucial aspects like naming conventions, metrics, color codes, or folder structures before level designers get busy in the real levels. I primarily focus on layouts and scripts in this chapter, but a critical early step is setting up layers and having a unified standard across the teams. Most modern level editors allow more than one team member to work on a level by working in separate layers. However, layer misunderstandings and version control conflicts are some of the more common issues within a team working closely on a level. Therefore, agreeing on a layer structure and creating all relevant layers early on is crucial. It will not eliminate all issues but will greatly reduce them later on. Early clean setup also means other team members can faster join the level's production.

It is best practice to organize and unify naming conventions, metrics, color codes, or folder structures, not just layers, before the start of production. It is a realistic scenario that you end up switching to someone's level during a production cycle. For example, there is a serious bug, and you have to help out while the original designer is on vacation or sick. In such a case, the last thing you need is to learn the other designer's naming convention or dig through their confusing layer organization. However, the worst situation is when people don't have any organization and keep everything completely messy and random. Then debugging their levels and scripts can be a complete nightmare. Therefore, it is important to agree on a united standard to keep teamwork as frictionless as possible.

Even if you happen to be the only one working on a level alone, I highly recommend defining a clean naming convention, folder structure, and color codes. Working on your level will be dramatically cleaner, which you will especially appreciate when you debug a tricky issue. If it then does happen that someone else has to work on your level, for whatever reasons, it can be pretty embarrassing for you if they spend more time digging through your clutter than fixing an issue.

DOI: 10.1201/9781003275664-16

### 12.1.3 Layout Skeleton: First Scale Impressions

#### *12.1.3.1 Introduction*

A new level's number one aspect of getting right as early as possible is scale. Sure, some adjustments will always happen, but you have to get pretty close to the final size as early as possible because the more anyone works on the level, the more expensive are any later, larger changes.

Another important consideration is to evaluate if the designated space is too big or too small for all the gameplay and artist ideas. You could have a huge list of fantastic narrative ideas you want to bring across about this cursed mansion just to realize that you barely have the space to include the basics. You are sketching out in 3D the bare space for your industrial facility, just to realize that there is no way in hell that you can fill all those huge halls with varied, entertaining gameplay. It is perfectly acceptable for plans to go wrong once you translate them into 3D, but do the cuts or adjustments now; do not be timid at that stage.

Finally, production scope is the other crucial factor for evaluating the scale. For example, do you really have enough time and artists to work on the entire space? Were the previous asset call-outs accurate, or do you maybe need more or fewer assets? As the level designer, do you have the time to finish all the parts of the level to the expected quality?

#### *12.1.3.2 Open World: First Steps and Early Scaling Estimates*

First of all, most of the time, when you start sculpting terrain, it will be too big. It is just one of those "rules," which we all keep observing over the decades and happened to me several times, too. It gets better once you add many objects for size references, such as houses, cars, bridges, and trees. Just be careful with trees, vegetation or rocks because their scale is not always relatable, especially in a fantasy, sci-fi, or stylized setting. However, the final most important step is to place roads and drive or walk over your terrain. Only the combination of realistically scaled objects and traversing through the world is giving you the correct impression. Therefore, I would not wait till your terrain looks all nice, but instead, as soon as possible, place objects, roads and move around. Even if it happens on a perfectly flat map or very crude sketched-out mountains, just make sure that you can easily remove the objects you added for scale, for example, by putting them in a special layer.

Suppose the foundation of your mission or level is largely terrain that I recommend importing, projecting, or re-drawing your map drawings on the terrain, of course in scale. It quickly gives you an idea of the true size of your locations or mission space coverage. This step would be a must, especially if you designed your map sketch with realistic measurements in mind. For example, a typical commercial airfield runway is at least 2.4 kilometers long, but that is not easily feasible in many games.

Again, once you have the mission sketched on the terrain, add a few simple objects at the main locations. Those objects just act as 3D markers and do not have to resemble the mission's context. A massive exclamation mark is all you need, but if the object also helps to get a feel for scale, then even better. If your locations are bigger than around a hundred meters, adding such objects to each corner or other key points makes sense to get a better idea of the scale. Afterward, move around in the space and see how it feels.

Terrain-based locations which feel too big at that stage will likely be way too big later on. If it feels just right, it is likely still a tick too big. However, if it starts to feel a tiny bit too small, I would recommend stopping with downscaling. Adding objects later will make the environment feel smaller than when it is empty, but many open-world locations in games are typically smaller than in the real world. Again, think about the airfield runway.

Certain size relationships between objects have to stay intact, especially when it is about the distance between relatable objects like doors, humans, or cars. So, we would spot if something is wrong with, for example, the distance between suburban houses, petrol pumps, or parking cars. However, for example, the exact size of space, like a parking lot, horse pen, rocket silo, or amusement park entrance, is often a lot smaller in games because they would feel massive if they follow realistic measurements. Relationships between known objects translate very well, but not distances per se. For example, even if players move in-game a lot faster than normal humans could run, covering several hundred meters on foot is simply not fun. Further on, sniping distances in many games is way shorter than in real life, but that can also have tech reasons.

No strict, general answer or number defines how much smaller a real-world location has to be to fit in a game. It all depends on your game, the movement speed/types, fighting types, weapons, and perspective. I have worked on multiple very similar first-person shooters, and seemingly, what was considered "long-distance sniping" was drastically reduced over time. With this change, the location's actual size often also got smaller, but not necessarily the player's perception of scale. The only general advice I have is to benchmark and prototype differently scaled environments as soon as possible and use your guts to determine a "maximum long fighting distance"? What is the maximum size for a combat location (especially considering your maximum AI count) and other typical distances in your game?

If your mission has multiple locations in an open world, then you have to travel between them early on, multiple times. First, you should move directly between them and then on the intended road/path/trail network. If you use any elements like waypoints or clear landmarks, you can expect most players to go directly between the locations. However, at that stage, make sure that the time spent traveling, depending on your intentions, is not too long but does not feel too short either. A three-minute car ride can be okay if the mission is all about a slow-paced road trip. However, if it is just about connecting two seemingly random locations, five minutes of driving without any other entertainment can be a stretch. Of course, ignoring what I said when driving alone in your game is one of the core fun pillars. I cannot give a simple number, but you have to navigate your world as soon as possible and feel comfortable with it.

Again, when the open world is still very empty, and the game is not very exciting, it is better if the tour feels a bit too long than too short compared to your intention. Driving through an empty open world will always feel more boring than driving through a finished packed one. Therefore, the feeling will become shorter the more the world's visual progress, even if the physical distance does not change. Also, more objects close to the road will make the traversal speed feel faster. Driving through an empty world always feels like a drag. However, avoid anything that feels extremely long, but you can only achieve a good feeling timing with trial, error, and benchmarking.

Those estimates might sound contractionary, making open-world locations a tick smaller than bigger while making traversals a tick longer. However, one is about the perception of time and the other one of space. In many games, one hundred meters feels way longer in real life even if you can traverse it faster. However, driving through a boring environment will always appear longer than through a dense, entertaining, visually dazzling space. Also a "tick" is a highly subjective measurement.

#### 12.1.3.3 Interiors and Complex Locations: First Steps and Early Scaling Estimates

Some companies call it white, gray, orange, or random color boxing. However, the process is essentially the same: You build interior-dominated levels or larger complex locations out of pre-made boxes. The boxes should represent the metrics of the game and include common architecture elements such as walls, stairs, ramps, floors, cover blocks, or walls with various windows or doors. The color of the boxes defines the name of the process, so for example, if the objects are gray, it is called gray-boxing.

This "boxing" process allows level designers to quickly sketch out complex locations or interior spaces which follow the metrics. Then ideally, the objects can be exported, so artists quickly have the location's base proxy, further speeding up the workflow. Flexible, scalable objects or a BSP-based level editor (BSP=Binary Space Partitioning to quickly block in kevel geometry) certainly allows for more flexibility, but sticking to metrics requires extra diligence. The more your game relies on clean metrics, the more I recommend building and using such a box-set.

I typically just placed floor pieces of the entire level to get a feel for distances. For example, especially for multiplayer levels this is an essential step because five seconds difference can make a huge difference here. However, I recommend adding at least walls, windows, stairs, ceilings, and doors for singleplayer levels to your first layout version because the feeling for scale is vital here. The wall or the resulting ceiling height significantly impacts how big or small a room feels, which you can later on still modify with lighting and wall textures. However, your intentions or expectations should be clear early on during the first layout phase.

For interiors, the real world is not the best reference for size. First of all, your game's metrics will dominate, especially minimum distances. For example, it is not uncommon for games to feature a minimum hallway width of two meters, often more in certain third-person games. Secondly, what feels comfortable in real life is not necessarily comfortable in your game. For example, I would consider a one-and-a-half-meter-wide hallway very spacious, but in most FPS (First Person Shooter), some would consider it tight. Therefore, the better you define your metrics and feel what distances are tight, comfortable, and spacious, the better.

When we talk about room sizes, even if you use relatable elements like doors or windows, your empty rooms will always feel too big initially. First of all, you need a lot more relatable objects with the correct scale in the room to make a proper estimate. Secondly, many interior rooms or locations are covered or filled with many objects, further making rooms smaller again. Trust me, it is frustrating to hear that you build your rooms too big, directors ignore all your arguments, and you have to make them smaller, just to hear a few weeks later that they are now too small with objects inside. Therefore the faster you can fill your rooms or locations with objects at spots where you imagine them later, the better. Even some simple orange boxes are better than nothing, plus you already get an early feel for cover. It will not only help your lead or director to make better calls but, more importantly, yourself. However, if you get feedback about empty rooms or doubt yourself, I can only recommend delaying any bigger changes until you can place enough objects for scale. Shelves on the walls or tables in the middle of a room can quickly make the playable space a lot smaller. Therefore, by default, an average empty room that feels a bit too big will likely be just right later on.

Huge flat floors are another potential problem when distances go beyond about 30–40 meters. First of all, such large empty spaces are rare in interiors if we are not talking about basketball fields, impressive entrance halls, mysteriously empty warehouses, or alike. Ideally, you try to break them up with stairs, columns, or other larger objects. The goal is not to take away the feel for their sheer size because this is often precisely what you want. Instead, partially compartmentalizing the space will make navigating or fighting in such spaces more interesting. Especially when filling a large flat floor with crates is the only option left. Sure, there is always an expectation for the rule. However, think about such topics early on if that is really what you want, because splitting up the floor or adding larger objects significantly impacts the space-feeling of a room.

### 12.1.4 Skeleton Script

#### *12.1.4.1 Initial Block-Out*

After you block out the base skeleton layout, the next step is typically a skeleton script. It is not always an official production step for every company or project, but I recommend it at least individually.

First, all required script files, folders, containers, or whatever your engine uses should be created. They have to follow the mandated folder structure and naming conventions. The initial, even almost empty, script creation has to be incredibly clean.

Secondly, you should add all planned primary mission objectives and ideally all level-loads to create a connection between the levels. If your game is rather open-world, then you of course don't have level-loads but likely a master script managing the missions and their objectives. Again the implementation has to happen as clean as possible following the mandated script standards. You have to be especially careful keeping everything clean if the mission objectives have tight-ins into some type of game-spreading meta-script.

As a third step, you add triggers for all objectives at roughly the right location with very simple and fast means, such as a proximity trigger or button. If the correct locations are not available, just place the triggers/buttons next to each other. The goal is that you can start and finish each level as early as possible. Therefore, it is ideally possible to also play the entire game from start to finish. Sure, walking through some invisible triggers is not fun per se, but regardless it is a key achievement. You do not only place basic objects during the skeleton layout phase for scale. Instead, often you also place them to find your quickly placed trigger boxes.

This process is crucial because any walkthrough breaks within the mission blocks must always be found and fixed as fast as possible. Any of such fundamental issues have a severe impact on productivity, reviews, playtests, and especially testing. Especially if the game might have, for example, issues with continuously loading levels or with any meta-scripts, it is crucial to find them as early as possible so you have enough time to fix them.

Except for rare temporary exceptions, your level should always be playable from start to finish, and fixing a walkthrough-break always has top priority over everything. Setting up a clean, solid, and working skeleton script and layout is, therefore, the foundation for a less stressful production later on. Once everything is set up and working, you can keep expanding the script complexity step-by-step, but you know it does work at its core.

It should go without saying that you have to keep scripting standards like commenting best practices, visual script direction, naming/grouping conventions right from the get-go.

#### *12.1.4.2 Further Skeleton Scripts*

In the classic sense, any script past the crude mission objective implementation is not a skeleton anymore. However, I would argue that certain games with strong emphasis could go a bit further. For example, racing games could add the first checkpoints or a shooter some super simple AI spawning. Ultimately there is no strict skeleton definition, and each project should handle it how it sees fit. However, the core definition of the skeleton phase remains: You can play from start to finish and set the foundations for layout, script, and team, so everyone has a solid foundation to get started for real.

### 12.1.5 From Skeleton to First Intention

#### *12.1.5.1 Initial Priority List*

Once you have a skeleton and everyone can start due to a solid foundation, it is essential not to lose focus when aiming toward your first iteration showing the imagined intention. The key is to balance between the right priorities and to cover as many relevant aspects. Focusing on just one aspect like AI scripting only means topics like layout or mission objectives fall behind. Alternatively, focusing on too many topics simultaneously likely results in none of them getting done in time. Below is a list of level design priorities I would recommend for most projects going from skeleton to the first iteration.

1. The most important work is always to fix walkthrough breaks. If nobody can play the level from start to finish, then reviewing and testing the level is hindered. Sure, occasionally, cheats can bridge the time till you have time/resources to fix it, especially if you rely on unfinished features or assets. However, it is common best practice to aim for a level that is always playable from start to finish.
2. The next most important tasks are all the ones that unblock a close team member. If everyone in your level's team follows this rule, you set the foundation for way more frictionless teamwork and way less frustration. For example, if an artist desperately waits for you to finish blocking out a building so he can work on the real model, then you rarely have arguments not to consider it as a priority. It gets tricky if you block several team members or you start doing nothing else than supporting team members. In such cases, sort it out among each other or involve a lead/manager. Also, keep in mind there is a significant difference between someone needing something from you and being completely blocked by you. The last one has top priority, while the first one can typically wait a tiny bit longer.
3. Anything connected to primary mission objectives would be my third highest priority. Mission objectives are the core player experience, plus often connected to key or unique features. The sooner you implement even placeholder features, the faster the feature owners/creators can get feedback and therefore have more time to adjust them.
4. The next important point is the foundation or requirement for any essential features in the levels. For example, you first need to build an adequate space for a boss enemy before adding it to the level. You could add it for basic testing purposes, but in my opinion, you better do it in

separate test levels. Once anything major gets implemented in a level, it should be possible to give relevant feedback, requiring a correct foundation.

5. Therefore, adding any essential features or major assets from other team members is the fifth priority for the same team-oriented reasoning from priorities two and three. For example, it should not take long for you to implement a new AI archetype or replace your basic block covers with the first iteration of cover assets. The real levels are typically the only valid environment to evaluate a feature or asset.
6. Close to number four is any foundation for basic features. For example, if your AI is very cover-centric, then at least some cover is more important than adding the AI because otherwise, the AI would behave so wrong that it won't give you relevant information. Generally speaking, the layout has, therefore, a higher priority than scripting. The skeleton also starts with a basic layout for a feeling of scale before adding the skeleton scripts.
7. Surprisingly low are any other fundamental features, even if they are at the core of the game. For example, a shooter needs things to get shot. However, even in a shooter, I would recommend implementing all the above points before adding AI. The exception, of course, is AI, which is essential for mission objectives or major features.
8. Finally, it is all about adding any "nice to haves." For example, they could be light switches, secondary objectives, collectibles, ammo boxes. Essentially anything necessary to show your level's intention, but can either be skipped in a pinch or cheated, like ammo or health.
9. Anything which is not helping you to show the intention of the layout should be last. Essentially, you would work ahead at that stage, toward the second pass or even alpha already.

#### *12.1.5.2 How to Use the Priority List*

I cannot recommend reciting the previous priority list or any similar list; that would be madness every few minutes. Instead, check against it, for example, early in the morning before or during your team chat or stand-up. The exceptions are the first two points since they have a severe teamwide impact.

The next three points are typically not very long-lasting or do not come up with high frequency. Sure, they have a higher priority if they come up, but it does not mean you should drop everything right away and jump on the new one. In many cases, early on during production, many big key defining features are not fully developed anyhow and, therefore, often do not take too much of your time. However, if you send days of prototyping and testing instead of working on the level, make sure that you talk to your lead first.

Priority point six and seven are typically the bulk of a level designer's work while working toward first intentions. You further block out or already refine the layout and add as many basic features as available. For example, you make sure all triggers work, AI spawns correctly, AI has a suitable environment, player-leading foundations set in, and the general mission flow comes to life. It is completely okay that the whole level exists only out of gray/orange/white blocks. The terrain is still rough-in, large assets only exist as crude placeholders, AI archetypes are placeholders, and the level can break if you play "wrong."

I need to clarify that no normal level at that stage is already "playtest-able," meaning that any random player could play the level without breaking it by accident. You aim for first intentions, meaning whoever evaluates them knows how to play the level. It is the wrong time trying to break the level. Additionally, you, or at least the lead, are typically present during such reviews and can hint if an action would break the level or script. As described as priority one, walkthrough breaks are only the ones that occur during the intended walkthrough break. For example, breaking the missing by leaving the mission area is not a priority, but not triggering the next primary objective is.

The last two points on the priority are really just bonuses. You should only work on them if any of the previous points are blocked, or you are in really good shape timewise. Sometimes, there are features, like a really cool little idea, that are not essential to sell the level's intention, but you have a personal connection to it. However, try to fight the urge to jump on it too soon. At that stage, there is no need to spend days making an overly complex script and layout by covering for an edge case that does not occur during any reviews.

#### *12.1.5.3 Must Haves—Should Haves—Can Haves*

Ideally, you sit together with your lead and manager and agree on which parts or aspects of your level are the "must-haves" required to sell the level's fundamental intention. The primary gameplay experience, mission objectives, and layout to scale are common candidates.

Then comes the "should haves," which help sell the intention. Typically, this is all the other space, encounters, navigation, puzzle, narrative, sections between the few previous "must-haves" key moments. For example, those are all your other combat encounters, layouts, cover setups, important optional objectives, and play-leading aspects.

Finally, come up with all the "can haves," which are not required to sell the level's intention. However, they might put a smile on the reviewer's face and give some bonus points in your favor. Still, they should never be your priority, and you can only work on them if there are no must or should haves left. At that stage, those could be, for example, certain edge cases, not-so-important optional objectives, environmental storytelling, or obscure side routes.

I recommend categorizing your tasks into those three categories, not just for this phase but in general. It helps to set clear expectations between your leads, directors, and managers throughout production. With time, you should better understand how they think and operate, and you can act accordingly even before they look at your level again.

### 12.1.6 Iteration and Post First Intention

Game development is inherently a creative, iterative process. Therefore, expect change because it is part of the job. Toward the first intention, the number of drastic changes is typically rare because it is the point of this first step to get a feel before evaluating if changes are required. Small changes are common during this phase, but anything bigger means that the initial idea was incorrect or something big happened, like a severe shift in production capability.

However, once you reach the first intention, expect some bigger changes. It does not have to happen, but it is always good to manage expectations. Once the first intentions are playable, ideally, all future tasks or feedback from leads, directors, peers, and yourself should aim now to reach alpha and ultimately gold.

The biggest danger are drastic shifts that require major reworks, restarts, or entire cuts. They can happen because even the bigger picture of the entire game is going through the same iterative creative process, which is impossible to predict in all its inherent complexity and detail. However, they have to remain the exception and require incredibly good reasoning. The lack of credible reasoning defines iteration for the sake of only change.

The risk comes from the pressure we put on ourselves or higher-ups put on us. Believing that this one more change is making it all so much better is very common. However, the associated costs and risks will quickly outweigh the imagined improvement. There will come a time in every product where cutting a problematic level, or part of a level is more work overall than fixing the part itself. Therefore, it is a sign of seniority accepting that a game has to come to an end, the number of changes slows down, new features after alpha should be an exception, and any final direction should not come up a few weeks before beta. However, even if they do have to happen, they need to be communicated very clearly. Trying to sneak in new features during the closing phase just because you believe your department came too close is simply unprofessional.

Another bigger topic is the pressure we level designers put on ourselves. I know a few level designers who were famous for never stopping iterating the layout or scripts. They could not stop trying out new ideas and see if they could push the envelope further. Sometimes I catch myself wishing that more designers have this self-drive because it is admirable. However, the problem starts when they cannot stop when it starts getting too late. A classic result is surprise changes in reviews, which never look good for everyone, especially if the new idea is not great. As much as level designers need consistency, communication, and stability from their leads, peers, managers, and directors, as much as they need it from the level designers.

## 12.2 Product Management

### 12.2.1 Introduction

This chapter is not necessarily intended for managers or producers but for level designers better-handling production. Production can be a wild ride, and you can reduce many issues with better expectations and fewer assumptions on all sides. In this chapter, I will cover some basic management topics that directly affect us, level designers, regularly.

### 12.2.2 About MVPs and Backup Plans

#### *12.2.2.1 MVP and Level Design*

The acronym MVP stands for "minimum viable product." For a level, it is the least feasible version you could ship. The level is reliably functioning, has no walkthrough breaks, but will never win any design prices. It has all the core aspects to have a place in the game because it needs the level. However, an MVP level lacks the full breadth of stunning art, memorable gameplay, or unique features to be an amazing experience. A broken level is not an MVP; it is just a buggy level, which you should never ship—the same accounts for only a functional level. I mean, you would never ship the skeleton version of your level.

However, you rarely aim to make an MVP level or mission. Still, it happened to me a few times in my career when we quickly had to create a new level or mission very late. Therefore, we only focused on the core element of the level. However, we only had time to ensure that the rest was not broken, looked okay enough, and connected everything coherently. We did not expect those levels to be stunners, but they were important in the bigger picture. Without them, the game would have suffered in its totality or had narrative holes. However, we kept them short enough, so their not-so-amazing experience had no significant negative impact on the overall game experience.

Now, when you usually work on a level or mission, you should aim for the stars with the true intention to reach the stars—landing on the moon is just the backup. The big problem is that, unlike common feature production, you often cannot just first build an MVP level and then keep adding "cool" parts till you run out of time. Instead, you plan for the most fantastic level within the allocated predicted expectations. However, we all know that prediction in game development is inherently complex. Long-term predictions are like one-month weather forecasts—regardless of how much smart brains and raw computing power you put behind it.

Therefore, you should have your original plan and multiple backup plans, with the MVP being your last. If your level ever has to drop below the MVP version, it is a severe cut candidate! However, shipping an MVP version is never a failure.

#### *12.2.2.2 Backup Plans for Level Design*

In my world, it is entirely okay to plan with a level that is a tick beyond the expectations and available resources because there is always a chance that you and your peers could pull it off. The feeling of shipping an extraordinary level against all odds is unbelievable. However, as incredible as it feels, it is even more important to accept and prepare for the more realistic, lower outcome right from the get-go. Getting emotional about not overachieving is not professional.

Therefore, we have our primary plan and a backup plan, or rather multiple backup plans. Typically, the still feasible dream version is the gold version, then silver, bronze, and finally, tint. Some projects or companies start with platinum, diamond, and go down from there. The gold (or however you call the highest one) is your semi-realistic dream version of the level, while the tint (or however you call the lowest one) is the MVP. All the other steps are in between.

However, when you start working on the level, you should not start with first completing the MVP. The point of having backup plans is that if things don't go according to plan, you can take a step down at a time. Reducing expectations, cutting beats, and replacing a unique feature with something simpler are usually ways more feasible than building upwards, adding beats, or replacing common sections with stunning ones. Removing or downscaling is usually easier than adding or upscaling.

I typically went very nervous when we had no backup plan for a level, or the lowest plan was still risky. It is never a good feeling to have no alternatives, and the only option was an all-out-victory. Too often, such levels then bind many resources only hoping that the team can still finish it somehow without guaranteeing that it will be a success. Alternatively, facing the reality that you only have a gold version, or an MVP creates a similarly bad feeling. It always creates the impression that the dream version holds the team hostage. This case is especially true if the gold version is way more unrealistic to achieve than just "semi-realistic." In both cases where there is no bandwidth for multiple alternative steps in between, I can only recommend going back to the drawing board.

Table 12.1 helps you to come up with four common different backup plans.

So, the saying "Aim for the stars, land on the moon" is, for me, just talking about backup plans, and you likely just wanted to trick the investors by reaching the stars, to give you enough money so you can land on the moon.

It is important to note that this is a production approximation of how I prefer to work personally. Many companies have their versions of a similar model or a very different approach. Still, reaching consent between producers/managers on how to approach level design production is a necessity.

#### *12.2.2.3 Example for Backup Plans and My General Approach*

Let us take one of our previous examples as an initially bland base: The player must rescue a hostage while staying stealthy, or enemies will execute the hostage. Then the player has to defend the hostage till your NPC buddy arrives. Finally, you have a wild ride behind the mounted gun of the get-away vehicle while your buddy drives.

I also define that the core aspect of the mission is to save a hostage because the hostage will play a major role in the future story of our game. Anything else is making the mission more memorable and better for the player.

Below is a Table 12.2 breakdown of what would be the difference between the different versions.

Typically, I start with something between silver and gold in my head and call it "realistic crazy." I then purposely go a bit more wild and crazy for the gold version because it should get everyone motivated without worrying too much about producers or managers, and who knows, maybe we can pull most of it off? I then slightly tone down the "realistic crazy" and define it as the silver—the "still motivational, yet conservative" version. Then I take a deep breath and define the MVP as the tint. I know it is painful, but I also know that it will give me safety and producers/managers sanity/sleep. Finally, I try to find a middle-ground between the conservative silver and the MVP.

**TABLE 12.1**

Four Common Backup Plans for a Level

| | | |
|---|---|---|
| **Gold** | The level's dream version which is just a tick unrealistic with the expected resources. It typically requires some luck or minor miracle to pull off. | You reach the stars. |
| **Silver** | The level has as many special, core, unique moments, art, and gameplay implemented as the predicted resources comfortably allow. No sacrifice on the level's unique core aspect. | You land on the moon. |
| **Bronze** | The level has as many special, core, unique moments, art, and gameplay implemented as half the predicted resources comfortably allow. No sacrifice on the level's core aspect, except it likely is not overall unique anymore. | You reach the international space station. |
| **Tint** | The level reliably functions from start to finish, the one core aspect works as a minimum implementation (not unique) and the level shares the same bug density as the rest of the game. | You have lift-off, reach space, see the earth is not flat, and safely return. |

**TABLE 12.2**

Example of the Backup Plans for a Mission

| | |
|---|---|
| **Gold** | • The stealth section is systemic. Upon detection, AI has to systemically run to the hostage to kill it.<br>• The location's layout is very complex with several buildings, multiple levels of verticality, all interiors are accessible, many vertical connections around and between the buildings, ziplines, and various upper (roofs) and lower (short sewers) stealth routes.<br>• Enemy AI during the stealth section has a wide range of patrols, idle animations, and conversations. Several idle animations and conversations are unique to this mission and serve the narrative.<br>• Upon rescue, the hostage picks up a gun from the enemies, can defend itself, and follows the player.<br>• Reinforcement enemy AI systematically searches the parameter for the hostage with a mix of search dogs, helicopters, short- and long-range (on roofs) archetypes.<br>• The buddy AI with the get-away vehicle arrives and then drives systemically while the player is behind the mounted gun.<br>• The extraction drive is very long, with a mix of static enemy roadblocks, helicopters, tanks, and fast-chasing vehicles.<br>• The buddy switches routes depending on how fast the player takes out roadblocks. Alternate routes become more difficult.<br>• The drive goes through a mix of open fields, bridges, small villages, jumps, dense forests, along shallow rivers, next to trains, and overall medium to high elevation changes. |
| **Silver** | • The stealth section is systemic. Upon detection, AI has to systemically run to the hostage to kill it.<br>• The location's layout is fairly complex with several buildings, all interiors are accessible, and various upper (roofs) and lower (short sewers) stealth routes.<br>• Enemy AI during the stealth section has a wide range of patrols, generic idle animations, and conversations.<br>• Upon rescue, the hostage gets a gun by script, can defend itself, but stays in one of the buildings.<br>• Reinforcement enemy AI systematically attacks the hostage's building with a mix of short- and long-range (on roofs) archetypes.<br>• The buddy AI with the get-away vehicle arrives and then drives systemically while the player is behind the mounted gun.<br>• The extraction drive is fairly long, with a mix of static enemy roadblocks and fast-chasing vehicles.<br>• The drive goes through a mix of open fields, bridges, dense forests, and overall medium elevation changes. |
| **Bronze** | • The stealth section is not systemic. Upon detection, the player has X seconds to kill the AI, which would shoot the hostage by script.<br>• The location's layout is simple with several buildings, no interiors are accessible, and various upper (roofs) stealth routes.<br>• Enemy AI during the stealth section has a wide range of patrols but only a few generic idle animations.<br>• Upon rescue, the hostage hides in one of the buildings without the ability to defend itself.<br>• Reinforcement enemy AI systematically attacks the hostage's building with short-range archetypes.<br>• The buddy AI with the get-away vehicle arrives and then drives on a scripted spline while the player is behind the mounted gun.<br>• The extraction drive is fairly short, with only roadblocks or other on-foot AI.<br>• The drive goes through a mix of open fields, dense forests, and overall low elevation changes. |
| **Tint** | • The stealth section is not systemic. Upon detection, the player has X seconds to reach the hostage or the mission fails.<br>• The location's layout is very simple with several buildings, no interiors or roofs are accessible, but features various stealth routes between the buildings.<br>• Enemy AI during the stealth section has only various patrols.<br>• Upon rescue, the hostage hides in one of the buildings without the ability to defend itself.<br>• Reinforcement enemy AI semi-scripted attacks the hostage's building with short-range archetypes.<br>• The buddy AI with the get-away vehicle arrives on a scripted spline and the mission ends without an action-packed vehicle extraction. |

In reality, you will not likely reach an exact gold, silver, bronze, or tint version. It will always be something in between or, most likely, something even more different. For example, you might have a tint version but with more systemic elements because your game supports it well, or you have the tint version with the vehicle extraction from the bronze variant. However, the different backup plans and in-between steps give you the safety to go a bit nuts initially without causing a huge risk. Trust me, knowing that you do not crush to rock bottom when the dream fails is quite reassuring.

### 12.2.3 About Benchmarks and Prototypes

#### *12.2.3.1 Introduction*

Both benchmarks and prototypes are classic assignments or mandates during pre-production. Prototypes can still happen occasionally later during production, but benchmarks are getting rarer later on.

The primary goal of level benchmarks and prototypes is to get answers which you do not know yet. The primary difference is that benchmarks aim to a final or almost final quality level, while prototypes just want to prove or experiment with an idea as fast as possible. Therefore, prototypes very rarely push for high quality and often include many hacks to keep their production plus turn-around cycles iterative and fast.

#### *12.2.3.2 Benchmarks*

With level design and environment art benchmarks, you try to answer classic questions like:

- What does the close-to-final art direction look like in-game?
- Following the art direction, what is the maximum art detail, and can we still run on our target platform at 30fps?
- How much do we have to adjust the art direction and quality expectations to reach the performance goal?
- What is the ideal workflow to create high-quality assets?
- How long does it take to create a standard location with all gameplay ingredients reaching skeleton, first intention, close to alpha, and close to beta?
- How much AI can we afford in a standard, close-to-final location performance-wise?
- How can we impress the press/clients of our game at a convention within only ten minutes of playtime?
- What tools do we need to create a fully fleshed level?

In reality, many benchmarks are more art-oriented, and the few gameplay benchmarks you create are also typically demos for pitches, press, expos, or other types of highly important reviews. In many cases, such gameplay benchmarks are art benchmarks at the same time. However, in my experience, it is hard to learn anything about production speed from benchmarks because, early on, you lack fully established production tools and workflows. Additionally, the team often lacks experience and potentially smooth corporation. Therefore, in many cases, you create gameplay benchmarks to achieve exactly that: Gain experience taking a game's small chunk close to the final. This experience is crucial before starting production to avoid any ugly surprises when you are supposed to go full force with the entire team.

It is more common for more senior- or intermediate level designers to work on benchmarks. However, overall I can only recommend that you work on a benchmark if you have the opportunity, even juniors or leads. It allows you to gain a lot of relevant experience getting through production. After all, you can only make good calls about the future if you have a valuable clue about how it could end. Theoretical or only opinionated predictions are rarely fruitful, and that is why benchmarks are so vital.

The biggest issue of benchmarks is that typically most of it is throw-away work. For most developers, this should be clear, but it is worth reminding everyone occasionally, just to keep expectations real. Still, it is hard to push for a close-to-final result knowing that most of it will not find its way into the final game, except usually the experience, a few assets, and maybe a small segment.

Another problem with early benchmarks is that you commonly cannot realistically reach an accurate final version. Above, I always wrote "close to final" because you usually do not have all the tools, features, experience, tech, or assets in pre-production. This situation is especially true for gameplay benchmarks. Ultimately an early benchmark remains an estimate and the best effort assumption. For example, it is nearly impossible to gain early performance calls when your engine is in production while working on the game. In such cases, the best you can do is create your stunning dream benchmark, accept the initially low performance, and hopefully get an idea of where and how to optimize the engine. However, you have to keep maintaining the benchmark level in order to track performance optimization progress. The problem of maintaining a throw-away level is that it is not always the most fun task.

#### 12.2.3.3 Prototypes

The primary purpose of prototypes is to test or experiment with situations or features. For example, you want to know how to make a feature/situation fun, what values feel balanced, what layout is most suitable for a specific feature, or what are still okay jumping distances with different movement speeds. You want to find answers with isolated and comparable cases which would cost too much to find in real levels.

Therefore, the primary factor and consideration of prototypes is speed. If a prototype is highly elaborate and requires a ton of resources, then either it is one of the game's key features, or something went wrong. It is a common mistake to polish prototypes too much or too long because designers start to enjoy it too much. As much as this is a good sign, I recommend switching to the real levels as fast as possible. Only real levels provide a final realistic environment to evaluate a gameplay scenario or feature. You use a simplified, fast-loading prototype level to get your answer, but once you feel comfortable, you stop prototyping. You may have to go back because the prototype was great, but then the feature had severe issues in the real levels. For example, AI worked great in a prototype environment, but we could not create consistent and believable environments like that in real levels. We had severe performance issues in a proper game environment once all features came together, or the feature started to have serious issues with all the other features of a real complex level.

In most cases, prototypes happen in separate test levels. Ideally, the levels are almost empty and, therefore, quick to load, especially if programmers work with them and want to load the level in debugging mode because then everything is a lot slower. Typically keeping a prototype clean is not a big necessity, as long as the messiness does not affect the real levels. Also, hacks and some questionable scripting are okay as long as it helps to make prototyping faster and there is an agreed plan on how to implement them in the real levels correctly.

Another important consideration for prototypes is a fast iteration cycle. If you cannot iterate quickly, then you are not necessarily prototyping in the original sense. I have experienced several layout prototypes where the layouts barely changed for weeks. A common reason for slow iteration speed is that designers either wait for something else or believe it is "good enough." If you wait for something, then as fast as possible, move on to the next task or prototype. Further on, believing a prototype's result is "good enough" can only be said if you exhausted all feasible options or you run out of resources/time. Declaring yourself that something is "good enough" while you still have further options, resources, and time left is lazy.

Good engines allow level or game designers to prototype most ideas without the help of coders. Advanced and scripting tools are therefore a necessity. It is great fun to prototype ideas and features with a powerful scripting language and often an excellent way to become better in scripting. Additionally, it is a good feeling to be part of the game's original creation. A massive amount of fantastic ideas come from developers just playing around with ideas. I would say more ideas come from prototyping than from meetings! I cannot go into details, but I am proud to say that several game-defining features came from junior level designers prototyping.

Also, a good prototype nullifies the need for many wasteful meetings and endless theoretical design documents. Back in the days, when people still printed design documents, we saved thousands of trees with prototypes. I am a strong advocate of light level design documentation because we have such fast tools nowadays—the same counts for prototypes and design documentation. Therefore, in my opinion, most (game) designers who cannot prototype are not designers but writers with questionable narrative skills.

## 12.3 Third- and First-Person Perspectives

### 12.3.1 Introduction

In this chapter, I want to share some considerations for making levels for a first or third-person game. In first-person games, the camera is where the eyes of the player's protagonist would be. Nothing is obstructing the player's view except a weapon or tool held in their hand. However, the player does not see the character, except typically the hands and maybe feet when they look down.

In third-person games, the camera is behind the player's avatar, either further back or close to the character's shoulder. The player can clearly see their protagonist from behind, blocking some parts of the player's view.

### 12.3.2 Scale for Perspectives

I've mentioned it a few times already but objects are not necessarily up to scale compared to the real work. However, the scale of objects, in believable settings, is only slightly bigger because players can compare them to what they know. For example, if a basic car is suddenly 20% bigger than an average-sized human, we instantly notice such even small differences. It is a bit different with objects defined by a "distance" like windows or doors because for most games they are at least wider than the norm. For example, an average door width is somewhere between 0.7 and 0.8 meter while in games it typically starts with at least 1 meter, if not more.

The real important factor is the distance between objects and there are even more crucial differences between first- and third-person games. I've already hinted at some aspects in Table 12.3, but I think it helps to look at a clear example. As a base let's look at a very simple small restaurant room with four tables and six chairs each.

In real life 0.7 meter is usually enough space between wall and table. Between the tables, in the middle of the room you usually need at least 2.5 meters so guests and waiters have enough space. A common table size for six people is around 1 by 1.6 meter. Therefore, the room dimensions are $0.7+1+2.5+1+0.7=5.9$ meters width and $0.7+1.6+2.5+1.6+0.7=7.1$ meters. With a bit of rounding this is an average 6 by 7 meter room or 42 $m^2$. Yes, the example is faulty because you don't build a room for your furniture, but let's stay with it to show the difference between real world, first- and third-person scaling.

When we translate this room into a first-person game, then we keep the idea that you can walk around all tables, at all sides. However, the distance between objects in first-person games is way bigger than you could squeeze yourself to a table in real life. Let's take a minimum distance metric of 1.5 meters for our example, a not uncommon value. We do not scale the size of the tables or chairs, plus we push the chairs close under the tables, but we still give it 0.1 meters to have a bit of wiggle room for a semi-organic look. Therefore, the room dimensions are $1.5+0.1+1+0.1+2.5+0.1+1+0.1+1.5=7.9$ meters width and $1.5+0.1+1.6+0.1+2.5+0.1+1.6+0.1+1.5=9.1$ meters. With a bit of rounding, this is an 8 by 9 meter room or 72 $m^2$. The floor size has almost doubled, and the width and length of the room increased by around a third. I purposely did not touch the distance of the middle hallway between the tables because I saw no need for it so far.

Finally, we translate this room into a third-person game. We increase the minimum distance metric to 2.5 meters, an almost conservative small value. We scale the tables and chairs (except the height) by around 20% because otherwise, they might look too tiny in the huge space. We keep the chairs pushed close under the tables with the previous 0.1 meters for wiggle room. We also have to make the middle hallway bigger or lose the scale contrast to the hallways on the side. Therefore, the room dimensions are

**TABLE 12.3**

Main Differences between First- and Third-Person Level Design

| First-Person Games | Third-Person Games |
|---|---|
| Levels allow for more accurate engagement, especially at a more extended range. Fighting at close distance in first-person games is rarely pure joy. | Levels allow for more melee combat opportunities or, overall, a closer engagement combat distance. Essentially all sniping and often aiming in third-person games is in the first person. |
| Engagements can be more twitchy and fast-paced, except melee combat. Melee combat can still be fast and frantic, but then it is rarely a delightful experience. However, the price is the lack of combat awareness, which means players can quickly get overwhelmed/frustrated when many enemies attack from many different, opposing directions. | Overall, engagements are usually slower, except for melee combat. The higher camera angle allows keeping combat awareness, allowing level designers to create more viable attack angles or enemy numbers without overwhelming players. |
| The camera position allows for a more immersive experience. However, the typical field of view is 70° to 90°, which is way lower than the ~120° of a human. As a result, players have less situational awareness. It is much easier for designers to surprise or shock players, direct the exact view of players at, for example, in-game events, or recognize more hidden clues. | The higher-up camera position gives players a better understanding of the environment and situational awareness. As a result, players are more likely to recognize, for example, in-game events, environmental threats, or environmental storytelling. However, it is also a lot harder to surprise or shock players. In many games, a rotating third-person camera can look around corners and spot threats, which the avatar otherwise could not see. |
| Ceilings or other obstacles above the player's camera can get very low. For example, crouching through air ducts is typically more comfortable in the first than third person. | The higher camera position typically requires a higher ceiling or less obstacles close to and above the character's head. The lower the camera, the more the character is blocking the player's view. |
| Players can navigate tight spaces without confusing camera switching, especially when their back touches the wall. | When the character's back is close to the wall, the camera is pressed against it, too, and it has to go somewhere, typically into the character's head. However, this is often a sudden and confusing switch that is not very comfortable for many players, especially when it includes glitches. |
| The camera is closer to the ground, or players can move the camera close to objects, allowing players to spot or watch more minor details a lot easier. That fact can be an essential consideration, especially for environmental storytelling or puzzle design. | The camera is further away from the ground, making it more difficult to spot tiny details on objects ahead or on the ground. However, players can better understand the overall environment from a higher view angle, giving different opportunities for environmental storytelling or puzzles. |
| The more horizontal camera angle allows for a bigger focus on distant events/objects and the sky/ceiling itself. This observation is significant for any threats, events, or player-leading elements at a distance or above the player. | The typically more downward-pointing viewing angle reduces the impact on distant events/objects to some degree and certainly on anything above the character. Especially above and close is difficult to deal with. |
| Metrics for the minimum distance between objects is, in my experience, at least 25% to 50% smaller compared to third-person games. The first reason is that a closer camera distance to the environment allows for more precision and details. The second big reason is that in first-person games, typically protagonists/AI need less extensive character animations. The previously mentioned camera issues are another one. | Metrics for the minimum distance between objects is, in my experience, at least 25% to 50% bigger compared to first-person games. Precision due to the camera distance is one aspect, but also occasional imprecision due to the protagonist's movement animations. After all, you can see the character's feet very clearly. Another big reason is that player characters often have extensive character animations which need much space, like dragging and stabbing enemies over cover. The previously mentioned camera issues are another one. |

(*Continued*)

**TABLE 12.3 (*Continued*)**

Main Differences between First- and Third-Person Level Design

| First-Person Games | Third-Person Games |
|---|---|
| The player has no feet awareness. Therefore if they look straight forward they do not know exactly where they stand. This is especially crucial for navigation challenges, especially jumping or balancing. I can only recommend to reduce jumping challenges in first-person games to a minimum, never make them nail-biting difficult, and failure should not be drastic. | The player has an excellent feet awareness of his character. This fact allows them to create challenges where exact foot positioning is required, for example, jumping or balancing. |
| The player has very little body awareness, and the camera is tied closely with the character's movement. Therefore, any crazy movements like rolling, zero-G floating, swimming, or walking on walls can very quickly lead to confusion or nausea. Additionally, complex full-body actions, like climbing, are not as easy to execute as in the third person, especially when keeping the overview or looking out for the climbing route. | The player has excellent body awareness, and the camera is independent of the character's movement. Therefore, it is much more comfortable to let the character do rolls, swim, walk on walls, float in zero-G, or climb. This wide range of options has a significant impact on navigational opportunities for level design. Characters can also get a lot closer to large objects without losing orientation, for example when climbing large walls. |
| Due to the lack of overview, losing orientation in first-person games is easier, especially in tighter environments with a lot of twists and turns. Therefore, player-leading has to be very strong in such environments, or the sections are preferably more linear. | Due to the heightened spatial awareness, it is typically easier to stay oriented in third person, even if the space is getting a bit tighter, as long it does not cause camera issues. |
| The player can't look around corners or over certain objects without exposure. | A third-person camera allows players to safely look at the space ahead around corners or over certain objects. This is especially crucial for stealth games. |

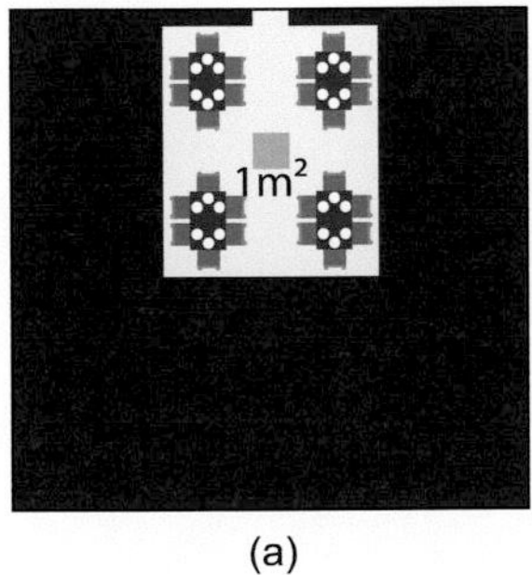

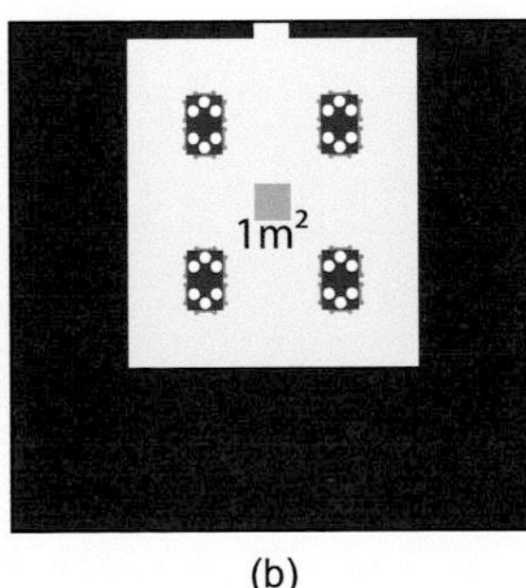

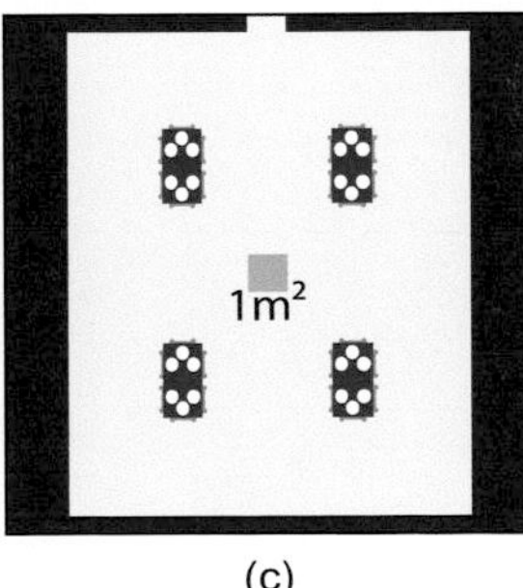


**FIGURE 12.1** (a) Real-world scale of a minimum-sized example restaurant room. (b) First-person layout of the same restaurant room. (c) Third-person layout of the same restaurant room.

$2.5+0.1+1.2+0.1+3.5+0.1+1.2+0.1+2.5=11.3$ meters width and $2.5+0.1+1.9+0.1+3.5+0.1+1.9+0.1+2.5=12.7$ meters. With a bit of rounding, this is an 11 by 13 meter room or 143 $m^2$. The floor size is almost a factor 3.5 larger, and the width and length of the room doubled.

I hope this example shows you how quickly a relatively small 6 by 7 meter restaurant room becomes bigger than most people's rental apartments. It should also show why you have to be so careful with taking real-world maps and translating them into your game world. However, the scale relationships ideally stay the same. For example, see the above figure, if the restaurant's tiny kitchen was only half the size of the restaurant then it shouldn't be much bigger in our game, if not even smaller.

# Section V

# Practical: Layouts

# 13

## *Cover, Flow, and Player Leading*

This chapter goes into detail about how we shape the environments for our players. It is very cover-centric because cover is one of the primary level design layout elements in action games. It has a huge impact on most combat, stealth sections. However, additionally understanding cover as a tool to manipulate the second-to-second gameplay greatly impacts transversal gameplay blocks, placing any layout elements, and learning a lot about flow itself.

When we talk about flow, we must talk about player leading. It is one of the core crafts of any good level designer. Without good player leading, players will get frustrated and likely stop playing while blaming your game.

Games nowadays are so incredibly complex and different, but my goal with this chapter is to establish a mindset about cover and player leading. Ideally, this mindset translates to your game's unique possibilities and gameplay options.

## 13.1 Cover Mentality

### 13.1.1 Introduction

This chapter aims to bring a cover-centric mindset across—essentially, my fundamentals of approaching cover placement. I try to keep the concept rather abstract and less game-specific, yet with practical application in mind. Ideally, this means you can easily apply it to your game and needs, both single- and multiplayer alike. I will discuss the most common layout cases and how I would approach them in terms of cover.

### 13.1.2 The Corner

The corner scenario is probably one of the most typical situations in any action game and an excellent example to get the fundamentals across. A corner, by definition, provides two covers, in the picture below, pointing south and east. This doesn't give a lot of options, and as a result, both players and AI are very predictable and limited.

Then often, designers or artists place a crate right at the corner. Despite likely looking a bit better, it doesn't really increase the number of options by much. Additionally, and that is the worst part, it creates an awkward flow around the corner. If going around the corner is a valid option for our player or AI, then this is a bad cover placement.

A better concept is to place your cover further away from the corner, providing enough space between corner and the new cover. This means you keep the swift flow around the corner while you add four, not just one, more cover options.

A secondary cover object, a bit further away from the corner, allows the players to change up the attack angle, commit to the space ahead more comfortably, provide cover from all sides and increases the players' unpredictability.

In the case of AI, it allows more than one of them to go around the corner simultaneously because they now have two cover options toward both corner's main directions. This is vital if your AI is very cover-centric. Otherwise, you have many stupid AI running around the corner and getting shot like lemmings.

DOI: 10.1201/9781003275664-18

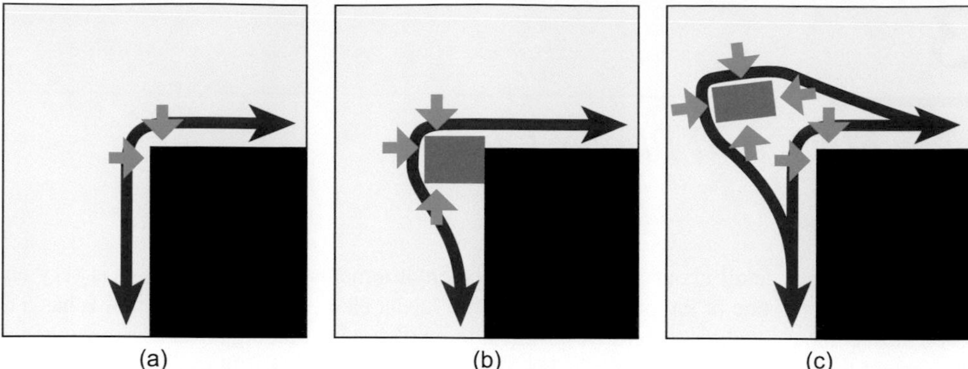


**FIGURE 13.1** (a) Original corner. (b) With added cover object touching the corner. (c) Cover object further away from the corner.

Essentially you created an additional lane going around the corner. This is quite crucial, and I'll talk more about lanes further on. You can even expand the number of covers here, providing even more options, and more options (within limits) is always better than funneling the decision-making.

### 13.1.3 The Wall

So, when approaching cover placement at walls, it is common for designers and artists to place cover objects along its side. In the context of a believable world, this is not wrong per se, but let us see how you can make it work better cover-wise. The main issue now is that going from cover to cover creates a very uncomfortable flow and is just a singular lane.

So, the first common reaction is to move one of the cover objects further away from the wall. The distance between the wall and cover objects needs to be wide enough for players to rush through comfortably. Transitioning from the cover object at the wall to the one further out should be very smooth and equally comfortable to go back to an object at the wall.

This change is good because we now improved the flow while adding cover options in all directions. If all objects are next to a wall, then there is no cover pointing outwards. However, if the distance cover is not enough, then it likely causes visibility issues from cover to cover. The more high cover you used, the more relevant this case is, and visibility directly relates to the line of engagement between the covers.

In such a case, my recommendation is to move it even further away from the wall. I mean, if you moved it already by a few meters, then a few more should not be a big issue. We have a better flow, clear visibility between the cover objects, and still more cover options in all directions. However, there are, of course, cases when you want to block sightlines with cover, especially in slower-paced and or stealth parts.

### 13.1.4 The Hallway

Hallways are another classical scenario for cover placement. Furthermore, I do not just talk about hallways in buildings here but any kind of linear stretch or corridor in any setting. It can be, for example, walkways, valleys, bridges, tunnels, or ridgelines.

The typical cover placement in hallways is on the sides, providing the well-known leap-frog flow between them. Now, by default, there is not anything wrong with some leap-frogging between covers, but if your corridor is wide enough, then let us think about an alternative setup.

First, provide cover on both sides, then a cover in the center, and repeat the pattern from then on. Now, the result is very impactful because it creates more cover, meaning more options for players. Additionally,

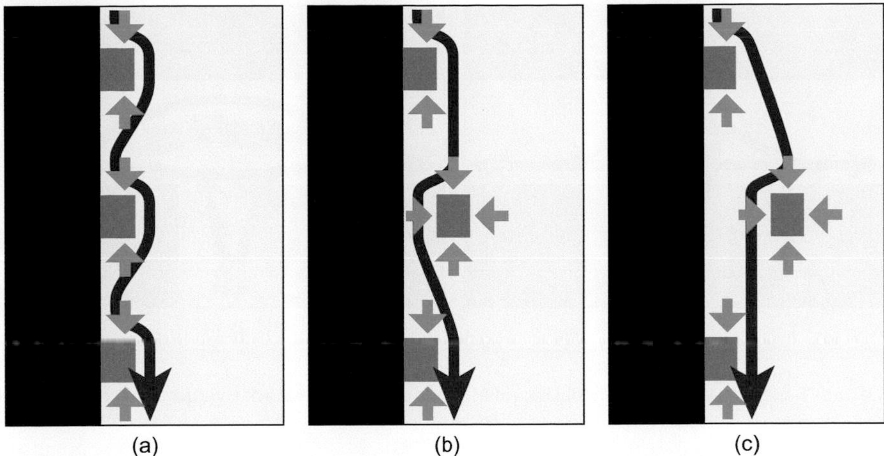


**FIGURE 13.2** (a) Original wall with cover objects. (b) One cover object moved away. (c) No cover object blocks sightlines between.

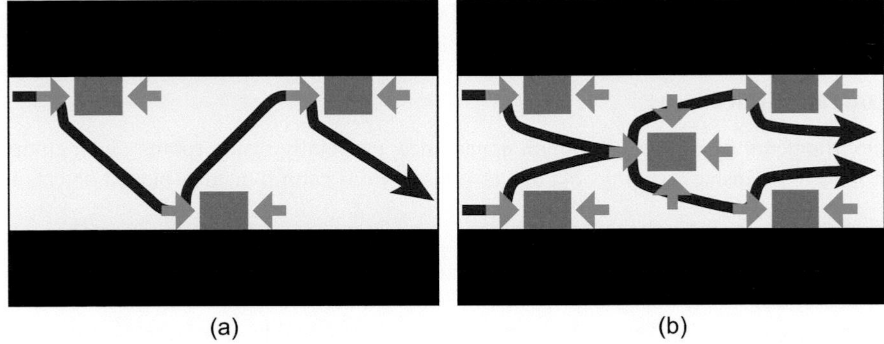


**FIGURE 13.3** (a) Hallway with classical cover placement. (b) Hallway with improved cover placement.

this directly translates to more AI flowing through the hallway simultaneously because often (systemic) AI requires a lot of cover to move efficiently.

Secondly, you keep a nice flow through the hallway, but please keep in mind that it can get a bit tighter and can slow down your game speed, of course.

Finally, one of the more significant differences is that it creates two lanes through a previously linear space. It is even better because, at every second cover, the players can switch between them. That is especially important for multiplayer maps. AI has a hard time predicting players' actions, but human opponents can do very well.

The last comment is that I recommend keeping the central cover objects only medium-high to keep some sightlines intact. Of course, change it up from time to time, but if your space appears to be too cramped, then your hallway quickly might feel more like a room.

### 13.1.5 The T-Junction

Like the hallways, the t-junctions should not be limited to just interiors since such setups can appear in any, more linear, environments. By now, I hope most of you expect me to place the cover objects more central to the t-junction, away from the walls. This assumption is correct, but I would like to elaborate on it a bit more.

First of all, it creates many cover directions, it does not affect the original flow much or not at all, and it makes a new lane. So far, so good; this is already a significant step in the right direction.

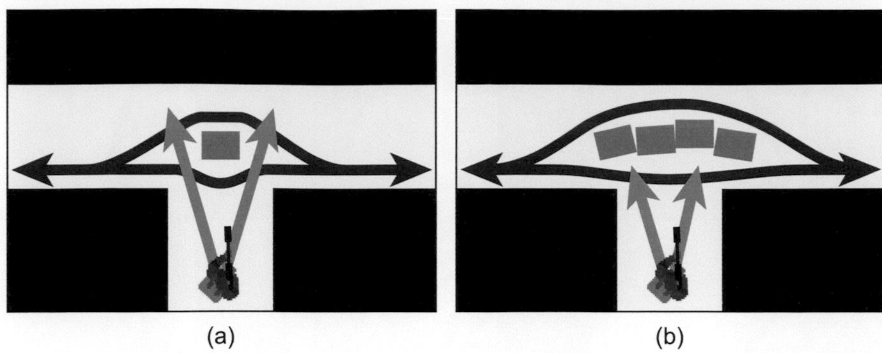


**FIGURE 13.4** (a) T-Junction with one cover object. (b) Multiple cover objects block sightline from the corridor below.

At that moment, I would like you to think about optionally extending the cover further, left and right, so you can sneak by the top hallway completely unseen. It might matter less if there is AI in the intersecting hallway. Its reaction time likely will not trigger detection for any players rushing by, but it can mean a lot in multiplayer. Purposely blocking sightlines is an essential consideration in such cases. After all, it makes a massive difference if your human opponents know if you use a lane or not.

### 13.1.6 Concave Spaces

Concave environments have a very common appearance, especially inside rooms. Such environments do not just have to be inside buildings but can also result from natural or man-placed objects in bigger spaces.

First of all, a room needs to be big enough to feature any cover, or it gets merely too cramped, and of course, the cover is not very relevant. Now even if your room is big enough, having the cover on the walls might be unnecessary, simply because it will be implausible that there will be a fight between two parties along the common room walls. To clarify, I am not talking here about huge halls or gigantic warehouses but reasonably sized or even larger rooms in buildings.

If a room is big enough to feature cover comfortably but is too small to require cover along its walls, then covers should be placed inside the room, away from the wall, especially providing cover toward the entrance of the room, the most likely threat direction.

Keep in mind that a cover object inside a room can often look odd or get very cramped, especially in smaller ones. In such cases, do not place any cover and remember that the door frames provide cover, too, but more about doors soon.

Suppose a room has more than one entrance or features a more complex shape, like L or H-shaped. In that case, it is essentially just a combination of corners, hallways, or t-junctions, and I have covered them already previously.

### 13.1.7 Convex Spaces

Concave environments are often around larger round shapes like around a big rock or gas tank. Placing the cover objects away from the wall can help, but there are better scenarios.

First of all, let us look at the scenario with all covers placed away from the convex wall. You have many cover options in all directions, multiple lanes, and opportunities to switch between them. Still, the flow going from cover to cover is not ideal due to some harsh angles. It isn't bad per se, but to create more believable environments and improve the flow, let us think about better solutions.

A good alternative, in my opinion, is to alternate between cover at the wall and away from it. You still keep cover options in all directions available. Furthermore, more importantly, it creates a nicer flow going from cover to cover.

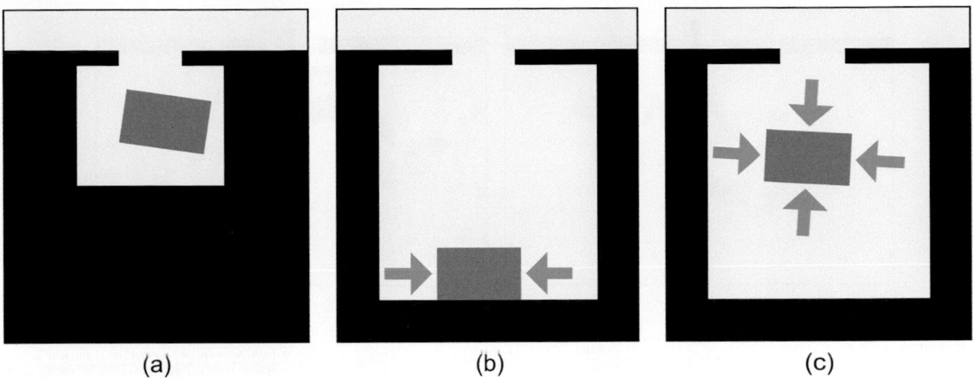


**FIGURE 13.5** (a) Room is too small for cover in the middle. (b) Room is too small for cover on the walls. (c) Cover object in the center of the room.

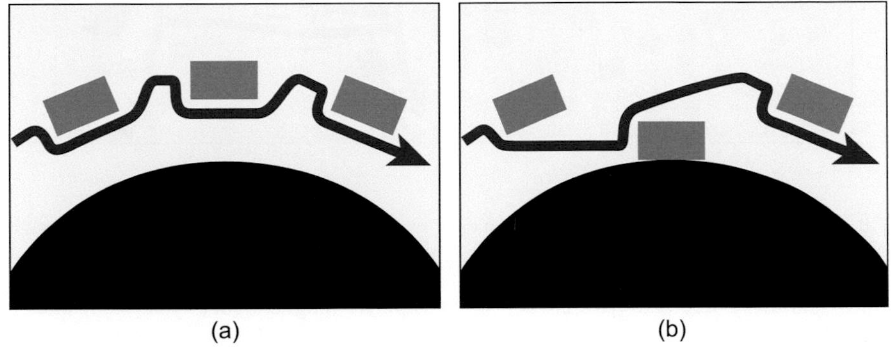


**FIGURE 13.6** (a) Cover objects are away from the convex wall. (b) Every second cover object is away from the convex wall.

Sometimes it is okay to have fewer options for the sake of a better flow. Granted, it is very case by case. There is no 100% strict rule to follow, but instead, develop a good sense and mindset with time, and play your section a lot!

### 13.1.8 The Door Frame Problem

It is time to discuss the infamous door frame. It is a bit of a particular case, but it haunts us, level designers, for eons. Essentially the eternal problem is that players prefer to stay outside of the room. They rightfully use the security of the door frame to kill everyone in the room. Furthermore, first, experience your beautifully designed combat space when they can rush through it in safety. There are many ways to approach this issue but let us see what cover can do.

The first option is to provide cover close to the door frame, which is better than the door frame. The players could better observe the room the scene ahead, a better sniping spot, or a great place to lob grenades from. There are many possibilities, but it all greatly depends on your available space and your game itself.

Secondly—and it is not the nicest one—you can use cover to block the sightlines for the players from the door frame. Door frames are only valid spots to attack if you can see the enemy. So blocking the player's view even just a bit can be an okay incentive to lure him in.

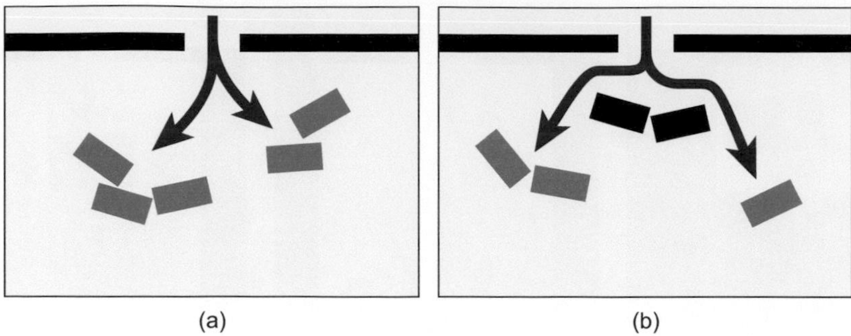


**FIGURE 13.7** (a) Cover objects as player-magnets. (b) High cover objects make the door frame less attractive as cover.

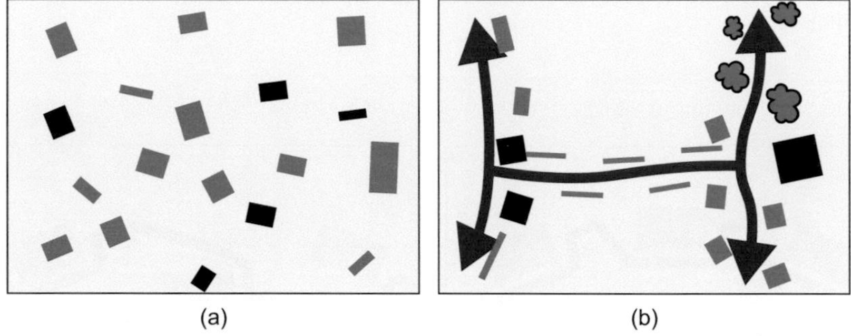


**FIGURE 13.8** (a) Randomly placed cover objects in an open space. (b) Cover objects form a clear network in an open space.

So the main takeaway here is to treat cover objects as player-magnets, ideally stronger ones like their beloved door frames. Otherwise, we can use cover to weaken the advantage given by the frame. Of course, none of those options works well for smaller rooms, and that is just fine.

### 13.1.9 Cover Placement in the Open

Any object placed in an open location is heavily contextual to the environment. Nevertheless, let us stay in our abstract level design headspace.

The most important advice I have about cover placement here is to avoid an even-ish distribution without going through all possibilities. Even a large forest or crate factory should show some patterns and structures represented by the cover. Think about it in terms of a cover network and less about just filling up space with objects. Each path should have a character, or at least speak to different player types. Some lanes are more aggressive, faster, sneaky, tricky to navigate, or harder to spot. A simple path setup providing a clear left or right path is better than just some loveless, random distribution.

Cover is one of your primary ways to guide the player through your fictional, action-packed, and tense worlds. By no means waste that personal opportunity to craft a wonderful experience for your players.

### 13.1.10 Closing Words

I could keep talking about more scenarios, possibilities, or different unique situations. Still, the chapter is more to bring a mindset across than to explain every case. However, I hope my mindset approach to cover will make you think a bit more consciously the next time you drop a crate.

By no means, please do not strictly follow all those guidelines one-to-one, all the time, or it can create some very gamey and artificial worlds. Still, I believe the more often you can follow this cover mindset, the more likely your AI will work better, and—more importantly—your players will appreciate it. Cover is one of the most fundamental level design aspects for pretty much any action game. So spending some severe thoughts about flow, lanes, cover direction, and switching options will go a very long way.

Finally, especially when it comes to cover, always stay in sync with your fellow friendly environment artists. Any miscommunication about such a crucial ingredient can only cause trouble.

## 13.2 Cover Types

### 13.2.1 Introduction

In this chapter, I want to dig a bit deeper into the commonly used cover types, how to use them, what to consider, and my general thoughts about them. A clear understanding of the different types is fundamental for any further cover design consideration. After all, like every artisan, every level designer should know his tools.

Even if this chapter will not cover every cover type, I hope it gives you insight into the basic classes so you can apply similar thinking to your unique game-specific covers. Too often, people just think of the cover as crates. However, the more you are aware of its many types, the better your world will look while making a better layout.

### 13.2.2 Block, Medium, and High Cover

Let us start with the most common type, the block cover, with extra focus on half and full height. Essentially the objects are typically blocks or round shapes providing cover from at least three to four directions, if not more. AIs or players can circle it reasonably quickly, so large buildings or mountains are not block cover in this context.

The difference between half and full cover is that half (or sometimes I say medium) cover only protects if the player or AI is crouching. Full—or high—cover is then providing cover even when the player is standing. They are the level designer's bread and butter of cover.

Classic examples are our infamous crates, barrels, and containers. Nevertheless, it also includes anything else like cars, outhouses, rocks, trash bins, large blocks of frozen dolphin kidneys, and bigger trees.

Of course, block covers are very versatile because they provide cover in essentially all directions, and this versatility creates a particular safety in uncertain situations. They are so common because they resemble widespread objects in our worlds.

Their presence on the battlefield means they can easily create new clear lanes and form a cover network. Their downside is that their versatility restricts your power as a designer to control the actors or impact their behavior. However, I will talk more about controlling cover types a bit later. Still, if you do not care about controlling the player or AI too much, this cover type is a safe bet. Plus, too much control is often not a good case, especially in more systemic games. Ultimately, their versatility creates a strong feeling of safety for the player. Most AI systems heavily rely on them as well—after all, the player is super random for the AI.

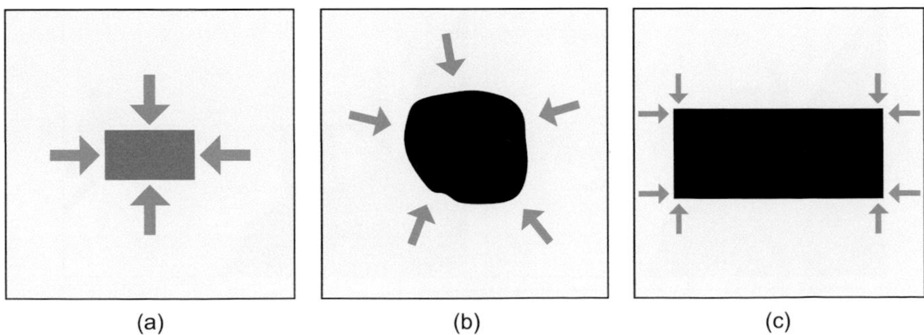


**FIGURE 13.9** (a) The humble crate. (b) A thick tree trunk. (c) A shipping container.

However, things start to get interesting when I compare half and full covers for first- or third-person action games when it comes to this feeling of safety. In third-person games, you can easily look over half cover, which means you do not lose awareness ahead. Moreover, good awareness often directly translates to a faster speed. Hustling from medium to medium cover is a breeze in third-person games, especially if they have a good cover mechanic.

It starts to become different in FPS games, where half cover blocks most or all of my view. You might have gotten a glimpse ahead but that was a momentary view. Additionally, players do not feel too super safe because they could be targeted from the top if an enemy is a bit higher or very close. Additionally, crouching is an additional action players have to perform. Ultimately this combined discomfort means that players often do not stay here very long. However, they are still better than nothing in most cases and by no means a bad design choice—especially in slower-paced and or stealth sections.

AIs do not have such consideration, plus they are often welcomingly visible going from medium to medium cover. Meaning, in heavy action sections, I would say that half cover is probably more commonly placed by level designers for AI than for players. For third-person games, there is not such a perceived differentiation.

When you now look at high cover, then things are again a bit different. Full cover still provides a strong, if not stronger, sense of safety in third-person games, but it lacks the ease of awareness. You can still usually pivot the camera around the corner. Nevertheless, it is an extra conscious action and generally not as revealing as looking over half cover. As a result, I would say that high covers, compared to half-high ones, slow down the flow in third-person games a bit while still providing an excellent sense of safety.

In FPS games, high cover is a bit more preferred. Awareness is reduced but that's similar enough compared to half cover. You typically gain your basic awareness during the approach anyhow. However, safety is top-notch, and I have to run/walk there; no extra crouch action is needed, and those are the primary kickers for me. High covers are stronger player-magnets in FPS games than half covers, which occasionally directly translate to a faster game flow. Sure it drops slightly due to potentially reduced awareness, but the attraction is still stronger in high cover.

For AI, the primary consideration is that they are safe behind high cover. Meaning, unlike with medium cover, there is no off-chance that their head is poking up, leading to a headshot by the players. Otherwise, AI is not aware of their body parts poking out, meaning they can appear stupid or useless cannon fodder, which should not be your intention.

### 13.2.3 Cover at Slopes

So when I am talking about cover at slopes, the primary problem here is with medium-high cover. The first set of problems with them is with slopes that are so steep that they do not generate cover on the upper side and also they are practically useless in multiplayer.

The only practical solution you have is, first of all, to flatten the space behind the cover object, but that obviously might not always work or it might look incredibly gamy. The second solution is to use high covers and hope that your animation system will make feet and legs still look good enough.

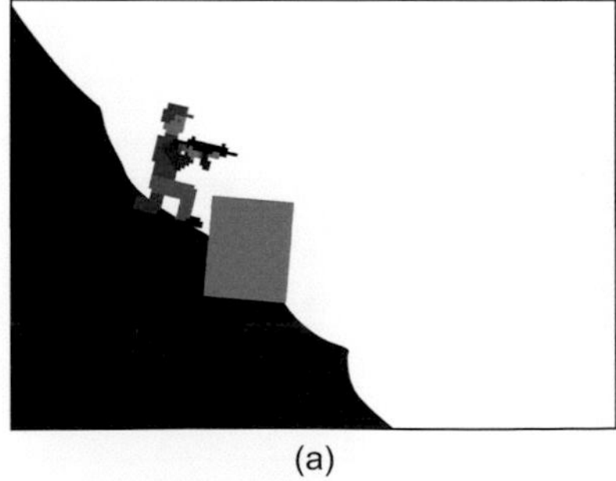

(a)

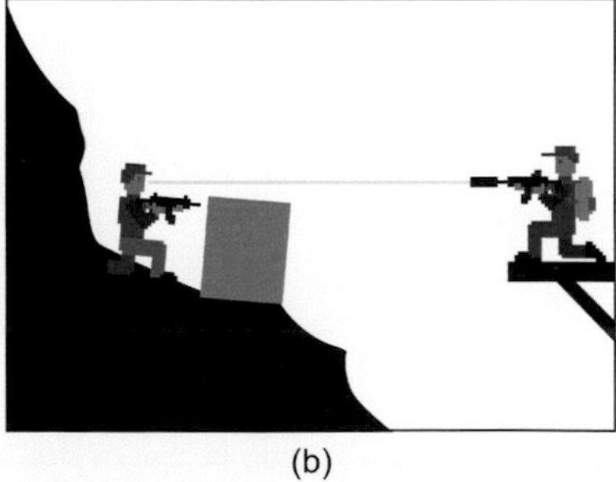

(b)

**FIGURE 13.10** (a) The slope is too steep to generate any valid cover. (b) The slope is gentle enough to generate cover but the head can still poke out.

The next problem with cover at slopes is when it just does generate cover. However, the slope still pushes the character's head over the medium-high cover object, which can look quite stupid. Of course, switching to high cover is again a solid solution—if you can. Otherwise, massaging the slope behind the cover is often more feasible in such cases since the impact is often relatively minimal to the already modified terrain. Sometimes a bit of cover object rotation can do the trick as well.

Finally, I have mentioned high cover several times. So I quickly want to say that a medium-high cover can feel like a high cover against anyone from below within the right circumstances. So, for example, medium-high bushes can quickly conceal standing AI if the players come from below. Just something to keep in mind because it also goes both ways.

### 13.2.4 Thin Cover

The following commonly used cover type is what I call: Thin or two-sided cover. Essentially, the objects are so thin that they only create cover on two opposing sides. Moreover, they exist in medium to full height, but height aspects were already covered previously.

I think good examples are our conveniently placed pieces of corrugated metal along walkway railings, stone walls, really crazy tough and upright wood pallets, or simply your everyday gamy bulletproof solid fence. As you noticed, based on my examples, they often do not reflect everyday real-world objects and their natural properties and their ability to not stop bullets. They certainly are a creation of games and movies, but that is fine.

Despite their unrealistic behavior, as a designer, I do like thin covers quite a lot, and that is because of their ability to control movement. If my thin cover points in the right direction, then I know the player or AI feels safe here, and that can slow down the game speed. Nevertheless, if the object does not point in the right direction of the threat, I can strongly assume that the players and or AI will move. Either they cross the cover-less section quickly, retreat, or find a better cover.

A classic example of this situation is industrial walkways. If the threat is ahead, players cross them as fast as possible or stay on the other side and only cross once the threats are dead. However, if the threats are on the sides below the walkway, then crossing it is slower, using the thin cover in the railing to safely take out enemies.

As you see, they do control the player and AI because if I would have placed crates along the walkway instead of thin cover, then players' behavior would have been very similar for threats ahead and on the sides.

I also like them to guide the players along lanes, affecting their movement and often even their view. A good example is a random cottage in the woods. I only have a few random trees around in the first version, meaning players can move around freely everywhere. However, as I said, they could move anywhere because they have enough cover options around and feel equally safe everywhere. They might not even circle the hut at all.

In the second version, I remove a few trees close by and replace them with a fence around the hut. Sure, you might say that removing the trees would have been enough to guide the players around, but

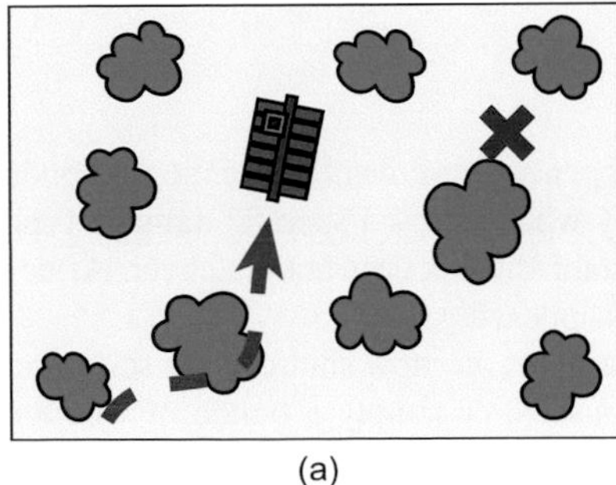

(a)

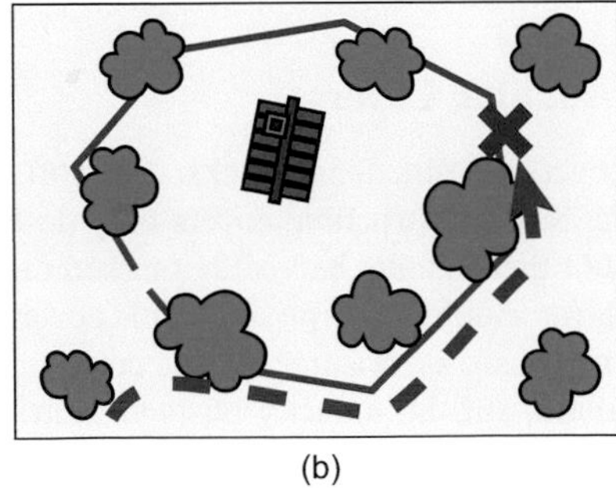

(b)

**FIGURE 13.11** (a) Cottage without fence and subtle players control. (b) The fence around the cottage can guide the players to a specific spot.

the fence adds a level of precision. There is a way higher chance that curious players stick along the fence while circling the building instead of some random trees. Meaning I could, for example, guide them to notice some creepy clues about that cottage making the whole experience way more exciting without any forced hand-holding. Please keep in mind that this is just an incentive and will not work with every player.

Thin cover is so versatile for us level designers because it is so non-versatile for players - but of course, that only works well if the players need safety.

### 13.2.5 Soft and Penetrable Cover

The next type is soft and or penetrable cover. By definition, the objects are not really cover in the classical sense but rather concealment. But anyone who often gets into firefights will explain to you that in lack of cover, concealment is better than nothing. Essentially, they are any large enough objects which hide your presence but barely, or not at all, stop projectiles.

The main difference between soft and penetrable cover is that softcover does not affect the lethality of projectiles. At the same time, penetrable cover can reduce the damage but only to some degree. So they are pretty comparable, and therefore I have grouped them for this chapter. Classic examples are your typical drywalls, infamous car doors, creepily giant teddy bears, unlucky hostages, or simply a leafy bush.

First of all, most better AI systems can read and understand soft cover well enough—within limits and edge cases. Still, most do not know how to handle penetrable cover. Both work the best in multiplayer games, given that low render settings do not ruin vegetation.

Another issue with soft covers is that I am only aware of very few AI systems that systematically consider soft covers as backup covers if there are no hard ones available. After all, concealment is better than nothing, plus it kind of looks smart when AI rather runs from bush to bush (as most humans would) than straight through the open.

Together it means that you need to educate yourself on how your game handles such cover types. How they interact with AI and how you can debug them if some funky edge cases show up.

So, the following statements only reflect games I heard of or worked with.

- Penetrable cover is a feature for players and only accidentally for AI.
- Penetrable cover can add to the realism of your worlds and creates small memorable moments for the player.
- Especially in multiplayer maps, penetrable cover can add extra depth for the more experienced players, but be careful not to overdo it or create too random or frustrating situations.
- Softcover is affecting AI's perception but differently than the human eye would see it. Typically, there is a convex object which affects the AI's raycasting and not, for example, the individual pixels of the plant's leaves.
- Softcover, therefore, is again a cover type attracting primarily players, especially for stealth sections or paths.

### 13.2.6 Destructible Cover

Destructible covers are functional blocks, thin, soft, or penetrable covers. Once they get enough damage, they dismantle. Some destructible covers only destroy when hit by a specific damage type like explosives. Still, all of them should be visibly marked or established as destructible cover. After all, during a firefight, no player should be surprised by his cover disappearing.

Classic examples are surprisingly brittle concrete barriers, window shutters, ice sculptures from your narcissistic villain, still an unlucky hostage, brittle bushes, or simply a bunch of wooden planks. Of course, their use resembles their original cover types, which I have discussed already previously; the destruction is just an additional layer of complexity.

I like to use destructible cover if I want players to move around during combat because often players have their favorite cover spot, and then they sit there till everyone is dead. Destructible cover is one way to approach such a typical situation. Essentially players eventually lose their favorite spot and have to find a new one.

This approach is all good and obvious, but the trick is to guide the player to the next ones you had in mind. Ideally, you guide them to the side or front and not, in the worst case, to a cover behind. Essentially, it comes down to nudge players committing to your space before you use more destructible cover.

Paths of inviting softcover, a well-placed thin cover network, or way bigger gaps behind are cover-centric examples of how you can make players commit. Another trickier way is to mix up the destructible and non-destructible covers, but the solid objects are not the best cover or are less ideal spots. Meaning players do not want to stay here long but keep being drawn to them if their previous, better cover got destroyed. That is easier said than done, especially if your environment has world-building restrictions. For example, suppose your game has destructible vegetation, and you build a forest. In that case, you have to accept that most of your cover will not last long. That is part of the job.

On the flip side, if your game or environment does not support destructible cover, do not force it. Every level designer I know who then started hand-scripting destructible environments was not happy for long. Of course, special scripted events are an exception since I was talking about fake-systemic one-offs, which, again, are very wrong.

### 13.2.7 Bulletproof Glass

Another uncommon type is bulletproof glass, a type often forgotten to be considered as cover. While every previous cover type was at least always concealment but not always real cover, bulletproof glass is the opposite: 100% cover but no concealment. So by definition, you can see through but not engage through this type.

Typical examples are force fields, magic shields, tactically enhanced transparent sugar sheets, or simply, of course, actual bulletproof glass.

The big obvious problem is that I'm not aware of any systemic AI system that can handle such a case very well or at all. At best, any AI behavior was faked with a good script. This circumstance means this cover type is usually only valid for non-combat situations or multiplayer.

It is a classic tool in each level designer's toolbox to allow players to observe an in-game event while preventing any possibility of messing with it. I will not now get into the whole topic of controlled and uncontrolled cutscenes. Still, bulletproof glass has its uses in such cases, but the trickiest part is its justification of existence.

A sci-fi space station having bulletproof glass or force fields is plausible enough, but not an ordinary flower shop from the 1960s. Especially consistency is a big problem. Why is that big house window bulletproof, but the ones in the bathroom are not?

In multiplayer, I would use it carefully at smaller key moments to allow players to get a safe sneak-peek at the opponents. Alternatively, connect it to a specific particular object or exotic environment. However, I would keep its heavy use out of central bigger battle spaces simply because it can quickly become frustrating when used too much.

Finally, make sure that the player language should be very clear. It is pretty frustrating to empty half a magazine into a glass to realize that it is bulletproof.

### 13.2.8 One-Sided Cover

A one-sided cover is an object or terrain which generates only cover toward one direction. Besides the fact that developers often underestimate this cover type, it has an extensive range of appearances. For example, it could be a rock embedded at the bottom of a slope, a simple triangle from the side, or a block cover with all sides but one covered in annoying small objects to prevent any AI cover generation.

Its use is a more controlling one than even the thin cover. You essentially deny the opposing side to use the same cover object. At the same time, you are very deliberate in which single direction to use the cover object. So again, it is a very controlling, almost surgical cover type, which I would be cautious about within a systematic game. Especially systemic AI functions better the more cover is available in most directions.

I see two primary uses for it in a level. The first is at crucial moments where you need the mentioned control or reduce the chance of systemic misbehavior. The second one is its natural appearance. For example, you do not have to justify yourself if a blocky rock, stuck in terrain to create a climbable ledge, only makes cover in one direction. Certain architecture can create similar situations as well.

## 13.3 Cover Flow

### 13.3.1 Introduction

#### *13.3.1.1 Cover Flow Definition*

My core definition of cover flow is that players continuously and smoothly transition between cover objects with the intended speed and face appropriate difficulty.

The continuous and smooth aspects are one of the basic general flow definitions. However, in the context of a game, we have to look beyond it. Therefore, speed and difficulty come into play. Speed in the context of cover, for me, is a mix of distance and rhythm. Finally, the difficult aspect is so crucial because cover without a threat is kind of meaningless. Striking a balance between transition, speed, and difficulty is one of the main challenges dealing with cover.

In this chapter, I focus solely on the flow of singular cover lines because it is easier to explain. However, in reality, you should branch out your lines, creating a cover network. The same methodology applies, just that it features more than one option. I will go into more details about cover networks in general later on, while in this chapter, I focus on the flow alone.

#### *13.3.1.2 When and Why Is Cover Flow Important*

Cover flow might sound intriguing, but it is, first of all, essential to understand that it is not always needed. As I already mentioned, if you do not have an adequate threat, you barely have to think much about cover, and certainly not about many covers connected by a good flow. For example, coming around a house corner and shooting only two minion grunts does not require a lot of cover consideration. However, a threat does not always have to come from action but can, for example, also come from a tense stealth setup.

Secondly, the threat has to last long enough and ideally cover a certain amount of space to be worthy of lengthy flow planning. For example, facing a tank would likely be a challenge, but if it only takes two well-aimed/timed RPG shots, then the fight might be over way too fast. However, suppose it would require careful navigation around the tank under constant enemy fire. In that case, this sounds more like a worthy cover flow consideration. Finally, when I mentioned that it needs space, then I primarily meant space for the player. Depending on the AI system, cover flow can be a significant factor for AI but is most important for the player. Again, it all comes down to providing options again.

However, once we consider all those previous points, the reason why cover flow is so crucial is to guarantee a coherent, smooth and continuous experience in situations where cover is imperative. Combat or stealth situations are already inherently stressful, often complex, and can quickly get messy. Ideally, level design should not worsen it by providing a choppy, confusing, and frustrating experience. Additionally, a good flow feels great for the player, especially when the overall difficulty is high. Finally, it also allows us designers to guide players during intense scenes when we usually "lost" much control over players.

As a general term, many elements play together to achieve wider game flow, and the cover flow is just one of many aspects. However, my general train of thought is that low-level layout is the foundation for all other low-level elements like scripting, pacing, and other game mechanics.

### 13.3.2 Cover Transition

#### *13.3.2.1 Connecting Angle*

The minimum requirement to achieve a smooth and continuous flow between covers is that players must know that there is at least one other cover option available. Therefore, the connecting angle between the

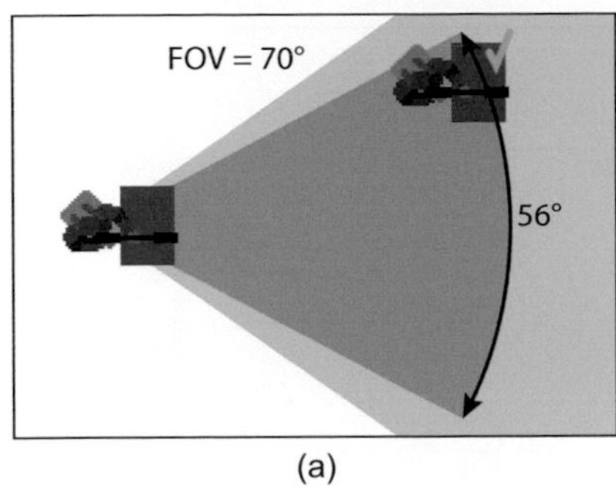


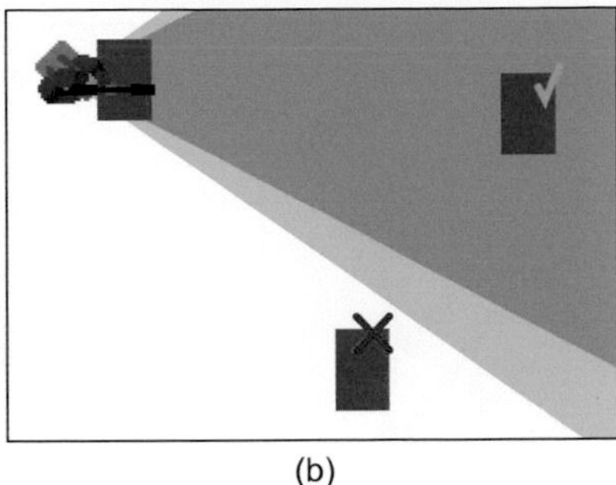


**FIGURE 13.12** (a) The player can easily recognize the next cover objects because it is within their FOV. (b) The player likely misses the cover object to their right because it is outside of their FOV. Therefore, the player unfortunately might transition more uncomfortably to the cover ahead of them.

cover objects is key. Ideally, it is smaller than the field of view (FOV) of your game. So even if they arrive at a less ideal angle, they can still see the next option. For a smooth transition, I recommend placing the following cover objects within a maximum viewing angle of 60% to 80% of the game's FOV. The faster the transition speed, the smaller this angle should be.

In the example graphics above, we have a first-person console game with a common FOV of 70°. Therefore, ideally, the next cover objects should be within a FOV of 56° (= 80% of 70°). In the left picture if the player comes from the left and stops at the first cover object, they can easily spot the next one. However, in the right picture, they might not quickly see it and won't transition to the cover at the bottom. Instead, more likely, many will transition to the one on the far right ahead, even if the distance is a lot further.

In reality, it is not that strict, and I do not remember level designers planning cover flow with a ruler. In the example above, the player could have remembered the bottom cover and then transitioned there. Essentially it all means place the cover objects first as you see fit, then jump in the game and make sure that the next intended cover object is always well and clearly visible from the current one. The 70% to 80% is a guideline and tight buffer to stay on the safe side. The only reason to look at it a bit closer during the first layout is that if you have to move one cover object a lot, you might cause a more considerable ripple effect along the line.

The argument that players remember cover from afar is a very valid one. However, I would be careful relying on it too much because many players understandably quickly forget such elements in the heat of a battle. The vast majority of players are not pro-gamers or what we as developers unfortunately might consider/hope to be average.

Another argument is that players are not still arriving at cover. Of course, they will look around a bit more left and right instead of being stuck straight behind the cover object. However, to keep the flow as smooth and fast as possible, I recommend staying on the safer side. Still, in very slow-paced games with, for example, a strong stealth and exploration focus, I think you can go above even above the FOV, but I would be careful with anything beyond 180° because then it is a backward movement.

### *13.3.2.2 Orientation at Cover*

If we look at the direction players look toward at cover objects, there are a few important factors. The most dominating ones are any attractors, like any immediate or pressing threats or strong player-leading elements. If you can control such elements, you know where players are looking and place the next cover accordingly to keep the flow intact.

However, in many games, such precise control is not realistic. Especially in systemic games, AI tends to be all over the place, even though the general direction is still possible in several cases, when, for example, players attack or defend a location. Still, the next defining element you can rely on is the approaching vector. Essentially the angle of how players would approach the next cover object coming from the previous one. However, I would not be too stringent about it because players can still strafe, especially when the attractors are in a very different direction.

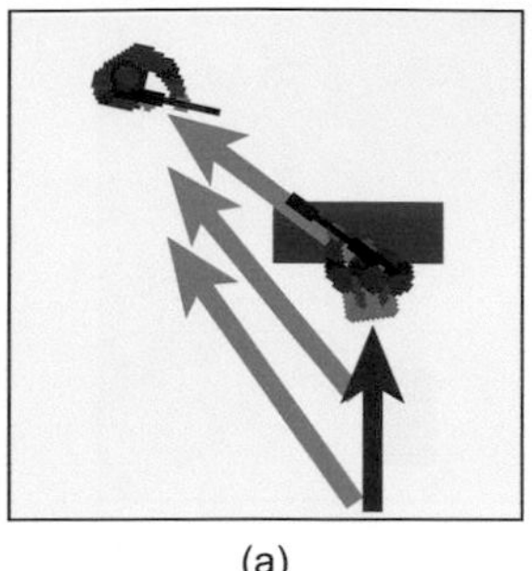
(a)

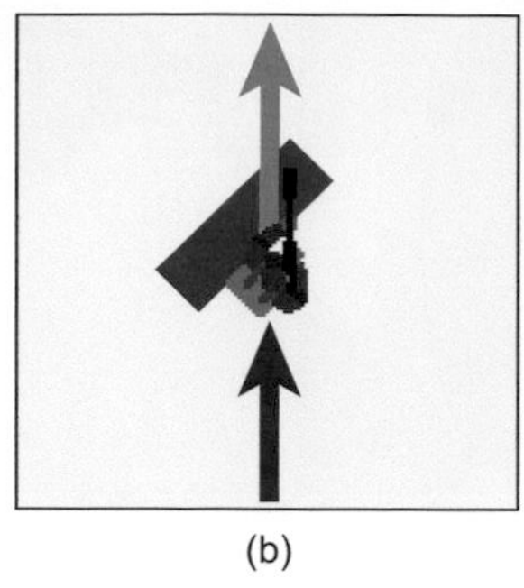
(b)

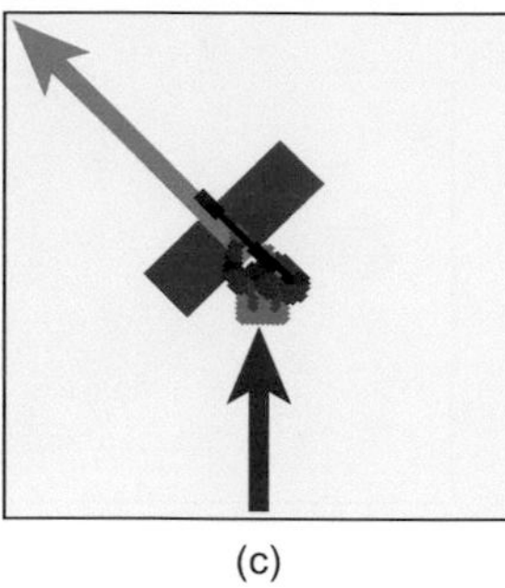
(c)

**FIGURE 13.13** (a) A strong attractor like a threat is the primary reason for players to rotate the FOV at cover. (b) The arrival vector is the next strongest factor that affects the FOV at a cover object. (c) Finally, many players rotate themselves perpendicular to the cover object at arrival.

Another softer yet still functioning factor is the orientation of the cover object itself. Especially in slower-paced or cover-centric games, players often orient themselves perpendicular to the object's surface they face. It is not the most decisive factor, but I have also seen it happening in more frantic scenarios. This factor works well if the cover object is flat because players typically prefer the longer side over the shorter, less safe feeling side.

### *13.3.2.3 Cover Placement Considerations*

If the initial cover object allows full view, you, as the level designer, have the complete FOV available to create a proper cover flow. However, if the cover is blocking the view and the player can only see limited parts of the battlefield ahead, you must consider that players will not look perfectly straight ahead. Expect players to only properly see or understand what is further away from the direct straight line. This realization is especially crucial with larger high cover, for example, larger structures. Therefore, do not expect players to use cover within the wall, especially if it is an opening.

However, you often want players to follow large walls as a guiding element and often guide them into a building. Therefore, I recommend placing a cover object in front of the opening. Such a cover object acts as an attractor till players recognize the opening next to it, plus it provides a good starting block going forward if any player or AI wants to leave through this opening. Alternatively, you can place a cover object in front of the opening ahead of the opening. From here, the player can see the opening, too, and you do not obstruct the straight flow along the wall.

### *13.3.2.4 Transitioning between Covers*

I have already covered this topic in the previous "Cover Mentality" chapter, but it is important to mention it again in more detail in the context of cover flow. By definition, a cover is typically a place of safety. Therefore, leaving it to get to the next POA should be as smooth as possible for a good flow. A transition is choppy the more rotations players have to perform, and the larger the rotations are. Typically the longer distance between the cover objects, the smoother the transition, but distance also has considerations (see further below). Any larger rotation is a chance to lose orientation or awareness of threats ahead temporarily. However, players could counter this issue if they strafe, but the more strafes you add to the transition, the more difficult you make it again for certain players.

If the next cover object is precisely in front of the current one, and if the player only uses 90° rotations, they have to rotate four times in total 360°. However, this is not how most players move in reality. Anyone more comfortable with the controls will typically have at least one or two strafes and an angled transition. However, if you look at the movement curve above, it is not very straightforward either. Additionally, never blame players for not connecting cover in a smooth flow. Instead, offset the next cover to reduce noise in the player's movement, including vaulting or jumping over cover. That is also the reason why arranging cover for leap-frogging is so popular, despite its limitations.

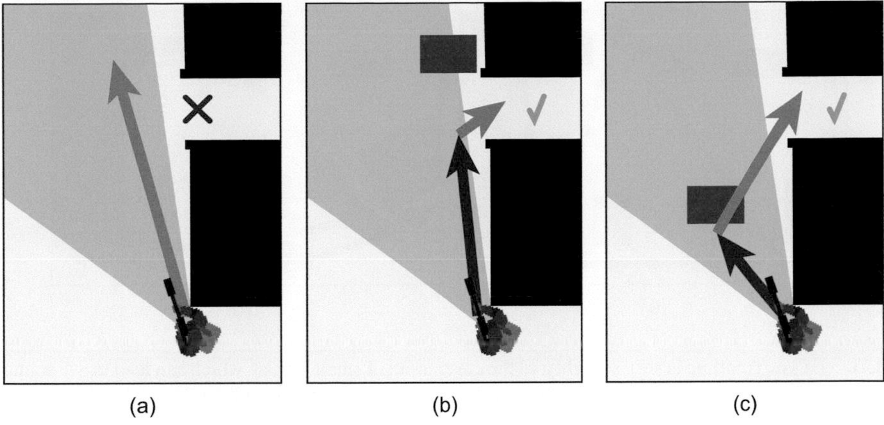


**FIGURE 13.14** (a) From the corner the player has trouble to spot the entrance to the right. (b) The cover object attracts the player to go along the wall and as a result they spot the entrance. (c) Alternativly, players could spot the entrance from a cover object ahead of the entrance.

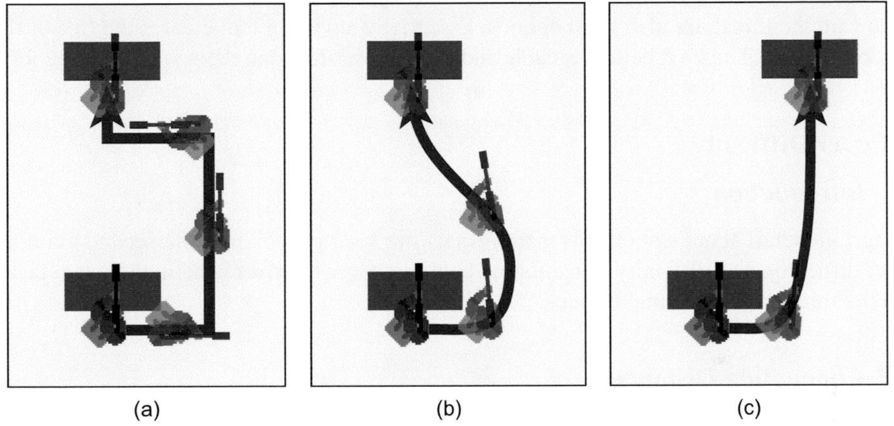


**FIGURE 13.15** (a) Four 90° rotations to get to the cover straight ahead. (b) One strafe to the right, then forward movement with another strafe to the left to the cover straight ahead. (c) Only one strafe to the right and then forward to the cover offset ahead.

### *13.3.2.5 Flow with Frontlines*

Frontlines are very common cover constructs in action games. First of all, a frontline in level design is defined by cover going left and right while the threat is ahead. However, they bear considerations regarding smooth transitions because the cover is on their sides, outside their FOV looking at the threat. However, if you introduce the frontline early enough, players can remember and understand the cover layout concept. Still, this only works well if the frontline and its cover options are well visible and clearly readable so the player has enough time to grasp the concept. Remember to not count on players remembering a single cover object outside of their FOV. In the case of a frontline, it has to be a lot bigger and more covered to stay in players' minds.

Further on, if possible by world-building, I recommend orienting the frontline not perfectly straight but covered toward the threat. It makes any movement, whether rotating or strafing, a lot more comfortable if it keeps pointing toward the threat. Even a slight curve is already helping to make transitioning between cover options more enjoyable—think about a lens focusing on the threat.

An important consideration building frontlines is the style of cover. The ideal cover is anything that follows the frontline, highlights its sideways direction, and makes transitioning between positions

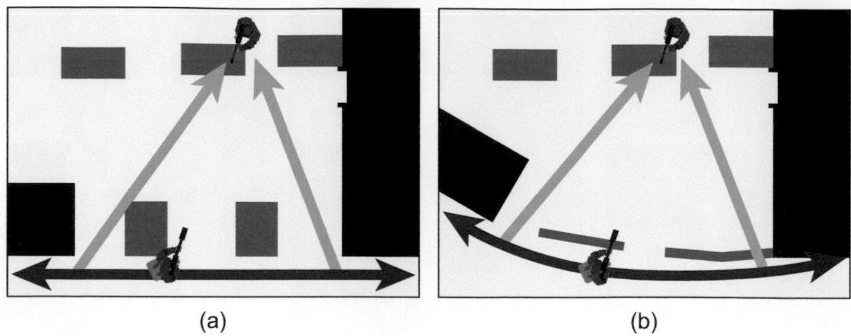


**FIGURE 13.16** (a) The frontline is very straight and the cover is out of small blocks, which can lead to a less smooth cover flow sideways. (b) The frontline is curved inwards toward the side of the threat(s) and the thin, curved, and leading cover helps to have a smoother cover flow sideways.

smoother. Of course, a classic example is trenches, but in the reality of most games, I think an extended thin cover is the better option. As I previously mentioned already, they are ideal for guiding players along a line, and in this case, especially sideways. Alternatively, any lengthy cover objects with long sides pointing toward the threat are also good options. Essentially anything that creates the line of the frontline with cover helps to make it better readable and easier to strafe along them while aiming forward.

### 13.3.3 Cover Difficulty

#### *13.3.3.1 Introduction*

After going into detail about smooth cover transitions, we have to look into the second main aspect of cover flow: difficulty. The difficulty transitioning between cover-to-cover is defined by two factors: distance and the threat traversing the distance.

#### *13.3.3.2 Connecting Distance*

Let us start with the two problematic cases, too-short distance and too long distance. A too-short distance is by tendency very safe to traverse, but it often feels pointless, and often the transition is not very smooth due to many tight movements in a short time. Therefore it either feels out of place or like a hick-up in the flow. Therefore in many cases, players skip the closer options but then feel forced to use the long distance, potentially missing other options visible only from the skipped cover.

A too long distance to the next cover has issues as well. Often players do not even recognize it because it is too far away or if they do, they consider it too risky. Therefore, players often stop and start looking for an alternative, safer route, consequently dropping out of the flow and losing focus altogether. If there is really no alternative route, running a long distance between covers can feel like I missed something, I am playing the game wrong, and it does not make me feel smart.

I recommend testing out what is a good cover distance in your game. As an average base time for action games, I usually say three seconds plus minus one, at maximum speed. I recommend not playing too perfectly to simulate more realistic player actions. Therefore, have a few turns instead of only strafing or do not sprint perfectly the entire way.

Anything above four seconds can already be long in a firefight, and two seconds is borderline too short. Anything longer than five to six seconds starts feeling way too uncomfortable for my taste, and it better comes with a proper POA like a compelling shooting position, powerup, or flanking position. It gets especially tricky in vast open worlds where it is absolutely impossible to provide cover every three to six seconds. My given times above are solely for dedicated combat zones. For stealth, scenarios feel free to deduct one or two seconds from the upper limit, but first, get a feel for your particular game!

#### *13.3.3.3 Connecting Threat*

However, the distance alone is irrelevant without looking at the threat traversing between covers. Sprinting for seven seconds to the next cover can feel like a lifetime in an insane bullet hail, but it is just a plain boring, at best mundane, action with no severe risk.

The worst outcome is especially the risk of absolute failure, like upon detection in a forced-stealth scenario or straight-up death. Failure upon detection traversing between covers should absolutely be a deterministic risk for the player, but timing can become tight before reaching the next safe spot. A cover distance where on average, players lose above two-thirds of their health is a very high risk, regardless of their distance (and I'm thinking about games with regenerating shields/health).

However, on the one hand, longer transition times could give players more options to mitigate incoming damage by, for example, killing enemies along the way, sliding, smoke grenades, force fields, or covering fire. Of course, that doesn't mean that long distances are safer now! Also, players have the same options at shorter distances, but they do not always feel necessary. On the flip side, longer distances also give enemies more time to react and engage the player. Especially when you fight AI, reaction and detection time are crucial when evaluating the threat from cover to cover. Therefore, in many games, the transition between covers is, on average, rather a small risk because the AI is slow to react, being an adequate risk.

I would consider losing one to two-thirds of health between covers medium to high risk, depending on if players have health regeneration and how fast it is. Consequently, zero to one-third of health loss is medium to low risk.

Still, my estimates above are for the heart of the combat zone, but it should all start a bit more collected. Most combat or stealth scenarios start with a low threat to ease players into the player flow. The deeper players progress within your cover flow, the higher the threat can be. The initial short phase was primarily there to lure them in and give them a sense of safety until it is too late, and they then have to deal with the threats. Once players eliminate the threats or they reach the end of the beat, the difficulty drops again, of course.

Looking at the pacing of your level or mission, you have the ups and downs of beats, then comes the internal rhythm of each beat individually, and then even micro intensity curving switching from POA to POA. By no means should anyone map out such pacing in detail! However, understanding that each part follows a rhythm and melody from the macro to the micro is crucial in creating a coherent flow.

### 13.3.4 Cover Speed

#### *13.3.4.1 Introduction*

After going into detail about smooth cover transitions and difficulty, we have to look into the third and final aspect of cover flow: speed.

Essentially, any cover that players might consider relevant in the current threat situation slows down the speed. At cover, players stop for at least one second or more, and therefore they slow down. Any section where they do not have such a cover object or other similar POA, they tend to move faster, will not stop, and instead, bridge the space quickly.

#### *13.3.4.2 Why Control Speed*

It is important to control the cover speed because, at times, I want to slow down players or want them to cross a space quickly. It does not only help to establish a good rhythm, but it also directly correlates with distance and difficulty. I want players to slow down to give them an advantage against threats ahead.

However, I also do not want them to overcommit or rush ahead because otherwise, they might miss crucial environmental clues (e.g., narrative, alternative routes, or gameplay elements like explosive barrels, ammo, sniper spots, mounted machine guns, or hidden enemies/mines). It also helps control the pacing of space because, like with the pacing of beats, you need some low-intensity moments to cherish the fast-paced ones.

One reason I want players to accelerate is that I want them to commit to a space ahead, either to reduce the chance of luring too much AI in a disadvantageous situation, reduce the chance of them moving backward again, or so they run into a trigger I need for the next script. Another reason comes down to rhythm and pacing again. It is hard to create an action-packed or tense stealth section without the occasional risky mad-dash.

Speed control is also crucial if you want to balance out long and shorter paths, as I mentioned in the abstract mid-level chapter of this book. However, the type of balance is essential. Sometimes you want to keep a longer path fast, but that also makes it less safe, or you want to reward players taking the long path by making it safer, even if that makes it slower. The same counts for the shorter, often middle routes or shortcuts. Often a well-designed fast yet unsafe middle section intensifies the control fight for the heart of your map. Alternatively, you can make the shorter route slower to balance out the faster, longer flanking routes.

Therefore, the interworking of high and slow speed is essential for a good flow. For more linear experiences, slow down before a bigger moment, or for more open/multiplayer experiences before entering a significant location. It is like the calm before the storm, but a storm would be quite lame if the storm never comes.

### 13.3.4.3 Abstract Understanding

In my opinion, the best way to work with, visualize, or explain cover speed is to go back to some more abstract thinking. I start by drawing cover lines along the main cover direction. If players in a certain direction have to move through many lines, I know that the cover speed is slow here. If players move along or between the lines, I know they likely move a lot faster here. I can apply this thinking either reactively or proactively—I can do that to analyze an existing location or set a location's fundamental cover direction.

The red arrows represent slow yet safe traversal between bases A and B. The blue arrows are fast segments. Of course, the arrows are the opposite if players would move or fight from side to side. The simple

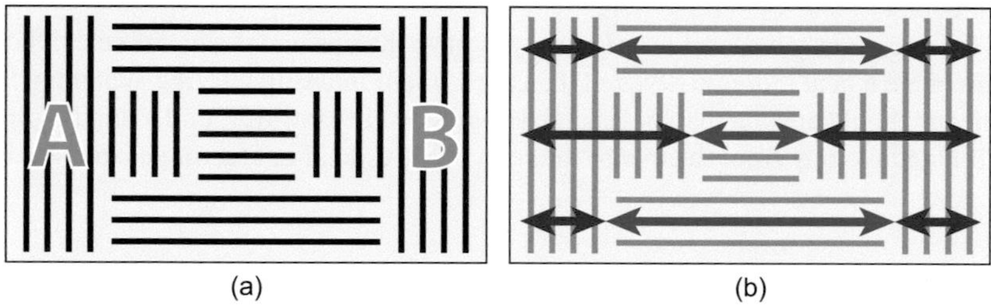


**FIGURE 13.17** Cover orientation and how it affects player speed going between A and B.

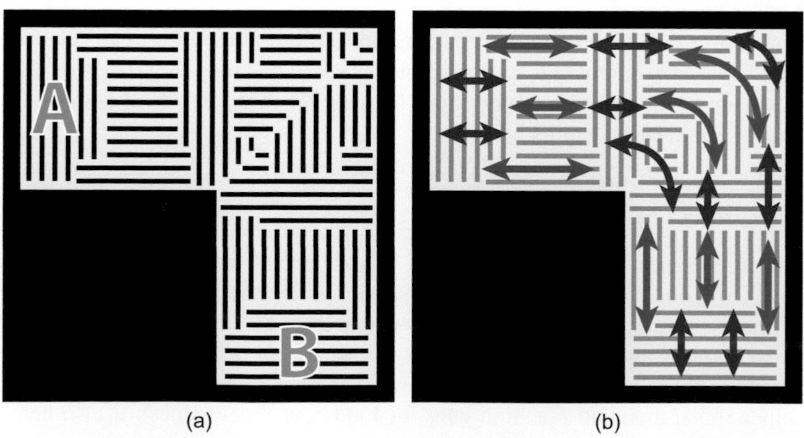


**FIGURE 13.18** Cover orientation example in a L-shaped room and how it affects player speed going between A and B.

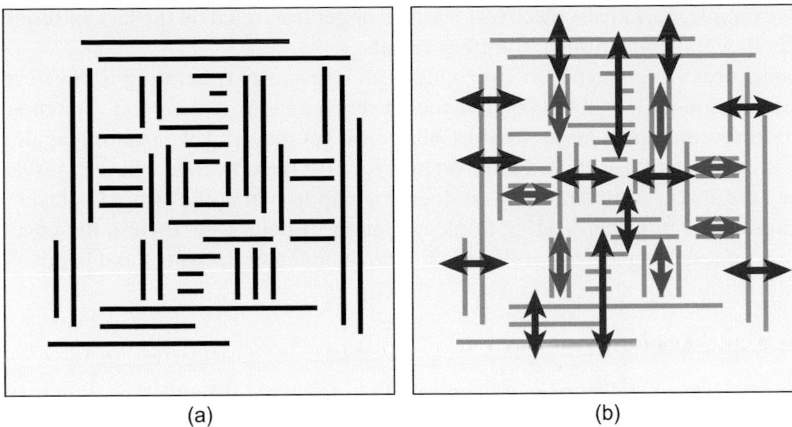


**FIGURE 13.19** Cover orientation example of an open-world location and how it affects player speed coming from the four main sides.

example above shows two fast flanking routes to balance out the longer route while the middle only has a small quick segment, accompanied by two longer slower-paced parts toward the heart of the bases.

The example graphic above is a loose recollection of an airsoft field where I helped the owners redesign their arena. Their problem was that their field was an L-shaped warehouse and that they did not have much space. They had two bases A and B, which I represented by the respective horizontal lines because they had to offer a strong defense against any attackers. In front of the bases, the cover speed should have been fast, requiring any attackers to prepare and make one last rush to enter the bases. However, the cover orientation here also allowed it to attack from multiple sides without too much exposure from both flanks. Before, the mad-dash zone had to be some staging cover with therefore slower speed. It was important to slow down the speed even further along the short connection at the field's inner corner because it was the shorter one and a key spot to control the middle of the field. However, the longer path through the middle should have been faster again to compensate for the longer route. The slow upper right corner had the purpose of creating a staging ground for any sneaky long-distance flanking on the outer edge of the field. All long and short routes between the two bases were now a lot more balanced and offered different types of playstyles.

The example graphic above shows a quick cover speed sketch of a small open-world location. For simplification, I kept all arrows at 90°, but of course, they can be at any angle. Several slow covers surround it as staging grounds, vantage points, or sniper spots. Then there are two slower routes to the central location for either sneaky players or AI to leave the location safely. Otherwise, the routes from the outside to the location are fast. Reversely they can act as cover for AI or players fighting on the sides. Otherwise, the central location has a much dense, slow cover protecting the location. After all, the defenders' goal is to stay safe, and they have no severe need to traverse outside, leaving their objective area.

## 13.4 Player Leading

### 13.4.1 Introduction

Player leading is by many considered another core level design skill. It is an art form to guide the player through space how you, the designer, had intended it without the player noticing a "higher creative force" involved, especially the infamous waypoints. It gets increasingly more complicated the more things the player should do while the intensity and distractions arise.

Especially early playtesting levels exist to investigate how successful the player leading is. Suppose players do not recognize all of your level's elements successfully. In that case, they likely fail to understand, for example, narrative, objectives, features or get frustrated by the lack of progress and success. Plus, likely they miss out on some stunning visuals.

On the flip side, observing playtesters over video can be equally frustrating for us developers. You created the most stunning art up in the sky, and the players only look at their feet. You thought you created an easy-to-understand path far around the obstacles, yet players keep running against it. Players keep staring at all your carefully crafted hints on how to solve the objective, but they just keep on moving and say they are stuck. At that moment, it does not help to blame the "stupid" player, but instead, you should reconsider your player-leading implementation. If done well, then in the next playtest you magically have a lot less "stupid" players, but just more competent designers and happy players.

### 13.4.2 Moving and Looking

Before I start to go deeper into the topic, it is important to reinforce the understanding that player leading is about guiding both the look and the movement of the player. However, both intentions have very different tools at their disposal. In some cases, the methods overlap but it is important to differentiate them during the design process.

Make it clear in your head if you want the player to look at something or go somewhere. Then think about all the different methods and apply the correct ones in your current context. Depending on your game or the players' situation those tools can heavily vary.

As much as possible try to avoid expecting too much from the player at the same time. In recent years, game mechanics and worlds increase in complexity and it is not fair to take it for granted that players look up at the right spot, understand the puzzle's solution while also grasping the deep narrative's impact in the same moment. Break it into easily digestible bites and have some breaks in between. You make it easier for yourself and ultimately for the player.

### 13.4.3 "Sins" of Player Leading

#### *13.4.3.1 Introduction*

When I am writing here about "sins," then I mean player-leading tools and solutions, but the ones which, in my opinion, we should avoid, or at least try to reduce. They are either very gamy solutions that remove players' feeling of succeeding or relying on developers' unrealistic expectations of the players' attention (span).

However, many of the methods here are well established in certain games or genres. Therefore, first of all, it is not easily possible to remove them. It requires much effort from the developer side and I recommend changing the game fundamentals only during the initial conceptual time. It is especially unrealistic to successfully remove or reduce any of those tools in the middle of production because the game's direction has shifted too far. More often than none, the game still ended up with those tools again, despite wasted time and effort.

Secondly, players have expectations, too. If, for example, the last ten installments of your game worked with a certain tool, then it is tough to remove them in the next sequel successfully. Potentially it might cause fan confusion or even frustration and should be carefully introduced and, more importantly, well justified. I am all for reducing or removing those "sins," but it cannot go along with lots of (wasted) development time and too many unhappy fans.

#### *13.4.3.2 Waypoints*

Let us start with the most obvious and probably most common player-leading game element: the waypoint. To quickly clarify, we are talking about points set by the game, not by the players themselves. They are head-up display (HUD) elements marking a spot in the 3D space of your game and occasionally include a distance indicator. The use of waypoints as a development guide-tool is controversial among certain developers, which it is for a good reason.

First of all, it takes away any agency of the players to go where they want. For example, objectives update, and then a dot shows up on the players' screen, telling them where to go. Now, the players have no choice but to go where the game tells them to move, or their objectives will not progress. The players never had a chance to figure it out by themselves. Of course, non-arguably many players do not want to figure it out by themselves and instead enjoy such hand-holding, especially in larger (open-world) games. Again, as I previously mentioned, it heavily depends on your game type, player audience, and your game's legacy.

Secondly, very often, players are so used to being guided by waypoints that the vast majority runs straight toward them. I stopped counting playtesters running against walls or jumping down a cliff because they followed a waypoint. As frustrating as it is to watch as a developer, the players felt very frustrated as well. Unfortunately, often due to production time and game restraints, the main developer reaction is to add even more waypoints, guiding the players along a tight chain of dots.

In my opinion, depending on the context, game, and especially scale, it is okay to use waypoints. Using a waypoint to guide the player to a location several kilometers away is acceptable because teaching all players to become girl or boy scouts using a compass, clues, and a map is not always practical for players and developers alike. Ideally, players have a choice whether they want some hand-holding or not. Still, if you use any waypoints, expect players to run toward it in a straight line, regardless of whether a mountain, minefield, or evil flushing maelstrom is in between.

However, the problem arises if you use too many waypoints in short succession. The more waypoints you use, especially in smaller, confined environments, the more agency you remove from them. In such cases, I firmly believe we have better tools that do not give the impression that we think the players are "stupid" and need detailed guidance. Still, I understand it is tricky because much better tools are not easy to add to your level at the times it typically makes sense to have playtests. It often requires major reworks, which are then too costly, and you have no other choice to go back to more waypoints again.

Therefore, you need to think about player leading right from the beginning. Set yourself the goal to use little or even no waypoints at all. It is comforting to know that you have it as a backup solution, but if you do not try to avoid them from the beginning, you will rather end up with way more than a few acceptable ones. Kudos to every game which made it with no waypoints. Sure for some, it is a lot easier than for others, but it should remain our goal as developers to give as much agency to the players.

#### *13.4.3.3 Compass*

I am talking here about usually a HUD element, typically a bar on the top of your screen, which indicates the direction you are facing. There is, of course, nothing wrong with such an element. However, it gets tricky when it includes, for example, objective markers, NPC position, harvesting spots or vehicle locations—essentially waypoints and more.

Not only does it include similar problems like the classic waypoint on your screen, but it also gets worse if it gets too crowded with markers while it typically lacks any decent feeling for distance. Additionally, if the objective marker is much above or below the players, the compass struggles to be a decent helper because it is typically horizontal oriented. In such cases, it can be especially frustrating and confusing for the players.

Therefore, my recommendations are the same for waypoints. Additionally, limit the number of marker types and the number of markers at the same time. I appreciate the notion of decluttering your screen, but only if it is reducing the problems, not adding more or different ones.

#### *13.4.3.4 Minimap*

Like the compass, the minimap has similar issues to the waypoint. It is another game-centric tool to precisely tell players where to go with little to no agency for them. Commonly it is in the corner of your screen indicating the direction of the next objective marker, and once they are close, it shows where on the map the target is located.

Like the compass, it quickly can get too cluttered if the game fills the minimap with way too many other game elements. Additionally, if the waypoint is too far away, getting a distance-feeling is not always possible. It is also not always easy with a minimap to indicate if an objective marker is far above or below the players. A unique problem for minimaps is that often players do not pay much attention to it because it is so small in the corner of their screens, or they focus on it too much ignoring what's happening on the rest of the screen.

If your game relies on waypoints and features a minimap, they should be combined and support each other. However, address topics like icon density early. I would recommend not relying exclusively on the minimap for level design, except we are talking here about elements that are otherwise way too messy to realize. For example, this could be, displaying a precise zone or showing icons for which you do not want to use the infamous waypoints.

#### 13.4.3.5 Text Briefings

Giving the players a lengthy text briefing with much vital player-leading information at the beginning of a mission or level is a bit old school but still not uncommon, especially for lower budget games or when for example, text notes come into play. The problem arises when you, as a developer, assume that the player remembers any bit of critical information on how to navigate through the challenges ahead.

Accept that most players will not remember or make notes. Even if players can re-access the text during play, in some menus, it is still far away from ideal in relatively fast-paced action games. It can work in the context of slower exploration of role-playing games, but I would be careful not to use it too much for main quest lines. You know that something went wrong when most players use more external sources from the internet to find their objective than the in-game tools.

Again, especially in action games, I would avoid using text briefings as a medium for critical information, especially for player leading. You have better, more elegant, and modern methods at your disposal.

#### 13.4.3.6 Cutscenes

Like, text briefings, cutscenes at the beginning of a level can include a load of vital player-leading information. Again, the problems start when developers assume the player paid close attention to details, and even worse, believe that they remembered them.

There are so many reasons why players ignore or miss parts of cutscenes. They might be annoyed by them and want to go back to play, get distracted by siblings, pets, parents, or babies, want to have a bit of a break, or are simply tired. I have seen playtesters taking off their headphones every time they watched a cutscene. I do not know why they did it, but those things happened.

This reality should not prevent developers from adding important information to cutscenes, but nobody should expect all players to remember details from them ten to twenty minutes later in the level. Instead, reinforce and repeat the information in other forms or shapes such as objective texts, dialogs, radio messages, or other visual means.

#### 13.4.3.7 Audio

Unfortunately, audio is another "sin" of player leading. However, it is absolutely not a sin to use audio, of course! The problems arise when you exclusively rely on audio as a player-leading tool. This case could be anything like an informative radio call, objective-updating NPC dialog, or a noise supposedly guiding the player to a collectible or treasure.

It saddens me to say, but in theory, using audio for such cases always sounds great because audio is unfortunately often underutilized. However, way too often, players miss such audio clues, have their headphones off, get distracted, or even have audio off. Of course, it is also a matter of accessibility since deaf players should also enjoy your game. Therefore I can only recommend not exclusively using audio for player leading.

Instead, use audio in conjunction with other methods. It is excellent to reinforce other player-leading elements, for when players pay attention, but if they don't, then there should be other clues around to help them going forward.

#### 13.4.3.8 The One Solution

I've already hinted at this case when I talked about exclusively audio for player leading. The reality is that you should avoid using only one player-leading element exclusively. Players in modern games are often so overwhelmed with the amount of information and visual fidelity we put on their screens that it is not unrealistic to assume that they miss crucial clues about where to go or what to do. Therefore, I recommend consistently applying multiple player-leading tools.

For example, the players might miss the guiding NPC going around the corner, but then you also pay attention to the flow of the environment, have light coming around the corner, and have the NPC shout from around the corner. Every element you add and combine with the others increases the chance that the players catch one or more of them.

I agree; the infamous waypoint is one of the rare player-leading tools which can work exclusively. However, the big advantage is that the more other elements you combine, the less likely you might need more waypoints, especially at shorter distances—and I believe every waypoint we prevent saves at least one kitten and puppy!

#### *13.4.3.9 "Left Corner"*

There is the "rumor" floating around the internet and among certain developer circles that most players prefer to go left, instead of right. It might have come from playing a lot of Dungeon & Dragons or thinking early developers of 3D shooters build their levels from left to right. Some think it has something to do with controllers as most players are right-handed. The point is that there is not enough clear evidence. So, feel free to treat it as fake news, level design conspiracy or simply superstition.

I never followed such a rule and never had any issues with it. I saw countless playtesters going right because most level designers don't give players two 100% equal left or right opportunities. Any decent level designers or environment artists add some hints which path they would prefer the players to take—even if it is just subconscious or accidental. Therefore, I can only recommend you to ignore it as well, but if you do follow it then manage your expectations.

### 13.4.4 Layout and Flow

#### *13.4.4.1 Funneling, Angles, or Macro Flow*

This classic player-leading concept uses big shapes, angles, and a mix of large rooms and small exits to push the player in a direction gently. Essentially it is the level design equivalent of a fish trap. You are attracted to a small exit/entrance and enter a bigger space, but you already clearly identify the next exit/entrance when you enter the wider area.

The almost instant introduction of the next exit is key. The players always know how to progress when they enter a new space. Space can be a tight apartment hallway, large warehouse, huge train yard, or a massive island in a pool of hot steaming devil excretion. Regardless of the scale, the rules are always the same.

First of all, the transition between the areas makes sure that players are already looking ideally in the exit direction. Secondly, when they enter the new space, the players have a moment to rest to have enough time to recognize the exit. Thirdly major shapes are pointing or are angled toward the exit; comparable

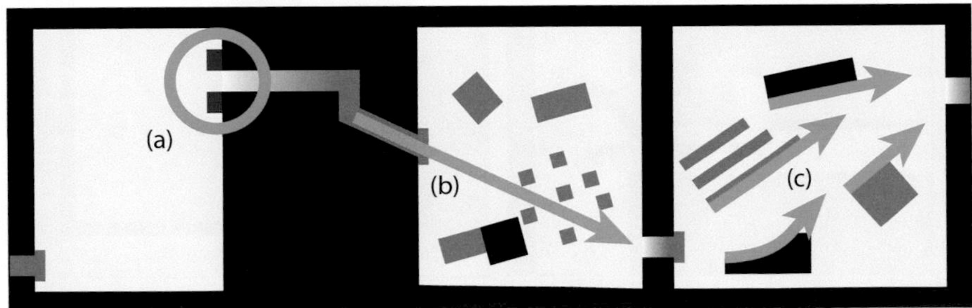


**FIGURE 13.20** (a) The exit stands out from the background or is marked by a significant landmark. (b) The transition guides the players' look toward the exit. (c) Macro composition aims the players' look toward the exit.

to composition elements point toward your focal point in a painting. Fourthly the exit is clearly recognizable as an exit or at least stands out. Either your game has a certain player language that indicates transitions or exists, or at least the exit correlates to a unique, memorable, and standout asset. This asset could be, for example, an elevator, a bright glowing exit sign, an open, massive repair hall gate, or a jump-pad surrounded by a tornado of sparkles.

The more rules you can apply, the more solid your player leading will be. Keep in mind that this method is not limited to enclosed, connected arenas but works in open-world contexts, too. However, you might have to be more strict since quickly, players might get distracted and leave your orchestrated space.

#### *13.4.4.2 Micro Flow*

This player-leading tool is all about using smaller objects to make careful player orientation adjustments, making a big difference. It happened so often that I saw players entering a room, looking around a bit from the entrance, maybe going to the dresser to loot it and then leaving again. Most of them have not recognized that the right corner includes a window that leads outside—and all that because most of them turned right and not left after looting the dresser.

The reasonable assumption is that players rotate rather toward the obtuse angle instead of the acute angle once close to an object. It is simply a human thing and a matter of smooth flow of movement and view. Our goal as level designers is to use objects or small architectural modifications to affect the before-mentioned angles. So, for example, a shopping cart on the left side of the hallway means that players have to move on the right side and, moving forward, look slightly more toward the left. In my next example, I could add a bed in the room to affect the angle when approaching the dresser or move the room's entrance. Of course, there are other methods to get the players out of the window, but the microflow is an exquisite one and works well in conjunction with other player-leading tools such as light, animations, or audio.

#### *13.4.4.3 Architecture*

Okay, just saying architecture is a player-leading tool is very broad. In this context, I mean a players' familiarity with common architecture and their resulting expectations. For example, toilets are typically dead-ends, restaurants have a kitchen with a back entrance, supermarkets always have a warehouse and a larger store-front with shelves, or underground parking lots have separate exits for cars or passengers.

Of course, there are always exceptions to such otherwise accepted standards. However, it is okay to rely on the fundamental rules accepted by our society. So, for example, players can expect that if they enter an underground parking lot by the car-ramp, to find a door and a staircase. You can be certain that most players will look for it and go there at least once.

However, make sure that you follow local cultural rules depending on your level's location and audience expectations. A dingy restaurant in the northern mountains of Thailand might not follow the same rules as a neighborhood hipster BBQ joint in Toronto. Also, I was primarily referring to standards known

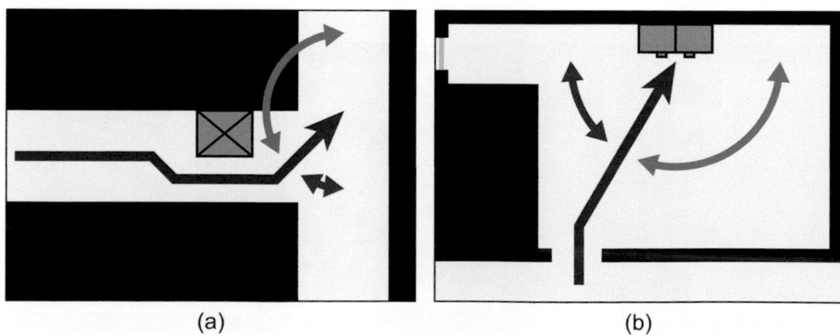


**FIGURE 13.21** (a) More players likely going left here because the crate changed the angle. (b) Players likely won't see the window on the left if attracted by the dresser.

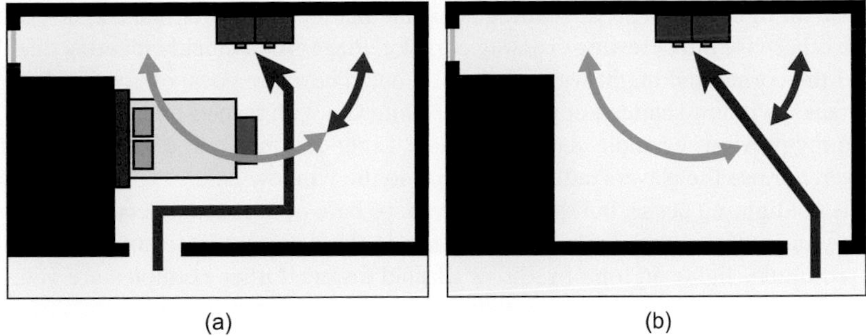


**FIGURE 13.22** (a) The added bed changes the approach angle to the dresser, increasing the chance to spot the window. (b) The new entrance position changes the approach angle, too.

to wider "western" societies, but they can alter if your audience is very unfamiliar with them. I must recommend being culturally sensitive and doing your research.

Additionally, be careful about changing such rules. If suddenly all bathrooms in your downtown LA goth clubs are not dead-ends, then do not expect most of your players to know just because you are an active clubber in that scene. Still, if well introduced and justified, then breaking the rules can, of course, be very refreshing and memorable. Just be careful, do not overdo it, and, again, make sure you did your research before—not every broken rule is cool, unique, and still makes sense.

#### *13.4.4.4 Vantage Point = Player Teaching*

The vantage point is not necessarily a player-leading tool, but I want to reinforce its significant role to teach the player where to go. It is a calm moment at the beginning of a new action bubble or around an open-world location. Here, ideally, the players should not just make plans to elegantly murder every AI down there but instead also plan how to progress or traverse the location.

For that matter, from vantage points, you should provide the players with the correct, clearly identifiable traversal indicators. After all, it is often reasonable to climb a tree in a survival situation to see where to go. The same goes for vantage points and player leading.

If, for example, from a higher-up billboard around your gas station location, you show players an inviting sewer hole. Then players should expect that they can crawl through it and likely infiltrate the center's location. Hiding that sewer entrance or only making it visible from odd angles drastically decreases the chance that players will use, hence this would be bad player leading. Ideally, all main navigation options and paths are visible from your location's outer or inner vantage points. Here you can teach players about the location, and they can make educated decisions.

### 13.4.5 Art Elements

#### *13.4.5.1 Lighting*

I want to believe that lighting is the first art-related player-leading tool for most of us. It is so incredibly versatile and striking. We might not be moths, but we humans are certainly drawn to light, too. Light for player leading has three primary uses.

The first one is to highlight an area, character, or object. For this method to work effectively, most of the surrounding environment needs to be relatively dark because otherwise, the highlight does not create enough contrast. There are many reasons why bright spots attract players in the dark. One reason is, of course, that it is the only thing they can see, so naturally, they want to investigate it. The second one is that it is simply a common language in games; developers highlight things for players to investigate. This could be anything ranging from lit research facilities in a desert night, light in a particular door, to sunbeams highlighting an otherwise hidden button in a dungeon.

The second use for lighting and player leading is to hint that there is more. The classic example is light shining from an otherwise uninteresting crossing corridor. Players can quickly identify that there should be more around the corner and might want to check it out. The same goes, of course, for light coming from outdoor cracks, window shutters, or that creepy white van with turned-on headlights. It would have worked great in my previous example about microflow. Light coming from a streetlight or moon could work equally well to raise the players' attention to turn to the window here.

The last use is not lighting per se, but the glare, beam, or flare of it. It is not necessarily realistic, but it works acceptably in games, especially because it works in the daytime. For example, I am talking here about the big red blinky lights on top of radio or airfield towers. Other examples are your classic red/green card reader next to gates, sunbeams in a dusty dungeon, or the blinky reflection of a sniper. Any such highlights can draw additional attention to an otherwise easy-to-miss element in the background. Modern games are so busy and vibrant in graphical fidelity nowadays that any help is welcome. Of course, such use is even more effective in darker environments.

#### 13.4.5.2 Landmarks

Another classic art tool of player leading is landmarks. Essentially, they are large iconic objects in your environment that are clearly and far visible from their surroundings. They are so favored by artists and level designs alike because, if done well, they are not obstructive or gamy. Our world is full of landmarks, and humans are used to navigating with them. Typical examples are gigantic unique rocks, clock towers, radio masts, big, dense smoke, colossal satellite dishes, or your common aircraft carrier crashed on a mountaintop. The important aspect, besides its visibility, is its absolute uniqueness. For example, just a massive rock on a mountain in the mountains is not different enough, except it is unique in any form or shape.

The idea of a landmark is that players either use it as a go-to target to go or as an orientation helper. The first case is simple. It is essentially a big waypoint in a 3D space which is way less intrusive than a HUD element. They might not see it in every circumstance, but if done well, then it should not be hard for them to see it often enough. Especially if the journey is long, it can help get a feeling for distance to the ultimate goal. If the same landmarks exist in multiple levels, it can also tie the spatial context of the different levels together.

If players are supposed to use the landmark for orientation, then it gets a bit trickier. First of all, then the landmark should have identifiable directions or sides. Without clear sides, the players might have difficulty identifying if they are on the left or right of the landmark, making orientation very difficult. Your generic radio tower is not good enough, but massive satellite dishes are a better solution because they point in a clear direction. If such objects are not available or do not fit the setting, then the next best answer is to have multiple landmarks. If the level is small, then two might be enough, but three is the better number for a proper triangulation. However, I would be careful to expect that every player will perfectly triangulate their position based on landmarks. It is something which I would instead rely on subtly and ideally combine with other player-leading elements such as roads, rivers, or signs.

Since most landmarks are at higher positions, they not only act as guidance for players around, but once players are on top, they can show surrounding locations. Essentially, they are mega vantage points of the surrounding lands. Therefore, I would make sure many locations you want the players to find are well visible from up here.

#### 13.4.5.3 Signs

Adding a sign where the players should go or where they are always sounds like an easy solution, but it is not that clear cut. Especially in fast-paced action games, I saw many players not pay too much attention to signs. However, that should not discourage you from using signs, for example, the floor number inside a deep bunker, an arrow directly pointing toward the ship's bridge, or indicating that the armory is behind the door. I'm a big fan of using signs if there is an apparent world-building reason as they make sense in this context.

Suppose they are position markers like floor level or building number. In that case, I recommend not to shy away from making them bigger than life or putting some extra attention to them using dialogs, light, or particles. It is tremendously satisfying to hear playtesters talk out loud about how they navigate through your space using your signs. It is not easy to establish complete sign language for big installations like nuclear power plants or military bases, but it certainly pays off. It also helps to make your world a more believable space since such large compounds would, of course, have signs in real life, too.

The next use of signs is to hint a location to the players. The classic road sign indicating a gas station or an arrow pointing toward the bathrooms are good examples of how well it works in real life. Not all such signs have to be official ones. For example, fellow underground fighters left inconspicuous signs, or gangs use graffiti on walls.

In-game maps on bus stations or tourist attractions are another type of sign. However, not always easy to justify, and sadly without encouragement from the game, not all players are easily drawn to them or are quick to read them effectively. Still, I would recommend adding them as much as possible, even if it is just for world-building and environmental storytelling.

Last but not least, the "stay away" sign is something I previously advise you to consider. Depending on the game's context, most players, if they see a sign saying something like "Do not Trespass," then they are even more encouraged to have a look. It is a clever use of reverse psychology, which can fit well together with any world-building.

#### *13.4.5.4 Explosions/Animation*

By nature, we humans pay extra attention to movement in our view. Therefore, it is an excellent player-leading tool, especially if we want players to look at something specific. Once they recognize it, you can either let them enjoy a fantastic scene or potentially hope for other consequences you want from the players. Classic examples are fly-by helicopters, a burning, and crashing plane, a crossing bison herd, a collapsing building, a waving woman on a rooftop, a mortar barrage, or a bedsheet hanging out of a window in the wind.

First of all, there is never a guarantee that players will look at them, regardless of how much effort you put into them, and that can be pretty frustrating. I have spent hours scripting and animating helicopters flying over the players' heads, but there were always a few guys in playtest looking anywhere but up. There are a few ways how you can increase the chance that players will look at your scene.

The first is a bit of preparation or buildup, but the scene triggers by a look-at trigger. Of course, you need a backup in case the players never look at it. For example, the buildup can be particle effects coming down the ceiling, any fitting audio effects, or soft trembling screen shakes. Essentially anything which tells the players, "wait, something is about to happen, look around." The look-at trigger is a nice touch but not necessary, does not always work, or is not available in every engine.

The second solution is to have several similar events play out, hoping that eventually, the players will look at them. This method works especially well for fast and short scenes, which do not allow for a more extended buildup like jets roaring over the players' heads. So in this example, treat the first jet fly-over as a warm-up, then come the more important ones and add two to three more for good measure. I had a good experience with that method, especially in large open-world maps where it is challenging to guide the player otherwise precisely. However, creating such scenes is not always quick and easy, especially if they also drop some bombs or do other environmentally sensitive actions. Therefore, I created prefabs, copied them around the large map, and then adjusted the individual details. Different engines and tools ask for different methods, but if you use the same scene multiple times, look for ways to make your life as easy as possible. If done well, creating the illusion of a big war fought around the player by letting 12 jets bomb the living hell out of everything around does not sound too scary anymore.

#### *13.4.5.5 Indirect Guiding Elements*

Not every player-leading tool points directly at its target. Many indirect methods can be exquisite and excellent for world-building yet require the players to think and make a few educated assumptions.

Typical examples are train tracks eventually leading to something like a train station, power lines leading to civilization, or the suspiciously red cable that might lead you eventually to the puzzle's solution.

As a developer, you indirectly guide players with their assumption of the game's context or real-world expectations. By nature, they are more subtle but intensely satisfying for both players and developers when they work out. Their use and variety are endless, which also means you have to be very careful around them. As much as possible, reinforce them with in-game messaging from NPCs, signs, or lore texts. Do not be afraid to remind the players that following roads typically means finding structures. However, even with reinforcement, indirect elements are not a solid guarantee that players will find their way or not get lost. Therefore I would recommend using them for less vital objectives or targets but primarily build them for more exploratory players and missions.

## 13.4.6 Lure and Bait

### *13.4.6.1 Enemies*

In most games, enemy AI is a clear indicator that the players have not been there yet and should deal with them. Especially in action or shooter games, this is almost a fool-proof method to attract players, mainly because AI often stands out from the environments, and fighting them is hopefully intrinsically fun. Essentially, they are glowing, fun-infusing player-magnets. Of course, this method does not work well for games with routinely respawning AI, when fighting them is frustrating, or they are well hidden.

Still, I would not recommend placing all AIs with player leading in mind. Of course, there are many other more important reasons to place enemies. However, placing AI to attract players here and there is undoubtedly a good practice. Especially when you want to guide the players around certain corners or in a particular direction, it does not need many of them or has to be a difficult fight. Still, all the player attraction is fruitless if players do not recognize the new direction or target before, after, or during the fight. Therefore, I suggest using cover, AI behavior, movement, idle-actions, or other game ingredients to nudge the players' direction on approaching the encounter. Ideally, the approach direction points them toward their next target or path.

So far, I have only referred to static enemy AI as player-magnets, or at least AI, which had no very long guiding patrol paths. However, another good use of enemy AI for player leading is to guide the players to a particular zone, building, or more relevant enemies, by letting the AI walk, run or drive over an extended distance. Following an enemy through a crowd, observing them steadily from rooftops, or chasing after them are typical examples of that type. Essentially, the AI character replaces the waypoint icon, which then dynamically steers the player until the player catches the AI. Still, depending on your game and engine, scripting such scenes can be very time-consuming and requires careful planning, especially considering layout and other departments.

Another important yet often underutilized use of enemy AI is not to attract players but to repel them. Essentially the players understand that they should not go there, or instead, they cannot progress here yet. Ideally, they remember to come back once they are strong enough. Games with player levels and other roleplay mechanics use this method more commonly. However, I cannot recommend it for semi-realistic games or with systemic AI. It is incredibly difficult to create an AI encounter in such games which reliably stop every player with a 100% guarantee. There is always one player who finds that one glitch in your AI system or abuses a wired combination of systems. That is all fine and part of the game, but you as a developer for such games should be aware that you cannot stop players with AI, and therefore plan around it.

### *13.4.6.2 Friendlies*

Not only can enemies attract or guide players, but friendly AI can do it as well, of course. I am talking here, for example, about the classic waving and shouting quest giver on a roof, the local trapper guiding you through the wilderness, or the usual cheeky fairy trying to lure you to a treasure it wants for itself. Essentially it is like the moving enemy AI as a player-leading tool, just that players should not kill them.

The long-distance variant is especially so interesting because the friendly AI can tell players a lot about your world while guiding you. It is a great storytelling mechanic, and if they can also fight with the player, the better. However, scripting the enemy version can be tricky at times, then scripting a friendly AI doing the same, plus fighting and talking, can be even more complicated. I scripted and directed my fair share of such scenarios, and they were rarely a walk in the park.

#### *13.4.6.3 Reward/Loot*

Treasures, loot, power-ups, collectibles, resources, or any other type of item rewards are great, no-brainer player-leading tools. If the reward is enticing enough, then players are drawn to them like flies to honey. The stronger they are recognizable, especially from a distance, the better player-magnets they are. Hiding loot can be part of the puzzle, but then you need other ways to attract the players. Ideally, they stand out from the environment using, for example, particles, shimmer, audio, glow, or other gamy tools. If your game does not support such effects for various reasons, adjust the environment, so the reward object still stands out, creating contrasts of quality, quantity, saturation, complementary, or light.

However, they are only a leading tool to attract the players to a point. It does not provide any guidance on how to get there. Of course, a pickup on a table is simple, but it gets more interesting when used in the context of puzzles or if you want players to explore the full environment. For example, you notice that players barely use the rooftops of your location, then placing a well-visible reward item on the roof's edge can cause wonders. Now players see that the roofs are a valid place to go, and once they are up there, they might see even more paths and options. Using such rewards carefully, like breadcrumbs, work way more elegant than a tight chain of waypoints or on-the-nose hints.

### 13.4.7 Player Teaching

#### *13.4.7.1 About Player Teaching*

Any player-leading tools guide players through your game environments, and therefore players better understand, read, and experience them. The important factor here is that by continuously teaching the player how to read the environment, we also help them use it to its full potential and reduce possible frustrations. However, it does not always have to be with self-evident means like waypoints, objective texts, or blinking objects. The more subtle we can achieve this, the better because the player emerges more in the game's world without any artificial-gamy elements, which otherwise break the illusion.

A classic example is doors—the ones players can open and the ones which they cannot. Many games establish rules like: if it has a doorknob, then they can interact with it, and if they do not have a knob, then they are just a "wall" looking like a door. Typically, this is never explained to the player directly, but it is implied that eventually, players learn it. Now, later in the game, if the players enter a hotel hallway with many doors, they are not frustrated trying out all doors but are drawn to the ones with knobs. Essentially, we taught the players how to read the environment and then used that learning to guide them.

#### *13.4.7.2 Player Language*

A key factor in successfully teaching the players to navigate and experience your space effortlessly is establishing a clear player language, especially for interactions and navigation. It is crucial that player language is clearly recognizable by the players and used very consistently. A too subtle or even hidden player language does not work very well, except the player has, for example, total freedom of movement. The more muddled it is, the less likely players will use it, or otherwise, it leads to frustrations on both players and developer sides.

Navigational player language often conflicts with art direction if it wants to archive a more believable looking world. Marking every climbing hold or vaulting option with saturated color, particles, white caulk, or tape is not helping to establish a convincing semi-real world. Still, they might be a decent enough option to more jarring alternatives. HUD or other gamy markers are another solution, but they can also be jarring to declutter the game's screen from gamy elements. Ultimately this is not a topic for level design per se. However, it is a level design concern to use any player language tool consistently, especially to ensure where players cannot navigate. For example, if players typically can climb walls, think early on in development about what elements prevent climbing. Such elements could be, for example, barbed wire, spikes, overhangs, or even hedges.

Continuing, establish clearly and early in development the player language of interactables. Most interactables are similar player-magnets like loot or rewards. The same rules for consistency and clear visibility apply here, like for navigation player language.

Another exciting feature to teach the players what they can do in an environment is vision modes. Once turned on, they highlight the players' possibilities while typically toning down other aspects of the environment. It is a less intrusive way to explain players their environment without otherwise potentially glaring player language. However, I still absolutely recommend keeping consistency in place and clear visibility to a degree. For example, players should not always have to use the vision mode to identify climbable pipes and which ones are not. The second problem with vision modes is to guarantee that players do not stay in the mode all the time, or otherwise, players might never see all your beautiful crafted worlds. However, solving this problem is not necessarily level design.

#### 13.4.7.3 Play Styles

Another exciting way to encourage players to use your designed environments fully is to promote different play styles. After all, a stealth player will look for very different environmental clues and paths than a more action or even long-range player. How you encourage players to play different styles, especially when replaying the same environment, is very different from game to game. Some incorporate it with different achievements or in-game consequences. For example, successful stealth run triggers no alarm, or long-range engagement could trigger more helicopter reinforcements or mortar fire.

Giving the players much freedom to play your game is excellent, but sometimes even hinting at alternative playstyles might allow players to fully explore the total options in your game. Maybe they even find new styles or tools they never thought they would enjoy. If that goes hand in hand with using most of your designed environmental options, the better.

### 13.4.8 Player Leading Context

#### 13.4.8.1 Lighting Context

Previously I have stated that light attracts players. However, this is not true in all situations or games. In games where being in darkness or shadow provides a significant advantage, the light will not draw players toward it—instead, they will want to stay in the darker areas as much as possible. For example, the sun could damage, shadow provides concealment, or enemies cannot follow players in the dark.

The important consideration is that this only affects players' movement, not their looking direction. Once in darkness, they will still be attracted to watch anything in the light because it is either highlighted or humans tend to simply watch lit objects/scenes.

The opposite case is again, of course, the case in games where darkness is a threat. Either because, for example, it damages you, monsters live here, or some evil aliens use it to sneak up on players. Now players want to do anything but strictly stay away from darkness, way more than in other games that do not have such a context.

Again, vision modes or other features such as flashlights (for players and enemies), searchlights, fires, glowing swarms of living shadows, or dynamic lighting can bring some variation into play. Understanding the lighting context and experimenting with how the possibilities create interesting level design opportunities is key for doing a great job as a designer.

#### 13.4.8.2 Lure and Bait Context

In most games lures and baits work very well, especially in games that aim to provide a faster paced almost cinematic experience. Players are taught to continuously move after each new attraction, and that is great and fine.

However, rules change in slower-paced games where not everything which seems like an attractor has the best interest for the players. Horror games come to mind, where it is not necessarily advised to trust everyone and everything. In such contexts, lure and bait is certainly not seen like honey for flies. Playing with this ambiguity opens a lot of interesting possibilities for level designers.

#### 13.4.8.3 No Player Leading

The whole chapter was all about player leading, but there are situations where too strong player leading is not desired. I'm in particular looking here at certain survival games or some games with procedurally generated worlds. Games that do not require the players to follow a certain story and its threads often want the players to explore instead of running after waypoints.

Still, indirect guiding elements like train tracks, rivers, roads, or the occasional landmark are of course still relevant here. However, often they are rather a consequence of believable world-building than placed solely as strict player-leading tools. Creating worlds that just lead the player with subtlety is very challenging to design, but even more so rewarding once you see players enjoy exploring them.

#### 13.4.8.4 Flow Context

Leading players using flow and layout elements toward a particular direction or target is not always beneficial. This consideration is especially crucial when the game or section has an exploration focus. Instead, disperse the players' attention using elements like micro and macro flow. If you funnel the player too much, then potentially, they might not experience the entirety of the space. The more you push players in a particular direction, the less likely they understand that there was a space to explore, collectibles to find, hidden routes to explore, narrative clues to find, or rewards to be collected.

However, the goal should not be to make players feel lost or lose orientation. Instead, use flow elements to guide players to vantage points. Here they can get a grasp of the section's totality. At such inner and outer vantage points is the perfect time and place to introduce to players the player-leading art elements like signs and landmarks. They are essential to keep a strong sense for orientation, objectives, AI actions, and eventually the final exit of the space. Such vantage points are also ideal for showing narrative elements like in-game events or AI actions and hinting at rewards in the space ahead.

Player leading is not always to "aggressively" push players through levels to their goals as fast as possible. More importantly, once mastered, they are tools to properly control the game's speed and making sure that players make the best out of your designed space. Otherwise, developers spend weeks, if not months, to craft a vast world, and players rush through it in minutes or seconds.

#### 13.4.8.5 Other Game Mechanics

This book is about level design, but a chapter about player leading should mention other player-leading tools, particularly gadgets or narrative elements. Essentially, I highly recommend exploring any other opportunities to guide players, preventing any of the previously mentioned "sins," especially waypoints. I will not write about any element but instead, touch on three types I have used the most.

First, let us start with narrative clues. I am talking here about written or verbal clues where to go. They typically include descriptions using in-game world elements such as landmarks, compass directions, or other world features. For example, it could be "the treasure is on the island between the two twin lakes in the northwest," "the gangster boss travels between the Italian restaurants close to the south-east beach," or "the dragon's lair is lit by the morning sun under the highest peak of the Dogan mountains." They are an elegant way to give the players to find their target using non-gamy tools, and they have to spend time reading your world, which deepens their understanding and connection to your world. However, make sure that the descriptions are neither too much on the nose nor too vague. If they are too precise, the player might feel cheated for their smarts and exploration. If they are too vague, it leads to frustration, and likely they end up using external guides to find their target.

Secondly, let's look at tracking devices, which give a sense of direction and distance indicator. Typically, this is achieved with a tool in the players' hand or HUD using sound and small screens/lights. For example, the gadget indicates if the players face the right direction and indicate their distance by beeping more intensely. Such tools are essentially in-game waypoints without being so on the nose, more immerse, and often less precise. However, because they are comparable to waypoints, the same issues apply, just that potentially players might run less/more straight toward them and stop more often to reorientate. Therefore, make sure that the journey is enjoyable and fascinating, gives time for a break, and focuses primarily on the challenges along the way. After all, just running straight to a point without anything entertaining is not worth the effort.

Finally, let us talk about tracks leading through the world. For example, footsteps in the snow or blood drops. They are small clues on the ground that players can follow, leading them to their target. Often a special ability or vision mode is required to see them. They are another great way to keep players immersed in your world, especially if you use the journey to feed players narrative and world-building information. Additionally, I recommend interrupting the tracks from time to time, or otherwise, the players likely look down on the ground the entire time. Instead, make them stop and look around from time to time. Tracks work great when combined with the above narrative clues to strengthen the players' connection to the world further and lead them to the next set of tracks.

#### *13.4.8.6 How to Improve Waypoint Handling*

It is not a secret that I'm not the biggest fan of waypoints. Therefore, I would like to share some ways to improve working with waypoints, especially if they are an unavoidable part of your game's core feature set.

Using waypoints for far-distance targets or to tiny, hard-to-find objects can be acceptable. However, having a waypoint on a visible NPC, which is ten meters away from you, can be jarring and is arguably unnecessary. As much as possible, I recommend hiding the waypoints if the target is at close to medium distance and only turn it on when the players move far away. Essentially, the waypoint guides the player back to the target, but they should be off once the player is in the direct game space. The exact distance depends on your game and environmental situation, like the noisiness of the background, the size of the target, and space's lighting.

Another way to prevent too many on-the-nose waypoints is large areas that mark the target's location. A waypoint can lead the players to such a zone, but they do not show the target's exact position. It is still a gamy element, especially if the zone is, for example, marked in minimap, but at least players have a higher feeling of success finding it. However, on the one hand, a too-small area is essentially a waypoint again and should be avoided. On the other hand, a too large zone can quickly feel frustrating. The exact size of the zone depends on your game, environment's complexity, and target's detectability.

For example, a big, loud tank in a small village should not need a waypoint. It is enough if the players find the village. However, the search zone for a tiny key in a huge castle should not encapsulate the entire estate. Finding the right, fair, and challenging balance for such a zone or when to turn on/off waypoints is critical here. If you, the very knowledgeable level designer, think that the turn-off distance is a bit too close and the zone is just a tick too small, then you have a good starting point. Playtest should do the rest to fine-tune it.

# 14

# *Scenarios and Location Types*

This more extensive chapter describes classic and standard level design scenarios and location types. It describes how to approach them from an initial design perspective and especially talks about common problems and how to solve them.

Detailed design directions for such scenarios are difficult because games are so incredibly diverse. However, I do believe that many core problems are universal. Therefore I put an extra focus on issues and solutions. After all, it is an excellent start if a gameplay section has little to no problems, you understand the basic design and then just add your game's specifics.

It is important to note that all those sections, locations, and scenarios overlap. Nothing is strictly black and white. For example, you will find ideas, concepts, and design principles from the open-world part, which you can apply to linear attack scenarios. Singleplayer considerations mentioning AI might spark an important breakthrough for your multiplayer map, or what works in co-op could lead to an exciting fresh singleplayer puzzle. My goal was to write my design considerations in the part where it is the most relevant. However, as long as games are ever-changing and are a creative and interactive medium, all thoughts are connected and often interchangeable. The same goes, of course, for any design thoughts from other designers.

## 14.1 About Attack and Defense Sections

### 14.1.1 Introduction

I am combining both attack and defense because they are both two sides of the same coin. If one faction is attacking, then another is defending and vice versa. Of course, player-facing (meaning how they are perceived by players) they are fundamentally different, but the more AI advances, the more we can learn from both types by looking at the two topics together. The primary difference between attack and defense is that in one scenario the player is moving toward the enemy, while in the other the enemies are coming toward the player. Additionally understanding attack and defense layouts are the building blocks for most multiplayer maps, where such roles often switch fluidly.

In this chapter, I want to cover some basic understanding of setting up battle zones and combat networks. Those basics are essential for most other sections in this overarching chapter of scenario and location types because many of them include some type of attack or defense. Then we look at how to approach layouts and pacing for both attack and defense scenarios.

### 14.1.2 Combat Zone Basics

#### *14.1.2.1 Introduction*

A combat zone, or battle area, is a place in a level where any fights are common or expected. Therefore, all learnings about basic combat zones apply to both attack and defense layouts. For example, this could be in hot spots of your multiplayer map, around mission objectives, or you scripted an encounter in a specific location. Such zones are the bread and butter of every shooter game.

It is important to view every aspect of this chapter through the eyes of players and AI at the same time. For example, it might be an objective mission zone for the player, but the AI uses a network, frontlines, or a network of frontlines. The roles between attacker and defenders can quickly switch, and you should always design them from all involved factions' perspectives.

DOI: 10.1201/9781003275664-19

Most attack combat zones are built with few directions in mind, like a linear attack section. In contrast, defense zones are built with multiple directions in mind, like a defense encounter with attackers coming from multiple angles. In the open-world scenario chapter, I will go in more depth about such specific layouts. Further on, consider the different elements described in this chapter as building blocks for defense and attack scenarios.

#### *14.1.2.2 List of Considerations*

I have covered many combat zone basics in some form or shape previously in this book. Therefore, I collected a condensed summary list of important aspects of building a good combat zone.

- You should always provide multiple routes into a combat zone; otherwise, you or the enemies become too predictable. Defeating a predictable enemy only provides short-lived satisfaction. Alternatively, being predictable does not make anyone feel smart. However, defeating an unpredictable enemy or outsmarting your opponent is satisfactory and makes you feel smart. Keep in mind that unpredictability due to randomness is not the same as unpredictability due to smarts.
- Avoid bottlenecks that are not clearly recognizable as such. It is a frustrating experience taking a path to feel smart, only to realize that the level design robbed you of all options or set wrong expectations.
- Camping spots are problematic in multiplayer maps, but they are problematic in singleplayer as well because a camping player turns the combat into a very static and likely boring experience. Except the design intends not to call for a static player, like at mounted guns or sniping, you ideally want players to use as much of your combat zone as possible. One way is to always think in loops, even at low-level layout execution. Secondly, every powerful camping POA must have at least one, better two, counters to push out potential campers. Ideally, those options are outside of the primary FOV of the player so nobody can fully feel 100% safe.
- Sweeten every path you want players to take with suitable covers or other POAs. For example, there should always be cover close or right away when entering a combat zone. Ideally, those initial covers are all part of a cover network with a good connecting flow.
- You can apply everything you applied to the high and medium-level layout to the combat zone layout. Especially never forget to think in loops.
- Give players and AI a rich number of options within the combat zone. It makes the zone more fun, and the same rule about unpredictability entering the zone counts for within, too. As much as possible, provide a rich amount of paths, POAs, and options within the zone. Additionally, never forget about verticality above and below.
- Support as many playstyles as your game supports. It is good to give each zone a gameplay and layout theme. However, generally speaking, it is bad practice if you create a very singular

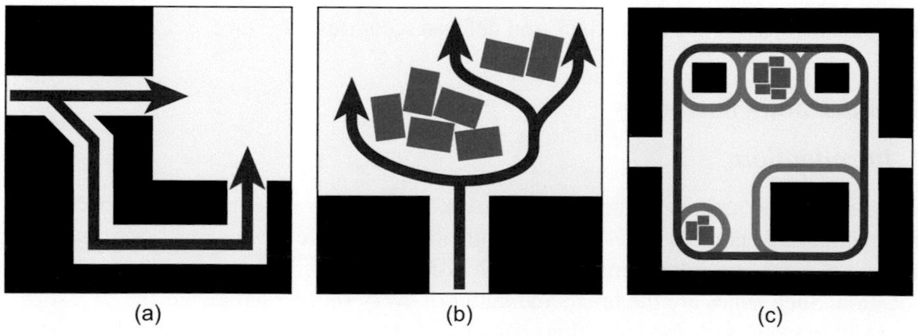


**FIGURE 14.1** (a) Alternative paths into a combat zone increase the unpredictability. (b) Cover at the entrances further increases the unpredictability and provides instant safety to enter the space. (c) Loops always keep playing an important role even in smaller combat zone around a single cover object.

experience. For example, if your game supports stealth and you want to build an action only scenario, then regardless, I recommend adding at least one stealth option. It does not have to be the most obvious or most accessible, but forcing a playstyle on players should be the absolute exception. Otherwise, you alienate a large fraction of your players.

### *14.1.2.3 Combat Network*

The network in a combat zone is the connections of covers and POAs. Largely the connections follow the same rules like cover flow. Planning out this network or web is essential because it gives players some orientation and flow stability, gives your AI a sense of purpose and safety, and is a strong tool for soft-controlling players. I already explained the basics of creating such a network when I wrote about POAs and cover flow. However, now I want to go more practical in the context of attack and defense.

The concept of combat networks is usually best used when the combat can happen from multiple angles, player or AI can freely roam, or you generally design for a very open and systemic game.

AI and many players typically prefer to take the shortest route toward their goal. A suitable way to guide them to alternative paths is to either attract them with POAs to other paths or repel them to other paths because the shortest route is very disadvantageous or straight-up deadly. For example, players with a sense of safety or systemic AI (that understands cover) are more likely to take a path with covers than running over the open. Alternatively, for example, a lava sea in the middle is a solid repelling reason for players and AI to not run straight through the zone.

However, typically the further a path is away from the shortest route, the less likely anyone will take it. For example, hidden fringe flanks at the furthest edges of your massive combat zone are potentially only visited by the exploratory or lost players. In general, I would be careful creating too many paths or a too complex network because it can quickly turn into a waste, except the space has high replayability or is for a large number of players/AI.

The paths of a network must be readable before players commit to it, or for example, stealth players might end up in sniper spots, or action players end up in a bunch of sneak air ducts. The common expectation is that the direct paths are more for the action-oriented players, the outer ones are more stealth or speed-oriented, and the higher ones are for snipers. However, occasionally it is nice to switch it up and surprise players, but only if they know it in advance. No player will go into a sewer for some sniping action, except you drop some clear hints.

The lack of a clean POA network typically results in a messy and confusing game experience. It is like moving around in a tense, unknown scenario without a manual, map, or compass. Any decently balanced attack or defense scenario is usually already intense and stressful for the player; the last thing they need is to also deal with layout confusion. However, to be clear, it is not about player leading alone, even if a clear POA network does positively impact player leading. Instead, it is about the order in the chaos.

A solid and clear network acts as a subconscious guide for players and shows them how to navigate your designed environments. It is very frustrating to see people only playing a fraction of your space you

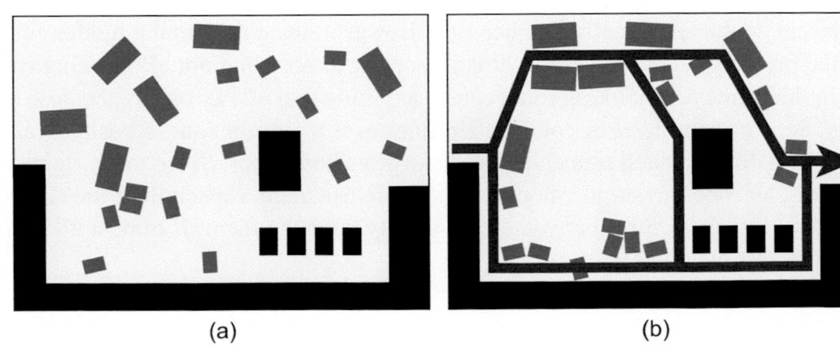


**FIGURE 14.2** (a) Not a clear cover (gray boxes) network. (b) Clearly readable cover network by arranging the objects along lanes.

spend days or weeks designing. Instead, you want to guide them so they can enjoy long enough the full beauty and brilliance of your carefully crafted layout.

However, I do not mean an overly obvious pathway when talking about a clear cover network. Often subtle hints, the courage to leave empty space in your layout, and emphasizing or strengthening existing otherwise incomplete networks are enough. For example, instead of placing a single artificial line of cover between two buildings, first, check what you have already from the perspective of world-building. Using a less clear line yet of world-fitting objects might not be exactly what you thought it should be, but it works well enough for gameplay, fits your world, and removes any artificial feeling design.

#### *14.1.2.4 Frontlines*

While combat networks can lead in any direction through large complex areas, frontlines are often smaller and more local. Frontlines are formed when two opposing forces meet and spread out along cover to both sides. In level design, this is typically two cover lines parallel to each other at a fighting distance. Sometimes the cover lines have multiple stages supporting a large number of opponents, are above each other, or are at different engagement distances. The line's cover can be a wide mix of, for example, trenches, houses, cars, crates, or whatever else is believable in your game world. However, I would be careful making such frontlines too obvious; the better they blend in, the better.

Frontlines are crucial for level design for multiple reasons. The first one is that they slow down gameplay. The slow down happens first because players feel safe and are motivated to not rush forward, and secondly because the enemy is also safer behind cover. The slow down means players spend more time in your environments, essentially affecting the ratio between your time spent creating the space and time players spent playing in it. Secondly, a frontline gives players time to explore multiple options and therefore feel smart. For example, such options could be a speedy flanking route, a crazy zip-line, or a sneaky stealth route leading behind enemy lines. Rushing through a linear chain of encounters typically only offers limited options, but a good frontline is about the breadth of options.

An essential part of every frontline is the death zone between the two frontlines. This empty strip of space hopefully forces both parties to stop, spread out, and look for other means to take out the enemy. Crossing the death zone means you expose yourself without cover to all the enemies behind cover. Additionally, you are likely moving, and the defenders are static, further tipping the odds against the attacker over open ground. Therefore, without the death zone, you do not have a slow-down, no spread out, and no need to look for other options. Of course, players could just stay behind the first cover they find and try to take out enemies from here, and that is okay, just probably not very fun. The key for you as a level designer is to present and "sell" the other options well enough, so players are intrigued to explore them. However, it is crucial to investigate how you can control AI staying behind the cover, not running over the death zone in the middle, and at least pretend to understand the concept of frontlines.

One other key part of frontlines is flanking routes. It is simply incredibly satisfying to outsmart, surprise, or outmaneuver the enemy, show up behind or next to them, and take them out swiftly. This feeling is stronger, the stronger the enemies are. Therefore, it is not wrong to design a frontline encounter that the most players could never really win head-on. However, once they find a hidden route, they can flip the tide of the previously doomed battle. It is important to note that not all flanking routes have to be at the sides. In this context, a flanking route can be anything that allows one to get close to the enemy in relative safety. So, for example, they could be zip-lines over the death zone, a bushy stealth pass right through the middle, a dingy crouch tunnel below, or surprise jump pads. Since many fights are resolved over flanking routes, level design should motivate players to use them, especially if the combat difficulty requires it. Additionally, make sure that you create variety between them. If almost all flanking routes are zip-lines, then it gets old quickly.

Alternatives to flanking routes are other types of POAs that give players or AI advantages, essentially anything which might give you the upper hand over the opponent on the other side. For example, this could be advantageous sniping spots, mortars, mounted machine guns, or that one angle from which you can hit that obviously placed gas tank in the back of your opponents. This type of POAs is a strong tool to give your frontline a prominent theme.

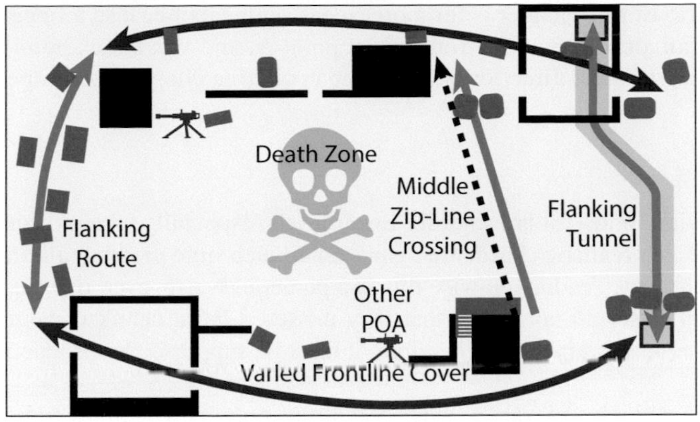


**FIGURE 14.3** Example of two opposing frontlines (purple) frontline with multiple flanking or one-way routes (green) to cross the death zone.

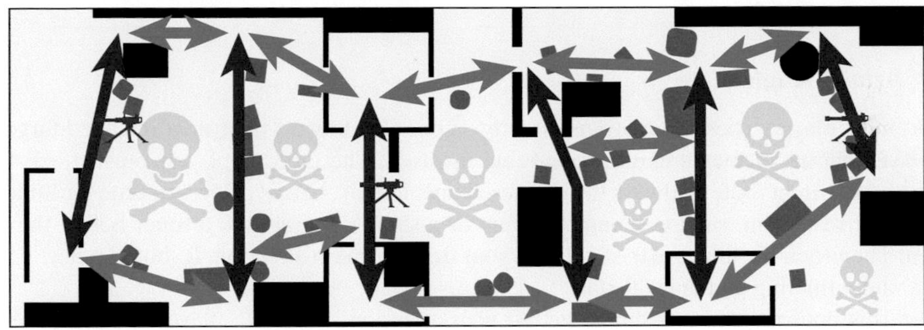

**FIGURE 14.4** A compressed example of multiple frontlines (purple) connected by (green) routes forming a frontline network.

Not all frontline setups are only two opposite cover or POA lines. It is a lot more complex. Looking back at trench warfare, we also had multiple layered frontlines connected by a complicated network. The layering plus network approach allowed troops to retreat to trenches behind or allowed supporting troops to move to the front. You can apply the same logic to larger combat zones with multiple connected frontlines. They either can hide troop reinforcement, prolong the fight further, or allow for a multi-staged fight.

Lastly, do not skip the 3D aspect of frontlines, especially when you work on a more complex combat zone with multilayered frontlines, then always consider verticality. You could have multiple frontlines above or below each other. Walkways, rooftops, stairs, ladders, ramps, zip-lines, or jump pads can give an additional dimension to a frontline. Especially after several frontlines back-to-back, players might face certain fatigue of simple 2D setups, and verticality is one of the easiest ways to keep such layouts fresh.

### 14.1.3 Attack Fundamentals

#### *14.1.3.1 Introduction*

The attack scenario has such a massive number of variations, but typically it comes down to killing/destroying one/multiple static/moving targets. Classic examples are destroying a few anti-air guns, killing the VIP, destroying the nuclear reactor, or simply killing all. For the context of this chapter, I keep it very general because adjusting to each type and its variations would make this large chapter unnecessarily complex.

The attack scenario of this chapter is for more linear segments because a linear direction defines the core concept of an attack scenario. You start at point A, and you attack point B. For a complete free attack approach without a direction, wait for the upcoming chapter about open-world locations.

#### 14.1.3.2 Branches

I would be careful with far distant branches for linear levels, especially with a strong directional focus for the player. There is a realistic chance that you spend much time creating alternative paths, which many players will not play. Production-wise this is a potential waste, even if it sounds nice on paper. Additionally, players either do not notice that they missed a large chunk of your level, or they get confused trying to explore everything. Therefore, it must be supported by production and the game's vision.

Instead, if you want to give players a wider breadth of options, I recommend creating one wider area. Players do not have the impression that they have missed something major, and for you, it is generally easier to create one large space (aka a very "fat" branch) than two far separate medium-sized ones. However, if the world or design requires multiple branches, keep their numbers as low as possible. Far distant branches have their place, especially in sandbox games, just be careful.

#### 14.1.3.3 Attack Angle

By default, most players chose to move as directly as possible toward their next intended target, especially if player-leading elements like waypoints are involved. Therefore, if players must attack someone or something, the direct route is always the most used one. Ideally, before players initiate the attack, there is a stopping or rest point, such as a vantage point or a short warning like a timer before the elevator doors open. Therefore, the direct path should get your first and main attention. It should reflect your main intention and dominating gameplay theme.

However, this does not mean it should get all your attention! After all, players should have options to attack. Even if your section only offers very limited space, player-facing-wise, it is possible to play with different engagement distances, playstyles, and verticality. Further on, you can give players ever-changing options by giving them different challenges, even if the environment is the same. For example, players are drawn to different options when facing rifle guys, attack dogs, or snipers.

The direct path remains the primary choice for most players till you change the odds. If you establish a frontline with a dead zone, you can use it to steer player attention to the sides, below or above, away from the direct path. Alternatively, you can affect the odds with strong attractors catered to the different playstyles. For example, if the right side features some higher-up walkways, it could attract players favoring long-range gameplay.

In the context of a linear attack scenario, it is unusual to go for a complete 360° around the target. More than 180° is rare. However, it can happen, especially around objective areas, large fights, or very attractive and sneaky flanking routes.

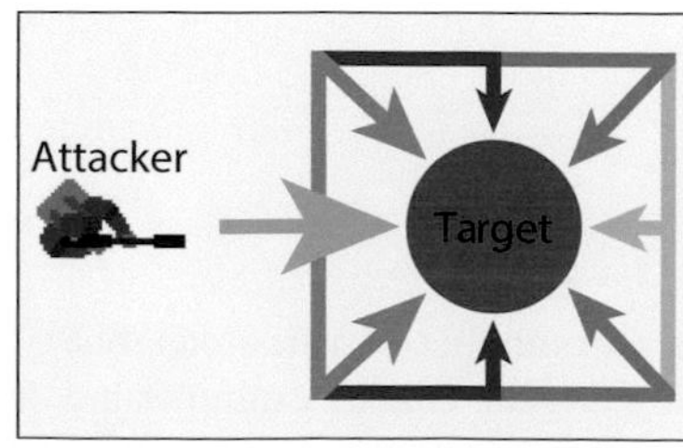


**FIGURE 14.5** Most players attack the target head-on, many from an angle, few directly from the sides, but it is very rare for players to attack from behind in a classic linear attack layout.

#### *14.1.3.4 Attack Layout Rhythm and Pacing*

An attack scenario is defined by players moving from A to B and taking on several threats along the way. Players are coming to the threat, not the way around. This simple-sounding statement is crucial to understand because we do have less direct control over the player's actions in an interactive medium. If players decide to stare at a wall for five minutes while the AI is desperately waiting for them, then this is their choice.

One of the basic motivators for players to move forward is the intrinsic fun to play your game, curiosity about what is next, general wish to progress within the game, plus standing around is usually quite boring. Therefore, a good attack layout is about chaining together the different encounters in an entertaining and exciting way. Now, when we talk about the flow of an encounter chain we can apply our basic understanding of variety, pacing, and rhythm.

Of course, serious time pressure, with serious consequences upon failure, is an option to control player speed. However, I would be careful with this approach because it is not always easy to justify and can feel very forced. Instead, another concept, without actual time pressure through failure, is to push players through a level with heightened intensity or speed to fake the pressure on a pure narrative layer. For example, players might hear someone keep reminding them to run or hurry up over the radio. There is no serious consequence to slow down or even stop and it might feel contrived, but often it works. However, do not do it too long or with too high a frequency because it can quickly become annoying.

Back to layout, the basic layout building blocks for attack scenarios are network, frontline, mission area, and passage.

I wrote about all four points previously except the "passage." The passage is a narrower section, with reduced scope, limited breadth of options, and restricted complexity, yet still featuring dedicated action. Do not mistake it for traversal connectivity without dedicated combat. Instead, examples of passage action sections are linear sewer battles, fights on top of trains, or along lengthy house corridors. They are essential to creating diverse, contrasting, ever-changing, and fresh experiences.

It is important to note that the transition between a network, frontline, or objective space can be seamless since, for example, a network can feature objective areas or an objective area can have multiple frontlines. Still, it makes sense to keep thinking about chaining them up following their first appearance along the golden path.

However, not only the type of layout is an important factor of the layout pacing, but also the size and complexity. Now by no means do we always have to start small/simple and end big/complex. What matters is the associated intensity or what exactly is happening there. For example, it is often difficult to have an intense gameplay climax in a large complex space because it is hard to focus all AI on the player who could be anywhere. However, if the large complex space features several attack helicopters, the intensity is high again, even in a larger space. Alternatively, objectives are another excellent way to control players, and then it makes good use of a large space with lots of AI.

Once you chain them up, it matters to look for patterns. For example, do you have too many frontlines of the same size and complexity, are all your passages of similar size, or do you always feature a network before a mission area? This consideration does not just count for one larger action section or layout but

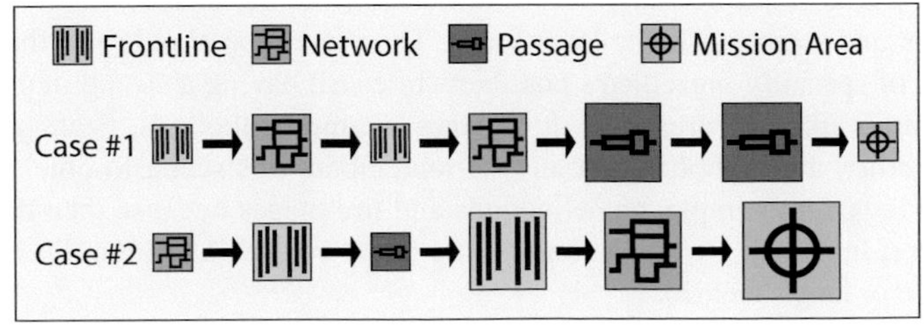


**FIGURE 14.6** Case #1: Starts with a very repetitive pattern, continuous with two very similar-sized passages, and ends with a very small mission area (no climax). Case #**2**: No repetitive patterns, steady increase in sizes leading to a big mission area.

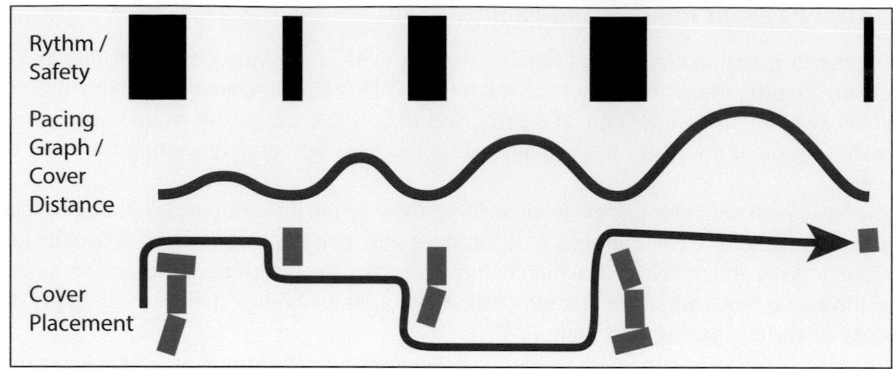


**FIGURE 14.7** Safer/bigger cover creates long beats, while longer cover distance increases difficulty/intensity comparable to music.

the entire level or game. Spotting repetitive patterns is a key process to guarantee a diverse experience for the player.

You can apply pacing and patterns to the individual cover connections, too. Crossing a long-distance or getting to a small cover object is usually more intense/difficult than traversing a short distance to a large high cover object. This consideration is interesting if you want to gradually slow down players through safety or accelerate them by applying the cover flow fundamentals. For example, the last section of a cover network should be more difficult than the middle of the combat zone, where you prefer players spending most of their time during the fight.

### *14.1.3.5 Attack Ingredients and Intensity Pacing*

The layout can have a significant impact on an attack experience. However, it is only half of the equation. The second crucial important is the actual target that should get attacked. In a lengthy chain-of-attack scenario, pacing will play, once again, an essential role hand in hand with the layout.

When you build an attack scenario, and it is time to think about the ingredients, then it is time to ask yourself a few questions: What are my basic or bread-and-butter ingredients? What ingredients make my scenario special, stand out, or even unique? How many specialty ingredients do I even need? How well do they fit my layout?

The bread-and-butter ingredients are your main fillers. You start with them, and they should be between 2/3 and 3/4 of your main elements. For example, your fillers could be your base grunts, the common infantry orc, or the cliché street fighter. You can have some gameplay variation between them, but they should remain similar, like guys with submachine guns and shotguns because they behave similar enough and fight at comparable distances. However, snipers and baseball guys likely don't belong to the same bread-and-butter group, but that severely depends on your game.

Secondly, we come to the special, stand out, or unique element. If you use more than 1/4 to 1/3 special elements, they tend not to stand out anymore. Additionally, the more different elements you use, the more the ingredients and scenario theme loses focus. Therefore, you should use the least amount and least different types of specialty ingredients possible while still having a strong impact. If you mix, for example, specialty units like necromancers, fire mages, raging hellhounds, healing priests, and drug-infused demons together, it is doubtful that anyone remembers this scenario other than it was a wild mess: Instead, just focus, for example, on hellhounds and fire mages because then the whole scenario's theme is all about fire. In reality, I would not mix more than two specialty ingredients and maybe go up to three if it is a huge or long scenario.

A common question is: Is the layout defining the ingredients or the ingredients the layout? The short answer is: It is complicated. In reality, they influence each other, but what truly matters is whether your game is world or gameplay-driven and how much good compromise can both parties achieve. For example, you could favor the world side a tick more till you see bad patterns appearing for gameplay or vice versa. If one side must suffer massively just for the other one to look a bit better, then it isn't worth it. For example, as much as I love a beautiful gameplay pattern, I would not want it in a boring, bland world. Alternatively, most worlds can easily adjust to a network or frontline setup, even if it isn't ideal in a particular case.

In my examples, I primarily mentioned AI archetypes as the main gameplay ingredient because, after all, it matters most what you attack in an attack scenario. However, other classic ingredients are, for example, explosive barrels, mounted weapons, portals, jump pads, or vehicles. However, if they do not directly affect or cater to the attack scenario, then at best, they are on a different layer of themes, like a navigation theme layer. The primary issue is that too many ingredients of any kind will dilute the overall experience and make it all forgettable.

After you set the foundations, it is time to see how we all mix and pace them together. Below is a common base encounter-chain pattern I recommend:

1. As a first encounter start with a few bread-and-butter ingredients as a warm-up.
2. Next encounter, escalate with bread-and-butter ingredients up to a medium challenge.
3. Add your special ingredient while keeping a similar challenge level. Feel free to use bread-and-butter ingredients as well, but make sure the specialty ingredient truly stands out and is hard to miss. However, do not use the specialty ingredient to the maximum of 1/4 to 1/3 yet.
4. If you have more than one special ingredient, you can feature separate encounters to use them. If it is very long, you can have some pure bread-and-butter ones in between. I would only recommend mixing multiple specialty ingredients early on if the chain is short.
5. Depending on the length of your scenario, escalate it up to your maximum of 1/4 to 1/3 at the final encounter with mixed specialty ingredients.

I would only safely recommend breaking the 1/4 to 1/3 limit if it is a unique moment, like, for example, a unique mass-sniper fight. However, like everything, it is complicated, especially in conjunction with the layout. You might have a short passage section in between where it makes sense to use 100% melee units, even if they are considered your specialty units. Therefore, consciously breaking the rule can be okay at times, but you have to see it within the bigger picture and context. Case by case, a great player experience always trumps sticking to guidelines; just help yourself by involving your leads and directors before you do the actual work.

### 14.1.4 Defense Fundamentals

#### *14.1.4.1 Introduction*

Production-wise defense scenarios are very smart because the players spend a long time at one location. The ratio between the time it takes to create such a space and the time players spend here is typically favorable for the developers. However, such defensive scenarios have the reputation of putting players in a purely reactive state instead of being the active ones driving the game's progress. Still, at times, I prefer a good defense setup over another attack because, as a player, it is variety in pacing, I can get used to an environment, and fully enjoy playing the totality of its layout.

For the context of this chapter, the defense objective is a static one, like a PC getting hacked, cowering hostages, or a fixed arena that needs to stay enemy-free for an extended period. I will cover any defensive objectives which move around in the upcoming separate escort section.

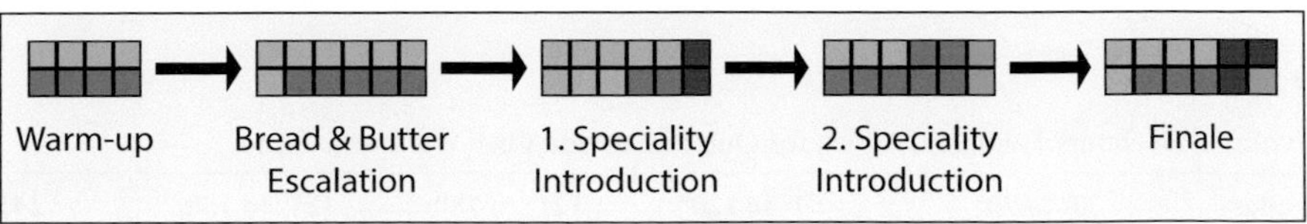


**FIGURE 14.8** Example introduction of specialty AIs (red and green blocks) among bread-and-butter AI (grey blocks) in a chain of encounters.

### 14.1.4.2 Defense Angles and Difficulty

When you defend one or multiple points, areas, NPCs, or other entities, the key factor starts with: Where are the attackers coming from, or which angles do I need to defend? From a developer perspective: From what angles should I let the attackers come, and how many at the same time? In the context of this sub-chapter, the attacker is a reasonable challenge, which can be one or multiple enemies suitable to your layout.

Let us start with one player defending, and attackers come from one direction at the same time. In order to be semi-challenging, the angles the player must defend should be bigger than his FOV, or ideally bigger. My general rule of thumb with FOVs lower than 90° is that defense angles between 90° and 120° are an easy defense. 121°–180° is a medium difficulty, 181°–240° is difficult, while attackers coming from all around is very difficult, and usually not recommended early on in a game. The difficulty is increasing because players must cover more angles, and a broader coverage also means more attack lanes. My rule of thumb is one attack lane per 60° plus one for extra spice at unusual angles or one angle less if enemy count is very high. Look at Table 14.1 for a brief overview.

It varies between games but for example you could create such a table below, for one player and one wave at a time.

It is difficult to exactly quantify this chart because wave" is a very subjective term here and severely varies depending on the used enemy types, of course. Therefore, consider each "wave" in this context as an average to easy threat. Feel free to adjust this chart to your game's reality, especially if later waves meant to send more difficult enemies.

The one thing you should ideally avoid as much as possible is that all continuous waves come from the same direction; in other words, the player can always see all threads within their FOV, regardless of how many attack lanes you feature. Instead mix up the attack lanes as much as possible.

Without touching the individual wave difficulty, itself you can make defense setups more difficult by sending multiple waves simultaneously or closely staged from different attack lanes. The bigger the angle

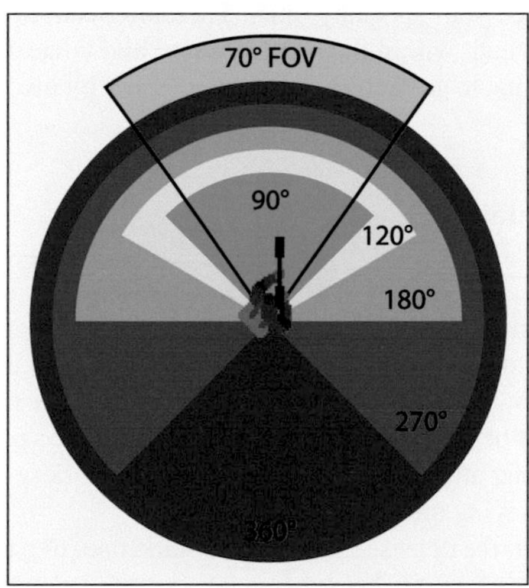


**FIGURE 14.9** Different angles covered by a player for a defense scenario.

**TABLE 14.1**

Table to Evaluate Different Defense Angles for One Player and One Wave at a Time

| Defense Angles | 70° to 90° | 91° to 120° | 121° to 180° | 121° to 180° | 241° to 360° |
|---|---|---|---|---|---|
| **Difficulty** | crazy easy difficult | very easy difficult | easy difficult | medium difficult | difficult |
| **Attack Lanes** | 2–3 | 3–4 | 4–5 | 5–7 | 6–8 |

**TABLE 14.2**
Table to Evaluate Different Defense Angles for One Player and Two Waves at a Time

| Defense Angles | 70° to 90° | 91° to 120° | 121° to 180° | 181° to 240° | 241° to 360° |
|---|---|---|---|---|---|
| **Difficulty** | easy difficult | medium difficult | difficult | very difficult | very high difficult |
| **Attack Lanes** | 2–3 | 3–5 | 4–6 | 6–8 | 7–9 |

**TABLE 14.3**
Table to Evaluate Different Defense Angles for Two Players and Two Waves at a Time

| Defense Angles | 70° to 90° | 91° to 120° | 121° to 180° | 181° to 240° | 241° to 360° |
|---|---|---|---|---|---|
| **Difficulty** | crazy easy difficult | very easy difficult | easy difficult | medium difficult | difficult |
| **Attack Lanes** | 3–4 | 4–6 | 5–7 | 7–10 | 9–12 |

difference between those lanes the bigger the difficulty impact. Let's look at how that could be like if we use the previous table and example, but this time with two waves simultaneously (Table 14.2). Of course, the more waves you want to send, the more attack lanes you need. This is even more important if you want to be unpredictable.

If you have two players in co-op you can knock down the difficulty by two or three levels depending on your game. Since one of the primary defense challenges is to cover multiple angles, just one more player can significantly impact the difficulty. More players also mean more attack lanes, to stay unpredictable. For example, let's take our previous table with two simultanous waves, like in Table 14.3, but this time with two players.

Keep in mind that such assessments are purely subjective and based on my personal game experiences! It can be wildly different for your game. Another significant factor is any features that help the defender, such as buildable fortifications or a wide arrange of freely placeable tools like mines, turrets, summons, or other types of traps. I would be careful with cases where enemies come from very opposing angles or enemies coming from (almost) all directions simultaneously. This might only be a rare case or best left for coop games. Lastly, in more systemic or multiplayer games, the attack lanes only describe a general direction or wider path, especially if a wide cover network or frontline is available.

### *14.1.4.3 Defense Layout Types*

After the defense angle, the next important consideration when building a defense scenario is the layout type. The layout types affect both defender and attacker options. I tend to split them into four main types: open, block, hollow, and spread. In this subchapter's context, I consider lanes available 360° all around but feel free to adjust it to your needs.

The open type is where you have one or multiple objectives to defend, but they are close together, and nothing really obstructs the view in-between significantly. In its most simple form, the player could stand at one spot and could shoot at all attackers by simply rotating. It is a straightforward type and often associated with abstract defense objectives like defending an area for domination or simply surviving. Alternatively, it could also be associated with a single defense objective like a single PC downloading data or a single NPC cowering down. The defense objective doesn't have to be in the center of the layout but could be close by. The point must be easily accessible from as many sides as possible. If the number of simultaneously used attack lanes is low, then this type is easier. However, it quickly rises in difficulty when the numbers go up because the player is in the open and more exposed to multiple attack angles standing in the middle. Getting swarmed by hordes of enemies from all sides can quickly turn frustrating.

The block type is where you have a large blocking object at the center forming a loop around it. Therefore, you cannot observe all attack lanes from one spot and move around it to cover all angles. It is a classic yet simple defense layout that can work with many different defense objective types. However, the blocking element has a significant impact on situational awareness and likely delays the detection of any incoming attackers. Therefore, it can quickly become frustrating if you do not have other means to

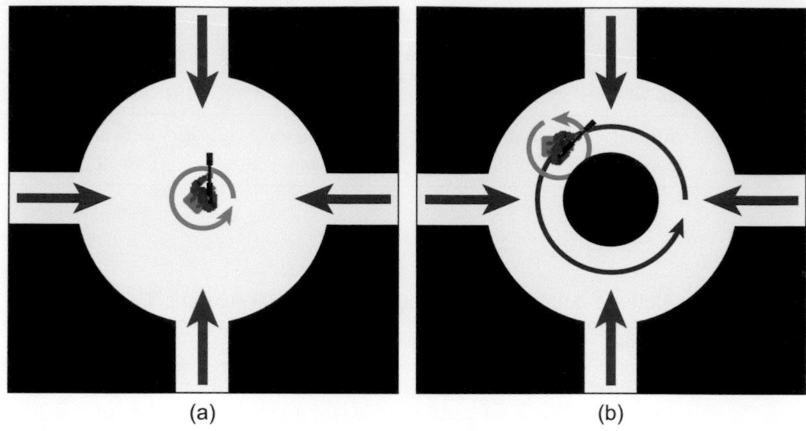


**FIGURE 14.10** (a) Open defense layout type. (b) Block defense layout type.

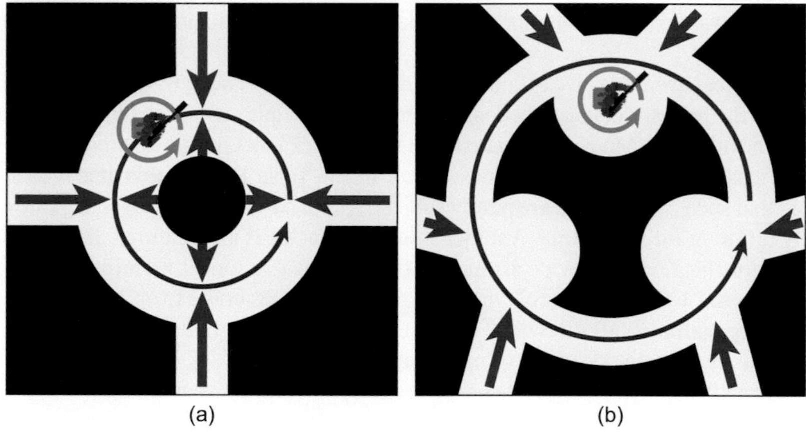


**FIGURE 14.11** (a) Hollow defense layout type. (b) Spread defense layout type.

signal active attack lanes. This messaging is especially crucial for a single player and multiple simultaneous attackers in a 360° scenario. However, the central block is a good opportunity to use it as a landmark, adding a loop, or for a narrative and world-building tie-in.

The hollow type is where the attackers do not just come from multiple outer sides but also come from central positions. You can combine this type also with the block, spread, or open type regarding visibility. The classic example has a tunnel opening in the center, interdimensional portals, or enemies continuously dropping from the sky. As a result, enemies could be anywhere at any time, which can quickly become very stressful and hectic. Therefore, this is rather an uncommon defense layout type and should be handled with care.

The spread type means that your defense objectives or ideal defense spots are far spread out without clear sightlines between. As a result, the player must constantly move around to check a large amount of space continuously. The primary difference to the block layout type is the complexity of the environment and the distance. While it is enough when playing the block type to circle a single object, it requires several turns and time to play the spread type. Classic examples are multiple hostages, downloading PCs, or bomb spots in multiple rooms. It is a more advanced type, yet still common, especially when it is okay if a few defense objectives are allowed to fail.

The layout of the attack lanes is the same as those of the attack scenario without the mission area. Passages are typically used for streamlined, faster ways to the defense zone, especially if only limited space is available. Networks, frontlines, or a combination are suitable if you have much space, but I would especially consider frontlines close and facing the defense zone.

#### *14.1.4.4 Defense Intensity Pacing*

The approach of pacing and ingredient mix is like the attack scenario. Therefore, focus only on a few specialties and memorable elements. Gradually introduce them, have some dips in intensity, and end with a strong, impactful climax. However, there are a few crucial aspects unique to defense pacing.

Other than for the attack scenario, your script is defining the pacing a lot closer in a defense scenario. You control how close the AIs are spawning, how short the intervals are between new attackers spawning, and how fast it takes them to reach the defense objective. The player can only affect pacing by taking out enemies either fast or slow. Therefore, you as a level designer can design highly intense pacing with a noticeable increase in intensity. If you have a static or clear defense mission objective for the attackers to deal with, you have another important factor for the AI to stay focused and less chance for the player to affect the pacing.

When we talk about spawning new attacking AIs, it is important to consider when you spawn the next wave. I recommend two options. The first is to spawn the next wave with a noticeable delay in between as a breather. However, breaks can also feel gamy or overly scripted. The second option is to spawn the next wave when you have about two to three enemies or ~10% to 20% enemies left of the current wave. A bit of randomization here is undoubtedly a nice touch, too. How many of the current AIs are still alive before you spawn the next ones is another essential pacing factor because you do need some dips in the intensity for the next escalation to be noticeable. I usually cannot recommend a steady stream of AI continuously pouring to the defense objective. I would also never spawn the next wave instantly after killing the last one of the current one.

Lastly, I highly recommend focusing on the final attack wave, the climax. Ideally, it has a noticeable increase in the total amount of AI and specialty AI. Now is the time if you have anything that can act as mini-bosses like vehicle enemies or advanced versions of AI archetypes. Additionally, try a slightly lower dip in the intensity curve than usual between the final and the previous wave to make the last wave's impact even more noticeable.

### 14.1.5 Problems and Solutions

#### *14.1.5.1 The Anti-Climax AI*

I wrote several times that a good attack or defense scenario should end with a climax. However, if the player must kill several enemies, it gets very quickly anti-climactic, the fewer AIs are left at the end. Scraping up the last few leftover enemies is everything but an exciting high note. It is especially problematic if the AI is systemic, players can hide easily, and the combat zone is large. If now players must search the enemies instead of sweating to survive, then the climax is ultimately ruined.

The first way to approach this common problem is to redefine climax in this context and set realistic expectations. If your game is inherently systemic, then such an experience is part of your game, to some extent. In such cases, I would define the climax by fighting the last final wave till the enemies are too weak for a climax. Therefore, this last encounter or wave must be a serious threat with a noticeable spike in difficulty but not with higher numbers of AI because then we go back to the original problem. Instead, this spike in difficulty happens with more difficult AI, ideally not only hard-hitting enemies but especially long-surviving AI. Classic examples are the mini-boss tank, the super demons, or crazy armored special forces. It should be an enemy which lasts so long that ideally, they are the last threat players must defeat. Of course, they can be accompanied by other lighter enemies which ideally get killed before finally finishing the very tough one.

However, if you do not have such a tough type of AI or using them is not as consistently reliable as described above, you need to get rid of your leftover enemies as fast as possible. Depending on your game, tech, and context, you have a few options:

- You can let the AI flee, and once they are far away, they do not count anymore.
- You can send the AI to a specific area in the map where players can kill them quickly and fast.

- You can kill the AI, either by suicide or other means (tricky).
- You can send all AI to the player, directly, searching, or only in their rough proximity.
- You can mark them for the player, so they do not have to search the last ones for too long.

Sometimes, a combination or different escalation levels are possible. However, the goal remains to keep this last phase of wiping out the last remaining enemies as short as possible. This method, in conjunction with some much stronger archetypes, should do the trick in most scenarios.

#### *14.1.5.2 The Start Is the Challenge*

It is common that if players attack a prominent location, like a military base filled with enemy AI, then the initial perimeter clash is the only primary challenge. However, usually we want players to fight throughout the entire space and not just at the outside. This issue is especially a problem for systemic games because all AI in the area quickly rush to the player. Once the player kills all enemies, they can stroll through a now-empty location which took you way more effort to build than placing a fence around your base.

The primary solution is to control the active AI and stagger the spawning based on player progression. Initially, you should spawn the AI guarding the perimeter and only a few inside to fake the impression that there is "life" throughout. Once the player enters the base, spawn the next group safely, so players have no chance to recognize their spawn location or even notice that they just spawned in. Instead, it should feel like they just came out of a building or bunker. Staying undetected should get rewarded with less freshly spawning AI and ideally still in an idle stage. However, if the player got detected at any time previously, feel free to turn up the heat. Depending on how many layers your location has, you can repeat this method with increasing difficulty. Keep the enemy spawn locations and the triggering in mind because at no point should the players be aware that moving through invisible triggers is triggering the next wave. One way to reduce this possibility is to keep a consistent stream of respawning "hunter & killer" reinforcements upon detection, independent of the player progression within the space. Their purpose is to keep some soft pressure on players, but the actual escalation happens by progressing through the space. This reinforcement approach and layered enemy scripting are a good foundation for games with less systemic AI, too.

However, keep in mind that this methodology only works if the location is large enough. It certainly does not work for small locations. A rule of thumb is that the location must be at least three times larger than the average engagement distance. Therefore, if the location is very dense with objects, it is easier to spawn new groups of enemies undetected than in a very open and lofty location. However, if the location is too small or very sparsely populated, you can only spawn enemies coming from the outside as reinforcement.

#### *14.1.5.3 Players Do Not Play Correctly*

You carefully designed your cover network, placed well-planned frontlines, and measured the precise distance for the perfect cover flow. Then during playtest, you realize that most players do not follow your precisely crafted design.

First, let us accept that it is perfectly fine if players do not play as we had it in mind because that is the nature of an interactive medium. Sure, some players purposely want to break your level, but we do not design for them and should spend much time caring about them.

However, if most players completely ignore your layout or another type of level design setup, it makes sense to have a closer look. First, players can only use what they know exists. Therefore, you need to give them time and space to understand what is ahead of them. It does not always have to be a perfect vantage point, but the more complex your setup, the more time and overview they need. Secondly, players only use your setup if they consider it as an advantage. If you had a trap in mind or wanted to lure players into an extra challenge, then expect them to "smell" it. Also, always expect players trying to use all their gear to "cheat" their way through your combat setup. Even if it is not true in most cases, it is a healthy design mindset. Thirdly, players only use your setup if they need it. If the threat is too minimal for average players, then, of course, they will skip it.

All in all, it typically is not the players' fault if your setup is not functioning as intended. It is a mix of lack of readability, felt disadvantage, and simply need in most cases.

#### *14.1.5.4 Enemies Lack Purpose*

One reason why I like objective-based defense setups is that here the AI typically has a clear purpose. Killing the players is not their primary purpose but killing or destroying whatever the players have to defend. Attacking players along the way only happens if they pose a threat, but if the players are not visible, they continue with their original goal. However, if players are the attackers, then in many games, the only goal of the AI is to attack, too. If AI only exist to kill or be killed, it reduces the immersion fighting intelligent opponents and consequently reduces the chance for players to feel smart in return. It might work for some hell demons, braindead zombies, or raccoons with rabies, but not for anything smarter.

The solution is to give attacked AI a goal beyond attacking the player, even if it is short or temporarily. This purpose can be in their systemic behavior like running to an alarm and calling for reinforcement, healing their friends, or providing force shields. However, such actions are not really objectives, just something else than attacking. Instead, I recommend you think about what is the purpose of the attacked AI? In many cases, they are defending something or someone. Therefore, what are your game's tools to display such an objective? For example: Can you make them retreat? Can they regroup, can they join with other AI, or try to gain fire superiority? Are there any dialogs or animations you can play to show their objectives to the player? Anything you can do to make the AI have some purpose during combat, other than getting killed or killing the player, will make your world a more believable place.

#### *14.1.5.5 Surviving Is Not Fun*

When I previously stated that I do enjoy simple defense scenarios, there is one type that requires extra careful attention: When the players only must defend themselves or simply survive a certain amount of time while staying in a specified area. The problem is that the AI typically does not know where the player is, and if the player is hidden, they just search around. It requires a lot of careful scripting, good layout, and well-balanced game mechanics to be exciting for players, so they constantly must switch positions and constantly feel the tension. Such a setup becomes especially tiring to work on if the defense area is large and changes still a lot during production.

My first recommendation would be to give the AI another purpose than only hunting the player. In other words: Give the player something to defend, which the AI knows. Even if you give players much leeway, it is better than nothing. However, if you cannot do it, then I recommend keeping the defense area as small as possible. Next up, I would change the objective from "survive X time" to "kill X enemies" because essentially, if players killed enough threats, they defended themselves successfully. The survival aspect can remain in the narrative treatment. However, gameplaywise, players are again in an active role. Alternatively, you can cheat a bit and give the systematic AI a loose player location. It can work in a pinch if the location you provide the AI is not too precise. The player should never feel cheated, just conveniently pressured enough.

## 14.2 About Open-World Locations

### 14.2.1 Introduction

The core definition for an open-world location is a space that players can access from all sides. However, at times large structures or natural formations can block the full 360° access, like a cliff wall, game world borders, inaccessible large buildings, or lava lakes. There is no strict rule, but I would treat any location with less than 180° access rather like a wide linear space or sandbox, but the transitions and interpretations are fluid and depend heavily upon context. For example, a mining entrance at a cliff might only appear to feature 180° access, but then it might also feature a hidden back entrance.

Any location in an open-world which only features an entrance to a linear section is not a true open-world location. In such cases, the open-world merely acts like an expensive menu to linear levels. For me, the 360° access remains the fundamental definition of a true open-world location. Therefore, level designers must design their location for players attacking from any possible angle and playstyle, making it one of the more challenging yet very rewarding layout types.

Despite the name, non-open-world worlds, such as a sandbox or large multiplayer levels, can also feature such layouts. The previous chapter focused more on attacking along linear sections. This chapter focuses more on the general design attacking open layouts, their flow considerations, and different types. Defending such a location was already covered in the previous chapter as well. Similarly, ingredient pacing and mixes from the previous chapter apply here as well.

### 14.2.2 The DNA of an Open-World Location

#### *14.2.2.1 Surrounding Path and Vantage Points*

If the core definition of an open-world location features 360° access, then it also means that you can move around every such location. Cliffs, walls, or structures might occasionally allow only one-way traversal or force players to hike long ways around. Still, as a level designer, you should always try your best to provide players a path around an open-world location. However, they do not have to be actual paths, easily found, easy to traverse, or at the perfect consistent distance to the location.

The path can be as wide as possible or as tight as needed but let players see occasionally the target location for orientation. I recommend designing multiple purposely placed overviews or vantage points along the path. They allow artists to present and frame the target location nicely, but at the same time allow players to get an understanding of their options and observe the AI ahead. Especially the idle animations of the local AI are good narrative tools to bring a location to life, give it purpose and context.

Therefore, such vantage points are close enough for the AI to be active and observable by players, but also distant enough for players to not easily get detected. Common vantage points are higher than the location's ground, but occasionally other angles can provide a similar overview or rather an insight. The exact minimum and maximum distances depend on your game and what archetypes are present at the location. For example, snipers on watchtowers require players to stay away further or stay in bushes compared to a location filled by blind toxic slimes. Keep in mind that the distance greatly affects the exposition possibilities. For example, overhearing conversations about war crimes in a well-guarded prison camp, surrounded by watchtowers and snipers, will be very difficult from the outside.

For a small open-world location below a hundred by a hundred meters, I recommend at least three vantage points as the absolute bare minimum. However, my recommendation for such locations would be four to five vantage points. The fewer vantage points you provide, the less likely players will find them. Bigger locations need, of course, even more vantage points.

You can increase the chances of players going for such vantage points by making them clearly stand out. Classic examples are nearby water towers, huge rocks poking out of a forest, large billboards, or conveniently accessible rooftops on the other side of the road with a big neon sign screaming for attention. In an urban environment or when the target location is huge, the vantage points can be part of the actual location. For example, your target environment is a large factory, but the actual gameplay space is only a subsection of the industrial complex. Therefore, you can use parts of the surrounding factory-like train wagons, towers, rooftops, or conveyor belts as vantage points. An open-world location does not have to be an isolated structure or area. Instead, it makes it look even more artificial and gamey. This topic is especially crucial in urban or other large complex environments/worlds. The more a location can blend in the surroundings, the better.

Do not expect all players to move around your location. Some careful, exploratory, or long-range loving players might do so. However, the primary function of the surrounding path is to give every player, coming from any direction, a fair chance to find a vantage point and then find their way in. You should not underestimate the player-leading nature of such paths. I would even go so far and design player-leading

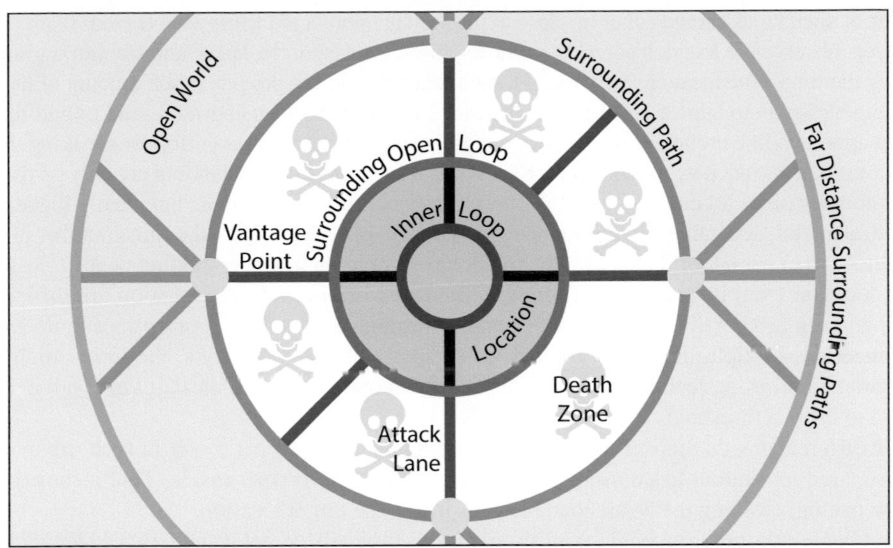


**FIGURE 14.12** Schematic, abstract, basic open-world location diagram: Far distance paths lead to vantage points surrounding the locations. The surrounding path connects all vantage points. Attack/Sneak lanes connect this surrounding path with the location. The location is surrounded by an open loop which has lanes leading in the inside with an optional inner loop.

elements even further outside the surrounding path pointing toward it. Such far distance surrounding paths and elements have the primary purpose to lead to the actual closer surrounding path—essentially, player-leading to player-leading.

Once players are at the vantage points, it is important to note that such observation points should not be excellent combat spots, especially not for sniping. It might sound confusing since you are supposed to observe the enemies but not engage them. Of course, players can snipe them from here, but they should quickly find them at a disadvantage because typically, you want players to play your well-crafted location and not just the surroundings. Once they engage here, they should either have a very tough sniping game, commit to the location ahead, or retreat. One semi-reliable way to achieve this is to provide very little cover protecting against threats coming from the location, forcing players to move and act quickly. However, suppose the player has the means to engage from a distance without the risk of detection, like with suppressors, drones, or summons. In that case, I recommend discussing solutions with game design. This case is also very different if your game has a strong long-distance combat focus or none.

#### *14.2.2.2 Attack Angles and Way In*

Once the player has scouted out the location long enough to their liking, it is time for them to commit. Ideally, this means a movement toward the location after none or only a limited number of long-range engagements. The following considerations are important to convince and guide players into open-world locations.

As stated previously, a typical open-world location is accessible all-around. Still, I recommend thinking about attack angles or lanes comparable to the previous defense scenarios, just in reverse. For example, running over an open field is not considered an adequately designed attack lane. Instead, add lanes that stand out enough that players should consider them good options and chain of POAs compared to the rest.

Such lanes are so important because there is typically empty space around an outdoor open-world location. Now, such paths allow players to cross this empty space in relative safety, like a flanking route, while providing the level designers to guide players.

The start of such lanes should either be close to the vantage points or clearly visible from them. The idea is that players observe the location ahead from those points, plan, spot the lanes, and smoothly transition to move along them into the location. Still, ideally, such lanes should not provide a rich amount of hard cover or other suitable spots to start a big firefight. Instead, I recommend focusing more and providing a safer undetected approach like crouching through high grass, using a zip-line on a rooftop, or sneaking through a short sewer tunnel. As much as possible, search for vertical solutions for the lanes and not only on the ground level. The number of such lanes should be at least the number of vantage points but ideally higher. It feels predictable, artificial, and gamy if every vantage point always provides exactly the same number of lanes.

In a tighter urban open-world, you usually do not have a consistently surrounding death zone isolating the target location from its proximity. Therefore, the lanes leading into the location are different, too. For example, I am talking about the sneaky backdoor through the kitchen, rooftop access, underground sewer connection, or ziplining over a busy road. In such tight environments, the lanes might not all have the same committing feeling, like sneaking across an open field with bushes, but you still have the impression to cross a threshold.

Another difference is that most enemies are not staged at the outer perimeter in such urban environments, compared to outdoor locations. Instead, most of them are further inside. That means the initial lull, or low pacing, crossing the death zone happens inside the target location.

Once combat breaks out in an outdoor location, players typically do not want to run back over the open field but stay inside. However, in the case of an urban location, players are ideally already way deeper in the location when combat breaks out. Therefore, it is crucial to provide enough options for players as soon as they are inside and where combat typically breaks out further inside. Otherwise, they might quickly run back out again if it feels like a trap.

#### *14.2.2.3 Outer and Inner Loops*

If we go back to loops, then a generic outdoor open-world location always has a surrounding open circle. This case means that you can circle the entire location once you cross the death zone staying on the surrounding loop. In urban or other complicated environments, the circle might be fully closed or partially closed, and players should be able to circle the location rather inside than outside.

Regardless of open or closed, this surrounding loop is crucial to allow a fluid connected movement of local AI, reinforcement, and players, for a natural flow within the location and gives players reset or get-out of fight options in case it gets too heated, without leaving the location. If the pressure gets too high and players do not have options to slip out sideways, they will likely rather go back to the surrounding layer.

From the surrounding layer, you have multiple pathways leading deeper into the location or going up or down. Conveniently placed ladders, quick stairway access, or shallow crouch tunnel entrances are

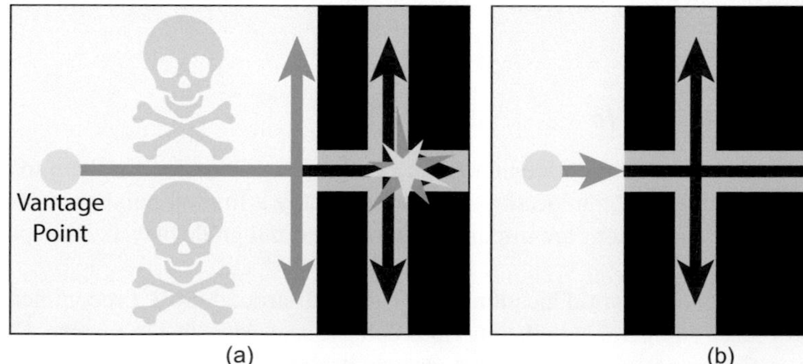


**FIGURE 14.13** (a) **Outdoor open-world location:** Clear death zone between vantage point and location, open surrounding loops provide sideways options around the location, common combat encounters appear soon after entering the location because death zone, and open loop keeps player close enough. (b) **Urban open-world location:** Usually no death zone between vantage point to location, inside closed surrounding loops provide sideways options, common combat encounters appear later after entering the location to keep players inside.

classic examples of alternative routes into the location. Ideally, you can also see such specialty options already from the vantage points acting as additional player magnets. The way into the location leads to the potential mission objective or provides AI to sweep through the location quickly, too.

How many dominating inner loops you have in addition to the outer one heavily depends on the environment. Smaller outdoor locations typically have none, while smaller urban locations should have one. Larger variations have multiple, for example, layered inner loops like an onion or connected ones like an eight, two overlapping loops, or the Borromean rings. More about base layout types and their loops further on in this chapter, but it all comes back to inner and outer loops again.

Lastly, open-world locations do not have to resemble very circular or square locations but can have almost any shape. For example, harbors going around a small bay or lengthy bazaars are perfectly acceptable, unusual shapes if they don't go too extreme. It also gets exciting if an open-world location has multiple horizontal layers vertically above each other, such as a street, rooftop, and underground level.

### 14.2.3 Basic Enemy Setup

#### *14.2.3.1 Introduction*

If you build linear or even some sandbox layouts and start populating the world with enemy AI, you typically know where the player is and in what state (alerted, relaxed, etc.) the world is. Therefore, you can spawn your AI very controlled, well timed, and have a good grip on pacing and difficulty. However, open-world locations are such wide playgrounds that they require a different mindset working with AI.

#### *14.2.3.2 Parameter and Overwatch AI*

The first AI players see at an open-world location are guarding the outer parameter or keeping overwatch from the inside. Classic examples are your pesky guard dogs sniffing around, circling guard patrols, bouncers at key entrances, or snipers on high spots. Besides guarding the place, their function is to tell players: Here is danger.

The key is finding a balance between guarding the place difficult enough and encouraging players to get in. Dangerous enough to be intriguing and provide an appropriate challenge, yet easy enough that players commit to and engage the location within your design intention.

Players should never see all AI ahead from any vantage point. I would stay between 40% and 70% maximum visible AI at each vantage point, but depending on the context, visiting each vantage point could allow players to observe all AI eventually. However, I would not use more than 30% to 50% of your AI guarding the parameter or keeping an overwatch because they are the most exposed and will likely die first. Exposing more than half your present enemies to a likely quick or silent death is not ideal. However, the trick is to effectively guard a location with the lowest amount of AI. This number greatly varies between games and engines. In most cases, you can lock down a smaller, isolated location with three rotating snipers. However, you do not always have a small, isolated location or always want to use lots of snipers.

Alternatively, you can use patrols or guards; however, there are a few important considerations. First, do not let them perform too long patrols or the openings are so long that some players might not even know there is a patrol. However, if your max AI count is high enough, you can work with overlapping patrols. Secondly, if you really want to use a very long patrol, make sure it travels fast, like a vehicle circling the location. Thirdly, avoid any static guards because they are too easy targets. Instead, let them do a few little animations or small patrols forcing them to move around a bit. For example, the bouncer switches from leaning against the doorframe to his favorite smoking spot to occasionally shouting something to the crowd. Fourthly, do not forget that patrols can do other things than just walking and stopping. If they stop and look around, let them smoke, urinate, chat, yawn, or scratch their backs. Ideally, you have a combination of observers at high points, medium-long patrols, and some slightly moving guards. Each one protects one part, so each part of the outer rings is checked at one point. There should be no always guaranteed safe passage into an open-world location, except it is a cool and hard-to-find stealth path.

### 14.2.3.3 Inner AI

The first function of the inner AI is to bring life to the location. Players observing them from the outside or sneaking inside should see a wide range of animations, overhear intriguing conversations, get immersed into the world, and expose the function and purpose of the location within the world and narrative. As much as possible, AI on the inside should not just all scratch body parts, yawn, urinate, and smoke, but their actions directly link to the location's function. So, for example, if the location is a black site prison, guards should torture some prisoners, or a secret toxic laboratory should include soldiers carrying toxic waste barrels. I only mentioned potentially threatening enemies and not harmless civilians because if your overall active AI count is limited, you need to tell all that narrative with more enemies and with fewer or no civilians.

The second function for inner AI is to act as local and almost instant reinforcement for the outer guards. Likely the outer guards or the ones keeping overwatch will die first, but if the AI is lucky, they could still alert the remaining AI. This situation should create an instant spike in difficulty and pacing because several AIs start swarming toward the player. However, I recommend placing the inner AI further away from the outer parameter, delaying their arrival a bit because if the wave of enemy AI hits the player too fast, they might be motivated to retreat while they are still on or close to the outer surrounding loop. Instead, giving them some time allows players to make a few more steps inside or get a better idea of their options.

If players successfully sneak around or kill enemies undetected, they should be rewarded, especially witnessing more of the world and narrative. For example, they could overhear some lore-relevant conversation or observe further narrative animations. However, I recommend exposing your key narrative or most relevant idle animations already from the outside, so more players have a chance to notice it.

### 14.2.3.4 Additional AI

In many cases, the present local AI is not enough for a lengthy firefight, a suitable challenge, or a longer mission. Therefore, you need to bring in new AI as reinforcement. The trigger for the spawning of additional AI varies between games and could be, for example, detection, alarm, finding dead AI, or mission objectives.

How many AIs you can spawn additionally depends on how many active AI your game can handle performance-wise. Often this means you can only spawn new incoming AI in small groups once some AI gets killed. I severely recommend never instantly replacing a single dead AI character with a single new one. Instead, always work with small groups of two to four AIs. Such groups or waves ideally have an increase in difficulty for pacing.

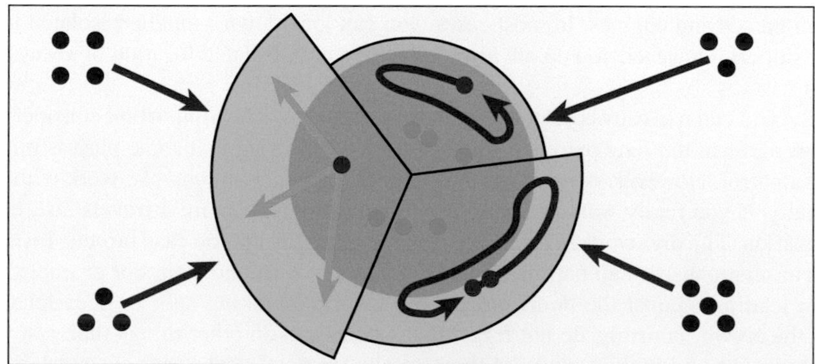

**FIGURE 14.14 Basic Open-World AI Setup Schema Example**: Parameter AI (red) is 40% of the total initial present AI split into three sectors. Left is a sniper, top right a single patrol close to the location (gray), and bottom right is a two-man patrol a bit further out. Sixty percent of the initial AI is inside (green), doing idle animations chatting or patrolling. Additional AI (blue) comes in from the outside in case more AI is needed.

If you pick the archetypes for the additional AI, make sure that they fit their spawn position. If they spawn far outside, they are ideally fast movers which come close and not slow moving long-range or heavily armored enemies. If they appear close or within the location, such as dropped by helicopter or arrive by truck, slower well-armored troops can work well again. Long-range troops that tend to stay outside the location are often less ideal, except the player is aware of them, or they are a serious, reliable threat to the player. Often such long-range troops stay too far outside the location and the player ends up searching for them. However, reinforcement should come to the player as fast as possible whenever possible.

Spawning AI outside a location is not always easy because they must spawn far away to make sense but close enough to arrive on time. They also must spawn unseen, which means behind large enough objects which are not too absurd. If players see ten AI characters suddenly come out behind a thicker tree, they will certainly raise some eyebrows. Lastly, they still must arrive in time and often must cross a death zone. I will cover the main problem around this topic later. However, for now, I highly recommend designing any open-world location right from the beginning with ideal spawn positions for reinforcement. Adding large rocks or buildings later just to spawn AI behind often feels very shoehorned in.

Therefore, it is tempting to spawn AI inside the location. However, I would be incredibly careful with this approach! As a golden rule in level design to never spawn AI at locations the player recently visited or knows is closed off. You should also never spawn AI too close to the player because there is a realistic chance that the layer might observe them spawning. Therefore, if the location is small, do not spawn inside, and if the location is large enough, then still be extremely careful and better to have a script in place always to pick the spawn points furthest away. Such a scenario is especially a nightmare in co-op. A location is large enough for such "inside" spawning if at least three times larger than the average engagement distance. I also cannot recommend mysterious doors that only open from the inside, but an endless stream of AI is continuously coming out of them (=monster closets). As much as possible, try to let AI come in from the outside if you deal with open-world locations. Again, this is game dependent, since, for example, certain aliens of demons have more flexibility.

### 14.2.4 Basic Layout Types

#### *14.2.4.1 Introduction*

This chapter will share my general thoughts about some of the more common, simple open-world layout types. I focused on relatively small location types rarely exceeding a hundred by a hundred meters. Much bigger location layouts quickly become too complex to observe repeating patterns or, in most cases, are just a combination or variation of the simple ones.

#### *14.2.4.2 Single Structure*

One of the most common types is a location focused around a single structure or building like an abandoned hotel, an occupied gas station, or a decadent mansion full of vampires. Other structures or objects can be around, providing cover, but the main building or structure is the dominating layout factor.

The main flow within the location is around the building and going through it. It has no secondary outer lanes or loops because the location's dominating aspect is simple. The inner structure can have multiple floors, all types of shapes, and several accesses, but it is important to have access to as many sides as possible to keep a fluid flow here. All lanes connected to the surrounding one, going through the main building, create more and more sub-loops. They are crucial to bringing complexity to an otherwise very simple layout.

The graphic shows a simple cross of connecting lanes going through the central structure. However, it can be more complex with more lanes, secondary paths on the mid and low level, and even an inner circle if the building is large enough. The most important factor is recognizable ways into the buildings for attackers and easy and fast ways out for the defenders. If your central structure has multiple floors, make sure that each floor has at least two connections to the outside for a more fluid flow. How well the location itself is defendable depends on the context of your game and location.

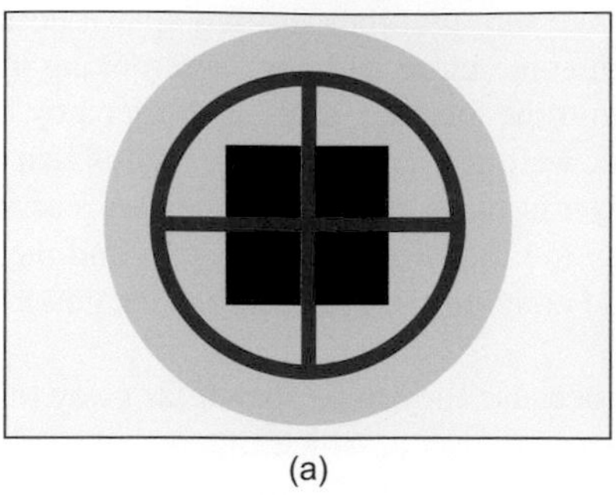

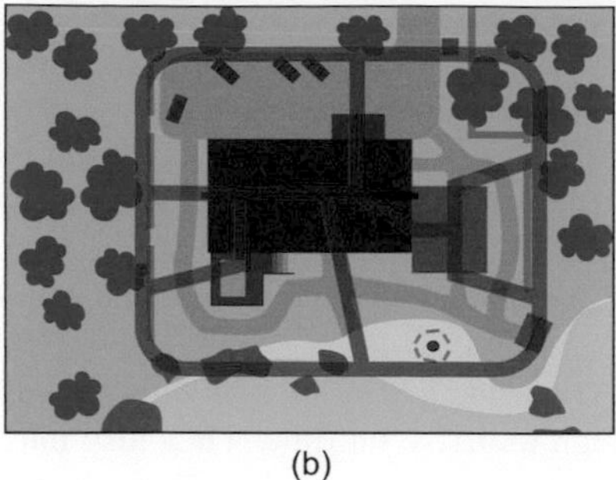

(a) (b)

**FIGURE 14.15** (a) Abstract, basic single structure layout. (b) A small countryside hotel as an example for a single structure layout. The horizontal lane has a few more options due to the attached restaurant building and the pool-patio but otherwise it stayed fairly simple.

However, the circle around is equally important to the lanes going through the central structure. By default, the central structure provides a huge cover to the outside. However, for attackers to effectively use the outer lane, they need plenty of covers and ideally a few bigger ones as footholds and orientation. Depending on the size of your location and inner structure, I would not recommend forcing but only motivating players to go inside. The close surroundings might open up many interesting navigational opportunities all around or provide some unique options for firefights, environmental storytelling, or traversal challenges. Without an outer loop around the structure, you need to create such loops within the structure like in certain urban environments. However, usually it is a lot easier to feature a loop outside than crafting one inside a building.

### *14.2.4.3 Multi-Structure Flow*

The next one is creating the flow connecting multiple medium-sized structures or buildings, forming one large loop. Typical examples are workshops with scrapyards, farms with multiple buildings, small military bases, or random depots—any other smaller objects in between connecting the main ones to create the outer bigger loop. The center typically stays empty.

The primary focus is a huge loop going all around, connecting all the main structures. The number of such structures is not crucial, but it should be at least three. Usually, players stop in one of those structures, fight, and when the pressure gets too much, they slip out to one side, soon finding themselves in another structure. This flow repeats till players complete the objective. It works well in both aggressive and stealth playstyles.

The secondary loops outside the structures and in the center are merely routes that come automatically with this type of layout. Sometimes, you can enhance them, especially when it is unsuitable for making your structure very strong or dominating. It is not realistic to expect perfect available buildings all the time for every location. However, if possible, your primary focus should be on the flow directly connecting the structures. You can achieve this by, for example, placing the only open doors and windows exactly at the right spots, arranging covers slightly angled to guide players between the buildings, funneling them back from the other (pink) loops into the buildings, and keeping the center a death zone. Larger locations could feature multiple such interconnected loops.

Such structures must be relatively safe spots providing combat, stealth, and navigation opportunities to as many directions as possible. They do not always have to be buildings with interiors but can also be denser collections of cover objects if they support the flow and are recognizable.

Also, the distance between the structures is key. If they are too big, it is harder for you to connect them with cover, and players will likely not follow your flow. Therefore, when the location can feature many buildings, it is better to have a shorter distance than a too long one between the buildings.

Many locations use this type of layout, but unfortunately, with a broken or very choppy flow. Too often, players get stuck in a structure, feel trapped with no way out than to retreat, or die trying to reach the next

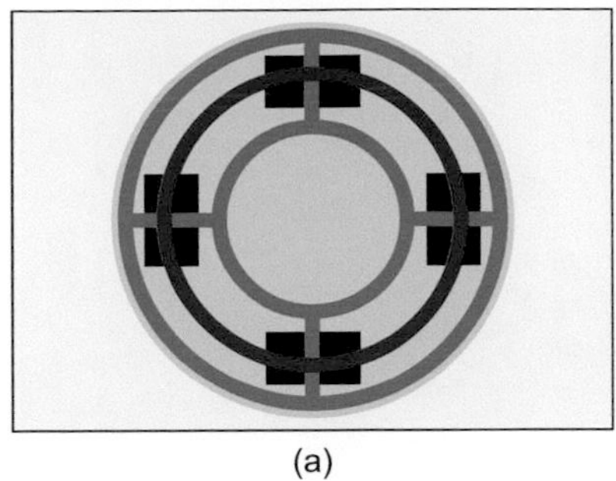

(a)

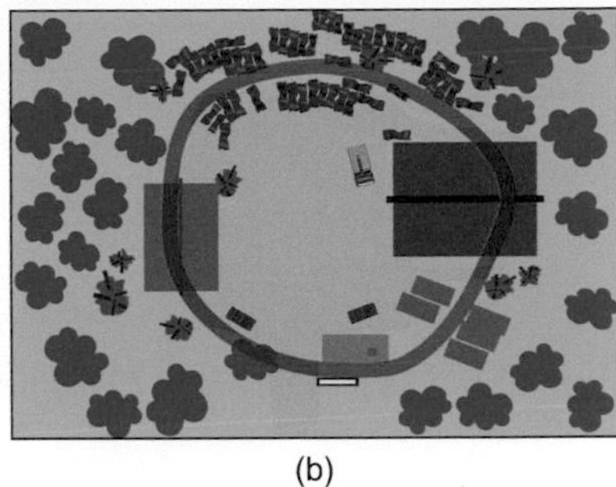

(b)

**FIGURE 14.16** (a) Abstract, basic multi-structure layout. (b) A small garage with a scrapyard. The main loop goes along: the rusting cars at the top, the main garage right, a bigger storage building right, and a larger container for the office at the bottom. The office container doesn't have to have an interior, it is just there to complete the flow.

one. Trying to enjoy the spaces can feel incredibly choppy and rough because not enough attention was spent on flow, guidance, and funneling. Every little carefully rotated object or added opening matters that prevent players from getting stuck or skipping a crucial path. I am aware that at first, such a layout might appear gamy looking at it from the top, but it very quickly vanishes once you are in the game. It truly feels great to have firefights in all directions, quickly swap position to another safe spot, and repeat. All while staying within the same location.

### *14.2.4.4 Separate Structures*

This type represents any layouts featuring structures so distant or disconnected from each other that there is no fluid flow between them. Typical examples are leftover fortress towers, distant buildings on an airfield, or observatories with two or three telescope buildings. Any additional objects are around the key structures or buildings to lure players out and support some secondary flow around them.

Usually, I have encountered such layout type with two to three large structures but rarely with more due to space limitations. Also, the more buildings you add, the more likely you end up with a choppy multi-structure flow, due to a mismatch of intentions and layout reality. Now, the secondary loops around the separate buildings result from separate structures and vary from setting to setting. Of course, those structures do not have to be buildings again but can also represent any other type of denser collections of assets, with ideally some verticality again.

The base pattern for playing such a location is one structure at a time. Players take care of the threats of one building, observing the next one and looking for a way to the next. As you see, there is a noticeable dip in pacing, quickly followed by a spike, which starts with the transition to the next one. While the previous two open-world layout types have more continuous pacing, this one has some clearer ups and downs for most players.

Essentially this layout type creates a death zone with frontlines between the dominating structures. There is no fluid flow between them like the multi-structure flow. Therefore, you have to play and plan well to transition from building to building. This type lives from the tension between the strongholds and waiting for the right opening, finding the hidden path, or just running through the death zone like a mad person. So even if there is the main lane connecting the structures more likely players look for the slow flanking routes. Another way to see such a layout is to consider it a center axis layout. However, the two sides should still be within your game's engagement distance, or it might feel like two separate locations. Some proximity is required to establish a relationship between them.

### *14.2.4.5 Spiral*

As the name preludes, this layout is a main linear lane going in a spiral. It is a relatively uncommon type, and I have not used it too often. Typical examples are your wide and strangely shaped tower in a fantasy

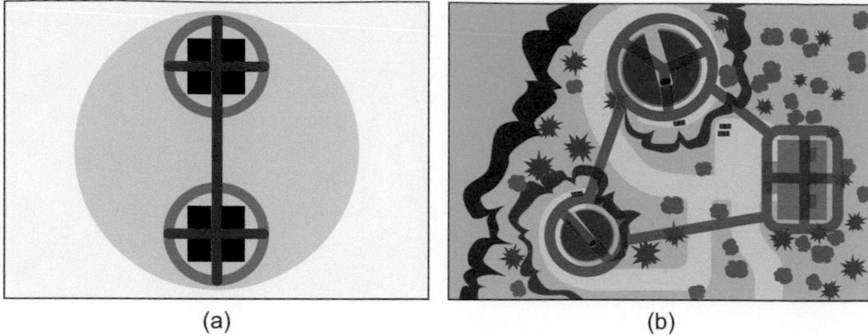

FIGURE 14.17 (a) Abstract, basic separate structure layout. (b) An observatory with two telescopes and one research building with a cliff downwards on the left. Each building has their secondary loop around, and the primary ones are connecting the buildings without directly forming all the flanking options.

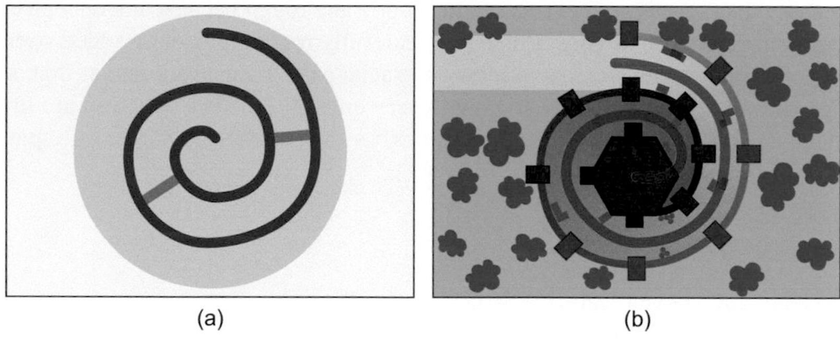

FIGURE 14.18 (a) Abstract, spiral layout with two optional in-between connections. (b) A generic fantasy tower with a spiral path leading up to the center tower.

game, the corn maze in a horror game, a smaller open-pit mine, or a military forward operating base on top of a mountain.

If the center is much above the surrounding floor, you have secondary paths going down from the center, and if the center is below the surroundings, then the secondary paths are the way around. If the whole location is primarily on one level, then any cross-connections are going both ways, or there are few such connections. A spiral layout on the same level is particularly tricky because likely players lack a good overview or close landmarks for orientation, especially when the walls are very close together.

The primary problem with this type is its inherent linear nature. Therefore, if I use this type, the center is usually elevated, additionally acting as a player-leading element. Additionally, any player coming from the outside must fight their way up or occasionally find a carefully placed hidden shortcut. Always let players work their way upwards if you have much good content along the way and let them jump and skip parts downwards.

Open-pit mines or other layouts where the inside is much lower are tricky. First, they are difficult to fill with lots of good content all the way around. Secondly, players can skip the spiral by jumping downwards. Therefore, give them clear advantages to fight along the spiral, or rather make it very disadvantageous ending up at the bottom with enemies all around.

### 14.2.5 Problems and Solutions

#### *14.2.5.1 Not Enough AI*

We level designers love making our locations too big because we have so many ideas, world-building requires it, and we keep getting told to give players lots of options. Additionally, nowadays, better production pipelines and technology remove many previous limitations. Therefore, our locations became not just better looking but also grew in size. However, the number of active AI did not grow at the same rate in many cases. Therefore, almost the same amount of AI has to fight in increasingly larger space. Too little AI in too much space is a common issue.

My first recommendation is to check how feasible it is to reduce the location's footprint. Remember that such a reduction does not have to be just deleting objects but also a reduction in gameplay importance. For example, you might be hard-pressed to reduce a larger hotel complex further, but you certainly can reduce the cover density of the open space around the pool, golf course, or parking lot. Essentially you reduce the space in which gameplay is possible and happening without touching the main building's footprint. Usually modifying buildings with interiors is lots of work, while arranging cover outside is not.

Secondly, restrict the AI's presence to a smaller area. Look for the most suitable smallest space in which the AI can tell the same narrative, and about ~40% of them can still realistically guard the location. I like using the "40% AI guard" criteria because if I need much more AI, the location is usually getting too big or too complex. Complexity is important to factor in as well. A small, yet very complex location, can quickly run into the same problem as a large but simple one.

The question is now, what do you do with the rest of your large location if you restrict AI only to a small part of it? The answer is that you use it for the players. I would see if you can reduce their complexity, but otherwise, they might allow for some unique and exciting stealth lanes, vantage points, or attack angles. We would have often never considered putting so much effort into such points and paths, but after we shrank the AI-occupied area, we had the other space and assets already available, and they were a blast.

#### *14.2.5.2 Players Only Stay Outside*

I am talking about players not leaving their comfortable sniping spot and finishing off all enemies without putting a step into your elaborate layout. This issue is frequent in open-world games or larger sandbox levels. By default, players should have the freedom to play how they want, and if sniping is part of your game's playstyles, then it would be wrong to punish it. However, like with many topics, it is a matter of balance. The problem becomes relevant if sniping is always a lot easier than going down in the layout.

Let us look at this issue, ignoring game balance and individual player skills, only from the level design perspective. First, every sniping position is part of your layout, and not just the location players are sniping at. I know it does not change much, but it is a matter of mindset. Therefore, do not be sad or angry that players do not play your "layout" if they indeed do so.

Secondly, if sniping is seemingly overpowered, then ensure that the location's surrounding layout does not provide advantageous long-range shooting positions. For example, you provide little to no cover or lots of exposure. Therefore, players can initially observe in peace but can only do about one or two shots before they must change position. In my opinion, a semi-continuous moving player is okay because then they are playing your surrounding layout.

Thirdly, it matters what counter tools you provide to the enemies. Do they have snipers themselves? Can they engage indirectly via artillery or mortars? Do they have fast-moving archetypes that put some serious stress on sniping players, like attack dogs or quick-flying imps? Can the enemies retreat to a safe position? Are there safe passages with cover for the enemy to rush the sniper? The questions are just examples of ideas on how to strengthen the defender. Another, less nice solution favors reinforcement spawn points close to sniping players. I would not advocate this solution until you exceed all others and still have serious camping issues. It is especially a huge no-go if the spawn positions are very close to the player! Just because players seemingly "abuse" the system does not justify you being unfair to them, especially if they just play your game.

In the end, in my opinion, sniping is not the issue. It is a legit playstyle, which only becomes a problem if players can camp and exploit. However, the exploit issue is not related to sniping alone and is often the cause of problematic game mechanics and layouts. Therefore, level design will most likely find the best solutions working close together with game design.

#### *14.2.5.3 The Reinforcement Takes Too Long*

As I have mentioned previously, reinforcement or other types of outside-spawning AI is often crucial for open-world layouts. However, it is a common issue that they take too long till they arrive because we do not want to spawn them ten meters behind the player.

Helicopters or other vehicles are an obvious solution. However, if players can take them out with wildly available rocket launchers, they can quickly take out all your arriving enemies with a few explosives. Another problem is that vehicles typically must spawn further away due to sound and visibility, especially helicopters.

In all seriousness, the most proven solution is to consider such spawns from the very beginning. You should know from the documentation phase that you will need such spawners and how close they should be. Therefore, your larger layout should incorporate safe, close enough, and several backup spawn positions. Dropping large, gamey-looking rocks around your military camp just because you need safe spawn positions is not a good indicator for a solid planning phase.

If it is an outdoor map, think early about terrain features like trenches, small valleys, or close hilltops that allow you to spawn AI close enough and provide some safety and justify why and how AI could appear so close. The same counts for urban maps with, for example, alleys, subway exits, or rooftops. Often, outside AI, which takes too long to arrive, is a layout topic and not a game mechanic one. However, good mechanics make it easier for us level designers to address this issue.

Lastly, I recommend planning for at least two more backup spawn locations so your script or game can always pick the ideal positions for your AI to spawn. The primary reason for such backup positions is that players should never see AI spawn, but it can also spawn the fastest to arrive yet safest position.

## 14.3 About Stealth Sections

### 14.3.1 Introduction

The typical stealth gameplay loop is: plan, execute, vanish, then repeat. This loop means the players need, first, a way to oversee the situation, typically a vantage point of some type. Then they can execute their plan and vanish without ever getting detected. However, if the plan goes south—and that is okay, especially on higher difficulties—then they need fair enough opportunities or space to adjust their plans. No plan survives the first contact with the enemy, but fairness for the player is very relevant in a game's context. This is even more important if detection means instant or imminent failure.

For the player stealth setups are all about careful timing to avoid detection, reading, and maxing out the environment to its full potential while considering equipment and abilities. Ultimately, they are an art form of level design because they include a huge array of different interwoven design elements, with such a small margin of error for the player. This chapter covers the foundation and most common mistakes and how to address them.

If you can incorporate most, if not all, solutions below then you very likely have a very solid stealth setup. A lot of further considerations are heavily game dependent or are covered in other chapters of this book. Also, when I talk about stealth setups in this chapter, I mean the purest form that does not allow any detection and avoids killing AI when possible.

### 14.3.2 Stealth Foundation

For me stealth in video games is comparable with a music rhythm game, just with drastically different controls, characters, camera view, and that you first must figure out the song. Essentially it is a chain or string of actions the players must perform within the right timing to complete a stealth section.

Some of those actions can be sneaking through shadows, jumping off a balcony, waiting while hanging on a ledge, crawling through an air duct, or knocking out an enemy. The amount of leeway, timewise, the player must complete this chain of actions is a significant difficulty factor. Another difficulty factor is the sheer number of actions, the number of different types of actions, and the speed at which the actions switch.

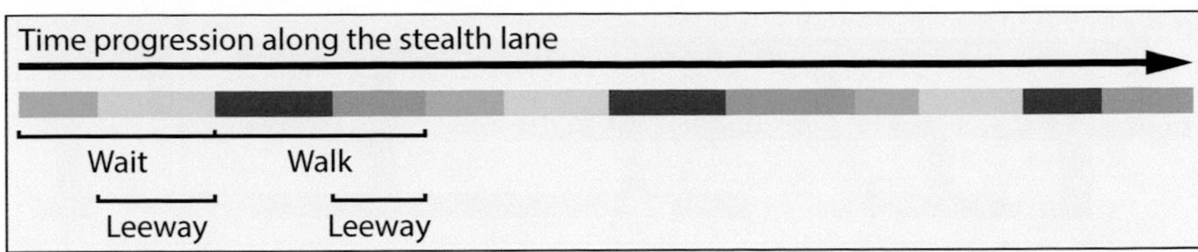


**FIGURE 14.19** Easy example.

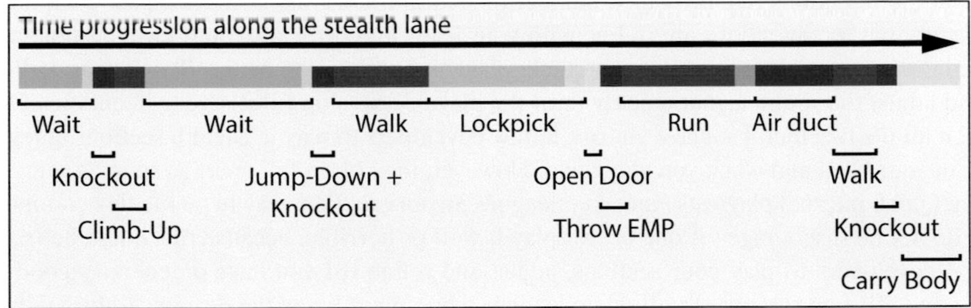


**FIGURE 14.20** Difficult example.

An easy example is a simple chain of walking and waiting in cover while a few guards walk in circles. Just two types of actions, the player only must do them three times, and the players can wait three to eight seconds—much leeway—because the guards walk so slow and stop smoking a lot. It is a very forgiving and easy example.

As a difficult example, let's imagine a scenario where the players must time a guard's knockout precisely to the second, then quickly climb back up a pipe. Then use the corpse to attract another guard, jump down for a knockout, then lockpick a door with the perfect time to avoid detection and slip through the door. After the door, instantly throw an EMP grenade to temporarily disabled an otherwise protected camera, get in an air duct because a guard is coming to investigate the noise. Now rush through the air duct to get behind the guard in time, knock him out, and carry away his body before the camera turns on again. Timing is incredibly tight, the amount and types of activities are very high, and they all switch fast.

Those below strings of actions represent the different lanes you designed throughout the space. Ideally, you have multiple such strings through your stealth sections, and as much as possible, they should connect. The goal is a connected network of such lanes because, without any crossovers, the players have way fewer choices. Stealth games are typically not about mighty players dominating their enemies with ease, but the players should be at least in control of their options. Sometimes if I look at the abstract visualization of especially stealth paths, then it reminds me of the music rhythm games.

I've mentioned it already a few times, but another essential part of any stealth setup is the planning option for the player—the vantage point. A classic vantage point is a high observatory spot at the start of the stealth section, from which the players have a good view over the location. Up here, they can plot a plan, observe AI movement, and look for unique routes or other gameplay ingredients. Typically, they do not have time pressure sitting at such points. However, I recommend occasionally breaking the norm, especially in later levels. For example, vantage points can be from below or through a camera; they can be from hanging off a pipe; they can be deeper in the stealth section; they could be multiple smaller and less powerful vantage points; or they face some time pressure. The various options are endless, but unfortunately, it all comes down to trial and error without any planning option for the player. Learning a section by failures and retries is not a highly entertaining experience, at least not for good and fair stealth games.

**FIGURE 14.21** Example: Main lanes go through a stealth section with interconnections.

As a developer, I would be careful planning out each lane too much in detail on paper. I recommend planning out the intentions like difficulty, number of stealth routes, list of ingredients, complexity, and length. Ensure that the intentions are in line with your leads and directors' high-level design and directions. Then the sooner you can rough out a quick, playable version, the better. Play it repeatedly, adjust timing, and adjust the rough layout quickly until the playable version fulfills your intentions. Once you are happy, it all fits together, I suggest you ask fellow developers to play it. Stealth sections quickly work flawlessly in your head and when you play them. However, they often fall apart as soon as someone else plays them. Quick internal playtests among colleagues are an excellent way to tackle this common issue. However, do not be discouraged if one or two play it well or horrible, because that could be (bad) luck. Get several developers to play your sections, adjust and refine till you have a generally good feeling. However, you will soon run out of willing colleagues who do not know the design. Additionally, do not rely on such tests too much. The quick internal tests are great to get rid of the rough edges, but there is a reason why big playtests with non-developers and specific reviews exist for more detailed refinement.

### 14.3.3 Problems and Solutions

#### *14.3.3.1 The Avoidance Path*

All right, let us start with a widespread occurrence that not everyone seems to identify as a problem per se. I call it the "Avoidance Path." It is essentially one path through a layout that enemy AI never contests. It might be a very complex path, but once the players know it, they never care about timing or patrols. The name of this problem describes why this is bad: it allows the player to avoid any challenge. Finding a 100% safe path might offer a bit of a navigation puzzle, but good stealth setups involve dynamic pressure in some form or another.

The minimum solution to fix it is straightforward: make sure that enemies are at some point seeing each part of the layout. Pay extra attention to the ideal path and make sure that AI contests them, at least occasionally. Remember that the "ideal" path is likely the easiest and not necessarily the one you want the players to take.

Your desired difficulty then determines the frequency of enemies challenging a specific part of the path. Also, consider this does not mean they have to check every last spot in the layout but instead contest the main lanes, which lead to completing the stealth section.

So, ensure that, from time to time, the player must consider the enemies, look around a bit, stop, wait for AI to do their sweep, and then keep moving. If players must stop and wait, even on the most straightforward path, then you avoid this problem.

#### *14.3.3.2 The Vantage Point*

The next one is a classic issue in stealth or action games: "The Vantage Point Problem." It describes the situation where the players can oversee the upcoming challenge from a particular spot to do his planning, aka from a vantage point.

The problem appears when the vantage point is too powerful because, for example, it has elevation, ready cover, or inviting shooting lanes. These are just a few examples of how such a point can hurt the balance of the setup, lead your players to walking through a now-empty layout, and throw all your work to build and script the space in the garbage.

**FIGURE 14.22** Simplified example for an "Avoidance Path" with static AI. At least one of the AIs should move in this example, this section could easily become quite difficult and features very likely no "Avoidance Path."

There are several different solutions to fix "The Vantage Point Problem": First, make the vantage point a terrible fighting position. For example, make it very exposed, with no cover. Alternatively, create the space so that the players can only observe the scene through something like bullet-proof glass.

Second, you can introduce reinforcements once the players push deeper into the layout or kill a set number of enemies.

Third, make sure the players cannot kill all enemy AI from this spot by restricting those AI to certain areas even when combat breaks out. Important note: the logic of the space must support this and do not have AI stop at an invisible wall.

Fourth, break up your layout so that many more minor vantage points cover it. Several less relevant vantage points avoid the issue of the first vantage point overseeing the entire space and force the players to break up her plan-execute-vanish cycle into smaller discrete chunks. It also has the added benefit of allowing you to spawn your AI in smaller chunks as well.

In most cases, you will need a combination of these solutions to address the vantage point problem in a way that supports your game mechanics and direction.

#### *14.3.3.3 The "AI Waiting to Get Killed"*

I think we all have seen the next one in a game: "AI waiting to get killed." Characterized by a few—or even one—AI standing around, with their backs to primary navigation routes, whose only reason to exist is to be assassinated by the players. Outside of tutorials, these setups do not make players feel smart or powerful because there is no challenge to overcome.

The solution is simply to have the AI moving or looking around. They can still be easy prey, but at least they do something. To be clear, by no means am I saying that all AI should always move around and never stop. Instead, they should occasionally stop in order to create openings for the player. The player can read such an opening with the usual AI idle actions like talking, yawning, urinating, and smoking.

The goal is to create a good blend of actions. Let them move around, at least rotating, and periodically stop to do something. It means that players will have and see opportunities while maintaining a plausible scenario and a decent challenge. Stealth setups are ideal scenarios to showcase narrative with AI because they are slow-paced and ideally not interrupted by the players.

#### *14.3.3.4 The "Crazy Difficult Setup"*

At least one level designer in each level design team always creates "The Crazy Hardcore Setup." It is so difficult that even your best testers have trouble beating it. However, of course, the LD keeps insisting that it is "super easy" and then proceeds to show you.

Keep in mind, most developers play their levels so often that they become myopic regarding the difficulty of their content. However, players straight up stop playing levels that are frustratingly difficult and then rightfully blame you, the developer.

There is a simple solution for the issues you do not catch internally: lots of playtests and iteration. There are excellent reasons why most companies run playtest sessions. However, do not let the developers disregard the results and blame the playtesters for not being pro-players. Remember to "Love the player," at least a little bit, and give him a balanced challenge. It can range from super easy to super tough, depending on your game, but it should always be fair.

#### 14.3.3.5 The "Messy Setup" Problem and Solution

The main difference between "The Crazy Hardcore Setup" and "The Messy Setup" is that the latter is not about skill but luck. Essentially, it is about relying on randomization to determine if players can sneak through a section or not. The best players will fail if they get an unlucky dice roll, while terrible players can luck right through.

Randomization in stealth sections is a very tough sell, especially if the consequences of detection are drastic. Arguments for replayability fail when the setup makes advanced skills irrelevant or rewards terrible play. In both cases, it removes any feeling of accomplishment.

The solution is quite simple: Keep stealth setups deterministic. However, if you want randomization, keep it to less gameplay-relevant things like what idle animations guards will play or what idle dialog they use, but for example, not the direction they are facing. If you feel you must randomize, then make sure to give the player enough time to react to an unpredictable outcome. Be fair if you must randomize—do not hate the player. Remember: randomization without reaction time is a big no-go in level design.

#### 14.3.3.6 The "Tools or No Tools"

As we said at the beginning of this chapter, stealth games are famous for featuring many toys, abilities, and gadgets. For level designers, this gets a bit tricky if the players can unlock them in an uncontrolled order or choose not to equip them for a mission.

If a stealth section requires the player to have access to a specific gadget or ability, and the game does not force it, we create a situation where the players cannot progress or get detected. Almost as sad is the situation where a stealth section is super cool and fun, but only if the player has a specific gadget or ability.

Ideally, players' essential gear and abilities—the ones they always have with them—allow them to complete each stealth section. Of course, the right gear should make it easier—that is the whole point of their existence, but the wrong loadout should never force a failure on the player. Proper design planning early on and rigorous testing dramatically helps to avoid such situations.

Another solution is to give the player the gadget in the mission or an option to re-equip. The downside is that this can feel entirely "on the nose." Even giving strong hints during the mission briefing is no guarantee. Systemic games suffer a lot when you have to tell the players how to play to have fun. Again, make sure that the minimum player loadout is enough to enjoy completing the section. This frees you up to see optional gadgets or abilities as an additional layer of fun and difficulty.

#### 14.3.3.7 Unfair AI Scripting

I have already talked about messy and difficult setups, but it is now time to turn our thoughts to unfair AI scripting. These classic setups are Hallmarks of frustrating conditions, which you should avoid at all costs.

The first one I call the "Quick Turner." The enemy walks a long path—Let us say in a hallway—The player follows him for a stealth takedown when suddenly the enemy turns around 180 degrees and instantly detects the player. The players had no chance to know that this would happen, and this frustrating moment has robbed them of a satisfying kill.

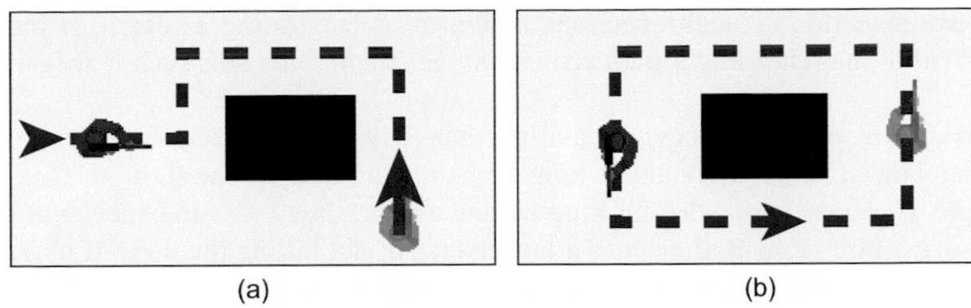


**FIGURE 14.23** (a) Avoid linear back and fore paths for AI, especially straight ones. (b) AI should walk on circular paths, and never rotate 180° on the spot.

The solution is simple: Never create linear back-and-forth patrol paths. As much as possible, let them walk in circles with at least three to four points. Now, if the AI turns, it does not look right away at the players, and the players can disengage or keep following him. Along the same lines, if you must use a linear layout, for whatever reason, then have the enemy turn slowly to warn the players and give them time to react.

The second one is "Seeing the code." For example, this case happens when an unintended player action—like walking through an invisible trigger—spawns a new group of AI for no discernible reason. It gets even more frustrating if those enemies spawn in very close to the players and look at them right away. While true that we must control the number of AI for tech reasons, it is also true that there are better ways.

Now, first, there ideally should always be a player-facing reason for AI to enter the same gameplay space. An alarm, reinforcement call, or the players opening a gate to new sections are classic reasons that soften the blow of spawning enemies close by. If those options are not valid, then at least give the player a fair warning that, for example, an elevator is approaching, and make sure the signs of this warning are apparent and known to all players. In short, we can solve this problem with either good reasons, ample warning, or both.

### *14.3.3.8 The "No Puzzle Puzzle"*

Stealth setups are essentially puzzles, a puzzle where finding the right path and strategy is one of the primary keys to success. It is no longer a puzzle if you only have two options: the intended correct path and apparent failure. However, it can get even worse if it is a single path from the get-go, with just a bit of timing challenge along the way. We often see this in games that are not stealth at their core but use stealth sections as exotic flavors.

The intention is noble, but a single path and a timing challenge is a poor stealth puzzle. By the way, the same thing applies if only 1–2 options are recognizable, especially from the beginning of a stealth section. Why go to the trouble of making other routes if no one can find them?

The solution is simple: provide enough options visible from the inner and outer vantage points—essentially spots in the layout where the player can plan without constantly worrying about being detected. Then three to five main paths are a good number. Plus, combinations of smaller paths allow the player to switch between the main valid stealth lanes. Spatially, try to separate the paths: two or three on the ground and then the same amount, where possible, higher or lower.

### *14.3.3.9 The "Left Door Right Door"*

I usually say that choices for the players are great, but only if they have at least a sense of the consequences. Sure, some surprises are nice here and there, but high-impact, frustrating ones are usually not.

Imagine the players arriving at two doors. The left door allows them to continue, and what is behind the right door will certainly kill them. Essentially, they now have to make a blind choice where one option is death. That is just a mean and horrible design. The same goes for stealth options, of course, because detection in stealth sections is almost as frustrating as death. If the players do not have fair warning that choosing a path will likely get them detected, such a scenario is highly frustrating.

Solution: if all stealth options look equally inviting, then they should remain valid stealth. Sure, some can be harder than others, but there should be hints about the difficulty at the start.

So, for example, if players hear a dog barking behind a door, they know to expect a dog. If they do not like dogs or are afraid of them, they have a fair chance of not taking the door. If players still take the "dog door," then it is their fault and likely will not blame the developers but themselves—fair game.

#### *14.3.3.10 The "Vanilla Setup"*

The second last topic is the "Vanilla Stealth Problem." Now, we already talked about the typical richness of gadgets and abilities in stealth games. However, relying on them is a problem, but so is not supporting them at all. One of the worst examples of this is not providing enough vertical navigation in a game that features a rich set of 3D transversals. Players should expect that levels support the full range of available features. So, if your game supports drones, but most of your levels are no-fly zones, then you have done something wrong.

The solution is obvious: make sure all features are supported. Okay, granted, this is easier said than done, especially when we know features will arrive late in a development cycle. Still, create checklists early on; ideally, integrate them in your game-wide progression sheet. It is a sad day for level design when we must tell other developers that we failed to integrate their hard work into our maps.

There is nothing wrong with certain levels having more or less love for particular gadgets or abilities. It would be boring if all levels were equal in this regard, so work on the previously mentioned global progression sheet. Such a document helps you ensure that your levels' totality covers all features, introduced, specially featured, and not supported. Regardless—prohibiting any feature aggressively for extended periods should remain a big no-go and only used as an absolute exception—otherwise, why did you make the feature in the first place?

#### *14.3.3.11 The "One & Done"*

Finally, let us talk about the One & Done problem. It is a simple, straightforward one: When something is too simple. Essentially when a stealth setup has one super obvious option, and that is it.

These easy setups have their place in tutorials and maybe in very early levels here and there, but they do not have a place anymore after that. A player will feel cheated and betrayed, rather than satisfied and proud, for solving a puzzle without challenge. Finding the right level of challenge is incredibly tricky, for sure, but just as extreme difficulty is not a good option, neither is making something superficial and shallow.

One of your key achievements in game development should always be to make the player feel clever. The proud feeling of having solved a stealth section with a carefully crafted challenge easily beats the hollow reward of a game where you never have to think. Make the player feel proud again, and they will keep coming back.

### 14.3.4 Closing Words about Stealth

Good stealth setups are complicated to design, and just alone avoiding such common mistakes goes a long way. The crucial last lesson is that stealth setups are not just for pure stealth games! Hardcore stealth setups can be a niche, but I promise you that they are not going away any time soon.

However, the basic understanding of great stealth level design sets a fantastic foundation for most modern systemic action games, where stealth is just one of many playstyles. They are fun and satisfying to play if done well and allow you as a developer to tell an emergent narrative without strong hand holding or even cinematics. They are a great tool to showcase, for example, some of your game's or engine's prime features, animations, special effects, or audio.

## 14.4 About Traversal Sections

### 14.4.1 Introduction

This chapter will cover some of the common, challenging types of players traversing through space. Many games feature such segments, either because they want to switch up the gameplay experience or as a modifier to existing gameplay. Essentially traversing in games can be split into four main categories: time pressure, speed, exploration, or skill. In some cases, it is a combination of those categories. Each segment in this chapter covers representativity, one of those main categories.

### 14.4.2 Time Challenge

#### *14.4.2.1 Introduction*

Let us start with a classic case where the player must reach a certain point within a certain time. Alternatively, it can also be multiple points chained together. Classic examples are a cross-country checkpoint race, reaching the antidote in time, kill-house with time pressure, or reaching the bomb before it explodes. Some types are more forgiving, like certain checkpoint races, because you have a chance to catch up again, while others, like the bomb scenario, are more absolute.

#### *14.4.2.2 Checkpoint Types*

If you have checkpoints or similar scenarios, consider if you want the checkpoints to add time to your available time or reset the timer till the next checkpoint. Alternatively, a combination of the two types is possible; for example, small checkpoints or stunts could give you bonus time, while the big checkpoints reset it to a new value. The two checkpoint models are not just relevant for classical races, but act as a foundation model for most other time challenges.

The reset option is arguably more player-friendly because if you just barely made it, you still have a fresh start for the next segment. Small mistakes are completely ignored each time you reach a new checkpoint, and it does not matter how many mistakes you made in total if you reach the checkpoints.

However, the additive method requires players to continuously perform well because, after a few too many accidents, the later checkpoints will not give enough time to reach the end. The core root of success is to continuously keep the speed up throughout the entire challenge. A lot of small mistakes which slow you down will still make you fail.

Therefore, if you want non-stop performance and pressure, pick the additive option. However, keep in mind that the rest option is easier to maintain and balance later because you only must adjust the time for the next segment and not have to keep the entire race in mind. This time-balancing aspect is especially crucial if playtests come late, or the track keeps changing throughout development.

#### *14.4.2.3 Other Considerations*

Below are some of my considerations and lessons learned with designing various types of time challenges.

- Always have a good understandable reason for the time pressure. Only in sport contexts would I accept an abstract HUD timer. I would expect an understandable reason for the player in all other contexts, like a bomb timer or the time till the poison reaches the heart. However, make sure that the players have a believable way to know or get reminded about the timer.
- Let your counters count downwards because it puts more pressure on players. It is easier to directly see how much time you have left. The other way just forced players to make math under pressure. This case is especially relevant if you have mechanics which grant you bonuses for doing well because it is always better to add for doing great than to subtract.
- Keep in mind that the intensity for time challenges is going up right at the start. There is no slow easing into time pressure, even if the player would have much time. Therefore, do not

expect players to do anything else than achieve the time challenge as fast as possible. Do not expect them to do much else.

- I recommend increasing the difficulty only moderately along long-time challenges. It is incredibly frustrating to have the hardest nail-biting skill challenge at the end of a 15-minute-long race. Performing well for an extended period under stress should be the primary challenge and not a wild ride along the difficulty curve.
- Consider other means to gain back time than reaching a gate. For example, finding vodka bottles could give you more time to find the antidote, or driving over zombies grants some bonus seconds. Any such ideas allow you to extend a time challenge section more entertainingly, with an extra layer of gameplay, instead of simply giving more time.

### 14.4.3 Chase

#### *14.4.3.1 Introduction*

If the player must catch up with someone or something, we have a chase. Common examples are running after a cat burglar over rooftops, chasing after that purse thief, or trying to grab that elusive mountain goat that stole your antidote and now runs along dangerous cliffs in the Swiss Alps. It is a classic, high-speed action movie trope, and it is no wonder that it found its way into action games, too. However, as quickly as they feel, they are slow and time-consuming to design and build. There are several lessons I learned and shared in this chapter.

Like with time challenges, the player must move quickly, but it is less about time pressure than distance or speed pressure. Players want the distance to their target to go zero, and they achieve this by overall moving faster than their target. However, this is not always the truth in games since there are two types of chases: continuous and segmented.

The continuous chase is the classic type, which we also know from real life if we ran after someone. Our target was continuously moving, slowed down, accelerated, or even stopped at times. However, despite us occasionally losing sight of it, we know it never teleported or stopped for us to catch up. This teleportation is one of the key differences between the continuous and segmented chase types. The segmented type cuts the chase in subsections, and if you reach certain triggers in time, the target starts running again. It teleports or resets out of the player's sight in many cases.

I compare them to the two checkpoint types: additive and reset, for a better understanding. Like in the continuous chase type, you need to perform continuously great in the additive checkpoint type. If you are too slow, too often, you lose because, at some point, the time you gain by reaching the checkpoints is not enough anymore. In contrast is the reset checkpoint type where upon reaching the checkpoint, the timer resets to a new value, like with the segmented chase. Therefore, the continuous chase is about keeping or even increasing speed, while the segmented one is more like a resetting time challenge. Still, since both chase types share so much with time challenges, many of their considerations apply for chases, too.

#### *14.4.3.2 Continuous Chases Considerations*

- The continuous chase heavily relies on mechanics like a systemic AI for the chased target. You can do with less systemic features, but the more complex the environment or events are, the harder it gets to hand scripted it.
- Pick the continuous chase type if you do not care where the chase exactly ends.
- It will be difficult to trigger complex scenes like cutscenes at the end of the chase because you do not know exactly where it ends. You can do it to some extent with enough effort, but you must be aware of the often drastically increased costs. I do not recommend making an arbitrary, jarring teleport to a seemingly random spot for your end-chase cutscene. Instead, I would consider adding an extra objective like bringing something from the caught target to a location and then playing the cutscene.
- If it is an option that the chase never ends, then you need a large amount of space for a lengthy loop.

- If you have reliable systemic systems and ideally a large open world, this type is a strong contender.
- I recommend reducing randomness during such a long chase, but depending on the robustness of your system, some randomness is possible, which is a unique aspect of this chase type.
- Ideally, the threats/challenges along the way are all scripted, but because it is inherently a rather systemic segment, I recommend introducing incoming threats very early. Otherwise, very likely, players might miss them, especially if they do not look at the right spot or are faster than you anticipated. Therefore, this extra buffer for introduction will be very crucial. Any bigger impactful surprises have the chance that the player will lose the target.
- Even if this type can end at any point, I would still recommend looking into some basic control features like controlling speed or damage resistance. Otherwise, the chase can last less than a few seconds or will last for hours.
- For average players, with enough robust speed control features, you can hopefully have a semi-precise end-point while players enjoy the continuous chase, with its systemic, continuous feel. Essentially you accelerate the target if the player gets too close or slow down a bit if the player gets too far behind. Only getting too far behind would trigger the failure. Some players might sense the rubber banding, but if it ends with a smooth experience, most will not mind or not even notice.

#### *14.4.3.3 Segmented Chase Considerations*

- If you want the chase to end reliably at a specific point, you ideally use the segmented chase type. This chase type is especially beneficial if you want very location-specific events to happen at the end, for example, a cutscene.
- This type can work in larger open worlds or sandbox arenas, but I believe this type is especially shining in very linear games or linear sections.
- Usually, the segmented chase type is very deterministic with no randomness because each segment is a carefully crafted and ideally a very cinematic experience.
- Do not let your target disappear too often, and only let the target disappear for a short amount of time. Ideally, the player can see the target for as long as possible.
- Do not let the target disappear, and then let it do a long-distance teleport if the time between disappearance and appearance is very short. It is a jarring experience noticing that the game cheats, and you can never catch the guy till the game decides so. You will never get it tweaked perfectly for all players, but if timed well, then most will not mind.
- Let the AI occasionally stop, wait for the players, perform, for example, taunts or attacks. It gives the players time to catch up without feeling cheated or losing sight of the target for too long.
- Every time the player loses the target, make sure that the player looks and is guided in the right direction toward the target again by naturally following the linear layout. Use every trick out of the flow-player-leading book because you want to avoid chasing a waypoint at all costs.
- Be careful with other, potentially time confusing, threats/challenges along the way because the timer is arbitrary, and players do not know much time they have to deal with the threats/challenges along the way. For example, it sounds cool to have some enemies during the chase, but I would not consider adding them if players cannot kill them fast. Therefore, any challenges should be light and quick to overcome.

#### *14.4.3.4 General Chase Consideration*

- Only use a waypoint if the target is far away.
- Expose the target as often as possible. For example, let it silhouette against the sky on a hilltop, a lengthy run far below the player, or let it carry a flare/flashlight at night. The better the exposition, the less likely you need waypoints, at least at a close distance.

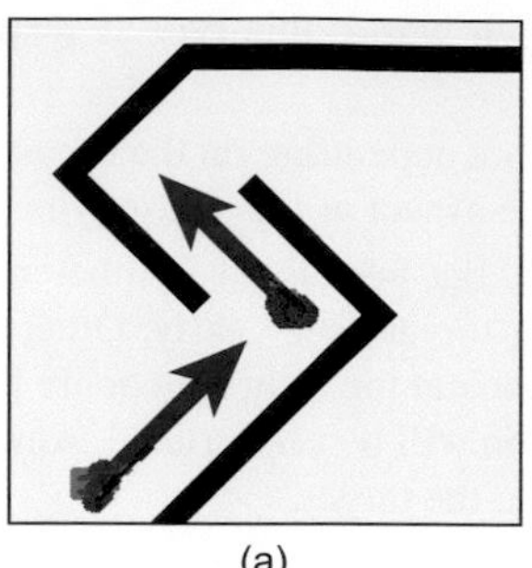
(a)

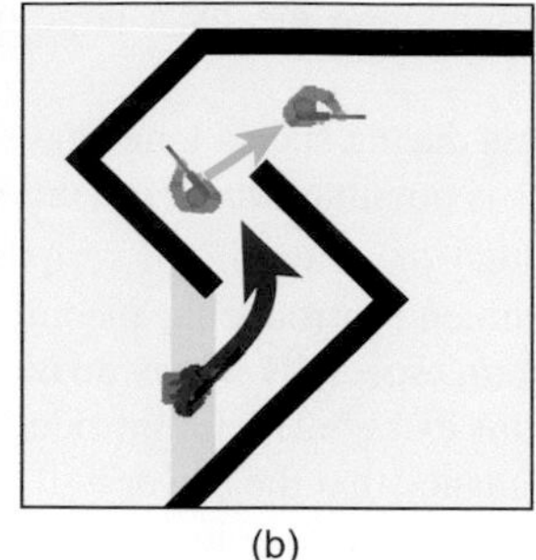
(b)

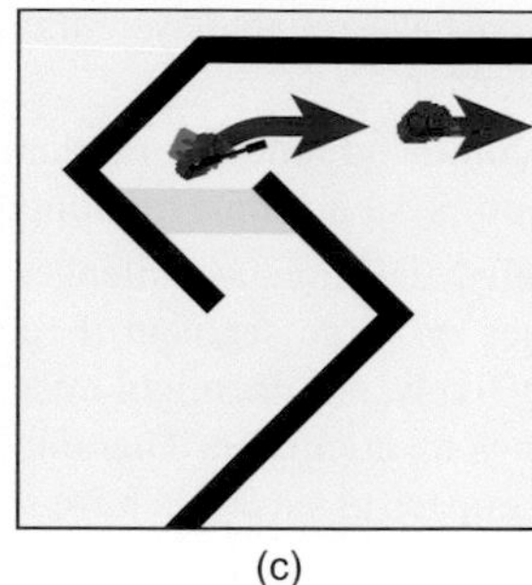
(c)

**FIGURE 14.24** (a) The player chases AI, AI runs away, around a corner. (b) Once the player cannot see AI (yellow trigger), the AI teleports away to next position. (c) Once the player walks through next trigger (yellow), AI starts running again (always a bit before the player could see it).

- Absolutely avoid any path angles larger than 90°, especially for on-foot chases. If possible, even avoid the 90° ones, especially when they happen at a high frequency in tight spaces. If you must have 90° angles, give the player enough space for a long smooth movement curve. For a smooth high-speed chase, I would primarily stay under 45°. The rule of thumb is that the higher the speed, the smaller the angle. This point is crucial, starting at the very first layout planning.
- If you think the chase's difficulty feels just right, it is likely still a bit too difficult for most players.
- Try to change up scenery multiple times during longer races. It heightens the feeling of progress while at the same time appearing less monotonous.
- Like with the time challenge, I recommend avoiding any massive difficulty spikes, especially at the end. Instead, I recommend creating nice pacing focused on intensity, not suddenly increased by difficulty. For example, the last segment of the race goes through a burning forest, the music gets intense, a hailstorm of ambient explosions all around, or the speed goes up because the last part simply goes only downhill. However, some increase in difficulty is, of course, fine, or have at least several save-points along the way.

### *14.4.3.5 Being Chased*

Next up is the case the player is the one being chased, or they get chased while chasing someone else. Classic examples are running away from lava, hordes of zombies, the police, a boss vehicle, or a sentient angry boulder.

You could see "being chased" sections like checkpoint time challenges, just that you don't move to meet a timer, but you move to stay alive or win the objective. Like a time challenge, you can structure it segmented or continuous, with their usual benefits and consequences. This mindset is especially crucial for production, scripting, and designing the chase's individual segments.

However, being chased is significantly different from just chasing a timer because there is an actual threat chasing the player. Therefore, as a level designer, you should use this opportunity to make it a seriously intense scenario. Think about how you introduce the threat, why is it a serious threat, how can you intensify the threat factor during the chase or any close calls? Do not forget the basics of pacing, which means occasionally letting the chase intensity cool down to come back even stronger. Make sure that the end is a true highlight, go as intense as possible, and do not spend your best moments early on. Especially because you are usually in control of the threat chasing the player, you should be also able to control the pacing a lot better.

The type of chaser has a significant impact on your chase setup. If you have a horde of less unique entities chasing the player like zombies or police then you can "cheat" because, they could show up anywhere, even in front of the player. Independent from other engine restrictions, they are usually easier to script, yet lots of work. It is common to let enemies spawn endlessly till the player moves forward, then

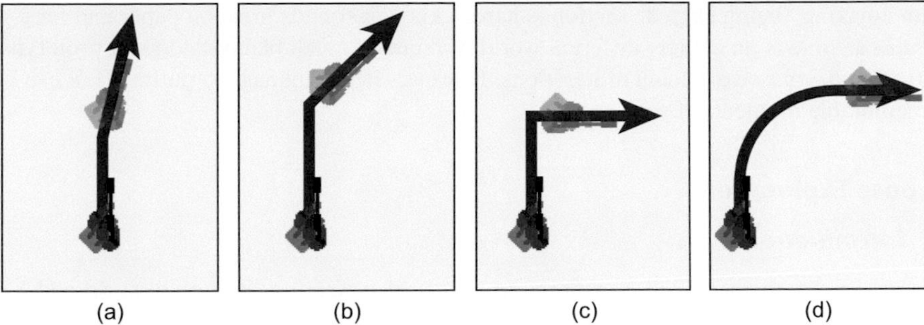


**FIGURE 14.25** (a) High speed means only low angles. (b) Medium speed means ~45°. (c) At low speed you can go up to 90° but never more and ideally less than 90°. (d) If you have a 90° angle, then try to provide a long curve instead a sharp angle.

slow or stop it once the player moves into the next segment. However, I am not a big fan of endlessly respawning enemies, except it is clear to players that they cannot win this fight.

The next case is if the player is chased by one or a few unique entities, like a boss police vehicle, a flock of three named dragons, or a huge nameless boulder. Keeping the pressure up for an extended period and controlling the pacing with a limited, unique element is difficult to script and to stay exciting. Therefore, I recommend applying the segmented approach because it allows you to reset the chase based on player position. Occasionally let the threat disappear, just to let it reappear based on player position when everything is aligned again for another intense moment. The disappearance also works great for a pacing dip and allows for an even more spectacular re-entry. However, ideally, you have another environmental factor, threat, or objective keeping the player moving. For example, the player is falling or sliding a lot, the house is on fire, the water in the underwater station keeps rising, or they must reach the shuttle before the space station explodes. While all those examples already sound like an intense situation, imagine being chased by something way worse.

The last types are natural catastrophes or similar events, which are a mix of the previous two. It is very taxing on production, yet it is not necessarily strictly a single chasing entity. For example, water or lava could pour out from anywhere around the player, or meteors or artillery grenades can impact all around, too. However, executing the believable destruction is usually exhaustive production.

However, the biggest problem by far for any "being chased" segment is that the threat is usually behind players because, by definition, they mean to run away from it. It is incredibly difficult to gauge the distance to the threat or even see it as a threat if you do not see it. Sound, VFX, and other aspects can play a factor, but they cannot replace seeing it. In movies, it is easy because the camera perspective can shift and rotate around, making such sections very exciting. However, in games, this is not easy to achieve. Therefore, I recommend being very careful if you consider such a segment and seriously plan it out in more detail than I usually would.

- Primarily you should think and plan how you can keep showing the threat to the player a lot?
- Can it reappear at the side, pushing away the player and changing course?
- Can you non-forcefully move/rotate the player to become aware of the threat again?
- Can the threat overtake the player, so players need to change course again?
- Can the player run backward the entire time to keep an eye on the threat continuously? I am asking this question to tackle some potential edge cases, especially if it is the segmented type.
- What other tools do you have to increase the threat's presence if the player cannot see it?
- Will it become monotonous at some point and how can I use the element in new refreshing ways?
- Do you have other ideas to spice up the scene besides the threat?
- How flexible are you with timing the threat's appearance, or can you control the speed of the threat dynamically adjusting to the player's movement? The less tight your scripting, the less hassle you have, but it might impact the cinematic feeling.

Creating an amazing "being chased" section is hard. I know it sounds great on paper and for a pitch but executing it in a game is an entirely different world. It requires much planning, lots of prototyping, tons of playtesting, and a massive amount of iterations. However, if you manage to pull it off, it can be one of the most memorable moments of your game.

### 14.4.4 Loose Exploration

#### *14.4.4.1 Introduction*

This chapter is more about the loose exploration aspect of traversing through a world and less about finding a specific location based on a loose description. The last point resembles more of a puzzle which I will cover in the next bigger chapter. Instead, I want to motivate players to explore a world. Exploring often has little rewards because missions and alike usually give the better loot. However, in this chapter, I purposely want to ignore some of those facets and approach the topic more from the perspective to create an intriguing world.

This topic is very relevant for open worlds, somewhat relevant for sandbox levels, and lesser so for linear games. However, I believe some interesting ideas and lessons are relevant for all types.

#### *14.4.4.2 Player Magnets*

The obvious choice is ideally some more prominent distant elements that are unique enough, so players consider them for a visit. Essentially, I am talking here about landmarks that I have already covered in the player-leading part of this book. However, player magnets, first, have to stand out more than a simple landmark. For example, a unique rock in the mountains can help players orient, but it is not enough to attract anyone. However, if huge glowing crystals uniquely cover that one rock, this might raise a few eyebrows. Ideally, you want the players to become curious and ask questions. For example: What are those crystals? Why are there crystals? Can I get some of those crystals? Is there more to it, like some unique creatures, dungeons, spells, or other wonders?

Secondly, the landmark needs to be attractive. For example, early in your game, a massive, evil, menacing dragon warming her belly on a volcano might not be welcoming, but certainly later in the game. It also depends on what players expect from a location within your game's context or familiar tropes. For example, if players see the ruins of a small castle, then they probably expect to find some loot and maybe even a dungeon. If they do a few of those in your game but never find anything, then you can bet that they will not visit any others for those reasons. Therefore, they must know that exploration is rewarding. However, the more you want players to explore, the wider you need to spread your reward types. Some players are satisfied finding some hidden lore to dive deeper in your world-building but do not forget the other players are only looking for gameplay rewards.

I recommend featuring at least three player magnets visible from each location. You should have at least three because one is likely the one you came from, and the next minimum of two gives players a choice. If they can just see one new, it feels like following a pearl string. Also, the more options you offer, the higher the chance that players spot at least one because, often, the current landmark itself or its close surroundings obscures the view to other landmarks. I also recommend varying the distance between landmarks to appear more natural, for example, featuring smaller landmarks like huts and farms closer, and bigger ones like castles and dragon nets at larger distances.

Essentially you can imagine it like a network of various sized and distant landmarks, connecting all major hot spots in your world, and let's not forget the little ones, too. However, ensure to continuously check their visibility in the game after finishing the terrain and vegetation.

#### *14.4.4.3 Traces and Foreshadowing*

However, in the reality of even just a semi-believable world, it will be incredibly difficult to guarantee enough visible landmarks from each other. Therefore, you need hints, traces, and for the extra layer of thrill and spice: foreshadowing.

Traces and hints are indirect hints that indicate something of a certain type, but players don't know exactly what. For example, if players see a smoke plume, then they know something is on fire, but it could be a house on fire, cultists burning a mass grave, a plane crash site, a very hot and smoky gate to hell, or simply a pitmaster who ruined his BBQ. To a large extent, this unknowingness makes it so intriguing, exciting, and irresistible.

A less urgent or event-based method is more subtle traces or hints, like telephone cables or train tracks. I have covered them briefly in the player-leading chapter, but I would like to add the extra element of mysterious exposition. For example, train tracks leading straight to a mountain create a different curiosity and expectation than train tracks along a valley. The one leading to the mountain could end up being a simple tunnel. However, maybe it leads to a secret underground military base which is either an alien gate leading to the stars, or it got repurposed and is now an eccentric millionaire's BDSM dungeon.

The main point of such clues or traces is to connect locations if landmarks are not suitable or visibly blocked. High and dense vegetation or mountains often prevent level designers from relying on landmarks. Additionally, it feels strange, artificial, or gamy if every second mountaintop is a big shiny something. Sometimes, just follow the subtle footsteps in the sand, or maybe your game has a special view mode to see traces.

The concept of foreshadowing in world-building is to slowly give players a few hints or clues which get them excited or worried. However, many such clues do not give a clear sense of direction of distance, just that you are in the right area. For example, if your mission is to kill a spider queen, you know you are not too far off when you see a lot of large nets and once the number of nets intensifies, you are likely going in the right loose direction.

Alternatively, foreshadowing can attract to something the player is not actively looking for yet. For example, the player is in the area for a mission to hunt venison but then stumbles over several mutilated, rotten human corpses along the shoreline of a stream. Players follow the stream upwards, and might find some corpses which get fresher and fresher till they find a hut at the stream's shore belonging to a mass murderer, specialized on lost hikers.

At that moment, I must mention the particular use of sound because audio and foreshadowing go so well hand in hand. For example, the spooky howling winds, bone-shattering screams of eldritch witches, or loud moaning of some undead gothic monks can undoubtedly enhance the dreadful emotional impact of getting closer to a location without seeing it yet.

If possible, layer your clues and foreshadowing elements. Start subtle, and the closer the players get, the clearer the clues are. However, the clues can also switch in tone. In the beginning, it might be more about hinting about the presence of the location, while the closer ones strengthen the additional narrative layer. It is like layering up the flavors in a complex dish—it all comes down to the right mix and timing for a great experience.

What makes such experiences so special is that it was not the game telling players to go and look for around. They felt smart reading the world, following clues, got wrapped up in the intensifying chain of clues, and finally revealed an exciting plot. There is rarely a guarantee that foreshadowing works as intended, but it is certainly a very memorable experience if it does.

### 14.4.5 Skill Challenge

#### *14.4.5.1 Introduction*

A traversal skill challenge is your classic jumping section, balancing, or wingsuit canyon. Usually, navigational skill challenges are at the core about reflexes or, in other words: mastering the game's controls, mechanics, and player movement. I purposely leave out time pressure and the puzzle aspect because they are covered in other parts of this book, but you can certainly can combine them of course.

#### *14.4.5.2 Basic Approach*

Make a list of all your fundamental navigational challenges. Classic examples are distant jumps, dodging swinging blades, or balancing over thin objects. Each game usually has its own set of common or unique navigation types and different values. Therefore, before you start building a traversal skill challenge, get a feeling of an easy, medium and difficult challenge for each navigation type separately. For example, if you want a jumping challenge, test different horizontal distances, jumping with different movement speeds, jumping forward and upwards, or jumping forward and downwards. Note down your observations. In many cases, game designers should already have such large levels for you to get a feeling.

It would be best to gain experience and feeling about any reactionary elements of such challenges, especially in connection with tight timing, character movement, and reflexes. In some games, animations or other game/environment factors negatively impact reaction speed or tight movement control. Especially play around with chaining up traversal actions like jumping or climbing with basic movements like moving, strafing, or rotating. I recommend getting an excellent feeling of how all the different elements play together in any combination possible. Therefore, if you build a more complex navigation skill challenge section, make sure you stay in close contact with the game designers. The tighter your skill challenges' margins for error, the more you rely on that the control values don't change, and the sooner you want to know if game design changes anything during the development process. Additionally, game designers might inspire you for some interesting combinations, as well.

One big factor for navigational skill challenges is the perspective. Essentially any highly excruciating challenge which benefits from the body and especially foot awareness is usually a no-go in first-person games. Only guessing where exactly your feet are and then still making incredibly tight jumping challenges are highly frustrating. I know level designers can build and well play such challenges, but that is not a reason to implement them. I would only recommend such challenges in first-person games if the consequences of failure are minimal, or the challenge is very forgiving. Overall, for navigational challenges in first-person games, I would focus more on the puzzle and exploration aspect and keep the foot awareness skill part easy. In other words, leave all the other crazy skill parts, which for example, require very precise or long distant jumps, for the third-person games.

Lastly, as usual, keep in mind that what feels easy for you is likely a tick more difficult for most players out there, at least within the earlier levels. In later levels, you might go a bit more challenging.

#### *14.4.5.3 Implement and Mix Them*

Now that you have a perfect feel for navigation in your game, know each element and how they feel chained together, it is time to design your actual section. To be clear, when I write about a skill challenge, I mean lengthy sections and not just one or two simple jumps.

First, you want to avoid even loosely comparable repetition within the same game because it not only bores players but also because it feels uncreative. Therefore, you need to be well aware of the work of your fellow level designers and communicate well together.

Secondly, know your challenge's location within the game and its intended difficulty, available skills, and complexity. It might sound obvious, but it happened multiple times that we had to cut down beautiful, crafted navigation sections because they were too early in the game and featured abilities players did not possess yet. Therefore, if you have a very elaborate section, keep in close contact with game designers so they know it, play it a lot, and are aware of the consequences if anything changes.

Thirdly, we know the complexity, the features, difficulty, and what combinations we should not repeat, now it comes to the actual mixing. I would start with the key highlight or the combination of navigation abilities that make your section stand out. If the idea allows for further escalation or scaling of complexity/difficulty, this initial segment should be in the middle, otherwise the end. Ideally, the start is a bit of a warm-up and acts as the player's commitment to the section. If it is a lengthy section, make sure that there are breaks in-between segments.

I would be careful to combine too many navigation abilities on one continuous segment. If multiple segments create your section, then each segment can, of course, feature a different mix, but ideally, short breaks separate the segments.

As much as I am not a strict worshipper of rational design, I do prefer using it as a foundation for mixing up navigational abilities. However, I then modify it to my needs, the world-building context, and the emotional impact I want to achieve. For example, the design might ask for a mellow, safe feature introduction, but if players happen to fall out of an airplane, they better learn fast. However, first introducing them to your game's parachute and free-fall mechanic in a safe space will likely take away most of the thrill and dullens the narrative.

## 14.5 About Puzzle Sections

### 14.5.1 Introduction

In this chapter, I want to talk about classic navigation, physic, game feature, or abstract puzzles. Classic examples are finding the key to open a door, how to use the teleport gun to overcome a lava sea, or how I can catapult myself on the upper floor. Still, you can apply many fundamentals of this chapter in conjunction with more action elements like boss fights or very tricky combat challenges.

The less your puzzle relies on systemic mechanics; the less likely it is that there is more than one solution. Classic puzzles have one solution, but some puzzles often have more than one way or multiple degrees of "solution effectiveness." For example, you can solve some puzzles with a range of steps where the fewer steps you need, the higher your score or the faster you solve it.

In limited narrative games, like classic "point & click" adventures, players often only have one specific solution for a puzzle. For example, you first had to find the ingredients for the Molotov cocktail, then combine them, and use the cocktail against the wooden door to open it. However, in systemic action games, the puzzles are more about overcoming a problem that often offers many different solutions. For example, to open a wooden door, players could select a Molotov cocktail, explosives, roll down barrels to shatter the door, or maybe even guide a raging bull to crush it open.

I recommend clarifying your game's actions or verbs suitable for easy and advanced puzzles. If destroying a wooden door is a simple player action, it needs some modifiers, it is only an easy puzzle, or it is one of many steps within a bigger puzzle.

When designing a puzzle section, I prefer to cut it down to three steps: introduction, comprehension, and execution. Compartmentalizing those three player phases allows me to avoid common design pitfalls and unblocks some initial hurdles because, otherwise, approaching puzzle sections can be daunting.

### 14.5.2 Step 1: Problem Introduction

It might sound banal, but the essential initial step is to guarantee that players understand that there is an actual puzzle. It happens way too often that players are stuck and have no idea if they just forgot to do something trivial before, only missed the next clue where to go, stumbled over a game bug, or actually faced a puzzle.

Any exposition you have at your disposal can help clarify that now it is time to think for the player. Classic examples are spelling it out in objective text, a radio voice tells you, cutscenes introducing the puzzle or clear player language. For example, if players face a door with a red light and previously learned that they can open red-lit doors, they can guess that there is a way to open the current door somehow.

It is easier if your game has several puzzles, and the player reencounters a familiar setup. However, avoid repeating similar or even the same puzzles. Of course, player language, which tells the player that it is now puzzle time, is excluded from that guideline.

It gets a lot trickier if players encounter a new fresh puzzle challenge, especially if it is either incredibly complicated looking or very subtle. The complicated part is instead part of the next step: comprehension, but the subtle one must be tackled already during step one. Therefore, if you do not have the apparent "sledgehammers" of expositions like cutscenes, objective texts, or radio dialog, try to think about all kinds of hints, clues, sounds, VFX, little objects, environmental storytelling, music, or in-world voices. Essentially you should make it abandonly clear to players where they want to go, and that something is blocking their progression. Therefore, when you design a puzzle section, avoid any distractions where to go. It is imperative that whatever is blocking the progression should not hide the puzzle either. If a dead-end only looks like a dead-end then don't expect that players treat it like a puzzle (excluding hidden rooms, of course).

A significant factor is your game's context. For example, high octane action games or very narrative-focused games typically have very different approaches to puzzles. However, in both cases, the puzzle must fit the context, and if done right, it dramatically helps to introduce it seemingly in your game world. For example, in a generic fantasy game players could rearrange the magic symbols on the crypt's door to break the protective spell, and not play Tetris instead.

Lastly, the intensity of the puzzle introduction greatly matters. It makes a massive difference if players solve a puzzle under a constant threat or in a calm environment. It should go without saying that the higher the threat or its frequency, the easier the puzzle itself and the more apparent its introduction should be. Realizing that I should have solved some hacking puzzle in a few split seconds during a high-speed chase is rarely a welcoming fair challenge. Therefore, in such situations, I would keep puzzles very light and their introduction with a massive number of hints and foreshadowing. I suggest keeping the inventive, creative puzzle masterpieces for the calm moments where players have all the time in the world.

### 14.5.3 Step 2: Environmental Comprehension

#### *14.5.3.1 When, Where, What Is Going On?*

After the player realizes in step one that they must solve a puzzle, it is now time for them to understand what is going on? What type of puzzle? What are the tools or actions I have at my disposal? What is the space in which I solve the puzzle? The more you help players answer such questions, the more you help them or increase the difficulty. I recommend messaging the puzzle type very clearly, like if it is a simple open-door problem, a machine to turn on, or finding a key. Often, this question is already answered during step one.

The array of available actions should also not be mysterious because clearly understanding the possibilities is essential for solving a puzzle. However, they can be hidden at odd viewing angles, behind destroyable objects, or hard to reach by navigation. For puzzles, there is a strict difference between understandable and viewable. Therefore, once players find the location of an important action, it should be apparent and not easily misread or missed entirely. For example, players must jump down a dark pit to find the next grapple point. You, as the designer, placed many hints on top of the cliff that this is a valid, yet risky option because otherwise, nobody would dare to find. Overall, I would be careful with such puzzles where minor mistakes can lead to death, and the chance of misunderstandings is so high.

Following this, players should get a good sense of which space and time they should solve this puzzle. If you expect players to search several square kilometers or remember hints from four hours ago, then you likely make it unnecessarily difficult or rather frustrating. I recommend keeping the puzzle space "reasonably local," meaning that the context of the puzzle sets the space. For example, a puzzle about a forklift in a warehouse should not exceed the warehouse's rooms and outer court, or a puzzle about a steam engine should not exceed the range of its pipes or closest sources of coal and water.

However, the previous examples primarily covered puzzles with strong physical connections. It is a matter of time and less space when it comes to narrative or some abstract-based puzzles. In my experience, any hint older than about ten minutes becomes tricky for many players to remember. Instead, I would rather stay within a maximum two-minute time window for action games if the puzzle is mandatory to progress. Remember, if players are stuck because they do not remember the previous hint, they will start looking around for a while, but I would not expect them to go back more than a few minutes to recognize a hint and connect the dots finally. More than ten minutes can be an option for elaborate side quests, activities, easter eggs, or other optional shenanigans.

#### *14.5.3.2 How to Solve the Puzzle?: Step 2.1—Exposition*

Now players have a subtle feeling where to potentially look for clues to solve the puzzle ahead. They should also know what type of puzzle it is, and if they find anything relevant or essential, they can clearly recognize it. The puzzle is also logically fitting in the game's context and the current environment. All those steps are important to consider during the design process because they set the foundation for the most crucial step: finding the solution.

It starts with the clues and subtle hints you provide for the player. I recommend approaching them like a good narrative exposition which shows more and tells less. Therefore, never tell straight up any step to solve the puzzle. Instead, give environmental or narrative hints, which players still first must understand and combine to be a clear hint, but it must happen in the player's head, by themselves. They must feel clever, not you. Any strong handholding would cheat them from the reward of self-discovery.

#### *14.5.3.3 How to Solve the Puzzle?: Step 2.2—Actions*

Puzzles are all about mechanics wonderfully interwoven with the world. Therefore, picking the right mix of mechanics, ingredients, verbs, or actions is the key. You want to avoid repeating a too similar mix of actions within the same game. You also want to make sure that the difficulty and complexity of the chosen ingredients fit your game and the puzzle's position within the game's progression, but more about difficulty soon.

Ultimately each puzzle should bring something new. Taking an existing working puzzle, including getting inspired by similar games and evolving it, is, of course, the easy option. However, coming up with a completely fresh idea is the holy grail of puzzle design. I recommend working on a separate test level and just toy with all the available features. Change settings, combine them in unintended ways, try reversing their function, or see how your scripting language allows you to modify, alter, move, link, and reverse the features—especially lookout for anything that somehow creates momentum or damage.

The momentum or movement can apply to both objects, AI or players. Essentially if you find a new innovative way to move an entity, you can investigate how you could use it in a puzzle. Similarly, you can find new ways to inflict damage, or other "aspects" unique to your game like electricity, fire propagation, creature summoning, light & darkness, or some gravity-altering, sticky slime. Usually, the development team comes up with a few basic puzzles with the game's unique ingredients, and then it is time to experiment with alterations. Then out of those experiments, "new basic" ideas grow, and so on.

If your puzzle is comparable to other puzzles in the same game, make sure that it features a unique twist. For example, the basic puzzle is about shooting a rope, so the crate falls and crushes the grate below. One advanced version requires a trick shot to shoot the rope. Another idea could be to lower the water below so the crate can properly crush on the grate. Occasionally, such an evolution of basic puzzle ideas can create completely new basic ideas or spark completely random yet refreshing puzzle directions. I would certainly recommend as a team to always enhance existing puzzles and collect them till you have an abundance of ideas ready for any situation to come. Pre-production is a great time to create such collections.

When thinking about all the crazy feature combinations, often people forget the simple ones, like movement, jumping, and looking around. I am not talking here about the element of a skill challenge, but simply about exploring unusual viewing angles for clues or following the right trace to a hint. The first classic example is to follow the red cables to turn on the electricity for a machine. The second one is to look up/down in a location where people usually would not look up, like in an air duct or other tight spaces. Sometimes something like jumping on a narrow rock, carefully balancing, and then turning around, plus looking up, is all the challenge you need for an in-between puzzle step.

Another neat feature in some games is a special "detective" view mode. Usually, it allows you to see tracks, clues, smells, or highlight elements like heat, blood, or other unspoken fluids. Ideally, the view mode has some drawbacks, so players only turn it on occasions. Such a view mode adds an extra layer to any puzzles, including narrative, physical and abstract types. However, I recommend not always relying on the view mode to be the magical design solution to solve most puzzles. Mix it up a lot since it should be just one of many tools in your toolbox to craft puzzles.

If they are not part of your game's core, approach any abstract one-of puzzles with caution. Of course, puzzle games should not shy away from them, but they need to balance their production impact. The more complex and unique they are, the more likely any playtest feedback will force changes, but changing anything complex late in development is always facing high costs and potential friction. I recommend keeping them both modular and simple for the longest time till you spend serious effort to polish and finish them. I have seen too many level designers pour their heart and soul into some incredibly complex yet brilliant puzzle setups—just to break the designer's heart later by simplifying it to oblivion. To further put salt in the wound: it required much overtime to adjust.

Ultimately, for me, the secret sauce finding the most innovative and exciting feature combinations for puzzles is a design-hive-mind. Asking a handful of designers from all types of specializations or experience to come up with many crazy puzzle prototypes for a week can be mind-blowing. The focus should be on quantity and out-of-the-box ideas. You not only learn a lot about the individual personalities, but likely everyone will also get a ton of amazing inspirations. You would be surprised, sometimes one of the game-defining features comes from juniors or people without an "official creative" job expertise/title.

### *14.5.3.4 How to Solve the Puzzle?: Step 2.3—Difficulty*

So far, I have mentioned a few puzzle difficulties affecting aspects like the visibility of the actions or the size of the area. However, the difficulty of puzzles is one of the most challenging parts to get done right. Judging the difficulty of a combat setup or orientation challenge can be evaluated by looking at statistics but determining it for a puzzle is based mainly on opinion.

Ultimately for me, the difficulty of a puzzle is affected by the following main elements:

- Clarity and visibility of actions or clues
- The size of the area required to solve the puzzle
- How much time has passed since the first necessary clue
- The complexity and number of ingredients in total
- The complexity and number of ingredients per each step of the puzzle
- The unique or overuse of the ingredients or their combinations
- The exposition clarity, or in other words: How much do players must think outside the box to figure out the solution with the given clues?
- The implementation of the puzzle and its solution in the logic of the world, or in other words: How consistent/coherent is the puzzle within the game's context/world?
- Comprehension fairness of the solution

The last point is likely the most crucial one and a summary of the points above. However, it is also the worst one to judge as a designer. You can create loose metrics to quantify the difficulty of the challenge with some of the points above. It is a decent starting point for a foundation. Still, a rational design approach for puzzles will only get you so far because any rigid system will have issues dealing with such a subjective matter. For example, the number of steps does not include the difficulty of each step. If you then start quantifying each step, you need to take its previous uses, clarity, visibility, and its place within the exposition's totality into consideration. It just gets messy combining factual elements like counting with subjective elements, and all you end up with is spending much time developing guesswork.

However, there are some quantifiable rules to avoid, which you, later, can adjust to your game and turn into clear directions:

- It is problematic if a puzzle's design intention includes the idea of a lot of trial and error/death. Any puzzle should be solvable by some smart players at the first try by applying logic and never luck.
- It is problematic if a puzzle's design intention includes too many actions, clues, or ingredients per step. Each game has its unique maximum set of ingredients it can use per puzzle step. You need to prototype and playtest early to figure out your maximum acceptable number.
- It is problematic if barely anyone in the development team can solve your puzzle, and it is so tricky that even after solving it once, they still must ask you for the solution again. If you are lucky, players will look up the solution on the internet and not stop playing your game.
- It is problematic if players can easily die while exploring or solving the puzzle, especially if the last checkpoint is far behind—either reduce the puzzle's deadliness or add more smaller checkpoints in-between.

- Stay away from puzzles whose solution is based on a game limitation. For example, your game has regular melee attacks, but none underwater. Therefore, the puzzle's solution should not lower the water level first to break a grate with a regular attack.

In my experience, if you think the puzzle is "just a bit too easy," then it is likely alright for now. However, that largely depends on your puzzle design skills and where the puzzle's location is within the game's totality. Also, later it is a lot easier to make a puzzle harder than the way around. Simply removing hints is usually trivial compared to coming up with new ones.

Lastly, the most crucial step to determine and tune a puzzle's difficulty is lots and lots of playtests. For puzzles, I recommend starting first with individual playtests where users express their thoughts while solving the puzzle. What do they see or recognize? How do they interpret the clues and hints they detect? What is their chain of thoughts attempting to solve the puzzle? Based on such and more questions, start tweaking your puzzle's difficulty. After you feel good, it is time to initiate the playtests with larger numbers. All you then care about then is how many solved the puzzle and their final thoughts about design and difficulty. Another factor is how many playtests the game's budget can afford and focus on puzzles. Since people are so incredibly different from each other, the quantity approach is crucial after you iron out the rougher edges of your puzzle during the initial quality approach.

### 14.5.4 Step 3: Executing

The last step is to consider when designing puzzles is how players meant to execute them. I have previously covered topics like deadliness, space, and time required to solve a puzzle, but I recommend revisiting them once again for this last step. Make a very conscious decision if solving the puzzle, executing it, or both to be the challenge. However, when you combine a difficult puzzle and a difficult skill challenge, it can be overwhelming or frustrating for players. It is incredibly difficult for you as the designer to judge because you know the solution and how to play the game. Therefore, take this consideration seriously and in doubt, tone down one of the aspects.

If the execution can fail, it is a matter of how forgiving the failure is. If players just fall a few meters and try it again in a few seconds, then it is usually not a big deal. However, if players can die close to the end and must replay 15 minutes of a mix of skill challenge and puzzle, then it certainly does not sound enjoyable. I prefer shorter difficult segments with checkpoints or other types of forgiveness than lengthy, less difficult segments, which can still trigger a lengthy reset at the end. If checkpoints in-between is not possible due to technical or other reasons, think about other ways to make them fairer. Can you rewind time? Can you make the falling damage not deadly? Can I climb out of the hole again? Can it get easier after multiple retries? Still, remember, at the core, a pure puzzle should be more about finding the solution than executing the skill challenge flawlessly.

It gets a bit trickier when the execution is a one-off, and the failure does not trigger a reset like death. This case significantly affects physics puzzles or puzzles relying on limited resources. The example was my previous crate hanging on a rope, which falls when the player shoots the rope to crush the grate below. However, what happens if the crate misses the grate for some reason, like something blocks the crate touching the grate or the player swings it before shooting the rope? In such a clear case, my first advice is to drastically reduce the chance that the player might accidentally cause failure. For example, I recommend making the grate very large, increasing the crate's weight unnaturally so it does not swing much, or blocking the environment around so players cannot accidentally park a car below the crate. My second advice is always to implement a failsafe by a script. This script should guarantee that the grate always collapses if the player shoots the rope, and the grate does not collapse within two to three seconds. It is not very elegant but, in most systems, easy to implement. If you followed advice number one very well, then the chance that it still happens should be incredibly slim. Therefore, you should not spend a ton of resources and time on a rare edge case. The same counts for players who purposely try to break their own game experience. The priority remains to avoid accidents.

The second example is about a puzzle, which, for example, requires explosives. In this case, players only have a limited number of explosives, meaning they cannot progress once they waste and miss with all explosives. First, that can be okay if the puzzle is optional. However, if it is mandatory to progress, you as a designer need to provide a way to provide players with an unlimited number of explosives. It does not always have to be a magical refilling ammo box, but some continuous respawning enemies can drop such explosives in a pinch. If such solutions are not an option, such a puzzle should not be mandatory to progress. However, providing unlimited resources of something often has a very gamy feel, especially in games with a believable theme. However, some solutions can feel less gamey than others. In some cases, even a magically refilling ammo box is not a huge deal, exploit, or often is not even noticed by many players, especially if the execution of the puzzle is easy.

Lastly, solving, especially a challenging puzzle, should feel rewarding for the player. It does not always have to be a ton of loot or an expensive cutscene. However, I certainly recommend chatting with various artists, animators, writers, and sound designers to guarantee that the finish does not feel like an empty pad on the back. For example, the evil machine explodes in a firework of particles and a symphony of screeching metal while cursing you to robot-hell, or the crate crushes the grate with incredible satisfying noise and a huge puff of smoke.

A lot of the additional artistic, narrative, and audio flavors can cover up a lot of gameness or a too strict following of design methodology during the execution or at its end. In many cases, puzzles should be implemented harmonically in the world, and in the worst-case scenario should feel whimsical. However, if they feel stale and shoehorned in, then either cut them early or spend some time with other experts what else you can do. The nature of puzzles usually includes many disciplines anyhow, so better to chat and work with them early than too late. Plus, the more people you involve, the more refined the puzzle will get at the end—It is all about teamwork.

## 14.6 About Escort Sections

### 14.6.1 Introduction

When players and multiple AI characters must reach a location alive, you have an escort section. Essentially it is a moving defense scenario. The core variants are: the player is following the AI character, or the AI is following the player. It is not uncommon for players and AI to reach multiple locations in a row to succeed in the mission objective. Classic examples are bringing freed hostages to safety, following a local scout through the jungle, helping a prince/princess escape a lengthy dungeon, or protecting a trader reaching the next village harmlessly. However, if the AI character is only optional around the player, then you can ignore most points in this chapter.

However, because it involves many complex parts with a very high fail rate, it leads to infamous frustration for both the designers and players. It always sounds great on paper because it has so many narrative possibilities and features refreshing gameplay to the usual killing, destroying, go-to, and interacting. However, many senior developers dread such sections for very good reasons. It requires a lot of experience, vigilant planning, carefully managed expectations, and very solid game mechanics to pull it off and turn it into an enjoyable, memorable experience for players. Often, such sections get cut early or simplified down to oblivion.

Therefore, I would like to share some insights in creating such escort sections, and it starts by splitting them into the types I know best: systemic-follow AI, systemic-lead AI, conditional AI, and spline AI.

In this context, systemic means the AI's brain is given a goal to reach a certain point or stay close to a certain entity like the player. However, other stimuli along the way can change the AI's priority, for example, reacting to incoming threats. Usually, level designers often have little impact on the AI's brain directly since most of its core decision-making happens in code.

Conditional is the more scripted variant where more elaborated scripting fakes the "smarts" of the AI. In this case, level design has more control, but it increases their workload and potential bugs. The spline variant is a less common version where the AI stays on a spline.

Other types exist, but in my experience, they are a combination of the ones above or game-specific variants. For simplicity in this book, I'll keep the number of escort AIs down to one and focus on single-player only. More AI and Co-op scenarios make describing the cases unnecessarily more complicated to describe.

The layouts for escort scenarios usually combine attack, defense, and traversal sections. Therefore, I will not focus much on layouts in this chapter but cover the complications, problems, and solutions of such an escort scenario.

### 14.6.2 Systemic-Follow AI

#### 14.6.2.1 Introduction

In this variant, the AI follows the player systemically, and depending on the AI's code and navigation abilities, the experience is either great or highly frustrating. For example, hostages run straight through a hail of bullets, something keeps emitting "suspicious" sounds that keep the AI in an endless "investigation" pattern, or the AI's brain shuts off completely, and players must then reload the last checkpoint.

Without a doubt, this variant is one of the most difficult ones to get right, especially if the environment is complex and dangerous. The primary problem is that the player could guide the AI into very problematic situations accidentally or on purpose. As a level designer, you have little control over where the AI ends up. Additionally, you need a very robust systemic AI system, lots of code support, a deep understanding of your scripting language, and often strong nerves. Therefore, I would be careful recommending this type.

#### 14.6.2.2 Risk Reductions

Below is a list of ideas on reducing the risk with such a scenario. Some aspects involve game design considerations because a good AI design dramatically impacts the success of this level design.

- Be careful with follow-AI, which is both fighting and very aggressive. Often, such archetypes tend to charge into combat, often ahead of the player, and then die in less glorious and highly frustrating fashion. Keeping the AI behind the player is also problematic because players want to see the character they are escorting. However, if technically possible, I recommend that in combat the AI prefers to pick points behind the player during combat but once combat is over, they go and stand again ahead of the player.
- If playing stealth is a valid playstyle for the player, you should insist that the AI has a silent weapon, is not initiating unprovoked combat, and has some enemy detection reduction. It is incredibly frustrating if you design an exciting combat setup, the player wants to stealth-kill everyone, and the following AI goes crazy with his machine gun as soon as he sees an enemy. It is also very frustrating if the enemy AI keeps spotting the friendly AI because it positions itself continuously in the open—therefore, the detection reduction for the friendly AI.
- All player paths should be accessible by the AI. I would be very careful if the player can traverse a location, but the friendly AI does not. The result, at best, could be that it stands around doing nothing. At the worst, it might take the alternative route straight through the entire enemy camp. AI follow-teleportation can help, but I would not recommend relying on it solely.
- If the AI can follow the player anywhere in the level, I recommend keeping the overall environment simpler. In my experience, most AI issues during development are not code-related but connected to unclean layouts (or bad scripts). Therefore, if you work with a very finicky and complex system like a systemic escort AI, keeping the layout simple is even more important because keeping it clean will be a lot easier throughout the level's development. I'm talking here about a tick larger shapes, clear go or no-go slopes, no high density of small objects that affect navigation, consistent, smooth floor navigation, and generally being careful with any layout experiments.
- This type of gameplay can be incredibly difficult in an open-world context without any further limitations. Therefore, I would not necessarily recommend it in such a context and only consider it in linear levels or controlled sandbox arenas.

- I recommend a tool where you can mark areas where the escort AI will not move into; ideally, you can turn it on and off via script. So, you can prevent it from moving into unfortunate locations even if the navigation would usually allow it otherwise. It just gives you some additional control over its movement, for example, keeping it further away than normal from cliff edges, preventing it from running over the open, or other environmentally sensitive areas that would be unwise for it at times. Such a tool could also allow traversing larger areas or even open worlds because you could control the wide path the AI would not leave.
- Unfortunately, if the player can push the escort AI around, you need to ensure that your space is very safe. However, I would not spend a lot of time on players who want to ruin their own game experience but instead make sure that no player can accidentally push the AI in unfortunate situations. This is either much work for you, creates some odd environmental solutions, or ends with bland "super safe" locations. In general, I would not recommend supporting push-able escort AI characters because the layout consequences and the debugging are not enjoyable.
- Instead, I usually recommend non-push-able escort AI characters. However, this solution will not come without drawbacks, either. The primary problem is that they can block a player's progression if they stop at tight places like door frames. Therefore, you ideally avoid having such tight spots at bottlenecks, which is not always easy in any believable urban or similar environments. Ultimately there is no perfect solution or answer for this topic, just case-by-case considerations.
- I highly recommend adding some reset mechanics. This mechanic can be a player-centric one like a revive when the AI is down. Alternatively, a passive example is a teleport if the AI gets stuck and the player is not watching. If escort sections are inherently frustrating due to breakage, you should always design early on with reset and backup options in mind to prevent any hard walkthrough breaks.

I recommend also looking into the risk reduction of the other escort variants, especially the systemic-lead type, because they might help in your case, too.

### 14.6.3 Systemic-Lead AI

#### *14.6.3.1 Introduction*

In this variant, the player is following a systemically leading AI. Usually, it stops when the player is too far behind or accelerates if the player is ahead. In some cases, it might move insanely fast or even teleports if the player is not watching. Like with any systemic cases, they are great if they work since their systemic reactions are more natural and consistent. However, they are similarly frustrating like the follow-type if they do not work. Therefore, we have the usual examples, as AI stops for no understandable reason, runs off in the wrong direction, or is stuck in an endless loop.

I am close to saying that this type is less frustrating than the follow-type because at least you as the designer can somewhat control where the AI ends up. The AI might be systemic, but at least you, as a level designer, control where it wants to go. If the player is not following the AI, it stops or catches up. Therefore, I would carefully recommend this type conditionally if the AI code is solid, you are a confident scripter, and level design has good support from the programmers.

#### *14.6.3.2 Risk Reduction*

Below is a list of ideas on reducing the risk with such a scenario. Most points from systemic-follow AI are relevant for this type, but the ones listed below are especially crucial for leading AI cases.

- Since you have more control in this variant, I recommend avoiding any random encounters along the way, which could quickly waste this crucial advantage. Depending on how quickly your systemic AI brains get scattered or distracted, such random encounters can break your escort section, at least long enough to be frustrating. However, the core advantage of systemic AI is that it can handle such random encounters, but it simply increases the risk for a random breakage.

- Then trying to overwrite the systemic AI brain with a more enforcing script or even turning off the AI's sensory stimulus might work initially. However, the strong point of a systemic AI brain is to react to such threats or inputs. If, for example, an AI character ignores fire, gunfights, or nearby enemies, it will create an inconsequential and non-immersive experience. In a pinch, I would rather temporarily make AI invincible than blind, deaf, or not feel anything, except for a unique, super important, and strictly scripted sequence.
- The more likely something can go wrong during the journey following the AI character, the more frequent checkpoints you should add. Therefore, if push comes to show, your escort AI character is stuck somehow, and the player must restart from the last checkpoint, they will not lose too much progress. It still is not great, but it is better than continuously replaying 15 minutes until the AI finally makes it.
- Ideally, invest in some overwrite-switch that forces the AI to move or get reset, especially if the player is not looking or is very far away. It should not kick in in the middle of a firefight with the player close by observing the AI. However, if the AI is stuck or distracted by "butterflies" (= anything random we do not know right away without much debugging), again, a brain reset is a good idea. If the player managed to get far ahead, a backup teleport is a good alternative solution. Of course, that might not be immersive, but I believe players appreciate them more than a braindead/confused escort AI somewhere in the back.

### 14.6.4 Conditional AI

#### *14.6.4.1 Introduction*

The movement of the AI is triggered and controlled if certain conditions are met. The most common conditions are "all enemies dead," "player stepped in an invisible trigger," or "gate is open." For example, a hostage only moves through the room once players killed all enemies. Then it stops at a safe spot, waiting for the next threats to be eliminated, and so on. The conditional approach can work for both leading and following types. It does work with less advanced systemic AI brains, but if there are threats and stimuli around it can get tricky to hand-script each case and combination. This type works well in very scripted linear experiences, ranging from non-combat to very combat-oriented AI archetypes. However, it has strong limitations regarding flexibility or in anything but a linear section.

#### *14.6.4.2 Risk Reduction*

Below is a list of ideas on reducing the risk with such a scenario. Some points from systemic AI types are relevant for this type, but the ones listed below are especially crucial for conditional AI cases.

- Keep the conditions simple and avoid anything too complex. It is important to steadily keep such a section going and not consistently stop the flow with difficult puzzles or other distracting challenges from the escort experience. However, if that is what the game is asking for, I recommend toning down the escort aspect and focusing on only one and not two major gameplay elements simultaneously.
- Keep the locations in which the player must meet the conditions small. For example, running around a huge temple complex looking for that last demon priest to kill before your friendly AI moves again is not fun. Instead, keep those spaces tight and controlled.
- Try to have a high frequency of small conditions and steps forward instead of rare yet larger progress. In the perfect world, it feels like a continuous flowing cinematic experience. However, asking the player to complete a ten-minute long-lasting section for the friendly AI to move once again can be seen as a slow drag.

- At times consider adding backup options to resolve the conditions by script. For example, the player progressed far ahead without killing every enemy in the previous segment. Depending on your game, you might want to automatically disable the last enemies or let the AI go to the player and let your friendly AI move again. Not great solutions, but also another reason why you should keep the segments small or prevent the player getting far ahead.
- If the escort AI cannot defend itself against enemy threats, consider a fail-safe mechanic to avoid instant failure. For example, a temporary shouting match at gunpoint, several melee attacks, or even an arrest attempt. Ideally, this gives players still the time to react and prevent failure.
- In the case of very combat-skilled escort AI, I recommend a feature that controls their lethality. On the one hand, you do not want the escort AI to kill all the enemies for the player, but on the other hand, you will likely have moments where you want them to take care of the threats and move on quickly. For example, if the player progressed without killing all enemies in the sections, the escort AI could take care of them instead of you killing them via script. Another issue is if the opposing AI factions can't kill each other fast because it simply looks odd if two fighters keep shooting at each other at two meters for minutes.

### 14.6.5 Spline AI

In this variant, the AI is navigating along a spline, laid down by level design. Depending on the game, there can be rules that allow the AI to go away from the path a bit to get behind cover, interact with something, or get to a better shooting spot. If it is a leading escort section, then the AI would try to be ahead of the player, and if it is a follow one, then, of course, behind. Alternatively, you can still mix it up with conditions to further control the AI. The advantage of this system should be very clear because you can work very precisely, and it is hard to mess with the AI. It can play the correct animations at key moments, say the right lines, and rarely gets stuck, especially if players cannot push it.

It is a great solution for very cinematic or narrative sections, but it can have serious issues in larger game spaces of sandbox or open worlds. If such limitations are not a problem, this is a solid alternative that can certainly reduce some of your headaches. However, be prepared to likely spend a lot of time scripting all such details. Many risk reduction advice from the previous types still apply.

## 14.7 About Co-op Level Design

### 14.7.1 Introduction

Designing levels for a co-op game requires adjusting particular layout and gameplay aspects. I can already hint that it is a lot more than just providing more space. However, it is not rocket science if you follow a few basic principles and reflect on your own co-op gaming experiences. Instead, many co-op design considerations are very much valid in singleplayer, too. However, badly executed design basics are highlighted in the more complex co-op environment.

In this chapter, I would like to share my experience and learnings working on several co-op projects and their impact on level design. I will primarily focus on two-player co-op for simplicity, but it should be straightforward scaling up for more players. I will also keep topics very generic so you can easily adjust them to your game's specific nature and needs.

### 14.7.2 Space in Co-op

#### *14.7.2.1 Introduction*

When I started my level design career and faced co-op level design the first time, I was told: "Just provide more space, 100% for each player." It should go without saying that this rule was severely flawed. Therefore, let us start covering some basic layout fundamentals concerning co-op.

However, before we go into specifics, I must stress that all previous layout concepts in this book are still valid. Sure, some of them must be adjusted or need a stronger focus. However, if anything, flaws in such basic level design principles become more glaring in co-op. Unfortunately, in my experience, topics like environmental storytelling, exploration, or anything too strongly focused on narrative take too often a backseat in co-op level design, primarily because in most cases, you focus more on the (gameplay) experience with your friend than taking your time to enjoy the game's depth and details.

Another important consideration is that most of the points here are also valid for multiplayer maps. After all, spatial adjustment for multiple players or improved coordination between them applies very much to them, too.

### *14.7.2.2 Options over Space*

As I have hinted previously, co-op does not necessarily mean more space per se. Most decently designed singleplayer layouts offer plenty of room for at least one more player. The reason is that even basic single-player layouts usually offer at least three options or paths to navigate through a basic (combat) space. If two players enter that space, one player has three options initially, and the second still has two, which is still acceptable. If one player is ahead, the second player behind likely again has three options available. Sure, ideally, we have a few more, but we do not need that massive amount in a usually faster-pressing co-op reality. As a rule of thumb, I would go for the following formulas.

- Minimum number of options = Number of Players * 1.5 (rounded up)
- Appropriate number of options = Number of Players * 2
- Comfortable number of options = Number of Players * 2.5 (rounded up)

Of course, there is a limit of options once the number of players goes up, and the believable world forces limitations on you. For example, for a four-player co-op game, it is not reasonable to always provide six to ten options all the time, especially when we are talking here about bottlenecks, hallways, tight alleys, or tunnels. Consider it as a guideline and be aware of the consequences if you break them. Case and point, several co-op games specifically feature such bottlenecks to force co-op gameplay because here players are more vulnerable here against specific threats.

Also, keep in mind that the above options do not always mean paths. It can also be, for example, a mounted gun, a sniper spot, another good firing position. It is also important that players can quickly, easily, and often switch between the options.

More or adjusted number of options in co-op also means you do not have to adjust your distances significantly between all objects, especially not anything rooted in world logic like doors, windows, streets, or excavator stairs. However, it is a nice touch to increase the distance between objects which previously only allowed one player to get through simultaneously, if the world reality allows it. It simply prevents one player from blocking others in case of a struggle or miscommunication. The blocking topic is especially crucial at bottlenecks or very hectic combat spaces. This issue also means you should try to avoid having, for example, regular doors as bottlenecks, but instead pick a wider gate, if world-building-wise possible, or provide an alternative route.

### *14.7.2.3 Splits at Battlefields*

Providing options early at the beginning of a battlefield is a staple layout aspect in singleplayer, but it is even more critical in co-op. First, provide some safe space for them to chat about who does what now. Then they need enough space to fan out and understand the options available. Nobody should be able to block any player or cause any messy chaos. Ideally, multiple paths offer each player multiple options for their favored play style.

The beauty of co-op and early path-splitting is that you, as a designer, have a higher chance that players use your entire layout. However, it is also essential to avoid too-distant fragmentations where some paths lead players far away from their buddies. On the flip side, a too strong restriction to one tight path could result in some players further back not even being aware of what is going on ahead.

#### *14.7.2.4 Front Lines in Co-op*

When you design combat spaces, front lines and especially the flanking routes are even more essential in co-op. First, you lack clarity of space under stress with more partners because it is another potentially confusing factor requiring coordination, a potential source of distraction, and requires additional awareness. Secondly, in my experience, the need to keep pushing forward in co-op games is higher than playing a combat scenario which you can play at your own pace. Therefore, good flanking routes to keep the momentum going are even at a higher priority in co-op than in singleplayer.

A chaotic frontline setup or lack of it will likely result in a messy gaming experience and reduce meaningful coordination between players. The clarity topic is especially important in stealth scenarios or when many enemy AI is involved.

#### *14.7.2.5 Cover Flow in Co-op*

Like with front lines, a clear cover flow is essential in co-op. Coordination between co-op partners in a chaotic environment with no clear cover network and flow is once again a recipe for potential chaos. At best, players get lucky, but in my experience, it becomes more a matter of individual skill than cooperation. Therefore, for a smooth co-op experience, a well-thought-out cover flow following basic methodologies is essential.

As usual, do not judge the cover flow and cover networks from the top view. Instead, only judge and validate it in-game. Ideally, you test it in co-op during in-house playtests and ask others if they feel similarly about your cover setup.

#### *14.7.2.6 Reset Options*

If things go wrong in combat and you are still alive, it is always great to have an option to reset, tactically retreat, come back smarter, and ideally on a different route. Ideally, good combat layouts allow such options. The layout requirement for retreat options is another reason why path-splits at the beginning and within a battlefield are crucial. In co-op, they are even more essential because the chance that something goes wrong is dramatically increasing with each other player. For example, a two-player co-op stealth setup has twice the number of players which can get detected, or if all enemy AI, balanced for two players, focus their fire on just one player at a time, meaning double damage. As you see, in many cases, co-op might make everything more fun, but it certainly does not always make it easier. Instead, more likely, things go wrong, and at least one player should have the option to get out again, reset and come back to save his buddy, or initiate a completely new attempt.

However, make sure that players who retreat have new ways to come back. Otherwise, their retreat feels shallow, or they might leave the battlefield and lure enemy AI in unfortunate positions.

### 14.7.3 Communication and Layout in Co-op

#### *14.7.3.1 Introduction*

A crucial aspect of any co-op game is communication to coordinate your actions. The stronger the co-op focus of your game, the stronger the requirement for coordination to overcome the co-op tweaked challenges ahead. Therefore, every element of your game should support communication, including layout.

#### *14.7.3.2 Have a Break*

In singleplayer, we should design levels with low and high pacing in mind. The low-intensity beats are essential for players to catch some breath and increase the next beat's impact. In co-op, such breaks are even more crucial for multiple additional reasons.

First, they allow players to meet, communicate and plan ahead. It does not always have to be a vantage point, but even just a calm hallway can be enough for a quick chat. The second reason is for other players to catch up. Somehow in co-op, one player is often faster than the other, usually the more experienced or inpatient one. Such low-intensity beats can allow the other player to catch up if the faster player happens to be nice and waits. Alternatively, so-called co-op gates can help, but I will cover them a bit further down. However, without breaks in layout and scripts, the distance between the fast and the slower player tends to get larger and larger. This results in a disjointed experience, aka the opposite of co-op.

#### *14.7.3.3 Inner and Outer Vantage Points*

I have already hinted at vantage points just now, but vantage points in co-op are even more essential, and they have special requirements. First, vantage points are important planning spots, and planning together is even more crucial, or it just becomes an individual skill-based free-for-all. Without the option to plan actions together, it tends to feel more like a singleplayer experience where you happen to play with another partner. Outer vantage points must be unique. You have especially difficulty in open-world games to describe your location if all vantage points look similar. For example, if five similar-looking large hills surround your fishing village, then it needs extra effort for players to describe them. Instead, give each hill a unique, glaring difference, and players will thank you. Of course, it also helps primary player-leading since they act as landmarks.

Additionally, in co-op, vantage points outside of battlefields are crucial and vantage points inside larger locations. Such inner vantage points allow for readjusting coordination and realigning plans together. Designing such inner vantage points is not easy because they should attract players and are unique but not act as exploits either. However, they are crucial, especially in games with large combat areas, like huge open-world locations with a strong stealth focus or other coordination needs.

Lastly, ensure that any vantage point is big enough for all players to fit on them comfortably without getting detected. After all, it is hard to coordinate anything together if only one player can see the location ahead.

#### *14.7.3.4 Unique Locations and Landmarks*

Player leading requires another co-op consideration. In order to clearly communicate about movement, all landmarks or other stand-out locations must be unique. No, I am not talking about subtle differences like, for example, various differently rotated rooftops of various churches. Instead, you should have only one church within the vicinity without any chance for misunderstandings. Especially in public matches with unknown co-op buddies, clear communication is crucial. Otherwise, your game's community must come up with their own names, which are only known to the frequent players. Unfortunately, any development of exclusive, outsider language development can lead to community fragmentation, and the learning curve for new players gets steeper.

### 14.7.4 Gameplay in Co-op

#### *14.7.4.1 Introduction*

The layout is not the only level design aspect that considers the unique possibilities and challenges of co-op design. Instead, most co-op-centric games would do a bad job focusing on layout considerations alone. In my experience, you must have strong co-op-centric gameplay features and scenarios to use the potential of co-op fully. Otherwise, just playing a more difficult singleplayer game with a friend can be more fun than playing alone, but otherwise can also feel stale or like an after-thought.

#### *14.7.4.2 Classic AI Setups for Co-op*

Dealing with AI enemies in co-op is a classic coordinated gameplay moment. This coordination requirement is especially relevant in games with a strong stealth focus or when the enemies are so tough that precise planning is necessary. Below are a few essential basic AI considerations, specifically tuned to the co-op situation. Ideally, they can provide a foundation for your game's unique needs.

- Clear AI Groups: Any groups or individual AI enemies need to be clearly visible and clearly recognizable as a group. This clarity is essential in singleplayer but even more crucial in co-op because otherwise, it makes communication and coordination even more difficult.
- Visibility Blockers: Further on, keep AI groups separate from each other. Seemingly random detection or alarm propagation, due to unforeseeable sightlines of different AI groups, is annoying in singleplayer, but it worsens in co-op. The whole situation with other players is inherently messier and more chaotic. Any unnecessary and unpredictable noise from the AI and poorly designed environment taints any co-op experience.
- Timing Puzzles: Any enemy AI encounters that rely on well-timed actions between the co-op players are great moments. For example, taking out enemies quickly while other AIs look or walk away. However, the clarity of AI movement and rotations needs to be very clear, or any coordination between co-op players is in vain and will only lead to increased frustration.
- Co-op Takedowns: Such takedowns or co-op fighting maneuvers require coordinated actions between at least two players to take down or damage an AI opponent. The classic example is where one player is distracting the AI while the other player uses the opportunity to shoot the enemy's weak spot at the back. For an introduction, such encounters are fine in a simple arena-like space, but I strongly suggest incorporating more advanced environments or navigation later. For example, reaching the back requires dodging raining lava, well-timed grapple swings, or other special gadget use. In such instances, as level designers, we often rely on AI behavior alone to create fun, but we instead should push the challenge and fun coming from the layout, too.

#### *14.7.4.3 Co-op Gates*

So-called "co-op gates" are moments where all co-op players must be present to proceed. Classic examples are a safe door that only opens if two players turn two keys separate from each other, an incredible heavy rock that requires all players to push, or a surprisingly heavy shop gate that requires two super spies to lift.

Their main gameplay purpose is to guarantee that no player can rush forward, leaving the others behind. There is also a technical reason for streaming limitations in many cases. Such gates would safely unload the environment behind and load the next one. If the co-op gate is also a lengthy procedure, it helps streaming even more. Still, the gameplay reason will remain relevant, but it allows for a wider variety of flexibility in finding such gates. The ones required for streaming always include variants that guarantee that the previous segment was completely sealed off and not visible anymore.

I recommend investigating the technical feasibility of co-op gates at the expected level of quality early in production. Opening a gate by script when two players are at the same time in an invisible trigger shape is the easy part. However, it quickly gets tricky with synchronizing animations online or when you face many edge cases in a wildly systemic game environment. Therefore, I suggest keeping such gates far away from enemy AI encounters, destructive environments, large amounts of physicalized objects, or other complicated shenanigans. This also means it is vital to plan for their safe and calm locations during the documentation phase. Squeezing in co-op gates later during production always means a noticeable drop in quality and a significant increase in production cost.

Finding co-op gates for two players is not always easy but manageable. Two characters doing things like lifting, pushing, or turning are mostly within reason. However, if it requires four players to lift a gate, it raises some eyebrows. Additionally, such gates must be huge, accompanying all four players simultaneously. Therefore, it gets unreasonable to find believable solutions and always enough space in every game environment when too many players are involved. For all those reasons, if you have more than two to three players, I recommend looking for abstract or gamy solutions like the previously invisible triggers, or other ones unique to your game. If your game already has an arcade touch, it should be even easier.

Another difficulty, even with two players, is to come up with enough ideas of such gates without the impression of repetition and strange coincidences. There are simply only so many gates to lift, so many safe doors requiring two keys, or so many heavy objects to push. Eventually, it can feel artificial and annoying to the players because it feels rather gamey than immersive. Therefore, I strongly suggest that you come up with at least five or more very different co-op gates which can be used in almost any of your game's expected environments early on during pre-production. It is better to have solid yet maybe generic ready-to-go solutions than to rush creating potentially cheap co-op gates later in production. Then once you know the likely final environments, you can come up with several unique ones, just for those specific spaces, if time and resources allow it.

Production-wise such well-executed co-op gates can quickly become expensive. Therefore, the earlier you plan for them, the better. Also, in many cases, the (technical) actions themselves are very similar, just the animations are different. For example, a synchronized key turning is very similar to a synchronized button pressing for the scripters, designers, and coders.

Another often forgotten solution is a "narrative co-op gate." For example, an NPC only opens the next gate when every player is here. This NPC could also just exist on the radio and remote control everything from afar or exist in your game space. However, if the NPC exists in the same space, then make sure that he reliably opens the gate and, for example, cannot get killed, can get too distracted, or only exists "on the radio." It can be a bit convenient and appear lazy design-wise. However, if your game allows it, I will certainly recommend that you consider it because if embedded right, then most players will not mind it occasionally.

### *14.7.4.4 Unique Co-op Gameplay Moments*

Playing games with other players, ideally, friends, is usually already more fun than playing alone. Basic co-op considerations, which I have listed above, are the basics. However, the key essence of a serious co-op game is unique co-op moments beyond simply more challenging sections. Those moments rely on mandatory coordination and often communication.

Unique co-op moments are so closely connected to your game's particular mechanics. Therefore, I offer a basic list of considerations when designing your own unique co-op gameplay moments.

- Carefully elaborate your co-op pacing, meaning when and how many unique co-op moments of what intensity you need for your levels and your game's totality. Such pacing planning ensures that, for example, you do not have too many moments too early in your level. It also guarantees that the most intense ones are instead at the end of your level, and the most intense ones are at the end of your game. It also helps create some low co-op intense breathers in between where players focus instead on their individual skills. As usual, a good mix and increasing intensity are the foundation for a good overall game experience.
- Go through your game's features and mechanics and investigate their use in a co-op context. Even seemingly non-co-op features like melee attacks or climbing can be incorporated in co-op gameplay. It is all a matter of context and challenging the status quo. A lengthy free-for-all brainstorm and prototype phase can do wonders here once you temporarily lift all creative limitations.
- Create a list of basic "bread and butter" co-op moments you can plug in almost anywhere if your co-op- pacing requires some more coordination, but you have nothing too unique in place. Usually, such basic actions rely on simple level design or a single feature like a tough AI enemy, which requires distraction to get to the weak spots or where players must coordinate separate actions.
- Once you have a list of such basic co-op gameplay moments you can plug in anywhere, start developing advanced versions. They require more steps to complete, have a modifier, more complex layouts, or combine multiple co-op moments. Ideally, the basic list and their advanced variants should give you a solid foundation for most moments, and you have more time to develop level agnostic ones.

- The tighter the required timing and the complexity of the coordination/communication, the more difficult is the co-op moment. I highly recommend keeping such values easy, tunable, and the complexity modular. It is realistic to assume that co-op moments require more balancing, iterations, and fine-tuning after playtests than your comparable singleplayer sections.
- It should go without saying at that point, but prototype early and a lot. Once you have a wide set of promising ideas, it is less about new ideas but about challenging the prototypes about production feasibility. Now is the time to collect solutions for edge cases, investigate how expensive the co-op moments are to ship and how excited the development teams get. The more edge cases you can eliminate, the better. However, in pre-production, I would not spend too much time solving them all, if you are aware of them and have a plan to tackle them.
- You have to playtest them a lot more than singleplayer. First, you only get half the reports for a two-player co-op game compared to a singleplayer game from a playtest lab with a fixed number of stations. Secondly, since two players are involved, the information from each data entry is less "clean" since you do not know if both players contributed equally. Therefore, you need a lot of playtests, and it does not get better since not all playtest labs are well prepared for co-op sessions due to the increase in setup complexity and technical difficulty.
- Most dedicated co-op moments are either about splitting up players or getting them close together. Therefore, to coordinate their actions when separate or initiate the sudden separation, they must communicate closely. Classic examples are one player controlling a crane while the other hangs on the hook shooting buttons, or one player instructing the other over a monitor. Alternatively, they must get close together and coordinate tightly. For example, when one player is driving while the other one is at the car's mounted machine gun, or one player must carry a wounded VIP while the other one defends them. Just make sure that one player is not doing something very dull for too long while the other one has all the fun. For example, one player being defenseless and slowly pushing a cart while the other one is killing hordes of monsters is only fun for one. Advanced versions require players to perform multiple actions separate, close together, unite/spread quickly, or a combination/chain of it altogether.

# Section VI

# Practical: Technical Aspects and Game Design

# 15

# *Scripting and Technical*

Even if some people believe level design is all about layout, scripting is usually an equally essential part of level design. In many cases, it is all particular level designers do as their day-to-day job, without even being specialist technical level designers. Especially advanced scripting skills allow for quick prototyping of most gameplay concepts, blurring the lines between design roles. Therefore, I consider scripting as essential for any practically-minded designer. After all, there is the famous saying from Tom & David Kelley: "If a picture is worth 1000 words, a prototype is worth 1000 meetings."

However, technology is advancing rapidly, and gaming technology is absolutely no exception. Additionally, tech and scripting are often unique to the different games and engines. Therefore, I will not explain every scripting language unnecessarily but keep it as broad yet useful as possible. Therefore, I will focus on a quick scripting-type overview and the essential mindset approaching technical topics including basic problem-solving. However, it is best to learn more about your unique scripting tools or languages from other explicit sources related to your specific project or engine.

## 15.1 Scripting Types

### 15.1.1 Introduction

This chapter will give a brief overview of the three main scripting types commonly used for level design. However, once again, I will not go into too much detail since better sources explain the details of each individual scripting tool or language.

### 15.1.2 Text-Based Scripting/Programming

Any type of text-based scripting or, generally speaking, programming is a realistic possibility for any designer. Lua, C++, and C# are just common examples for bigger gaming engines like Unity, Unreal, or CryEngine. Also, languages like JavaScript can act as a quick prototyping tool. Even some deeper knowledge of Excel and its macro language can be helpful in general design processes. It does not mean every level designer has to learn to program, and many will never have to in their careers. However, some basic understanding and familiarity with source code editors like Visual Studio Code or Notepad++ certainly do not hurt. For example, it can allow level designers to create their own nodes for visual scripting tools. Additionally, even if your engine does not require any text-based scripting for level designers, in my experience, even some basic scripting/programming understanding helps you to establish rapport and empathy with coders and other technical folks.

I am well aware that any text-based scripting, especially programming, can appear daunting at first. However, rest assured that if you have a good mentor or tutorial and start easy with a motivating achievable goal, you will get into it quickly. It is an incredibly satisfying skill to learn, which I cannot recommend any higher.

In my professional career, the exposure to text-based scripting/programming was limited since I always had more experienced programmers around, and we were never required to do anything in text. However, I managed to acquire more and more skills after work, and the more I spend time in the game industry, the more I find a use for some quick prototyping, which often happens text-based. Let it be game jams or some quick meta-flow prototypes in JavaScript. It does not have to be always about level design, but sometimes simply about being a team player and game developer.

DOI: 10.1201/9781003275664-21

### 15.1.3 3D-Scripting

I am using the term "3D-scripting" for any type of scripting which happens in the 3D space of your editor. In such instances, for example, you connect AI spawners with a trigger in your editor viewport instead of linking them via a visual or text-based script in a separate window. Each entity usually has a vast number of options to adjust them individually, like giving them factions, animations, or light patterns. Typical examples for such a scripting method are Quake 1/2/3, HalfLife 1/2, FarCry 1, or many in-game editors like DOOM SnapMap.

It is a great way to do simple scripts quickly, intuitively and relatable because it happens in the actual game space. After all, many people scripted many great games that way. However, it is limited to the often restricted, available possibilities and is not comparable to the vast complexity that, for example, visual scripting usually allows for prototyping. I am not saying that you cannot do some insane scripts with this method because many have done so. It is a very convenient way, especially for quick basic scripts, which cover a large amount of our day-to-day work as level designers. However, once you reach a certain level of complexity, other tools might be better suited.

Another important topic is the clarity of the organization of such scripts. Usually, it is very clear for the one who created it, but debugging someone else's rather complex 3D-script can be painful. Therefore, I strongly suggest establishing standards early on. For example, all non-object-related 3D-scripting elements like logic boxes are stored in the center of rooms or above the middle of outdoor locations. I spend much time chasing entity links just to find those elements deeply buried under terrain or in objects. Also, a strict naming convention, layer organization, and color code will do great for you, even if you work on your level alone. Very quickly, 3D-scripting can get very messy. Therefore, anything that helps you quickly orient yourself and fellow developers in all the calculated chaos will dramatically reduce your stress level during debugging or when you want to extend or modify your scripts.

### 15.1.4 Visual Scripting

In recent years visual scripting has become the norm for most AAA level designers. Essentially, in a separate window, it connects the input and output of various nodes visually in a graph. The graphs are either separate files or are "inside" an entity in your game world. The spatial, graphical arrangement allows many users to grasp the context quicker and easier, without being a programmer. Classic examples for level designers are Unreal Engine's Blueprint or CryEngine's Flowgraph. However, more and more engines like Dunia, Anvil, Snowdrop, Unity and various game-making kits support visual scripting.

The main advantage over 3D-scripting is that you can keep your nodes and related entities a lot more organized and logically connected. Therefore debugging and creating more complex scripts becomes a lot easier without losing too much ease of use compared to 3D-scripting. Additionally, the node graphs usually offer a lot more power and control compared to common 3D-scripting because, in many ways, it offers similar possibilities like working with text. At the same time, it is a lot easier to grasp and understand compared to the more abstract ways of text-based scripting.

However, you still need programmers or tech-savvy folks to create each node and support them with the main code and game. Therefore, you do have limitations and potentially a bottleneck. Still, once your engine grows a fair deal, many nodes are usually available, providing a lot more powerful possibilities than 3D scripting while being way more accessible than text. Therefore, I consider it today's norm of level design scripting, even though many things can still get very messy and complicated, but more about that in the upcoming chapter.

## 15.2 Scripting and Database Basics

### 15.2.1 Introduction

In this chapter, I want to cover the fundamentals of working with technical level design aspects like database work and scripting. As I have mentioned, I will keep this topic engine agnostic, yet I will focus on visual scripting since it is, in my eyes, the industry standard for level design scripting. The similarity between many visual scripting systems should allow you to quickly switch between the different engines once you know one well enough. Of course, each scripting system has its strengths and quirks, but none of them is impossible to learn. However, what is more necessary to learn initially than the in-depth knowledge of a specific scripting environment is the right mindset, which I am trying to bring across here.

## 15.2.2 Approach to Problem Solving

### *15.2.2.1 Introduction*

In most cases, solving technical challenges is about the right problem-solving mindset. Initially, certain issues or tasks might sound daunting and crazy, but they will be significantly more manageable with the right approach. It is worth noting that this basic approach works for most types of problem-solving, not just for scripting, but I apply it here most frequently and consciously. I will use the following challenge as an example case to explain this approach:

As a level designer, you have the task to populate a large village with a lot of AI, but the engine only supports a maximum of ten AI at the same time. By far, this number is not enough for the village size, barely enough to spend on the outskirt defense alone. The engine does not support different types of AI, which are less CPU taxing at different distances. Plus, the AI presence has to work for pre-combat (idle) and for combat.

### *15.2.2.2 Step 1: Understand the Problem(s)*

Essentially usually, you have a technical challenge or restriction, which at first sight clashes severely with the intended creative vision. Instead of instantly reacting and saying "no," it is crucial to explore all options and attach a price to them. Sometimes this price is just more time, additional needed resources, or an increase of complexity, leading to a more complex debugging phase at the end of the project. However, to propose different solutions, you need to take your time to think, dig deep, and formulate a detailed list of problems before you find individual solutions. In my experience, the initial knee-jerk reaction to say "no" is primarily connected to this lack of problem seeking, personal issues involved like a strong ego, insecurity, differences in creative vision, or tiredness. I will ignore the last set of problems and rather focus on the solution-oriented approach.

Going back to our example, I can split it up into the following problems:

- You can only work with ten AIs without the option to spawn cheaper variants at a distance.
- If the straightforward solutions (= spawning enough AI) are not supported by the engine, you have to fake their numbers or rather create an illusion for the player.
- The script has to work for both the idle and combat state.
- If the AI has to respawn, the player should not feel surrounded by gamey spawn points ("monster closets").
- I will have many repetitions in my scripts because I do seemingly similar things with ten AIs.

### *15.2.2.3 Step 2: Compartmentalize*

While the initial challenge might be daunting, you are already on the right track once you break up the initial task into smaller core problems. Suddenly, individual problems are a lot more realistic to solve than their totality. However, if a problem is still causing you a headache, keep breaking it down until you reach enough manageable chunks. The concept of compartmentalizing bigger challenges into smaller feasible ones is a general approach to solving problems, but it takes practice and often patience.

I recommend you start writing down your individual steps because each step to solve the problems usually directly translates to a group or larger block in your visual script. For example, we know that our script at some point has to handle idle and combat cases. Therefore, we can already visually sketch out that we have two separate large blocks for the two cases at some point.

Let us go through our script example and break it down:

1. You have to initialize the script and spawn the first set of AI on the outskirts when players approach the village in an idle stage. This initial step is basic scripting as we know it.
2. Since we cannot spawn enough AI, I would split up the village into multiple areas to populate only the current area the player is present. Therefore I need a script group that determines the current player zone.
3. I only have ten AI, and all the following scripts have to work with them. So I make sure that the script is AI-ID agnostic. The detailed execution depends on your engine, but usually, engines can work with relative AI-IDs through some type of token, broadcast, linking, or variable system.
4. Once the player is inside the village and the AI is still idle, I send all alive AI to random points inside the current player sector. They will continuously patrol it and occasionally perform idle animations like smoking, conversations, pissing, or yawning. As long as players stay undetected, there is this subtle group of AI around them, and ideally, they never notice that they are being followed due to the AI patrol randomness and the slow stealth speed of the player.
5. If the AI switches to combat, I will also send them to the current player sector, but once inside the zone or if they detect the player, I will let their systemic combat behavior take over.
6. If AI dies either while the AI is still idle (player stealth kill) or in combat, I have random respawn points prepared outside of each village sector where I know players cannot see them from within their current sector. This step is quite some work, but it guarantees safety, so players never see AI respawning, and it has to happen at a safe distance and behind a large cover so that players do not feel surrounded by a gamey spawning system.
7. I have to design the layout so there are enough non-destructible large objects in the village for the AI to spawn safely. I have to work with the involved environment artists closely so they understand the importance of those objects and structures.
8. If an AI character spawns during the idle case, I slot their ID in the already existing random idle patrol script. Therefore, every new idle AI starts coming into the zone and joins their idling AI friends. I do the same with the specific combat script if it happens during combat. Depending on your engine and AI system, they would run into the current player zone either in a dedicated combat zone or a random patrol point. Some systemic systems don't need any such guidance during combat.
9. If players switch zones during combat, and they know the player's position, I will let the AI follow the players systemically.
10. If players switch zones during combat, but the AI does not know the players' position to follow them systematically, I have to create backup scripts for the search behavior. This behavior is very engine and AI-system-dependent. Some games require an additional search script from level designers, while others can handle this more subtle and automatic.
11. I check for any repetition in the script and see if I can translate some in some type of multi-use containers, script prefabs, shared libraries, or whatever else your engine has to offer. The idea of such systems is that if you fix or modify one, then all the other ones change as well. This step will significantly speed up your iteration and debugging game, plus it keeps your script clean.
12. Lastly, I need to add a script that defines when this whole spawning stops because every script needs an end case. This case depends on completing player objectives or other creative directions.

As you see, it is not a trivial list of scripts all working connected. However, none of them is longer impossible once you break it down into smaller steps after clearly identifying the core problems. You can also see that several problems and solutions appeared once I broke down the initial set of challenges further.

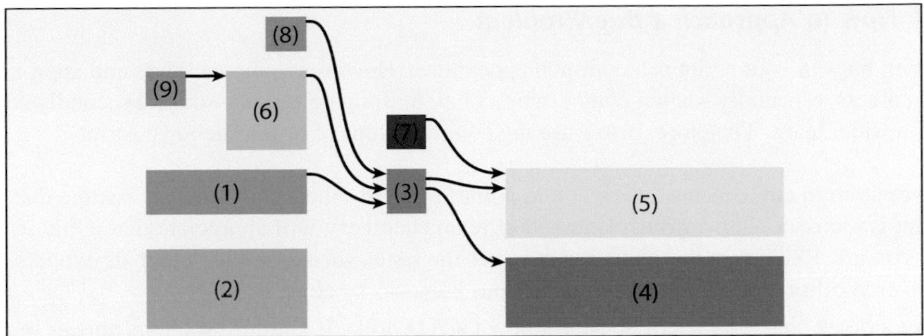


**FIGURE 15.1** (1) Initial script, only triggers once, (2) Script which determines player zone, sets script-wide variables, therefore not connected with the rest of the script, (3) Checks if AI state is idle or combat, (4) Random, looping idle AI patrols, (5) Random, looping search points for if not active combat state (for example: search or investigating (depends on AI system)), (6) Respawning of previously killed AI at random points outside of current player sector, (7) If AI loses player the script activates the search/investigate patrol in the current player sector, (8) If player switches sector this script resets the current idle patrol or search points, (9) The "win" condition of this gameplay block stops the respawning.

In reality, with some practice step one and two will happen more and more simultaneously and not after each other.

Also worth noting is that many solutions are engine-specific. My example stayed very generic. Especially handling AI in different states like idle, combat, or search is handled very differently from AI system to AI system.

#### *15.2.2.4 Step 3: Involve Your Team*

Even when you successfully script a very complex script, it does not mean you finished the job. Instead, there are many reasons why you should involve your team and peers now, and ideally earlier already.

First, there is no reason why you should not involve other developers if you are stuck and do not know further. This situation can be already during the planning phase when the problem or individual chunks overwhelm you. Trust me, it is more shameful to not ask for help and struggle in silence than admitting you need help. Or in other words: You show strength, trust, and integrity if you reach out to your colleagues. Remember, you all sit in the same boat. Do not expect yourself to know everything, especially if you are new to the job. Even seniors can't know everything.

Secondly, expect that someone else might have to work on your script at any point. For example, because you have to work on another level, you are sick, on vacation, or you ramped off the project, and others have to debug your script. Therefore, you must add a ton of comments for better comprehension, that you keep everything tidy, and separate your visual script in as many groups as feasible for better clarity. I will talk more about production scripts later on, but for now, also keep in mind that you benefit from a clean script, too. Like any design work, expect that your script will change, get cut, and extended. If your initial script is messy, it will only get worse. However, keeping your script clean, all the time, will make upcoming iterations a lot faster and easier for you.

Thirdly, once you have finished a more extensive, complicated script, take the time and go through it with a fellow tech-savvy designer. Not only might they spot some improvements and you learn something new, but likely their questions to understand your work might spark some further improvements. Further on, just explaining it to someone will very likely spark some "Aha" moments for you, things you have not considered before, which will dramatically impact your debugging phase later on—like explaining it to a living "rubber duck." Additionally, they might learn something and might return the favor. I have not always done this last step myself, and I regret it. Some of my old scripts had to get removed and redone way simpler because it was simply too complex for others to debug when I was already off the project.

#### *15.2.2.5 How to Approach a Bug/Problem*

Dealing with bugs in your script is a common appearance. However, some methods and approaches are better than others, especially when it comes to first of all finding the actual issue and secondly within the context of a wider team. Therefore, below are my common steps of how to debug a script.

1. Never jump to any conclusions right and point fingers at others. It is safer to assume that your script is the issue than anyone else's—your team chemistry will appreciate that. Only if, later on, you are 100% sure that your script is not the issue, then approach other developers. You keep credibility if you first have done all your homework below.
2. Have a quick chat with peers or your fellow QC/QA folks if similar problems appear in other levels or circumstances. Alternatively, check any emails, chats, boards, or other means reporting issues. If it is a known global issue, you can skip a more thorough investigation because others have done it already. However, maybe you can help further?
3. Go through the script slowly, step by step, as if you explain it to someone else ("rubber ducking"). Maybe the problem is obvious, especially with the bug's description. However, I recommend including all parts of the scripts, including the ones which might not be directly connected with the bug. Many times, other non-directly related parts cause issues down the line.
4. Add breakpoints, debug messages, or other means after each node. It might be tedious at first, but you need to find out when the script breaks. Yes, after each node, because it is dangerous to assume that every node reliably outputs even if you use them all the time. In such cases, it is better to be safe than sorry—or in other words: better to go through your script thoroughly once instead of sloppy one or even two times and then still do a thorough round at the end. If the script is huge you could break it up in bigger chunks first.
5. Test it in a separate, clean, and simple environment once you find out which node, feature, or entity is causing the issue. For example, if a light doesn't turn on in your level's script but in a test level, the problem is likely in your script. However, if the light does not turn on anywhere, then it starts to make sense to involve a tech-savvy person, especially if it seems not to be a known global issue. It also makes sense to check any project/build changelogs to see if that particular entity, system, feature, or node underwent some changes recently. For example, if you cannot even turn on the light in the editor without a script, it is likely a code problem and not a level design script issue.
6. If your script works several times on your machine and cannot find the issue, you must compare the context. For example, if the bug happens in a retail build or on a different platform, then check, for example, aspects like streaming, physics, or AI. Likely programmers or other tech-savvy people can help you shed some light on the issue or help with investigating the true source of the problem. Also, do not forget your friendly neighborhood QA/QC people to narrow down the cause of the issue.

Depending on your engine and team setup, expect some steps to be more granular. For example, you could break down step #4 into smaller ones. However, I hope that this quick overview will help you debug your problems since the pattern is usually very similar.

### 15.2.3 About Databases

Before we start a deep dive into scripting, I think it is essential to have a few quick recommendations on dealing with databases. Classic examples for designers and artists are databases containing your game's weapons, vehicles, AI archetypes, asset prefabs, dialogs, or mission objective properties.

Pretty much any even slightly complex project will eventually end up with databases. Additionally, databases are usually very centrally accessible to many developers within the entire team, which makes clear guidelines even more critical. However, if one developer messes up a database, it can cause grave issues to the entire team and negatively affect the entire project. A single bad entry can stop internal game reviews for hours, if not days.

By default, I highly recommend assigning one, ideally, two developers in charge of each database. Two developers are better because one could, for example, be sick, on vacation, or stuck in traffic. Of course, those two can be in charge of multiple databases, but they should be very reliable and know what they are doing. If any other developers would like to modify the database, they would ask those two chosen ones. If the change request is approved, then whoever is skilled, trusted, and available makes the change. Potentially only the two chosen ones make changes on the database. However, if everyone could modify the databases anytime they like, you likely quickly end up with a chaotic mess, an erosion of standards, bloating the database due to obsolete entries, and working with it will become much more difficult for everyone. Having many more database owners would only add more noise and water down the intention behind the guideline to keep it tight, clean, and tidy. If the team is huge or you have separate teams, for example, in separate studios, you should have more owners for each sub-team, but they must stay in tight sync.

However, especially in smaller teams, it is reasonable that the two owners are not the only ones allowed to modify the databases. Still, I recommend first getting approval or sending a message to them about what you have modified if they are not available in time. Even if you are allowed to modify them, they have to be aware to fix any entries eventually or know what is going on. A few times in my career, it happened that we unintentionally created many very similar AI archetypes, which took quite some time to adjust in the databases and reassign the correct archetypes in our levels.

Lastly, writing down the established standards, conventions, and owners of the databases is a recommended step. This step will allow newcomers to get a quick idea of what databases exist, whom to reach out to if they have change requests, and if they happen to modify a database themselves, they know which strict rules to follow.

### 15.2.4 Scripting Foundation

#### *15.2.4.1 Introduction*

I know many level designers who primarily define themselves as scripters and barely worked on any layouts. However, this is the wrong book to teach every different scripting language for every engine. Therefore, I will only focus on essential aspects of visual scripting, which every level designer should follow in my opinion. They should help to learn a new visual scripting language faster, make fewer mistakes, improve your debugging and iterations, and ultimately improve your collaboration in a team. I would consider them the absolute basics and a must in most cases. Depending on your engine, tools, and project, you want to adjust or extend them. However, communicating them to everyone involved is imperative to establish team-wide consistency, standards, and efficiency.

I know enough level designers who considered themselves "advanced" scripters yet struggled following such fundamentals. As a result, it had a severe impact on their career, their work, and the project as a whole—learn from their mistakes.

#### *15.2.4.2 Continuous Left to Right*

Let us start with a simple basic step to keep your visual-script clean. Arrange any continuous nodes that happen after each other from left to right. There should be no exceptions since almost all nodes of every visual scripting tool have their input on the left side and their output on the right side. Therefore, if they go from left to right, your connecting lines or links stay simple, clean, and more or less straight without any intersections or winding curves.

Another initially seemingly less crucial step is to keep the top of all continuous nodes in one line within the grid. Keeping them in a perfectly straight line further increases the cleanliness of your visual script and makes it a lot easier to read. After all, most of us are not used to reading wobbly horizontally but in straight lines. Yes, cleaning it up later takes some time, but placing them correctly from the get-go barely takes no time. The top nodes on the top row are ideally the most defining ones.

A simple example is if you initiate a script, then comes the first trigger, which spawns the AI, and then after the spawning it is sent on a patrol. All those nodes should be on one straight line going from left to right.

#### 15.2.4.3 Same Time = Below

Next, to keep your visual-script clean is to place all nodes that happen simultaneously perfectly under each other. This vertical order ties nicely with the first direction to keep continuous nodes going horizontal left to right. All of them together make reading a script very easy for yourself and others—the same counts for variable inputting data in nodes.

For example, if you spawn multiple AIs simultaneously, all the AI-spawn nodes are under each other, and their individual patrols happen on their respective right sides. Other usual examples are the vertical spread after randomizations or other conditional branches.

#### 15.2.4.4 Least Amount of Overlapping Connections

If your script has many connecting lines between the nodes, arrange your nodes with the least overlapping connections. Essentially you entangle your script to keep it clean and read fast. This step is critical if some of your nodes have many inputs or many outputs. If you have such messy connections, it is vital to either rearrange your nodes while still respecting vertical alignment if they happen simultaneously. However, in such cases, usually, it matters less which node is on top or bottom as long as there are no overlapping connections. Alternatively, you can try to rearrange the order of the inputs into a node to reduce overlapping links. Sometimes it also helps to rearrange nodes to avoid links going through/below other nodes or do any other convoluted paths if the links in your tool go around nodes. A bit of moving them up, down, left, or right can go a long way to keep your script looking clean and tidy.

However, often there are limits to how far you can prevent any overlapping, especially if the node input positions are fixed. Therefore, you often have to make a judgment call when to stop entangling for the sake of overall order. Your overall script readability has priority over individual overlap prevention. However, try your best to reduce overlaps to the absolute minimum. As usual, doing it right from the beginning is a lot faster than cleaning it up later. Therefore, excuses like "don't worry, I will clean it up later" should never count.

For example, there is no reason why variable-nodes cause intersections or why you should not neatly arrange them cleanly.

#### 15.2.4.5 Group Closed Steps

Once you follow the first three guidelines, you should arrange your script in clearly separate groups. Ideally, each bigger or smaller step in your script should form a recognizable group in your visual script.

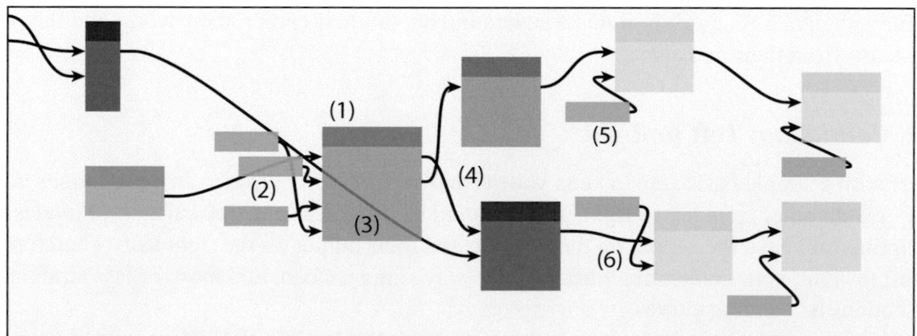


**FIGURE 15.2** (1) The continuous nodes (bright blue, orange, etc.) are not in a clean horizontal line, (2) Variable-nodes are not vertically clean placed and have man intersecting connecting lines, (3) A connecting line goes through another node, (4) Simultaneous triggered nodes are not cleanly aligned vertically, (5) Variable-nodes are not in front of their main node, (6) Lines coming from variables should not intersect other lines.

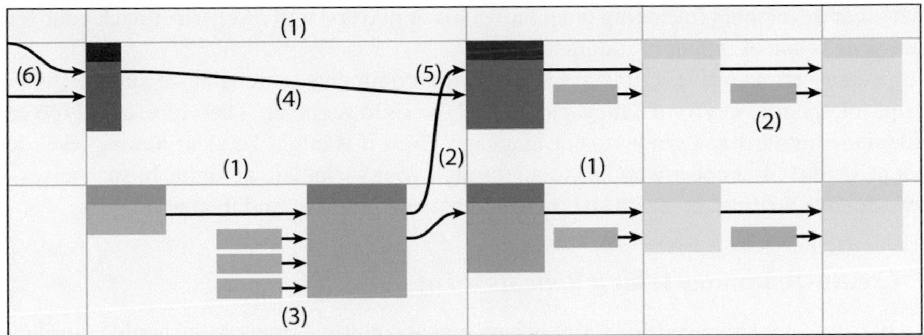


**FIGURE 15.3** (1) Continuous nodes are cleanly aligned horizontally, (2) Simultaneous triggered nodes are cleanly aligned vertically, (3) Variable-nodes are cleanly arranged in front of their main node without overlapping lines, (4) Line coming from another script segment is no longer intersecting another node, (5) Sometimes it is not avoidable to prevent intersecting lines—that is fine, but keep it to the minimum and still cleanly readable like above, (6) No more interconnecting lines.

In the previous chapter, you can see this compartmentalization approach when I wrote about problem-solving. It allows you and others to understand which script group is doing what quickly, and if they look for something particular, they know where to look and where not. It also keeps your thinking compartmentalized, allowing you to focus on just the problems of this specific step. Since this scripting type is such a visual medium, it is essential to use their strengths to your advantage and not lean into its chaos potential.

Common examples for separate groups are first initiations, AI patrols or spawning, conditional logic blocks, distinct control actions, or mission objective handling. The more they are mixed up, the worse the script's readability. In doubt, first, have rather too many too small script groups instead of too few too big ones. It is a lot easier to unite groups later on than it is to entangle them.

Suppose you have extensive scripts with many, especially simultaneous, script groups; I suggest adding nodes that help you organize the visual readability. I am talking here about very cheap (performance-wise) nodes with many inputs or outputs with no other function. Place them at the beginning or end of your script group to have a clear end or beginning to keep everything well organized.

Another recommendation is to look into your tool to group or highlight such sub-scripts. Typical examples for such features are groups that you can enlarge/minimize or color their background. It just further helps to keep everything cleaned up and not right away overwhelming. However, make sure that you name your groups reasonably for anyone else to quickly understand them.

### *15.2.4.6 Comments*

By default, you should rather comment too much than too little in your script. However, there are a few simple guidelines below to follow.

First, comment why you are doing a script, or in the case of larger groups, what this group is about; for example: "Check to determine at what distance the waypoint should appear for each co-op player" or "AI spawn group A." Anyone going over your script can get a rapid overview of your script. It is also helpful for yourself if the script is huge or you have not worked on it for a while.

I cannot recommend that you comment on the obvious. You should not comment on anything readable by looking at the script for a second or two. For example, do not add a comment over a randomizer-node "random outputs." Instead, the larger group could have something like "Group to determine random spawn points for AI." As much as you should be liberal to comment on pretty much anything else, such obvious comments are just clutter.

Also, keep out anything personal or which is not necessarily helpful. For example, skip comments like "this script is for dummies," "this script is a complete mess," "backup script in case the player is too stupid to get the puzzle," or "if you are lost, write a mail to myname@companymail.com." Always keep in mind that other developers (including potentially fans or players) will likely read/hack your scripts and do not share your sense of humor or judgment.

Lastly, especially in extensive scripts, try to keep your comments searchable. If anyone should search in your script for specific keywords, they should find the right segment. Therefore, avoid too cryptic or project-wide non-standardized synonyms or language. Even if it might be clear among level designers, it might not be trivial for a coder who has to go through your script late at night. In such cases, instead, spend a few seconds writing too much so others do not need hours to find it later.

#### *15.2.4.7 Create Templates Which Repeats a Lot*

Like with any piece of written code or script, which repeats multiple times, you should consider creating universal templates, functions, or adding them to a global script multi-use library. The exact use, ways to do it, and terminology depend on your script language. However, essentially it should allow you to have the same repeated piece of script existing only at one place, and you only "reference" it with its context-specific inputs and outputs in your actual scripts. If you happen to fix or modify your template, it will affect them in all your scripts. This approach is a massive time-saver, drastically reducing the complexity of the individual scripts and decreasing the chance of bugs because you only have to fix it once.

In reality, however, it is not always easy to recognize such patterns, because many scripts are similar but not exactly the same. In such cases, try to either give your universal scripts some flexibility and customizing options or even accept some limitations. In the end, it will likely pay off for developers to have a bit limited script if the project as a whole stays cleaner and less infested by bugs. I know it is not easy to accept by every highly self-proclaimed "script-god" out there, but trust me, the vast majority of players will not notice all the different small nuances in your scripts.

However, there is no reason to make every little bit of script into a global template. Anything trivial, straightforward, and small script snippet does not have to become a universal template. If something like that really repeats a lot, I would instead recommend talking to programmers if they have a better idea, like making a new node instead of a script library entry.

#### *15.2.4.8 Always Have Backups in Your Scripts*

Every script should have a clear start and a clear end state. Both have to be connected to make sure that there is a guarantee that the script starts reliably and ends. Therefore usually, if I start with a script, I start with whatever initiates it and then directly connect it with the end state. Then I test it just to make sure that even this super basic flow works. If my end state does not exist yet for production reasons, I use a placeholder like a debug message, light, or similar.

Most bugs happen in the sections in-between once the start and end state work. For example, if you rely on AI to do anything essentially, deal with streaming, specific player actions, physics, or other potentially unreliable features, things can go wrong (very engine/tool dependent!). In all such cases, I strongly recommend that you start adding backup scripts. Common backup solutions are time delays that happen simultaneously in your script's background. However, this severely matters case by case because you should resolve not every backup solution with a time delay. Alternatively, avoid relying too much on all nodes' output to work smoothly. Additionally, I recommend that you trigger all major key parts of your scripts with console commands or button presses during the development process. This step is especially important for mission objectives and cutscenes. A bug in such systems/scripts should never be a walk-through break during a review. For example, we had to cancel many big reviews because a cutscene did not end, and there was no way to skip it otherwise.

For example, you want that once the player arrives at a house in an open world, an AI character greets the player, goes to a point, and opens the gate to the next dungeon. So many things can go wrong here. Let us go through a few cases:

- The AI/entity has not streamed in yet because of a random hitch since the player-movement speed in the final build is a tick faster than in your editor or another glitch or hick-up with streaming. As a result, the script stops because a non-loaded entity cannot continue the script—If streaming is a reality for your game, add in your script that it only continues once all relevant entities are loaded before the script relies on them.

- The AI might get killed, run away, an object blocks it to go to the point to open the gate, or anything else preventing the go-to command—Add a time delay, so the gate opens after X seconds if the AI did open it not yet otherwise. It is not a pretty solution, but I believe players likely prefer a magically opening door over not progressing.
- For whatever reason, the AI does not finish their dialog, maybe it gets distracted. Therefore, the next part of the script does not trigger—Never rely on less fundamental aspects like dialogs or animations (sorry, audio, animators, and narrative folks!) if they can get interrupted or stopped otherwise. Instead, add a backup script (usually time delay) running simultaneously, which guarantees that the next part triggers even if the AI somehow gets distracted. However, keep an eye on, for example, dialogs in case they change length throughout production.

Many bugs which are hard to debug are connected to such issues. They are the typical suspects of "it works on my machine." Always consider that the final game environment behaves a tick differently and is usually faster than your development environment, especially if an editor, a build-process, and compiling are involved. Also, never rely on AI to be a reliable tool to trigger anything crucial except it is a cutscene, and even then, I would sleep better with a backup. Physics engine tends to be a bit different too, in a release build environment. Same counts for streaming and even script execution. If you then add the differences between platforms you are in for a treat.

Lastly, often the engine is not executing every node with the same speed, which in the end, after some debugging, results in a lot of "0.01-second time-delay nodes" in some people's scripts to guarantee that the ideal order stays intact. However, each engine has its own method and quirks here. Therefore, if you script anything more advanced, it makes sense to know a bit more about your engine's node costs and how truly simultaneous it executes nodes in your scripts. For example, if you use a lot of simple nodes to organize your massive script, you should know that they have a tiny cost, too. This case is especially crucial if you rely on anything conditional that happens simultaneously or sensitive time-wise, even if it makes no sense at first glance.

#### *15.2.4.9 Follow Conventions*

Any team-wide conventions or standards are a must to follow. Such criteria/norms could be anything from consistent color-coding script groups, any naming conventions, or what nodes to only use during prototyping. However, this also affects anything related to your scripts, like consistent naming conventions of entities or color-coding of like AI spawners, patrol points, or area shapes.

This point also means that such standards must be determined and communicated at the beginning of a project. The later anyone establishes such conventions, the more unnecessary work scripters have to do later. That is why usually experienced level designers establish such norms early on.

### 15.2.5 Scripting Mindset

#### *15.2.5.1 Introduction*

In this chapter, I briefly want to cover some scripting mindsets that people often misunderstand, are not taken too seriously, or do not separate enough. Not every scripting approach makes sense for every stage of a project which is often the cause of friction, bugs, and lots of avoidable extra work.

#### *15.2.5.2 Dig Deep*

When you are learning a new visual scripting language, of course, start doing the usual tutorials and experiment around a bit yourself in test levels. However, I recommend going through all nodes. You do not have to use them all, but at least get a good feeling of what is available. If you have the time and idea to use more nodes in further prototypes or experiments to learn the system further, the better.

Each scripting language has its own quirks—get to know them. Especially get very familiar with the logic and math nodes, how it handles various variable types (for example, level-wide, game-wide, script local), and how the system ties in with databases and world entities. Once you know those, look into the different input types like booleans, integers, or strings and how you can modify them using math, logic, variables, or other inputs. It will significantly benefit you if you can comfortably modify all the nodes' inputs and variables when you do any complex gameplay prototypes. Essentially you should quickly learn how far you can push the limits and where a hack ends and production scripts start, but more about them below.

#### *15.2.5.3 A Prototype Is a Prototype*

If you prototype or hack anything quickly together, you are your own expert, judge, and curse. Therefore, it is up to you to follow any script guidelines or how clean you want to keep it. However, I highly encourage you to keep it clean and well commented if there is even a remote chance that your script might turn into something useful for the project or others have to deal with it. Also, any clean prototype is better/faster to iterate on than a messy one.

I am saying it here because I worked on many prototypes/hacks myself or collaborated with many level designers doing similar work. People often commented about how messy the script was, which was annoying because it was just my own quick test or exploration. However, it got even more annoying once the prototype found traction in a few instances, and I had to clean it up before moving into a production environment. All it means is a matter of experience when you should script fast and messy and when a bit slower but clean. However, others should similarly be careful with quick judgment about other people's prototype/hack scripts. A hack is a hack, is a hack—just mark and communicate it accordingly.

#### *15.2.5.4 Production Script Standards*

Let us start with the obvious. A production design or level script has to be clean, well commented, and follow the project guidelines. Channeling your inner OCD is not a bad approach here. As much as possible, use universal libraries by ideally working with tech-savvy central developers. Remember, such script templates used by many other developers must be extra clean, very flexible for project-wide use, and solid/reliable. Additionally, any script, with or without global library use, has to be reliable under any circumstances, meaning backup scripts, for even slightly risky scripts, are a must from the get-go. It is better to be overly cautious early on than lengthy, painful debugging later on. Therefore, important global script templates are typically in the hands of a few specialized technical (level) designers/scripters.

It is not uncommon for some hasty scripts or experiments to creep into production scripts, especially if the initial ideas were not 100% certain yet or they originate from pre-production. Likely, such less-production-ready scripts cause issues down the line or need iterations. In such cases, fight the urge to hack the hack. It is imperative to take your time and clean up the specific scripts, and if it means redoing large parts of it, then so be it. You will thank yourself later, and in the worst case, you learned something for later.

At any time, expect that the ownership of your scripts can shift to other designers for various reasons. Also, at any time script reviews by your leads, peers or other tech experts can happen. Therefore, once again, it is crucial to keep your scripts clean and easily understood by others. Assumptions or your personal understanding of common sense will not be your friends. Instead, I recommend you comment too much, ferociously follow project conventions and keep your scripts tidy. Ultimately, you, your peers, and the project can only benefit from your diligence.

# 16

## *Working with Ingredients*

We level designers work with all kinds of gameplay ingredients daily. After all, one of our key defining pillars is to be assemblers. Modern games feature a wide periphery of gameplay features, and it is not possible to talk about each one of them. However, I can only talk about some of the more common and the ones I am more familiar with to give you an idea of how to apply or tweak them for your game. After all, many basic lessons and methodologies are either comparable or adjustable.

Good game designers are not the ones who have many great ideas, but the ones who make them work well and harmoniously in the game's complexity without alienating their peers in the process. However, just adding a few AI archetypes, exploding barrels, or health packs is not enough for good level designers either; therefore, learning to use those essential ingredients correctly while dodging the common pitfalls is one of the primary foundations for being a level designer. This chapter will share some of my fundamental rules, guidelines, and directions, assembling common design ingredients to make even better levels.

## 16.1 Basic AI and Design Rules

### 16.1.1 Introduction

This chapter is a wider collection of various design guidelines and best practices about working with gameplay ingredients. While it stays generic in several aspects to accommodate your game needs, I will focus on AI since they are usually one of the level designer's most tricky yet most important ingredients.

### 16.1.2 Basic AI and Combat Guidelines

#### *16.1.2.1 Never Rely on AI*

It always sounds great when designers have ideas like "that tank is blocking the base's entrance, so players have to do all the other objectives to unlock the back entrance" or "that final boss is so powerful, that players have to level up for days till they can defeat him." However, countless YouTube videos of very difficult games have proven that there will always be a few players who can defeat such AI challenges.

Therefore, especially if you design levels for less difficult AAA games catered to a broader audience, AI is not a reliable way to stop players. This fact is even more accurate the more systemic the AI system is. There will always be some unforeseeable exploits, glitches, or simply great players who use the game's full arsenal to overcome any AI challenge. In many cases, players bypass the AI and do not even defeat them, and if they have to defeat them, then exploits are a common practice. Modern games are commonly so complex that it is almost impossible for all developers to accommodate every circumstance and combination.

If you want to stop players, I recommend anything absolute, like a closed gate, or an NPC that must show up to transport players to the next segment. In rare instances, you design AI as an absolute blocker for players, but then they are specially designed one-offs or specific to your game's vision, type, or genre. After all, some games don't care if you can defeat the final boss right after the game's start, but you all have to be in agreement about that.

#### *16.1.2.2 AI Brings Life to the World*

I already wrote that AI should not exist to be killed by players in other contexts. I mean, sure, in certain games, that is a legit reason for their existence, especially straight-up action games, and that is fine.

DOI: 10.1201/9781003275664-22

However, if your game has even the slightest mandate to feature a believable world, the AI's initial player-facing goal is to bring your world to life, not only friendly AI NPCs.

Sure, the main purpose of enemy AI is to provide a gameplay challenge, but before they start engaging the player, they should have a purpose in their life. Even some guards defending a seemingly meaningless warehouse full of crates have a purpose, and it should fit your world's direction and vision.

Therefore, once you have figured out the challenge factor and your main gameplay tools, plus the appropriate layout, it is time to ground the enemy NPCs in your world. How would they behave here? How would they behave if attacked? How can they teach the player something about the world with dialogs, animations, behaviors, or sheer presence? What is the one thing even the least unattentive player spots right away?

Further on, purely relying on standard systemic or other global behaviors will ultimately mean that combat encounters for players can start to feel very similar. Still, the key is first to infuse the encounter with initial world-building aspects but then give them purpose during combat. For example, let them shout different context-specific dialogs, let them retreat occasionally, or do not make them call for the same reinforcement all the time. Giving them purpose should not end with the first detection.

#### *16.1.2.3 AI Archetype Combinations*

Knowing the individual AI archetypes is good and essential, but knowing their combinations is even better. Like with food, you want to have a great mix of different flavors and avoid too much doubling up. For example, multiple melee archetypes attacking the player usually do not give you the desired combat profile or mix. Combining simple close-range shotgun guys with mid-range rifle soldiers is better but likely not strongly noticeable by the player. However, for example, mixing snipers and attack dogs is a classic and proven combination because they each challenge the player differently and complement their attack styles.

A good combination of archetypes can increase their difficulty beyond their individual strength. For example, in many games, two snipers and two attack dogs are way more challenging than four snipers alone or four attack dogs. Of course, the environment and layout have to be in their favor as well.

If we go back to the example of combining shotgun and rifle enemies, then they could be a good combination if they have noticeable secondary abilities which complement each other. Common examples here are, for example, various grenades like a flashbang, explosives, or smoke. Essentially one archetype's weapons and abilities force movement/stop on players while the other AI archetypes benefit from it. For example, the enemy sniper benefits from players getting held by dogs or pushed out of cover, while shotgun enemies benefit from disoriented players after a flashbang.

Learning such combinations is crucial for exciting and challenging combat experiences, especially if the number of AI actors is limited. I recommend researching what combinations work well in what environments and designing the archetypes with synergies from the get-go.

#### *16.1.2.4 AI Needs to Answer All Player Actions*

Not every AI archetype works well in every environment, which is usually acceptable within reasonable limits. However, the AI must answer every player's action somewhat. For example, if players are in a tank or at a spot the melee AI cannot reach, they should have a way to react to it. A definitive solution for this situation is throwing grenades, both for unreachable players or the ones sitting in a tank. However, it gets complicated when the enemies are melee-only (animals), and players can quickly jump on objects where the AI cannot reach them due to navigation limitations.

It does not have to be a perfect reaction, but at least they should not appear to be stupid, broken, or braindead. The minimum reaction is to run away or perform some foolish/heroic action, but ideally, the AI can make some difference/damage. If your solution is less than ideal, it is also important to tweak your environment so that such situations will not happen or will not happen a lot. Edge cases of accidents are hard to avoid in complex, believable environments, but you should avoid allowing easy exploits. Most experienced players will go for the easiest and fastest solution, even if that might (unknowingly) "cheat" them about their fun game experience. Therefore, try to break your AI, find exploits, work with game design, and ultimately avoid layouts that show certain archetypes in their worst light.

#### 16.1.2.5 Factions

If your game features opposing factions, then featuring any AI factions fighting against each other is always a nice touch bringing your world to life. Of course, it reduces the encounter's difficulty, especially if players can watch and observe the fighting resolve. However, those circumstances can be solved with additional reinforcement. Otherwise, you can introduce them early in the game where a low difficulty is okay, use it to show the strength of a certain enemy type, or generally use such fights to introduce a new AI archetype. Generally speaking, they are a great narrative, introductory, and world-building tool.

Additionally, it is a great way to keep the pacing exciting without every event always being about the player in the center of attention. Sometimes it is nice just to sit back and watch an exciting battle unfold. It gets even better if players have ways to manipulate the battle's outcome without being directly involved, especially if a direct, open involvement would be incredibly difficult.

#### 16.1.2.6 Less Ideal AI Archetypes

Often, we level designers face the situation where we have to feature AI archetypes that are not ideal. Such archetypes could be flawed because they are subjectively/objectively limited in features, have strong limited use in the available environments, or are simply not fun. However, we have to use them for reasons like narrative, world-building, lack of available alternatives, or game progression.

In such cases, I recommend first trying to tweak the environment and layout in their favor. Some minor tweaks can often make a noticeable difference, even if that means sacrificing some minor world-building or believable aspects. Secondly, possibly pair them with other archetypes with which you can pair them to either mask their flaws or maybe even compliment them enough to be somewhat semi-exciting. Thirdly, limit their use and avoid using them repeatedly after each other. For example, suppose you have a whole set of problematic AI archetypes. In that case, I recommend not featuring levels/missions with only such enemies but mixing in as many better enemy archetypes in between. Essentially, you try to mask their "bitter taste" with other "flavors" in a food analogy.

#### 16.1.2.7 AI Encounters as a Puzzle

This point is very game-dependent, but usually, the direct head-on approach to engage enemy AI should be more difficult than finding alternative solutions. Finding such different solutions is commonly referred to as the "action puzzle." The trick is to make such alternative ways easier than the direct approach. For example, often sneaking around and killing everyone undetected one-by-one is more complicated than running into the room head-on with a big machine gun. The individual player skill and preferred playstyle are enormous factors here. Therefore, you should design the layout and the used gameplay ingredients to almost aggressively hint and favor such alternative solutions above the direct approach. I have covered the case of selling options to players multiple times in this book before, but it should remain a vital design step for every encounter.

After marketing such alternative solutions, it is time to think about making the direct approach more difficult. The solutions can be in the layout itself, cover placement, placement/rotation of enemies, or other ingredients like machine guns/mortars/reinforcement in the back, making the direct assault solution a step closer to suicide.

#### 16.1.2.8 Spawn AI Ahead of Time

A standard level design mistake is to spawn/initiate AI too late. As a result, fast players can see them just coming to life when they rush forward, conveniently see multiple AI guys come around a tiny, tall crate, or even see them spawning directly. Therefore, you have to stress-test your spawn-triggers at the maximum possible speed, and once you cannot see any issues, you still give the AI some additional buffer time. Give your AI enough space and time to comfortably populate the combat space and avoid players observing that this scene was visibly scripted.

This timing/triggering adjustment also includes having enough physical space or time between combat encounters. Therefore, either tweak the layout accordingly, so you have enough space to trigger them early enough, or let the AI enter the space from the outside. For example, the courtyard is unpopulated when the player sprints forward, but then a jeep arrives, and multiple enemies debark and search the space. However, keep in mind that in such cases, often, a single well-placed player grenade/explosive can end the fight before it begins.

#### 16.1.2.9 Layer Your Combat Encounters

I know I have many food comparisons, but also any bigger combat encounters (in contrast to small combat snacks) should have layers of flavor. A good combat encounter has a mix of different ingredients, not only AI. For example, some very tough slow enemies that keep pressure on players, some fast chasing and flimsy AI types, plus some environmental flavors like explosive barrels, lava pits, mortars, lots of climbing options, or many sneaking routes. Like the previous mix of AI archetypes, I recommend researching and listing ideal and less ideal ingredient and layout combinations beyond the AI archetypes.

Further on, you can consider layering in flavors step by step by bringing in some of them after each other. For example, start with something big and tough, which draws a lot of player attention to take down, but then follow up mid-way with something fast or long range. Another example is starting with an enemy with lots of explosives but then adding an enemy that can pin down or disorientate players. It becomes a valid player strategy to quickly take out the explosive-handling enemies because they are way more difficult to deal with once the pinning-down enemies arrive.

By layering up the combat flavors, you allow the fight to develop in exciting, refreshing ways and reduce frustration if an all-at-once combination is overwhelming. It is a gentle way to control pacing.

#### 16.1.2.10 Plans Go Wrong

This point is not about accepting that many players will not play your combat encounters the way you had in mind because we have already covered that case in this book. Instead, I suggest you carefully look into some execution flaws of your enemies—let them make some mistakes, too. Now, I do not mean scripting them to have accidents, especially if players play the same section more than once, such scripts feel too artificial. Of course, I also don't mean adding bugs.

However, you can encourage mistakes by preparing the environment and ingredients. For example, a group of reinforcement soldiers runs aside some gas tanks which the player can shoot, lava pits are dangerously close to the preferred yawning spots of hell demons, or the main combat area has many physicalized objects to stumble over. The more systemic your game and AI system are, the more you can create some of those moments. However, use them carefully, or it either makes your enemy AI look too stupid, or it leads to easy go-to solutions. For example, there should not always be a pit with spikes each time players face some kickable flesh-golems.

The nice part is that such a setup can also lead to entertaining mistakes on the player's side. However, this is another reason why you should not overdo it, or it might lead to frustrations, the setup loses the novelty factor, and the win/loss for the player might feel too orchestrated.

#### 16.1.2.11 Surprise and Break Rules

I wrote a lot of basic guidelines on how to use and mix AI ingredients. However, to stay fresh, occasionally surprise players by breaking such directions. For example, once in your game, let the player get attacked by only close and melee enemies, and instead of sending in some snipers midway, spawn right from the get-go. A win for players feels stronger if they had to stay on their toes. If each combat feels too designed by the book, the wins feel too shallow, and players will not feel smart. If you want players to keep playing your game as long as possible, give them a reason to keep getting surprised gameplay-wise, and not only by visually stunning scenes, or a good narrative.

### 16.1.3 Ingredient and Gameplay Pitfalls

#### *16.1.3.1 Items as Triggers*

To some more arcadey, gamy, or particularly sinister games, the concept of triggering events when picking up items certainly fits. However, if it is not part of your game's core DNA, I would strictly avoid triggering threats like traps or spawning enemies when a player picks up a goodie like ammo, health, or a weapon. Essentially you teach the player that picking up something good triggers something bad, which reduces the warm feeling of a reward.

Another classic example is enemies spawning when players get behind a mounted machine gun, so they have targets to maw down. It was especially common in older, very linear games where you usually did not have the space or advanced AI to feature mounted guns as a systemic tool. However, nowadays, we do not have such limitations or excuses.

However, if you work on games that feature such behaviors, I recommend surprising players as much as possible in a satisfying yet relatable way. Therefore, there should never be a guarantee that always the same happens, and the less likely players expect it, and the more surprising the reaction, the better.

#### *16.1.3.2 Items as Hints*

A profound collection of weapons, ammo, and health packs is another classic item-related trope indicating a tough battle ahead. Now, there is nothing too wrong with setting up players for success before a big fight, but I recommend hiding it a bit if possible. For example, you can slowly oversaturate the player's ammo and weapon choices in longer sections before the boss fight, instead of providing a concentrated collection before the last door.

#### *16.1.3.3 Actions and Consequences*

If players have to make meaningful choices, it has to have meaningful consequences. Ideally, the consequences are known for players; otherwise, it becomes a lackluster guessing game. What counts for big decisions within the game's narrative or progression also counts for smaller decisions like: Do I run to the MG? Do I try to sneak? Do I try to lure the enemy to the gas tank? Any choice you give to players should have a consequence with their risks associated. Waiting for enemies to walk by the gas tank is not a guarantee, but if it works, it feels fantastic. If players get to the MG but just at that moment there are no enemies in front, it should be their fault, not the game's. Especially in systemic games, the consequences do not have to be an assurance each time, but there should be a fair chance when playing the game's systemic nature.

However, if sneaking is doomed to fail regardless of how hard players try, it feels stale. The same case counts for MGs at positions so useless that neither AI nor players ever want to use them. Therefore, picking such offered options either results in frustration, emptiness, or no meaningful consequences.

#### *16.1.3.4 Exploits vs. Making It Easy*

Occasionally you create challenges or mission objectives that can be incredibly easy and fast to complete once you know the right way. However, I would not raise a red flag in most cases if it is not a common occurrence in your game. Therefore, occasionally it is better to accept such a loophole for a few players than to sacrifice the experience for the majority. However, I would be careful if such an easy solution is a straight exploit skipping a large section of content or making it easy because the player is smart.

If players figure out a very clever way to overcome a gameplay section seemingly trivial, then it is not a big deal in my book. After all, the game should reward cleverness, as long as you stay within the game's core rules. However, by definition, being clever is not easy. Especially in very systemic games, it is also a reward for us developers to see what innovative solutions players come up with. However, I would get a bit worried if it is trivial to skip large sections—especially potentially exploiting an issue in your setup or script. I would consider such exploits as bugs and work closely with QA/QC to find and hopefully eliminate them. Sure, you likely end up with a few of those in your released game, but hopefully, they remain rare and are difficult to find. The real problem is instead if you know such exploits, they are easy to spot, you cannot address them accordingly, and your game is meant to be highly replayable.

Having an adversarial mindset to spot such issues early is a big bonus; work closely with QA/QC and try to break your own setups and scripts seriously. After all, you, the creator, should know the flaws the best, and the sooner you fix them, the more time for tweaking and polishing you have later on. Also, remember, we usually do not build our games to make speedrunners' life easy because they need their challenges, too.

#### *16.1.3.5 Randomization*

By default, I would be careful with randomization if your game isn't meant to be highly replayable. Also, dying a lot and therefore being forced to replay the same section is not a sign of replayability in all games. Many difficult games purposely avoid randomness, so players have a chance to learn the levels good enough to beat them eventually. The main problem with randomization is that it is not usually worth the extra production costs compared to the player experience. Still, that severely depends on your game, of course, but let us assume you do not work on, for example, a rogue-like.

Script-wise, adding randomization is usually not a huge deal. However, that is not where the costs are hidden. The production costs are in testing all the variants and debugging them if things go wrong. Sure, a few random patrol points is usually not a huge issue. Still, small randomization is usually not picked up by many players, but if it is safe to do so on your side and does not add much production time. I believe giving the nod to the attentive players is a nice gesture. Sometimes it is the little things that make the difference. However, if you are an inexperienced designer, I strongly recommend playing it safe and solid first instead of trying to show off with small randomization. The more experienced you are, the better you know if they are worth it.

However, imagine the case of random layouts and your AI shows buggy behavior. Now, reproducing it for QA/QC and later on for the developers within the exact circumstances will get incredibly tricky. It worsens if you have several random elements like AI archetypes, big layout aspects (=major pathing differences), spawn points, and small layout aspects (= object orientation/size). Now you would need a system that can go through all the variants and recreate them on demand, and it still means someone has to test all variants each time it goes through meaningful changes, potentially daily. This step is a serious undertaking and should be greenlit by production early on. Many games start with such noble ideas and then wastefully cut them throughout development. If randomization is not at your game's core, do the right, yet tough, call and skip it early.

#### *16.1.3.6 Ingredients Flavor Your Layouts*

When I design a layout and do not feel a good connection with it early on, I often make the layout about a specific ingredient. It is so common to give layouts some underlying flavor that you often find "ingredient flavors" as part of each level design documentation. However, I strongly recommend limiting it to only one or two ingredients; otherwise, no ingredient clearly stands out.

For example, if your layout is about propane tanks, place many of them conveniently placed at key spots for some entertaining explosions. However, it also should motivate you to rethink some layout aspects to create such beautiful moments. Just adding a few propane tanks in a generic layout is not suddenly making it extraordinary. The ingredient, whatever it is, forces you to give your layout consideration a clear purpose which can lead to some even better ideas along the way.

For example, you have an underground bunker with an extensive network of tunnels, and the chosen ingredient is a mounted machine gun in the hands of AI. In order to overcome this deadly threat in the tight hallways, you could design a network of air ducts around it, something which might not have come to your mind without the addition of the MG.

Another example could be if the layout is a bit boring but features many height differences, then grappling, zip-lines, double jumps, wall running, or other means of 3D navigation come to mind and tweaking it for the perfect use. However, this also means the layout does not always have to feature the ingredient directly. It is often enough to tweak a layout for one or two specific player abilities, weapons, or gadgets. Not all players might pick up on it, but often it is enough for you, the level designer, to have some sparks, direction, and inspiration for a particular layout. Even if players do not use the "correct" ingredient or ability, they will still likely feel that the designer built the layout with purpose.

## 16.2 Working with AI Types

### 16.2.1 Introduction

Covering all types of AI types would be a bit too crazy in the context of this book. Instead, I want to keep the AI types generic, focus on the main groups, and primarily cover the ones I have the most experience with. I will not go very deep into the game design of each AI type but instead focus on their impact on level design.

In my experience, the level design consideration, which counts for most different AI types, also counts for players in multiplayer with similar sets of weapons and abilities. Therefore, what sounds like a chapter primarily catered toward a singleplayer experience you can also apply for most multiplayer games.

### 16.2.2 Melee AI Types

#### *16.2.2.1 Introduction*

In its basic behavior, melee-AI types move toward their target and attack it with a melee weapon. Some feature special movement types like jumping, dodging, moving in other strange patterns, flying, swimming, climbing, or vaulting. Classic examples are common zombies, guys with baseball bats, knights swinging swords and shields, and of course, most animals.

What unites them is also their common weakness: the lack of range attacks. This deficiency means they cannot attack anything they cannot reach with a melee attack. Sure, some types have some type of backup range attack, but it is uncommon and often still limited. Therefore, I want to focus on basic types like classic zombies or animals.

#### *16.2.2.2 Level Design Considerations*

By default, the expected player behavior facing such enemies, besides engaging them, is to move backward or to safe spots. Ideally, they are looking for choke points limiting the movement of the AI enemies. Therefore, it is vital that the layout focuses heavily on loops and features no dead-ends.

As another essential factor, you should avoid players wanting to retreat too far backward, even leaving the battle area entirely, except the enemy AI is very fast. Usually, you drop or teleport players in the middle of a space or first initiate the fight very deep/late into the given space. Alternatively, you can give players POAs ahead or at the sides that appear way more beneficial than moving backward.

Often such POAs are safe spots where melee enemies cannot engage the players. However, they come with a big problem because no threat also means not much challenge and arguably no fun. Therefore, try to keep those environments as much as possible free of such 100% safe spots, except players cannot fully engage melee enemies from here. I know it is not easy to create such layouts, especially in believable environments or open worlds, but even just trying it as much as possible is already helping. Ideally, you only allow such 100% safe spots with AI, which can retreat or otherwise can defend itself when the player is unreachable.

Instead, I recommend you look into temporary safe spots. Those locations are safe for some time, but eventually, melee AI can get up and force the players to move again. However, prolonging very repetitive movement around the same spot(s) should be avoided as well (avoid a "kiting" exploit). Alternatively other threats like range AI pushes the player out from there. Ideally, players benefit from using as much of your designed play-space as possible, therefore, using at least three to four of such spots in one combat space.

All the points above are about longer engagements with the melee AI type either because it is a horde or because they take a long time to take down. If there are only a few and they die fast, then it is all about the presentation or introduction. It is more a matter of surprise at shorter distances that you staged impactful. The classic example is the zombie behind the toilet stall door or the tiger jumping out of bushes. However, I recommend not overdoing such encounters because they quickly become old and predictable.

Another important consideration is with smaller melee enemies like wolves, badgers, or angry turkeys. Many players have trouble hitting lower targets that cycle the player fast at close range, especially when playing with a controller. Therefore, do not use too many of them continuously or simultaneously. Instead, I suggest occasionally using them as a "spice" element, especially in conjunction with other harmonizing AI archetypes.

### 16.2.3 Mid- to Close-Range AI Types

#### *16.2.3.1 Introduction*

In many action games, those AI types are your bread-and-butter AI attacking players with, for example, rifles, shotguns, fireballs, sub-machine guns, arrows, spears, or lightning bolts. Their range attacks allow them to attack players in almost every circumstance while staying within a comfortable distance for players to engage them as well. Common differences are, for example, the attack range, if they seek cover, their type of damage/attack, their health, navigation type, and other unique abilities like throwing grenades, teleporting, shields, or calling in airstrikes.

#### *16.2.3.2 Level Design Considerations*

This group is incredibly diverse, making it very difficult to give practical level design considerations. However, most of the time, when I covered AI in this book, I have talked about this particular type because they are essentially the norm for most action games. Also, typically what is good for players with similar capabilities is good for them, too.

Suppose their behavior is heavily cover-based, then. In that case, a good cover setup is essential but equally important is a good cover setup for players engaging them from a distance and moving with purpose and options. With or without a firefight, this cat-and-mouse game is one of the key fun factors engaging with this AI type. The more you give both players and AI the necessary space and options (and cover) to unfold their full behavior, the better. There is nothing worse than sending a bunch of mid to close-range AI down a tight hallway without any cover or options. Even just having such sections in your level or area can become problematic if players can lure them into such death traps. Lots of navigation options and POAs are essential when designing space for such an AI type, regardless if they are now cover-based or not.

Pairing up close and mid-range AI, for example, shotgun and rifle troops, is a classic solid mix. The shotgun guys usually rush to get close enough while the rifle guys pressure players. In many ways, such close-range types are like melee enemies, just without the extreme limitations. The layout benefits from similar considerations, but it does not have to bother with the design problem of small safe spots on large crates or rocks to jump on.

### 16.2.4 Long-Range AI Types

#### *16.2.4.1 Introduction*

I am talking here about the classic snipers but including any related types which, for example, shoot rockets, lightning bolts, or railgun slugs. They commonly do not move a lot except when trying to keep a distance from their enemies. Some can switch weapons at close-range or feature other extra features like distracting abilities such as smoke, flashbangs, or teleportation.

Real-world sniper methodologies usually include staying hidden or switching positions after each shot. However, in games, many players do not appreciate it when they get shot by an almost invisible enemy. Therefore, many snipers in games feature gimmicky red lasers or scope flashes.

#### *16.2.4.2 Level Design Considerations*

The role of an AI sniper in games is to either engage players into equally long-range fights or to get them closer under mainly cover. In both scenarios, players need to have a chance to spot the long-distance threat. How high the chance should depend on your game and, to some extent, how dangerous snipers are in general. Brutally getting killed by one shot by an almost invisible enemy at 1,000 meters might not be everyone's cup of tea, but snipers which never hit and barely do any damage are neither. However, usually, snipers are a severe threat because then players have to take them seriously and switch up their gameplay pattern, which is what we want to achieve as designers.

In the first scenario (= long-range firefight), players need various spots, either soft, destructible, or hard cover, from which they can return fire against the enemy sniper. Ideally, they can switch between the spots unseen to outsmart the AI during this often deadly cat-and-mouse game. The challenge and fun here are to land deadly, precise hits before the enemy does it. It is a lot easier when you know exactly where the enemy is, and the same counts usually for enemy AI snipers, too. Therefore, the unseen switching of cover is important before appearing again. If this is the case, then design your layout with that tactic in mind. Try to provide a careful cover network for long-range stealth gameplay with many hidden connections between good counter sniping POAs. How obvious such connections define the difficulty of your combat encounter. Also, the direction of this network is important; do you want players to stay at a similar distance or you want them to get closer?

For the second scenario (= player moves closer to sniper), it should be even clearer that players need a cover network. The type of cover can be anything from soft, hard, or destructible. The last one can be especially fun if the enemy fire destroys them quickly, forcing players to move forward continuously. A classic example is running from tombstone to tombstone while the enemy sniper is in the church's bell tower. Well-designed cover flow and pacing are crucial to continuously increasing the intensity and distance between the objects. Lastly, make sure that the enemy sniper has a way to react and do something meaningful when the player gets close. Just standing there paralyzed, with eye contact, waiting to get shot, is not the ending such a previously formidable foe has deserved.

Another important game-wide consideration is to clarify what a long-range engagement in your game is? I have worked on games where this type of combat started at 70 meters and only went up to around 120 meters, while others went up to several hundred meters. Many such considerations have a lot to do with the target platform and used engine, especially streaming and, of course, the type of game. All that makes it so important to clarify it ahead of time.

### 16.2.5 Tough AI Types

#### *16.2.5.1 Introduction*

I mean your classic heavily armored enemies, walking tanks, or just massive bullet-sponges with this AI type. Usually, they walk slowly and get more deadly the closer they get to their target. Typical weapons are machine guns, rocket launchers, flamethrowers, massive melee weapons, or even suicide bombs. They are essentially almost immune to common campers and need much damage or often a take-down from behind to finish.

Their existence is usually gamey, but they have a crucial function in games. The main gameplay purpose of such AI types is to pressure players and flush them out of otherwise well-defendable spots. That is why they work so well with other enemy types that usually fall for camping player. Sure, they fall for such simple luring traps, too, but they usually do not die right away. Additionally, they are a great tool to prolong fights and a good foundation for more minor boss fights. However, if they are too "bullet-spongy," not an incredibly deadly force, and therefore a chore to take down, their use is minimal. Hopefully, they can do more than just walk toward enemies and shoot. Classic examples here are some types of shields, grenades, mortars on the back, severe push attacks/stomps/swings, or some type of incapacitating the enemy up-close.

#### *16.2.5.2 Level Design Considerations*

Their ability to apply pressure on players and force them to move makes them an excellent choice for any complex layouts, especially when the environments feature a lot of chokepoints, tight corners, or camping spots. However, when you want to push the player around, you need to ensure that the player has ways to escape. Therefore, the loop is your friend again. The size of the average loop here depends on the engagement distance and health of your tough AI type. The longer their attack distance and the higher their health, the bigger the loop can be. Otherwise, players have too much space to engage before getting into challenging trouble. Also, long distances mean players have more time to apply damage to their enemy. Of course, a fast movement AI speed can compensate to some extent, but then we are moving away from the core principle of this type.

As useful as this type is, it also comes with a trap. Level designers tend to add them to almost every fight because this AI type gives the other involved archetypes enough time to show their abilities and apply damage. This case is especially valid if you mix them with weaker enemy AIs. The tough guys draw much attention from players for an extended period, acting as the NPC variant of a classic player tank in RPGs. However, it is essential that you, as a level designer, can create enemy encounters with archetype mixes that do not include a tough guy. It starts with the layout but continues with other gameplay ingredients, which allow for setups, excluding any tough guys. For example, pure long-range engagements with a few melee fast-mover AIs, lots of area-of-effect denying enemies with Molotov cocktails paired with snipers picking off panicking players, or the use of vehicles to replace the tough AI archetypes. Such AI cocktails require game-specific layouts, which you can complement with other ingredients such as mounted guns, mines, traps, or teleporters. Therefore, no one always needs tough guys, even, of course, they could work well here, too.

### 16.2.6 Hordes and Fast AI Types

#### *16.2.6.1 Introduction*

Another classic AI appearance is hordes of enemies or swarms. Usually, they are fast-moving enemies who die fast under enemy damage. Typical examples are large groups of zombies, swarms of fast-moving aliens, wolf packs, or other types of light demons. Just because they appear in larger groups, it does not mean they are limited to melee attacks only. Instead, many of them can feature ranged attacks, even though they are usually limited to a closer range like spitting acid, throwing knives, or grenades.

#### *16.2.6.2 Level Design Considerations*

For players, any bottlenecks in the layout or other chokeholds become key points to lure enemies toward, essentially any points where the enemies cannot fan out and surround enemies while players can concentrate fire on the enemy horde, and also, any spaces where area-of-effect weapons like explosives or fireballs have maximum effect. Since such environmental key positions are important, many players will move in their proximity. Therefore, you can use it to your advantage to give enemies surprise flanking routes or to place additional ingredients like mounted guns or traps.

Large areas where the AI can surround players are essential in your layout, and usually, that is where players encounter such hordes. However, players should have options to counter such moves by deploying a massive array of explosives or moving to more advantageous positions like the previously mentioned choke points. Such provided opportunities in your layout are a key aspect to define the difficulty encountering hordes.

If your setup features a never-ending stream of enemies, you need to message players that this is a nonstop respawning threat and what they have to do to stop the onslaught. Otherwise, they will just waste much ammunition/time and ultimately frustratingly get overwhelmed. For example, are there any gates to shut, any portals to close, or is simple advancement through some obscure invisible triggers enough? It is the same as with any other type of puzzle. First, players must understand the problem and then have a fair shot to figure out a solution.

Another important consideration is any fast enemies with ranged attacks. Usually, such enemies have to look at the enemies to shoot at them. As a result, if they move around, especially sideways or away from them, they cannot attack. Therefore, your layout has to be clean enough to allow them to keep engaging the players and not keep turning continuously. On the flip side, players can use that to their advantage and lure them in environments where exactly that happens, but then it is a clever strategy and should be rewarded. However, I have worked on games where enemies always looked toward the player, which resulted in much crazy strafing and backward running AI. As effective as it was, it also looked very unnatural.

## 16.2.7 AI Groups

### *16.2.7.1 Introduction*

The holy grail of advanced AI is to showcase advanced group behaviors, for example, any staging in front of a door before breaching it with flashbang grenades and dogs, officers yelling commands, or any coordinated movement while providing covering fire. In many cases, such behaviors are fake because either the commander is yelling out commands the troops would have done anyhow individually, or the cool-looking actions are heavily scripted. However, in some rare instances/games, such coordinated actions are indeed true systemic behaviors.

### *16.2.7.2 Level Design Considerations*

As impressive as such group behaviors look in test levels or game trailers, they are hard to conceive in the reality of a game environment. Often when I tested a new presented group behavior on a developer's PC, I killed them before they could show their newly learned tactics or moves. Not that I was such a great player, but instead, the problem is that once you take out a few members, there is not much of the team left to showcase any visible coherent maneuvers, especially if you consider the player's perspective in a natural game environment with a few view-blocking objects and not "developer view" from above where the troops all move nicely. Once a few enemies die, their group pattern disintegrates, and while players keep taking out enemies, the AI system has trouble continuously adjusting. During playtests, it was even worse because the playtesters did not know what to look for and had especially no mercy leaving AI alive so they could showcase their new group behavior.

Therefore, if you have such advanced and shiny AI systems, I think it is only fair to give them some space initially. Bulletproof glass, initially touch enemies, or a severely weak player situation comes to mind, which forces the player to watch and observe more than right away engaging. Once players are aware of the AI's potential, they hopefully keep it in mind the next time they encounter them, and a lot will happen then in their minds, even if the AI systems have trouble catching up.

Ultimately, environments for group behaviors have to be well-tuned to showcase this exact behavior. It would be best if you designed the layouts where they appear first so that it is not easy for players to take them out quickly. Give the AI enough space, and include backup buffer zones at all sides and not obscure them entirely. For example, a dense jungle is not the right environment because players cannot see what is happening while the AI is swarming them from all sides. Usually, a denser cover network with lots of medium cover or lots of thinner tall covers works best here. Elevation differences and alternative paths at different heights are also good additional considerations as long as the player can observe the movement very well. Still, players should see the enemies move but not always have easy and fast kills.

Another less level design-related topic is the use of commanders of officers. Generally, I would not recommend connecting any group behaviors with the existence of such archetypes. It is okay if they provide other buffs or advantages to the group, but it should not be behavioral. It is already tricky enough to show such team tactics, but it would be even easier to disrupt it by taking out a single enemy, even if they are some tougher guys.

## 16.2.8 Boss Fights

### *16.2.8.1 Introduction*

Writing about boss fights in a sub-chapter is honestly not giving them justice. It is an immensely complex topic and incredibly game-dependent. Therefore, whatever I write here is barely scratching the surface. It is a complicated endeavor between game design, level design, narrative, art/animation, and of course, game code plus other tech-savvy departments. The narrative sets the mood, game design/code sets everything in motion, art/animation makes it look stunning, and level design provides the appropriate layout and supported script. Since I can only cover some basics about boss fights, I will focus on the level design mindset alone.

#### *16.2.8.2 Level Design Considerations*

For me, a good boss fight is more than a big mean enemy AI in a large flat arena. A good boss fight always considers the environment, which makes it so much more challenging and rewarding. However, the environment comes in two flavors: one for the boss and the other for the player.

Often big boss enemies appear only on simple ground because of their unique movement, navigation needs, and many technical animation restrictions. Then their movement is less dynamic, and often very limited, scripted, hand-animated, teleports, flies, or the boss is rather static. Boss enemies that rely on new complex systemic AI navigation usually cannot be massive because developing a complete unique movement system for such rare AI types is usually too expensive. Therefore, most bosses are variants of existing AI types or their navigation is rather simple. Therefore, sorting out such topics is crucial when designing a boss fight for level design. Even if you planned some fancy solutions, I highly recommend planning safe backup solutions. It would not have been the first time that we had to cut big chunks of a big boss fight because the boss could not handle the final environment at the end of the development cycle. After all, cutting a boss's feature or stage is, unfortunately, easier than rebuilding a huge, by then finished, and polished environment.

The second flavor is the layout for the player. It counts for both cases, the environments that are player-only or the ones shared by boss and player. However, since boss fights are meant to be tough, I suggest building the environments first boss-friendly and then considering player needs. Usually, suppose the environment plays a crucial role in defeating the boss. In that case, first make sure that the boss works well on its own. Then start adding a wide variety of layout options for players like more cover, flanking routes, access to ingredients, or simply good attack spots. Then start chipping away such options till you have the desired difficulties without interrupting a good flow. Usually, it is easier to remove than to add, especially in later stages of development.

However, I do not mean making the fight super difficult too early, rather the opposite. Instead, anything should be catered to the boss so there is no space where the boss cannot function well. Through iteration—and your boss fight will go through a lot of it—the combat space will change, but if your mindset from the get-go is always to think boss first and player second, you reduce the chance that exploits or other tricky spots sneak in. Again, this is less about difficulty per se but rather making sure that the boss works as designed and remains impressive at each corner of its arena.

Once I had to design a boss fight that was meant to be so hard that only one person in QA could defeat it. Sure the design approach already sounds bad, but in the end, the only way to beat the fight was using certain corners as exploits. Needless to say that we then ran out of time for further tweaks, and the game shipped with that fight. With the more experienced mindset I stated above, I certainly believe I could have done better.

In the end, for a healthy level design mindset the boss's feature should matter less—it is about using them well and give them a stage to shine. Any boss fight is a highlight, and it always weakens the player experience if the battle is dominated by unclean features, bad execution, seemingly minor yet plenty bugs, or exploits. The one thing level design can help here is to provide a clean boss-friendly environment and a properly executed script. As usual, this mindset and tight collaboration with other departments set the foundation for everything else.

## 16.3 Working with Different Gameplay Ingredients

### 16.3.1 Introduction

In this chapter about ingredients, I am looking at types like pickups, vehicles, fixed ingredients, and navigational ones. Like with all the previous ones, they are very game-specific, so I keep the information more general and level design-centric to have the maximum use for you and your game.

## 16.3.2 Pickups

### 16.3.2.1 Small Ones

A typical smaller pickup is anything that is usually not game/match changing but more about giving you that slight edge in a fight. Typical examples are small ammo boxes, minor armor shards, or anything which only gives a bit of health. Usually, you see them seemingly randomly sprinkled among levels, hidden in drawers, or often dropped by enemies. However, if you, as a level designer, placed them thoughtfully, they can have a significant impact on player behavior.

In multiplayer, they usually have two purposes. The first is a quick top-off of health, armor, or ammo. However, their second purpose is more interesting if they allow their associated player values, such as health or armor, to go over the usual maximum. Usually, it is not much, but when similarly skilled players meet, and one has 5% more maximum armor, this can mean the difference. They carry a lot more value for high stake matches among experienced players. Therefore, I would place them either far away, for example, away from other big armor pickups. Alternatively, place them right around the corner of any bigger fighting spaces.

Another huge factor in multiplayer is their sound when players pick them up. Especially in more advanced matches, predicting the enemy's movement via sound is significant. Therefore, you should consider placing them in hallways or other long stretched paths which allow enemies to guess where they are heading. Placing them at intersections makes predictions a lot harder than in sections that only have two ways in or out. So, the combination of their value mixed with the drawback of potential predictability is what makes them such an exciting tool to use for level designers.

In singleplayer, their use is usually less dramatic. Usually, in such circumstances, small ammo or health is to keep players going and not to deplete some of their resources completely but keep them stagnating or only swindle slower. For example, a level primarily features rifle and shotgun enemies, meaning no sniper rifle ammo drops. Placing a few sparse and small sniper ammo boxes still allows some players to keep their preferred playstyle occasionally without abusing it too much.

### 16.3.2.2 Big Ones

Compared to small pickups, any big ones are potentially game/match changing or give players a significant advantage at times. Typical examples are temporary damage boosts/invulnerability, big weapons, or hefty armor. Placing them is a very conscious decision and significantly impacts early design stages. Therefore, I recommend making a list of the big pickups before you design your layout, or at least work on the list once you have an initial layout idea/sketch because often you build layouts around such big items.

When we design locations for impactful pickups, we have to think about risks vs. rewards. Yes, that also includes risky dead-ends for once and other aspects like exposure, predictability through sound, and very central locations. Expect such locations to gain lots of traffic, meaning they should either feature many options directly or close to their access routes.

Additionally, you should balance their associated risk with their type of reward. For example, a very open map usually supports long-range gameplay with sniper rifles or railguns. Therefore, the biggest risk of picking up a suitable gun is getting sniped yourself. Those circumstances mean such weapons should exactly be exposed to such long-range engagements because it fits the flavor of the map and, therefore, its main risk. Alternatively, they are in a tight underground tunnel, which is the polar opposite because the risk for long-range players is usually higher in tight close combat. Your choice depends on the quantity of such placed weapons on the level and the intended gameplay flavor dominating the map. If there is only one such weapon in a multiplayer map, then I suggest making it very exposed, but at the same time, do not place much ammo for it. Fighting that one unique gun becomes a significant factor and one of the map's focus points. On the flip side, if the map features a lot of long-range weapons, then I suggest instead placing them at safe, close-range spots, so more players have equal chances. The whole match is long-range dominated by most players, but some players will use that dominance/imbalance to their advantage by moving fast with devastating close-range guns.

Big pickups are usually strong influencers for the upcoming gameplay and pacing in singleplayer. If players get their hands on a powerful sniper rifle or machine gun usually foreshadows the next segment's gameplay. Therefore, such pickups are less about their immediate location and more about what comes next. For example, giving players a rail gun with a powerful scope and then sending them down a tight underground tunnel network sends a mixed message. Like multiplayer maps, such big pickups or gadgets have to be part of the initial design of your level since they have a significant impact on your map's core layout and vision.

#### *16.3.2.3 Collectables*

Collectables are a bit of a special case since they usually don't add any immediate gameplay difference. However, it is worth noting that players should never be able to mix them up with other, more dangerous types. For example, players might see a collectible with a red blinking light as a proximity mine because red lights usually indicate something dangerous in games. Therefore, make sure that your player language is consistent and switch it to a green or white light.

For their placement I would treat them either like puzzles or to encourage exploration. Their puzzle difficulty depends on your game's direction and possibilities. If their purpose is to motivate players to search every corner, then start placing them wherever you assume the action will be very low or which has no other gameplay advantages. Ideally you adjust their placement after some playtests after your assumptions have either proven to be correct or needed modifications. It often happened that some of the best hidden collectibles were found first but the ones in almost plain view were missed. In such instances playtests always beat early developer assumptions.

### 16.3.3 Vehicles

#### *16.3.3.1 Introduction*

This chapter will talk about vehicles as the center of attention. If the headline of the sub-chapter includes "Player," then it is about vehicles driven by players, and if it includes "Friendly AI," then friendly AI is driving it with the player on the passenger seat or, for example, at a mounted gun. "Enemy AI" means the player is attacked, chased, stalked by such vehicles. In my experience, land-based vehicles are the most common ones in typical action games, covering many basic vehicle level designs, including important considerations for the other types of air and water. However, once again, that is very game-specific.

#### *16.3.3.2 Land: Player*

Suppose a segment is about players driving a land-based vehicle. In that case, first, you have to manage design expectations because usually, it is hard to predict what players do with their given vehicles or what could happen to the vehicle in the gameplay segment. A classic issue is when designers expect players to acquire a vehicle as a mission objective because it is required to jump over a big gap. As beautiful as it sounds on paper, it quickly runs into problems once players lose the vehicle. Forcing a game restart if the vehicle gets destroyed is already not an elegant solution. However, it is worse if you fail the game if the vehicle gets stuck, which additionally is not easy to detect with common scripts. Then usually, players have to restart the next checkpoint by hand, which sends a rightfully frustrating signal.

Therefore, I would be cautious when designing a segment requiring a player-controlled vehicle. Some games feature very robust mechanics, do not shy away from many mission failures without death, or have very simple/safe environments. However, if you are not 100% sure, I suggest treating vehicles only as the dominating flavor in all other cases, but always with a backup option on foot. Still, by all means, design your segment vehicle first and anything else second, but it needs secondary options. Alternatively, essential vehicles might respawn, which is an excellent option to keep such key-vehicle moments alive, but it has to fit into your game. Continuously respawning a unique vehicle with strong narrative ties can be jarring and is not always the best suiting option.

The design of the driving environment should, first of all, take any leanings of what I wrote about "Connection Between Open-World Locations" previously. Secondly, expect that players will drive how they want, preferably directly to the waypoint or any relevant prevalent landmark. Ideally, some types of roads, trails, streets, or other guiding open stretches of land are going in a similar direction as an additional guiding element. If you have the space, I recommend having more than one route toward the goal.

This route's track and encounter design should follow the common pacing and ingredient mix guidelines. However, any lower pacing segments in-between are less for narrative or chilling but about reorientation and realignment. Typically, these are open, straight segments in which players can breathe a bit, get their barring, and focus on getting up to speed again. In between, you can add challenges like fights, stunts, or some light speed-based puzzles. However, as usual, start small and seriously consider that the attention to smaller events or elements is close to zero at higher speeds or risky moves requiring lots of concentration. You have to introduce anything way ahead of time that players should pay attention to. It must be over obvious and expect that many will still miss it. This over-exposure also counts for any narrative elements or mission objective updates. Players are usually so focused on driving and not crashing that they will completely miss minor changes on their HUD or pay little attention to crucial dialogs. Instead, I recommend designing driving sections for driving alone and leaving additional layers for calmer, slower moments.

Plan out your track on paper or draw it directly on your terrain. Separate the straight segments and which ones are more curvy or challenging to drive. If you have lengthy (semi) straight sections or easy curves, consider adding any challenges here, as long as you have reorientation parts before and after. If you have too many challenges after each other, reconsider adjusting your track. At that point, I would like to suggest that at no point does your track have to be a continuous "official" route, street, or path. Going off-road, vertical, or other risky short-cuts to connect two separate "official" paths is a great way to spice up your driving section and make it feel more like an action movie. For example, you are going downhill, but the official road would be long monotonous serpentines. Cutting straight downhill is faster, crazier, and way more adrenaline pumping and feels improvised. However, you as a designer should prepare this route, cleaning it up for an inviting drive with no small obstacles like tree stumps, stones, or guard rails. Once it works for driving and player-leading, spice it up with elements like suicide ATV guys, herds of crossing deer, or the obligatory attack helicopter.

Providing precisely targeted challenging encounters during a driving section is a massive problem, especially when players can roam freely in an open world. Some games have a random encounter system in place. However, I recommend not relying on it since they are usually inherently meant to flavor the world, are random by default, difficult to adjust to your specific design needs, and rarely provide meaningful difficulty. Instead, you usually want to design and script hand-crafted events.

By default, start looking for any natural choke points or any other areas players have to visit due to mission objectives. Once you have exhausted all such options and feel it is not enough, it is time to look at the more open segments. Usually, you then start with very wide trigger shapes, ranging far left and right. Whatever you spawn should be fast or have a long engagement distance. If your triggers have to be so wide that the enemies loosely spawning at its center have no realistic chance to attack fast-moving players, you have to split them up into more individual scripted encounters. Also always spawn any enemies way ahead of players so there is no remote chance that either player can see them spawning or they are not ready, yet. The faster the players can move the bigger should be your hefty buffer.

I am aware that this can become a chore, especially in large open worlds. Therefore, one solution is to work more with prefabs, including the triggers and scripts, which you can quickly distribute over your world in areas players are most likely to frequent. Especially use fast movers with long detection radiuses, which are environment independent, like planes, flying aliens, dragons, off-road vehicles, or helicopters come to mind here. However, the less systemic your enemy AI is, the more linear your driving segments have to be, or otherwise, you script way too much with not enough gain.

If you do not want to rely only on fast-moving vehicle-based enemies or your game does not support them, then look at what other archetypes your game has to offer. However, any enemies on foot are essentially static compared to a player in a fast vehicle. Additionally, they have to threaten the player's vehicle and the player inside. For example, a guy with a shotgun can do pretty much nothing against a tank. Therefore, you should apply them ideally at segments where players have to slow down, drive straight toward the foot soldiers for a lengthy period, or have to leave the vehicle. If you do not have such layout segments, maybe consider building ones.

Another nice change of pace and provide some gameplay variety during a lengthy vehicle section is to force players to leave the vehicle, do something on foot to continue, and then continue in the vehicle again. The classic example is a gate that players have to open away from the vehicle before continuing. Not only is it providing some different gameplay variety in between, but it also allows you to feature different AI archetypes than you usually could during a pure driving segment.

### *16.3.3.3 Land: Friendly AI*

Occasionally, I enjoy it as a player if a friendly AI character takes over the wheel and I focus on shooting or enjoying the ride. Within the bigger picture of a level, it is a nice change of pace, especially after some very slow-paced segments where players had to think a lot. Now it is all about just all-out action and less thinking. However, in the even bigger picture of your game, do not use them too often because due to their simplicity, they tend to stale faster than other more complex gameplay types.

The huge advantage is that you know where the player is where they go, and therefore you can script events a lot more reliably and more detailed. Most important from the get-go is to come up with a good mix of different challenges you throw at the player. Otherwise, you end up with a tiring, repetitive chain of roadblocks and chasing enemy vehicles. Alternative examples are many explosive gas tanks along the road mixed with some grunts, shenanigans with physicalized objects, any possible vehicle stunts, driving next to a train covered in enemies, or sometimes even just standing around for a bit while the player and driver have an argument about where to go next.

The second crucial aspect is timing. When do you spawn what type of enemies are already in full swing and ready when the player comes by? Timing events for fast-moving players is entirely different from when players are on foot, especially when streaming and AI are involved. I highly recommend working with comfortable buffers because whatever might work well in your editor tends to be a bit different in the final optimized build, or some minor glitches are a rare possibility.

Since you know where the player is, at all times, you can spawn threats, usually a lot closer to the player's vehicle. However, you still need to spawn them hidden behind objects, terrain, dense vegetation, buildings, or way ahead of time. Therefore, besides timing, you should consider such safe spots during the paper design phase. Adding large objects only to spawn enemies behind is usually evident to players already, but it is worse if such massive objects are added late during the development cycle. Also, early planning such spots makes creating a believable world easier for the environment artists compared to dealing with shoe-horned-in huge objects or strange looking bumps in the terrain late during development.

In such segments, the time it takes to deal with threats highly depends on your game, the weapons, and the vehicles involved. However, expect players to take way longer than you because they will not know where the threat is coming from when it appears, and they will most likely not look in the right direction. Therefore, add some extra time buffer for players, especially to your slow-paced segments in between, for them to catch up; they will appreciate way more than you do.

### *16.3.3.4 Land: Enemy AI*

Using enemy AI vehicles correctly is not easy because they are usually quickly destroyed if players have anti-vehicle weapons or a too tough nut to crack if they have inadequate weapons. This topic becomes even more tricky if the game gives players much freedom about their weapons, ammo, and resupply. For example, shooting three RPGs at a tank or once at a car is not usually highly challenging, but it gets frustratingly complicated if you have no RPGs or explosives. Anything in-between is the design challenge. Ultimately, this discussion starts with game design, but how can level design play an important factor here?

Level designers need to deeply understand vehicle behavior and navigation—especially their possibilities, limitations, and where they tend to behave buggy. For example, vehicles often use a different navigation system than humans, which usually means they need more space. Additionally, they might have trouble with specific environmental conditions. I worked on games where AI-controlled off-road cars could barely get up small steep hills because the AI brain could not shift gears fast enough or understood the concept of taking an extra boost before. In another game, tanks occasionally got stuck on small corners, like sidewalks. If players controlled vehicles, such issues rarely exist. Therefore, you must know such complications and adjust your environment to guarantee that such issues do not surface regularly. Of course, it is impossible to create the perfect environment, especially if the AI behavior is very systemic but let's at least avoid the most glaring ones. Let us also assume game code and other departments try their best to do their part to make the whole experience a smooth one.

However, I recommend that design, in general, should overthink their systemic approach occasionally. I worked on a lot of very systemic games, but the ones with the best vehicle AI was the one that had the option to reduce the systemic brain and required level design to do more work instead. Instead of relying on a systemic AI brain to find a suitable path through very complex environments, we level designers placed suitable paths. In the end, it looked way smarter and worked way smoother. Sometimes less is more and players don't usually care if the AI brain is systemic if it gets stuck on every second street sign. A reliable non-systemic system will always beat a broken systemic one.

The next big topic for level designers in such combat setups is to create opportunities for both enemy vehicles and players. I am talking here about attacking, retreat/defense, and safe navigation opportunities. I recommend sketching out the opportunities for one side in your documentation, ideally the ones with the more active/dynamic objective. Once you finish the ones for this side, you work on the opposing/countering opportunities since no tactic or spot should be perfect. Where are good (attack) spots regarding the objective? Where are any fixed ingredients like mounted rocket launchers, mortars, or crates with mines? What are good routes to retreat from such attack spots? What is very safe, and where are semi-safe routes to switch between the different attack spots? Especially the last consideration is often overlooked but crucial to create a good flow.

The number and quality of opportunities are the primary level design factor in prolonging or shortening fights against enemy vehicles. If three RPGs can destroy a tank, you should not expect a fight to last long if players have a tight network of perfect attack spots and tons of rockets. A fight against even a single tank can be a longer, thrilling experience if you sacrifice some good attack angles/spots, RPGs are sparse, and have more unsafe routes. Also, do not keep the network too small or short, but do not spread it out so long, so it becomes a drag navigating it. Lastly, topics like tank health, weak spots, or ammo/weapon management are something you should discuss together with game design.

#### *16.3.3.5 Water: Player*

I will only focus on the unique aspects of water vehicles since most basic aspects are comparable to land vehicles. Let us start with the fact that fast corners need a lot more space on the water and that you cannot really break quickly. If you expect players to drive fast with a water vehicle, give them a lot of wiggle room and safe space, especially in the corners. I recommend way more than what you consider enough. Also, do not forget that most water sections are on a flat surface, which means players have a limited view about events ahead, unlike going up/downhill on land. Especially if the race is along a river or between obstacles, it gets tricky, and your original paper planning from the top-view is quickly proven wrong with fresh players. Therefore, in such circumstances, instead plan in with too much water space than too little. Usually, later it is easier to remove water access/space by dropping in a few more rocks, debris, or trees than extending a riverbed.

Open ocean or large lakes have their own unique challenge: boredom. Cruising a straight line without many obstacles to steer around and, at best, fighting a few random boats, helicopters, tiny kraken, or sharks with lasers is only fun for so long without any environmental stimulus or factors. It is like constantly fighting enemies in nothing but a flat arena. At some point, it simply gets boring due to repetition. If adding environmental aspects like large rocks, shipwrecks, cliffs, maelstroms, massive waves, or storms are not an option, then the best you can do is to control the enemy.

This reality means, for example, not to use all enemy boats and helicopters in the first few fights. Carefully stretch it out. Let players ease into the illusion that they have mastered fighting certain enemies, and then give them a curveball with a new, very different enemy type. Also, never use too many different enemy types simultaneously and try to mix them up as we did with usual AI archetypes. Of course, this strategy has limits, too, because usually, many games do not have an endless supply of boats attacking enemy types. However, it is way better than an uncontrolled wild mix of enemy ingredients which ends up like "brown sauce" again.

Another complication of large water bodies is to spawn enemies safely. Usually, the view distance is far, and the number of obstacles to spawn enemies behind is limited. It also looks very gamy if ten speed boats come around a single small rock. If enemies spawn outside of the view distance, they usually take a very long time before they reach the player, and a lot can happen in that time. I would usually recommend spawning enemies at a mid-distance outside of the player's field of view in such scenarios, like behind or on their side. It is not ideal by far, but we can rely a bit on the observation that many players on a boat usually do not look around constantly. So spawning enemy boats behind or at the sides is often not considered glaringly gamy because it could be reasonable that they came from here unnoticed. Alternatively, if you know where the player is heading, consider ideally spawning enemies ahead and sending them directly toward the player. Often mission objective locations on water feature big enough objects to spawn enemy boats or occasionally even helicopters behind.

Going back to rivers, we should talk about slopes, white waters, or waterfalls. Usually, placing long stretches of water splines or planes with a slight angle requires a lot of careful planning and terrain work. Depending on the river size, complexity, or specific dependency of the river banks to other crucial locations, it is also susceptible to changes and they quickly become more expensive than expected. However, good tools, careful planning, and a solid engine significantly reduce stress.

Going upstream with a motorized boat is usually not a big deal in games, but it becomes strange when it is easily possible to go up rapids. I have experienced many games with no strong connection between river current and vehicle speed. In many cases, it was even possible to glitch up waterfalls. Unfortunately, this means you should be careful about such otherwise visually stunning river features. The main recommendation is to use a lot of rocks or similar obstacles, which reduces the chance that players can glitch upstream like a horny salmon.

It is usually an absolute joy to jump waterfalls or white waters with a boat in games. However, like with all boat ramp actions, be aware of the physics-meshes of boats and the rocks/ramps. Often it leads to crashes, tipping boats, or very goofy jumps at best. Especially the V-form of most boat bodies rarely harmonizes with convex rock shapes or even with flat ramps. We usually placed many invisible proxy meshes, which only affect vehicles, to guarantee movie-like jumps. It is one of those little tricks many players appreciate unknowingly. However, even if they notice them, I believe most players appreciate a smoother experience with a "modified reality" over a finicky annoying, unspectacular one. You can use the same shapes to fix other iffy sections where boats usually get stuck due to not very responsive boat controls, like next to complex shorelines or many small objects.

Besides enemies and ramps, you can add many other ingredients to make a water journey fun. First, think about explosives and fire, like mines, floating explosive barrels, or floating oil slicks on fire. Secondly, when you design your ramps, always consider some additional explosions, or that not every landing has to be on the water. Sometimes grinding overland with a boat for a few seconds is a nice change of pace. Next, think about everything which can crash into the water. Usually, crashing objects into water is easier to realize than anything crashing on land because the impact and deformation are hidden under a lot of water VFX. Then most of the object is under conveniently murky water. So, consider how many of your towers, bridges, or precious Maya ruins could fall into the water, but at least let it be a few boulders, trucks, and trees. It is one thing to dodge generic floating water mines, but it is a different level of crazy if someone keeps throwing school buses at you while you pace down the Mississippi with a speed boat. Making water sections fun is difficult, especially in games that mostly play on land. However, they also offer many unique options, which are usually too crazy/expensive on land.

#### *16.3.3.6 Water: Friendly AI*

I would certainly consider adding a section where friendly AI controls a boat because it is a really nice refreshing change of pace. For example, players could run around on the boat doing various things like mounting various guns, throwing mines in the water, or taking pictures of yawning hippos. In my experience, such gameplay is not very common, but maybe that is precisely the reason why we should look at adding more.

If it is not a slow river cruise, then make sure that the friendly AI has much space in curves. If you thought players had issues controlling boats in fast, tight corners, then usually AI is way worse and needs much leeway. It is especially crucial if the boat can accidentally get stuck stranding on riverbanks or beaches. It is quite anticlimactic sitting in the gunner seat of a riverboat when it gets stuck on a sandbank, and the driver AI does not even realize it. Therefore, give them way more space than you would give players, and ideally avoid river banks on the outside of curves where the boat could beach. Instead, use more rocks or cliffs and occasionally cheat with invisible vehicle-only proxy meshes. Be overprotective of your friendly AI once they are in boats. Nobody cares if an AI-controlled car leaves the road on land for a bit, but this could be a walkthrough break on the river.

Let us also not forget that other forces can push a boat around. For example, that could be other boats, explosions, waves, or the previously mentioned school buses. However, often AI has trouble compensating for such impacts, and you as a level designer have to give them more wiggle room the more often such instances can occur.

Once they traverse long routes over open oceans or large lakes, you have the boredom problem again. It is especially prevalent here because the AI will take the most straight and direct route. However, you have at least a good idea of the AI's route. Therefore, you should plan accordingly and make the best out of it. So, for example, surfacing submarines, crashing meteoroids, awakening Cthulhu, or a horde of giant turtles can be introduced a lot more spectacularly than if players are driving the boat themselves.

#### *16.3.3.7 Water: Enemy AI*

By default, most of the learning from the previous chapters about vehicles, especially boats, stays relevant. Especially when I wrote about spawning enemies, mixing them up nicely, and giving AI boats much safe space to maneuver.

For starters, be careful planning any water environments where enemy boats have to make U-turns in tight environments. For example, enemy boats come toward the player on a river, but then the player passes them, and AI now has to turn and catch up with the player again. As you can imagine, they need a lot of space. Otherwise, they take much time going back and forth or getting stuck completely. In most cases, they are not a threat to speedy players. In reality, if you want boat vs. boat fights on a river, you need very wide rivers or enemies can only come from behind/sides. If such wide rivers do not fit your world, plan for other challenges along a river ride and keep the boat vs. boat fights for the bigger lakes or oceans.

Next, think about cool ways to introduce enemy vehicles because players are restricted to the limited water surface, which you can use to your advantage. Think about, for example, boats jumping over bridges/ramps, planes flying dangerously low over the water, or helicopters dropping speed boats. Depending on your tools, game, and engine, consider "cheating" a bit with animations to make it look more spectacular instead of relying on an AI system to perform one-off stunts.

Be careful when players can shoot the gunner and driver of boats separately. An enemy boat without a driver but with a gunner is, at best, a very angry sitting duck. However, an enemy boat with a driver but no gunner is usually very useless and wastes performance resources. Therefore, talk early to game designers and coders on how to resolve such issues and free up resources fast.

I would not recommend a situation when players are on land, and the enemies are on boats. At best, the enemies can perform one attack before they have to make a bigger circle before they come back again. Alternatively, they slow down or even stop. None of such ideas is very spectacular or highly entertaining. In such circumstances, enemy boats are best used to drop reinforcement troops, or in scenarios where you know, players have to stay close to the beach for extended periods. Otherwise, enemy boats are best used against other water-based vehicles only.

#### *16.3.3.8 Air: Player*

Many basic learnings from the previous vehicle types are also relevant about planes, helicopters, flying carpets, and alike. Especially topics like spawning enemies or limited enemy AI ingredients. However, let us start with the common observation that it sounds already exhilarating if we talk about flying. However, flying in games and reality are two completely different experiences. For example, I would shit my pants jumping down a cliff with a parachute, but in games that is business as usual.

If your air vehicle has no combat capabilities, the flight is ideally short and gorgeous or has a navigational challenge. Navigation usually means flying around obstacles, close to the ground, or whatever else your game has to offer up in the air. Even some floating, gamy rings, or other types of checkpoints are better than nothing. Long, non-gorgeous and non-challenging flight sequences should be avoided.

If your air vehicle has combat capabilities, it matters if the targets are in the air or on the ground. Developing a sophisticated air combat AI is not trivial, and featuring enough combat and enemy variety is even trickier. Production-wise, it gets worse if your game's primary focus is fighting on land while the dogfight in the clouds is just to spice up the game experience. If your ingredients for aerial combat are limited, then I recommend keeping such fights sparse, spread out your few ingredients and their mixes, and try to make the environments more challenging. For example, have the first fights against easy enemies high up in the air, and at the end use the most difficult ones close to the ground, in some canyons, plus supported by anti-air ground units. It might also help to not bundle up the majority of air combat in one segment in your game but spread them out. Therefore, they truly act as a spice element here and there to break up your game's core experience.

Once the player's enemies are on the ground, we face two key issues. First, if players missed their attack or did not destroy everyone already, it takes a while till they can perform the next attack. Usually, this depends on the speed and maneuverability of the player's vehicle. However, even if you are in a fast mover like a jet, you distance yourself from the target location before the next attack. Depending on your game and the actual distance, this could mean enemy troops are not rendered anymore, it might unstream, their AI brain turns off, or the whole script might reset completely. However, keeping all the units "alive" in the system might be taxing performance-wise. However, this is more a topic for programmers and other tech-savvy folks. The critical aspect for us level designers is to, first of all, be aware of such a maximum distance and if they are too small that type of fight might not be feasible. Then we should make sure that players are not inclined to get distracted by other events, enemies, or locations while engaging the current ones.

Secondly, enemies on the ground need to detect the player's air vehicle fast enough and still react appropriately to be an actual challenge. If players are in a tank, your "only" problem is to make sure that the AI has tools to damage the tanks. However, once players are in a very fast air vehicle, enemy AI, which is tuned for ground combat, often cannot detect fast enough or even look up properly. Once again, solving these core issues is not a primary level design topic but something we need to be aware of because it severely impacts what enemy troops we place and where. For example, if primarily RPG, machinegun, or sniper AI can damage player helicopters, but they have a limited range, we would need to place many of them on high towers, rooftops, or tall rocks. However, this could also severely impact players who come on foot if your game offers such freedom. Creating two separate enemy setups and scripts, one for the player on the ground and one for the player in the air, is not what I would recommend by default. It is the last resort option if other systems in your game are not flexible enough and you need a specific catered experience for both cases. However, maintaining, debugging, and iterating two separate AI setups and their scripts is not trivial in the long run.

#### *16.3.3.9 Air: Friendly AI*

As a level designer working on friendly AI controlling an air vehicle while the player is in an observatory or gunner role is usually easier than if the vehicle is on the ground or water. No dynamic objects could suddenly block the path, or no physic impulses can push the boat on the shore. The flying path is usually unobstructed with little to no hindrances, besides, of course, destruction of the vehicle itself. Therefore, you can put all the focus on scripting the ride, from a unique perspective, as entertaining and stunning as possible.

#### *16.3.3.10 Air: Enemy AI*

Let us start by talking about flying enemies when the player is on the ground. Such enemies are great to add variety, can be fast and heavy hitters, can drop reinforcement, and are fantastic to change the player's focal plane. Usually, most enemies are mostly on a horizontal plane, but now players have to look up and likely also engage them with a different set of weapons or tools. If they are special in your game, then make sure you do not overuse them because otherwise, they stop being unique, and their fresh nature becomes quickly stale or even obnoxious instead.

One of the essential aspects you as a level designer have to understand is how they navigate. Usually, the flight navigation grid is very chunky, blocky, and by far not as precise as ground AI navigation. Therefore, a few, unfortunately, placed tall vertical elements can block large chunks of that grid, and as a result, flying AI vehicles have a hard time coming close to them. Usually, their behavior also means that they prefer to stay away from objects they could bounce against, and as a result, they will stay far away. Therefore, you need to debug the flight navigation grid and move your objects accordingly so they do not occupy too much space in the grid. This consideration is especially crucial if you, for example, want AI air vehicles to fly between towers or along a canyon. It is also crucial to involve environment artists early in this process so they do not block the entire air space with, for example, long radio/flag poles, industrial chimneys, or thin ivory towers. It is common that a single telephone pole, radio antenna, or similarly thin object blocks a huge otherwise empty field for helicopters to drop reinforcement or perform similar actions.

The next consideration is how frequently can flying enemies attack players? For example, a plane usually does a strafing or bombing run and then has to make a big turn before attacking again. During this turn, many things can happen. Ideally, you give players many options to hide or prepare for the return. Fighting a plane on an open, empty field is usually less fun due to the lack of options. However, if the environment is too dense and complex, then enemy AI has trouble spotting the player in time and still adjusting its flight path to engage.

Helicopters or similar slower and more static flying enemies have it a lot easier. Usually, they can operate better in more complex environments, as long as you keep the previously mentioned flight navigation very clean. It is not a huge issue for a plane if it does not come too close to a tower, but if a helicopter, in a video game, keeps staying away 30+ meters from every taller object, it quickly looks a bit odd. Fighting such more persistent air enemies requires more options for players to dodge attacks, hide, and pop out again for an attack, compared to fast movers in the sky.

If players are in an air vehicle themselves fighting flying enemies, they need to be very careful about the different flying speeds. For example, the speed difference between a plane and a helicopter in games is so high that planes commonly overshoot a helicopter, and it is almost like the plane is fighting a static target. Like in real life, the speed of an air vehicle is one of its greatest defenses. However, if speeds between the opposing parties are similar, you need a good, nimble dogfighting AI or otherwise, it becomes a chore with many frustrating turns where not much is happening.

### 16.3.4 Fixed Misc Ingredients

#### 16.3.4.1 Introduction

Fixed miscellaneous ingredients are non-navigational tools placed by the level designers that players can use but cannot move or only barely. So I am talking here about your usual arsenal of mounted guns, mines, gas tanks, cameras, trip-wires, AI turrets, or explosive barrels. They either deny specific player actions, like cameras or mines, or enable new player options, like explosive barrels or mounted weapons. Therefore, they are essential elements to give a section its unique flavor, next to layout, scripting, objectives, and AI composition.

#### 16.3.4.2 One-Use

The one-use ingredients are, as expected, not usable anymore once they get enabled, activated, or used. The classic examples are mines, explosive barrels, or claymores. Their common use is either against enemy AI, players, or both.

If they are against enemy AI, start your best guess where they are not most effective but most likely to be spotted and used by players. The best-placed explosive barrel has no use if no player ever shoots at it. However, shooting an explosive barrel is already a lot of fun, even if it rarely kills a lot of AI in one boom. Classic spots for such shootable explosives like gas canisters, propane tanks, oil drums, or ammo crates are next to cover because they attract AI. The non-combat version of this placement is next to spots where AI hangs out for talks, smokes, or yawns. However, I think it tends to be too cheap if you overuse it. Instead, consider not just your usual corners but also long straight lines, which AI often takes during a firefight or idling patrols. Shooting an explosive barrel just at the right moment when an AI passes by is, in my opinion, way more satisfying, than killing clueless sitting ducks with explosives.

If they are meant to be used primarily against players, then I recommend placing them as much as possible in front of players, where they can see them, or at least the explosion. Since it can be quite frustrating getting killed by a seemingly random explosion behind you just because the enemy AI managed to get a lucky shot and hit that inconveniently placed explosive barrel—the same counts for mines or similar trap-like installments. Ideally, players have at least a slight chance of spotting them before they instantly or seemingly randomly get killed. Ideally, players should blame themselves if they step on a mine and not the game, especially if it happened more than once. Therefore, I cannot recommend randomly located, invisible mines, even if that makes it "more realistic."

In both cases, playtests are vital. Your initial assumptions need to be verified by an audience that does not know all the mines and explosive barrels placements. I worked on many locations meant to have a certain explosive or fire flavor, but surprisingly nobody used them as effectively as we did. Our main takeaway was: If you think you placed enough anti-AI explosive barrels, add some more, and if you think you placed enough anti-player mines, remove some.

#### *16.3.4.3 Multi-Use*

The multi-use ingredients can either be used multiple times by players or do not turn off, explode, or shut down once AI has handled them. For now, I ignore the fact that many of them can have health, and players eventually can destroy them. Classic examples here are various mounted guns, cameras, or AI-controlled turrets.

Mounted guns in most games nowadays can be used by both AI and players. However, in most cases, they are rather placed by AI, and players get to them and use them against their original owners. Therefore, I would start by placing them where they logically make sense if you happen to be the defender. For example, a mounted gun at a roadblock, on a rooftop, or at the end of a long road/funnel can make sense. However, placing the mounted guns inside an enemy camp or the back of a warehouse makes little sense, even if that means players can kill lots of AI from here. A mounted gun, conveniently placed by enemies to kill as many of them as possible, is a bit odd. However, once you find a believable spot from the enemy's perspective, you should consider tweaking their position or surrounding objects so that some effective player-use is still reasonable. After all, most grunts are not tactical geniuses and make some mistakes, just no huge blunders. Of course, if the player is in a defensive situation then the opposite counts. Still, always consider enemies to have solid counter options or to not place the machine gun at a too powerful position. I recommend to motivate players to move around and use other POAs.

Cameras are a classic tool in games with stealth elements. Performance-wise their cost is low, they either deny player navigation or make it more difficult, and their player language is usually well established. Their placement is the key trick. If players can spot them from too far, then it might be too easy for them to destroy them without any risk. However, if players cannot spot them in even a slightly fair way, cameras can get frustrating. Therefore, I recommend playing a lot with audio, movement, and alternate vision systems to give players a fair chance to spot them, even before they have direct sight but at a closer range. However, a camera alone is usually not exciting enough. For example, just putting cameras over entrances unattended is not enough. Ideally, combine them with enemy AI patrols, and the cameras complement their movement patterns. Cameras alone are typically not a primary threat; at best, they are indirectly dangerous, but they can watch over key spots while the AI is gone or act as a second/third eye on idling enemies. Additionally, carefully plan out the direct threat they can trigger because cameras have even less value if detection is meaningless.

In contrast to cameras, which usually only trigger detection, enemy AI turrets are a serious direct threat. Usually, they have a decent amount of health, can dash out massive damage, and detect fast.

Therefore, a tactically well-placed turret can feel abusive yet lumpish at the same time. However, I would always recommend placing a turret at crucial key spots that initially appear to be abusive and then refining player-facing counter options. If, instead, you place a turret at a bad spot first, it usually requires way more work to make them meaningful. The player-facing counter options are not paths that avoid a turret. Instead, they offer players the option to outsmart the turret while often putting themselves in danger. Given the usual simple brain of a turret AI, the outsmarting part is not the key consideration. However, think more about the spots from where players can engage the turrets, how the spots are connected, how well the connections are protected, and the distance between them? For example, continuously engaging a turret from two opposing directions is a proven, safe tactic, yet it can become very tedious. If taking out a turret feels like a safe, boring job, it is time to remove some safety and add some spice.

### 16.3.5 Navigation Ingredients

#### *16.3.5.1 Introduction*

Navigational ingredients provide a natural movement action. The ingredients are anything which is not covered by the basic movement actions like stairs, ramps, falling down, or running. Instead, most of them only require a navigation action like a jump, move, step, while others require some less direct navigational ones like a grab or throw. Classic examples are teleporters, ladders, crawl tunnels, water, grapple (free and contextual), and dangerous ones like lava lakes or spike walls. Many other navigational aspects in the context of puzzles or skill challenges were covered previously.

#### *16.3.5.2 Fixed*

Talking in detail about every type of fixed navigation ingredient would get out of hand. Therefore, I will focus on some of the more typical ones, representing the mindset of how to approach the rest and often very game-specific ones.

I want to believe that ladders are one of the most common navigation ingredients. I include here all variants of ladders like climbable vines, ropes, or pipes. Essentially separate objects which designers can add that allow players to move vertically. In my experience, they become unfortunately very popular among designers if they realize that they need another lane to a higher spot. Usually, this happens because the initially planned paths were not enough, or adding something normal like stairs does not fit the world. Classic examples are walls of medieval castles or rooftops of stand-alone buildings because usually, the number of normal, believable accessways is limited or not possible at all. So adding lots of ladders is the last option. Especially if the building asset is close to being finished by artists, it is usually too costly to add a stairway. Then it is a lot easier to add a few ladders on the side. The primary problem with ladders is the vulnerability of the user. Some games allow fighting from ladders, but you are still somewhat locked, predictable, and usually limited in your options. Especially AI on ladders is easy prey. Therefore, I recommend avoiding planning with ladders in the early design stages. In my experience, if you plan with many ladders early on, you end up with even more in the end. Instead, try to initially design a space without ladders, except where you really cannot avoid them. In the end, you likely will add a few more here and there anyhow, but then they feel less shoehorned in. To be clear, I am not against ladders, but they should either make absolute sense world-building-wise or be a last resort design option.

Working with teleporters can be a lot of fun as a level designer. Teleporters are one of the most powerful navigational ingredients. However, with high design responsibility comes high player expectations. If your game and level features teleporters, I would start designing my layout with the teleporters in mind from the get-go. Once you have the basic layout idea in place and all teleporters are absolutely justified and well-integrated into the bigger layout concept, first, then I would design the rest of the detailed layout. For example, why bother with the detailed column placement if you can skip the entire room with a teleporter? That is why the justification for teleporters is so vital. Teleports should never allow people to skip large parts of your layout but offer instead an alternate route that has to enrichen your layout. You have to integrate them into your bigger picture of options and lanes and treat them accordingly, especially their speed and risks. Especially the high speed and low risk makes their integration tricky.

Therefore, think about other risks you can associate with them, like placement away from other power-ups, visible exposure, or at least add strong audio clues. Alternatively, you can place them further away from the main lanes to add some extra time component to them but be careful that it does not feel too arbitrary punishing. At no time should teleporters feel like an afterthought to fix an otherwise flawed layout. More likely, you might end up with an even more flawed layout but now also with a sour taste.

Water for non-vehicle navigation is another huge topic, so let us only focus on the most critical aspects. If AI can swim and use water to traverse, one of the first things to master is the connections between water and land navigation. Usually, those connections have either many restrictions or behave very finicky. AI might calculate very odd and long paths if the connections are not flawless. Also, make sure that you have more than enough backup connections like multiple ladders or long beaches if some of the connections are blocked or occupied. Another important consideration is how well water acts as concealment in your game. For example, how deep does a player have to swim underwater to stay undetected by enemy AI? Thirdly, understand how AI navigates in and below water. If your game is not very water-focused, it can be that the true navigation for underwater creatures remains 2D, but they just have the option to go 'down' while still following the 2D grid on the water surface. If you checked those key points and have good answers for any potential issues, I generally recommend using a fair amount of water in your maps. Too often world restrictions do not allow us to use a lot of water in maps, but in the few opportunities where we can, then rather plan with a bit too much than too little. Water can open up many unique opportunities, especially a new aspect of verticality. A village on stilts on top of a lake is a classic example because you have stealth navigation under the water, potentially over the rooftops, and of course, on the village's normal "ground" floor.

Fixed, contextual grapple points or similar climbing/swing spots to quickly traverse vertically or horizontally are another classic level design navigation ingredient. As much fun as they are to use, first check if AI can use them, too. Suppose they cannot then make sure that AI has alternative ways to follow players, or it is somewhat okay that players can leave them behind. It might become an easy way to skip many fights or to exploit the AI limitations if it does not come up with other disadvantages for the player, like no weapon usage while grappling. Still, I would be extra careful using them in highly contested combat spaces. Next up, experiment with them a lot in a separate test level, especially when it comes to swinging, transitioning between different movement types, and gaining momentum. For example, check if you can grapple out of water? How does sprinting, jumping, or free-falling affect the grapple swing speed? Can you transition out of a driving vehicle to grapple? What is the maximum distance you can catapult yourself using grapple, straight and around corners? Answering such questions should become your foundation when building various difficult grapple sections. You certainly want to avoid just chaining up some generic straight swings because usually, the feature is way too cool to be used in boring ways.

Lastly, let us touch on crawl tunnels, like air ducts, small sewer pipes, covered ditches, or underfloor grates. Usually, they are great for exploration or are alternate stealth passages to bypass threats or avoid detection. Depending on your game's stealth and exploration focus, their entrances should either be more or less hidden. Still, ideally, players should not first notice the network of crawl tunnels after completing a section in your level. One way to give players a fair chance is to apply some basic world logic. For example, air ducts usually do not randomly exit out of the ceiling and then on floor height. Instead, they are somewhat consistent within the same building. Especially with air ducts, you have to be careful not to create some random connections between rooms. Sure, design can have some leeway over world logic, but it has limits. Ideally, world-building guides game logic and not the way around. The same counts for crawl tunnels under the floor, but usually, they are easier justifiable by architecture than the consistent use of two-meter-long air ducts between rooms. Also, if you use many air ducts, do not forget about the room's doors and the flow for "normal" people in your game space. Developers can always lock doors, but if the only way into a room is through crawl tunnels, then the original "architect" of the building made some embarrassing mistakes.

#### *16.3.5.3 Free Use*

The use of free navigation tools like free-grapple, double jumps, rocket jumps, or free-use short-distance teleportation is technically not a level design ingredient. However, it is something level designers have to be very aware of. Sure, by now, it should be clear that you, as the level designer, should have experimented with such features a ton, tried to exploit them, combined them with as many other features as possible, and stretched out their possibilities to the max. However, even if you think nothing more extreme is possible, some players will beat you in finding even more extreme combinations, especially in very systemic games. Accept it. That is okay, do not worry. Many cases that look like "bad" design exploits are often rooted in late-game tweaks from the game design side, but then it is too late to check all levels or tweak all environments. That is also okay; that is part of game development. Please do not blame game design now because it is not all that simple.

However, if you know all those realities and how little you can prepare for all the late-game changes or fringe feature combinations, at least you can add some extra safety. I once checked all my cliffs, making sure that no vehicle could get up and leave the playable space. However, I still added some invisible walls on top to prevent any "accidents" and added some extra kill zones in case some players find even ways behind the walls. Of course, some players tried and managed to get up on the cliffs, but they could not get over the invisible wall. Then some players had some freaky physic-bugs and were catapulted over the walls by accident. Lucky my kill zone made sure that they were not stuck behind the invisible wall. Sometimes death is more merciful than wandering endlessly outside of the play space.

Therefore, expect the unexpected and have more than one backup. Also, do not spend too much time preventing fringe cases, freak accidents, or people purposely trying to ruin their game experience, but more about such general cases later.

#### *16.3.5.4 Threats*

The last navigational level design ingredients are locally placed threats that do not need activation. I am talking here, for example, about lava lakes, acid pools, or spike walls. Merely touching them or falling into them can mean serious harm or death. By core definition, such elements deny space or make navigating near them more dangerous. However, engagement distances and threat positioning is key here. For example, nobody cares about a lava pool in the middle of a room if the fighting distance happens over a long range. Therefore, besides world logic reasons, seriously consider adding them only if they actually propose a threat to players or AI.

As level designers, we need to work with powerful POAs next to such threat zones to motivate players considering to come close. For example, good cover options, destructible covers keep pushing players forward, power-ups, or other fixed ingredients like mounted guns. At least, by players avoiding such threats, they should expose players more than usual when navigating between POAs. However, always double-check the relevance of such threats and either do not bother implementing them or rather modify the environment and POA network accordingly.

Of course, the same counts for enemy AI, too. There is a certain satisfaction kicking a powerful enemy into an acid lake or against a spike wall. However, carefully manage expectations. Therefore, do not always place an enemy in front of spike walls so players can kick them into the spikes. It is fine to orchestrate such circumstances for tutorial reasons but let players work for their quick and easy kills in later levels.

# Section VII

# Closing Topics

# 17

# *Closing and Shipping*

The common saying "The last 10% take 90% of the effort" is very much true. In the beginning, everyone is jolly, excited, and fantasizes about how amazing the new game or level will be. Then comes the lengthy development cycle; many dreams had to get crushed in the process, and then you still had to run a few unexpected "Mogadishu miles" to finish it. It is human nature to be fed up at the end, and they just want to have it out of the door. However, a key difference between experienced and inexperienced developers is not how they start a project but how they finish it. Knowing how to close a project severely affects how you start one and how you pace your energy in the often year-long process. In this chapter, I want to share some experiences about the three main topics at the end: balancing, bug fixing, and general closing mindset.

I am touching here on many production basics because every level designer should understand such topics and crucial development phases. However, I will keep it light enough because, after all, this book is not aimed to go in-depth about such topics, per se, and several aspects will likely differ from your project, company, or studio.

## 17.1 About Balancing

### 17.1.1 Introduction

#### *17.1.1.1 Overview*

In the balancing process, you want to ensure that your intended difficulty matches your game's reality. So, for example, the first levels of your game are very easy, the last level is very hard, and the ones in the middle of your game are something in between. Then you have difficulty fluctuation within your level where bosses or special gameplay highlights are more difficult than your lower paced or narrative segments. So far, so good.

The biggest problems with balancing are that it is very subjective and that testing it is very time-consuming. Therefore, many developers either just went by feeling, large audience playtesting, or developed some scientific measurements. In my experience, it requires a bit of both, and I want to share some of my observations.

#### *17.1.1.2 Balancing Is Not Pacing*

Let us first clarify that gameplay pacing is about intended intensity but not only about difficulty, while difficulty directly affects pacing. So do not assume that your carefully constructed pacing graph directly correlates to balancing intentions, even though it can overlap at many parts. Therefore, I highly recommend keeping those two graphs and their data entries separately.

#### *17.1.1.3 Details of Balancing*

I do not mind planning pacing a bit more granular, especially when I involve pure gameplay intensity and narrative or coop focus. However, whenever I planned out difficulty with the same granularity, it felt like a waste at the end. To be true, nobody is truly checking later on if that fight here was now a four or a five in difficulty. Pacing and difficulty exist in different granularity levels because the pacing is an early intention, but difficulty measurement happens more at the end of development.

DOI: 10.1201/9781003275664-24

Early on, aspects are there to sketch out a detailed picture without doing much work yet. However, if some of its early detailed intentions do not find their way into the final product, it will still ship, and likely nobody will notice. Also, if it is not inherently flawed or broken, and pacing is just a tick off, nobody usually will make much trouble about it sometime after the alpha milestone.

However, it is a lot different with difficulty. If a boss fight is too easy early on, nobody should really care. It is perfectly fine, as long as everyone is aware of the target difficulty and we have ways, plans, and features to tweak it later on. Later on in the production, of course, tutorial levels have to become incredibly easy, and the boss fights a tough nut to crack. However, usually at that point, nobody is going through detailed documentation anymore. It happens over broader strokes, like "This level or segment is too easy/difficult" or "This enemy type is way too easy/difficult." It is not about each individual micro encounter because it is blurred together into large experience segments and a large portion depends on who plays it how. It is way too complex and subjective to micro analyze or plan every bit.

Of course, again, if something smaller truly stands out in a very negative way, then it should be pointed out, but that does not mean we need to plan it in the same granularity. Instead, design difficulty per level, not per beat, and make broad comments on which level parts are a lot easier or way more difficult than the level's average difficulty. Too much granularity either in difficulty levels or separating them into too tiny chunks will not help you save time in the end.

### 17.1.2 The Sum of All Parts

#### *17.1.2.1 The Core Issue*

One of the biggest problems about difficulty is that many factors are affecting it. An encounter with a single AI can be affected by various player character stats, AI stats, layout, exposure, and we have not even talked about the individual player skills yet. Then if you identify a segment as too difficult/easy, the discussion usually starts if it is a level or game design issue, or both.

Usually, if the issue is isolated, it is level design, and if the issue is global or appears in multiple segments, it is more a game design topic. However, it is not always that simple. Usually, I would work more with game design at the start of the balancing process. Then once the balance between the individual features starts to feel okay, I would shift more focus to level design, balancing the individual segments, and finish it off with some last simple global game design tweaks. Usually, changing global damage or health modifiers is safer to modify, close to gold master, than messing with level content again. Still, any late-game changes are risky.

However, I would start with game design because if the ingredients compared to each other do not feel right, and they start getting tweaked, level design will keep adjusting forever, and that wastes much time. Therefore first, game designers should finish their basic balancing "homework" before levels get tweaked in detail. In reality, the transition from game to level design balancing is fluid and overlaps, but the intention and mindset count.

#### *17.1.2.2 Balancing Timing*

One of the biggest mistakes about balancing is when to initiate the process and to what degree. By default, my advice is not to start any severe balancing passes till your game is not content and feature complete. Usually, this happens around the alpha milestone.

I would consider any detailed balancing before this period a waste of time. Of course, you should address any outliers or super obvious balancing issues to keep reviews practical. However, I would not consider this an actual balancing pass. However, as long as big content blocks are changing, it is not really possible to judge the game's difficulty in its totality—the same counts, even more apparent, for unfinished features and their use in the levels.

Before or after the alpha milestone, outsider playtests are usually possible, and ideally, such first more significant playtests are the target for the first balancing pass by the devs. From then on, playtests become your continuous balancing guide.

#### 17.1.2.3 Developers Do Not Count, Almost

By default, you as a developer can set difficulty expectations but you shouldn't be its judge. You have been playing the game for months, if not years, and you know the levels and game's details inside out. However, it is all a matter of context.

For example, you should not evaluate the difficulty of a linear action single-player game based on developer performance or skills. The knowledge of the levels, game, and the fact that replayability is not in focus, disqualifies developers from fairly judging the final difficulty of such games. This observation especially counts for early levels. However, arguably in later levels, you could expect a more advanced knowledge of the game and will to explore the levels in great detail, comparable to developers.

Another example where developers can certainly set the standard is any game with high replayability. Raids in MMOs, multiplayer shooters, or "souls-like" games come to mind. Arguably, and entertainingly in many cases, developers are often not even good enough to set the difficulty high enough for the most hardcore players. We seriously thought we set the difficulty high enough when we worked on such games because we developers struggled to beat the segments. Still, soon after the game was released, an embarrassingly high number of players complained that it was too easy.

#### 17.1.2.4 Playtests and Balancing

Using playtests to evaluate difficulty is an excellent method. However, it does not come without issues. First, the playtest candidates do not necessarily represent the average audience of your game. Some playtest labs do a fantastic job finding suitable candidates, but in my experience, a session rarely exceeded more than 20 candidates. Such numbers are barely representative enough, in my opinion. Also, the type of people who, for example, join for one week, 25–40 hours of playtest sessions are often not representative either. I would never downplay the importance or the candidates of a playtest; just do not take every result as absolute fact.

Secondly, you should be careful with facts and data because of the interpretation. A common mistake is to jump to conclusions too early after watching playtests. Seriously, try to restrain yourself from jumping to conclusions. First, take your time to do your proper research about why certain things happened. Ideally, discuss it together in a group after you get all the data and not just jump right away into action just because you saw the live feed of one single candidate.

For example, a high number of deaths is not a direct indication that a segment is too difficult. I would only look at such data together with the perceived difficulty assessment of the candidates, their gaming background, and watching the footage. Another classic example is the urge to place more waypoints because players seemingly got lost. With some digging, we often found out that players were not lost but wanted to explore or lost because of other player-leading aspects that more waypoints would not address.

Thirdly, working with a good research lab, internally or externally, makes a huge difference. Their observations and interpretations will be already very helpful, but they also make sure that the test's context is valuable. Unfortunately, I also had to work with research labs that did not generate meaningful results, either because the test's circumstances rendered the results useless or because their report was incredibly faulty. If you are lucky, you get the raw data and videos to do your own research, but that is usually very time-consuming. Working with a good research lab is absolutely worth it, especially if you can cater the test precisely to your needs.

## 17.2 About Bug Fixing

### 17.2.1 Introduction

In this chapter, I want to write more about a bug fixing mindset than exactly how to fix bugs. If the bug is difficult, I recommend following the problem-solving steps I outlined in the previous chapter about scripting.

### 17.2.2 Bug Fixing Approach

#### *17.2.2.1 The Foundation*

Usually, you should check your bug-tracking tool early in the morning before you start any more significant tasks. If your team has stand-ups, make sure that you check them before so you can bring up any new bigger issues. Often bigger QA/QC teams do a test run of the game before the rest of the other developers start their workday, or they work in a different time zone. Therefore, if that is the case, certainly expect new bugs to come in early.

Next up, make a quick glance over your list to see if you have already spotted any outliers or concerning patterns. For example, check for any major walkthrough, game, or build breaks, bugs that obviously should get assigned to another person, or bad prioritization. Essentially make a quick clean-up of your current list without spending too much time and be aware of anything major on your plate. If there is nothing with absolute top priority, focus on the obvious issues you can clean up quickly before even loading up your engine, tools, or game. Remember that other people rely on you to check your bugs, especially if they were wrongly assigned.

#### *17.2.2.2 A Common and Ideal Approach*

After you clean up your list, it is time to work on your bugs, assuming that bug fixing currently has priority. A very common approach is to fix as many small little issues as possible. After all, checking off many bugs in your list is incredibly satisfying, and your bug-fixing statistics will look amazing. Not many developers get judged by their bug-fixing speed, but it is good for the ego if you know you killed a large number of bugs. I bet most developers have done that and occasionally are still doing it, including myself. However, this is not the ideal approach.

First of all, the ideal approach is to respect the assigned priorities by QA/QC, starting with the highest, of course. High-priority bugs should be fixed first for good reasons because they usually have a higher impact on the overall quality of your game. You as a developer should typically not change the priorities yourself because QA/QC usually has strict guidelines about it. However, if you spot anything out of the ordinary, talk to the appropriate person, so they can correct it and hopefully make sure that it happens less often in the future.

Besides priorities, start your day with the big and complicated issues. At times I would even ignore the bug's priority compared to a big and complicated one if I knew how to fix a higher prioritized bug quickly and safely. The reason for starting with the bigger and more difficult ones is that my brain is usually fresher in the morning and I have more time to consult my colleagues throughout the day. Later in the day, I am usually tired, and so are my fellow developers in case I need their help. However, everyone has a different energy flow throughout the day, but it is also not very nice to approach people with a big messy problem when they are about to leave.

Later in the day, when I am getting more tired, I go back to the quick and easy bugs. I don't want to add more bugs while fixing them, so keeping the safe and easy issues for the end of the day is a good strategy. It also ensures that you do not go home thinking over a complicated problem that might rob your sleep. At least, that is what was happening to me very often. Also, ending the day with a nice bump in your bug-fixing statistics is a good feeling and usually shows better teamwork and energy strategy than starting the day with it. Getting rid of many bugs at the end of the day can also reduce the perceived pressure a lot of bugs on your list can have on you. Even if you still have some bigger, higher priority bugs on your list, I recommend fixing smaller "lighter" ones in the last hour to feel good before going home and especially not to think about fixing them overnight. Attempting to fix bigger issues at the end of the day can also lead to even more bugs.

#### *17.2.2.3 Bugs vs. Tasks*

A big question is always, when do you start fixing bugs while you still have tasks on your plate? First of all the transition is usually a smooth one, except the bug load is so high that you have special bug-fixing days or weeks. Also, close to milestones, the focus usually shifts for most developers from tasks to bugs.

However, I would not focus too much on bugs before the alpha milestone while the game is still in heavy development. There is a real chance that the segment, layout, or script will change. Ideally, nobody should report smaller bugs at that stage anyhow.

The primary bug-fixing focus in the pre-alpha period is on bugs that negatively affect the work of others. For example, if a game does not start, the AI cannot shoot, a cutscene does not start, or a broken shader does not allow artists to do their job. Remember, a core pillar of good teamwork is that everyone prioritizes unblocking others. Very importantly, this includes reviews, meaning the game needs to be in a good enough state so people can give constructive feedback. Unfortunately, reviews are often canceled because the game is too buggy, which means days, if not weeks, of no feedback for the developers. Of course, a stretched terrain texture, floating crate, or placeholder material will not prevent constructive level design reviews but too many of them may impact the art feedback. It is always a matter of perspective, context, and expectations.

Usually, after alpha, the expectations rise, especially when we talk about bugs. Ideally, the alpha build has not a large number of serious bugs, hence usually a few weeks of stabilization aka bug-fixing before. At some point between alpha and beta usually comes the closing period, with a stronger focus on bugs, but tasks will remain a reality up to a point. However, I will talk more about closing in the next chapter.

Bugs take over tasks if their priority is higher than those of the tasks. Ideally, such tasks become fewer and fewer the closer you get to the beta milestone. However, project reality and director/lead discipline to generate fewer tasks can greatly impact such an ideal reality. At that stage, the better directors have some empathy for production or management, not those who demand changes until the bitter end while risking the entire game's quality. In my experience, it is a gradual transition, and many feedbacks at the end are rather bugs than tasks, with the occasional task masked as a bug, but those are less than ideal.

### 17.2.3 Etiquette

#### *17.2.3.1 Forwarding Bugs*

Each time you assign a bug, or task, you should include a meaningful comment. Usually, forwarding a bug to someone without a comment is rude. Sure, some blatantly wrongly assigned bugs or crazy obvious issues do not need a detailed comment, but even then, a quick comment is a nice touch.

The comment should help the recipient to quickly understand why they got the bug and hopefully how to address it quickly without being patronizing. If the bug is not clear-cut, the recipient should not have to do the same in-depth research you have done already. Therefore, add your findings and why you assign the bug to another person in the comments. The comment should save the overall team's time management. You might be annoyed that you got the bug and spend time on it just to find out that you cannot fix it, but that does not mean your college has to go through the same frustration. This topic is especially crucial if the recipient might also think they are not the ones meant to fix the bug. Without good comments, bugs often go back and forth between the same people till even more people get involved, and the bug is still not fixed.

#### *17.2.3.2 NAD, AD, WNF, NMI, and CNR*

Let us go through some standard methods to react to bugs (or certain tasks) besides closing it as "Fixed," or setting the bug as "Duplicate." The exact wording of such other reactions might differ in different bug-tracking tools, but they should be similar among most.

"Not a Defect" is your reaction if a bug is not a bug. However, I do recommend consulting with someone else before you close a bug as NAD because QA/QC might disagree, and it can start an argument. There are always such fringe cases where people can argue if it is a bug or not. Regardless, you definitely need to close it with a good description of why this bug is not a defect.

"As Designed" is similar to NAD, except that the bug is not only not a bug but a feature. Reacting that way can be perceived as "cheeky" because it has the meme-nature of "It is not a bug, but a feature." Therefore, if you are not 100% sure, consult with a peer, manager, lead, or director and add a reasonable comment, ideally pointing at the specific design documentation.

"Will not Fix" (WNF) is a reaction if you accept that it is a bug, but you do not want to, or more likely, cannot fix it. The most common time for this reaction is at the end of a project when attempting a fix might introduce worse issues, or you lack the resources to do so. I highly recommend consulting with a manager, director, or lead before you WNF a bug because it means the project will ship with another known bug. Be aware that some projects or companies statistically track the WNFs because a high WNF-rate usually means a lower accepted quality for the end product. It should really be the last resort and should never be a single person's decision. Of course, it has to go with a detailed comment.

"Need more Information" (NMI) is a common reaction if you do not understand the bug's description or you can't reproduce/find the bug. You are passing the bug back to QA/QC, asking for more detailed information about the bug. However, you are still keeping the bug "alive" compared to "Can not Reproduce" (CNR), which is more of an attempt to close a bug because, according to you, the bug essentially does not exist anymore. A CNR bug can still be re-opened by QA/QC because certain bugs have low reproducibility or only happen in certain circumstances, build-types, or platforms. By default, rather try NMI first after you have done everything on your side to reproduce the bug or you do not know further. Closing a bug as CNR just because "it works on my machine" should result from certainty and proper diligence and should not create the perception of laziness.

#### *17.2.3.3 Bad Bugs*

You sometimes get bugs that you could describe as "bad," and I do not mean a severe issue per se, but a bad description or report. It can range from a not specific description, lack of important information/screenshots/coordinates, or occasionally design suggestions. I can understand why you could especially perceive the last one as annoying. However, folks from QA/QC are just game developers, too, and in theory, it should not matter who has a good idea. They might miss a lot of contexts, and therefore their idea is likely not feasible or good. However, react professionally, write a calm response, and only if it happens more than once, involve the appropriate managers or leads.

The same counts for any other occurrences of "bad bugs." A one-time hick-up is not a reason to react harshly—we are all humans. However, if there is a pattern emerging, involve the responsible managers, leads, or directors. Still, do yourself a favor, be a decent human, and never let out your anger toward QA/QC, even if it is late at night or you are under a lot of pressure.

## 17.3 About Closing

### 17.3.1 Introduction

Not every company or project has a clearly defined closing phase, but regardless there is such a phase anyhow. However, the quality of closing can vary. It is a switch in mindset when we change from expressing our creativity to finishing what we have. This switch is hard. We designers are constantly being pushed to be creative, and we have to stop now. Sure usually, the transition is gradual, but it still happens. Also, as a quick reminder, I am talking here about ideal cases, yet, every project has its own reality, and it will differ in more or less detail from what I am describing here.

It is the time when you run out of tasks and get a lot more bugs. It is the time when directors argue with managers about that one last task and then another. It can be frustrating because just around the alpha milestone, when all the different game's parts come together and you start to see the full picture, you are meant to stop changing. However, it is not usually all that extreme, but without a good closing strategy, it can also turn into a never-ending story of changes, and then suddenly, you have to ship what you have. Both cases, absolutely no more changes post-alpha and never stop iterating, are awful. Therefore, I want to share some personal insight into hopefully closing a project a bit smoother and still fulfilling.

### 17.3.2 The Role of Creatives and Managers

Loosely said, creatives are the main leading force of a project initially, but once closing kicks in, it is the managers. The transition usually happens somewhere between the alpha and beta milestones. In the beginning, it is all about having the most amazing ideas, while in the end, it is about finishing what you have started. If creatives were in the driver's seat the entire time, then the game would get iterated and polished forever, but never ships.

Therefore, such a switch is hard. You have to accept that the project will come to an end. You will wish you were smarter earlier, but it is a lie in most cases. You had to make mistakes in order to know what was correct. After all, it is a creative process, and, within limits, waste is part of it.

However, managers who were with the project for a long time are often heavily connected and, therefore, even they have difficulty letting go, too. Therefore, some companies use special "closers," project-external managers whose main job is to close a project because they do not have a personal connection with the project. They meant to make hard calls to guarantee that the game ships on time and ideally with the expected quality. However, in my experience, they are not cold-blooded project-killers and are still humans with empathy. Sure, they have a job to do, but they are still reasonable, and nobody wants a bad product either. Still, the fact that such roles exist shows how difficult this process is.

An essential role of higher-ranking creatives like leads or directors during closing is to advise how to fix bugs. Less from a technical, but certainly from a creative perspective. For example, can you remove the object here, or is it vital for cover? However, there comes a time when creatives should leave and leave the entire project to be finished by the trusted hands of managers and tech folks, which is okay.

### 17.3.3 The Stages between Alpha and Beta

#### *17.3.3.1 Grace Period*

As I stated previously, closing starts somewhere between alpha and beta. However, ideally, it does not start right after alpha. First, give the creatives some time for the last bigger changes once they can enjoy a feature and content complete game. It is the first glimpse at the totality of the final product, so of course, some changes have to happen. However, if alpha is not fully complete in terms of features or content, this phase between alpha and closing is usually larger. Unfortunately, it is not uncommon to have a partially incomplete alpha. Secondly, usually at that time, you have a lot of feedback coming from playtests or larger reviews, which again means a lot of important changes.

Usually, this last "grace period" of larger changes is between one-third to a quarter of the time between alpha and beta. However, if you only have a few months between alpha and beta, you quickly get into time issues because you still have to polish and bug fix. Unfortunately, we all know games that shipped without sufficient polish and bug fixing but great potential.

#### *17.3.3.2 Closing Phase*

So after this initial short grace period, usually closing kicks in. However, it is not like someone turns off the light of creativity because there might still be exceptions, and you still have to polish. The main difference now, everyone should only work on tasks or bugs if they have a correlating entry in your issue-tracking software. Furthermore, each such entry must be approved by a selected, small number of selected managers. In theory, creatives can request as much as they want, but nobody should work on it if the key managers are not approving it. Those critical steps might sound drastic at first but are essential to successfully close a project and bridge the transition from iteration to a solid shipped product. It also purposely slows down the incoming task speed.

Often you can only check-in your work in your version control software if you have an approved task in your issue-tracking software. This step is important so developers do not secretly keep changing bigger aspects of the game and potentially do not introduce more bugs and ultimately more work. It is also the time of so-called "ninja tasks" where developers use the task or bug of another issue to submit further unapproved changes. It is controversial because some small adjustments by senior people are usually very safe. However, they set a bad standard for less experienced developers, and this practice erodes the trust in the managers.

When you start to optimize it severely depends on your game's current performance, your goals, and your team's experience. However, usually, you can start some performance testing and optimization once you are content and feature complete. Unfortunately, any bigger creative changes will likely make previous performance investigations questionable. Suppose you recognize severe performance issues early on during closing. In that case, this has to be a huge factor in approving any last more significant changes since they are not just a risk in themselves by adding potentially more performance problems but also take away time to optimize. Therefore, do not wait too long with performance tests. Ideally, start with the first ones close before alpha, just to get an idea or spot trends.

#### *17.3.3.3 Polish Phase*

Typically, you still do a lot of small polish work during the first part of the closing phase. However, I am talking about small, risk-free polishing like more details in textures, rearranging the objects on a shelf to be more lively, or adjusting idle animations. The tricky part is that polish can still have performance impacts, and any polish means less bug fixing.

Therefore, most importantly, you should only polish it if it is risk-free, have approval from the appropriate people, and be aware of the potential performance impacts. For example, adding new idle animations can mean an increase in memory. That is why it is so important that any task gets first approved, and the approving manager gets advice from experienced developers. If a task like that gets spotted, they can give clear guidelines on what to look out for.

The polish phase overlaps with the "grace period" and the bug-fixing phase. Essentially this means the less bigger tasks and bugs you have, the more time for polish you have. The exact ratio depends on your game's quality state, the available time, and the assessment of the responsible managers. Most games have seemingly never enough time to polish everything. That is the unfortunate reality of having limited time and resources. However, you should allocate a fixed time for polish which only gets reduced if the game is in big trouble due to core design flaws or overwhelming amount of bugs. Further on, focus more on polishing the first levels/missions and anything you need for marketing. Unfortunately, many players don't finish all their games and at first it is about selling a game than it is about polishing levels which not many players will reach anyhow. I'm not proud to make the previous statement, but with more experience you will make less grave mistakes and plan with a longer time between alpha and beta. Ultimately both will lead to still more overall polish time at the end.

#### *17.3.3.4 Strict Bug-Fix Phase*

At one point during the closing phase, managers should stop approving tasks, and every developer fixes only bugs. Once again, that is an ideal case. At a later stage, even bugs should get through a strict approval process. Certain bugs are simply not worth fixing anymore in the end because they might introduce more issues. The closer you get to beta or especially gold master, the more WNF issues you have. Even big and severe bugs are not approved anymore in the end if they are too risky. Instead, they usually are already designed for day-one patches and alike. However, depending on the game and used tech, level design bugs are not always included in patches because updated worlds or levels can make the patch file size very large.

### 17.3.4 About Tasks, Bugs, and Empathy

#### *17.3.4.1 Still Big Tasks?*

So what bigger tasks or changes are still okay to get into the game during closing? The answer to that question is the balance between potential newly introduced risks and the gain for the game. This balance is a call the key closing managers have to make because they approve any changes. However, they have to gather all the relevant information from especially tech-savvy people and, of course, have to listen to the arguments from the creatives.

Usually, bigger risks closer to the beta milestone are a no-go, whereas the occasional big change is still okay at the beginning of closing. Tech people are the main advisors about the involved risks here because they are knowledgeable people, and they might also be the ones cleaning it up if it goes horribly wrong. If a creative change is worth it is the more tricky topic. My main methodology was: "Will we gain another percentage point in the reviews, or will it cause someone to write positively about it?" If the answer was "no," the change was likely too minor or not significant enough. However, you should also ask, "Will someone recognize it negatively?" and, of course, try to fix/improve it if the answer is "yes."

Of course, this process is very subjective and can lead to some arguments between creatives and managers. However, in many cases, it allowed me, as a member of the creative team, to accept that this task would not get in. This acceptance, on both sides, is crucial to keep a healthy and productive relationship between everyone during this vital phase.

#### *17.3.4.2 Manage Expectations and Empathy*

When I previously wrote about acceptance, we also have to be absolutely clear about managing expectations and developing empathy toward managers. It is not their role to "kill your creative babies." Instead of fighting them, the more we "creative folks" support them, the more we get a smoother collaboration and a better product.

In my experience, the more you support and understand the closing managers, the more they are willing to listen to your reasons, too. It is in nobody's interest to make a bad or crippled product. It just happens that those managers have the job to close the project, bring it to an end, and ship it at a high quality. You, a creative person, had your time to shine previously. Now it is your responsibility to support the closing process, whatever it contains.

Experience shipping a few games is crucial here. If it is your first time, you might put yourself under much pressure or even panic a bit. Time is running out to make the last big changes, but you are told that the time for big changes is over. However, the more experience you have, the more you realize it rather matters how you react to and deal with issues than trying to prevent them all from happening. You can never perfectly design or plan out any iterative and complex process like lengthy game development early on.

#### *17.3.4.3 Edge Cases*

You will encounter edge cases not only during the closing phase, but it is the time when they tend to pop up in higher quantities. Edge cases are bugs or other issues that have a rare appearance but often have a significant impact on the game's quality while are also often expensive to fix. Common examples include strange results involving physic engines, specific player gear setups, rare hardware flukes, or AI systems, essentially elements that are seemingly very random, complicated, complex, or outside of your control.

First of all, we have to separate them into two categories. The first one is the edge cases every player can stumble over by accident. These are the bugs and issues I highly recommend fixing if you have the resources. For example, if players happen to drive with a highly optimized end-game vehicle so fast in an enemy encampment that the key VIP does not load and the game is broken. It can happen to everyone, and it can very negatively impact the game's experience, especially when players spend a great deal of effort playing the game at a high-level of sophistication.

The second category of edge cases is where players purposely try to break the game. For example, if players keep piling on vehicles at a cliff and then use an explosion to get catapulted out of the game world. This breakage was not an accident; the players tried to break your game and potentially his own experience by purpose. However, addressing such bugs is not only very costly, they are often also tough to find. Just look at all the glitches of speedrunners of otherwise seemingly very well-made games. You could spend days, if not weeks trying to fix them "the correct way," and often the fix would ruin the experience for all other players. In our example, it could mean raising all cliff walls to ridiculous heights.

Therefore, my main recommendation is to "not spend 98% of your time on the 2% of the players who purposely want to ruin the game" and their own game experience. Either let them have the glitch if there is no competitive element involved or fix it with the simplest solution on your side as long as it does not affect the rest of the "normal" players. In our example, I would fix it with nothing else than invisible walls and maybe an additional kill trigger. Sure, invisible walls and arbitrary kill triggers are not elegant ways to fix problems, but they are quick and easy solutions and it is okay since most players will never experience them.

Additionally, you gain time to focus on improving the game for the remaining 98% of the players. This mindset has saved my colleagues and me so much trouble and time and prevented countless arguments between us developers.

# 18

# Becoming a Level Designer

In this chapter, I would like to summarize some of the most common questions I get from students or other people who would like to become professional level designers. Besides my own career as a designer, I also hired countless level designers in several studios and companies. Therefore, I like to share my experience on how to become a level designer and advice regarding portfolios, resumes, interviews, and level design tests.

Please, keep in mind that this is based on my personal experience and does not necessarily establish an industry-wide standard. Therefore, if you follow all my advice, there is no guarantee that you will get a job. However, I interviewed a vast number of designers and artists in the last 20 years, in many studios and different companies, together with many colleagues, so what I am sharing here should have a wide foundation.

## 18.1 How to Get Started

### 18.1.1 Introduction

There are usually three common ways to become a level designer: Getting hired straight from the mod or modding community, from a university, or transitioning to level design from QA/QC. There are other ways, such as transitioning from environment art, game design, or even coming from the movie industry. However, such transitions are very specific and severely dependent on the particular context and therefore are not a standard procedure.

### 18.1.2 Mod Community

I have a soft spot for the mod community folks because it is my origin. I jumped from the Quake 3 community straight to a level design job at Crytek, working at Far Cry 1. However, there are many mod communities besides Quake, like Unreal, Crysis, Skyrim, and Half-Life. There are similar communities, less about a specific game, but around engines like Unreal Engine, CryEngine, or Unity. However, having an existing game as a base usually makes making a new game or level easier than a barebone engine.

The mod community is such a fantastic way to get into the industry because you can show skills, true passion, and teamwork. Remember, mod community work is for free usually. So you spend a huge amount of your precious free time creating such modifications or total conversions and release them to the public. It takes a huge amount of dedication to learn all those skills, and it shows us, the professionals, that you can finish a product and, remember, finishing something is the hardest part.

However, that is only applicable if you do release and finish something. The internet is full of mod teams who announced something cool but never released it. Therefore, you absolutely want to make sure you release something. Either by joining a trustful team or working on your own. If you do not release anything, you have difficulty getting the professionals' attention or using it in your CV. It is common for game companies to reach out to mod community members who stand out with their work. After all, it is ideal to hire developers who are already familiar with the company's tools.

So how do you get from the mod community into the professional industry? Once again, pick something you believe you can finish. At the start, go for something very easy and very manageable. It could be just a small level. It does not matter, but get it to be released. If it is bad, just do not add it to your portfolio, but you have to get the experience of releasing something. Once you are comfortable with the

DOI: 10.1201/9781003275664-25

process and get your first feedback from the public, pick the next project but hopefully a more ambitious one. Keep going and growing on your own, or ideally, try to find and join a decent team.

Releasing a quality mod project or even a total conversion as a team and you being one of the level designers is, in my opinion, the best way to show that you have what it takes to land a job in the industry. Not only did you hopefully do a good job as a level designer, but you also showed you could work effectively in a team. Additionally, coordinating a mod team with seemingly random individuals, often spread over half the world and in different time zones, shows great organizational skills. Further on, it deserves respect if you are working on your mod project for free in your spare time. It can really show that you have what it takes. However, make sure that the team's ambitions are realistic. I would usually recommend staying away from teams that search for many essential people because they will likely search for them forever, and you do not get to release your work together with the rest of the project.

Once you have a few interesting releases, you can add them to your portfolio and start applying for jobs. However, I highly recommend standing out from the crowd. Often, just making a few basic levels isn't impressive or unique anymore. For example, see if you can bend some game rules, have unique scripts, experiment more with cinematics, have unique art assets, or extend the existing narrative. Still, the most important is quality. Nobody wants to hire a messy level designer who makes many bugs and whose level is hard to work with by other developers.

### 18.1.3 University

Another method is to find a suitable university for level design and then apply for a job with the finished degree. However, the bigger problem is finding a suitable university because most of them are rather about game design or generally game development. Therefore, at least try to find some that have semesters focused on level design or have many projects together with other students where you can be the level designer or similar role at times.

When you look for universities to become a game developer, try to find one where the teachers have relevant game industry experience or at least have many guest lectures from industry veterans. It is not uncommon for good universities to have tight, long-lasting collaborations with gaming studios. It is a win-win situation because the universities gain professional insights and useful lectures, and the game development studios have access to well-taught students once they are done with their studies. Now, during your studies, it can allow you to build a relationship with a gaming studio and a better chance to get hired by them later on. However, game studios usually only initiate such collaborations if the university has a solid track record and foundation, which on the flip side should help you identify a proper school.

Further on, investigate why the teachers are not in the game industry themselves or never even joined. Some genuinely prefer teaching, while others cannot find a job in the game industry for various less-than-ideal reasons. There is a significant difference between universities and their teachers. Therefore, some solid research on your part is certainly important for you to find a good university.

In general, I always preferred to hire students who worked in small teams on several projects during their studies and, of course, were level designers. Such small project teams are comparable with mod teams, just that you have a teacher involved and you usually pay for the university. Still, an interesting aspect of such projects is the variety and the time limitations. If you can show as a level designer that you can design anything from drone racing stadiums to haunted houses to an arena shooter, you are on a good track.

Nobody expects to hire a fully fleshed level designer, perfectly catered to your unknown game, straight from university. We were looking for potential. Someone who, once again, stands out from the crowd, has a creative mindset, is not shy to learn new things, takes some calculated risks, has variety in his work, and ideally shows great teamwork and team fit.

### 18.1.4 QA/QC

Not everyone has the opportunity to start right away as a level designer because not every company is comfortable with always hiring people without any industry experience. I mean that not every company or studio sees level design positions as entry jobs, except in cases where the designers show a lot of talent and potential. However, often a foot in the door is all you need. Therefore, a common easier entry to the industry is to start in a QA/QC role because the base requirements are usually less. Of course, I am not talking here about expert testers or leads, but QA/QC on an entry job level.

Further on, I recommend going for such positions in a studio that also hosts the other game developers. Switching from a dedicated testing facility to a separate game development studio is way harder than if you are already in the same building. It can work, but I have seen it way rarer.

Ideally, you get hired as a "development tester" (exact titles can vary) because they are directly embedded with the other developers, preferably in the same room. Therefore, you can absorb a lot more game development experience and knowledge while sitting with the others. They also get to know your personality and, when the time comes, can recommend you as a great team fit.

During the interview, I would not start by saying, "I only want the QC job to become a level designer." Usually, companies hire people for QA/QC to be primarily testers. Of course, you can mention that down the line, you would be interested in growing in a different direction, but it should not be your main pitch. I remember people not getting hired for QA/QC because they considered their job just a necessary evil to become a designer. It does not go well with the present QA/QC members and leads. However, especially your lead or manager usually has to be on your side for you to transition out of QA/QC but that's a topic for another day.

Once you have the job as QA/QC, I recommend not mentioning all the time to everyone around that you want to become something else because it can become quite annoying, and it might show a bit too strong that you dislike your current job. Instead, try to work out a fair transition plan with your manager or lead and what you have to do/show for it. It also helps to build some solid rapport with the present level designers. See if you can help them out here and there, show reliability and that they can trust you with even sensitive tasks. Ideally, you should also have access to the engine and level design tools. Not every company allows QA/QC testers to work on their own training levels during work hours, but maybe during downtime or outside of work time? You can often strike a deal if the company is interested in growing their level designers from within.

Unfortunately, there is no guarantee that it will work out as planned or as fast as you have imagined it. You need to find a trustworthy company and leadership, which is not always easy as an industry newcomer. Getting any transition plans in writing is ideal but not always common because often such transitions are not time but context-specific. For example, it could happen at the start of the next project, but the previous project keeps getting delayed, and you never get your chance in a respectful time. Therefore, companies are usually careful with too strict promises.

Despite all the complications and uncertainties, I would encourage you to take the step to apply for QA/QC because I know and have hired a large number of fantastic level designers who transition out of it. Also, some of the best and most respected producers and managers I know share this background, too. You learn a great deal about the industry, and it prepares you very well for the pitfalls of game development. Overall, I believe developers coming from QA/QC have a stronger sense of balancing risks, avoiding many issues, and having a very solid game development understanding.

## 18.2 A Good Cover Letter, CV, and Portfolio

### 18.2.1 Introduction

The use of cover letters, portfolios, and CVs varies heavily between different companies. Not every company expects all three. For example, I have never applied for a job with a cover letter, and not every company I have interviewed for asked for a separate portfolio. This observation is also a good reminder that everything I write here is highly subjective.

### 18.2.2 The Cover Letter

I do not see a cover letter as the breaking point of a good application. It can add extra flavor to the application, but I have yet to see anyone being rejected because of a cover letter alone.

The primary point of a cover letter is to show your personality and soft skills, but it is less about your professional experience or hard skills. It should reflect you as a person, why you are ideal for the new company, and your uniqueness. However, mentioning the standard aspects like team spirit, hard worker, problem solver, or fast learner is not necessarily unique because pretty much everyone writes that about themselves. Of course, you should or can mention them, but it will not make you stand out.

Instead, the majority should be about what makes you special. Write a bit about your hobbies, background, why you have a passion for level design, your favorite games, or how you learned level design. Give some short examples of why you truly have such soft skills, even if they sound standard. A good cover letter is a great foundation for an interview chat. If it only covers the previously mentioned basics, the interview might potentially be only basic and less memorable.

Also, keep it short, less braggy, avoid cringy quotes, be humble, and let it be entertaining to read. Nobody wants to read a long awkward, cocky, or boring essay about someone's life story. I have yet to read a good cover letter longer than one page. Remember, those going through your application material might go through several applications a day and do not have much time allocated for the process. Therefore, be on point, memorable, and show passion and personality.

### 18.2.3 The Resume or CV

#### *18.2.3.1 Basic Setup and Essentials*

In my opinion, a resume should give the reader a quick overview of your professional and life experience. Therefore, do not mix up the CV with the lengthy portfolio. I always welcomed resumes that fit on one page so I could easily print them out and, during the call, did not have to search through multiple pages to find interesting talking points—the same counts for scrolling through multiple pages on a screen when I do not print it. Many people think a lengthy CV means much experience; the opposite is true!

If it happens to go over the first page, it is not the end of the world, but still, try to keep it brief. Especially I recommend keeping the work history on one page so the reader can easily follow and compare your experience.

First of all, a CV should contain all the relevant information for HR because recruiters or HR are often the first ones looking at it and do a first filtering process. So it must include your name and a way to reach you, usually an email and telephone number. Nationality, (higher) education, spoken languages, and social status (only if you would relocate with a partner or children) are individually optional. You do not have to mention them, and certain countries can have different laws—I'm not a lawyer! However, likely they will come up during the interview process when relocation or visa applications are a topic. However, only add them if you feel comfortable, especially if the CV is accessible online for everyone or you fear discrimination.

Second, before I forget, make sure your resume is printable. A homepage with your work history is all nice, but it is not very sufficient without a downloadable document in a standard format like.doc or.pdf. This aspect also counts for the cover letter, CV, and portfolio.

#### *18.2.3.2 Work History*

Next is the most significant part: your work history, including the company you worked for, what was your title, the game you worked on, and how long you had the specific job/title. Potentially it makes sense to add the country or city of the studio. I recommend keeping the job description light but on point. If you have a separate portfolio, you can go into more detail here but only add as much in the CV so it still fits on one page. Try to fight the temptation to write everything you did here in detail. Focus on the important big pieces and try to combine points rather than make a separate bullet point about each small aspect.

For example, an entry could be like:

- XYZ Game—ABC Studio (Berlin)—Senior Level Designer (April 2015–May 2017)

- Layout and script of the multiplayer map: "Random Map" and "Other Map"
- Mentored and managed three junior level designers

Other important bullet points, as long as the CV fits on one page and there is no repetition

I usually would recommend that each game is one entry. I would not recommend that each studio/company or position be one entry because it can quickly raise questions like: what games did they work on while in this studio or in what position for how long? You could list them, but it can get confusing if you got a promotion during the same game or switched studios while working on the same projects. Therefore, in my opinion, sorting it per game keeps it more straightforward for the reader. In my opinion, your title or position of a game is always your last one on the given project. So if you got a promotion at the end, that is your title for this game's entry. If you do not have games or larger projects on your belt yet, do not worry. For example, you could list each level or prototype as an entry. Later on, once you ship a few games, those initial entries can become a single encapsulating one.

I, as a reader, want to see your personal growth. How fast have you progressed? Does the progression look legit, or are there any holes or oddities? Did you work on games that stand out and maybe even fit ours? Do you show expertise which we are interested in? Did you work in studios where I might know someone, too? How long have you stayed at the same company or game project? I will not detail all the potential red flags we usually could spot right away in work history, but make sure that it is accurate. The industry is small, and the truth will always come out eventually.

### *18.2.3.3 Skill Section*

A small skill section indicating your hard skills, engines, or other software you know well is a nice bonus. I usually do not make a huge deal out of them because you can see most in the work history. If you worked on a game using the Unreal Engine, it is clear what engine you know. If you wrote, you did much documentation; some basic text editing software is usually a given, like Microsoft Office or Confluence. They are essentially standard by now and don't make you stand out. I would only add them if you have enough space or move them to your portfolio.

However, if you, as a level designer, have anything more unique like advanced video editing skills, drawing, 3D art, or programming, then certainly add them to your list. In the portfolio's optional hobby or interest section, you should list potentially less game development relevant skills like photography, free climbing, horse taming, or medieval gospel. I recommend keeping them out of the resume. Still, make sure that you are comfortable sharing your interests because some can lead to unintended misinterpretations by less professional or experienced recruiters or hiring managers. For example, some might consider horse riding as "too girly" or competitive shooting as "fanatic politically charged weapon freak." Those generalized assumptions are, of course, completely unprofessional, but unfortunately, there are still people out there with such thoughts.

### *18.2.3.4 Finishing Touches*

Like the cover letter, your resume should stand out and be memorable. Remember hiring managers usually go through many resumes at a time. Therefore, simple text on a white sheet of paper is not enough. A few graphical lines and a neat table are the minima to show a base organization foundation, and it shows you are tidy. If a document is messy, then most likely the work too.

However, the minimum to stand out is the rare splash of color, maybe some different background color of certain document parts or colorful bars. Make sure you use only one, maybe two colors, to ensure that your document does not turn into a Christmas tree. Also, since someone could print your resume, make sure that most of the background color is paper-white. It is always uncomfortable to print a whole page of black with white text just because it looked "cooler" on screen. The number of colors also counts for the number of used fonts. Only use one, maybe a second one for headlines, but that is it. Further on, the font should be simple and easy to read. Keep the fonts professional and stay away from anything too stylized.

Also, if you are not a gifted documentation formatting person, then it can make sense to get inspired by resume templates. However, I recommend never directly using any of the templates because it is often apparent and sloppy, and some can interpret it as laziness.

However, a single graphical element or illustration can help you be more memorable and spark interest. If you have the space, you could, for example, add an undead, giant space hamster wielding a frozen chicken as a weapon to show a bit more about your unique personality. Alternatively, it could be the logo of your YouTube channel, modding homepage, or similar. However, keep it small, it should not dominate the entire page. Instead, in my opinion, keep it connected to your personality plus keep it clean and graphical. I also recommend staying away from screenshots on your resume.

Lastly, make sure that you spell and grammar check your text. It also helps a lot if you ask someone to go through it and give you feedback. This review process counts for all your submitted documentation. If we spot spelling or other mistakes in a resume, cover letter, or portfolio, always send mixed messages. It is even more embarrassing and shows a lack of care if it comes from a native speaker.

### 18.2.4 The Portfolio

#### *18.2.4.1 Content*

The portfolio is where you can go way more detailed and in length. Here you can add many screenshots and links to any videos, channels, or homepages. Essentially, it is the extended version of your resume for whoever is more interested in detail about what you have done after the CV or cover letter spiked their interest. The main difference is that you could print the CV while you usually do not print the portfolio due to its large size. However, I will come back to this point in a moment.

In the portfolio, you can go into more detail about pretty much everything and not just your work but also topics like side projects, hobbies/interests, or specific education/skills. For example, you could move your entire skill section and list of known software to the portfolio.

Essentially replicate your CV, add everything else, including previously mentioned side or smaller projects, and flash out each entry with a list of bullet points, screenshots, and maybe even video links. Then you add topics like skills, known software, hobbies/interests, and anything else you consider relevant and feel comfortable to share. However, just because I have said you could go all out here does not mean you should bore people with a massive list of screenshots and an intimidating wall of text. Each picture and each bullet point must absolutely count. Avoid repetition in your text because it might feel like you just want to show off with text volume. Focus on the most relevant and exciting details which make you stand out—the same counts for screenshots. For example, seeing the same mansion from eight different angles will not make a better impression, or usually the opposite. Pick one that shows your design intentions the best, and then let it be. Remember that you are applying for a level design position and not necessarily as an artist. Therefore, the design has to have priority over a pretty-looking picture or at least keep a healthy balance.

#### *18.2.4.2 Delivery*

Now I previously said that portfolios are usually not printed. However, I would still expect that there will be someone out there who maybe wants to print it. Therefore, I recommend skipping too colorful and dark backgrounds and providing the portfolio in an easy-to-print file format. I recommend the.pdf file format because it works in most common browsers (as part of your optional homepage), but it is also easily printable. I would not recommend a separate homepage portfolio and another one for printing because you have to keep another file up-to-date, which only invites errors.

If you decide to keep your portfolio online only on a homepage, make sure that it is comfortable to read, easy to comprehend, and not confusing. I saw way too many homepages with a black background with dark fonts, huge gaps between the pictures or text, inconsistent font usage, buggy Java/Flash plug-ins or scripts, and a lack of any structure to tie it all together. Such messy homepages give a bad impression. Therefore, I recommend keeping it simple, organized, dense enough, and only going fancy if you know what you do. Remember, you are applying for a level design position, not as a web designer. Creating a fancy and wanna-be memorable homepage is all nice, but it can also quickly backfire.

The same thing I wrote about comprehension, readability also counts if your portfolio is a separate printable document. However, if you provide multiple files, I recommend that they are consistent in style, or at least in font and basic formatting. Delivering several wildly different documents can give a negative insight into your personality and cleanliness. While I usually recommend a resume or CV to stand out with deliberate formatting, I would tone it down a bit for the portfolio because your content should make you stand out, not the formatting, colors, or document design. Instead, a too strong visual document design could distract from your content and actual achievements.

Any videos showing your levels are a nice addition. However, either send some walkthrough videos of some good players who talk a lot and enjoy the experience or keep them short and on point if you made the video yourself. I would not recommend a lengthy flythrough with no commentary or explanation about your design thoughts. If you do not want to talk, keep it even shorter, around 90–120 seconds, like a trailer/teaser. However, even if you talk, I would be worried if your video is longer than three to four minutes. Usually, the people who review candidate portfolios do not have time to watch a 20-minute video about your level and will therefore fast-click through it themselves. This likely means they might miss some important bits. Therefore, rather keep them short enough so nobody wants to skip parts and you can show and focus on the important bits.

#### *18.2.4.3 Level Design Portfolio*

If you apply for a level design position and your portfolio includes only a few individual levels, which is common for entry level design positions, you should detail your design intentions. If you worked on bigger, more well-known games, it is easier because we likely either played the game or read about it enough to understand it. However, if that is not the case, you need to sell what you have even stronger. Of course, you can still outline your intentions even if you worked for known games but it is even more important the less known your project was.

We, as reviewers, want to know how your design brain works. What is important for you? How do you approach a level and its design? What do you have in mind for the player, or what do you expect them to do? Maybe include your initial sketch and original vision and then show how it changed, especially why. It is always a bit fishy if a junior level design applicant seemingly nails his perfect design vision right away. Expect professionals to likely notice if you hide or fake anything. Being honest, especially about your failures and learnings. Often mistakes and their lessons learned count more at the beginning of your career than your successes.

However, what counts for junior level design applicants, can easily apply to any other seasoned level designer. It is not always easy to figure out someone's design approach during an interview or test. Therefore, I always welcomed it if even senior designers went into more detail about their design approach and thinking of their later levels. It does not always have to be a GDC talk, but just some commentary during a short video or a breakdown of your level's iterations (so far, NDAs allow it) is a nice touch that can make your portfolio stand out. At least, I always enjoyed reading them and therefore spent a lot more time with that candidate's application, which is what you want.

## 18.3 The Test and Interview

### 18.3.1 The Test

#### *18.3.1.1 Introduction*

Level design tests are ubiquitous as part of a level designer's application. Usually, there are two types of tests. The ones they send you to solve externally and any test they ask you to do on-site. Expect to deal with both types because both have different focuses and reveal different things about you. In my experience, an external test happens before a lengthy round of verbal interviews because it is an excellent foundation to dig a bit deeper into your design thinking.

### 18.3.1.2 External

A classic level design test is to provide documentation for a level, usually connected to a game of the company you are applying for. For example, design an open-world location, a linear level, or a deathmatch map. Usually, the only thing you know ahead of time is how long the company expects you to finish the test, like 24 or 48 hours. Then you tell them when you would like to start, you get an email at your selected time and date, and then you have to upload the result in time. In most cases, people obviously pick weekends, but then you remove the option to ask questions if anything is unclear. However, that happened very rarely in my experience.

First, read it very carefully once you get your test, ideally two or three times. Then make a very clear list of the deliverables. We were continually surprised how many people already failed during this first step even though we provided the deliverables to them with clear bullet points. For example, if we expected to get visual illustrations of the map and answer certain level design questions, they instead wrote 20 pages about the background lore, attached a game design pitch about some random artifacts, or detailed character biographies for NPCs nobody asked for. A bit of bonus and extra depth is okay, but it should stay the minority. Focus on those deliverables and nothing more.

Even though you usually have to provide common level design documentation, in doubt, go in more level design detail than you usually do. Remember, when it comes to level design documentation, I wrote that individual cover placement is too much because it will change anyhow during iterations. However, in the case of a test, it helps us, reviewers, to see if you understand cover placement or similar more detailed design aspects like patrol paths, AI placement, or pick-up locations. Therefore, you should certainly go into such detail, even if it doesn't represent common documentation practices.

Speaking about granularity, do not be a know-it-all. For example, if you try to explain to the hiring manager or reviewer that you can skip going into detail because details will change during production, do not expect that you will pass the test. If the test asks for certain aspects, I recommend you provide them, and in doubt, you over-deliver. It is okay to explain that you delivered extra material because that is how you get inspired or because it was not clear to you. However, showing any attitude is rarely good advice, especially not when trying to get a job.

Next up is the actual design itself. As with the resume, you have to find a way to stand out because the reviewers will get many applications, and you want them to remember yours for all the good reasons. My main recommendation is to first go through all the clichés connected to your given test and instantly come to your mind. Put them on a list and ensure that your design does not even get close to them. For example, if the test asks for an urban defense location in New York City, you should never even consider a warehouse, container harbor, random sewers/subway, or construction site. Next are all the obvious famous locations of New York like the Statue of Liberty, Central Park, Rockefeller Center, or the Empire State Building. If you touch such cliché locations, your design must be absolutely spot on. However, I recommend researching deeper and looking for the fringe, rare, exotic, unique, and exciting locations of your setting. For example, it could be a drag queen club in Hell's Kitchen, an absurdly decadent multistore penthouse owned by a Russian oligarch overlooking Central Park, or a mission during a vivid acid jazz concert in the crypt of an upper Manhattan church. Essentially show that you spend more than "five minutes" researching your setting in Google and that you can clearly think outside of the box. You want to make reviewers smile and spike their interest in meeting such a creative person like you.

Another very important aspect is that you share how your design brain works, comparable to what I already hinted at during the previous portfolio segment. What were your design intentions? Why have you picked your location? Why have you designed the layout the way it is? What are your design philosophies? What do you expect players to do based on your design? Maybe add your initial abstract sketches or a bit of the design history? Show the human behind your design and remember you cannot be there to explain/defend your design when they review it for the first time. Therefore, everything has to be self-explanatory, but do not expect anyone to read long pages of text either. Usually, the more visual you can stay, the better.

Usually, tests only ask for some 2D illustrations and text. Sketching or modeling anything in 3D is a bonus but one I always welcome. Of course, always check the specific expectations, but in my experience, you can use whatever you want, like SketchUp, Unreal, or Unity. Sometimes people even added little videos of the levels in 3D. However, the best was providing playable levels of the company's game so far. Of course, if the delivery asks for an illustration (2D or a picture from something 3D), you can never skip it, but adding that bonus level or video always goes a long way. Do not be afraid if you do not have all the exact models or art for your layout. Walking the extra mile is what counts. It shows passion, dedication, and courage.

#### 18.3.1.3 On-Site Test

In my experience, a live on-site test is more about how and why you design things the way they are, instead of the actual creative outcome, unlike the external test. Therefore I highly recommend speaking out loud about what you are thinking. Why do you design it this way? What is your approach to tackling such challenges? What are your key inspirations? What other design considerations crossed your mind, especially why you would discard them. I was told I did not get my first level design job because I did design the best level but because they liked my thinking, approach, and mindset. I do believe that every decent interviewer will handle it similarly because being incredibly creative under pressure is not within realistic, human expectations.

Expect that they will throw curveballs at you. For example, suddenly the mandate changes, a section gets cut, or the task appears seemingly impossible. Again, it matters less that you have the perfect answer but how you approach such challenges and what is your train of thought. Trying to find the perfect answer will often hinder you from progressing, and you might even stall completely. However, when it comes to creative problem-solving in interviews, the journey is usually more interesting than reaching the perfect solution. After all, you, as a candidate, miss a lot of context. Therefore, talk a lot, explain your actions, ask a few questions, and always say why you decided in a certain way. As soon as you give them insight into your thinking, they might give you more context, essentially helping you find the correct answer. If you do not explain, they cannot provide you with the parts you could not know.

Another crucial piece of advice is to prepare for improvisation level design tests. Of course, you cannot prepare for their exact questions, tests, or challenges, but you can prepare to speak and design several basic scenarios, levels, or games. Those basics can then act as your building blocks, and with some adjustments and combination, you quickly have a good answer since you can focus less on the fundamentals but more on making them shine. It is all about stress management. For example, prepare several basic level design scenarios for defense, attack, stealth, racing, high octane scenes, or cool/exciting/unique/fringe settings. Think about your dream games or various settings and genres, even if you do not like them too much. The bigger your back-catalog, the more flexible you are, and the easier it is to adjust and combine them. Especially try to cater them to the games of the company you are interviewing for ahead of time. For example, if you apply for a famous company for open-world games and have no ideas for such locations or missions, it is only your fault.

### 18.3.2 The Interview

#### 18.3.2.1 Preparation

The most important thing you can do, like the on-site test, is go into an interview with good preparation. Believing you can improvise or freestyle everything rarely ends well. Let us start with the most basic interview questions, for example: Tell us about your career? What are your strengths and weaknesses? What is your favorite game, and why? What motivates you to go to work? Where do you see yourself in five years? There are countless lists on the internet about such fundamental "HR" or "trick" questions. You just need to adjust some of them to the games industry slightly. You have no excuse for struggling to answer such questions, and if you do, it might look as if you do not care too much because you are badly prepared. However, be aware that you do not give too many "by the book" answers, telling what you believe the interviewer wants to hear. Any good interviewer will notice it and might discard your answers. Therefore, you should as much as possible personalize your answers. Honesty always beats seemingly "fake, yet perfect" answers.

Next up is to research the company you are applying for. Not only what games do they make, but also who are their top bosses, what are their values, and what is the company's origin story? It is not only embarrassing if it comes out during an interview and shows that you might not care too much. Further on, look for articles, presentations, or speeches given by the company's employees to understand how they approach design and general game making. This preparation especially includes research about the people who interview you. Often companies tell you their names ahead of time, or you can try to ask. A quick search on LinkedIn or Google can do wonders for your interview preparation.

After you are well prepared, I highly recommend rehearsing your answers. Ask your friends, partner, or trusted colleague to be the interviewer so you can train to speak out the answers out loud. Especially if you might be very nervous, and most of us are, any loud-speaking exercises can go a long way. However, if you do not have such a person quickly available, at least write down your answers and then read them out loud. You will appear way more confident and struggle less.

Additionally, you might find some interesting things about yourself when you write them down. Things you might not mention when you are nervous and feel under pressure. How often did we all finish interviews and realize we could have said way more or given better answers!

Lastly, very important, prepare your questions for them! Most interviews have that segment, at the end or between, where it is your turn to ask questions. First, it is a great opportunity to learn more about your potential future employer and if you actually want to work for them. Secondly, good questions show that you care, are interested, and think things through. It is always awkward if the interviewer asks, "Okay, do you have any questions for us?" and then you have none. Have a list prepared, and it is okay if you have them written down and just go through it during the interview. For example, how is their team setup, what is their management setup or reporting line, what is their overtime, sick-leave, holiday, or bonus policy, do they have a mentorship program, what social activities are common among the team, or why the interviewer believe it is such a great company to work for? Never go into an interview without your questions. It might be that they already answered many of them during the interview. However, you should have a long list and always include some more personal ones, like what is your favorite game, what are your expectations about me, or where do you think I have done well or bad during this interview?

#### *18.3.2.2 The Interview*

You are well prepared, and now comes the actual first interview. First, let us be very clear, it is okay to be nervous. The better you are prepared, the less nervousness might impact you, but still, nervousness is human, especially if it is one of your first jobs. Still, I have interviewed incredibly anxious senior developers, and it turned out to be fine for them. Do not forget to breathe, speak slowly, have some sips of water, and if you need time, repeat their questions; plus, do not be afraid to say that you are nervous or need to think for a second or two.

Now, when the interviews start, expect several phone or video calls or a lengthy session with multiple sessions on the same day on-site because there are usually many people who want to talk to you. It commonly starts with HR or recruiters getting the basics done like salary expectations, relocation needs, or visa topics. Usually, this first session is also the first screening, just to ensure that the basic expectations match and that nobody wastes much more time later on. For example, if salary expectations do not match, further interviews are likely fruitless for both sides. Then comes a few rounds with various developers with a mix of managers, directions, leads, or future team members.

During the interviews, they want to know more about you as a person, but especially about your soft and hard skills. Are you a good team or culture fit, or do we want to work with that person? Do your previously shown test or portfolio and your present hard skills match up? What are your true motivations for joining this company? Can we work around the candidate's shortcomings, or what else do they bring to the table? If you prepared well and looked through common interview questions, you quickly realize that most questions probe for a lot deeper answers than they might appear on the surface. For example, if they ask you about a previous mistake, they are likely less interested in the specifics of the mistake but how you handled it and how you present it now. Do you excuse yourself a lot? Do you try to justify it rightfully? Do you blame others? What did you learn from it? Is it a "good" mistake, or does it sound like a "weak" one just so you appear like someone who barely makes severe mistakes? How honest do you indeed appear? It can quickly get complicated, but the key here is being yourself, honesty, and good preparation. If you come across as too fake and non-genuine, you severely reduce your chances. In this spirit, in my opinion, it is better to say that you expected such a question than to give an almost too well-rehearsed answer for a complex question. We have often noticed such behavior and always appreciated honesty instead.

Lastly, stay away from lengthy monologues. Usually, a single interview session is not longer than one hour. True story, but once a candidate wasted 30 minutes talking about their career. It is okay, at times, to give lengthy answers but come to a point soon. In doubt, say that this will be a lengthy answer and invite them to stop you if they get what they want from you. However, keep such cases at a minimum. Do not rush it either, but in that one hour, you rather want them to run out of questions than the way around. After all, if they run out of questions, they get to know what they want, and you have more time to ask your questions or have a bit of a friendly social chat at the end. The strategy to suffocate the interviewer with lengthy answers so they cannot ask too many questions rarely pays off. Instead, they will get the impression that each time they have to work with you, it results in long monologues, which is usually not something too many people are looking forward to.

Again, be well prepared, get to the point, and stay genuine. If you need time to think, you are nervous, or you are about to give a lengthy answer, just say it. You want the interviewers to get to know you because if they believe you would not fit, you likely will not be happy ending up working for them either. Lastly, never forget you are interviewing them, too. If they fail to convince you that you should work for them or sense any red flags, like toxic or burn-out work culture, during the interview, make the intelligent choice and respectfully step away from the offer.

### 18.3.3 Rejection

Now ending this book covering rejection is certainly not the most elegant way, but unfortunately, it is part of our reality. Most likely, throughout our entire careers, we will not get all the jobs we want.

Let us keep in mind that they interview you because they need someone like you, so it is not their agenda to make you feel bad. If it does not work out, the company more likely found someone who they believed fitted better their team, culture, or skill expectations. It usually does not mean that you are a lousy level designer! This case is especially true the longer the interview process lasts, and you still drop out at the end. However, even if they reject you early on, it does not mean you are unskilled. Unfortunately, luck, timing, misunderstandings, and other global/local factors out of our all control play a relevant role. There is no point in beating yourself over it.

If you apply for a new job, either send out many applications or only a few specific targeted ones if you still feel comfortable staying at your current job for longer. Betting all your cards on only one specific dream job is simply too risky if you are in a rush to leave or gain a job to begin with. It is not worth it because returning to your dreaded current job/situation after getting rejected by your dream job is way too devastating.

If you get a rejection, I would always try to ask for feedback about what did not work out or where you could learn something. Sure, not every company provides such feedback. Still, you can do it yourself to some extent. Take some time and reflect on what you could have done better next time. Even if you did everything well, there are certainly learnings you can use for the next time. For example, you might have learned some new interview questions you can prepare for, got a better feel for salary expectations, or each test you do will sharpen your skills and extend your level design back-catalog. Some people apply for jobs for the interview training alone because you quickly get rusty after years of working for the same company. Also, who knows? Maybe it accidentally opens up some great opportunities.

# *Index*

Note: **Bold** page numbers refer to tables; *italic* page numbers refer to figures.